INTERNATIONAL MARKETING: MANAGERIAL PERSPECTIVES

Subhash C. Jain
University of Connecticut
and
Lewis R. Tucker, Jr.
University of Connecticut

CBI

CBI Publishing Company, Inc.
51 Sleeper Street, Boston, Massachusetts 02210

46893

Library of Congress Cataloging in Publication Data

Jain, Subhash C. 1942–
    International marketing.

    Bibliography: p.
    1. Export marketing—Addresses, essays,
lectures. 2. Marketing management—Addresses,
essays, lectures. 3. International business enterprises—Addresses, essays, lectures. I. Tucker,
Lewis R., 1943- joint author. II. Title.
HF1009.5.J34   658.8′4   78-31876
ISBN 0-8436-0903-6

Copyright © 1979 by CBI Publishing Company, Inc. All rights reserved. This book may
not be reproduced in any form without written permission from the publisher.

Printed in the United States of America.

Printing (last digit): 9 8 7 6 5 4 3 2 1

TABLE OF CONTENTS

Preface   vii

Introduction: Perspectives of International Marketing   1

NATURE OF INTERNATIONAL MARKETING   23

1. A Conceptual Framework for Multinational Marketing
   Warren J. Keegan   25

2. Dimensions of Multinational Corporations
   United Nations   37

3. Industrial Marketing in the International Setting
   C. P. Rao   56

4. American Investment Abroad: Who's Going Where,
   How, and Why
   Booz, Allen, & Hamilton   66

5. New Worlds for Marketers: Speculations on Marketing's
   Origins and Future
   Richard F. Wendel   73

iii

46893

ENVIRONMENT OF INTERNATIONAL MARKETING   85

6. Patterns and Parallels of Marketing Structures in
   Several Countries
      Susan P. Douglas   87

7. Competition Encountered by U. S. Companies That
   Manufacture Abroad
      Robert B. Stobaugh   99

8. Is Antitrust Sinking U. S. Trade Effort?
      John H. Sheridan   110

9. Canadian Attitudes and Policy on Foreign Investment
      John Fayerweather   125

10. His Master's Voice
      Karl Sauvent   144

ANALYSIS OF OVERSEAS OPPORTUNITIES: CONCEPTUAL ISSUES   153

11. A Multi-Level Approach to Researching Overseas
    Markets
      C. P. Rao   154

12. Methodological Considerations in Cross-National
    Consumer Research
      Robert T. Green and Phillip D. White   167

13. Special Wrinkles in International Marketing Research
      Lee Adler   180

ANALYSIS OF OVERSEAS OPPORTUNITIES: APPLICATIONS   187

14. Marketing Opportunities and Marketing Strategies in
    Japan
      Masaru Yoshimori   188

15. The Marketing Environment in Saudi Arabia
      Jack G. Kaikati   200

16. Expansion of the European Common Market and its
    Effect on the Euro-United States Trade
      Venkatakrishna V. Bellur   218

17. Marketing in Eastern European Socialist Countries
      Charles S. Mayer   229

18. The Coming Leap Forward in China Trade
   Julian M. Sobin 239

PRODUCT STRATEGIES 245

19. Multinational Product Planning: Strategic
   Alternatives
   Warren J. Keegan 246

20. International Product Policy: The Role of
   Foreign R & D
   Vern Terpstra 255

21. Product Life Cycle as a Determinant of Global
   Marketing Strategies
   Jose de la Torre 268

22. Technology Transfer to Less Developed Countries
   Jerry R. Ladman 281

DISTRIBUTION STRATEGIES 293

23. Selecting Sales and Distribution Channels
   United States Department of Commerce 294

24. The International Expansion of United States Franchise
   Systems: Status and Strategies
   Donald W. Hackett 303

25. Planning and Control in International PD
   L. Soorikian 316

26. TRW Datacom: A Better Idea for Overseas Distribution
   Art Detman, Jr. 321

COMMUNICATIONS STRATEGIES 329

27. 33 Caveats for the Prospective Overseas Marketer
   Richard Manville 330

28. Coordinating International Advertising
   *Dean M. Peebles, John K. Ryans, Jr., and
   Ivan R. Vernon* 344

29. Effect of National Identity on Multinational
   Promotional Strategy in Europe
   S. Watson Dunn 355

30. Multinational Positioning Strategy
   David R. McIntyre 369

PRICING STRATEGIES   375

31. Multinational Firm Pricing in International Markets
    Jeffrey S. Arpan   376

32. Is Uniform Pricing Desirable in Multinational Markets?
    Peter R. Kressler   386

33. Commodities: Importance, Market Power, and Feasible
    Solution
    V. H. Kirpalani   393

PLANNING AND IMPLEMENTING MARKETING
PROGRAMS   409

34. Guidelines for Developing International Marketing
    Strategies
    Yoram Wind, Susan P. Douglas, and
    Howard V. Perlmutter   410

35. A Conceptual Model of Long-Range Multinational
    Marketing Planning
    Jagdish N. Sheth   424

36. Organizational Structure and Marketing Strategy
    in the Multinational Subsidiary
    William K. Brandt and James M. Hurlbert   433

37. Competitive Marketing Strategies for International
    Public Telecommunications
    Gary L. Jordan   444

PROBLEMS AND PERSPECTIVES   459

38. The MNC and the Public Interest
    Peter P. Gabriel   460

39. Analyzing Corporate Impact: Some Innovative
    Approaches
    Orville L. Freeman   474

40. What Happened to the Marketing Man When His Inter-
    national Promotion Pay-Offs Became Bribes?
    Subhash C. Jain   480

41. Solutions to Financial and Marketing Problems
    Commonly Encountered by Foreign Business Firms
    Marketing Products in the United States
    John R. Darling and Hussein H. Elsaid   494

Selected References   509

PREFACE

A special panel from the prestigious Brookings Institution recently observed:

The internationalization of business has so expanded international influences, even on domestic business, that all students of management should have a greater knowledge of these influences and how they affect business and management.[1]

Nowhere are these international influences more apparent and conversely subtle than in the field of marketing. Accelerating change in all quarters of the international marketing environment has created immense challenges for the prospective and practicing marketing managers. The very fact that international marketing is faced with increasing complexity requires a commitment among its participants to a process of lifelong learning.

The purpose of *International Marketing: Managerial Perspectives* is to contribute to that lifelong learning process through carefully selected readings that blend theory and application in the coverage of international marketing strategy. The theoretical material creates a framework for "students" of international marketing at all stages of development (those who are practicing and those who soon will be) to interpret and better understand the applications presented here or observed elsewhere. Thus, the authors and

---

1. *The International Dimension of Management Education* (Washington D.C.: The Brookings Institutions, 1975), p. 10.

journals that are represented by the selections in our book have been chosen for their conceptual and practical contributions as well as their timeliness and readability. The sequencing of the articles was undertaken with the objective of introducing concepts and techniques that would then be further developed through subsequent articles on practical applications. As a result, the reader will find articles from such diverse publications, as the *Journal of Marketing, Columbia World Journal of Business, Sales & Marketing Management, MSU Business Topics, The Marketing News,* and the *Journal of International Business Studies,* have been purposefully integrated in the ten sections that are contained in the book. It should also be noted that at the end of each article is a set of discussion questions that are designed to not only enhance the readers understanding of concepts but also generate an appreciation of their strategic implications.

The first section of the book introduces the field of international marketing. The complex environment of international marketing and the need to investigate its various economic, social, political and legal dimensions are addressed from a conceptual, methodological, and applications perspective in the following three sections. How these environmental implications must be factored into marketing programs are the subject of the next four sections each of which separately addresses international product promotion, place, and pricing strategies. Section nine focuses on the integration of marketing strategies through a treatment of the topics of international marketing planning, organization, and control. The concluding section underscores the turbulence of the international marketing environment through a discussion of emerging issues that are creating new problems and opportunities for international marketing managers.

We are greatly indebted to a number of individuals and organizations who have provided various kinds of support in bringing our efforts to fruition. We wish to extend our thanks to the authors and publishers who permitted us to reprint the articles that are included in this book.

We are also grateful to our wives and families whose patience, assistance, and encouragement made the completion of our tasks less difficult and more satisfying. We also wish to acknowledge the support of our colleagues and staff at the University of Connecticut.

It is hoped that these readings will in some small way stimulate all students of international marketing to extend the conceptual framework presented here through the design and conduct of bold and imaginative international strategies. In this way, the experiences of past, present, and future international marketers can be combined to create a greater understanding of a most challenging international marketplace.

SCJ
LRT

The following matrix can be used as a comparison tool for *International Marketing*.

International Textbooks Correlated with the Reader

PERSPECTIVES ON INTERNATIONAL MARKETING
Article Numbers

Chapter	Kahler and Kramer[1]	Cateora and Hess[2]	Keegan[3]	Terpstra[4]
1	1, 3, 5	1, 2, 3, 40	1, 3, 5, 39	1, 3
2	2, 4, 38	4, 5	4, 40	4, 5, 7, 15
3	7, 8	32	6, 7, 13, 14 16, 26	13, 14, 16, 17
4	—	6, 13, 14, 26	15, 16, 17	6, 13, 14, 26
5	22, 26	6, 9, 13, 16, 17	10, 11, 12	8, 9, 37, 38
6	10, 11, 12, 13 14, 16, 17	8, 37, 39	10, 11, 12	1, 2, 3
7	6, 7, 13, 14, 26	2, 7, 13, 14, 16, 26	18, 19, 20, 21	10, 11, 12
8	15	10, 11, 12	30, 31, 32	18, 19, 20, 21
9	33, 34, 35, 36	15	22, 23, 25	22, 23, 24, 25
10	22, 23, 25	2, 37	26, 27, 28, 29	26, 27, 28, 29
11	24	18, 19, 20	22	25
12	18, 19, 20, 21	3, 21	33, 34, 36	30, 31, 32
13	26, 27, 28, 29	26, 27, 28, 29	35	33, 34, 36
14	30, 31, 32	30, 31, 32	2	35
15	40	22, 23	37, 38	
16	8, 9, 37, 39	22, 23, 25		
17	—	24		
18	—	—		
19	—	33, 34, 35, 36		
20	16, 17	40		
21	—	—		
22	—	38		

1. Kahler, Ruel and Roland L. Kramer, *International Marketing,* Fourth Edition (Southwestern Publishing Co., 177)

2. Cateora, Philip R. and John M. Hess, *International Marketing,* Fourth Edition (Richard D. Irwin, 1979)

3. Keegan, Warren J., *Multinational Marketing Management* (Prentice-Hall Inc., 1974).

4. Terpstra, Vern, *International Marketing* (Dryden Press, 1972).

Introduction: Perspectives of International Marketing

The world has come a long way since Columbus discovered America. Today the economies of most countries are so intimately interconnected with each other that no nation can afford to isolate itself from the rest of the world. The United States, because of its economic and political significance, must be particularly sensitive to the interdependencies existing in the international market place. These articles provide a marketing perspective on both the obligation and the need of the United States to become economically involved in worldwide markets. Particular emphasis is placed on the past, present, and future role of multinational corporations and their role in the conduct of national marketing strategies.

United States Involvement in International Marketing

While many United States firms have long been engaged in foreign business ventures, the real impetus to overseas expansion came after the Second World War. In attempts to reconstruct war-torn economies, the United States government, through the Marshall Plan, provided financial assistance to

European countries. Since the postwar American economy emerged as the strongest in the world, its economic assistance programs, in the absence of competition, stimulated extensive corporate development of international strategies. It has been said that:

. . . in those halcyon years, nothing seemed more seductive to U.S. business than a foreign climate. American manufacturing companies of all types treked abroad in prodigious numbers, and wherever they migrated, their banks, advertising agencies, and accounting firms went with them. The book value of United States foreign direct investment swelled from about $12 billion in 1950 to more than $50 billion in 1966. It is now estimated at between $140 billion and $150 billion.[1]

Exhibit 0-1 not only provides an appreciation of the extensiveness of United States direct investments overseas but also indicates where American business has concentrated its efforts. It can be observed that 60 percent of United States investments overseas have been in Western Europe and Canada. However, as many underdeveloped countries (LDCs) gained political freedom after the war, the national governments of these countries also sought United States aid to modernize their economies and improve living standards. Thus, LDCs provided additional opportunities for the United States corporations, especially in those more politically stable countries where the United States foreign aid programs were in progress. It is apparent, though, that for a variety of reasons—cultural, political, economic—United States corporations found more viable opportunities in Western Europe, Canada, and, to a lesser extent, Japan.

In recent years, overseas business has become a matter of necessity both from the viewpoint of United States corporations and United States government. The increased competition facing many industries, resulting from the saturation of markets and the competitive threats from overseas corporations doing business domestically, has forced United States corporations to look to overseas markets. At the same time, the unfavorable balance of trade, partly due to increasing energy imports, has made the need to expand exports a matter of vital national interest. Thus, while in the 1950s and 1960s international business was characterized as a means of capitalizing on new opportunity, in today's changing economic environment it has become a matter of survival.

Modes of Business Overseas

The mode in which business is conducted overseas is a function of a firm's commitment to the pursuit of foreign markets. A firm's overseas involvement may be categorized as: (1) no marketing overseas; (2) infrequent marketing overseas; (3) regular marketing overseas; and (4) worldwide marketing operations. Given the tremendous opportunities and governmental incentives to

EXHIBIT 0-1
U.S. CUMULATIVE DIRECT
INVESTMENT ABROAD

Billion U.S. $

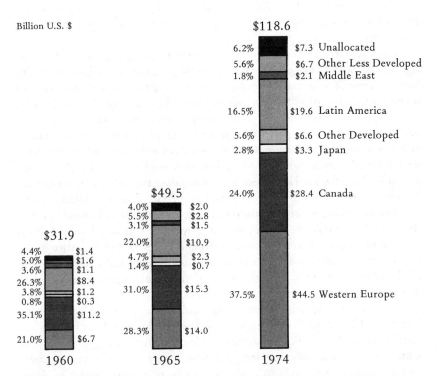

$118.6

6.2%	$7.3 Unallocated
5.6%	$6.7 Other Less Developed
1.8%	$2.1 Middle East
16.5%	$19.6 Latin America
5.6%	$6.6 Other Developed
2.8%	$3.3 Japan
24.0%	$28.4 Canada
37.5%	$44.5 Western Europe

$49.5

4.0%	$2.0
5.5%	$2.8
3.1%	$1.5
22.0%	$10.9
4.7%	$2.3
1.4%	$0.7
31.0%	$15.3
28.3%	$14.0

$31.9

4.4%	$1.4
5.0%	$1.6
3.6%	$1.1
26.3%	$8.4
3.8%	$1.2
0.8%	$0.3
35.1%	$11.2
21.0%	$6.7

1960   1965   1974

Source: *International Economic Report of the President* (Washington, D.C.: U. S. Government Printing Office, 1976), p. 66.

engage in overseas marketing, it is surprising that 92 percent of United States firms confine themselves only to domestic markets.[2] Often it is only through infrequent efforts to capitalize on an *ad hoc* opportunity that firms first become involved in foreign markets. For example, an overseas customer may approach a domestic firm to buy its product without ever being solicited by the United States operator. Alternatively, the firm during recessionary periods in the United States may look to overseas markets to liquidate its inventories. Regular marketing refers to deliberate attempts to serve the overseas markets on a continuing basis, mainly through exporting. A worldwide marketing operation is a stronger commitment where export activity is supplemented by assembly and/or manufacturing conducted on foreign soil.

Each level of involvement in overseas marketing can generally be associated with a specific mode of business. Four different modes of business are available to a company entering foreign markets: (1) exporting; (2) contractual agreements; (3) joint ventures; and (4) manufacturing. A company may minimize its risk of exporting domestically manufactured products by either a minimal response to inquiry basis or by systematically developing demand in export markets. As evidenced by a 20 percent annual growth rate since 1970,[3] a major part of the overseas involvement of large United States firms is through export trade.

Contractual agreements consist of several types: (1) patent licensing agreements, with managerial training included on either a fixed fee or royalty basis; (2) turnkey operations, which include plant construction, personnel training and setup of initial production runs, which are based on a fixed fee or cost plus arrangement; (3) co-production agreements, where the plant is built and operated with part of the output used as payment (most common in the socialist countries); and (4) management contracts, which involve a multinational corporation providing key personnel to operate the foreign enterprise for a fee until local people have acquired the ability to independently manage the business (currently widely practiced in the Middle East).

The remaining modes of business, i.e., joint ventures and manufacturing, represent higher risk alternatives in that they require various levels of direct investment. A joint venture between a United States firm and a native operation involves a sharing of the risk to accomplish a mutual enterprise. This, incidentally, is the most common form of entry once a firm moves beyond the exporting stage to a more regular overseas involvement.

One example of a joint venture is Ford Motor Company's partnership with a local Egyptian firm to establish a plant for the assembly of trucks and diesel engines. In Brazil, a subsidiary of Hercules, Inc., is engaged in a joint venture to build a polypropylene plant with three other firms. A multinational corporation may also establish itself in an overseas market by direct investment in a manufacturing and/or assembly subsidiary. Because of the volatility of worldwide economic, social, and political conditions, this form of involvement is most risky. Examples of a direct investment situation would include Chesebrough Pond's operation of overseas plants in Japan, England, and Monte Carlo.

Marketing Decisions and the International Environment

Not only are the risk factors underlying the mode of entry largely contingent on the nature of the foreign environment, but these environmental forces also influence the development of marketing strategies. Marketing decision making for the exploitation of international markets is strategically similar to the decision-making process guiding domestic marketing endeavors. More specifically, four marketing decision variables—product, price, distribution, and promotion—need to be as systematically addressed in the context of international marketing as they would be in domestic market segmentation strategies. What is different about international marketing, however, is

the environment in which marketing decisions must be made and the influence that environment has in shaping marketing strategies. The principal
components of the international marketing environment include cultural,
political, legal, commercial, and economic forces. Each of these forces
represents informational inputs that must be entered into the marketing
decision-making process.

Culture Culture refers to learned behavior over time, passed on from generation to generation. This behavior manifests itself in the form of social structure, habits, faith, customs, rituals, and religion. Each of these tends to
impact on individual life styles, which in turn shape consumption patterns in
the marketplace. Thus, what people of a particular country buy, why they
buy, when they buy, where they buy, and how they buy are largely culturally determined. There are five elements of culture: material culture,
social institutions, man and universe, aesthetics, and language. Each of
these elements will vary from country to country. The importance to marketers of understanding these often subtle variations has been illustrated by
Dichter:

> In puritanical cultures it is customary to think of cleanliness as being
> next to godliness. The body and its functions are covered up as much as
> possible.
>
> But in Catholic and Latin countries, to fool too much with one's body,
> to overindulge in bathing or toiletries, has opposite meaning. Accordingly,
> an advertising approach based on Puritanical principals, threatening French-
> men that if they didn't brush their teeth regularly, they would develop
> cavities or would not find a lover, failed to impress. To fit the accepted con-
> cept of morality, the French advertising agency changed this approach to
> a permissive one.[4]

Similarly, language differences from one country to another could lead
to problems, since literal translation of words often connote different mean-
ings. Several classic examples of marketing blunders include the famous
slogans "Body by Fisher," when translated into German meant "Corpse by
Fisher," and "Let Hertz Put You in the Driver's Seat," being literally translated into "Let Hertz Make You A Chauffeur."[5] Even the choice of color,
via packaging and promotional copy, may impact on marketing decisions.
For example, in the United States the bridal gown is often white and is
equated with purity. In most Asian countries, however, white is associated
with death in the same way that black is a symbol of mourning in the American culture. In short, culture could and has had far-reaching effects on the
success of overseas marketing strategies.

Politics The laissez faire era, when government both domestically and
overseas had little if anything to do with the conduct of business, is past

history. Today, even in democratic societies, governments exercise a pervasive influence on business decisions. In fact, it is not uncommon to find in many overseas countries that the government actually owns and operates certain businesses. For example, British Overseas Airways Corporation is a government owned and operated enterprise.

Although the degree of intervention varies across countries, recent developments in LDCs perhaps represent situations where government policies are most extreme. Therefore, to be successful overseas, an international marketer should determine the political climates most favorable and exploit those opportunities first. Robinson suggests that the degree of political vulnerability in a given overseas market can be ascertained is by researching a number of key issues. Positive answers to the following questions would signal political troubles for a foreign marketer:

1. Is the availability of supply of the product ever subject to important political debates? (sugar, salt, gasoline, public utilities, medicines, foodstuffs)
2. Do other industries depend upon the production of the product? (cement, power, machine tools, construction machinery, steel)
3. Is the product considered socially or economically essential? (key drugs, laboratory equipment, medicines)
4. Is the product essential to agricultural industries? (farm tools and machinery, crops, fertilizers, seed)
5. Does the product affect national defense capabilities? (transportation industry, communications)
6. Does the product include important components that would be available from local sources and that otherwise would not be used as effectively? (labor, skills, materials)
7. Is there local competition or potential local competition from manufacturers in the near future? (small, low investment manufacturing)
8. Does the product relate to channels of mass communication media? (newsprint, radio equipment)
9. Is the product primarily a service?
10. Does the use of the product, or its design, rest upon some legal requirements?
11. Is the product potentially dangerous to the user? (explosives, drugs)
12. Does the product induce a net drain on scarce foreign exchange?[6]

Legal Environment Given the best of intentions, it is not unreasonable to assume that differences will arise between parties doing business. What recourse exists for the resolution of differences and whose laws will apply are of vital concern to international marketers. While there is no simplistic solution to such a complex problem, it is important that marketers anticipate areas where disputes are likely to arise and establish beforehand agreements on what means will be used and which country will have jurisdiction in the resolution of differences. According to Business International, the following are the areas in which legal difficulties in marketing are most prevalent:

1. Rules of competition on (a) collusion, (b) discrimination against certain buyers, (c) promotional methods, (d) variable pricing, (e) exclusive territory agreement
2. Retail price maintenance laws
3. Cancellation of distributor or wholesaler agreements
4. Product quality laws and controls
5. Packaging laws
6. Warranty and after-sales exposure
7. Price controls, limitations on markups or markdowns
8. Patents, trademarks, and copyright laws and practices[7]

Needless to say, the marketer in conjunction with legal counsel should probe these areas and establish with the buyer various contingencies prior to commiting his organization.

Commercial Practices An international marketer must be thoroughly familiar with the business customs and practices in effect in overseas markets. Although some evidence suggests that business traditions in a country may undergo a change as a result of dealing with foreign corporations, such a transformation is a long-term process. Thus, local customs and practices must be researched and adhered to in order to gain the confidence and support of local buyers, channel intermediaries, and other business operatives. The specific customs and practices of a country may be studied with reference to the following factors:

BUSINESS STRUCTURE

Size

Ownership

Various Business Publics

Sources and Level of Authority

Top-management Decision Making

Decentralized Decision Making

Committee Decision Making

MANAGEMENT ATTITUDES AND BEHAVIOR

Personal Background

Business Status

Objectives and Aspirations

Security and Mobility

Personal Life

Social Acceptance

Advancement

Power

PATTERNS OF COMPETITION

MODE OF DOING BUSINESS

    Level of Contact
    Communications Emphasis
    Formality and Tempo
    Business Ethics
    Negotiation Emphasis[8]

Economic Climate Only a small percentage of people in the world approach the standard of living experienced in the United States and other advanced nations. The state of economic development of various countries can be explained and described through a number of measures. One common measure used to rank nations economically is per capita GNP. Exhibit 0–2 shows the per capita GNP of different nations.

According to Rostow, different countries of the world can be grouped into the following stages of economic development: (a) the traditional, (b) the precondition for take-off, (c) the take-off, (d) the drive to maturity, and (e) mass consumption societies.[9] By following Rostow's scheme, most African, Asian, and Latin American countries would be categorized as underdeveloped, having lower living standards, and limited discretionary income. The variability and importance of discretionary income is illustrated by the fact that a degree of effort must be exerted in different countries to earn enough to purchase the same product. For example, to buy one kilogram of sugar, a person in the United States needs to work a little over five minutes, while in Greece it takes fifty-three minutes of labor to earn an equivalent amount. In many African and Asian countries the effort needed to buy a kilogram of sugar, or for that matter other products, is even higher.

Another important determinant of economic development pertains to the expenditure patterns of people in different countries. In India, for example, there is one car for every 600,000 people. Algeria, despite its oil riches, has only 52 people in 1,000 owning radios. In the Philippines, only 23 percent of the dwellings have electricity.[10] Given the type of product being marketed, the poor living standards in developing countries represent both an opportunity and a limitation for United States businessmen. The economic health of a nation must be studied through such factors as those mentioned above, and others, before a marketer can decide if indeed an opportunity exists.

Foreign Trade: Past, Present, and Future

The effectiveness in which domestic firms have met the environmental challenge of international marketing as well as the changing nature of overseas markets can be partially assessed through foreign trade statistics and past governmental policies.

EXHIBIT 0-2

Gross national product per capita for major regions of the world and selected countries (in 1973 U.S. dollars)

	GNP/capita for countries	GNP/capita for regions
North America		$6,150
United States	$6,224	
Canada	5,485	
Latin America		810
Argentina	1,478	
Brazil	768	
Haiti	141	
Mexico	883	
Europe		3,790
United Kingdom	3,119	
France	4,775	
West Germany	5,600	
Italy	2,525	
Sweden	6,198	
Portugal	1,328	
Near East		850
Israel	3,094	
Turkey	555	
Africa		310
Algeria	503	
Egypt	260	
Ethiopia	90	
Kenya	186	
Nigeria	227	
South Africa	1,078	
Rwanda	68	
South and East Asia		440
India	130	
Pakistan	128	
Japan	3,765	
Indonesia	127	
Oceania		4,300
Australia	5,482	
New Zealand	4,032	

Source: *Yearbook of National Accounts Statistics,* 1975, vol. 3 (New York: United Nations, 1976). pp. 3–9.

Policy Perspectives   To gain insights into how foreign trade in this country has evolved to its current status, it would be useful to describe the major periods of commercial policy affecting the extent and conduct of United States trading activity.

An appropriate starting point is the mercantilist era, which spanned the years between 1500 and 1750. This period was marked by the emergence of many detailed regulations and controls over international business. All the world powers—England, France, Spain, and Portugal—attempted to gain trading advantage by following such a policy. More specifically, each power attempted to generate an export surplus to acquire precious metals (primarily gold).

Over time, this policy changed with the advent of the industrial revolution, the emergence of a true business class, and the influential writing of Adam Smith. The onset of World War I saw free trade again fall by the wayside as war needs forced greater protectionism and disrupted evolving liberalized trade patterns. Tariffs and quotas dramatically increased, and the world was thrown into general economic instability.[11] After a limited post-war prosperity, the 1930 depression struck, and tariffs again rose as countries tried to keep out foreign goods to protect jobs at home. Post-depression years witnessed the introduction of a series of major trade agreements and efforts to break down the existing barriers. In 1934, the Reciprocal Trade Agreements Program (RTAP) came into effect, which included among its provisions the Most Favored Nation Clause. RTAP resulted in a number of tariff cuts, many of which were quite substantial. For example, between 1930 and 1933 the average tax on a good coming into the United States was 53 percent. This was reduced by 1961 to 17 percent.[12]

In 1947, the General Agreement on Trade and Tariffs was adopted. Although it was not as spectacular as the RTAP, it at least set out the principle to meet and bargain in good faith for tariff reductions and to continue to use the most favored nations' concept to speed cuts. The European Economic Community and European Free Trade Association were formed in 1957. These pacts broke down most internal tariffs and quotas and thus brought a new prosperity to Europe. The Kennedy round of talks, involving more than 80 countries, from 1967 to 1972 via the Trade Expansion Act of 1962, were also very productive. As a result of these talks, tariff cuts took place averaging 35 percent over a five-year period, on 60,000 items representing 50 billion dollars in value. In addition, quotas were reduced, which further contributed to freer trade conditions.[13] Next, the United Nations Conference on Trade and Development (UNCTAD) opened markets of industrialized nations to less developed nations. This facilitated unilateral agreements with advanced countries in that it extended most favored nation status to less developed countries.

Currently, the Carter administration, at least in public statements, has stated that it plans to continue the established policy of vigorously pursuing free trade as a major national goal. This position has been taken despite the many protectionist sentiments of congressmen and senators who feel American jobs and businesses are being hurt by the inflow of cheap foreign goods and the relocation of many plants and facilities overseas. Thus, the general thrust in international trade policies has been towards less restriction. Although protectionist lapses have been experienced, most nations have come to realize the benefits of vigorous worldwide competition. In the long run, the profit potential for companies engaged in worldwide markets will be enhanced by the move toward greater international cooperation.

Foreign Trade Activity The precise nature of these growing opportunities, as well as the problems posed by free trade, can be observed in Exhibit 0–3. From the statistical overview of United States foreign trade activity contained in Exhibit 0–3, it will be noted that for the first time since 1881 a deficit occurred in the United States balance of trade in 1971. In recent years, the trade deficit has continued to grow and has reached alarming proportions. A major reason for the increasingly unfavorable trade deficit is the oil imports, which have risen from about three million barrels per day in 1970 to over ten million barrels in 1977. As a result of the trade deficit situation and its adverse impact on the value of the dollar, the government has become increasingly concerned and has taken steps to further stimulate United States overseas involvement.[14]

Exhibit 0–4 shows the composition of United States foreign trade. Almost three-fourths of our exports are capital goods and other manufactured products. Major imports are led by fuel, which alone constitutes over one-fourth of our foreign purchases. Capital goods and other manufactured goods are also major components of our import trade. On a country by country basis, Canada represents our most important trading partner, and in 1975 accounted for 20 percent of our exports and 23 percent of our imports. Three-fifths of our trade is with developed countries, while the remaining two-fifths is with OPEC and LDCs. Interestingly, the LDCs (other than OPEC countries), which account for about one-fourth of our trade, are the only group of countries with which the United States always had a favorable balance of trade. It appears that while the United States is facing its current trade deficit, the LDCs provide a better opportunity to turn the situation around.

The Role of Multinational Corporations in a Changing Environment

A most significant recent development with respect to foreign trade activity has been pervasive marketing impact created by multinational corporations. The multinational corporation represents the highest level of overseas involvement and is characterized by a global strategy of investment, production,

EXHIBIT 0-3

U.S. foreign trade [In billions of U.S. dollars]

	Exports[1]	Imports		Balance	
	f.a.s.	f.a.s.[2]	e.i.f.[3]	f.a.s.[2]	c.i.f. (imports)[3]
1950	10.1	9.0	N.A.	1.0	N.A.
1951	14.0	11.1	N.A.	2.9	N.A.
1952	13.2	10.8	N.A.	2.4	N.A.
1953	12.3	11.0	N.A.	1.3	N.A.
1954	12.9	10.4	N.A.	2.5	N.A.
1955	14.3	11.6	N.A.	2.7	N.A.
1956	17.3	12.9	N.A.	4.4	N.A.
1957	19.5	13.4	N.A.	6.1	N.A.
1958	16.4	13.4	N.A.	3.0	N.A.
1959	16.4	15.7	N.A.	.7	N.A.
1960	19.7	15.1	16.3	4.6	3.4
1961	20.2	14.8	16.0	5.5	4.2
1962	21.0	16.5	17.8	4.5	3.2
1963	22.5	17.2	18.6	5.3	3.9
1964	25.8	18.7	20.3	7.1	5.5
1965	26.7	21.4	23.2	5.3	3.5
1966	29.5	25.6	27.7	3.9	1.8
1967	31.0	26.9	28.7	4.1	2.3
1968	34.1	33.2	35.3	.8	− 1.2
1969	37.3	36.0	38.2	1.3	− .9
1970	42.7	40.0	42.4	2.7	.3
1971	43.5	45.6	48.3	−2.0	− 4.8
1972	49.2	55.6	58.9	−6.4	− 9.7
1973	70.8	69.5	73.2	1.3	− 2.4
1974	97.9	100.3	108.0	−2.3	−10.1
1975	107.2	96.1	103.4	11.1	3.8

1 Excludes Department of Defense shipments and includes reexports.
2 Imports are Customs values prior to 1974 and transation values for 1974–75.
3 Values for 1960–73 are estimates.

Source: *International Economic Report of the President* (Washington, D.C.: U.S. Government Printing Office, 1976), p. 149.

EXHIBIT 0-4
COMPOSITION OF U.S. TRADE, 1975

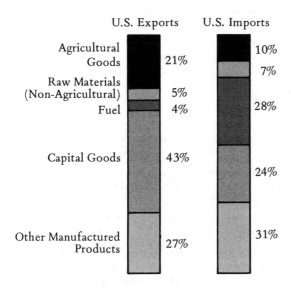

	U.S. Exports	U.S. Imports
Agricultural Goods	21%	10%
Raw Materials (Non-Agricultural)	5%	7%
Fuel	4%	28%
Capital Goods	43%	24%
Other Manufactured Products	27%	31%

Source: *International Economic Report of the President* (Washington, D.C.: U.S. Government Printing Office, 1976), p. 26.

and distribution. It has been observed that multinational corporations are the most viable economic force in the world today, in that:

MNCs are a desirable, even necessary, tool for helping create the economic balance which the times call for. With resources, capital, food, and technology unevenly distributed around the planet, and all in short supply an efficient instrument of quick and effective production and distribution of a complex of goods and services is a first essential.[15]

No other institution is more capable of successfully implementing this vital task than the multinational corporations. The decision making in these corporations transcends national boundaries and generates revenues and assets that, when combined, exceed the Gross National Product of many individual nations. More specifically, the value added by each of the top ten multinational corporations in 1971 was in excess of three billion dollars, or greater than the Gross National Product of over eighty countries.[16]

Ironically, due to their very success in sustaining rapid growth, concern has been recently expressed over their impact on foreign policy and the economic and social welfare of host economies. These concerns are evident in the introductory remarks made by then President Gerald Ford in the *International Economic Report of the President* to Congress in March of 1976:

Multinational corporations continue to be a highly visible and controversial factor in international affairs. Multinational corporations have made major contributions to world economic development and will continue to do so in the future. . .many developing countries actively seek investment by multinational corporations recognizing their potential contribution to economic development. . .we are participating in the development of an international code to provide guidelines for responsible corporate behavior.[17]

The more common examples of the "controversial" side of MNCs offered by critics include:

1. MNCs undermine ability of government to maintain employment, control money supply, and meet social needs by their enormous size and impact on small economies.
2. They promote the gap between rich and poor nations.
3. They misuse and misallocate scarce resources.
4. [They] use labor-saving devices that keep up employment in less developed countries.
5. Those firms that get more than 50 percent of their profit from abroad really don't care about United States economic interests.
6. Global giants based in United States avoid many taxes by using foreign companies. In 1958 they provided 25 percent of federal revenue, now they provide less than 15 percent.
7. Americans lose jobs when they go overseas.[18]

In short, MNCs are accused of investing great sums of money in the nations of the world, creating diseconomies at home and abroad and obtaining exploitive rates of returns. The United Nations, for example, has determined that between the period 1965 and 1968 the average return on book investment of United States companies was 7.9 percent from investments in the developed countries and a dramatic 17.5 percent in developing countries.[19] The United Nations study further suggests that, as of 1970, net monetary flows were much less favorable to the host country than would be expected. Specifically, the data showed approximately four billion dollars a year more was coming out of the host nations than was being reinvested.[20] It goes without saying that to the developing nations of the world four billion dollars could do a great deal to improve the existing quality of life.

Although many aspects of these corporate giants may well be negative, it is overreacting to push the panic button, as Barnet and Muller do below:

The excessive power of large corporations over the political and economic life of this country has all but destroyed the system of checks and balances in our society. . .the redistribution of economic and political power is the price of maintaining a democracy in America.[21]

Abuses certainly do exist, and they will never be completely eliminated. However, if the corporations with governmental assistance and foresight can stimulate appropriate business conduct then the benefits outstrip the costs in the long run. The multinationals are a fact of life, and we must learn to deal with them, not destroy them.

The specific manner in which government, at home and abroad, has attempted to minimize past MNC abuses varies greatly. In all cases, however, increased regulatory pressures have and will ultimately impact on the range and quality of opportunities available to MNCs now and in the future. For example, many foreign governments have gone to great lengths to control them by either forcing part-ownership by the host country or taking over established operations. Other controls include taxes, profit repatriation regulations, and exchange controls. The goal of these measures is to keep the host nation strong or dominant in order to insure as high a level of reinvestment as possible into its economy. In light of these regulatory developments, MNCs contemplating foreign investment must be extremely cautious about the countries they choose to be involved in.

Although the United States government has moved to curb power of domestically-based MNCs, it has at the same time also provided protection to businesses operating abroad in such areas as expropriation and in the use of economic and military aid pressures to bring about equitable treatment.[22] In addition, government and corporate leaders are beginning to learn that business, diplomacy, and foreign affairs are becoming so interdependent that both parties are now striving to create a better and freer flow of information and assistance.[23] The rationale for this kind of cooperation is the government belief that a number of actions favorable to the national interest can be brought out through the conduct of business by United States firms in foreign countries. Among the benefits cited are: (1) the businesses can demonstrate the superiority of United States technology; (2) these large firms, through acting responsibly and assisting the host country, can show democracy in action; and (3) these firms can foster better understanding and cooperation between countries.

A further indication of the efforts of United States government to constructively assist business is the formulation of a code of conduct for international dealings. This code of conduct not only spells out the government's position with respect to the overseas behavior of United States firms but also that of the host countries. The code includes:

1. Follow principles of good business practice
2. Be voluntary rather than mandatory in dealings with host governments
3. Governments should be nondiscriminatory toward foreigners in their country
4. Acknowledge principles of international law
5. Both business and government must respect contractual agreements made between them[24]

In summary, the present can be characterized as a time of high growth in the dollar values of investment and trade between all nations of the world.

The multinational corporation has served as a major impetus to this growth. However, fear of the economic and social pervasiveness of these giants has also put many nations of the world on the defense and has resulted in the institution of cartels, stringent laws, and other restrictive practices. Although nations are apprehensive of MNCs, and vice-versa, the growth continues, since MNCs continue to meet the demands of a highly interdependent world economy. Although environmental forces are rapidly changing, the world market is a large, profitable, and growing one. It is apparent multinationals will continue to exploit, albeit more cautiously, overseas opportunities. The simple fact remains that the MNCs need markets and resources, and the developing nations need technology and the financial assets these corporations provide.

New Challenges

The biggest challenge posed by the changing environment is one of addressing the inherent uncertainties created for decision makers. How can the multinational corporation operate when policies are in a state of flux at home and vary so widely among the many nations they deal with abroad? Several alternatives for confronting these challenges are outlined below. Basically, a company should strive to be a good citizen in the eyes of the host government and the general public. First, with respect to the dangers of takeover, the MNC has a number of strategies it can employ. Perhaps the best way to avoid or delay problems is to pursue corporate policies that are beneficial to the host country. Among the activities that should be considered are the employment and training of as many local people as possible and ensuring their advancement in the company. The purchasing of as much raw material and support supplies as possible also enhances good relations. Similarly, the promotion of export activity to create a balance of payments surplus would be positively received. Another move would be to enter into government and local ownership arrangements that involve the host in the decision-making process. Although these methods are not foolproof nor do they exhaust the list of possible alternatives, they have been effectively employed by a number of firms.

Second, a corporation should avoid being politically active in a foreign country, the reason being that public disclosure of such activity would place the firm in the middle of domestic affairs issues in which it would most surely end up a loser in the long run. There is enough recent evidence of bribes, campaign fund violations, and other practices to suggest that the risks of this type of company involvement far outweigh the potential benefits. Staying out of politics, however, does not mean the corporation should avoid actively developing favorable ties with governments. Efforts to foster open communications and a willingness to cooperate in the achievement of government goals or to assist in solving national problems would be steps in the right direction. Thus, if a detrimental piece of regulation is passed, the likelihood that the company and government officials could sit down and satisfactorily resolve any associated problems would be substantially raised.

Third, beyond the "good citizen" concepts cited above, the firm can attempt to make expropriation difficult by a variety of methods. The corporation can attempt to keep the level of technology so high and changing that the foreign government would not have the ability to run the operation economically. Or, if the host country did take it over, the future advances in technology would quickly pass them by and they would in a very short time lose their competitive advantages. In addition, the multinational corporation can attempt to make the foreign country operation so interwoven with the entire corporation that it cannot be removed from the parent and still function properly. This can be accomplished by the tying of management, supplies and natural resources, research and development, and technology to the parent organization. Although this approach has its merits, the very action of tying up the foreign operation in this way could provoke the host country into establishing stricter controls to protect its own interests. Thus, "tying up" should be undertaken within prudent limits in such a manner that the host government does not feel its interests are placed in jeopardy.

Fourth, the company can establish short- and long-term legal contracts with the host government as to rights, ownership, and taxes. This is perhaps the best preventative approach available, since it is the most explicit and least likely to result in misunderstandings. However, there is the risk of the country breaking the contracts, especially if a new government comes into power. The other problem with this approach is that it is based to a great extent on a mutual trust, which in many instances is lacking.

Finally, there are also various insurance coverages to protect against financial losses that can be purchased to cover war expropriation and other causes. The Agency for International Development (AID) provides insurance coverage of 200 percent of the value of the investment for companies owned predominantly by Americans in nations where the United States has special bilateral agreements. Firms can also obtain insurance for investments from other sources, such as the Overseas Private Investment Corporation (OPIC) and the Export Import Bank. In the event that a corporations's operation is taken over by the host nation, there are some legal avenues through various forums available. These include the use of existing treaties, international laws, and courts in the nation involved. In addition, the corporation can go to the World Bank Center for International Investment Disputes. As a last resort, a firm can ask the United States government to step in on its behalf if the business is owned by Americans in the "Espousal" process. When this is done, the government of the United States acts as the corporation's bargaining agent, and the corporation gives up all rights in an effort to get compensation and/or keep control of the enterprise.

The United States government can assist the multinational corporation in meeting its challenges in other ways as well. For example, the government can provide a great deal of technical information about a country's politics, resources, people, languages, and problems through its embassies and internal contacts, thus saving the corporation much time and money. Also, if the government provides solid backing against takeover by using its leverage in economic and military aid, the risks of takeover may go down to some extent, as countries will think twice about losses in aid and assistance that their actions could precipitate.

Finally, to stop the criticisms of many who point out the evils of the multinationals, the MNCs should mount their own public relations campaigns to show the public at home and abroad the good things they do, such as building schools, hospitals, and creating and training productive workers overseas. At home, they can point to cheaper imports, more products available, and the need to go worldwide for many resources that are not currently available in domestic markets.

Thus, the challenges are great, but they can be met and overcome by responsible, reasonable, and properly thought out actions by the multinationals. These organizations have a large array of ways to protect themselves in meeting overseas challenges. Which may be the most effective way used alone, or in combination with others, will depend on the firm, country, and business involved.

Future Outlook—Importance of International Business

The future outlook of international business and the role of the MNC is very difficult to predict. Different sources have different perspectives so it is perhaps best to simply relate some of the more widely regarded positions and their implications for the future. Keegan perceives the years ahead of the multinational corporation to be quite prosperous. He speaks in terms of a world orientation with a growing symmetry of power between the United States multinationals and non-United States multinationals, global markets, economies of scale gains, and emerging interest in marketing among the socialist countries.[25] However, he seems to totally ignore the existence of the less developed countries who may resist the multinationals, or the governments of developed countries whose politics may possibly lead to reinstatement of trade barriers in the future for certain commodities. The formation of cartels, and energy and mineral shortages, may also lead to serious difficulties for MNCs.

One emerging possibility is the advent of Soviet Union and Eastern Europe multinational thrusts into markets in which they have not been active. The existence of Soviet or Eastern Bloc state-run multinationals exploiting the world market may become a competitive reality. Obviously this would throw much of the current predictions of growth and power completely astray, because those countries have been totally ignored in the forecasting process.[26] The potential future impact, particularly with regard to less developed nations, should be kept in mind as resource needs of all nations increase and the supplies dwindle.

Another factor to consider is the changing roles of many countries and the future effect on world demand and supply. Iran and the other oil giants have now become the creditors of all the world.[27] What they will do with their money is of vital importance to the multinational corporations. If they buy goods and keep money flowing, the corporations will gain sales through exploiting the many opportunities created. Conversely, if they hoard it, the multinationals stand to gain little.

Finally, for the first time in history, the conduct of economic and commercial affairs has attained the same stature as military and political considerations in the formulation of foreign policy.[28] As a consequence, the possibility of developing long-term peace between nations could be greatly enhanced if mutually rewarding economic agreements can be affected between governments and corporations. The successful attainment of closer relationships, by taking advantage of opportunities to stimulate equal growth, prosperity, and improved standards of living, would serve to reduce past differences. Perhaps in this way a closer and better world could slowly evolve. Of course, failure to understand the nature of this interdependency could ultimately lead to international instability and military confrontation. Thus, as the late Senator Hubert Humphrey observed, with the future potential for global peace being so closely intertwined with the pursuit of international marketing opportunity, extreme caution should be exercised in the approach taken by MNC and host government alike.[29]

Strategic Implications

Now that the historical, present, future, and changes in the international environment of the multinational corporations have been explored, the question arises as to what strategies should be taken to chart the waters of an uncertain future.

The most important strategy is to formulate programs with greater flexibility. The days of the multinationals dictating terms, running the operation, and taking out exorbitant returns on their investments with little concern for the impact on the host nation are gone forever. All countries, regardless of their stage of development, have become keenly aware of the economic world around them and are not likely to accept arrangements characteristic of the past. Multinational corporations must be prepared for long, hard negotiations, often under disadvantageous conditions, and must be ready to make numerous concessions if they expect to gain access to foreign opportunities. Beyond gaining access, they must be prepared to actively contribute in ways never before imagined to the growth and prosperity of the host nation's citizenry. If the multinational attempts to do less than expected, the results will most likely be expulsion of the corporation and nationalization of its assets.

In addition, the multinational should be tolerant of and sensitive to the policies and desires of its own country. It is apparent that the home government can offer a great deal of aid to the multinationals in the form of technical and research data as well as insurance against the dangers of expropriation. Thus, the multinational should strive to undertake policies and strategies that are acceptable to its home government. The knowledge that a home government is supportive and protective of its MNCs will further enhance their position in dealing with foreign governments. To attain this end, the multinational corporation should also attempt to enhance its image at home and abroad by educating the public on the positive aspects of its activities.

Finally, MNCs must continue to grow and expand in the world and keep themselves competitive with multinationals of other nations. It is obvious that resource scarcities are here to stay so it will be the responsibility of the multinationals to use their financial strength and technical ability to undertake the exploration necessary to meet the demands of the world. It is vital that they follow a growth and development strategy to locate and extract resources cheaply enough to meet worldwide consumer and industrial needs.

In conclusion, the multinationals must develop strategies that stimulate their growth and competitiveness while at the same time stem public apprehension about the misuse of their inherent power. This is no easy task, but it must be done. The growth role of government will force MNCs to temper the strategies for the public good. Obviously, MNC and public objectives will often conflict, but the ultimate search is for the optimal strategic blend. Perhaps flexibility and constant change of individual strategies is the approach that will prevail rather than unwavering commitment to any one long-term strategy.

NOTES

1. Sanford Rose, "Why the Multinational Tide is Ebbing," *Fortune* August, 1977, p. 112.

2. *Seven Surprising Facts About Exporting* (Washington, D.C.: U.S. Department of Commerce, Bureau of International Commerce, 1977), p. 1.

3. *Ibid.*

4. Ernest Dichter, "The World Customer," *Harvard Business Review* July–August, 1962, p. 116.

5. "Translations Can be Tricky," *Sales Management* October 2, 1964, p. 40.

6. Richard D. Robinson, "The Challenge of the Underdeveloped National Market," *Journal of Marketing* October, 1961, pp. 24–25.

7. "48 Management Checklists for Foreign Operations," *Business International* January, 1964, p. 8.

8. Philip R. Cateora and John M. Hess, *International Marketing* (Homewood, Illinois: Richard D. Irwin, Inc., 1975), p. 176.

9. Walt W. Rostow, *The Stages of Economic Growth* (London: Cambridge University Press, 1960), p. 10.

10. *World Tables* (Baltimore, MD.: University of Baltimore Press, 1977), pp. 524–527.

11. D.A. Snider, *Introduction to International Economics* (Homewood, Illinois: Richard D. Irwin, Inc., 1970), pp. 166–170.

12. "Testimony of U.S. Secretary of Commerce Before House Ways and Means Committee in 1957," in *U.S. Government and Common Market* (New York, N.Y.: F.A. Praeger, Inc., 1962), p. 38.

13. D.A. Snider, *op. cit.,* p. 163.

14. *International Economic Report of the President to Congress* (Washington, D.C.: U.S. Government Printing Office, 1976, pp. 26–27.

15. J. Irwin Miller, "Future of the Multinationals," *The Management of International Corporate Citizenship* September, 1976, p. 4.

16. Department of Economics and Social Affairs, *MNC in World Development* (New York, N.Y.: United Nations, 1973), p. 13.

17. *International Economic Report of the President to Congress, op. cit.,* p. 111.

18. "A New Partnership Between Businessmen and Diplomats: They're Working Toward the Same Goals," *Nations Business* September, 1974, pp. 74–75.

19. Department of Economics and Social Affairs, *op. cit.,* p. 187.

20. *Ibid,* p. 193.

21. R.J. Barnet and R.E. Muller, *Global Reach* (New York, N.Y.: Simon and Schuster, 1974), p. 38.

22. *International Economic Report of the President to Congress, op. cit.,* pp. 80–83.

23. "A New Partnership Between Businessmen and Diplomats: They're Working Toward the Same Goals," *op. cit.*

24. *International Economic Report of the President to Congress, op. cit.*

25. Warren J. Keegan, *Multinational Marketing Management* (Englewood Cliffs, N.J.: Prentice-Hall, Inc., 1974), pp. 547–550.

26. Raymond Vernon, "The Multinationals," *Foreign Affairs* January, 1977, p. 254.

27. G. Hauge, "Preface to a Conclusion—World Trade," *Vital Speeches,* December 15, 1974, p. 145.

28. G.E. Bradley, "U.S. Government Business Cooperation—The Phenomenon of U.S. Business Operating Internationally," *Vital Speeches* March 1, 1977, p. 312.

29. H.H. Humphrey, "International Trade—A Summit Conference," *Vital Speeches* February 1, 1973, pp. 235–239.

NATURE OF INTERNATIONAL MARKETING

With advancements in communications and transportation technology the world has truly become a highly interdependent international marketplace. The tremendous explosion witnessed in international trade has created new opportunities and difficult challenges for contemporary marketing managers. The articles contained in this section have been selected to provide an overview on the nature of these challenges and how marketers have formulated strategies to tap attractive international markets. The first article, by Keegan, addresses the need to develop a conceptual framework for formulating multinational marketing strategy. Three basic dimensions differentiating multinational from domestic marketing are described and the implications for international marketing decision making explored. The recent growth of multinational corporations has greatly influenced the way marketers have operated abroad. The very success of these corporate giants in implementing marketing strategies has led to a wave of world-wide criticism. The second selection in this section represents a recent effort of the United Nations to report on the patterns of multinational activity abroad. An interesting contrast on the impact of MNCs across advanced, developing, and centrally planned economies is a major feature of this United Nations survey. The central theme developed by C.P. Rao's article is that industrial marketers are every bit as susceptible to the pitfalls inherent in exporting to foreign markets as are consumer products companies. The specific problems encountered by United States firms in the past, and guidelines for the development of international marketing strategies, are offered. The next article clearly illustrates

46893

through statistical data the importance of overseas involvement to United States firms. The study conducted by Booz, Allen, and Hamilton describes the pattern of concentration of United States investment as well as the modes of entry most commonly practiced. The section concludes with an interesting historical perspective, presented by Richard Wendel, on the conceptual underpinnings of international trade. The author also speculates on what the future of international marketing will bring in terms of new opportunities and new methods of operating abroad.

The growing involvement in international marketing has resulted in a greater need for conceptual frameworks to guide practice and programs. This article looks at the nature of multinational marketing in terms of its similarities and differences with domestic marketing. The transferability of marketing concepts across international boundaries is studied in depth.

1.   A Conceptual Framework for Multinational Marketing

Warren J. Keegan
George Washington University

A leading international businessman recently observed, "There is no such thing as a multinational market. We have domestic markets worldwide but no multinational markets. There are, to be exact, 142 national markets worldwide. Each one of these markets is unique in the sense that it is not exactly like any other market, and therefore each is a domestic market. Yet, any company which is marketing simultaneously in two or more national markets is involved in a process of international or multinational marketing."

The growing involvement in international marketing has created a need for a conceptual framework to guide practice and programs. What is multinational marketing? What dimensions, if any, distinguish multination marketing from domestic marketing? How should marketers conceptualize the task of multinational marketing?

There are similarities and differences in all markets, domestic and foreign, but the concepts of marketing science are universally applicable. Basic

Source: Reprinted with permission from the November–December, 1972 issue of the *Columbia Journal of World Business.* Copyright © 1972 by the Trustees of Columbia University in the city of New York.

marketing concepts such as the product life cycle and traditional marketing tools such as market segmentation are as applicable in Athens, Greece as they are in Athens, Georgia.

There are three basic dimensions of multinational marketing which differentiate it from domestic marketing. The first is environmental. Unlike his domestic counterpart a multinational marketer must respond to many different national market environments. At the beginning of a company's international involvement, activities outside the home-country market are referred to as "foreign" marketing and require the management of the same activities as domestic marketing, but in an unfamiliar national environment.

One company's foreign market is, of course, another company's home or base environment. France is a foreign market to a United States manufacturer who has never operated there, but it is the home market for all French-based manufacturers. To a United States company with operations in France, the country may be simultaneously a "foreign" market to the United States headquarters and "domestic" market for the company's French subsidiary. Over time, the United States company with operations in France may cease to think of France as a foreign market and consider it one of the company's market areas, no more "foreign" than an area in the United States. This occurs when French operations become truly integrated into the corporate operating structure, and the company has shifted in orientation from the binary domestic-foreign market concept set for operating markets to a unitary definition of operating markets in which they are all considered simply as "operating" markets. In such a company, "foreign" markets would simply be considered as markets in which the company has not yet established operations.

In a growing number of companies the concept of "foreign" is breaking down because of the growing involvement of the corporate headquarters in the company's marketing programs wherever they are located. ITT, for example, has product and functional specialists at headquarters who are responsible for marketing operations on a global basis. To these specialists, and to the president of ITT, there is no such thing as a "foreign" market in the psychological sense—there are markets in different parts of the world, at different stages of development, with different characteristics. Company operating units exist in each of these markets, and these units are expected to understand their own markets in depth. ITT knows as much about the French market for telecommunications equipment as it knows about the United States market.

A second dimension of multinational marketing that differentiates it from domestic marketing is the process of crossing national boundaries with a product, a price, or some aspect of an advertising, promotion or selling program. Crossing boundaries of sovereign nations requires passing through national controls that apply to goods and services. Some of these controls, such as tariffs and quotas, apply only to certain foreign-sourced goods.

Others, such as safety regulations, apply to all goods regardless of origin. These terms of entry apply not only to products, but frequently to prices, advertising and other aspects of a marketing program. A multinational marketer must know what these terms are in each national market and incorporate them as parameters of his international marketing plan.

The third dimension of multinational marketing arises because a company markets its products simultaneously in more than one national environment. This results in issues and opportunities which are distinct from those associated with the crossing of national boundaries. A multinational marketer must evaluate and compare respective national market opportunities. He must decide who should perform marketing functions in the organization. For example, to what extent should marketing planning and control be autonomously performed by subsidiary management groups? To what extent should headquarters be involved in country marketing analysis, planning and control? To what extent should control and delivery of marketing services, such as marketing research and advertising creative work and management, rest at headquarters? To what extent can lessons gained in one market be applied in other national markets? To what extent can practices and techniques be applied across national boundaries? To what extent should products, prices, advertising, etc. be standardized to achieve global optimization of net profits? These are just a few of the questions raised when a company seeks to relate its activities in multiple nations to each other in ways that enhance the effectiveness of each national marketing program and the effectiveness of the total world marketing effort. Without a conceptual framework answers are difficult, if not impossible.

The major factors that constitute the environment of global marketing are depicted in Exhibit 1-1. At the center of the diagram is the company, defined in four major dimensions: its products, its marketing skills (particularly the marketing skills of product, communications, distribution, pricing and marketing research management), other skills (production, R&D, financial and managerial skills), and its resources (manpower, financial and physical).

The company's products, skills and resources are the endogenous factors in the conceptual framework. The most important of these is the product(s) that a company offers in international markets. One useful way of looking at products internationally is to place them on a continuum of environmental sensitivity. At one end of the continuum are the environmentally insensitive products, that is products that do not require adaptation to differences in the economic and social environments of markets around the world. Typically, such products are industrial and are adapted to universal rather than local technology. A company with environmentally insensitive products will have to spend relatively little time finding out about the specific and unique conditions of local markets, since the product the company offers is basically universal. A computer line is an example of a relatively environmentally insensitive product.

EXHIBIT 1–1
THE COMPANY IN A WORLD OF CLUSTERS OF NATIONAL
MARKET ENVIRONMENTS

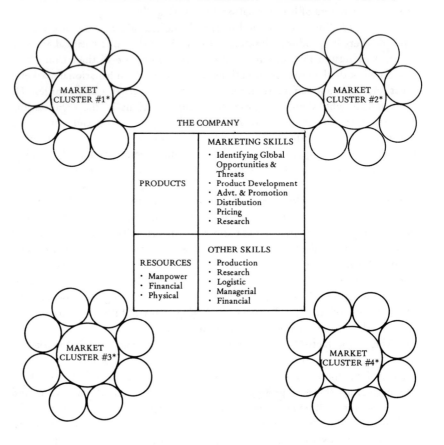

*Note: The number of market clusters shown here is arbitrary. In any specific situation, the number of clusters used for operating and analytical purposes will depend on the characteristics of the markets and the operating strategy of the company.

The objective in forming clusters is to maximize the within-cluster similarity of markets and the between-cluster differences on specific and weighted characteristics. These typically include such characteristics as location, income levels, market size, channel structure, language, communications infrastructure, etc. Each company must identify characteristics that are crucial to its own market success and weigh these characteristics. The weights of characteristics may be different in clustering markets for operating purposes as opposed to analytical purposes. For example, for operating clusters, distance and proximity may be the most important market characteristics because of a need to minimize transportation and communications costs. In the same company, clusters developed for analytical purposes might ignore distance and proximity.

At the other end of the continuum are those products that are highly sensitive to differences in economic, social and cultural, physical and governmental factors in national markets. The company in the business of marketing environmentally sensitive products will have to spend a great deal of time and effort to learn how its products interact with the environment of specific national markets. Convenience foods are an example of relatively environmentally sensitive products.

Skills are a second major category of endogenous resource. A primary skill of a multinational marketer is the ability to identify local opportunities and threats. When a company is entering international markets for the first time, the development of this skill is a first requirement. Since there are 142 different national markets, it is rarely feasible to study each of them in depth. In practice, a company must develop criteria for screening national markets in order to select those that present the greatest opportunity. As a company grows internationlly, an additional dimension arises: how best to allocate resources among existing markets.

Evaluating opportunities is not just a simple matter of finding the biggest existing market. Demand, competition, and the degree of market difference from known markets are each important considerations. The first step in evaluating local opportunities is demand analysis. Two types of demand must be considered:

Existing Demand   This is the actual current sales in a market. This consists of local production plus imports minus exports. Although such data are often lacking, various estimating techniques can be used.

Latent Demand   This is demand that would exist if a desired product was offered at an acceptable price. In the United States latent demand has historically been tapped by new product developments, such as the Polaroid Land camera. The demand for instant photography already existed before this product was introduced.

The international company has a unique opportunity to tap latent demand by taking a product it has marketed in one or more nations and introducing it to other national markets where the product has not previously been sold. If it chooses markets with enough similarity to those where it already has experience, it can apply that experience to the new market. Instead of marketing an entirely new product, the company is marketing a new international product. Skillfully done, this can substantially improve the chances of success as compared to those of new product introductions in a domestic market.

Demand levels of a product must be evaluated in the light of expected competition. The difficult choice is between large, often fast-growing competitive markets where the major challenge is the existing competition vs. smaller, less competitive markets. This is a strategic issue that must be resolved in the light of each company's appraisal of its best relative opportunity.

Another factor involved in the choice of new foreign markets is the degree of similarity existing between them and already-known markets. The greater the similarity to known markets, the less there is to learn and the more applicable is previous experience. One of the reasons United States companies frequently begin their international market expansion in Canada and the United Kingdom is that these markets exhibit many characteristics in common with the United States market, not the least of which are language and the legal system.

In the end, a company must compare opportunities and threats involved in global expansion of markets to its own capabilities and decide on whether to expand; and if so, upon a sequence of national markets entry. It must back this decision with a commitment of resources (people, money and facilities), the third endogenous factor in the conceptual framework.

Irrespective of the general nature of opportunities and threats, a company must have the skills to formulate successful marketing programs in each national market selected. Most companies find it necessary to assemble a national marketing staff as a part of each national subsidiary. These staffs are a major marketing resource of a global company.

The company exists in a world of 142 different national market environments. Each of these environments is unique. Yet each contains elements of commonality and similarity. The task of the multinational marketer is to recognize both similarities and differences. He can then respond to the unique dimensions of each market and still effectively transfer his marketing know-how to develop effective marketing programs. As a multinational organization develops, the transfer of know-how should shift first from a home-country to subsidiary pattern; then to an organic flow from within the multinational-country system. Regardless of the country of location, know-how and experience with potential applications elsewhere in the world should be exploited.

To break down the complexity of managing and co-ordinating large numbers of foreign subsidiaries, international managers have often adopted regional groupings that cluster countries exhibiting within-group similarities and between-group differences. The major dimension used has been physical proximity. Typical regional groupings would be the Americas, Europe, Asia and Africa, each combining countries that are reasonably similar in terms of broad environmental dimensions. Such regional groupings reduce the time and money costs of travel for the personnel involved.

These geographic groups, however, may be less useful for analytic purposes than groups or clusters based on other environmental dimensions. The marketer may find it more useful to cluster countries on the basis of market development as indicated by various economic, market and social measures. The clusters developed will depend upon the technique, the dimensions used and the weight assigned to each dimension. If stage-of-market development is specified as a major dimension, then the country clusters in Exhibit 1–1 would be based upon income. This would result in clusters of the respective high-, middle- and low-income countries of Europe, Asia, Africa and the Americas rather than geographic clusters.

Seven major dimensions of each national market environment are shown in Exhibit 1-2. These dimensions provide the exogenous influences or dimensions of a conceptual framework. Each of the dimensions is highly diverse from one part of the world to another. Stage-of-market development, for example, may be measured by per-capita GNP, which ranges from a low of $60 per annum in several African countries to the high in the United States of over $4,000. However, within this wide range of global per-capita GNP, there are clusters of countries at the bottom, in the middle and at the top which are sufficiently similar to provide a unifying influence.

Another important market characteristic is size as measured by total national income. The United States market, with over a trillion dollars in annual income, is enormous. Other industrialized countries with incomes on a per-capita basis quite similar or close to those in the United States are relatively small in the aggregate. A good example would be Sweden, whose per-capita GNP in 1969 was $3,553, but whose GNP was only $28 billion. At these extremes, the size of markets is a highly differentiating influence. The structure, information system and control system appropriate for the Swedish marketing organization would be grossly inadequate for an organization which obtains a comparable share of the United States market. A company that is simultaneously marketing in large and small markets cannot adopt a unified approach to both. If it did, it would find itself with organizations, information systems and control systems that were either inadequate or too elaborate for the size of the market.

Marketing facilities are highly varied. Television, for example, is unavailable in some markets such as South Africa, but it is the major advertising medium in Latin America. Food retailing is mainly via supermarkets in highly developed markets, but such outlets hardly exist in less-developed countries.

The legal environment, including tariffs, taxes, laws, regulations and codes, differs greatly from country to country. For example, companies marketing equipment used in the construction and building trades must face a welter of codes and regulations that differ not only internationally but also within local political jurisdictions. The purposes sought by these regulations is not always a reliable guide to appropriate action. Consider, for example, the situation of a crane manufacturer. In many countries cranes must have a free-fall capability for instantly releasing their load in order to make the cranes safer. A crane with the capability of a free-fall displacement of its load is difficult to tip over. In other countries, however, there is a requirement that a crane *not* have a free-fall capability. This prohibition against free fall is also motivated by a desire to increase the safety of the crane operation. The rationale behind the prohibition of free-fall capability is that any crane with

EXHIBIT 1-2

MAJOR DIMENSIONS OF A NATIONAL MARKET ENVIRONMENT: ABSOLUTE AND COMPARED TO OTHER NATIONS

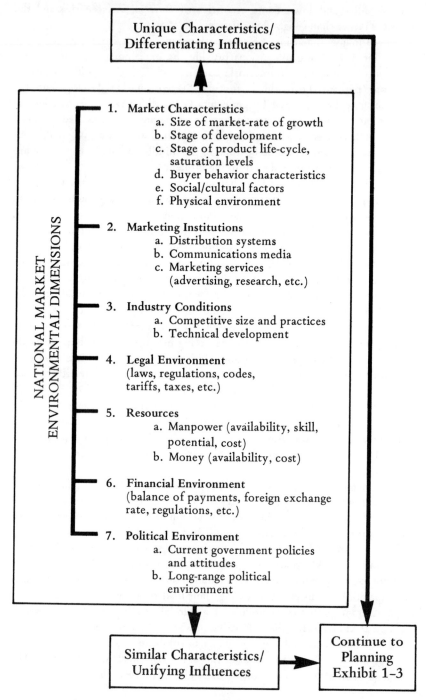

Unique Characteristics/
Differentiating Influences

NATIONAL MARKET ENVIRONMENTAL DIMENSIONS

1. **Market Characteristics**
   a. Size of market-rate of growth
   b. Stage of development
   c. Stage of product life-cycle, saturation levels
   d. Buyer behavior characteristics
   e. Social/cultural factors
   f. Physical environment

2. **Marketing Institutions**
   a. Distribution systems
   b. Communications media
   c. Marketing services (advertising, research, etc.)

3. **Industry Conditions**
   a. Competitive size and practices
   b. Technical development

4. **Legal Environment** (laws, regulations, codes, tariffs, taxes, etc.)

5. **Resources**
   a. Manpower (availability, skill, potential, cost)
   b. Money (availability, cost)

6. **Financial Environment** (balance of payments, foreign exchange rate, regulations, etc.)

7. **Political Environment**
   a. Current government policies and attitudes
   b. Long-range political environment

Similar Characteristics/
Unifying Influences

Continue to
Planning
Exhibit 1-3

this captability is liable to lose its entire load accidentally and thereby cause an accident. Hence, any company that wishes to market this product internationally must be able to offer both types of crane—those with a free-fall capacity and those without.

Each of the seven major dimensions of the national market environments shown in Exhibit 1–2 should be analyzed and evaluated in the process of formulating a local marketing plan for each national market. At the same time, the multinational marketer must evaluate each of the dimensions of the local market environment in relationship to the rest of the world and in its relationship to a cluster of markets. The analysis should focus on the unique characteristics of the market that differentiate it from other national markets and the characteristics which it has in common with other national markets.[1] This environmental analysis of differentiating and unifying influences is the basis of a multinational marketing plan that integrates each national marketing plan into an over-all multinational marketing strategy.

The objective of multinational marketing strategy is to optimize the utilization of company products, skills and resources on a global basis as opposed to national optimization, which results in a global sub-optimization.[2]

Perceptive response to the unique characteristics of each national market is the major task of the local staff of each country subsidiary. This marketing group must do what domestic marketers do throughout the world—analyze their marketing environment and subsidiary capabilities and identify products and services that can be sold at a profit. Since the subsidiary is part of a multinational system, a major potential source of subsidiary capability lies in the ability of the subsidiary to tap the products, skills and resources of its parent and of other subsidiaries in the system. The subsidiary shares with headquarters responsibility for searching for applicable products, skills and resources.

Headquarters marketers bear the major responsibility in a multinational system to search for similar characteristics and unifying influences that provide opportunities to standardize elements of the global marketing program. There are major benefits of standardization, including cost savings in product development and manufacture, in packaging and in advertising and promotional programs. Another major advantage of identifying unifying features is the possibility of exploiting good ideas and people on a global basis.[3]

One writer calls this "leverage."[4] There are three leverage opportunities for multinational marketers:

Program transfers   Multinational marketers can draw upon strategies, products, advertising appeals, sales management practices and promotional ideas that have been tested in several markets and apply them in comparable markets on a global basis. To the extent that a multinational company becomes successful in drawing upon its international experience in marketing programs it has an advantage over the purely domestic company, which draws upon its experience in only a single market.

EXHIBIT 1-3
THE MULTINATIONAL MARKET MANAGEMENT PROCESS

Key Questions for Analysis, Planning, and Control of Global Marketing

ENVIRONMENTAL ANALYSIS
of
NATIONAL MARKETS
(See Figure 1-2 for detail
of Environmental
Dimensions)

Environmental Analysis

1. What are the unique characteristics (see Figure 1-2 for characteristics) of each national market? What characteristics does each market have in common with other national markets?
2. Can we cluster national markets for operating and/or planning purposes? What dimensions of markets should we use to cluster markets?

STRATEGIC
PLANNING

Strategic Planning

3. Who should be involved in marketing decisions?
4. What are our major assumptions about target markets? Are they valid?
5. What needs are satisfied by our products in target markets?
6. What customer benefits are provided by our product in target markets?
7. What are the conditions under which our products are used in the target markets?
8. How large is the ability to buy our products in target markets?
9. What are our major strengths and weaknesses relative to existing and potential competition in target markets?
10. Should we extend, adapt, or invent products, prices, advertising, and promotion programs for target markets?
11. What is the balance-of-payments and currency situation in target markets? Will we be able to remit earnings? Is the political climate acceptable?
12. What are our objectives given the alternatives open to us and our assessment of opportunity, risk, and company capability?

STRUCTURE

Structure

13. How do we structure our organization to optimally achieve our objectives, given our skills and resources? What is the responsibility of each organizational level?

OPERATIONAL
PLANNING

Operational Planning

14. Given our objectives, structure, and our assessment of the market environment, how do we implement effective operational marketing plans? What products will we market, at what prices, through what channels, with what communications, in which markets and market clusters?

CONTROLLING THE
MARKETING PROBLEM

Controlling The Marketing Program

15. How do we measure and monitor plan performance? What steps should be taken to ensure that marketing objectives are met?

System transfers   Again, to the extent that multinational marketers can identify similar characteristics in national markets they can use planning, budgeting and other successful marketing systems previously developed and tested in national markets.

People transfers   As marketers in multinational companies acquire the expertise required to identify the potentials and risks of national markets throughout the world it becomes increasingly possible to assign skilled marketing people across national boundaries. A manpower pool with international rather than national dimensions is thus available.

To exploit leverage opportunities the global company marketing staff must necessarily work together. Each marketing staff group in the global company reports to a line manager responsible for a country, region, international division or the entire corporation. At the same time, there is a dotted line relationship symbolizing coordination and involvement of marketing at all levels in the organization. A major purpose of this multilevel coordination and involvement is to identify leverage opportunities. In addition, this coordination insures that marketing analysis is worldwide and not divided into unrelated national assessments.

The endogenous and exogenous elements of this conceptual framework are related in Exhibit 1-3 to a suggested process of marketing analysis, planning and control. Key questions for each step of this process are suggested. The sequence consists of environmental analysis and company analysis leading to a strategic decision regarding marketing objectives and resources (people, money and facilities) that will be committed. These strategic decisions must then be expressed in operational plans, and the whole organization must be structured to fit their requirements. Finally, auditing and marketing control is necessary to insure that actual and desired results are as close together as possible.

Multinational marketing management is one of the most dynamic areas in marketing today as the multinational corporations continue to extend their operations to the far corners of the world. The conceptual framework proposed relates the company to the global market environment and suggests a process for developing and implementing a global marketing plan.

QUESTIONS

1. What does the author identify as the three basic dimensions of multinational marketing?
2. What factors are involved in determining the author's concept of a market cluster?
3. Distinguish between latent and existing demand. What special opportunities with respect to latent demand exist for international marketers?
4. What is meant by the term "leverage" in multinational market opportunities?

NOTES

1. See John Fayerweather, *International Business Management*, New York: McGraw Hill, 1969.

2. It can be demonstrated that in any system of interdependent parts, the optimization of sub-systems makes it impossible to optimize the total system and, conversely, the optimization of the total system precludes the systematic optimization of sub-systems. See Russell L. Ackoff, *A Concept of Corporate Planning,* New York: Wiley Interscience, 1970.

3. See, for example, Robert D. Buzzell, "Can You Standardize Multinational Marketing?," *Harvard Business Review* November–December 1968.

4. Ralph Z. Sorenson, Associate Professor of Marketing at the Harvard Business School, first suggested the concept of multinational marketing leverage. Professor Sorenson is currently completing a study entitled *Multinational Marketing Leverage: A Study of Multinational Marketing Transfers Within Non-Durable Consumer Goods Firms.*

Multinational corporations have recently become the target of critics worldwide. As a result, pressure has been placed on individual governments and international forums, such as the United Nations, to enact measures limiting their power. To better understand the issues underlying the movement towards greater regulation of multinationals an appreciation of their nature would be helpful. This article empirically describes the structure of multinational activity in world markets in terms of their size and concentration, geographic and industrial distribution, patterns of ownership, growth and importance to advanced, developing, and centrally-planned economies.

2. Dimensions of Multinational Corporations

United Nations Department of Economic and Social Affairs

Size and Concentration

Although quantitative information on multinational corporations leaves much to be desired and the wide disparities in methods of estimation among corporations, economic sectors and countries introduce a considerable margin of error in the interpretation of all the essential economic magnitudes, a few general characteristics are discernible. A central characteristic of multinational corporations is the predominance of large-size firms. Typically, the amount of annual sales runs into hundreds of millions of dollars. Each of the largest four multinational corporations has a sales volume in excess of $10 billion, and more than 200 multinational corporations have surpassed the one billion level.

Indeed, for most practical purposes, those with less than $100 million in

---

Source: Reprinted with permission from Multinational Corporations in World Development, document No. ST/ECA/140 and corr. 1, pp. 6–23, Department of Economic and Social Affairs, United Nations.

sales can safely be ignored.[1] The very size of these corporations as compared with other economic entities, including the economies of many nations, suggests an important source of power. Moreover, there are strong indications that the multinational corporations have grown dramatically, especially during the last decade. As a result, both their absolute and relative size has expanded.[2]

Closely related to their large size is the predominantly oligopolistic character of multinational corporations.[3] Typically, the markets in which they operate are dominated by a few sellers or buyers. Frequently they are also characterized by the importance of new technologies, or of special skills, or of product differentiation and heavy advertising, which sustains or reinforces their oligopolistic nature.

Another characteristic of the very large multinational corporations is their tendency to have a sizeable cluster of foreign branches and affiliates. Although almost half of some 7,300 multinational corporations have affiliates in one country only, nearly 200 multinational corporations, among the largest in the world, have affiliates in twenty or more countries. The establishment of subsidiaries or the making of foreign investments, particularly in industries in which there is a high degree of industrial concentration, generally tends to be bunched in periods of relatively strong economic activity. These activities frequently reflect the need to react to or counter the activities of other multinational corporations.

A further central characteristic of multinational corporations is that they are in general the product of developed countries. Although the non-availability of statistical information on multinational corporations in many developing countries obscures the over-all picture, this fact in itself reflects the high degree of concentration of the location of parent companies in the developed countries. Eight of the ten largest multinational corporations are based in the United States. All in all, the United States alone accounts for about a third of the total number of foreign affiliates, and together with the United Kingdom, the Federal Republic of Germany, and France, it accounts for over three-quarters of the total.

The high degree of concentration of the origin of multinational corporations in the developed countries is even more clearly revealed by the distribution of the stock of foreign direct investment as measured by estimated book value. Of a total estimated stock of foreign investment of about $165 billion, most of which is owned by multinational corporations, the United States accounts for more than half, and over four-fifths of the total is owned by four countries, the United States, the United Kingdom, France, and the Federal Republic of Germany.

Moreover, foreign direct investment tends to be concentrated in a few firms within each home country. For the United States, about 250 to 300 firms account for over 70 percent. For the United Kingdom, over 80 percent of the total is controlled by 165 firms. For the Federal Republic of Germany,

82 firms control over 70 percent and the nine largest foreign investors alone control 37 percent of the total. In the case of Japan, although there are some giant firms active abroad, many small firms appear to have participated in foreign investment activities.

The size of affiliates varies with the sector and area of operation. In the natural resources sector, for example, affiliates appear to be three to four times larger than in manufacturing. In the petroleum sector and in trade the average size of affiliates is somewhat larger in developing countries than in developed. In manufacturing, the size of affiliates in developing countries is only half that in developed, whereas in public utilities it is double.

Some changes in this pattern appear to have occurred over the last two decades. The size of United States affiliates in developed market economies doubled between 1950 and 1966. In the European Community the increase was almost threefold and in Japan more than fourfold. On the other hand, no change was recorded in the average size of United States affiliates in developing countries, except in Africa where the United States presence had previously been very limited. A similar trend suggests itself among United Kingdom affiliates, where an increase in average size in the developed market economies has not been matched by an increase in the size of affiliates in developing countries. The pattern reflects the fact that affiliates in developing countries often serve the local markets only, especially in the case of import-substituting manufactures, while the relatively larger affiliates in developed countries frequently serve bigger regional as well as national markets.

The dramatic growth of multinational corporations in the postwar period has been accompanied by unprecedented growth in the number of affiliates, the levels of capital flow and the stock of investment. Between 1950 and 1966, the number of United States affiliates increased three times, from 7,000 to 23,000. The number of affiliates of the 187 main United States multinational manufacturing corporations increased almost 3.5 times during the same period. The growth of United Kingdom affiliates during this period was less dramatic, possibly a reflection, among other factors, of the sluggish growth of the economy and the longer history in the United Kingdom of direct investment abroad. In the first twenty years after the Second World War, the number of affiliates less than doubled. In contrast, the more recent entry of Japan into the field has been marked by a rapid rate of growth in the number of affilitates. Although no precise data exists, there are indications that the growth of French affiliates was somewhat higher than those of the United Kingdom, while affiliates of the Federal Republic of Germany are growing more rapidly than those of the United States.

The growth of foreign affiliates has been accompanied by an increase in direct investment and the accumulated stock of foreign direct investment. During the last decade, the flow of direct investment from 13 countries of the Organization for Economic Co-operation and Development rose from

$2.9 billion to $7.9 billion a year. Among the countries with an above-average rate of increase were Japan, the Federal Republic of Germany, Italy, the Netherlands and the Scandinavian countries.

The growth of investment flow has been reflected in the increase in its cumulative stock. Between 1960 and 1971, the book value of United States direct investment increased from $33 to $86 billion and that of the United Kingdom from $12 to $24 billion. The most dramatic increase, from less than $300 million to approximately $4.5 billion, was registered by Japan—a fifteenfold rise. Recent indications show that this pace has continued if not accelerated. Almost equally impressive was the performance of the Federal Republic of Germany, which exhibited an almost tenfold increase of investment stock to $7.3 billion by 1971.

Geographical Distribution

Although the network of multinational corporations is world-wide, the bulk of their activities is located in the developed market economies.[4] Over two-thirds of the estimated book value of foreign direct investment is located in this area where the advanced economic level and similarities in institutional and social structures have facilitated the spread of the multinational corporate system.

Although the developing countries have received only about a third of the total estimated stock of foreign direct investment, that is, only half as much as the developed countries, the presence of foreign multinational corporations in the developing countries is generally of greater relative significance, since their economies account for much less than half of that of developed market economies.

Among the developing countries, the western hemisphere has attracted an estimated 18 percent of the total stock of foreign direct investment, Africa 6 percent, and Asia and the Middle East 5 and 3 percent respectively. The distribution of affiliates (links) is roughly similar. Country variations reveal certain special relationships between the multinational corporations of some developed market economies and countries of investment.

The corporations of some of the smaller European countries with no colonial experience, such as Austria, Switzerland and the Scandinavian countries, have a limited spread in the developing world. Faced apparently with a limited domestic market, and at times with trade barriers, corporations in these countries have invested in other developed countries with a view to enlarging the market for their products. On the other hand, the developing countries' share in the number of affiliates as well as the estimated stock of investment is relatively high for Portugal, France, the United Kingdom, Italy, Belgium and the Netherlands. This pattern of distribution reflects the importance of former colonial ties. Thus, two-thirds of the French and Belgian affiliates in developing countries are in Africa, most of them in French-speaking countries. The more balanced distribution of the network of affiliates and stock of investment of the United Kingdom parallels to a large extent the geographical spread of the Commonwealth. One-third of United Kingdom affiliates, for instance, are in developing countries, 40 percent of them in Africa and 32 percent in Asia. Of the total stock of United Kingdom direct investment, 38 percent is in developing countries and is similarly geographically diversified. Sixty percent of it is equally distributed between Asia and Africa, 26 percent is in the western hemisphere and 13 percent—above the average of 9.5 for all Development Assistant Committee countries—is in the Middle East. The Japanese presence in the development countries is also pronounced. Sixty percent of affiliates and investment stock is located in these countries, with a strong concentration in Central and South America and Asia. Central and South America is also the preferred region for affiliates as well as book value of investment in the case of the Federal Republic of Germany. Canada, in particular, and Switzerland also, shows a high concentration in the developing countries of the western hemisphere, while the Australian presence is felt almost exclusively in Asia.

A little more than one-quarter of United States affiliates and of the stock of direct investment is located in developing countries. Central and South America account for about 70 percent of the number of United States affiliates and of the book value of investment in developing countries, with the rest more or less equally distributed among Africa, Asia and the Middle East.

Further light can be shed on this distribution of foreign direct investment among developing areas and the pattern of relationships between home and host countries by examining the distribution of investment by industrial sector.

Distribution by Industry: Natural Resources and Manufacturing

Historically, the activity of multinational corporations developed in the extractive and public utility areas before it became prominent in manufacturing. By the turn of the century, European and North American investors, attempting to secure their markets in petroleum, a field in which oligopolistic conditions were soon formed, and extended their vertical integration from the source of the supply to marketing. The entrenched United Kingdom and French positions in the Middle East were successfully challenged by United States corporations. Cartel arrangements concluded between multinational corporations before the Second World War were weakened in later years as the discovery of rich new fields in various parts of the world, in developing countries especially, encouraged the entry of new corporations into the field and brought about a large degree of market interpenetration among the largest multinational corporations in petroleum.[5] As the technology of production has become standardized and patents have expired, national corporations in developing countries, operating independently or in joint ventures with foreign multinational corporations, have been moving increasingly towards downstream vertical integration.

Market interpenetration and partnership have diluted the prewar international cartels in other extractive industries also, but the growth of multinational corporations experienced in the petroleum sector has not been matched by most metal industries. Where technology, economies of scale and market control by the multinational corporations do not constitute formidable barriers, and the geographical distribution of the raw material source is limited, as in the case of copper, host countries have at times succeeded in increasing their participation or even wresting control from foreign multinational corporations. In other industries, such as aluminium, where not all these conditions are present, multinational corporations continue to play a primary role.

Manufacturing activities abroad, on the other hand, appeared later than operations in natural resources, either as the processing of raw materials or as the production of consumer goods. It appears that, initially, manufacturing operations increased faster in developed countries, later in developing countries and in the last ten years their growth has again been more dynamic in developed countries, especially in western Europe. Industrial sectors involving high technical skills have witnessed the fastest growth.

Manufacturing is at present the major activity of multinational corporations. It represents a little more than 40 percent of the total estimated stock of foreign direct investment of the main developed market economies. Petroleum accounts for 29 percent, mining and smelting for 7 percent and other industries for 24 percent. A similar picture emerges from the distribution of United States affiliates among industrial sectors.

There is an asymmetry in the industrial distribution of multinational corporation activities in developed and developing countries. Whereas in developing countries half of the estimated stock of investment is in extractive industries and a little more than a quarter in manufacturing, in developed market economies half of it is in manufacturing, and about 30 percent is in extractive industries.[6]

Within a particular industrial sector, pronounced concentration in a few home countries is evident. Four-fifths of the estimated stock of investment in petroleum and in manufacturing originates in the United States and the United Kingdom.

Significant variations exist among major investing countries in the distribution of the stock of investment by sector. Although the largest investing countries, namely the United States and the United Kingdom, have a similar pattern in industrial distribution (one-third in extractive industries and 40 percent in manufacturing) both Japan and the Federal Republic of Germany show a different pattern of concentration; the former in trade and extractive industries, the latter in manufacturing. Japan's foreign direct investment appears to be aimed at securing raw material sources and export markets for the parent corporations. Even its investment in manufacturing (one-quarter of the total) is relatively heavily concentrated in lightly processed raw materials such as lumber and pulp and low technology industries such as textiles and steel and nonferrous metals. In contrast to the Japanese structure, almost 80 percent of the foreign direct investment of the Federal Republic of Germany is in manufacturing and high technology products such as chemicals, electrical products and transport equipment. When compared with the dominant position of the United States and the United Kingdom in petroleum, the Federal Republic of Germany's investment in this area is almost negligible (3 percent in petroleum and 5 percent in mining).[7]

Concentration in high technology industries is also a characteristic of United States investment and to a lesser extent that of the United Kingdom. Chemicals, machinery, electrical products and transport equipment account for half of all the manufacturing investment of the United Kingdom and almost 60 percent of that of the United States. The technological strength of United States multinational corporations in the major chemical and automotive industries has given that country a dominant position in these fields. Much of the expansion of United States manufacturing affiliates abroad has been in the production of "skill-oriented" products, in which research and development is relatively a high percentage of sales and where an oligopolistic structure is prevalent.[8]

Multinational corporations have also been active recently in the service sector, especially in banking, tourism and consulting. Banking in particular has grown spectacularly in recent years. Between 1965 and 1972, United States banks more than tripled their foreign locations from 303 to 1,009. In 1972 alone, United States banks opened 106 foreign locations (i.e., branches, representative offices and agencies, affiliates and subsidiaries) while in the same year Japanese banks opened 25 new facilities, bringing the total to 145. The total number of foreign facilities of United Kingdom banks in 1972 amounted to 192, those of the Federal Republic of Germany to 103 and those of France to 91.[9] Foreign deposits represent an increasing share of total deposits of United States multinational banks. For example, for the larger New York-based banks foreign deposits increased from 8.5 percent of the domestic deposits in 1960 and 33.6 percent in 1968 to 65.5 percent in 1972.[10]

The expansion of the Eurocurrency market to $100 billion by the end of 1972, coupled with the phenomenal expansion of overseas branches, especially of United States banks, provides a readily available source of funds that can be shifted internationally, as well as the mechanism through which such shifts can be made. At the same time, they provide an important source of credit in several areas of the world, over and above what can be supplied by local banks.

Ownership Patterns

By and large, multinational corporations exercise effective control over their foreign affiliates through complete or majority ownership, although at times such control can be exercised from a minority position. At least 80 percent of United States affiliates and 75 percent of United Kingdom affiliates are either wholly-owned or majority-controlled. In terms of stock of investment, these two countries have placed about 90 percent in affiliates that are at least majority-owned. This desire for majority ownership and control appears to be a general characteristic of multinational corporations from other home countries, except in the case of Japanese multinational corporations, where a somewhat more sizeable proportion of affiliates and stock of investment are minority-owned joint ventures. This difference in the ownership pattern is apparently influenced by differences in methods of control as well as in the industrial and the geographical distribution of foreign activities. The predominance of trading activities and light industries in the case of Japanese multinational corporations suggests that relatively small affiliates may be adequate in many cases. Moreover, since a relatively high proportion of Japanese investment—made mostly in recent years—is located in developing countries, the ownership pattern may also have been influenced by a tendency of some Japanese multinational corporations to maintain a relatively low profile in some of those countries. This geographical influence on ownership patterns is also suggested by the somewhat lower share of wholly-owned affiliates in the total number of affiliates of United States corporations in developing countries as compared with that in developed countries. Over the last three decades, a slight increase in the proportion of minority ownership, particularly in developing countries, is suggested by United States data. There is also an indication that the longer the life of an affiliate, the more likely is it to by wholly-owned. This tendency can, of course, be offset by pressures from host countries, as exemplified by recent trends towards increased local ownership in the OPEC and other countries.

Dimensions in the World Spectrum

The enormous size and steadily growing importance of multinational corporations are clearly revealed when viewed in the context of world economic activities. Although the usual comparison of gross annual sales of multinational corporations with gross national product of countries exaggerates the relative importance of the activities of multinational corporations, the general conclusion that many multinational corporations are bigger than a large number of entire national economies remains valid. Thus, the value-added by each of the top ten multinational corporations in 1971 was in excess of $3 billion—or greater than the gross national product of over 80 countries. The value-added of all multinational corporations, estimated roughly at $500 billion in 1971, was about one-fifth of world gross national product, not including the centrally planned economies.

International production, defined as production subject to foreign control or decision and measured by the sales of foreign affiliates of multinational corporations has surpassed trade as the main vehicle of international economic exchange. It is estimated that international production reached approximately $330 billion in 1971.[11] This was somewhat larger than total exports of all market economies ($310 billion).

Since the rate of growth of international production is estimated to have exceeded that of world gross domestic product or world exports, an increasing share of world output would be generated by the foreign production of multinational corporations if recent trends were to continue.[12] However, future developments will depend very much on the extent to which the problems raised by the operations of multinational corporations are dealt with by appropriate national and international measures that permit continued growth in desired areas and directions, or by restrictive measures which will obstruct further growth. In addition, changing relationships between different groups of countries, for example increased co-operation and exchange between developed market economies and centrally planned economies, will influence the direction of multinational corporation activities.

Dimensions in Developed Market Economies

If the world-wide integrative role of the multinational corporation is debatable, its importance to the interrelationship of the developed market economies is beyond doubt. Most of the developed market economies serve simultaneously as home and host countries. The United States, however, acts primarily as a home country, while certain others, such as Cyprus, Greece, Spain, Turkey, New Zealand, and South Africa, are almost exclusively hosts to foreign multinational corporations.

During the period 1968–1970, inward direct investment flows were on the average only 20 percent of the outward flows for the United States, 30 percent for Japan, 63 percent for the United Kingdom and the Federal Republic of Germany and 90 percent for the Netherlands. The reverse is the case with most of the other countries. In France inward direct investment flows were almost twice as high as the outward flows, in Italy and Canada a little more than twice, in New Zealand, three times higher, in Belgium, four times and in Australia, Spain, Portugal, and South Africa, 7.5 to 12 times greater than outward flows.

As far as the United States is concerned, the preponderant position in the economy is occupied by domestic multinational corporations, rather than foreign multinational corporations whose presence is not as yet significant. More than one-third of the manufacturing output of the United States is represented by the top 187 United States multinational manufacturing corporations. In certain industrial sectors, such as automotive, pharmaceutical and fabricated metal products, the consolidated sales of these corporations account for more than three-fourths of the sales of all United States firms, and in petroleum refining, chemicals, rubber and electrical machinery, for more than one-half. A larger group, of 264 multinational corporations, is responsible for half of all United States exports of manufactures. In 1971, United States multinational corporations generated an outflow of capital of $4.8 billion for direct investment abroad and an inflow of approximately $9 billion in interest, dividends, royalties and management fees. Furthermore, given the practice of extensive local borrowing, their control of overseas assets is substantially higher than the book value of long-term equity and debt held abroad.[13]

In contrast, the relative importance of foreign multinational corporations in the United States is limited. Foreign investment in the United States, while far from negligible, is mainly portfolio investment. The European investment in the United States, for instance, is about as high as the United States investment in Europe; but whereas 80 percent of the latter is in direct investment, 70 percent of the European investment in the United States is in portfolio form, almost equally divided between stocks and bonds. Thus, the book value of United States direct investment in other developed countries, with the exception of the Netherlands, is several times higher than the book value of direct investment of those countries in the United States.[14] Multinational corporations from the United Kingdom, the Netherlands and Switzerland are the leading investors in the United States, accounting for about 60 percent of total direct foreign investment. Although European and, more recently, Japanese corporations have penetrated the petroleum industry, manufacturing and the service sector in the United States, there is no single industry in which they have assumed a preponderant role.

With the exception of Japan, the reverse is true in the case of the other developed economies, where foreign affiliates account for an important share of output, investment, employment or exports.

In Japan,where regulatory policies have restrained foreign entry, firms with foreign capital participation represented in 1968 only 2.3 percent of total fixed assets and 1.65 percent of total sales in manufacturing. The share was much higher in the oil industry (60 percent) and in rubber (19 percent).[15] Given the recent Japanese liberalization measures, the share of foreign affiliates (more than half of which are joint ventures) must certainly have increased.

In Canada, at the other end of the spectrum, the presence of foreign multinational corporations is pervasive, representing one-third of total business activity. Foreign affiliates account for 60 percent of manufacturing output and 65 percent of output in mining and smelting. The United States accounts for 80 percent of total foreign investment and the United Kingdom for most of the rest. In the United Kingdom, United States affiliates represent almost 70 percent of the total stock of foreign direct investment. They account for 13 percent of total manufacturing output, employ 9.2 percent of the labour force and are responsible for one-fifth of all manufacturing exports.[16] In Belgium, foreign affiliates are responsible for a quarter of the gross national product, one-third of total sales, 18 percent of employment and 30 percent of exports. More than half of the total foreign direct investment is accounted for by United States-controlled affiliates.[17] In the Federal Republic of Germany, Italy, and France, foreign penetration is less pronounced, with the United States accounting for at least half of it, except in the case of France where its share is less than a third.[18]

The importance of multinational corporations in the developed market economies varies considerably by industrial sector. There is a high concentration in a fairly small number of industrial sectors characterized by fast growth, export-orientation and high technology, sectors which are also regarded as key sectors by the host countries. It appears that in most of the developed market economies foreign-owned firms own very high (75–100 percent) or high (50–75 percent) sector shares in industries characterized by high technology. Thus, there is very high or high foreign presence in the oil refining industry in Canada, the Federal Republic of Germany and Japan. Chemicals are under very high foreign ownership in Canada, high in Australia, and medium (25 to 50 percent) in the Federal Republic of Germany and Norway. The computer and electronics industries are under very high foreign ownership in the Federal Republic of Germany and the United Kingdom. Transport equipment is under very high foreign ownership in Canada and Australia, and medium in the United Kingdom. Electrical machinery is highly owned by foreign corporations in Austria, the Federal Republic of Germany and Canada.

The presence of United States multinational corporations is also more pronounced in some sectors than in others. For instance, they control more than half of the petroleum industry in Belgium, approximately three-fifths of the food, tobacco, oil-refining, metal manufacturing, instrument engineering, computer and technical manufacturing industries in the United Kingdom, and more than 15 percent of the production of semiconductors and 80 percent of computers and electronic data-processing equipment in the European Community. In the service sector, the United States presence is considerable in the hotel and recreation industries, consulting, public relations and banking. It is estimated that in 1970 there were more than 30 United States banks operating in Europe, many of them having established affiliates jointly with European banks.

Another indication of the importance of United States affiliates in developed countries is their share in the gross fixed capital formation of these countries. In Canada in 1970 it amounted to one-third, in the United Kingdom to one-fifth, in Belgium and Luxembourg and the Federal Republic of Germany to between 12 and 13 percent, and in France 6 percent. In certain industries, the share was much higher, e.g., in Canada it was more than 50 percent in chemicals, fabricated metals, machinery and transportation equipment.

Dimensions in Developing Countries

In 1968 developing countries accounted for about one-third of the book value of foreign direct investment as opposed to only one-sixth of world gross domestic product and one-fifth of world exports, not including centrally planned economies. Half of foreign direct investment in developing countries was in the development of natural resources, a little less than one-third in manufacturing and the rest in trade, public utilities, transport, banking, tourism, and other services.

Generally speaking, the relative importance of the multinational corporation in developing countries is rising in the manufacturing and services sectors and declining in the primary industries, in particular those connected with agriculture (plantations). On balance, the over-all importance of the multinational corporation is growing. As a source of the net flow of resources to developing countries, private direct investment flows from such corporations represented about one-fifth of the total in the 1960s. During the same period, this flow increased at an average annual rate of 9 percent. In six out of the twelve developing countries for which data were available, the stock of foreign direct investment increased faster than that of gross domestic product. In the second half of the 1960s, the slow growth of investment in some countries is attributable to the liquidation of foreign investment through nationalization.

The relative size of the accumulated stock varies by industrial sector and country, and the share of foreign affiliates' activity in output, employment or exports varies accordingly. In some countries, the foreign content of the local economy is very high and at times concentrated in one sector, while in others it is less significant or more diversified.

In the Middle East, which accounts for 9.4 percent of the total foreign direct private investment in developing countries, petroleum accounts for approximately 90 percent of the total stock of foreign investment.[19] In South America (36 percent of the total), on the other hand, 39 percent of foreign investment is in manufacturing, 28 percent in petroleum and 10 percent in public utilities. In Africa (20 percent of the total), 39 percent is in petroleum, 20 percent in mining and smelting and 19 percent in manufacturing. In Asia (15 percent), manufacturing has attracted 30 percent, petroleum 22 percent and agriculture 18 percent of the total foreign investment stock. In Central America (19 percent of the total), manufacturing has attracted 31 percent, petroleum 16 percent and trade 13 percent of the total.

This aggregate picture, however, does not reveal the fact that multinational corporations have tended to concentrate in a few developing countries. Only a few developing countries have a stock of direct investment of more than $1 billion. Thus, Argentina, Brazil, India, Mexico, Nigeria, Venezuela, and certain Caribbean islands,[20] account for 43 percent of the total stock of investment in developing countries, which is roughly the same proportion as that of their combined gross domestic product to the estimated total for all developing countries. According to OECD estimates for the end of 1967, in another 13 countries[21] in various developing regions the stock of investment was between $500 million and $1 billion, accounting for nearly another 30 percent of the total stock of investment in developing countries. This concentration is related to the sector in which foreign investment is predominant. In African countries and in Central and South American and Middle Eastern countries (Algeria, Libya, Nigeria, Zambia, Jamaica, Netherlands Antilles, Trinidad and Tobago, Peru and Venezuela, Iran, Kuwait, and Saudi Arabia), it is the extractive industries which predominate. In all these countries, the stock of investment in either petroleum or mining exceeds $200 million. In several other countries, manufacturing is the predominant sector, more than $200 million being invested in manufacturing in Argentina, Brazil, India, Mexico and the Philippines. In India and Malaysia, investment in agriculture exceeds $200 million.

The activities of United States multinational corporations represent half of the total stock of foreign direct investment in developing countries. In certain regions, however, such as Central and South America, the United States accounts for almost two-thirds of the total stock of foreign direct investment. The rest of the stock is represented by the United Kingdom (9 percent), Canada (7 percent), Netherlands (5 percent) and the Federal Republic of Germany (4 percent). In Africa, on the other hand, the United States accounts only for one-fifth of the total stock; the United Kingdom predominates with 30 percent, France following with 26 percent. Belgium, the Netherlands, and Italy account for 7, 5 and 4 percent respectively. In the Middle East, the United States accounts for 57 percent, the United Kingdom for 27 percent and the Netherlands and France for approximately 5.5 percent each. In Asia, the United Kingdom has the largest share (41 percent), the United States follows with 36 percent, France with 7 percent, and the Netherlands with 5 percent.

In some developing countries where the stock of investment exceeds $500 million, the foreign affiliates of a single developed market economy account for more than 80 percent of the stock of total investment.[22]

Data on the share of foreign multinational corporations in local production is limited. In Singapore, in 1966, affiliates from the main investing countries are estimated to have contributed one-third of the total value added in manufacturing.[23] It has been estimated that in the mid-1960s, sales of United States enterprises alone represented 17 percent of the gross value of industrial production of Mexico, 13 percent of that of the Philippines, and 11 percent of that of Argentina and Brazil.[24] In Central America, the output of foreign affiliates is estimated at 30 percent of the output of the manufacturing sector. Among the 500 largest manufacturing firms in Brazil, foreign affiliates controlled 37 percent of total assets.[25] In Mexico, among middle- and large-sized firms, weighted average foreign participation reached 45 percent in 1970. Foreign participation in the output of Mexican manufacturing industries, however, reached 100 percent in rubber products and transportation materials, and a weighted share of more than 75 percent in industrial chemicals and tobacco in 1970, while foreign participation in textile production was only 8 percent.[26]

Expenditures of multinational corporations on plants and equipment represent a varying share of the total gross fixed capital formation of developing countries. In 1970, the share of such expenditures by United States manufacturing affiliates was 9 percent in Mexico and 18 percent in Brazil. In some cases, such as electrical machinery in Brazil, the expenditure of United States affiliates on plant and equipment accounted for more than half of the total fixed capital formation in the industry.[27]

In addition to their dominant role in the export of products of the extractive industries, multinational corporations are in general playing an increasingly important part in the export of manufactures from developing countries.[28] There is evidence on an over-all increase in the exports of affiliates, both as a share of total sales and as a share of total exports by the host country.

Thus, exports of United States manufacturing affiliates in Central and South America accounted for 4 percent of their total sales in 1957, 7.5 percent in 1965 and 9.4 percent in 1968.[29] Their share in the total exports of manufactures from these regions, which was 12 percent in 1957, reached 41 percent in 1966. This share varies by country; thus, in Argentina, between 1965 and 1968, exports of United States affiliates accounted for 14.5 percent of total exports. In Mexico, in 1966, United States manufacturing affiliates accounted for 87 percent of exports of manufactures, and in Brazil they represented 42 percent.

Sporadic data suggest that despite their visibility and presence in key sectors, the contribution of foreign affiliates to the total gross domestic product of developing countries remain relatively small in most host countries. This is because the bulk of the gross domestic product of most developing countries originates in agriculture and the service industries where, on the whole, the presence of the multinational corporation is relatively limited.

Dimensions in Centrally Planned Economies

Although the centrally planned economies have attracted only a very small amount of direct investment and very few affiliates of multinational corporations, they are more involved in the activities of these corporations than a cursory examination of the standard data might indicate. The form in which the multinational corporations extend their operations in these economies differs from that taken in others. Equity participation in countries in which the private ownership of means of production is not congruent with the system is naturally uncommon. The major exceptions are a limited number of sales offices of multinational corporations and some minority participation, which is permitted by law in Romania and, on a very limited basis, in Hungary.[30]

Yet, apart from straightforward trade, the relationship between multinational corporations and the centrally planned economies has often involved co-operative arrangements in production, the development and transfer of technology, and marketing. Most of these arrangements are relatively recent in origin, reflecting the general trend in the centrally planned economies towards more outward-looking policies and a new emphasis on economic co-operation. Typically, a complex set of arrangements provides for technical help by the multinational corporation in plant construction (e.g., Occidental Petroleum and the proposed fertilizer complex in the USSR), exports and imports (e.g., the purchase by Occidental of the products of the plants, and sales to the USSR of Occidental products) and trade credit.

It has been estimated that there were about 600 industrial co-operation agreements with the developed market economies in force in Eastern European countries at the beginning of 1973. About one-third of these agreements have been concluded within the last two or three years, and continued fast growth is indicated. On the whole, these agreements account for a relatively small proportion of total trade with developed market economies. In some Eastern European countries, however, they already account for 10 to 15 percent of exports to the developed market economies in some branches of industry. In Hungary, for example, they are responsible for one-sixth of engineering exports to developed market economies.[31]

Similarly, while these agreements do not account for a significant share of the total output of Eastern European countries, they are important for certain branches. These are mostly industries requiring high technology or large investment. For example, over half of passenger automobile production in the USSR in 1975 is expected to come from Fiat, under one of the first industrial co-operation agreements negotiated with Italy. The current figure for Poland is two-fifths.

More recently, the role of multinational corporations in the exploitation of natural resources in the USSR has assumed particular importance. The copper project in Eastern Siberia being negotiated with multinational corporations would involve an investment of one to two billion dollars, with an annual production of several hundred thousand tons. The natural gas project in Siberia, also involving the active participation of multinational corporations, would account for a major part of the entire natural gas

production of the USSR by 1980. Moreover, as exports of these natural resources would continue to flow long after the initial foreign investments were
paid off, import capacity would be correspondingly expanded. A further implication of these projects is that because of the vast outlay and the scope
of activities involved, they will probably require the participation of very
large multinational corporations or a consortia of a number of them. Moreover, since many of these arrangements involve large deferred payments beyond the capacity of multinational corporations to finance, they will require
finance from banks or export credit institutions.

Similar co-operative agreements have also been made between enterprises
of the centrally planned economies and developing countries. Here, on the
other hand, the centrally planned economies are usually the providers of
technical aid, machinery and equipment and credits, to be paid off with the
products of the newly set-up plant.

In recent years, such co-operation has become a rapidly growing source
of development assistance from socialist countries. Among the socialist
countries' main partners are India and the countries of North Africa. Since
1971, there has been a tendency for a rapid spread to new partners in other
regions and continents.[32]

QUESTIONS

1. What factors underly the large size and concentration of multinational
   corporations?
2. Discuss the factors underlying the tremendous growth experienced by
   multinational corporations.
3. How does the growth patterns of multinational corporations differ across
   advanced, developing and centrally planned economies?
4. Discuss the positive as well as negative economic and social impacts
   created by multinational corporations.

NOTES

1. Raymond Vernon, *Sovereignty at Bay: The Multinational Spread of United States
   Enterprises* (New York, NY: 1971), p. 4.

2. See section on dimensions in the world spectrum.

3. Frederick T. Knickerbocker, *Oligopolistic Reaction and Multinational Enterprise*
   (Boston, MA: 1973).

4. The discussion of the distribution of affiliates in this section refers to affiliate
   "links", except in the case of the United States.

5. The nine largest United States multinational corporations in petroleum had crude
   oil operations in 1938 in forty countries and in 1967 in ninety-six countries. Over

the same period their subsidiaries in all types of operations relating to petroleum increased from 351 to 1,442. Vernon, *op. cit.,* p. 32.

6. Investment in petroleum in developed market economies is mainly in refining and distribution.

7. The radically different foreign direct investment structures of these countries reflect, to a certain extent, differences in endowments of factors and natural resources, in industrial competitiveness, and in business traditions' and orientation. In the case of Japan, the re-emergence of large trading companies and the desire to secure raw materials have played a determining role; in the case of the Federal Republic of Germany, the major factors were the competitive strength of the IG-Farben successor corporations and apparent disinterest in building up a major domestically-owned petroleum industry (approximateely 90 percent of the petroleum industry of the Federal Republic of Germany is foreign-owned).

8. Vernon, *op. cit.,* p. 63.

9. Data supplied by the Chase Manhattan Bank.

10. Frank Mastrapasqua, *U.S. Expansion via Foreign Branching: Monetary Policy Implications* (New York, NY: 1973), pp. 23–25.

11. Estimates of international production made in the literature vary according to the methodology used. J. Polk, on the basis of sales associated with direct investment and portfolio investment, estimates international production at $420 billion for 1968, see Judd Polk, "The Internationalization of Production", mimeo (United States Council of the International Chamber of Commerce, 1969); J. Behrman, on the basis of sales associated with direct and portfolio investment as well as licensed rights, estimates international production at $450 billion for 1971, see J. N. Behrman, "New Orientation in International Trade and Investment" in Pierre Uri, ed. *Trade and Investment Policies for the Seventies: New Challenges for the Atlantic Area and Japan* (New York, NY: 1971).

    Both authors, without adjusting for value added, evaluate the internationalized gross domestic product of market economies to be 23 percent for 1968 (Polk) and 22 percent for 1971 (Behrman). If the adjustment is made these shares will be considerably lower. S. Robock and K. Simmonds in calculating foreign production do not include portfolio investment or licensed rights; their figure for foreign production for 1970 is $230 billion, representing approximately 11 percent of market economies' gross domestic product. See S.H. Robock and K. Simmonds, *International Business and Multinational Enterprises,* (Homewood, Illinois: Richard D. Irwin, Inc., 1973).

12. Whereas between 1961 and 1971 gross domestic product of market economies at current prices rose at an annual average rate of 9 percent, international production, estimated on the basis of sales at current prices of United States foreign affiliates betwen 1962 and 1968, rose at an annual average rate of about 13 percent.

13. United States net capital exports for direct investment abroad as a share of investment outlays of United States affiliates vary considerably by year, sector, and area of investment. In 1968, in western Europe, the share was less than one-third; in a sample of 125 large multinational corporations (representing one-sixth of United States industry's ex-factory sales) only 6.7 percent of gross foreign investment was financed through a net capital outflow from United States parent companies, the principal source being foreign depreciation reserves, earnings and borrowings. Business International, *The Effects of United States Corporate Foreign Investment, 1960–1970,* (New York, NY: 1972).

14. The United States' stock of direct investment in the European Community is 3.5 times higher than the Community's investment in the United States; it is 7 times more in the case of Canada and almost 70 times more in the case of Latin America. Rainer Hellmann, *The Challenge to United States Dominance of the Multinational Corporation* (New York, NY: 1970).

15. Japanese Trade and Industry Ministry, *Special Report on Foreign Owned Firms in Japan* (Tokyo, Japan, 1968).

16. John Dunning, *United States Industry in Britain* (London, Economists' Advisory Group Research Study, Financial Times, 1972).

17. D. Van den Bulcke, *The Foreign Companies in Belgian Industry* (Ghent, Belgium: Belgian Productivity Centre, 1973).

18. The foreign share in the total nominal capital of firms in the Federal Republic of Germany was 19 percent at the end of 1968, and in Italy in 1965 15 percent. In France, out of a total of $707 million of direct foreign investment in 1967, the United States accounted for 30 percent, the European Community countries for 29 percent, and Switzerland for 22 percent. G. Bertin, "Foreign investment in France", in *Foreign Investment: The Experience of Host Countries,* I. Litvak and C. Maule, eds. (New York, NY: 1970).

19. The discussion on the distribution of stock of foreign direct investment in developing countries is based on rough estimates made by the Organization for Economic Co-operation and Development. See OECD, *Stock of Private Direct Investments by DAC Countries in Developing Countries, end 1967* (Paris, France, 1972).

20. Leeward Islands, Windward Islands, Bahamas, Barbados, and Bermuda.

21. Algeria, Libya, Jamaica, Panama, Trinidad and Tobago, Chile, Colombia, Peru, Iran, Kuwait, Saudi Arabia, Malaysia, and the Philippines.

22. In 1968, in Chile, Colombia, Panama, Peru, Philippines, and Saudi Arabia, more than 80 percent of the stock of foreign investment was owned by United States affiliates. In Zaire, 88 percent of total investment was made by Belgian affiliates.

23. H. Hughes and You Poh Seng, eds., *Foreign Investment and Industrialization in Singapore,* (Canberra, Austrailias, Australian National University Press, 1969), p. 192.

24. Economic Commission for Latin America, *Economic Survey of Latin America* (United Nations publication, Sales No. E.72.II.G.1), p. 293.

25. F. Fajnzylber, *Sistema industrial y exportación de manufacturas: análisis de la experiencia brasilera,* Economic Commission for Latin America, November 1970.

26. See C. Vaitsos, "The Changing Policies of Latin American Governments Towards Economic Development and Direct Foreign Investment", forthcoming in *Journal of World Trade Law*; Carlos Bazdzeseh Parada, "La politica actual hacia la inversión extranjera directa", *Comercio Exterior* (Mexico City, Mexico: 1972), p. 1012.

27. United States Senate, Committee on Finance, *Implications of Multinational Firms for World Trade and Investment and for United States Trade and Labor* (Washington, D.C., 1973).

28. The relative contribution of foreign affiliates may be affected by their orientation towards import substitution, which is enhanced by the restrictive tariff policies of host countries, and by the type of products manufactured in developing countries in connection with the global requirements of multinational corporations.

29. United States Department of Commerce, *United States Business Investment in Foreign Countries, 1960* (Washington, D.C.: 1960) and *Survey of Current Business,* October 1970.

30. Yugoslavia is a special case. It was the first socialist country to permit minority participation by foreign enterprises. A constitutional amendment of 1971 goes so far as to offer a guarantee against subsequent expropriation and nationalization, once a joint venture contract has come into effect.

31. United Nations Economic Commission for Europe, *Analytical Report on Industrial Co-operation among ECE Countries* (Mimeographed Document, E/ECE/ 844, 14 March 1973).

32. For further information, see "Centrally Planned Economies and the International Development Strategy" in *Implementation of the International Development Strategy: Papers for the First Over-all Review and Appraisal of Progress during the Second United Nations Development Decade,* vol. II (United Nations Publication, Sales No. E.73.II.A.3).

International marketing poses significant challenges to marketing strategists attempting to exploit foreign opportunities for industrial products. The scope of these opportunities is described in terms of growth trends and problems experienced by United States firms in the past. In addition, the author provides guidelines for dealing with such factors as competition, culture, the overseas image of American business in the development of pricing, product, distribution, and promotion strategies.

3. Industrial Marketing in the International Setting

C. P. Rao
University of Arkansas

Historically, foreign trade helped both the industrialized and the developing countries to expand and diversify their economic activity. Studies relating to the British and French experience in the second half of the nineteenth century, the United States, the Soviet Union, and the Japanese clearly indicate such economic growth through export trade.[1] After an extensive study of the interrelationship between export trade and industrial growth, Alfred Maizel arrived at the following conclusions, worth noting:

A general hypothesis advanced is that long-term shifts in relative competitive power in the widest sense may reflect changes in the rates of economic growth of the various industrial countries. Since exports are also an important part of the total demand for final output, in most industrial countries, a change in competitive power—which implies a change in export sales—will itself affect the rate of growth in industrial production. Thus, exports interact

Source: Reprinted from *Arizona Business* (March, 1974); Bureau of Business and Economic Research, College of Business Administration, Arizona State University.

in a dynamic way with the growth of the whole economy. There has, in fact, been a remarkably close relationship over the past 60 years in the relative growth rates of the main industrial countries and their shares of the world export market in manufactures.[2]

Among the developed countries there are wide differences with regard to the significance of export trade to their economic growth trends. For some island economies such as Britain and Japan, export trade contributes significantly to the total gross national product (GNP), whereas the same cannot be said about almost self-sufficient economies such as the United States and the Soviet Union. However, in an interdependent international economy the export trade would still be significant to countries like the United States, despite its marginal contribution to the total GNP of the country. This is particularly true if the country is experiencing an unfavorable external balance of payments position. In the United States case, the country suffered a negative balance of trade in 1971 for the first time since 1893. In the first half of 1972 imports exceeded the exports by three billion dollars. These developments intensified the export expansion efforts of the nation.

A careful analysis of the product composition of the United States export trade clearly shows that although the exports are expanding in absolute value terms, the relative share of the United States in the world exports is declining. The decline is particularly significant in the case of manufactured products, which constitute two-thirds of the country's total exports. The changing relative shares of the major industrialized countries in the world exports of manufactured goods show that the United States share has declined from 24.5 percent in 1955 to 18 percent in 1971.

A major portion of the manufactured exports from the United States involves industrial marketing in the international setting. Of the total United States exports in 1970, machinery of various types accounted for 27 percent and chemicals for another 9 percent. By including other types of industrial goods exports, it can be safely said that almost 50 percent of the total United States exports involve industrial marketing in the overseas markets; industrial marketing in the international setting is significant to the United States manufacturer-exporters not only at the present time but also in the future. In recent years exports of consumer goods from the United States have declined, particularly those of the labor-intensive type like the textiles. In both consumer durable and nondurable goods, the United States exports are being progressively priced out of the world markets. In view of these discernible trends in the international trade, future United States export growth can be expected mainly in the high technology industrial goods categories. Despite such overwhelming significance of industrial marketing for the United States export expansion, the subject has received very limited attention in the extensive literature dealing with international marketing aspects. Hence this paper examines some of the salient aspects of industrial marketing in the international setting.

Export of Capital Goods

Capital goods have certain special characteristic features that distinguish them from both the commodity and consumer goods exports. The manufacturer-exporter of capital goods has less worry about the idosyncracies of the foreign consumer than the consumer goods exporter. Capital goods purchases are generally characterized by the rational behavior on the part of the buyers; the capital goods are purchased by technical people who are trained for the job. The normal considerations in the purchase of capital goods, such as cost savings, service dependability, credit terms, and provision of spares, seem to be a universal phenomena. To the extent that there is uniformity in the buyer behavior in all the markets both domestic and overseas, the manufacturer-exporter of capital goods is better off than his counterpart in consumer goods.

Exporting capital goods, however, has its own special problems that are more difficult to overcome and require greater marketing ingenuity and efforts. Special organization approaches are necessary to make a substantial break-through in the overseas markets. An attempt will be made to identify some of these problems and suggest some organizational approaches to find solutions.

The Country Image Factor

Exporting in general and exporting the industrial goods in particular are very much influenced by a country's image in the world markets.[3] There is ample evidence to indicate that this image factor may help or harm the exporters' efforts in selling abroad. Individual countries enjoy great prestige as suppliers of certain products; for example, Scotch whisky, Swiss watches, French perfumes, and Japanese cameras, transistor radios, and other electronic goods are well known in all the world markets. These country images, other factors being constant, do certainly influence the customer preference and prejudices in evaluating the suppliers from various countries. It is reported that in the post Second World War years, Japan had to struggle hard to overcome its unfavorable prewar image as supplier of cheap and shoddy consumer goods.

It need not be emphasized that the United States enjoys a very favorable image as a supplier of technologically superior products. The United States leadership in the aviation industry, in the computer field, and in space technology have all contributed to the positive technological image of the country. Such an image of technological superiority is more significant in industrial than in consumer goods marketing. The favorable image solves many initial problems relating to the customer confidence in the suppliers' ability to deliver technically reliable and quality products. In selling industrial goods in the overseas markets, customer confidence in supplier's technical, delivery, and servicing abilities are very crucial. On all these counts, the United States exporters enjoy a distinctive advantage because of the country's favorable image as the producer and supplier of technologically superior products. Once the initial resistances are overcome and a few sales are effected in a given overseas market, the industrial goods exporter can hope for sustained sales growth in that market. Such a sales growth is facilitated by two characteristics of industrial goods marketing. First, once the psychological fears of "country's image" are overcome, the purchases of capital goods are made essentially on rational grounds. Second, in most cases of industrial goods the number of potential customers is limited, thereby encouraging more intensive efforts.

At the same time there are a host of export problems that are internal to the firm. These include the management's commitment and policy towards exports, and the development of an efficient export marketing organization so as to achieve the planned export targets. Resolving these problems is a prerequisite for successful exporting, and it is within the capabilities of individual firms. In the following pages we consider the nature of these export marketing problems and some approaches to resolve them. However, it needs to be emphasized that it is the combination of favorable external export environment and internal managerial efficiency that can achieve export expansion of the magnitude that would be optimal for the nation in the next five years.

Limited and Diffused Export Sales

For many manufacturer-exporters, export sales often form but a small proportion of their total sales. Even for leading exporters in each product category, exports seldom exceed 15–20 percent of their total sales. For most exporters, the exports constitute less than 10 percent of their total sales. Thus, although the bulk of the sales come from the domestic market, the exports contribute marginally to the total sales.

Related to the above characteristics of a firm's export sales is the fact that such limited export sales often come from a number of overseas markets. Each overseas market, therefore, on the average contributes a very small percentage to total sales of the firm. These two characteristic features of export sales—limited and diffused—have great significance for export marketing. In the first place these features limit the scope for efficient export marketing. The limited and widely diffused export sales lead to the following types of limitations in organizing overseas sales.

1. Problems of organizing presale advice and aftersale service
2. Problems of stocking and promptly providing the spare parts
3. Frequent and extensive foreign sales tours may not be justified by the volume of export sales
4. An extensive foreign sales organization may not be justified by the present or future potential sales in each overseas markets

5. The greater the diffusion of export sales, the higher the chances that export marketing efforts are less effective; this may restrict the growth of export sales and may result in greater instability

These characteristic features and the consequent problems call for greater marketing ingenuity on the part of management and for more careful planning and adaption of diverse marketing strategies to suit each or a group of export markets. Some of these strategies and approaches to export marketing will be considered later.

Intense Competition in the Overseas Markets

International markets are characterized by intense competition. Except West Germany and Japan among the developed, and among the developing, Libya and a few oil-producing countries, every country in the world is experiencing the problem of unfavorable balance of payments. While the developed countries like the United States and the United Kingdom are striving to maintain the leading roles of their currencies in the international monetary system, a number of developing countries are making all-out efforts to earn their foreign exchange requirements through export expansion. In the post Second World War years, the East European countries and China have also joined in the race for increased exports.

The result of these developments is that competition in the international markets is getting more intensified. In view of the current movement for trade liberalization, it can be safely asserted that this competitive intensity in world markets will continue. Because of such intense competition in the international markets, there is a great need for substantial commitment on the part of management that often is not justified by the level of initial export sales. However, unless the management is willing to commit resources for export efforts and progressively impart greater dynamism to their export organization, they may not be able to achieve any substantial results. In committing the resources in the initial years, management should take a long-term point of view. Only such an approach would enable the manufacturer-exporters to make the initial breakthrough into world markets.

The intense competition in world markets would require certain attributes on the part of management for success in overseas markets. First, there should be greater managerial flexibility so that quick decisions can be taken and implemented when necessary to satisfy the overseas customer. This managerial flexibility requirement is essential in dealing with both the internal and the external environment of the firm.

Some of the other problems arising out of intense competition in the overseas markets are:

1. Supply of quality products is often different from that supplied in the domestic market

2. Need for superior service and prompt supply of spares
3. Lower prices in the overseas market and the consequent need for a conscious export pricing policy
4. Use of credit as a promotional means
5. Need to appoint effective agents in the overseas markets

Cultural Factors

Cultural impact in international marketing has been well recognized in recent years. The cultural difference between the exporters' home country and his export markets may give rise to many a marketing pitfall. Generally, an understanding of this cultural milieu will be more significant in the export of consumer goods where closer attention must be given to consumer tastes, preferences, and prejudices in several export markets. But even in capital goods exports, an analysis and understanding of the foreign cultural patterns that have influence on business behavior will be crucial for export success. Even though business contracts and agreements can be generally expected to be uniform practices, empirical research indicates there are many variations with regard to the manner of entering into such business contracts, and in their implementation.[4] Furthermore, in dealing with foreign distributors, dealers, and other middlemen whose cooperation is of great importance in export marketing, a clear appreciation of their cultural differences is very important. The customers in different countries will display differences in cultural norms in such aspects as the following:

1. Tolerance to delays in correspondence and deliveries
2. Service expectations and promptness in providing such service
3. Negotiations and agreements
4. Services provided by the agents
5. Purchasing behavior of industrial goods buyers

An understanding of these cultural differences and the adoption of congruent marketing practices by the exporter will go a long way toward ensuring export success. The following observations uphold a universal truth and indicate the types of behavioral adjustments required in dealing with businessmen in various parts of the world.

Indeed the one trait that distinguished the American Businessman abroad from his forebears is that he has become the Great Adapter.

In the Orient he has learned to make points without winning argument—lest his adversary lose "face." In Italy he has learned to argue, so that the Italians will take him seriously. In Switzerland he has learned to be precise, because the Swiss take things literally. In Britain he uses "soft sell"; in Germany "hard sell". In Mexico he emphasizes price; in Venezuela, quality.[5]

Identifying Export Opportunities

A new manufacturer-exporter who wants to enter the export markets for the first time is confronted with a baffling number of countries that other manufacturer-exporters in the United States are supplying. The new entrants are often at a loss to know where to start and how to decide which of the several potential export markets should be selected for more intensive development.

A preliminary analysis of international and national trade flows with the help of published trade statistics would enable the exporter to get a general picture of trade prospects in the product category in which he is interested. For this purpose, the international trade statistics published by the United Nations, Organization for Economic Cooperation and Development (OECD), General Agreement on Tariffs and Trade (GATT), and the United States foreign trade statistics will be highly useful. In preparing statistical profiles of a number of potential export markets, the exporter may have to gather the following types of information for the last five years:

1. Balance of payments position of the country
2. Balance of trade position with the United States
3. Imports of the product or product category into the country, and from which countries
4. Analysis of economic statistics with regard to GNP, industrial production, or any other aspect that will be relevant to the exporter's product under consideration
5. Analysis of economic plans of the country particularly in the case of developing countries and centrally-planned Communist countries
6. Nature of trade restrictions, tariffs, import licenses, and exchange permits
7. Analysis of bilateral trade agreements with the United States, if any
8. Other restrictions e.g., declarations about imported goods, restrictions with regard to sales promotion, and opening of sales branches

To collect the above types of information the prospective exporter may have to use various sources. In addition to the statistical sources indicated earlier, reports of the United States Department of Commerce, correspondence with foreign country embassies or trade representatives as well as commercial attaches in the United States embassies in the overseas countries may also have to be utilized. Such country profile information can also be gathered from the research publications of research institutes or commercial research organizations. On the basis of such profiles, depending upon market potential, favorable market conditions, and the company's export commitment and resources, the potential export markets need to be short-listed for more detailed evaluation of markets and to ascertain the requirements for successful exporting.

Customer Analysis

Overseas customers may fall under various sectors. For capital goods specifically they may consist of government (federal, state, and local) departments or agencies, large industrial establishments, and replacement demand or smaller customers served by trading agencies. The exporters should analyze the requirements of the marketing problems in catering to each of these sectors and then decide which of the sector(s) they should enter. Such product-customer analysis would enable the exporters to identify the customer groups they can supply and service most effectively. Another consideration is that there may be stronger brand loyalty in certain segments than in others.

Analysis of Competition

The need for the exporter's understanding of the competitive environment in the overseas markets cannot be overemphasized; generally, competition comes from three sources—indigenous manufacturer in the importing country, exporters of other supplying countries, and other exporters in the exporter's own country. The competitive intensity in the overseas markets may differ from one segment to another. In general the capital goods exporter should compare his products and prices with those of the competing suppliers. These comparisons are not easy to accomplish. The products need to be compared with regard to their specifications, functions, and general differences that might be of interest to a customer. An analysis of such differences should enable the exporter to evaluate his product strengths and weaknesses vis-à-vis the competing products. Often such analysis is made difficult by the fact that the products are not identical except perhaps for their primary functional properties. Whereas the exporter's product may be restricted in the range of functions performed, the competitors' products may perform multiple functions, and vice versa. The industrial buyer's judgment is influenced not only by the functional properties of the product but also by other considerations, such as the operational and maintenance complexities.

Price comparisons are perhaps even more difficult than product comparisons. Apart from the basic problem of ascertaining the comparable price for identical products, price levels are influenced by the guarantees, service assurances, and credit terms. These difficulties accentuate the dangers of making hasty conclusions on the basis of price data that has not been properly analyzed.

In addition to product and price comparisons, the exporter should study the servicing policies and organization of the competitors. Similarly, if the products are sold through distributors, the commissions paid and promotional and other support provided relative to that of the competitors should be of interest to the prospective exporter.

Pricing for Exports

It is usually difficult to ascertain the competitive prices in the export markets; this is particularly so in the case of capital goods exports. Nevertheless, export prices have to be determined and quoted to the potential buyers. In the determination of export prices, consideration must be given to both the cost and non-cost factors. A careful analysis of these factors is a necessary prerequisite for systematic export-pricing; and there are many pitfalls in this process.

The normal tendency in the matter of determining desirability and possibility of export is to compare the domestic market price with the estimated FOB price realisable. Most of the time, FOB price compares unfavorably with the domestic prices. The process of comparison is made difficult because of the need to incorporate the direct and indirect export incentives provided by the government. Strictly in terms of cost analysis for pricing, the problem arises with regard to ascertaining what cost price should be compared with the estimated realisable FOB price. Many exporters adjust the domestic sales price in order to quote a lower FOB price, perhaps by reducing the profit margins. The domestic sales price is ascertained on full cost basis; as a general principle of pricing for exports, however, marginal cost pricing is more appropriate than full cost pricing. In the first place, exports form a small percentage of total sales, and, in the second, many of the overhead costs that are included in the domestic market price are not relevant for export pricing. Even when the firm is operating at full capacity, and a part of that capacity is utilized for exporting, there is no justification for apportioning the domestic marketing and administrative overheads to export business. Hence the costs to be identified with exports should be the direct manufacturing costs plus any marketing costs that can be directly identified with export marketing. For purposes of comparison with FOB price, the direct costs of manufacturing plus the directly identifiable export marketing costs (e.g., expenses of export department, costs of overseas trips) should be adjusted by deducting any available government incentives. If such an adjusted figure compares favorably with FOB prices, the exports will be making some contribution towards the exporter's general overheads.

In fixing export prices, as mentioned above, the non-cost factors must be ascertained. Thus, for example, the ruling competitive price in the overseas markets might make it imperative for the exporter to sell at the same price. For many manufacturer-exporters, who are not well known and who are relatively new entrants in the international markets, market entry problems might necessitate selling their products at below the market price. In other words the manufacturer exporters may be compelled to use price as a strategic element in the export marketing strategy.

The Export Marketing Mix

Through use of the strategic elements of product, price, channels, and organization, the exporter has to develop an appropriate export marketing mix that is consonant with his involvement in the foreign market and that takes into account the nature of its marketing characteristics. The development of a marketing mix involves determining the significance of each marketing element in the total marketing plan. The exporter will be able to develop a sound, suitable, and operationally feasible "marketing mix" only with a clear understanding of his resource constraints and with sound research to provide a knowledge of the foreign market.

QUESTIONS

1. How can a country's image factor impact on the opportunity of its businessmen to engage in foreign markets? How can this problem be overcome?
2. What kinds of problems do limited and widely diffused export sales pose for the international marketer's organization?
3. What causes can be attributed to the growing intensity of international competition? What problems does this create for firms involved in international markets?
4. Discuss the types of information, and where it might be obtained, that an international marketing manager would find useful in identifying foreign opportunities.

NOTES

1. See C.P. Kindleberger, "Foreign Trade and Economic Growth: Lessons from Britain and France: 1850-1913," *Economic History Review* XIV 2 (1961); F.D. Holzman, "International Trade and Economic Growth: The Soviet Union (1917-1957) and the U.S. (1869-1913)," A paper presented to the Social Science Research Conference, Princeton University, May, 1961; Leon Hollerman, "The Logistic View vs. the National Income View of Foreign Trade Dependence with Special reference to Japan," *Hitotsubashi Journal of Economics* 1, 1 (October, 1960).

2. Alfred Maizel, *Industrial Growth and World Trade* (Cambridge, MA: Cambridge University Press, 1963), p. 17.

3. See: *Products and People* (London: The Readers' Digest Association, 1963). This study gives interesting data on national images among the European Economic Community (EEC) countries.

4. See Edward T. Hall, "The Silent Language in Overseas Business" *Harvard Business Review* XXXIV, 2 (March-April, 1956), 119-127.

5. "Yankees Who Don't Go Home," *Business Weekly* (July 24, 1965), p. 48.

*The scope and importance of international
marketing to the United States is revealed
by this survey. Highlights of United States
expansion patterns include such facts that
high growth markets and American concentration of effort have been evidenced in developed nations with increased emphasis on
100 percent and majority ownership of these
overseas investments. The survey also observes that licensing appears to be less
favored by United States firms as a means
of conducting overseas activity.*

4. American Investment Abroad: Who's Going Where, How, and Why

Booz, Allen, and Hamilton

While spending record amounts on capital improvements at already existing
overseas installations, United States companies also inaugurated an impressive
number of new starts in foreign markets in 1970.

Nearly 600 firms initiated some 975 foreign investment activities in the
form of new establishments, mergers, expansions, licensing, or other types of
ventures. Though down slightly from the heavy surge of new activities recorded in 1969, the 1970 activities score tabulated by Booz, Allen, and
Hamilton researchers still contrasted sharply with the slackoff recorded in
previous years (see Exhibits 4-1, 4-2, and 4-3).

John Rhodes, senior vice president-international affairs for Booz, Allen,
and Hamilton, see the B–A–H scorecard of United States company activities
abroad as "encouraging. . .a continuation of the trend toward increased investment participation in overseas markets." The United States Commerce
Dept. survey of capital equipment expenditures by United States overseas

Source: Reprinted with special permission of Dun-Donnelly Publishing Corp. Copyright © 1971 by Dun-Donnelly Publishing Corp.

affiliates (a record $13.4-billion) in 1970 "bears this out," said Rhodes, who believes the intensifying competition in foreign markets requires United States firms to boost their stake in overseas investment and foreign on-site activity. What's more, Commerce estimates 1971 United States subsidiary plant and equipment expenditures will increase 18 percent this year, for a total outlay of nearly $16 billion.

Recurring comments by chief executive officers and other executives quoted in this year's editions of corporate annual reports also point to continuation of the thrust toward new overseas investment. More and more annual report booklets stress strong international themes—often in four-color layouts for emphasis—indicating how heavily companies now lean on sales and profits from entry into expanding markets to maintain corporate growth and offset dips and valleys in domestic activity as characterized by 1969-70 setbacks. Just as compelling is the widening recognition of overseas investment as a key weapon in combatting foreign competition not only in world but in home markets.

The statistical data accompanying this article comprise the 10th annual edition of United States overseas business activity as tabulated by the Chicago-based management consultant firm. Developed from official company announcements, press reports, and independent sources, the B–A–H tabulations provide an expanded basis for in-depth analysis of the developing pattern of United States overseas investment, particularly when viewed in pespective with the Commerce Dept.'s periodic surveys of American foreign business operations in terms of dollars invested.

The Booz, Allen, and Hamilton foreign-activity tables suggest some interesting trends in American business policies and practices in overseas investment.

As the charts indicate and as could be expected the developed countries and their major markets have been the focus of the majority of American business activities during the past decade. "American bubsiness continues to invest time, money, and talent in the developed, rather than the underdeveloped parts of the world even though exciting things are happening in Brazil, Africa, and other regions," Rhodes said.

Government statistics underscore this point. EEC affiliates of American firms boosted capital expenditures by 42 percent last year; another increase of 35 percent is forecast for 1971. In contrast Latin American investments may drop by as much as 5 percent in 1971.

But some interesting spot shifts could be in the making. In 1970, for instance, Brazil attracted considerable new attention from United States investors because of its booming economy, generally stabilized political climate, and booming economic expansion in key industrial areas. The B–A–H "total activities" table showed a 50 percent increase for Brazil, an interest also underscored by Commerce Dept. figures showing further heavy increases in plant expansion and equipment expenditures planned by United States manufacturing subsidiaries there in 1971.

EXHIBIT 4-1
U.S. FIRMS OVERSEAS—PATTERNS OF EXPANSION (1961-1970)

By Activity	1961	1962	1963	1964	1965	1966	1967	1968	1969	1970	Total
NEW ESTABLISHMENTS											
Manufacturing	382	445	516	507	426	398	363	371	524	469	4,401
Nonmanufacturing											
Establishments	178	139	202	254	259	190	182	202	348	275	2,229
Subtotal	560	584	718	761	685	588	545	573	872	744	6,630
EXPANSIONS											
Manufacturing	185	176	159	155	171	96	54	63	119	90	1,268
Nonmanufacturing	70	100	43	13	17	17	6	8	18	12	304
Subtotal	255	276	202	168	188	113	60	71	137	102	1,572
LICENSING AGREEMENTS	340	247	304	282	259	174	139	133	177	129	2,184
Total	1,155	1,107	1,224	1,211	1,132	875	744	777	1,186	975	10,386

By Region	1961	1962	1963	1964	1965	1966	1967	1968	1969	1970	Total
WESTERN EUROPE	597	559	597	598	554	473	369	394	595	480	5,216
European Common											
Market	332	319	325	334	291	260	204	210	325	284	2,884
Belgium-Luxembourg	38	54	57	61	61	46	35	38	85	63	538
France	101	64	67	72	54	53	48	29	52	71	611
Italy	63	74	73	63	46	50	37	42	56	27	531
Netherlands	48	42	44	64	45	33	23	41	38	40	418
West Germany	82	85	84	74	85	78	61	60	94	83	786
European Free Trade Assn.	246	209	226	210	170	154	131	148	224	161	1,879
Switzerland	50	34	37	23	12	19	13	17	32	20	257
United Kingdom	166	145	152	156	129	101	101	102	160	109	1,321
Sweden	15	16	11	15	17	17	10	18	16	13	148
Other EFTA	15	14	26	16	12	17	7	11	16	19	153
Other Western Europe	19	31	46	54	93	59	34	36	46	35	453
WESTERN HEMISPHERE	281	288	325	311	291	227	182	184	266	206	2,561
Canada	88	126	140	130	120	82	72	80	126	93	1,057
Mexico	52	53	71	65	49	49	37	27	47	27	477
Argentina	43	29	20	20	17	16	10	10	22	11	198
Brazil	25	16	10	9	23	10	22	14	16	24	169
Venezuela	18	22	17	9	13	7	7	7	6	7	113
ASIA	189	176	206	197	177	112	122	124	217	202	1,722
Japan	107	99	123	100	83	54	73	69	127	96	931
India	28	31	30	33	22	4	6	8	7	9	178
AFRICA	31	32	41	44	48	28	29	16	42	27	338
OCEANIA	57	52	55	61	62	35	42	59	66	60	549
Australia	54	49	53	54	56	34	39	54	63	52	508
Total	1,155	1,107	1,224	1,211	1,132	875	744	777	1,186	975	10,386

EXHIBIT 4-2
NEW FOREIGN ACTIVITY BY INDUSTRY (1961–1970)

1961–1970 Totals shown
in left hand columns

1970 Activity (584 companies)	New Establishments Manufacturing		New Establishments Nonmanufacturing		Expansions Manufacturing		Expansions Nonmanufacturing		Licenses		Total	
Farming	—	—	9	—	1	—	—	—	1	—	11	—
Mining	148	26	159	24	54	8	20	2	28	4	409	64
Construction	9	1	33	4	2	—	1	—	9	—	54	5
Food and kindred products	309	24	54	6	102	2	11	—	86	3	562	35
Textiles	111	9	13	3	12	3	2	—	91	5	229	20
Apparel	61	4	11	1	8	2	2	—	108	3	190	8
Lumber and furniture	65	6	22	2	9	—	3	—	37	4	136	12
Paper and allied products	138	15	25	3	47	2	4	—	54	3	268	23
Printing and publishing	67	8	27	4	8	—	6	1	16	—	124	13
Chemicals and allied products	729	68	153	11	260	17	27	2	210	26	1,379	124
Petroleum	73	6	33	8	27	1	4	—	18	—	155	15
Rubber and plastic products	96	9	23	—	61	3	—	—	59	5	239	17
Stone, clay, glass products	119	12	25	1	36	2	4	—	46	1	230	16
Primary metal products	231	19	57	7	57	4	7	—	97	6	449	36
Fabricated metal products	257	22	50	3	61	7	4	—	157	2	529	34
Machinery (except electrical)	571	66	196	24	147	14	29	—	374	23	1,317	127
Electrical machinery	473	57	148	19	97	5	18	—	270	9	1,006	90
Transportation equipment	342	35	91	6	115	8	12	—	227	17	737	66
Scientific instruments	210	33	85	16	63	6	13	—	70	5	441	60
Miscellaneous manufacturing (including ordnance)	134	16	35	10	24	2	8	—	100	5	301	33
Wholesale retail trade	95	10	129	18	22	—	25	1	33	—	304	29
Finance insurance	82	5	418	52	44	4	59	4	29	2	632	67
Transportation and business services	81	18	433	53	11	2	45	2	64	6	634	81
Total	4,401	469	2,229	275	1,268	90	304	12	2,184	129	10,386	975

The decade-long trend of ownership patterns demonstrated a continuing increase toward 100 percent and majority ownership of United States overseas investment as a percentage of total activity. "This may not be so surprising as it may seem," said Rhodes, "even though it appears to run contrary to popular opinion." He said the "interrelationship of many multinational companies may dissuade them from taking on new partners in every country. It would get too unwieldy." So for the present, at least, it looks as if American business still leans toward totally-owned activity.

The pressure being exerted by Latin American, African, and governments of other emerging and even industrial developed nations toward shared

EXHIBIT 4-3
WHERE U.S. BUSINESS IS LOCATING OVERSEAS (1961-1970)

1961–1970 Totals Shown
in Left-Hand Columns

1970 Activity (584 Companies)	New Establishments Manufacturing		Nonmanufacturing		Expansions Manufacturing		Nonmanufacturing		Licenses		Total	
WESTERN EUROPE	2,203	241	1,257	130	630	55	178	7	948	47	5,216	480
European Common Market	1,264	151	682	73	361	34	98	3	479	23	2,884	284
Belgium-Luxembourg	250	31	178	25	50	6	23	–	37	1	588	63
France	252	40	138	14	78	11	19	–	124	6	611	71
Italy	259	17	87	4	55	3	14	–	116	3	531	27
Netherlands	190	19	103	14	59	3	13	1	53	3	418	40
West Germany	313	44	176	16	119	11	29	2	149	10	786	83
European Free Trade Assn.	698	71	476	50	226	16	79	4	400	20	1,879	161
Switzerland	64	4	139	12	13	–	20	–	21	4	257	20
United Kingdom	527	55	252	27	188	13	44	3	310	11	1,321	109
Sweden	44	5	41	3	14	2	5	–	44	3	148	13
Other EFTA	63	7	44	8	11	1	10	1	25	2	153	19
Other Western Europe	241	19	99	7	43	5	1	–	69	4	453	35
WESTERN HEMISPHERE	1,168	99	433	65	455	19	70	3	435	20	2,561	206
Canada	478	56	166	25	240	9	28	2	145	1	1,057	93
Mexico	255	14	55	6	76	3	9	–	82	4	477	27
Argentina	69	2	28	6	31	–	5	–	65	3	198	11
Brazil	70	13	23	4	33	2	6	–	37	5	169	24
Venezuela	47	3	17	2	16	1	2	–	31	1	113	7
ASIA	691	85	304	56	78	7	32	–	617	54	1,722	202
Japan	307	40	118	23	24	3	10	–	472	30	931	96
India	109	7	12	1	15	–	2	–	40	1	178	9
AFRICA	127	11	103	8	30	3	6	1	72	4	338	27
OCEANIA	212	33	132	16	75	6	18	1	112	4	549	60
Australia	192	27	127	16	72	6	18	1	99	2	508	52
Total	4,401	469	2,229	275	1,268	90	304	12	2,184	129	10,386	975

ownership may not yet have exhibited its full potential effect, however. The ultimate trend could become evident in the next year or two and will be watched closely by international executives planning expansions into those areas. The trend toward majority interest by the United States partner in shared ownership situations seems unlikely to change in the foreseeable future.

Licensing appears to be losing interest steadily as a vehicle for United

States overseas activity. The number of licensing agreements recorded in the B–A–H tabulations has been decreasing constantly ever since the first survey was made in 1961 when 340 agreements were reported compared to only 129 in 1970, a low for the decade.

According to Rhodes, the "growing sophistication of European R&D" is a major reason for the licensing decline. Let's face it, he said, "more and more companies are doing their own thing."

Chemicals and allied products were the one category in which licensing activity registered a major increase (36 percent) over 1969 activity. Twenty percent of the license agreements reported were in this area. Non-electrical machinery licensing, while down approximately 40 percent from 1969, also accounted for approximately one-fifth of the licensing activity for 1970.

On a regional basis, most of the licensing agreements concluded were with Asian manufacturers and service industries, 41 percent of the total. As would be expected, Japan led all countries with 30, or 23 percent of the over-all total.

It is also interesting to note that nearly one-third of the licensing agreements involved small United States companies, i.e., those in the under $50–million annual sales category.

Last year many analysts had looked for continued, increased investment activity among smaller and medium-sized plants, particularly those in the $100–million range of sales activities. This advance failed to materialize, however. "There was a disproportionate amount of activity among the bigger companies"—especially manufacturers in the $250–million and up sales range—Rhodes noted, "as the economic situation tightened in the States."

In the $250–million to $1–billion sales range, for example, new manufacturing establishments comprised 50 percent of the total compared to about 38 percent in 1969. New installation by manufacturers in the up to $100–million category totaled nearly 35 percent of the total, down from 41 percent the previous year.

Activity by Industry

Nearly half (48 percent) of the total foreign activity last year involved the creation of new establishments of which six out of ten were manufacturing facilities. Comparing 1970 figures with those of the prior year, mining was the only industrial category showing a substantial increase (66 percent) though modest gains were registered in textiles, scientific instruments, and transportation and business services.

As a group, new chemical plants made up the largest proportion of manufacturing establishments announced during 1970—altogether 68 of the 469 involved. The chemical group also led all other industries in 1969. Machinery (both non-electrical and electrical) ranked next in the order as in previous years.

QUESTIONS

1. Why have American firms been more reluctant to exploit opportunities in developing nations?
2. If your company was involved in marketing small appliances what overseas markets would provide the greatest opportunities? Why?

The origins of marketing have been explored through a variety of historical perspectives. This article presents an intriguing alternative view based on the speculation that "marketing activities" were very much a part of ancient intertribal contact. The nature of marketing in a number of ancient societies is described and serves as useful background in addressing the future of international marketing in tomorrow's uncertain environment.

5. New Worlds for Marketers: Speculations on Marketing's Origins and Future

Richard F. Wendel
University of Connecticut

Alexander wept, legend tells us, on the banks of the Beas in India for lack of new worlds to conquer. Unlikely behavior for a man tutored by Aristotle—one who slept with copies of *Iliad* and Xenophon's *Anabasis* under his pillow.[1]

Alexander wept not for lack of new worlds to conquer, but, rather, because he could not persuade the commanders of his phalanxes to push forward across India to the Ganges and create access to the Bay of Bengal.

Like most of the well-educated Greeks of his time, Alexander believed the earth to be surrounded by the Endless Ocean. He told his followers ". . . down the river Ganges is the Endless Ocean. This sea, I assure you, you will find that the Caspian Sea joins; for the Endless Ocean circles round the entire earth."[2]

The promise of a splendid trade route extending from the mouth of the Ganges in the Bay of Bengal by water to the western shore of the Caspian was an attractive alternative to the long, hard caravan route, beset by bandits,

Source: Reprinted with permission of the Dushkin Publishing Group, Inc., Guilford, CT, from *Readings in Marketing 1977–1978*.

that wound back through Persia to Ionia. The water route would not only be safer, but quicker. The markets opened and the political ties secured through eight years of conquest could be maintained by such a route. Dependence on the land route threatened the permanence of the commercial and political domination established by Alexander and his *helots*.

More than a thousand years before Alexander, Queen Hatshepsut looked for ways to open trade with the Land of Punt. More than two thousand years after Alexander, conquest and exploration to secure new markets dominated the policies of nations.

Marketing's Origins

Alexander's concern for protection of the markets opened by his conquests, Hatshepsut's desire to reopen the ancient trade with Punt that the Hyksite invasion interrupted about the 18th century B.C., Prince Henry the Navigator's efforts to offset medieval Portugal's unfavorable balance of trade with the Arabs by eliminating the middleman between Europe and the riches of the heart of Africa and other historical examples argue that the traditional way of looking at marketing's origins may be less than a clear view.

Marketing's Origins: The Traditional View

In his posthumously published work, *Dynamic Marketing Behavior,* Wroe Alderson succinctly stated the traditional view of marketing's origins when he said, "The true beginning of trade was when the specialist began to compete with the generalist and gradually to replace him."[3] Adam Smith put forward this view more extensively in 1776 when he wrote:

> . . . *In a tribe of hunters or shepherds a particular person makes bows and arrows, for example, with more readiness and dexterity than any other. He frequently exchanges them for cattle or for venison with his companions; and he finds at last that he can in this manner get more cattle and venison, than if he went into the field to catch them. From a regard to his own interest, therefore, the making of bows and arrows grows to be his chief business, and he becomes a sort of armorer. Another excels in making the frames and covers of their little huts or moveable houses. He is accustomed to be of use in this way to his neighbors, who reward him in the same manner . . . a third becomes a smith or brazier; a fourth a tanner or dresser of hides and skins . . . And thus the certainty of being able to exchange that surplus part of the produce of his own labour . . . for such parts of the produce of other men's labour as he may have occasion for, encourages every man to apply himself to a particular occupation . . . and bring to perfection whatever talent or genius he may possess . . .* [4]

Smith used this view of the origins of trade to support his notion that men had ". . . a certain propensity . . . to truck, barter, and exchange one thing for another . . . ."[5] Smith's eighteenth-century Britain and the twentieth-century United States are both examples of what Robert Heilbroner has called the *market organization of society*.[6] But no all societies are so organized. Ancient Egypt was organized around what Alderson called "state socialism"[7] and Heilbroner a system of "command"—"organization of a system according to the orders of an economic commander-in-chief."[8]

Finally, there is in Heilbroner's system a third method of social organization: tradition. Societies organized around tradition make and allocate their goods "based on procedures devised in the distant past, rigidified by a long process of historic trial and error, and maintained by heavy sanctions of law, custom, and belief."[9] In tradition-bound societies, life may be rich in ritualistic forms, but it is rarely rich in material things.

Yet, even the most ancient of tradition-bound societies and those organized by command rather than market show evidences of goods from distant sources. Exotic goods from distant places have been found in archeological digs at the sites inhabited by Cro-Magnon man at the end of the last Ice Age. Mammoth-hunters of the Russian steppes used sea shells from the Mediterranean to decorate their clothing. In one Pomeranian dig site in northeastern Germany, an oaken box, looking for all the world like a modern salesman's sample case, containing Bronze Age tools of Near Eastern manufacture was found.[10]

Were these activities what would today be called marketing? They would appear to be closer to what contemporary enterprises involve themselves in than do the activities of Adam Smith's armorer, hut framer, smith or tanner. To see the differences between the traditional view and what may be called the "new" view, a review of contemporary definitions of marketing is useful.

Marketing Defined

What is marketing? One quick answer is that it is the work marketing managers do. While such a definition does tell us something of what marketing is and does, it does not, perhaps, give as much detail as we would like.

E. Jerome McCarthy has probably better defined marketing for more students than any other writer in the field. McCarthy's *Basic Marketing: A Managerial Approach* defines marketing as being on two levels. His first level of definition emphasizes the "macromarketing concerns" of "defining an efficient (in terms of resources) and fair (in terms of distribution of output to all parties involved) system, which will direct the flow of goods and services from producers to consumers and accomplish the objectives of the society."[11]

Because of his emphasis on marketing as a management activity, McCarthy stresses his second level of definition, which he describes as the "more active view," for it looks at marketing from the manager's point of view. This second level of definition reads:

Marketing is the performance of business activities which direct the flow of goods and services from producer to consumer or user in order to satisfy customers and accomplish the company's objectives.[12]

Judged by this managerial definition, the individual enterprises of primitive societies might qualify as marketing, but only to a limited extent. The primary limit upon using examples of internal trade from primitive societies is the extent to which their armorers, tanners, and hut makers think in terms of satisfying "buyer" demands. It seems that the orientation of the primitive trader is more likely to be to his product than to his customer. Customer-orientation is the heart of the way of managing enterprise that has come to be called the "marketing concept".

The Marketing Concept

The essence of the "marketing concept" is the conviction that enterprise decisions should begin with, rather than end with, the consumer. The focus of organizing resources should not be to make or obtain products and then sell them, but, rather, to make or obtain goods that meet the demands of the market place. To employ the marketing concept as a way of managing an enterprise requires not merely that the enterprise be customer oriented, but also that there be an organized and integrated effort to realize corporate goals.

In the business firm the usual goal is profit maximization, but as many recent empirical studies have shown, this does not always happen. Many firms look to survive, to seek growth, to maximize sales or to other goals rather than to maximize profit.

Not-for-profit enterprises usually look upon their reason for organizing in terms of their missions. Libraries may seek to increase circulation or borrowers. Hospitals may seek to improve patient care or to provide medical practitioners with better access to more sophisticated equipment. Ballet companies and symphony orchestras seek to raise the cultural level of the populace.

Whether profit-making or not-for-profit, enterprises seek to realize some objective through a planned, organized effort of many workers. It is the planned, integrated goal-seeking behavior of an enterprise that makes it what Alderson called "a system of action".[13] A secondary limit upon consideration of trade among members of primitive social groups as the precursor of modern marketing is the lack of evidence that it was a planned effort in anticipation of demands of the market place.

Marketing's Origins: An Alternative View

While trade within small, primitive groups by their members does not seem to explain marketing's origins, other behaviors, old-time out of mind, do.

Intertribal exchanges in various forms offer an alternative view of how marketing began. Until recently, the lives of most peoples of the world were shaped more by tradition than market. Who made what and who had claim over what goods were available was settled by non-market means.

The Indian village of the past was not a market economy. Each person performed his job largely determined by his caste, and shared in the village's produce on the basis of a complete system of shares. There was no market valuation of either the services of artisans or the produce of farmers, in such an economy there was no place for selling. The attitudes developed over the centuries of this type of . . . thinking cannot be changed quickly. Since 85 percent of all Indians still live in villages and many are still living partially in a communal system, this lack of understanding of a market economy is still a major force . . . . [14]

In tradition-bound societies, very little change is generated from within. External events—war, famine, political adventures and misadventures—cause them to wax or wane. The life of people in most tradition-bound societies of the past and present was and is short and brutish. Shortages of food, of clothing, of shelter, and of adequate health care have been everyday realities for most of the world's peoples from time immemorial. One age-old way to overcome shortages was to seek plunder through rapine and pillage.[15] Indeed, Wroe Alderson used to tell his graduate students that perhaps marketing's origins were to be found in its role as a friendly substitute for war. "Military" expeditions by contemporary primitive peoples continue to be one of the ways in which goods' shortages are overcome.

While among some early peoples pillaging gave way to "silent trade", some as Alexander's conquests indicate, were still pursuing a military solution to the vexing problems of material shortage.

In silent trade one party would put down its products at an appointed spot and then retire into the bush. The second party would then come up, observe what had been deposited and then put down what it regarded as goods of equivalent value. The second party would then retire to give the first party time to examine the proposed exchange. If satisfied, the visitors would pick up the goods offered in exchange and depart. If not satisfied, they would remain in the vicinity until the second party had sufficiently augmented the goods it was offering. [16]

Silent trade is the "international" marketing of much of Africa, South America's jungles and among the Aranta in Australia's outback.

But, not all societies evolved toward a system of silent trade and fixed places of exchange. When Homer tells us of "dark-prowed ships borne to Egypt by force of wind and wave" in trade southward from Minoan Crete, it is easy for us to imagine he is speaking of an ancient parallel to contemporary international marketing. Not so. Alexander carried the *Iliad* with him as a guide to conquest.

Will Durant has written that "It was as difficult to begin a civilization without robbery as it was difficult to maintain it without slaves in ancient times."[17] The prize won by Homer's heroes was the wealth of Ilium, derived by exacing tolls in kind from passing caravans and merchantmen. The "Gold of Troy" rather than Helen's face is most likely what launched the thousand ships of the Trojan wars.

Beyond the "silent trade" between tribal units and "marketing" expeditions like the Trojan wars were the state trading arrangements made by ancient national governments. The kingdom of Hammurabi in Babylonia and the New Kingdom in Egypt had little or no internal trade. Rather, the system of distribution used was one based on non-market factors. Rank, family, status in the prevailing religious hierarchy—all these and other bases were used as the basis of a system of what might be called "re-distribution" through which taxes and fees were levied in kind, stores elaborately catalogued and transferred to regional and national warehouses for consumption by ruling elites.[18]

Nor was the system of re-distribution limited to archaic kingdoms. In modern times this was the system found by Cortes among Mexico's Aztecs and by Pizzaro in the Peru of the Inca. Each of these new world societies had elaborate systems of distribution, but in neither case did the market play a major role. Indeed, nothing resembling a market existed in Peru at the time of its takeover by the conquistadores.[19]

Each of these despotic societies did, however, involve itself in international marketing. Most used state enterprises not unlike *Armtorg* the Soviet trading company used for international marketing dealings with the United States. Some established *ad hoc* trading missions of the type used by the contemporary Peoples' Republic of China. All aspired to *autarky* or economic self-sufficiency. The benefits of their international marketings were narrowly confined to small segments of their societies.

The inspiration of the Greeks of Homer in the sack of Troy may have been the overthrow of Crete by Theseus. When the Doric Greeks overcame Mycenaeans about 1400 B.C. they brought to an end an early sea trading culture whose markets covered the eastern Mediterranean.

Out of the ruins of the Mycenaean trade empire rose a group of trading cities populated by a people whom the Greeks called Phoenicians. Originally, Phoenician trade was based on a unique resource—the fabled Cedars of Lebanon. But as their trade increased, the Phoenicians began to make and secure goods in high demand among their trading partners.[20] It was to take advantage of the demand for grain among the warrior peoples of Greece and Italy that the Phoenicians founded the city of Carthage on the African coast in the 9th century B.C. It was from Carthage that the Phoenicians circum-navigated Africa in the 5th century B.C. At its height the Phoenicians trading empire was operated by the descendents of its Carthaginian colonists and stretched from the Tigris and Euphrates to, perhaps, Cornwall in the British

Isles. In the process of building their vast trade empire, these ancient merchants from the western coast of Asia Minor and the northern coast of Africa certainly invented the alphabet and, possibly invented what we now call marketing.

Marketing's Future

While the origins of marketing in intertribal and international trade may seem speculative, the internationalization of markets and marketing appears less so. In 1957 a Volkswagen ad carried the headline, "I don't want a foreign car, I want a Volkswagen." It then went on to ask, "Is coffee an American drink? Is hamburger an American food?" In mid-1976 Volkswagen announced that it was completing negotiations to makes Volkswagens truly American cars by producing them in New Stanton, Pennsylvania. In the ten year span between the ad proclaiming the Americanism of VW and the announcement of a transfer of production facilities from Wolfsburg to Pennsylvania, the future of marketing was reshaped.

It became obvious in the late 1950s that the system set up for increasing international marketing and finance at the end of the Second World War was breaking down. In 1958 the United States' share of world exports of manufactures stood at 27.7 percent; by 1972 it had declined to 19.2 percent.[21] Through the intervening period it became obvious that the dollar was overvalued in relation to the currencies of its major trading partners. Because the dollar was overvalued, United States' exports were unrealistically higher in price than foreign substitutes.

We must now look back at the trade and financial arrangements made at Bretton Woods in 1943 by the United States and its victorious allies. Their goal was to help overcome the devastation of World War II by setting up currency exchange rates in such a way that goods from those nations that had suffered most would be cheaper than international offerings of United States' firms. There were, in fact, two international programs of foreign aid set in motion: The Marshall Plan and these artificially rigged exchange rates. During the era of shortage that followed the war, the rigged rates made little difference. For a long while only the United States had the capacity to export anything or the ability to pay for imports from anywhere. But as the plans for economic recovery came to fruition, the competitive situation changed radically. Suddenly, underpriced market offerings from abroad began to take increasing shares of the United States market. Notable among them was Volkswagen. But, it was not just economy cars that began to compete successfully on a price basis. Every aspect of American daily life began to use foreign substitutes for domestic goods.

This substitution within United States markets could have been borne, but at the same time that foreign goods were competing successfully for domestic markets, they began to compete with increasing success in foreign markets. The United States experienced, at first, a decline in its favorable trade balance and, then, an outright deficit.

The same market conditions that made the United States an attractive marketing opportunity to foreign marketers began to attract American capital abroad. It became more profitable to produce for domestic markets in other countries than in the United States. Foreign investment by American firms seeking to compete in domestic markets with foreign marketers caused a further deterioration in the United States balance of payments. This was particularly the case when the Vietnam war inflation of the 1960s raised American price levels faster than those abroad. The dollar, which had been somewhat overvalued, became excessively so. Talk of a dollar crisis and the need for devaluation of the dollar became commonplace in the early sixties. Devaluation is not a popular course of marketing policy among Americans. Rather than face the electorate with such an unpopular decision, politicians kept trying to postpone the inevitable while the balance of payments of the United States continued to deteriorate, abridging marketing opportunity for United States firms both at home and abroad.

Finally, in 1971 a "sharp deterioration" in what might be called our international marketing balance took place. In the first nine months "the merchandise trade balance deteriorated by $3.3 billion."[22] A flight of the dollar developed. The time had come to alter the system of international marketing and finance set up at Bretton Woods. New policies were called for.

Among the new policies promulgated in August of 1971, the wage-price freeze attracted the most attention in the United States. However, the wage-price freeze was only one part of the package of proposals put forth. More important to marketers were: (1) final suspension of gold convertibility for the dollar; (2) "floating" the dollar to find its own value against other leading trade currencies; (3) imposition of a 10 percent surcharge on dutiable imports; (4) a variety of internal stimulatory measures including (a) a 10 percent tax credit on capital goods spending, (b) a 50 percent increase in personal income tax exemptions, and (c) repeal of the 7 percent excise tax on automobiles.

Not all these temporary regulations survived later international agreements, but their major impact did. First, the dollar was devalued by another 10 percent in Smithsonian accords a few months later and underwent a *de facto* further devaluation against such strong trading currencies as the German *mark* and the Swiss *franc* in the months that followed.

In addition to currency realignment, which made American goods more price competitive both at home and overseas, the United States government began to expand its efforts to encourage exports. Legislation allowing creation of a Domestic International Sales Corporation (DISC) was passed, allowing export marketers to defer payment of income taxes on profits of foreign sales. The Export Credit Insurance Program (ECIP) of the Foreign Credit

Insurance Association was created in 1971. With the creation of ECIP, American exporters could for the first time insure themselves against losses due to the political risks of international marketing. Devaluation, quota reductions, tariff increase, blocked accounts, and other political risks are now covered. ECIP is evidence that the United States, long the world's largest international marketer, was finally taking exports seriously.

Like selling refrigerators to Eskimos, improbable kinds of foreign sales began to take place. In 1971 the Bureau of Foreign Commerce noted in a full page *Wall Street Journal* ad that "A California wine producer has demonstrated that it's possible to market American wines in France." The winemaker is Paul Masson and their wines are served at Maxim's, one of Paris' most noted restaurants.

Have the new policies worked? Indeed they have! The market share of United States manufactures in international markets has been rising for three years.

The American marketers taking advantage of the new set of marketing opportunities presented rang up record export sales in 1975. The favorable trade balance of the United States in 1975 was $11.1 billion. In 1974 there had been a merchandise deficit of $2.3 billion.[23] Even that deficit was not so poor a showing as it might seem, for it came after the fourfold price increase in world petroleum prices by the Organization of Petroleum Exporting Countries and an increased dependence in the United States upon imported oil. Decreased imports as well as increased exports show the success of the new policies in making it possible for American marketers to compete more successfully at home as well as abroad.

New Worlds for Marketers

Future American marketing will be unlike its past. A major difference cannot help but be the new position of the United States in international marketing. For more than a century, the United States has been the world's leading exporter and importer in international markets. Despite this preeminence in world markets, American enterprises have treated foreign business as a minor area of marketing opportunity. It seems doubtful that the new worlds opened by the changes in national marketing policies will be ignored by future managers. International markets, now, must become as important to Detroit as they are to Wolfsburg and Tokyo.

It may even be that marketing has come of age as a policy science. Perhaps in future, marketers rather than economists will be called upon to advise government upon international marketing policy. Already there is some evidence that governmental attitudes are changing. In its probe of the pricing policies of import car marketers, the Treasury Department said in 1976 that it was seeking a "marketing agreement" with many foreign car marketers to the United States.

Evidence of the emerging new worlds for marketers in public life and in private enterprise comes with evidence of the final shift in the balance of trade between the United States and the Federal Republic of Germany. "Suddenly, it is the United States with a trade surplus in dealing with West Germany . . . . In 1974 the United States had a trade deficit with Germany of $1.3 billion. In 1975 the United States had a surplus of $451 million in its German trade."[24] In 1976, in 1977 and on into the foreseeable future it looks as if the United States merchandise balance of trade with Germany will be positive.

So, new worlds of opportunity for marketing lie ahead. The old order that prevailed for a generation after World War II is finished, except for its hold on our minds. Like those dusty *helots* of Alexander twenty-four centuries ago, marketers stand on the edge of discovering new worlds. Unlike Alexander's troops, we have little choice but to go forward.

QUESTIONS

1. Contrast the traditional views on the origins of marketing with the author's intertribal trade alternative.
2. Which of the factors impacting on the future of international marketing pose the greatest challenge to American marketers? Why?
3. Discuss how the United States has attempted to avert a "dollar crisis" through international trade policy.

NOTES

1. Mary Renault. *The Nature of Alexander* (New York, NY: Pantheon Books. 1975), p. 127.

2. Bjorn Landstrom. *Bold Voyages and Great Explorers* (Garden City, New York: Doubleday and Company, Inc. 1964), p. 37.

3. Wroe Alderson. *Dynamic Marketing Behavior* (Homewood, Illinois: Richard D. Irwin, Inc. 1964), p. 100.

4. Adam Smith. *An Inquiry in the Nature and Causes of the Wealth of Nations* (New York, NY: Random House, Inc., Modern Library Edition, 1937), p. 15.

5. *Ibid.* p. 13.

6. Robert L. Heilbroner. *The Making of Economic Society* (Englewood Cliffs, New Jersey: Prentice-Hall, Inc. Third Edition. 1970), p. 14.

7. Alderson, *Op. Cit.* p. 101.

8. Heilbroner. *Op. Cit.* p. 12.

9. *Ibid.* p. 13.

10. *Cambridge Economic History of Europe.* London, England: Cambridge University Press. 1952. Volume II. p. 4.

11. E. Jerome McCarthy. *Basic Marketing: A Managerial Approach.* (Homewood, Illinois: Richard D. Irwin, Inc. Fifth Edition. 1975), p. 18.

12. *Ibid.* p. 19.

13. Wroe Alderson and Paul E. Green. *Planning and Problem Solving in Marketing* (Homewood, Illinois: Richard D. Irwin, Inc. 1964), pp. 7–8.

14. Ralph Westfall and Harper W. Boyd. "Marketing in India." *Journal of Marketing* October. 1960. p. 15.

15. Wroe Alderson and Michael Halbert. *Men, Motives, and Markets* (Englewood Cliffs, New Jersey: Prentice-Hall, Inc. 1968), p. 58.

16. Alderson. *Dynamic Marketing Behavior.* p. 99.

17. Will Durant. *The Life of Greece* (New York, NY: Simon and Schuster, 1939), p. 10.

18. Karl Polanyi. *The Great Transformation* (Boston, MA: Beacon Press. Eighth Edition. 1967), pp. 50–51.

19. Hamilton Innes. *The Conquistadors* (New York, NY: Alfred A. Knopf, Inc. 1969), p. 101.

20. *U.S. Share of World Exports of Manufactures in Recent Years.*

21. Jack J. Bame and Evelyn M. Parrich. "U.S. Balance of Payments Developments." *Survey of Current Business* December, 1971. p. 35.

22. Brendan Jones. "Encouraging Exports." *New York Times.* May 16, 1971, p. 11.

23. Associated Press. "Probe of Import Car Sales Seeks Marketing Accord." *Hartford Courant.* June 18, 1976. p. 3.

24. *L.A. Times Service.* "Germany Loses Trading Edge." *Hartford Courant.* May 2, 1976. p. 47.

ENVIRONMENT OF INTERNATIONAL MARKETING

The differentiation of international and domestic marketing largely revolves around the nature of environmental forces impinging on the formulation of strategy. International marketers must be completely attuned to the environmentally conditioned sphere of operation in the overseas market in order to avoid the everpresent potential for failure. The readings contained in this section have been chosen to describe the numerous uncontrollable variables that must be addressed by marketers in assessing overseas opportunities, and in implementing and controlling international marketing strategies. The selection by Susan P. Douglas provides an excellent introduction into the complex arena of the international marketing environment. Critical environmental forces are identified, and the impact on marketing structures in different nations comparatively explored. The second selection focuses, in depth, on the often seemingly incomprehensible competitive dimensions of overseas markets. In this article Robert B. Stobaugh addresses the competitive factors underlying the slower growth rates recently experienced by United States multinationals. A partial answer to slower growth offered by Stobaugh is the different role the United States government plays as opposed to the role of foreign government with respect to multinationals. In the article by John H. Sheridan, the government's role in international marketing is further elaborated through perspectives on its antitrust activity. Contrary to what the United States business community has long argued, the author contends that empirical evidence of adverse impacts of United States antitrust statutes has not been offered. However, Sheridan does suggest that the relationship between the Justice Department and business needs to be improved through better communication.

The article by John Fayerweather provides a classic illustration of how a changing public sentiment can dramatically change the risk factor, hence attractiveness of a foreign market opportunity. The reasons underlying the Canadian's citizenry desire to establish more stringent foreign investment controls, and the implications for international marketers are addressed in the article. The concluding selection by Karl Sauvant focuses on the highly critical cultural aspects of marketing abroad. Sauvant explores the persuasive impact that multinational marketers can have on the social fabric of host nations. The dissemination of headquarters business values and practices through foreign affiliates not only creates additional marketing opportunities, but also affects the regulatory climate of the affected countries.

How similarly do environmental factors influence the marketing systems of different countries? This article identifies the major social, cultural, and economic forces affecting the development of marketing structures. A comparative analysis across five countries in different stages of development reveals only a weak relationship between these major environmental forces and the level of advancement and operating patterns of marketing channels of distribution.

6. Patterns and Parallels of Marketing Structures in Several Countries

Susan P. Douglas
Ecole des Hautes Etudes Commerciales

The theory that the development of the marketing system of a country is closely related to the development of its social, economic, technological, and cultural environment is widely held by many scholars.[1] According to this school a certain pattern of marketing structure in terms, for example, of the size and organization of firms, managerial attitudes, and channel structure may be expected to emerge at each stage of environmental development.

The precise nature of the relationship between environmental factors and the marketing system remains, however, a matter of some speculation. How far and in what ways does the level of environmental development affect marketing systems? Are marketing structures in countries at similar levels of development in fact similar? Can some process of market development comparable to that of economic development be identified?

Source: Susan P. Douglas, "Patterns and Parallels of Marketing Structures in Several Countries," pp. 38–48, *MSU Business Topics,* Spring 1971. Graduate School of Business Administration, Michigan State University.

The purpose of this article is to examine some of these issues through a comparative study of marketing systems in countries at different levels of environmental development.[2] The article focuses on the influences of environmental factors on marketing structures, in particular, and on channel patterns and relationships. Assuming that marketing is a universal social process that exists in some form in all countries, differences in marketing system characteristics may be attributed to differences in environmental development. Three sets of marketing system characteristics are examined: the size and organization of firms, managerial attitudes, and channel structure and relationships. It is hypothesized that environmental factors will affect channel relationships through their impact on the organizational and attitudinal characteristics of firms.

The article is divided into three sections. The nature of the relationship between a marketing system and its environment is examined. Findings of the comparative study are discussed and evidence concerning the hypothesized relationships between marketing structure and the level of environment development is analyzed. Certain conclusions are drawn concerning the relationship between the level of environmental developments and marketing structures.

Marketing activities take place within the framework of the social, political, economic, and technological systems of a country. Aspects of particular relevance to marketing decisions range from such economic and technological characteristics as the stock of public and private capital goods and the state of technology, to social and cultural factors such as behavior patterns, values, and attitudes.

Environmental factors affect marketing structure primarily through their impact on the individual firm. In the first place, the environment provides certain operating conditions that limit the scope of the firm's activity and affect its organizational structure. Factors such as disposable per capita income, cultural life-styles, and literacy of the population limit market potential and thus the scale of the firm's operations. Equally, economic and social conditions such as the availability of capital and the pool of managerial and labor skills determine the type of resources available to the firm and thus its mode of organization. Managerial attitudes are also affected by the marketing environment, since the values of the decision maker are to a large extent conditioned by the values of the society to which he belongs.

The impact of environmental factors on the organization of the firm and on managerial attitudes will, in turn, have repercussions on relationships between marketing firms and thus on the structure of distribution in a country. (See Exhibit 6–1).

In developing countries, market potential will tend to be limited by low levels of consumer expenditure. Technology is often relatively backward and financial resources of firms restricted. There will be little opportunity or

EXHIBIT 6-1
A SCHEMA OF THE RELATIONSHIPS BETWEEN
MARKETING STRUCTURE AND THE
MARKETING ENVIRONMENT

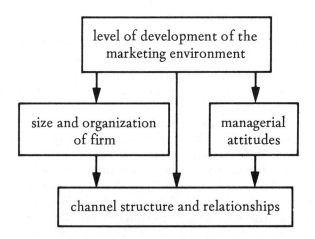

incentive to develop large-scale operations; markets are likely to be characterized by small family firms.[3] Individuals may feel little need to strive and compete, implying low achievement motivation, which may result in conservative and unenterprising management attitudes.[4]

Limited market opportunities and the small size of firms may lead to predominantly local distribution and long channels of distribution. Manufacturing firms may prefer to devote their limited resources to production, and
middlemen may assume an important and even dominant role in distribution.[5] Buying and selling relationships are likely to be transient as buyers try
to take advantage of variations in prices and conditions between local markets.

At advanced stages of development, increasing affluence will provide
wider opportunities, stimulating the emergence of large firms with professional management. More progressive and dynamic managerial attitudes also
will reflect a stronger achievement motivation.

Improved communications and transportation will facilitate a shift
toward broader geographic patterns of distribution and variations between
local markets may decline. A higher degree of routinization in buying and
selling relationships may develop. At the same time that an increasing proportion of effort is devoted to satisfying discretionary needs, conditions may
change from a seller's to a buyer's market and increasing emphasis is placed
on promotional activities; manufacturers may seek to establish and regulate
channel policy to obtain greater control over final sales and there may be
pressure to shorten channels of distribution.

Thus, substantial differences in the organizational and attitudinal characteristics of firms and in channel structure may be expected at different levels of development. The validity of this assumption is next examined on the basis of the comparative study.

Marketing Structures in Five Countries

A survey of the marketing systems of five countries with different environmental characteristics was conducted by the Marketing Science Institute. The information provides some empirical evidence to test the hypothesized relationships between marketing structure and the level of environmental development of a country.

The five countries, Japan, Chile, Italy, Ceylon, and Greece, were selected to represent different levels of economic and technological development as well as different cultural patterns. The level of economic, technological, and industrial development was evaluated on the basis of various classification schemes and indicators.[6] Sociocultural patterns at each level of development then were examined through a cluster analysis.

Japan and Italy were selected to represent two different cultural patterns at the most advanced stage of development. Chile was selected for its intermediate stage of development. Greece and Ceylon were chosen as examples from the semi-developed group of countries. Selected economic, demographic, social, and cultural characteristics for each country are shown in Exhibit 6-2.

The marketing systems of these five countries were studied through direct interviews with representatives of three categories of firms: manufacturers, wholesalers, and retailers. The firms were selected to cover typical channels of distribution for staple, semidurable and durable products. The exact number and specific products examined differed in the various countries but were representative of similar product categories, that is, the staple goods studied were rice, noodles or pasta, and canned goods (Exhibit 6-3).

The number of firms interviewed varied from country to country, ranging from 42 to 61 manufacturers, 22 to 109 wholesalers, and 162 to 346 retailers. The questions covered both functional and institutional aspects of marketing and examined attitudes and opinions of respondents as well as various aspects of the firms's marketing activities.

The data are subject to a number of limitations. A standard questionnaire for use in all countries was drawn up for each firm category. Few modifications were made so that the phrasing of questions was often not adapted to local conditions. This tended to generate some bias, for example, in the responses to questions on marketing research in semideveloped countries.

There were significant variations between countries in the number of firms sampled in each firm category, which limited comparability of results between countries. In many cases the size of the sample was small and any generalizations about a particular firm category in a country should

EXHIBIT 6-2

Selected economic, demographic, social, and cultural characteristics of five countries

Variable[1]	Japan	Italy	Chile	Greece	Ceylon
POPULATION					
1. Total population	97.0	51.0	8.3	8.5	11.0
2. Population density	680	445	29	168	431
3. Population growth	1.0	0.6	2.3	0.9	2.7
4. Active population	64.2	66.2	58.4	65.8	57.4
5. Agricultural population	40.0	29.0	27.5	48.0	53.0
6. Urbanization	43.1	30.3	46.3	38.4	11.4
7. Primacy	54.7	32.1	71.4	75.2	78.0
SOCIETAL					
8. Ethnographic diversity	7-9	1-6	7-9	10+	10+
9. Religious homogeneity	Heter.	Homog.	Homog.	Homog.	Heter.
10. Racial homogeneity	Homog.	Homog.	—	Homog.	Homog.
11. Linguistic homogeneity	Homog.	Homog.	Homog.	Homog.	Heter.
THE ECONOMY					
12. Total income	60.0	49.5	3.9	4.8	1.5
13. Per capita income	626	971	483	565	140
14. Electric power production	1610	1413	680	374	38
15. Energy consumption	1532	1570	1025	562	114
16. Steel consumption	258	245	73	63	12
17. Investment	40	23	12	19	14
18. Agricultural employment	40	29	27.5	48	53
19. Growth rate	11.3	6.1	3.5	6.2	—
20. Life expectancy	69	70	52	71	60
21. Infant mortality	23	35	120	39	52
22. Medical care	900	746	1600	800	4500
EDUCATIONAL LEVEL					
23. Literacy	95	87	80	82	70-80
24. Primary school enrollment	62	50	67	62	60
25. Secondary school enrollment	95	48	34	35	
26. Higher education enrollment	750	362	257	320	56
COMMUNICATIONS					
27. Newspaper circulation	420	101	119	121	37
28. Radio ownership	107	170	130	90	38
29. Telephone ownership	87	96	29	42	4
30. Television set ownership	183	56	< 1	0	0

EXHIBIT 6-2 (continued)

Selected economic, demographic, social, and cultural characteristics of five countries

Variable[1]	Japan	Italy	Chile	Greece	Ceylon
TRANSPORT					
31. Motor vehicles density	34	88	22	13	12
32. Road density	38.0	65.0	6.7	23.0	47.0
33. Railroad density	7.5	7.3	1.1	2.0	2.2
34. Rail freight utilization	59.9	32	28.0	5	2.8

[1]Details of the measures are: 1. total population in millions 1964, 2. population per square mile, 3. annual percentage rate of increase in population, 4. percentage of population of age 15-64, 5. percentage of total population in agriculture, 6. percentage of population in cities over 20,000, 7. population of the primate city as a percentage of the total population of the four largest cities, 8. number of ethnographic groups (religious, racial, linguistic, and ethnic) comprising at least 1 percent of the population, 9. homogeneous: one religion at least 75 percent predominant, 10. homogeneous: one major racial stock at least 90 percent predominant, 11. homogeneous: a common language spoken by at least 85 percent of the adult population, 12. total gross national product in U.S. $ billion 1963, 13. per capita gross national product in U.S. $ 1963 (Italy 1964), 14. kilowatt hour per capita 1963, 15. kilograms per capita 1963, 16. kilograms per capita 1961-63, 17. investment as percentage of gross national product 1963, 18. agricultural employment as a percentage of male labor force, 19. average annual rate of growth of gross national product, 20. years at birth, 21. infant death rates per 1,000 live births, 22. inhabitants per physician, 23. percentage of adults literate, 24. primary school enrollment as a percentage of population aged 5-14, 25. secondary school enrollment as a percent of population aged 15-19, 26. enrollment at third (higher level of education per 100,000 total population, 27. estimated daily circulation per 1,000 population, 28. radio receivers per 1,000 population 1964, 29. telephones per 1,000 population 1964, 30. television sets per 1,000 population 1964, 31. motor vehicles per 1,000 population, 32. kilometers per 100 square kilometers, 33. kilometers per 100 square kilometers, 34. million freight tons kilometers per 100,000 population.

Source: Bertil Liander, ed., *Comparative Analysis for International Marketing,* Marketing Science Institute (Boston, MA: Allyn and Bacon, 1967).

be interpreted with extreme caution. No attempt was made to trace a specific product through the channel from manufacturer to retailer. Inferences as to channel relationships and policy should be viewed as indications of probable trends.

Size and Organization of Firms

The survey revealed some significant differences between the size and organization of firms in each national sample. These, however, did not always correspond to what was expected from the level of development of a country, nor did countries at similar levels of development appear to exhibit similar characteristics.

In order to examine differences in the size distribution of firms in the

EXHIBIT 6-3

List of products studied by country

Item	Japan	Italy	Chile	Greece	Ceylon
Basic Staple	1. noodles 2. canned goods	1. pasta 2. canned tomatoes	1. pasta 2. preserves	1. pasta 2. tomato sauce	1. rice 2. canned fruit
Semi-durables	3. cooking utensils 4. soap 5. shirts	3. cooking utensils 4. soap 5. shirts	3. cooking utensils 4. soap 5. shirts	3. cooking utensils 4. soap 5. dress material	3. cooking utensils 4. soap 5. shirts
Durables	6. cameras 7. transistor radios or refrigerators 8. automobiles	6. mixers 7. transistor radios 8. refrigerators 9. automobiles	6. electric irons or blenders	6. electric refrigerators	6. stoves

various countries, firms were classified into three groups of small, medium, and large, on the basis of the number of employees and sales volume, as shown in Exhibit 6-4.[7] This exhibit shows that in Japan, a country at an advanced state of socioeconomic development, there was a significantly higher proportion of firms in the large-size class in all firm categories in the sample than in any other country. Equally in Ceylon, at the other end of the spectrum, the proportion of large firms tended, in general, to be smaller

EXHIBIT 6-4

Percentage distribution by size or firm in manufacturing(M), wholesaling(W), and retailing(R)

Size	Japan			Italy			Chile			Greece			Ceylon		
	M	W	R	M	W	R	M	W	R	M	W	R	M	W	R
Large	69	83	53	37	15	5	10	32	27	29	13	27	14	4	22
Medium	28	14	33	43	37	33	38	36	62	48	32	60	19	55	62
Small	3	3	14	20	48	62	52	32	11	23	55	13	67	41	16
Total percentage	100	100	100	100	100	100	100	100	100	100	100	100	100	100	100

than in most other countries. But in the remaining three countries there were significant variations between individual categories.

Although the level of development of Italy was comparable to that of Japan, the typical firm size was considerably smaller. The proportion of manufacturers in the large-size class (although higher than in Chile, Greece, and Ceylon) was substantially lower than in Japan. Similarly, the proportion of small wholesalers was comparable to if not greater than that in the other three countries and the proportion of small retailers was significantly higher than in any country, including Ceylon. The size distribution of firms in Greece was somewhat different from Ceylon, particularly among manufacturers, although both countries were semi-developed. In Greece, a higher proportion of firms sampled tended to fall into the large- and medium-size classes than in Ceylon.

Somewhat similar trends were observed with respect to the proportion of family businesses in each country. In Japan, a higher proportion of firms in all classes were incorporated than in any other country. Conversely, in Ceylon almost all firms in the sample were family firms. In the remaining countries a certain proportion of manufacturers sampled were incorporated but the large majority of wholesalers and almost all retailers were family firms.

Thus there did not appear to be any direct relationship between the size and organization of marketing firms and the level of environmental development. If environmental factors influence the size and organization of the firms, the impact is of an indirect and complex nature, which cannot be explained solely in terms of environmental growth.

Managerial Attitudes

The survey revealed few significant differences between the various countries with respect to managerial attitudes. Attitudes tended to differ between and within the various firm categories and with the orientation or focus of the attitude.

Most of the firms sampled were optimistic about future trends in sales, with generally a higher degree of optimism among manufacturers than among wholesalers or retailers. Manufacturers also tended to be more confident about their position relative to other channel members than were wholesalers or retailers. A substantially higher proportion of manufacturers in all countries, but notably in Japan, regarded themselves as in a strong position in the channel.

There was, in general, considerable variation in each country in the competitive attitudes of firms. In most countries there were some highly competitive firms and others much less so. The only two exceptions were Greece, where most manufacturers and wholesalers preferred to make agreements with competitors, and Chile, where the majority of both manufacturers and wholesalers preferred to compete vigorously.

The importance attached to sales as opposed to buying or producing tended to be low in all countries. In Japan most manufacturers were product oriented, although a substantial proportion of wholesalers and retailers were market or sales oriented. In Italy, Chile, and Ceylon less than one-third of the firms in each category were sales oriented. Wholesalers and retailers in Greece also exhibited a low degree of market orientation, although the proportion of sales-oriented manufacturers in that country was higher than in any other country.

Again, as with the organizational characteristics of firms, the data revealed no direct association between managerial attitudes and the level of environmental development. Factors such as the entry of foreign firms with sophisticated managerial techniques may influence the attitudes and policies of domestic firms in developing countries. Firms with a substantial volume of overseas business may assimilate the values and techniques of their business associates in more developed countries.

Channel Structure and Relationships

The findings of the survey suggest that channel structure and relationsips depend primarily on the relative size of firms at different stages of the channel rather than on the country's level of development.

There is little evidence to indicate that managerial attitudes significantly influenced channel policy.

In Japan, where firms in all classes tended to be large, there was considerable rigidity in channel structure and a fairly even balance of power at different channel levels. Traditional channels incorporating wholesalers were commonly used by manufacturers. Although a significant proportion of manufacturers appeared to be dissatisfied with wholesalers and felt that they hampered their (the manufacturers') competitive ability, there was little attempt to bypass wholesalers, who were regarded as an essential element in the channel.

In Italy, manufacturers who were large relative to firms at other stages of the channel tended to be dominant. There was a strong tendency, particularly for large manufacturers, to use direct channels. Correspondingly, there was less tendency to regard wholesalers as necessary and efforts to bypass wholesalers were fairly widespread. Since wholesalers were small, it was also fairly common for them to use agents for purchasing and selling.

In Chile and Greece, where most firms were either medium or small in size, there was considerable variation in the type of channels used by manufacturers. Some manufacturers made most of their sales to retailers and others made most through wholesalers. Attitudes toward other channel members also varied. Although most manufacturers thought wholesalers were necessary, attitudes toward their impact on the firm's success varied and there was little effort to bypass them.

In Ceylon, where many firms were small, there was greater flexibility in channel structure; few stable relationships were established.

Manufacturers often used both wholesalers and retailers, wholesalers sold to other wholesalers, and the use of agents by wholesalers was common.

Despite differences observed in channel structure and the size of the firm at different stages of the channel, distribution patterns appeared surprisingly similar in all countries. The overwhelming majority of manufacturing firms as well as most wholesalers in all countries (except in Italy and Greece) had nationwide distribution.

Variations in prices between suppliers tended to be moderate in all countries and few consistent differences were observed between countries with respect to frequency of purchasing or the unit size of purchase. Some differences were observed with regard to customer loyalty at the wholesale and retail levels, but not at the manufacturer level. The proportion of regular customers reported by wholesalers and retailers varied considerably in the various countries. In Japan, both wholesalers and retailers had a consistently high proportion of regular customers. In Italy, Greece, and Ceylon the proportion of regular customers reported by individual firms tended to vary, while in Chile, customer loyalty tended to be high at the wholesale level, but low among retailers.

If the hypothesized relationship is correct, the absence of any apparent relationships between channel structure and the level of development of a country may be accounted for by the lack of correlation between environmental factors and the characteristics of marketing firms. It is not entirely clear, however, to what extent characteristics of individual firms did affect channel policy. Of all the organizational and attitudinal factors examined only the relative size of firms appear to be related to channel structure.

Conclusions

Despite the comprehensive and scope of the survey there was little evidence to support the widely held theory that the development of marketing structure closely parallels that of the social, economics, and cultural environment. Except in certain respects in Japan and Ceylon, the level of development of the marketing environment did not appear to be an important determinant of the organizational or attitudinal characteristics of firms, or of channel structure and relationships. Nor were marketing structures of countries similar at comparable levels of development. In general, there was often a high degree of variation among firms within a country with regard to both firm characteristics and channel relationships.

These results suggest that the influence of environmental factors on marketing structure may be considerably less important than is frequently postulated. In particular, the variation among firms within a country suggests that individual firms may respond in different ways in varying degrees to environmental conditions. No consistent pattern of response emerged at the national level.

Alternatively, the relationship between environmental factors and the marketing system may be more complex and indirect than that tested. The timing of technological conditions may be a crucial factor. For example, the introduction of advanced marketing technology from a highly industrialized nation to a developing country may distort the relationship between the level of development and marketing structure. The appropriate methodology would be a study of the evolution of marketing structures over time in various countries rather than a comparative survey of countries at different levels of development.

In addition, aspects not considered in this survey—such as the concentration of economic and financial power and the rapidity of economic growth—may be important influences on the development of marketing structure. A more detailed investigation of the role of such factors and alternative methodologies is therefore necessary before it can definitely be concluded that environmental factors do not have a significant influence on the development of marketing structure.

QUESTIONS

1. What are the hypothesized relationships between marketing systems and environmental factors?
2. Which of these environmental factors would be most important to an international marketer?
3. How do you think the attitudes of American businessmen, on the issues explored by this article, would differ from those of their foreign counterparts?

NOTES

1. See, for example David Carson, *Internal Marketing* (New York, NY: John Wiley & Sons), 1967; Charles Kindleberger, *International Economics* (Homewood, Ill.: Richard D. Irwin), 1963; Leon V. Hirsch, "The Contribution of Marketing to Economic Development—A Generally Neglected Area," in W.W. Stevens, ed. *The Social Responsibility of Marketing, A.M.A. Proceedings* December 1961; Richard H. Holton, "Marketing Structure and Economic Development," *Quarterly Journal of Economics* August 1953; George Wadinambiaratchi, "Channels of Distribution in Developing Economies," *Business Quarterly* Winter 1965.

2. The author gratefully acknowledges the assistance of the Marketing Science Institute in making this data available.

3. Reed Moyer, "The Structure of Markets in Developing Economics," *MSU Business Topics* Autumn 1964.

4. David McClelland, *The Achieving Society* (New York, NY: D. van Nostrand Co. Inc.), 1961.

5. See, for example, D. Carson, *International Marketing*.

6. Bertil Liander, ed., *Comparative Analysis of International Marketing,* Marketing Science Institute (Boston, MA: Allyn and Bacon), 1967.

7. Manufacturers with less than 25 employees and under $2,200,000 annual sales, and with 26–50 employees and less than $160,000 sales, were classed as small. Other manufacturers with 26–250 employees and those with 251–1,000 employees and under $160,000 sales, were classified as medium. All other manufacturers (over 251 employees) were assigned to the large class. Small wholesalers were defined as those with less than 2 employees, and those with under 5 employees and under $480,000 annual sales. All other wholesalers with 3–15 employees and those with 16–25 employees and under $640,000 sales were classified as medium. All other wholesalers (over 16 employees) were classed as small. Retailers were classified on the basis of the number of full-time and family employees. All those with no non-family full-time employees were defined as small, those with 1–2 non-family full-time employees and less than 4 full-time family employees were classed as medium, and the remainder, that is, those with over 3 non-family full-time employees or over 6 family full-time employees, were classed as large.

How have American firms fared in the international competitive arena? Data obtained by the author suggests that United States firms manufacturing abroad have not only experienced slower growth than foreign competitors but also tend to be smaller in size no matter what measure is used. One explanation offered for this situation is the aid provided to foreign multinationals by their home governments far exceeds the efforts undertaken by the United States government to assist American firms operating overseas.

7. Competition Encountered by U.S. Companies That Manufacture Abroad

Robert B. Stobaugh
Harvard University

For some time it has been commonly believed that United States-based multinational enterprises are so large that they dominate their foreign competitors.[1] This belief is given support by a superficial examination of conditions that existed just a few years ago. For example, consider a tabulation of the worldwide sales in 1971, *including* those in the United States, of the largest ten firms (whether United States-based or not) in the nine industries in which United States foreign direct investment in manufacturing is concentrated. As shown in Exhibit 7–1, United States firms were the world's largest in seven of these nine industries; furthermore, 43 of these top 90 firms, or 48 percent, were United States-owned and these United States firms were concentrated in the first five ranks.

To be sure, a firm's activities in the United States can affect its competitive position outside the United States. But for the purpose of this article—that is, to determine competition encountered by United States companies

Source: Reprinted from the *Journal of International Business Studies* Spring/Summer, 1977.

EXHIBIT 7-1

Rank of U.S. firms among ten firms with largest sales in nine industries, worldwide including United States, 1971

Rank	Food Products (20)	Paper and Allied Products (26)	Chemicals and Allied Products (28, excl. 283)	Pharmaceuticals (283)	Rubber Products (30)	Primary and Fabricated Metals (33 & 34)	Non-Electrical Machinery (35)	Electrical Machinery (36)	Automotive (371)	Total No. of U.S. Firms
1		U.S.	U.S.		U.S.	U.S.	U.S.	U.S.	U.S.	7
2		U.S.		U.S.	U.S.		U.S.	U.S.	U.S.	6
3	U.S.	U.S.					U.S.	U.S.	U.S.	5
4	U.S.	U.S.		U.S.	U.S.	U.S.	U.S.			6
5		U.S.	U.S.	U.S.						3
6	U.S.	U.S.		U.S.	U.S.			U.S.		5
7	U.S.			U.S.	U.S.		U.S.			4
8	U.S.						U.S.			2
9	U.S.		U.S.				U.S.			3
10			U.S.	U.S.						2
No. of U.S. Firms in Top 10	6	6	4	6	5	2	7	4	3	43
Nationality of Largest Firm	U.K./ Neth.	U.S.	U.S.	Switz.	U.S.	U.S.	U.S.	U.S.	U.S.	7

( ) = Standard Industrial Classification of U.S. Industries.

U.S. = United States Firm

No entry in table = Foreign Firm

Source: *Fortune* "The Fortune Directory of the 500 largest U.S. Industrial Corporations," May 1972. "The Fortune Directory of the 300 Largest Industrials Outside the U.S.," August 1972. For list of firms, see report attached to testimony of Robert B. Stobaugh before the Committee on Ways and Means, U.S. House of Representatives, June 24, 1975, Table A-3.

that manufacture abroad—worldwide activities including those in the United States are not the best indicator. Worldwide activities *excluding* those in the United States are a more relevant basis on which to compare United States firms with their principal foreign competitors. We present such a comparison, along with two additional comparisons that seem relevant and for which we could find data.

The first of these additional analyses compares the size of activities of United States multinational enterprises outside the United States with the size of activities of non-United States multinational enterprises outside their respective home countries. We do this because the foreign competitors of United States multinational enterprises primarily are multinational firms themselves, mostly with headquarters in Europe, Japan, and Canada,[2] and the operation of a worldwide network of manufacturing facilities brings a somewhat different set of management problems than operating just in one country.[3]

However, competition takes place in individual product lines within certain market boundaries. Thus, the second additional comparison shows such data for United States firms and their foreign competitors.

Most of the above comparisons are available only for 1970 or 1971, so a comparison of conditions in 1970–1971 is presented first. Then, with the meager data readily available on a consistent basis between 1971 and 1975, we show what happened in this time period in order to assess trends in competitive strength.

Because we obtained whatever data were available to illuminate this little-known phenomenon, it is inevitable that we draw from a variety of sources, and it is not surprising that these sources used different measures of size. It has long been recognized that size is an imporant measure of competitive strength—it provides scale economies in management, research and development, marketing, production, finance and risk-taking.[4] Annual sales volume probably is the most widely used proxy for size; but others, such as book value, also are used. We use both annual sales volume and book value, depending upon which one was used in the original source of data. It is not surprising that our sources included not only different measures of size but also different samples of firms and different geographical areas. But it is striking that all the data seem to be consistent with a central theme—the foreign competitors of United States firms that manufacture abroad, on the average, are both larger and growing faster than their United States counterparts. And this same conclusion holds for the foreign activities of non-United States multinational enterprises compared with the foreign activities of United States multinational enterprises.

A Static View: Conditions in 1970 and 1971

If sales within the United States are excluded in a comparison, the results are quite a bit different from the competitive position depicted in Exhibit 7–1.

The United States firms drop substantially vis-à-vis their foreign competitors. The reason is simple: United States firms have a larger share of their sales in the United States than do foreign firms. In the same nine industries shown in Exhibit 7-1, we were able to identify eighty-seven firms that have an important amount of sales outside the United States—ten in each industry except rubber products, in which we could identify only seven. To be sure, the United States firms were well represented in this group, constituting 46 percent of the total (forty of eighty-seven), but they were concentrated in the lower five ranks. In only two of nine industries were the sales outside the United States by the leading United States firms larger than those of the leading foreign firms.

Further, in a number of the industries there were several foreign firms with sales larger than those of the United States firm with the largest sales; and there were eight in one case—primary and fabricated metals. Also, in some industries the sales of the largest foreign firm were substantially larger than those of the United States firm with the largest sales—they were fifteen times as much in one case (food products).

The classification of a firm as a multinational enterprise is somewhat arbitrary, and good data on its activities are difficult to obtain. We have used the definitions formulated by the Multinational Enterprise Project at the Harvard Business School and their data on the 187 United States firms and the 209 non-United States firms classified as multinational enterprises.[5] Sales data, however, being available only on the basis of all manufacturing industries aggregated, cannot be used to draw conclusions about competitive conditons within an industry. Still, the data are useful as a measure of the capability of non-United States firms to operate across national boundaries relative to that of the United States firms. Furthermore, there is some evidence that direct investment by non-United States multinationals tends to occur mostly in industries in which United States multinationals operate.[6]

The United States enterprises, on the average, are smaller than the foreign enterprises when compared on the basis of the total sales of foreign manufacturing affiliates. The United States average was $349 million, the non-United States average, $395 million (for 1970, the only year for which data are available; see Exhibit 7-2). Further, as the United States enterprises had a slightly greater number of foreign affiliates than did the non-United States enterprises (twenty-nine versus twenty-seven), the average sales of a foreign affiliate are smaller for the United States enterprises than for the non-United States ones ($12 million versus $15 million).

Although this analysis illuminated the foreign direct investment activities of the United States enterprises compared with similar activities for non-United States firms, two adjustments would be necessary in order to do a comparison on the basis of *all activities outside the United States*. First, the United States activities of the non-United States firms would have to be subtracted from totals; such sales were $14,800 million by 400 manufacturing

EXHIBIT 7-2

A comparison of the sales and number of foreign[a] manufacturing affiliates of U.S. versus non-U.S. multinational enterprises, 1970

	(millions of dollars unless otherwise noted)	
	U.S. Multinational Enterprises	Non-U.S. Multinational Enterprises
Total Number of Enterprises	187	209
Sales of all Enterprises Outside Their Respective Home Countries		
Total, All Enterprises	$65,300	$82,500
Average Per Enterprise	$ 349	395
Number of Manufacturing Affiliates Owned by Enterprise Outside Their Respective Home Countries		
Total, All Enterprises	5,490	5,640
Average Per Enterprise	29	27
Average Sales Per Affiliate	$ 12	$ 15

[a]In this context, "foreign" means outside home country of multinational enterprise in question.

affiliates, or an average of $37 million per affiliate located in the United States (Exhibit 7-3). Second, the home country activities of the non-United States enterprises would have to be added to the totals; such sales exceed by a large margin their $14,800 million sales on United States soil. Thus, these adjustments would increase substantially the average sales of non-United States enterprises, especially in Europe where most of them have headquarters. (Exhibit 7-3 shows the unadjusted figures; adding the headquarters-country sales of non-United States firms would push the $16 million European figure to a higher, but unknown level.) United States firms typically have smaller operations outside the United States than do the major non-United States companies with which they compete. Further, this conclusion seems to hold for all major geographical areas except Canada.

It would be desirable to know the total sales of each important seller within the boundaries of each market for each product line in which United States affiliates are competing. But such data are difficult to obtain, for they are considered by companies to be confidential and are seldom published. Within the time and budget limitations of this study, we were able to obtain through confidential interviews with United States firms, data on market shares in six well-defined product lines in the fifteen countries in which the bulk of United States foreign direct investment in manufacturing exists.[7]

EXHIBIT 7-3

Average sales per foreign manufacturing affiliate in selected geographical areas, U.S. versus non-U.S. multinational enterprises, 1970

| | | (millions of dollars) |
Geographic Location of Affiliate	U.S. Multinational Enterprise	Non-U.S. Multinational Enterprise
United States	$-	$37[a]
Canada	19	18
Europe	17	16
Western Hemisphere other than U.S. and Canada	6	13
Rest of World	6	9

[a]400 affiliates with total sales of $14,800 million.

For each of these product lines we attempted to obtain the following data for each country for 1971: (1) the size of the market; (2) the sales in the market of each of the major companies selling into the market; and (3) the nation in which each of the major companies is headquartered. We were able to accumulate sufficiently complete data to allow an analysis of fifty-nine out of the ninety cells of data potentially available; i.e., six product lines in fifteen countries.

On the average, the market share of the largest United States-owned affiliate in each market was only 80 percent of that of its largest foreign competitor. Furthermore, as shown in Exhibit 7-4, United States-owned affiliates had the largest market share in only 39 percent of the situations. Conversely, at least one foreign competitor had the largest market share in 61 percent of the cases. And most of these 61 percent were multinational enterprises—again providing evidence that the main competitors to American firms abroad are other multinational enterprises rather than strictly local firms. We, of course, do not know how representative this sample is. However, the fact that the 15 countries selected are those in which United States manufacturing activities are concentrated might well mean that the sample is biased in the direction of making United States-owned activities appear relatively larger than is actually the case.

A Dynamic View: Growth Since 1971

The only evidence available to us allows but two comparisons of the growth of United States firms compared with their foreign competitors since 1971.

The first of these is for the ninety firms—forty-three United States and forty-seven non-United States—that were the ten largest firms in each of nine

EXHIBIT 7-4

Categories of companies with largest market shares in fifty-nine product-country markets for which data were available out of a total of ninety product-country markets (six product lines in fifteen countries), 1971[a]

	Number	Percentage
Foreign Affiliate of U.S. Firm	23	39%
Non-U.S. Firm, of which:	36	61
Multinational enterprises	29[b]	49
Non-multinational enterprises	7	12
	59	100%

[a]With six products and fifteen countries, there is a possible total of ninety product-country markets. However, data on only fifty-nine of these were available to us. The product lines are automotive, diesel engines, ethical drugs, steam generators, tires, and wheeled tractors. The countries are Argentina, Belgium, Brazil, Canada, France, Iran, Italy, Mexico, Netherlands, Spain, Switzerland, Turkey, United Kingdom, Venezuela, and West Germany.

[b]Of these operations nine (15 percent) were inside and twenty (34 percent) were outside the home country of the multinational enterprise in question; thus, in 27 percent of the situations, a home-country firm had the largest market share.

Source: Interviews with headquarters of U.S. multinational enterprises. Supporting details are shown in report attached to testimony of Robert B. Stobaugh before the Committee on Ways and Means, U.S. House of Representatives, June 11, 1973, Table A-3.

industries in 1971 in terms of worldwide sales *including* those in the United States. Whereas, in 1971, United States firms (including their United States sales) were largest in seven of the nine industries (Exhibit 7-1), by 1975 they ranked largest in only five of the same nine industries. And the number of United States firms in the top half of each industry (that is, the first five ranks) dropped from 27 ·in 1971 to 26 by 1975. Furthermore, the average sales increase for the non-United States firms was higher than that of the United States firms in each of the nine industries (Exhibit 7-5).

The other information source provides still another clue about the relative growth of United States multinationals and their rivals: data on the book value of all foreign direct investment, regardless of industry, of multinationals headquartered in four foreign countries—United Kingdom, Switzerland, West Germany, and Japan. We do not have comparable data available for other foreign countries, but it has been estimated that, excluding United States-based foreign direct investment, these four foreign countries accounted in 1967 for about 59 percent of all foreign direct investment and ranked first, third, fifth and tenth among the ranks of countries.[8] The foreign activities of firms headquartered in these four nations grew much faster from 1971 to

EXHIBIT 7-5

Increase in worldwide sales, including those in the United States, from 1971 to 1975 of ten largest firms, both U.S. and non-U.S., in each of nine industries (as a percentage of 1971 sales)

Industry	U.S. Firms	Non-U.S. Firms
Food Products	69%	108%
Paper and Allied Products (26)	64	143
Chemicals and Allied Products (28, excl. 283)	94	106
Pharmaceuticals (283)	63	78
Rubber Products (30)	49	81
Primary and Fabricated Metals (33 & 34)	67	102
Non-Electrical Machinery (35)	88	111
Electrical Machinery (36)	43	86
Automotive (371)	36	82

Note: The ten firms in each industry were chosen on the basis of 1971 sales.

( ) = Standard Industrial Classification of U.S. Industries.

Source: See report attached to Statement of Robert B. Stobaugh before Committee on Ways and Means, U.S. House of Representatives, July 24, 1975, Table A-3.

1973 than the foreign activities of United States-based firms—51 percent for the non-United States firms versus 25 percent for the United States-based ones. (This growth is for a two-year period; thus, the average annual growth rates are 23 percent and 12 percent respectively.)

To be sure, certain biases might exist in this study. For example, some non-United States firms might have relatively more trading operations than United States firms and thus appear much bigger by a measure of sales than if another measure of size—such as fixed assets—were used. On the other hand, the size of some foreign firms might well understate their advantage over United States firms because many non-United States firms gain an additional source of competitive strength through their close links with financial institutions.[9]

A more exhaustive study is needed to explore such avenues; but in the meantime, one is left with the conclusion that our many different glimpses of the phenomenon support a consistent view. That is, United States firms face powerful foreign competitors and these competitors seem to be larger than their United States counterparts and growing faster.

The fact that the largest non-United States multinational enterprises seem to be growing faster than the largest United States multinationals is a continuation of trends observed for 1962 to 1967 by Stephen Hymer and Robert Rowthorn.[10] They offered two possible explanations to explain this finding: First, European governments were actively taking positive measures to strengthen their large corporations.[11] Second, the non-United States firms were smaller during that time; and smaller firms—both United States and non-United States—grew faster than the largest firms within any one industry.[12]

The statistics in our study seem to break new ground in that the largest non-United States firms still are growing faster than their United States rivals *even though these non-United States firms have passed their United States rivals in size.* We did not seek to determine the reasons for this, since such a study was beyond our scope. To be sure, the faster growth worldwide (including United States sales) since 1971 of foreign enterprises vis-à-vis the United States firms (as shown in Exhibit 7–5) can be partially accounted for by the fact that foreign firms have a greater share of their sales outside the United States and these sales were inflated because of the revaluation of foreign currencies relative to the United States dollar. However, there is no apparent way that this could account for the faster growth of non-United States-owned foreign direct investment, because the United States activities of United States firms are *excluded* in this comparison, whereas the United States activities of foreign firms are *included.*

It could be that Hymer and Rowthorn were correct—the aid that the home countries of non-United States multinational enterprises give these firms could provide a partial explanation.[13] For example, although the published tax rates faced by non-United States multinationals are comparable to published United States tax rates,[14] there is some evidence that foreign tax authorities are more lenient with the multinationals headquartered within their jurisdiction than are the United States tax authorities with United States-based multinationals.[15] Furthermore, less stringent anti-trust laws encourage non-United States firms to expand more via mergers within their home countries than do United States firms.[16] Of course, these close ties of non-United States firms with their home governments combined with governmental needs for employment and exports cause such firms to focus more on sales growth and less on profits than their United States counterparts.[17]

Aid to multinationals by their home government is an area in which systematic studies are needed. They are needed not only to provide scholars with greater understanding of multinational enterprises and United States business executives with knowledge about the nature of the competition they face, but also to aid United States Government policy makers in their grappling with a difficult subject.

QUESTIONS

1. Why is it important to exclude the domestic sales made by United States firms in conducting this comparative analysis?

2. Why has the United States been able to maintain competitive superiority in such industries as non-electrical machinery and automotive products, yet not fared well in primary and fabricated metals and pharmaceuticals?

3. What steps could the American government take to strengthen the position of domestic firms in overseas markets? Should it take such steps?

NOTES

1. The literature on this point is too extensive to be quoted here, but J.J. Servan Schreiber is perhaps the most articulate propagator of this view. See his *The American Challenge* (New York, NY: Atheneum, 1968).

2. For evidence, see Edward M. Graham, "Oligopolistic Imitation and European Direct Investment in the United States," unpublished D.B.A. thesis, Harvard Business School, 1975, Robert B. Stobaugh, et al., *Nine Investments Abroad and Their Impact at Home* (Boston, MA: Harvard Business School Division of Research, 1976).

3. Sidney M. Robbins and Robert B. Stobaugh, *Money in the Multinational Enterprise* (New York, NY: Basic Books, 1973), Chapter 2.

4. Scale economies of multinational enterprises are a central theme of Raymond Vernon, *Sovereignty at Bay* (New York, NY: Basic Books, 1971). Also, scale economies in management, production, finance, and risk-taking are discussed in Stephen Hymer and Robert Rowthorn, "Multinational Corporations and International Oligopoly: The Non-American Challenge," in Charles Kindleberger, ed. *The International Corporation* (Boston, MA: Ballinger, 1974). Scale economies in marketing administration are discussed in Ulrich E. Wiechmann, *Marketing Management in Multinational Firms: The Consumer Packaged Goods Industry* (New York, NY: Praeger, 1976). Scale economies in research and development are discussed in Raymond Vernon, "Organization as a Scale Factor in the Growth of Fibers," in Jesse W. Markham and Gustav F. Papanek, eds. *Industrial Organization and Economic Development* (Boston, MA: Houghton Mifflin, 1970), pp. 47–66.

5. James W. Vaupel and Joan P. Curhan. *The World's Multinational Enterprises* (Boston, MA: Harvard Business School Division of Research, 1973), pp. 2–3. This project initially collected data on United States firms and subsequently on non-United States firms. Based on the initial experience, the definition of a non-United States multinational enterprise is slightly different from a United States one. Furthermore, more extensive data were collected for the non-United States firms—hence, the project's data on United States firms had to be supplemented with data from other sources. But we believe that the use of comparable samples and perfect data would be very unlikely to change our basic conclusions.

6. Ibid.

7. These 15 countries for which we were able to get data are: Canada, Belgium, France, Germany, Netherlands, Italy, Spain, Switzerland, United Kingdom, Argentina, Brazil, Mexico, Venezuela, Iran, and Turkey. This list of countries comes from Peggy Musgrave, "Tax Preference to Foreign Investment," in Joint Economic Committee, 92nd Congress, 2nd Session, *The Economics of Federal Subsidiary*

Programs, a compendium of papers (Washington, D.C.: U.S. Government Printing Office, 1972) Part 2: International Subsidies.

8. This ignores foreign direct investment by firms headquartered in developing countries and thus is on the high side. However, the bias probably is not great. Calculated from United Nations, *Multinational Corporations in World Development* (New York, NY: United Nations, Department of Economic and Social Affairs, 1973), p. 148.

9. Hymer and Rowthorn, "Multinational Corporations," op. cit., p. 64.

10. Ibid., p. 70.

11. Ibid., p. 73. For a further discussion of assistance by European governments to large companies headquartered within their boundaries, see Raymond Vernon, ed., *Big Business and the State* (Cambridge, MA: Harvard University Press, 1974). Vernon is skeptical about the effectiveness of European governmental policies to date in developing high-technology industries, primarily because of their focus on domestic rather than worldwide market (ibid., p. 20); but he recognizes that state encouragement might have been one of the factors motivating European firms to invest abroad, especially in industries heavily dependent on raw materials, ibid., p. 22.

12. Hymer and Rowthorn, "Multinational Corporations," op. cit., p. 70. This reason is consistent with the idea that United States firms are leaders in product innovation, but that foreign firms, through copying or adapting United States products, gradually "catch up" with their United States counterparts as technology becomes more standardized within an industry. For an example of this loss of industry position by United States firms as technology matures in the petrochemical industry, see Robert B. Stobaugh, "The Product Life Cycle, U.S. Exports, and International Investment," unpublished D.B.A. thesis, Harvard Business School, 1968. For a discussion of the role of the product life cycle in foreign direct investment, see Raymond Vernon, *Sovereignty at Bay,* op. cit., Chapter 3.

13. Ibid.

14. National Foreign Trade Council, Inc. "Economic Implications of Proposed Changes in the Taxation of U.S. Investment Abroad," (New York, NY: 1972); and Arthur Andersen & Co., "Comments Regarding Proposed Regulations 1:861-8 and Analysis of their Effect on Competitive Position of United States International Business," mimeograph, November 15, 1973.

15. This is my impression based on interviews with both United States and non-United States multinational enterprises. Also, see Arthur Andersen & Co., op. cit. Furthermore, some are headquartered in nations that do not place a tax on profits repatriated from abroad; see Carl S. Shoup, "Taxation of Multinational Corporations," in *The Impact of Multinational Corporations on Development and on International Relations; Technical Papers: Taxation* (New York: NY: Department of Economic and Social Affairs, United Nations, 1974), p. 36.

16. For case studies in the steel industry, see Pedro Nueno, "A Comparative Study of the Capacity Decision Process in the Steel Industry: The U.S. and Europe," unpublished D.B.A. thesis, Harvard Business School, 1973.

17. For example, interviews as yet unpublished, by Dr. Henri de Bodinat in France, have revealed such a focus for French firms vis-à-vis American subsidiaries. Also, this lesser emphasis on profits is one likely explanation for the fewer divestments by non-United States firms compared with United States firms. See Business International, *International Divestments: A Survey of Corporate Experience* (New York and Geneva, December 1976), and a forthcoming study by the National Planning Association.

The business community has always been quick to argue that expanding regulatory pressures on domestic operations are detrimental to the long-term viability of the American economic system. The steady growth and importance of American overseas involvement now finds the same concerns being expressed by businessmen with respect to the constraints posed by antitrust statutes in international trade. However, the Justice Department contends that the adverse impact on international marketers, such as lost opportunities or discriminatory treatment, have not really been supported by empirical evidence. The author calls for an improved dialogue between the Justice Department and the business community in order to clarify what can be done to achieve a consistent national economic policy.

8. Is Antitrust Sinking U.S. Trade Effort?

John H. Sheridan
Industry Week

You're an antitrust lawyer for a United States company. One morning, the executive vice president summons you to a meeting in his office.

The firm, he explains, has been looking for a way to get a strong foothold in the European market. After some scouting, it has located a German company which is interested in selling a subsidiary. And that subsidiary has a product line similar to your company's.

"It will give us an immediate entry into the European market," he tells you, "a management team familiar with that market, and an opportunity to export parts made in our United States plants."

You mentally begin to search for a legal precedent. You're well aware that United States antitrust laws have a long reach. But you also know that case law involving foreign ventures is pretty sketchy.

You recall that another company once ran afoul of the Justice Department in making a foreign acquisition; the takeover was interpreted by Anti-

---

Source: Reprinted by permission of *Industry Week* (May 26, 1975). Copyright ©1978 Penton/IPC, Inc.

trust Division lawyers as eliminating a "potential competitor" from the American marketplace.

If your company consummates the deal involving that German company, perhaps the Justice Department won't intervene; the facts in your case don't directly parallel those contained in the precedent. But you simply can't be sure what the Antitrust Division's response will be.

Then the executive vice president fires the big question at you: "Could we be asking for trouble?"

What do you advise? Take a chance? Go to the Justice Department and ask for clearance? Or kill the project?

If you're like many company lawyers, legal uncertainty makes you uncomfortable. Chances are you'll answer: "We'd better not risk it."

Lost Opportunities

The Sherman Antitrust Act, the Clayton Act, and the Federal Trade Commission Act all include language extending their jurisdiction to commerce "with foreign nations." That extraterritorial scope, along with the interpretation put on it by the courts and enforcement agencies, makes the United States antitrust laws unique.

That long reach can be intimidating.

As a result, businessmen argue, many United States firms have passed up opportunities in the world marketplace. Facing the prospect—perhaps remote— of costly litigation, heavy fines, or forced divestiture, they've forfeited potentially lucrative export sales, technology licensing agreement, and joint engineering–construction projects—as well as overseas acquisitions.

In some cases, American companies have lost business to foreign competitors because the latter have been able to form consortiums and offer package deals, while the United States firms have had to bid independently. In other instances, the United States company's inability to enter into an agreement to divide world markets has scuttled plans to do business overseas.

United States businessmen see their foreign competition playing the international trade game under different, more lenient ground rules—without balance of payments suffering the consequences.

Says one multinational executive: "The United States economy is being had."

'So . . . Show Us the Evidence'

So far, businessmen haven't been able to argue convincingly enough to pave the way for a relaxation of antitrust laws or a change in the enforcement posture of government agencies.

Why? Because the evidence is mostly hypothetical.

Both the Justice Department and the Federal Trade Commission (FTC) express a willingness to listen to the evidence. But they want to know about

EXHIBIT 8-1

Court rulings with international clout

Case	Activity	Principle Established
DIVIDING MARKETS		
U.S. v. American Tobacco Co. (1911)	Agreement between United States and British companies to divide markets; a British firm involved agreed not to export to the United States	Allocation of markets illegally restrained trade; all parties to the agreement, including the British firm, were held to have violated the Sherman Antitrust Act.
U.S. v. General Electric Co. (1949)	Patent-licensing agreement between GE and a Dutch firm, N.V. Philips, which included territorial restrictions. (Philips agreed not to sell for import into the United States).	Licensing agreements that include restrictions limiting competition in the United States are illegal—and the application of the law extends to foreign firms, whether or not their intent was to restrain United States trade. (The court held the agreement strengthened GE's lamp monopoly in the United States).
Timken Roller Bearing Co. v. U.S. (1951)	Joint venture between Timken and a British bearing firm to create a jointly owned French subsidiary.	A joint-venture approach does not justify agreements between the partners to allocate world markets and restrict imports to the United States.
U.S. v. U.S. Alkali Export Assn. (Alkasso) (1949)	Agreements made between Alkasso, an alkali-exporting association of United States firms, and foreign competitors.	Export associations formed under the Webb-Pomerene Act antitrust exemption cannot execute cartel-like agreements with foreign competitors to divide world markets or to "indirectly" fix prices in the United States.
U.S. v. Imperial Chemical Industries, Ltd. (1952)	International joint venture between Imperial, a British firm, and Du Pont, involving use of patent licenses.	A joint venture, which in itself may be legal, cannot be cemented by "ancillary" agreements to divide markets.
BLOCKING COMPETITION		
U.S. v. Penn-Olin Chemical Co. (1964)	A domestic joint venture between two United States firms, Pennsault Chemicals Corp. and Olin Mathieson Chemical Corp., to produce and sell sodium chlorate in the southeast United States.	Section 7 of the Clayton Act, designed to thwart monopolies in the early stages, applies to joint ventures as well as mergers. Ventures that would eliminate potential competition between the partners—or create "barriers to entry" by outside competitors—illegally restrain trade. (The precedent is viewed as applicable to foreign ventures that diminish competition in United States markets.)
U.S. v. Falstaff Brewing Corp. (1973)	Acquisition by Falstaff of Narragansett Brewing Co., a major New England brewery.	The scope of Section 7 of the Clayton Act includes acquisitions that eliminate "potential" competition in a United States market. (Though Falstaff argued it would not otherwise have entered the New England market, the Supreme Court nonetheless viewed Falstaff as a potential competitor to Narragansett.)

EXHIBIT 8-1 (continued)

Court rulings with international clout

Case	Activity	Principle Established
RESTRICTING U.S. EXPORTS		
U.S. v. Minnesota Mining & Mfg. Co. (1950)	A two-pronged joint venture by nine United States abrasives manufacturers to: (1) establish an export association; and (2) create a foreign joint subsidiary in Europe. Parties agreed not to sell individually in Europe.	The Webb-Pomerene export association exemption did not "immunize" the joint venture in Europe from the Sherman Act, since the move would restrict exports from the United States. (The court also suggested the "intimate association" among the firms in manufacturing operations "may inevitably reduce their zeal for competition . . . in the American market.")

Source: Earl W. Kintner and Mark R. Joelson, An International Antitrust Primer (New York, NY: Macmillan, 1974). National Assn. of Manufacturers, "The International Implications of U.S. Antitrust Laws," 1974. Thomas W. Kauper, assistant attorney general, Justice Department, letter of April 26, 1974.

specific problems. They want to know which companies were prevented from doing what. Congressional committees also want specifics.

But specifics are the last thing company lawyers want to divulge. They shy away from anything that might attract the attention of the Justice Department or the FTC, especially the Justice Department's Antitrust Division. (If pending legislation to expand those agencies' investigative powers is enacted, these company lawyers will be even more reluctant to do so. Hearings were held this month on S. 1284, the Antitrust Improvements Act of 1975, which would do just that.)

"There is a built-in barrier against willing documentation of the problem," says Nicholas E. Hollis vice president of the National Association of Manufacturers (NAM) and manager of its International Economic Affairs Department.

"Businessmen, and especially their lawyers, say the last thing they want to do is to put their heads in a noose by stepping forward and showing examples of where they came close to the line and backed off. Somebody might want to know about other situations where they came close to that line and then decided to proceed."

An antitrust task force of the United States Chamber of Commerce found that to be all too true. Its study, which culminated in a report issued in early 1974, concluded:

American exporters and overseas contractors are unfairly and discriminatorily restricted by United States antitrust laws. Foreign countries, including Japan and the leading industrial nations of Europe do not impose their antitrust laws upon their export trade, and indeed often encourage their exporters and contractors to combine in the national interest.

But the chamber cited no concrete examples of United States companies which were hindered. "Lawyers for businessmen," it point out, "discourage speculative evidence [on what might have been transacted], since they are concerned about the possible overzealous reaction by the Justice Department in launching unrelated investigations."

Justice: No Sale

The chamber sent a copy of its report to Justice. Several months later it received a lengthy—and predictable—response from Thomas E. Kauper, the assistant attorney general who heads the Antitrust Division. The task force conclusions, he wrote, were "largely unfounded and unsupported."

Mr. Kauper pointed out that lengthy hearings were conducted by the Senate Judiciary Antitrust and Monopoly Subcommittee from 1964 to 1967, and that a number of private studies had been made. None of these exhaustive efforts has unearthed my real impediments to United States foreign trade arising from the operation of antitrust laws," he said.

Further, he stated, neither the Antitrust Division nor the FTC "has prosecuted a single joint venture or bidding arrangement to sell to foreigners in at least the last two decades." And, he added, "fewer than a dozen" domestic joint ventures have been challenged "out of the many thousands" formed during that period.

But no one can even begin to guess how many projects were scrapped before they ever got off the drawing board.

Often, export-related business decisions are abandoned without anyone recording the reason why," says Howard MacAyeal, director of corporate projects at Eaton Corp., Cleveland. "It's not like a lost order, where you can go back and document why you lost it or why somebody else got it.

"To say that antitrust isn't a problem in world trade is like saying that cancer isn't caused by a virus," says Mr. MacAyeal, who—along with Eaton chairman E.M. DeWindt—participated in an informal antitrust study group under the President's Export Council. "It's just that nobody seems to have very much real tangible evidence that you can get your teeth into."

At least one member of the chamber task force found the lack of hard evidence "very troubling." Peter D. Ehrenhaft, an attorney with the Washington law firm of Fried, Frank, Harris, Shriver, and Kampelman, says he considered filing a dissenting opinion.

In his work as an antitrust lawyer, Mr. Ehrenhaft says:

Never have I found a situation where antitrust laws have prevented an American firm from entering into the world market—where there weren't other reasons for the decision to stop or go.

That isn't to say that antitrust considerations don't play a role in deciding which of several options to take, or how to structure an investment.

But as a general rule I don't think one could make any kind of a showing that investments that should have been pursued were totally derailed because of it.

Mr. Ehrenhaft submits that companies don't regard possible Justice Department action as the "most worrisome aspect" of antitrust. "I think people are much more concerned about private, treble damage suits initiated by injured competitors. They have the knowledge and incentive. Triple damages are pretty adequate reward."

Keith Clearwaters, deputy assistant attorney general in the Antitrust Division, believes that companies frequently use antitrust as "an excuse not to support government policies"—such as urgings by the Commerce Department to increase exports. Often, he says, they're simply not interested in exporting, because the domestic market is quite large, easier to deal with, "and in some areas sheltered by trade barriers."

James Halverson, director of the FTC's Bureau of Competition, says: "Antitrust, particularly in the foreign market, is a great excuse for marketing failure. Many of our large companies do very well in foreign markets. The relatively inefficient companies don't do as well abroad."

Complaints from businessmen, he adds, "just haven't been that loud" compared with lobbying efforts on other issues. "You can probably find six or seven isolated instances [where antitrust has created problems], but you'd have to have a much more comprehensive analysis before you're likely to persuade us that antitrust exemptions should be broadened. . . . When you allow people to cooperate abroad, it somehow tends to slop over into the domestic market. Antitrust agencies are very skeptical of that sort of thing."

To unearth the kind of evidence needed to satisfy FTC or Justice, suggests Frederick Stokeld, associate director of the chamber's international group, "We'd need 500 people working on it full-time, I think."

But, he adds, the work of the chamber task force did accomplish one basic objective: "It got things stirred up."

NAM: Protecting the Witnesses

NAM has done a little more stirring.

An NAM study, published in mid-1974, generally agreed with the chamber's conclusions. But it went a step further in documenting its arguments: The report included nineteen case studies illustrating that companies have been inhibited in overseas ventures.

The names of the firms involved, however, were withheld; to persuade the companies to provide the needed information, NAM had to promise confidentiality.

In a number of the examples, overseas ventures were abandoned because companies found their hands tied when they tried to protect established markets.

Take "Company No. 10." It had developed a high level of technology, some of it covered by patents and patent applications. And it was looking for a way to capitalize on this technology in countries where it would have been impractical to build its own manufacturing plants. The logical answer seemed to be licensing its technology to a local overseas manufacturer.

But it didn't want the licensee to use that technology—along with low labor costs—to produce goods for export back to the United States or to the firm's other established markets. The United States firm feared it might be creating its own worst competitor. But antitrust laws, it concluded, prohibited entering into agreements to restrict marketing territories. Thus, a number of license negotiations were dropped.

NAM began its study with a survey. It received questionnaire responses from "several hundred" of the nations major companies. More than 70 percent said United States antitrust laws had injured their international competitiveness. Follow-up input helped to pinpoint six major problem areas:

> Difficulties with joint-venture formation
>
> Restriction on licensing arrangements (such as those Company No. 10 encountered)
>
> A serious problem of uncertainty, because "the boundary between legal and illegal action is ambiguous at best
>
> Inadequacies in the Webb-Pomerene Act (which provides limited antitrust exemptions for export associations)
>
> Restrictions facing United States firms doing business with state-controlled trading companies, such as those representing the USSR
>
> Difficulties in coping with "the monopolistic policies of emerging foreign resource cartels"

The last two problems have become significant in light of fairly recent developments in world trade.

"The drastic change in world economic realities over the last two decades requires a reassessment of United States policy directed at maintaining industrial competitiveness in overseas markets," NAM argues. Rising energy import costs and the overall balance of trade and payments problem add to the urgency of taking a hard, new look, it adds.

In six of the last seven years, the United States "current accounts" balance of payments has been written in red ink. Last year, the payments deficit was slightly more than $4 billion.

That slippage, after years of surpluses, is a "strong incentive" to continue exploring barriers to foreign trade, "whatever those barriers are," says Vincent Travaglini, director of the Commerce Department's Office of International Finance and Investment.

Mr. Travaglini isn't entirely convinced that relaxing antitrust curbs would make a significant trade difference. "Antitrust," he says, "is constantly cited

EXHIBIT 8-2
AS U.S. SHARE OF FREE WORLD EXPORTS SHRINKS,
THE PAYMENTS BALANCE DIPS INTO RED INK

U.S. Percentage of total
Free World Exports (including
exports to U.S. market)

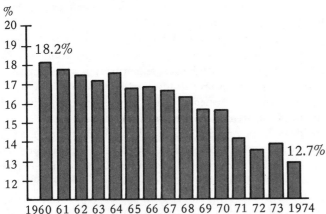

U.S. "Current Accounts"
Balance of Payments
(Billions of current dollars)

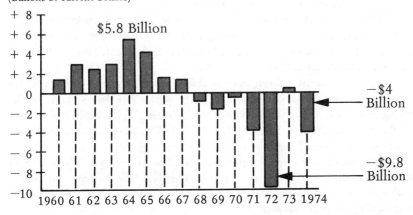

Source: Dept. of Commerce, International
Trade Analysis Staff

Source: Dept. of Commerce Bureau
of Economic Analysis *Preliminary

as one of the hairshirts companies are forced to wear. We ought to continue examining that argument until it is either proved or disproved."

Both joint ventures with foreign firms and acquisitions overseas can open up new export opportunities for United States-based companies. And both can lead to antitrust difficulties.

NAM found the foreign joint-venture problem to be the most common. When the foreign subsidiary is less than wholly owned, "there are considerable antitrust vagaries, particularly when the proportion of United States parent ownership drops below the majority level."

Eaton's Mr. MacAyeal points out: "When the affiliate is less than majority-owned, it is no longer considered part of the same company—But, rather, a potential competitor." And because antitrust law restricts interplay between competitors, the parent firm's participation in the day-to-day decision-making of a minority-owned affiliate may be severely limited— perhaps to the point of threatening the success of the venture.

With the trend, in Latin America and elsewhere, to limit foreign ownership to less than 50 percent, the likelihood of potential antitrust problems of this nature is increasing. "It's one area where the United States enforcement posture needs to be clarified," Mr. MacAyeal says. Where constraints inhibit foreign affiliations, the probable result is "an export dampening."

Many joint ventures and acquisitions have avoided legal snarls. But how can you know when you're treading on dangerous ground?

The key is whether the move will lessen competition, either in United States markets or between United States firms engaged in foreign commerce. More precisely, it's whether the Justice Department has reason to believe that competition will be lessened.

Even a move which eliminates "potential" competition risks an antitrust suit, depending on the other circumstances.

Justice has challenged several cases involving foreign acquisitions, but as yet no court rulings have been issued, notes Mr. Clearwaters, who is leaving his Antitrust Division post at the end of this month to enter private law practice with a Washington firm.

Domestic cases, however, have established the illegality of an acquisition that eliminates "potential" competition, he points out. In one case, Justice brought suit against Falstaff Brewing Corp., challenging its acquisition of New England's Narragansett Brewing Co. In a 1973 ruling, the United States Supreme Court found the acquisition to be anticompetitive.

With regard to foreign acquisitions, Mr. Clearwaters says, "There is really not much uncertainty. The same test will apply." The difficult question in such cases, he explains, is whether the acquired firm should be regarded as a significant potential competitor.

"The factual issues are the tough issues—determining such things as whether the acquisition will affect the behavior of firms already in the market, whether the market is concentrated, or whether the acquisition would make it difficult for other firms to enter the market," he says.

Although United States firms have to be careful that their overseas activities don't affect their competition at home, foreign countries are willing to overlook some degree of domestic impact—if they think the overall national interest will be served.

"The Europeans and Japanese tend to look at cartels, monopolies, and restrictive agreements in terms of the overall impact," says John Wagner, director of the Commerce Department's Foreign Business Practices Division. "Where it will help the country to achieve a particular goal, they'll allow it. The Japanese are probably the most pragmatic. They seem to go to the greatest extreme in looking at what's best for the country."

Articles 85 and 86 of the Treaty of Rome contain the European Community's (EC) "antitrust" restrictions. They are tighter than most of the individual EC countries' restraint-of-trade laws—and they do have an extraterritorial reach. But, many argue, they haven't been enforced as rigorously as the United States laws have been.

EC countries have "tolerated" agreements to restrict markets or to set prices "in some cases where a particular industry needs to be built up or protected from United States competition. Other countries do recognize that monopolies and restraint of trade can be damaging. But they also recognize in many instances the greater good—in improved efficiency—that may result from co-operation or joint action."

Japan's antimonopoly law, for example, allows exemptions for "rationalization" cartels or "antidepression" cartels.

Fred Byset, a staff executive with the United States Chamber of Commerce's Antitrust and Trade Regulation Committee, explains that rationalization cartels help to expedite production of goods for export: "A single industry may produce a product made of many components. Through the cartel, they'll tell one firm to produce what it makes most efficiently. And they'll tell the firm across the street to do what it does best. Then they put the product together at the lowest possible cost."

Because other nations are more dependent on export trade than the United States is, "they have adopted national development policies which have specific export-import trade principles involved," Eaton's Mr. MacAyeal observes. "And they administer those principles in a conscious manner, whereas we don't."

A 'Sandlot Philosophy'

An obvious question arises. Why is it unthinkable in the United States to permit some measure of domestic "spillover" from international ventures if the net result is a plus for the nation's economy?

The question reflects a "sandlot philosophy," says Justice's Mr. Clearwaters. "The theory behind the sandlot philosophy is that if the other guys are allowed to gang up, then we should be allowed to gang up, too—that we should form cartels to combat foreign cartels."

The problem with that theory is that a cartel does one of two things: Either it divides up markets or it raises prices above a competitive level. If you raise prices above a competitive level in international trade, by virtue of an American cartel, then you will probably wind up with less of the market than you had to begin with.

Mr. Clearwaters points out that the United States does have a "cartel program" of its own: the Webb-Pomerene Export Trade Act. "To that extent, we've gone along with the crowd. . . . But at least one Webb-Pomerene export association has been disbanded because it found that the purpose of the association, to raise prices, just wasn't realistic in the face of foreign competition."

Webb Exemptions: Narrow, Dubious

The Webb-Pomerene Act, adopted in 1918, was designed to put United States exporters on a more competitive footing worldwide. It provides conditional exemptions from certain antitrust restrictions for export associations, which must register with the Federal Trade Commission—and that must keep the membership door open. Participating companies can agree among themselves on prices and allocate world markets for exports, as long as competition in the United States isn't affected.

But the exemption is not widely used.

One reason for that, says William A. Bailey, is that the Antitrust Division "has made it as difficult as possible for anyone to use the act."

Mr. Bailey, a former assistant general counsel for the FTC, administered the Webb act for thirteen years until retiring from the commission last year. He says the frustration that built up over the years in skirmishes with the Justice Department contributed to his decision to leave his government post. He is openly critical of the Antitrust Division's attitude toward export associations.

"When it comes to Webb-Pomerene proposals, you can't get justice from the Department of Justice. They think that any time three people get together to do business outside of the United States, it's a conspiracy against the American people," Mr. Bailey says.

Justice, he believes, has gone to unreasonable lengths to block formation of Webb associations. And companies which do form export associatons are subjected to "surveillance" by the Antitrust Division. "They don't like that idea," he notes. Thus, many industries have shied away from forming Webb associations. And they view the antitrust immunity as hazy at best.

In other instances, willing companies have been denied Webb status because the enabling law is narrow in scope. It specifically exempts associations which are formed to export "goods, wares, and merchandise." But it doesn't mention anything about services, such as construction, engineering, financing, or management.

Justice: 'No Deal'

Mr. Bailey recalls one experience in which his interpretation of the scope of the law clashed with the Justice Department view. About ten years ago, he met with officials of the National Constructors Association (NCA) to discuss the possibility of a Webb association that would scout for joint engineering-construction projects overseas—such as erecting steel mills and petrochemical plants—and would coordinate participation by United States firms.

"They estimated that the opportunities we were losing amounted to about $2 billion a year in balance of payments," Mr. Bailey says. "Here we had the greatest technology in the world, but we weren't able to put it to work in foreign ventures because joint bids weren't permitted."

After reviewing the NCA request, Mr. Bailey concluded the proposed association would qualify under the Webb-Pomerene Act, "since about half the total cost of these projects involved manufactured goods. . . . Then Justice took a look at it and came up with the most specious argument I've ever heard."

Justice objected on the grounds that services would be part of the "package." As a result, the association was never formed, though NCA is hopeful that legislation will yet be adopted to expand the scope of the Webb act.

In the last session of Congress, a measure sponsored by Senator Daniel K. Inouye (D. Hawaii) was passed in the Senate as a part of a large export-related bill. It would have included engineering and construction under the Webb definition of "exports." The bill failed to clear the House, but Senator Inouye is expected to reintroduce his proposal in the present 94th Congress.

"We have lost business," the senator said during hearings, "because in many cases we have been outorganized, outplanned, and outhustled."

In one case, an NCA staffer points out, several United States firms spent more than $1 million preparing separate bids on the construction of a steel mill in Brazil. That money went down the drain when a Japanese consortium got the job.

Under a Webb association, he points out, the American firms could have put together a package deal, thus enhancing their chances of winning the contract. What's more, bid preparation costs would have been reduced considerably.

Another primary advantage, he adds, is that a Webb association could provide commercial "intelligence" to locate potential projects on a continuing basis.

Mr. Clearwaters says Justice would be willing to consider approving an association "to look for projects and cut bidding costs. But we'd have to look at whether or not there are spillover effects into domestic trade or United States foreign commerce."

If "spillover" were to be permitted, then the American consumer "would be subsidizing American firms who trade abroad—in the price he pays for goods," he says. "I doubt that the American consumer is ready to do that right now. And I wonder whether he should."

Is a Webb Association Needed?

It may be advantageous to form a consortium to build turnkey projects. Mr. Clearwaters believes. But, he points out, it often isn't necessary to form a Webb association to do so.

"If it is necessary to put a turnkey project together to get a contract, then certainly American firms should be allowed to engage in those kinds of joint ventures," he says. "And they have been allowed."

Mr. Kauper at Justice, in his letter to the chamber, emphasized that where the size of a project or the risks involved are so great that one company cannot undertake it alone, "it will be held to be legal . . . under United States antitrust law.

"It is when the joint venture is proved to have been a device for suppressing individual competition which otherwise could or would have occurred, or for excluding competitors, that the transaction will raise serious problems."

It would be reasonable, Mr. Clearwaters adds, to allow a joint undertaking—even in cases where separate bidding might be also feasible—if the joint approach will improve the American firms' chances of winning the contract.

If companies believe there is justification for a joint venture, but they're worried about the legality, they can get an opinion by using Justice's Business Review Procedure. "It's tailor-made for foreign construction projects," Mr. Clearwaters says.

Just as Justice is skeptical about what actually happens when companies are permitted to compare notes, businessmen are wary of the review procedure.

They raise three major objections:

> The time they spend waiting for an answer from the Justice Department might cost them whatever chance they have of concluding the transaction.
>
> If Justice does give a project a clean bill of health, there is no guarantee it won't renege at a later date. And changes in Antitrust Division personnel can bring changes in attitudes as well.
>
> Because of a 1974 revision in procedures, Justice will now make its Business Review findings public—in effect, tipping off the competition to what a company is up to.

"Generally," observes Mr. Bailey, "the review takes several months. And when a Webb association is involved, it may take a decade. By the time Justice is finished looking at a proposal for, say, a petrochemical plant, it will probably already have been built by the Japanese. "Even then, you'll probably get a letter which doesn't really give you an answer."

Several years ago, a group of engineering firms seeking to form a consortium to look for projects in Southeast Asia, received a letter from Justice which said: "The department . . . does not *presently* intend to institute any criminal antitrust proceeding." But it explained that civil action would be taken if "subsequent developments" warranted it.

Mr. Clearwaters contends, however, that the track record shows that "the Business Review letter is a strong commitment on the part of the government"—though it offers no guarantee against suits by private litigants.

"We've never brought a criminal case following the issuance of a Business Review letter," he points out. Civil action has been taken, however, to enjoin continuation of an activity on which the Antitrust Division later discovered it "hadn't been given all the facts," he adds.

Publicizing review information is "a serious problem," says NAM's Mr. Hollis. "If Justice makes your plans public, it tends to give your competitors an advantage. They'll know who you are, but you won't know who they are."

Mr. Clearwaters explains, however, that where disclosure of information poses a "substantial business risk" to the company involved, Justice has a procedure for keeping it secret. "But the company has to make a showing that it would create a risk."

Justice decides whether adequate cause for nondisclosure has been shown. "Few companies," NAM points out, "will be willing to entrust the Antitrust Division with the final decision concerning confidential business information in return for a Justice opinion of uncertain benefit or duration."

It's another stalemate, perpetuated by the mistrust between adversaries.

Business fears of fickle enforcement by the Justice Department have inhabited a common effort to measure the extent to which antitrust is a barrier to international trade—and to find ways to resolve the various problems.

Dialog between the business community and the Antitrust Division—in a nonadversary atmosphere—can help. And a start in that direction has been made by the President's Export Council's antitrust study group. In one session, top Justice and FTC officials met with business leaders for an informal, exploratory discussion.

"Perhaps," says the chamber's Mr. Stokeld, "the business community hasn't enough of an attempt to meet Justice halfway, to talk things out and explain what the problems are." He sat in on the Export Council session and concluded: "The people at Justice can listen—and there are flexibilities in the system." Through such exchanges, he believes, businessmen might become "a little less paranoid" than they have been.

"It is time," say NAM's Mr. Hollis, "for dialog [sic] not only between business and Justice—but also between Justice and other government agencies, so that Justice isn't operating in a vacuum."

The dialog, he suggests, should focus on two goals: giving business "a clear indication" of what it can do and establishing "a consistent national economic policy." It makes little sense, he thinks, for the Commerce Department to promote increased export activity while the Justice Department thwarts export opportunities.

"There is a tendency," Mr. Hollis says, "to look at antitrust with some degree of tunnel vision. We're not saying we want our system restructured to match the Japanese—but a more positive, more flexible approach is needed."

Mr. Clearwaters agrees there is a need to explore possible problems, and in ways other than the Business Review. Justice, he notes, participated in a Commerce Department effort to prepare a "white paper" on technology transfer and joint research affecting foreign commerce.

"If a misunderstanding exists, that's a problem," he says. "If an American businessman feels he's hampered when he really isn't—that antitrust is a tar baby that he just doesn't want to tangle with—then frank and open meetings can be invaluable."

QUESTIONS

1. What are the major court rulings impacting on international business activities?
2. How are these court rulings related to the major problem areas identified in the NAM survey?
3. "Antitrust . . . is a great excuse for marketing failure." Do you agree or disagree with this statement? Why?
4. How can the Justice Department and business community work more closely to achieve their joint objectives?

Political forces are perhaps one of the most volatile and unpredictable environmental considerations in international marketing. This article illustrates how changing national policies on foreign investment can dramatically affect existing and future market opportunities. Public attitudes underlying the decisions of Canadian political leaders are studied in depth as well as the prospects these attitudes hold for future investment in the Canadian economy.

9. Canadian Attitudes and Policy on Foreign Investment

John Fayerweather
New York University

The year 1972 was an important turning point in the evolution of Canadian policy on foreign investment. For the first time, a comprehensive cabinet level report on the subject was published. The report was prepared under the direction of National Revenue Minister Herb Gray and is a significant indicator of government thinking, although it is not an official policy statement. The Foreign Takeovers Review Bill, which was introduced in 1972, was the first piece of legislation to propose some degree of general regulation of foreign investment. Under this bill, all acquisitions by foreign investors of Canadian firms (above a size limit) would have to be proven to provide benefits to Canada in order to be approved.

While the Gray Report and Foreign Takeovers Review Bill convey some sense of official thinking about policy on foreign investment, many aspects of possible future action still are being actively debated. To assess this situation, during the summer of 1972 the author made an extensive study which

Source: John Fayerweather, "Canadian Attitudes and Policy on Foreign Investment," pp. 7-20, *MSU Business Topics*, Winter 1973. Reprinted by permission of Division of Research, Graduate School of Business Administration, Michigan State University.

resulted in a report on the major influences bearing on the future evolution of Canadian policy. Key observations from that report, with particular emphasis on attitudes, are summarized in this article.[1]

The evolution of Canadian national policy on foreign investment is a political matter—the product of decisions by political leaders responding to their perceptions of the desires and deeds of their constituents. Thus it is appropriate to focus this analysis on trends in attitudes, the quality of the attitudes, the goals underlying them, the range of attitudes among different Canadian groups, and their future evolution. This analysis will conclude with a look at the prospects for Canadian policy on foreign investment.

Trends in Attitudes

One of the few clear-cut facts in the current Canadian picture is the strong trend in recent years toward less favorable views of foreign investment. Two surveys provide quantitative confirmation of this trend. Gallup polls record the following change over an eight-year period in responses to the questions of whether Canadians feel they should have more United States capital.[2]

EXHIBIT 9-1

	Enough U.S. Capital	Want More	No Opinion
	(Percentage)		
1964	46	33	21
1967	60	24	16
1970	62	25	13
1972	67	22	11

A survey reported by J. Alex Murray and Mary C. Gerace gives the results of interviews with 5,000 Canadians over a three-year period.[3] In 1969, 34 percent of those interviewed replied that they felt United States ownership of Canadian companies had a bad effect on the Canadian economy; this number rose to 41 percent in 1970, and to 44 percent in 1971.

The trend in attitudes cannot be directly correlated with changes in the actual foreign investment situation. In 1948, foreign firms controlled some 43 percent of Canadian manufacturing but there was virtually no concern because of it and the government was energetically encouraging a greater inflow of foreign capital. The degree of control of Canadian manufacturing by foreign firms rose to 57 percent in 1958; the further increase since that time has been very minor, yet the rise in public interest has largely developed since 1958.

Therefore, we must attribute the trend in public attitudes to other factors. In part the evolution simply may be an indication of the time required to communicate a fairly complex subject to the people and to arouse their interest in it.

Another quite visible potential factor is the effect of United States economic policies in the 1960s, reinforced to some degree by adverse reaction to other United States affairs such as the Vietnam War and racial problems. Certain economic policies have had potentially severe implications for Canada, notably various efforts of the United States to correct the balance of payments deficit: the Interest Equalization Tax, the direct investment restraints, the 10 percent surcharge on imports imposed on 15 August 1971, and the creation of the Domestic International Sales Corporation (DISC) to foster United States exports by tax deferrals for one-half of the export profits.

A third line of explanation suggested during my interviews is more subtle but perhaps just as important; it relates to the general approach of Canadians to internal affairs. Traditionally it is said that government activities went along from year to year with little reexamination or innovation. As one official put it bluntly, "Life was dull." Then in the 1960s an awakening process gained momentum and a number of matters ranging from constitutional reform to economic policies came under scrutiny. As these reviews proceeded, foreign investment emerged in the minds of government officials and others as more and more important for two reasons: first, it was identified as a contributing factor in many of the internal issues being examined and, second, its character was a complication in many of the solutions being proposed.

The Quality of the Attitudes

To fully understand the nature of the attitudes one must look at the perceptions of Canadians of the effects of foreign investment and its importance compared to interrelated matters.

A broad picture of the perceived effects of foreign investment is provided by a recent attitude study. In late 1971, I made a survey of four elite groups (members of Parliament, permanent government officials, heads of business firms, and labor union leaders).[4] A related survey of a sample of the general public was made for me early in 1972 by a private organization. The results of the latter survey were not entirely satisfactory as there was a poor response from low income groups. However, the data from both surveys, confirm a quite consistent pattern of attitudes on the three main types of effects of foreign firms on Canada. The judgment of the cultural impact is essentially neutral; the economic effect both over-all and on the balance of payments are considered somewhat on the negative side; and the loss of control of national affairs is viewed as quite adverse.

This pattern may be considered with other evidence on the subject. Dr. Murray and Ms. Gerace report that those who were favorable to foreign investment mentioned most often its economic contributions.[5] Those with adverse views based them most often on the loss of control of national affairs. The Gray Report observes that

such studies as have been done by others—and they involve many qualifications—tend to suggest that the overall impact of foreign direct investment on economic activity has had a moderately favourable effect.[6]

Its economic criticisms are directed at specific multinational firm actions more than their total performance and again the critical emphasis is on the control aspect.

This evidence fits a generally perceived Canadian view that there is a trade off between economic benefits of foreign investment and loss of control of national affairs. The perception that greater independence through reduction of foreign investment would carry an economic cost leads naturally to putting that choice directly to the people. Such efforts have been made and the results provide some indicator of reactions. One general survey asked if people would accept a lower standard of living in order to keep further foreign investment out of Canada. More people answered "no" (46.6 percent) than "yes" (43.9 percent).[7] In another survey, M.P. Max Saltsman found that 95 percent of his constituents wanted more independence—but with no loss of standard of living.[8]

These results indicate the difficulty of determining clearly the degree of sacrifice Canadians are willing to accept as a cost of independence. Per capita income is now 25 percent less in Canada than in the United States. Thus, most Canadians are aware that they are paying a high price for independence. Without any pretense at precision one can simply imput from the surveys and other impressions that it is doubtful whether a majority of Canadians today are prepared to accept significant further economic sacrifices to reduce the role of foreign firms.

To assess the quality of the Canadian attitudes one also must know where the various elements fall in the priority scales of the people. Gallup polls reported the "main worry" of Canadians place the question as clearly subordinate to economic issues.[9]

This view was evident from the negligible role of the foreign investment question in the 1972 political campaign. While its minor role was due in part to the lack of significant differences between the two major parties that will be discussed later, in large part it confirms the relatively low priority given to

EXHIBIT 9-2

	1966	1972
	(Percentage)	
Employment	7	41
The Economy	35	14
U.S. Control	3	8

the subject. The decisions of the Conservatives and Liberals not to emphasize the issue were based on their private polls that showed that the subject had little voter appeal as compared to economic issues. The New Democratic Party made periodic efforts to push the foreign investment question to the fore but it also got little response. By comparison it apparently was highly successful with its basic theme, *the corporate welfare bums,* charging that business was reaping rewards of assorted government handouts while the people suffered from unemployment, inflation, and other economic troubles.

The conclusion to be drawn from the evidence is that in the crunch Canadians are far more concerned with the economic problems immediately affecting their lives than with the nebulous question of foreign control. Since actions to deal with the latter are perceived as having possible adverse economic effects, Canadians are generally hesitant about them. Thus, while the desires of many Canadians to limit foreign investment and reduce the degree of control it exerts are real, their quality as a factor in actual decisions is strongly moderated both by the ranking of the problem beside other issues and the effect of those issues on it.

The Quest for National Identity

The differences in attitudes on foreign investment and the changes in those attitudes over time are due in no small part to the difficulty Canadians experience in defining the goals of their nationalism. Virtally all Canadians will agree that they wish to preserve the "national identity" of Canada. But what does that mean? There are a variety of views underlain by differences in opinions as to what is desirable and what is feasible.

An excellent presentation of the thinking of those who regard the preservation of national identity as hopeless is found in George Grant's *Lament for a Nation.*[10] Dr. Grant's scholarly treatise develops at some length the nature of the impact of the United States on Canada and the evolution of the response to that impact. His conclusions are based on two main points. First, he observes that the basic purpose of life is consumption and that the benefits for consumption from economic integration with the United States are so overwhelming that the border is an anachronism.[11] Second, he argues that there is virtually nothing unique about Canada in its culture or other characteristics so its preservation as a nation is not only impractical but not even worthwhile.[12]

Dr. Grant foresees a considerable passage of time before these basic forces will deliver the final blow to Canadian identity: "Canada has ceased to be a nation but its formal political existence will not end quickly,"[13] he says. Inertia, the political decision-making process, and, ironically, United States resistance to absorption of Canada particularly because of the French Canadian problem will, he anticipates, defer for many years full political union with the United States.

Concepts of desirable and feasible national identity grade away from this in varied directions. So far as foreign investment is concerned, the main thrust is in the direction of formal and institutional aspects of industrial control. The extreme views consider that national identity requires that industrial decisions be entirely within Canadian hands including both top executives in business and direct government control. The more moderate views are satisfied that national identity is protected if the industrial decision-making structure is responsive to national desires which may be accomplished in a variety of ways, including limited regulatory measures, presence of Canadian nationals in management, or simply sensitivity of industrial executives to Canadian viewpoints.

Another approach looks more to the options open to Canadians in specific economic situations than to control of the whole economy. It accepts the fact that all nations, even the United States, are constrained in their overall economic control by international interdependence. The outlets for national identity therefore seem to lie in having sufficient control to realize fully the limited separate capabilities that each nation may have within it. This philosophy is concerned with preservation of sufficient elements of control in Canada so that the nation may exercise its identity when it so desires. Important objectives in pursuit of this philosophy are the support of Canadian entrepreneurs, the assurance that products appropriate to the distinctive life style of Canada can be developed, and the availability of opportunities for individuals to find employment within Canada according to their educational capabilities and personal inclinations.

It is in this context that the concept of the "truncated" firm emphasized in the Gray Report must be understood.[14] The truncated subsidiary is one in which key functions are absent, being in the hands of the parent organization. The deficiencies most often mentioned are top management, research and development, and exports. The question as defined by Carl Beigie, executive director of the Private Planning Association of Canada, is whether "foreign-owned enterprises have become so predominant—reaching a certain 'critical mass'—that important gaps have emerged in Canada's capabilities."[15]

To round out this discussion of the meaning of national identity, it is appropriate here to summarize an article entitled "Canada-U.S. Relations: Options for the Future" written by External Affairs Minister Mitchell Sharp.[16] Mr. Sharp concentrates on just a few central ideas. His main preoccupation is with "the continental pull," which has and will continue to draw Canada into greater ties with the United States. He observes that the consequent close interrelationship "even as an inadvertent process, has acquired a momentum that, as one American student of Canadian affairs has recently put it, is 'subject to profound internal growth.' " The logics of proximity and similarity lead naturally to cultural and economic integration and as the interaction proceeds, largely through the free action of private individuals and institutions, the ties between the nations become more numerous and stronger.

Mr. Sharp's analysis is guided by the dual criteria of distinctness and harmony. Accepting harmony with the United States as an obvious requisite, he focuses his main attention on distinctness. The problem in 1972, according to Mr. Sharp, was in a growing sense that "the underlying trend in the Canadian-U.S. relationship may be becoming less congenial to the conception of Canadian distinctness." He sets forth three policy options as possible responses to this situation. The first is that Canada go along as it has, reacting to problems as they arise, working out in each the best possible balance of results. He rejects this "reactive posture" as "not likely to represent much of an advance. On the contrary, if the continental pull is, in fact, becoming stronger, we may . . . have to run harder simply to stay in place."

The second option is to move deliberately toward closer integration with the United States. Mr. Sharp accepts the value of such steps that have been taken, (the auto agreement, for example) and apparently opens the door to some further movements in that direction—giving careful attention to their limitations. He feels, however, that the loss of economic and, possibly, political distinctness is a major deterrent if this approach is followed. He says that it is a "moot question whether this option, or any part of it, is politically tenable in the present or any foreseeable climate of Canadian public opinion."

"The third option would be to lessen, over time, the vulnerability of the Canadian economy to external factors—including, in particular, the impact of the United States and, in the process, to strengthen our capacity to advance basic Canadian goals and develop a more confident sense of national identity." This is the course Mr. Sharp prescribes as being both consistent with national goals and feasible. He stresses the "over time" aspect because the elements of national policy required can only evolve slowly given cost and other constraints. The guiding philosophy will be to build a stronger Canada with more varied world relations, better able to maintain its distinctness.

Mr. Sharp's views are probably as close as one could come today to the central tendency of Canadian attitudes on the meaning of national identity and the basic ways to pursue it. But, in light of the other views we have noted, the picture is not clear; that is probably the most important point to be observed about the whole subject. In Canada there is no consensus on the matter and there is unlikely to be one; this is because of basic differences in personal psychology and in individual circumstances and goals, and also because the feasibility of the options open to Canadians are so uncertain and changing constantly. The reality with which one must deal in assessing the situation is that a variety of viewpoints exist as to the extent and form of cultural, political, and economic identity which the country should seek to preserve as essential to the widely expressed desire for national identity.

The Spectrum of Attitudes

Of prime importance in the evolution of Canadian policy on foreign investment is this wide diversity of opinions. To get a feel for the spectrum of viewpoints the population will be sliced along three dimensions: opinion groups, socio-economic classes, and political parties.

Opinion Groups

In Canada one can find all manner of shadings of opinions on foreign movement. While the hazards of oversimplification in this process are real, there is a substantial clustering of people around several patterns of thinking.

At one extreme of this spectrum are the *radical nationalists* who advocate a socialist reversal of the foreign investment process. The organizational center for this approach is the Waffle Group, and the most conspicuous leader is Professor Melville Watkins of the University of Toronto. The Wafflers are determined that Canadians should have full control over their own economic affairs and that any significant control of industry by foreign firms is inconsistent with this goal. They do not believe that private enterprise is capable of reasserting control over industry or that there is sufficient private capital to purchase back control of foreign-owned subsidiaries. Thus, the only practical solution they see is nationalization of the foreign firms.

Numerically, the Waffle Group is a very small factor. It has a mailing list of only 2,500–3,000 people, according to Professor Watkins.[17] Geographically it is limited in large part to Ontario, particularly Toronto. The membership is drawn largely from the intellectuals in academic and, to a much lesser degree, labor circles. Its strength lies in the aggressive, articulate qualities of its leadership whose ideas are constant prods to the main body of national thinking. Undoubtedly their efforts have been a factor in moving Canadian thinking as a whole toward stronger nationalistic attitudes on foreign investment even though their particular solutions have only a very small following.

Moving back from the extreme end of the spectrum, we find a substantially large group who may be labeled the *strong nationalists*. Their organizational center is the Committee for an Independent Canada (CIC) formed in 1970. The CIC shares with the Waffle Group a determination to reassert Canadian control over the economy and a willingness to make sacrifices in the interest of Canadian independence. They differ from the Wafflers, however, in their intent to achieve their goals essentially within the established system of private enterprise and related governmental institutions.

In late 1972 the CIC appeared to be in the process of a major change in character and role. For its first two years it was guided by a general philosophy with little attempt at agreement on specific policy proposals. The membership covered a very wide range of views running all the way from some who were close to the Waffle approach to others with a mild concept of how the foreign investment question should be handled. The breadth of CIC influence at this stage may be measured by the fact that the group obtained 170,000 signatures on a petition to Prime Minister Pierre Trudeau in 1971.

In September 1972 the CIC held a policy conference in Edmonton, the outcome of which changes its image and will probably alter its membership. The delegates voted on some 202 specific policy proposals concerning foreign ownership, Canadian capital, trade unions, energy and the north, land, education, cinema and television, and the arts. Instead of the former vague philosophical image, the CIC now has a concrete program.

The program has a central character which can be concisely defined. The goal of reasserting Canadian control over the society is to be pursued by a wide range of specific measures—tax changes, investment controls, subsidies, land ownership regulations, and the like. In toto these measures add up to a substantial increase of social direction of national affairs, largely by the government. For example, rationalization is to take place by cooperative direction of government and industry councils; all foreign investments will be screened with the review covering all significant activities; the government should ask and, if necessary, require the chartered banks to devote more of their resources to higher risk enterprises, and unions will be detached from United States affiliation by several steps such as requiring small sections of internationals to merge with large units.

The CIC continues to differ from the Wafflers in rejecting outright socialism. But their program has moved closer to the Wafflers in philosophically accepting the assumption that the goals desired cannot be achieved without assertion of social intent through government intervention in the economy. In effect, the CIC brand of nationalism requires of its adherents acceptance of a cost in social freedom along with whatever economic costs may be involved in establishing the degree of economic independence sought. This clarified and tougher policy position will probably result in a smaller but more well directed membership. Some evidence of this was a report from the CIC in late 1972 that its membership drive having reached 8,000 was far below expectations.

The third group may be called the *moderate nationalists*. There is no organization representing them but they appear to comprise the majority of Canadians. The moderate nationalists do not generally speak in terms of a set of positive actions to reverse the foreign investment process nor of national sacrifices to achieve this goal. Rather, they advocate efforts to move toward more independence of Canadian industry by encouragement to Canadian firms, and making foreign firms serve the national interest better while protecting the Canadian standard of living.

They conceive of this approach as a form of "positive nationalism," which builds the national sector without significantly obstructing the foreign-owned portion. In reality, the appearance that this approach does not involve sacrifice by Canadians is not valid. The measures (such as subsidies and differential tax advantages) advocated by the moderate nationalists to support Canadian firms add a cost to the standard of living, but it is more hidden and smaller than the policies of the stronger nationalists which could result in direct reduction of new foreign investment.

The next three groups should be discussed together because, while their underlying attitudes are different, their positions on foreign investment are similar. The three may be labelled as the *internationalists,* the *non-nationalists,* and the *unconcerned.* They all tend to agree on laissez faire foreign investment policy. They are distinguished from the moderate nationalists in that they will not support the cost and complications of the special efforts to subsidize, push, or favor Canadian firms to build them up vis-à-vis foreign-owned ones. That is, they believe in a truly open, non-discriminatory economy in which the role of foreign firms evolves according to market forces without special nationalistically-oriented influences.

At the other end of the spectrum we find the *continentalists,* a term long established in the Canadian vocabulary to describe those who essentially believe in union of Canada and the United States. While in the early days, continentalism was often associated with political union, the advocates of full integration are very rare today. The majority of those described as continentalists essentially are advocates of a high degree of economic integration. Specifically, they favor a common market with a free flow of trade and investment between Canada and the United States and integrated handling of such matters as energy. Explicit advocates of continentalism are not organized like the CIC so they are harder to identify and count. Nonetheless, they would appear to be as numerous and influential as the CIC.

As one indication of this, we may note that in recent months the concept of the common market with the United States has been advocated by the Economic Council of the Maritime Provinces and the president of the Canadian Chamber of Commerce.

A true continentalist is by definition an antinationalist and that is a position of which society in general does not approve. To many Canadians continentalism is treason. Thus, in the visible give-and-take of political processes their influence is less than that of the nationalists of varying colors who are able to appeal to more popular emotional responses. The continentalists' influence accordingly is exerted rather in the less visible processes of government decision making reinforced by basic economic arguments. The future of their influence lies essentially in the strength of these economic considerations.

Socio-Economic Classes

Looking at the Canadian population along socio-economic dimensions, we find some distinct difference in attitudes. A basic statistical framework for comparisons here is provided by my surveys, to which illustrative evidence is added from a variety of published sources.

Data indicates that there is some differentiation according to social groups within the general public; those with an academic orientation and people lower on the income scale tend to have more negative views while those higher up on the economic scale give more favorable responses.

Among the key elite decision-making groups, the businessmen are most favorable. While some individual businessmen have a CIC-nationalist orientation, the business community as a whole tends to be relatively favorable to foreign investment. Businessmen are pragmatic by nature and, by-and-large, their experience with the economy dominated by foreign enterprise has been satisfactory. The adverse experiences seem to be most often directly related to competitive situations in which foreign firms are hurting the interests of Canadian companies. A good example of this apparently was provided in the debate in 1971 over the control of investment firms in Ontario. A case was made to the effect that Canadian development would be best protected if ownership of investment firms was limited to Canadians. However, a number of Canadian observers claimed that the main impetus for the efforts to resist foreign ownership came from Toronto investment houses seeking to protect their personal interests against strong competition from more aggressive and better financed foreign firms.

Opinions toward foreign companies of the two government groups are a little more adverse than those of the business leaders. Data also conforms to a logical expectation that the government leaders would be more concerned than businessmen with the difficulties of exercising control over the affairs of the country because of foreign ownership of business. Nonetheless, the government leaders are generally favorable in their appraisal.

Labor leaders in the elite group survey expressed a distinctly more adverse view of foreign companies than that of the other three groups. This difference was also noted in surveys in Britain and France and it seems quite likely that it is due in substantial part to ideological views about big business in general rather than any particular bias against foreign firms.[18]

In my interviews, I found that Canadians generally concurred that despite negative public statements about foreign investment, labor leaders took a rather pragmatic, essentially favorable view of foreign firms. Their overriding concern was for (1) more jobs, and (2) improved working conditions, both matters on which the foreign-controlled firms were favorably viewed. Their negative opinions were related more to specific actions (plant shutdowns, for example) than a general desire to check foreign investment.

Political Parties

The positions of the leading political parties on foreign investment can be discussed at two levels. Superficially, and for many practical purposes, the story is very simple. The Conservatives and Liberals have similar moderate nationalist views and the New Democratic Party (NDP) is strongly nationalistic. But the Conservatives and Liberals do have somewhat different positions and these differences will be significant for the future, especially in light of the uncertain political prospects coming out of the 1972 election.

As background for this discussion it is well to present a brief picture of the character of the main parties, synthesizing the analyses of several experts.[19] Both are essentially coalitions of mixed social, economic, ethnic, and geographic dimensions. They share basically similar conservative values, taking progressive positions on an opportunistic basis as circumstances direct them. The Conservatives have slightly more following among lower income groups and people with traditionalist, conservative leanings, especially in certain regions. But these socio-economic differences are small and may shift from election to election. Historically, the Liberals have been associated more with conciliatory relations with the United States, while the Conservatives have come to power three times (1911, 1930, and 1957) in periods of anti-American emotion.

With this background in mind we may look at the specific issues on which the Conservatives and Liberals have visibly differed. The proposed Foreign Takeovers Review Bill provided the only recent direct confrontation on a general foreign investment policy issue.

The official Liberal position was manifest in the decision to present the bill. That there was substantial disagreement within the party was also readily observed. Thirteen Liberal M.P.s endorsed the stand of the Committee for Independent Canada which declared that the bill was entirely inadequate.

The Conservative views were also divided. M.P. Gordon Fairweather presented the official opposition statement in Commons after the opening Liberal speech.[20] His statement was notably vague. The most specific indication of a position was, "I feel Bill C-201 in no way goes to the root of the problems created by direct foreign investment in Canada. This is not to say it is not a partial solution." Beyond this he dealt in very general terms with the constitutionality of the bill, the need for a general industrial strategy and guidelines for review, and the merits of other approaches to foreign investment like key sector expansion and international control. The concensus among people I interviewed in Ottawa seemed to be that the speech was indicative of the wide division of views within the party. The assumption was that the party caucus had failed to agree on a clear policy on the bill, so Mr. Fairweather had been instructed to say as little as he respectably could. Overall the indications are that the Conservatives accepted the takeovers bill but that because the moderating influences in their ranks were stronger than those among the Liberals, a somewhat milder approach was advocated.

Two other issues may best be discussed together. The Conservatives in their recent declarations have stressed Canadianization of boards of directors and greater financial disclosure. The Liberals have played down the former and indicated no interest in pushing the latter beyond the moderate requirements they enacted in recent years. The board of directors and disclosure proposals are apparently rather minor in that they would neither have much effect on performance of foreign firms nor cause them much operating complication.

There are two lines of reasoning that might explain the Conservative emphasis on these points. One is that they represent directions in which one can move at least a little to improve the performance of foreign-owned firms while still not interfering with the basic freedom of management decision making, as compared, for example, to the direct intervention in the screening process. The other rationale is that the position is strictly opportunistic. The Conservatives are under pressure to offer something different to counter the initiative gained by the Liberals in the public eye by pressing the screening approach. The board of directors and disclosure measures have some distinguishing features that are appealing. They apply to all foreign firms, not just the marginal group affected by take over screening. They appear to influence a much broader range of operational matters on a continuing basis. The Conservatives can make a fair case that these steps are, in fact, a stronger effort to deal with foreign investment than takeover screening.

Out of all this, what can we discern about the differences between the parties? Philosophically it would appear that the Conservatives have somewhat less inclination than the Liberals to favor government intervening in the economy and industrial management and, historically, at least, somewhat more protective nationalistic orientation. The opportunism of both parties seeking competitive advantage will lead them to some effort to differentiate their positions, although their essential conservatism (along with the specific aspects of the issues) will hold their positions within moderate limits. With this pattern of differentiation, one would expect the Liberals to give more emphasis to the direct influence on the operations of foreign firms and the Conservatives to stress more the general, indirect influences—but with both moving essentially in the same moderate nationalistic range.

Future Attitude Trends

The reflections at the beginning of this article on the difficulty of explaining the recent rise in nationalistic reaction to foreign investment are relevant to any consideration of the future. The overall trend of attitudes is hard to predict. It is useful, however, to note the outlook for three factors which may influence the attitudes: the character of foreign investment, Canada-United States relations, and basic nationalism.

The percentage of control of Canadian industry by foreign firms is not likely to increase much more because of deterrents within Canada and discouragement of foreign investment by United States policies. In addition, the performance of the firms is likely to be more satisfactory both because of increasing sensitivity of their managements to Canadian interests and measures taken by Canadians. Therefore, the concrete facts of foreign investment are likely to provide less basis for adverse attitudes.

It is apparent that there is a major change underway in Canada's relations with the United States. The days of the "special relationship" between Canada and the United States are past. Rather than treating Canada on a favored basis in trade and other matters, the United States government apparently is going to deal with Canada pretty much as it does with other friendly countries. External Affairs Minister Mitchell Sharp anticipates that the United States will be "an even tougher bargaining partner than in the past."[21] The Canadian American Committee, a responsible group of business, labor, and agricultural leaders from both countries, predicts that differences between the nations will grow deeper in the 1970s.[22] If disputes do intensify, the multinational firms would often be involved in economic issues between the nations and feelings toward them would suffer as a consequence.

Another source of possible adverse feelings is the course of basic Canadian nationalistic attitudes. There may well be a growing consciousness of the distinct possibility that George Grant's assessment is correct; if Canada has not already disappeared as a nation, it is close to doing so. If nationalism really has the emotional force approaching that of religious fervor, which scholars in the field believe, it would not be surprising to find the attitudes supporting it aroused to perhaps their greatest vigor when the substantive base for the survival of the realities of nationhood was actually or apparently in the process of being broken down.

The Future Tenor of Policy

What are the prospects for future Canadian national policy on foreign investment in light of these attitudes and other influences? At the risk of oversimplification, I believe that the answer to this question will be determined by just a few key factors.

A major factor will be the mood of the country. The progression toward stronger policies in handling foreign-owned business has up to now been largely motivated by growing public pressure. The continued growth of nationalistic pressure is uncertain but it is a reasonable possibility. On the other hand, the ranking of the foreign investment issue distinctly below other issues in public opinion priorities, may fall yet farther. One of the major results of the 1972 election was to elevate in importance the issue of national unity because it demonstrated that the Trudeau approach had not only failed but perhaps aggravated the English-French division among the populace. Employment and related economic issues are also in the forefront. These domestic unity and economic issues are far more pressing and immediate in the eyes of most Canadians than foreign investment, especially as the latter is for the most part considered a positive economic contributor.

There is a question here about the results of political instability on Canadian government action. In less developed countries, anti-foreign investment action is a common ploy of insecure governmental leaders. That possibility exists in Canada. Specifically, in an attempt to win over voters from the NDP, the minority government might adopt the CIC program. Lester Pearson pursued this strategy to a degree in backing Walter Gordon's foreign investment views when he had a minority government in the mid-1960s.

It is doubtful if any substantial shift of policy (as distinguished from political verbiage) is likely with this rationale. The Liberals lost more ground to the Conservatives than to the NDP and, in the long run, the recovery of Liberal strength lies in maintaining a firm center position—not swinging to the left.

Significant confirming evidence on this point is found in the first post-election statements of the three party leaders. All stressed that highest priority should be given to general economic problems. Mr. Trudeau and Mr. Lewis did not even mention foreign investment. Mr. Stanfield included Canadianization of boards of directors but it was low on his list.

The outlook was further clarified in the government speech at the opening of the 29th Parliament in January 1973. Primary attention was given to general economic measures. Foreign investment was treated briefly. The proposals made were: (1) takeover screening, (2) Canadianization of boards of directors, (3) improved access to foreign technology, (4) increased Canadian ownership for resource projects, and (5) consultation with provinces on measures affecting new direct investment. The second proposal will win Conservative support; the third proposal pleases Canadian businessmen; the fourth fits CIC-NDP goals, and the fifth will ease provincial relations. Most significant is the handling of the major issue of new investment—the prospect of new measures is held out to satisfy the NDP but the required consultation puts the onus for action on provincial governments with a strong probability of mild or quite gradual implementation.

The second factor is the growing conviction among a broad band of responsible Canadians that despite its generally beneficial character, foreign investment could be made to serve the national interests better. This is the maximizing-benefits psychology that pervades the Gray Report and current government thinking. It will provide a persisting momentum within the bureaucracy for continued movement to improve performance of foreign firms in such matters as exports and research.

The next three factors bear on the influence the bureaucracy and businessmen will exert. First, the great complexity of implementing general policies affecting foreign investment is increasingly clear to responsible people. The debate on the Foreign Takeovers Review Bill provided a vivid demonstration of this fact. A large portion of the Commons Committee examination of the bill was devoted to a multitude of side effects of the review system ranging from major points like fostering creation of new firms by foreign investors who were frustrated in takeover bids to minor problems like the status of mortgages of insurance companies. The obvious point is that in a country in which 60 percent of manufacturing is foreign-controlled, even measures of apparently simple and limited scope can have diverse effects and risks.

The second element is the lack of thorough knowledge of the economic effects of foreign investment. On the basis of the most penetrating study of the multinational firm yet undertaken, Raymond Vernon was able to conclude only that his findings

*suggest . . . that the impact of international investment is not necessarily
measured by such figures as yield on investment, payments to labor, and tax
payments. The effects recorded by these measures could be swamped by
those outside the recording net, especially if the effects run over a number of
years.*[23]

The Gray Report accepts the general conclusion of prior studies that foreign
investment is economically beneficial but in emphasizing that the studies
"involve numerous qualifications," it highlights their incompleteness.[24] Carl
Beigie, observes:

*The Gray Report is a disappointment for what it failed to include . . . the re-
port has added little to our knowlege concerning such basic and still un-
resolved questions as the overall impact of foreign direct investment on
Canadian growth, employment, prices, product diversity, and the balance of
payments.*[25]

The implications of this lack of full knowledge are clear. Responsible Canadian leaders are not likely to support substantial changes in policy affecting 60 percent of their manufacturing with such limited understanding
of the consequences.

The third, and perhaps most significant, element politically is the un-
abated quest of government leaders for new foreign investment. Just one
item suffices to affirm this point: after running up an impressive record of
actions relating to foreign investment in the spring of 1972, Premier William
Davis of Ontario spent much of August in Europe encouraging investors to
come to his province.

Finally, there are three elements of the national decision-making process
described in my full report which militate against strong action by the federal
government.[26] One is the traditionally limited role of government in business
affairs. Another is a reasonably close rapport between government and business at top levels that runs counter to decisions that are substantially at odds
with business thinking. The third is the economic policy strength of the provincial governments that deters the federal government from taking strong
steps that might be injurious to the interests of specific provinces. This latter
point is especially significant in consideration of any policy that would give
the Ottawa officials power to limit or direct new investment by foreign firms.
That would place power over jobs and other economic benefits in federal,
rather than provincial hands, something the provinces will resist strongly. The
net effect of these elements is a fairly slow pace of decision making and evolution of rather mild policies.

Putting these elements together one can make some reasonably logical
assumptions about the tenor of overall policy for the next few years. It seems
inevitable that, as a political necessity, the federal and provincial governments
must demonstrate that they are doing something about the foreign investment question. On the other hand, responsible behavior will restrain them

from strong action. The outcome under these circumstances will probably be very much a continuation of the recent pattern, that is, a gradual pace of new actions that provide visible evidence to the public that foreign investment is receiving attention but which are cautious enough so that costs and risks are minimized and there is a fair assurance of some tangible benefit, either economically or for perceived national values such as cultural identity fitting the prevailing philosophy among officials.

While numerous uncertainties have been observed in this discussion of the immediate prospects for Canadian foreign investment policy, the longer term prospects involve conflicting trends of basic elements whose resolution scarcely can be discerned.

Longer Term Prospects

On the one hand, there has been a steady buildup of nationalistic reaction to foreign-controlled business that has created growing pressure for action by the government. So far the actions have been of fairly limited nature. Some people have observed that they are so minor in nature that they simply postpone briefly the day when major actions must be taken; and, indeed, in permitting the main body of foreign investment to grow in strength they contribute to magnifying the corrective steps which ultimately would have to be taken if the strongest nationalistic feelings seen today were to become widespread. Thus, if one were to project the current rate of growth of adverse reaction to foreign business, one would have to anticipate a substantially more restrictive government policy within a decade. Because of the uncertainties discussed earlier one cannot project this trend with any certainty, but continuation of adverse reaction is a possibility one must consider.

On the other hand, there are certain solid indicators of basic trends toward international integration and especially toward closer integration with the United States ranging from George Grant's type of philosophical conclusions that Canada as a nation has already lost its identity through the functionalist concepts of non-nationalists to practical manifestations such as the continental rationalization of production and research in particular industries.

In a pragmatic free society, an evolutionary compromise between these two apparently opposing trends undoubtedly will be worked out in a reasonably satisfactory manner, though certainly with substantial tension and conflict. The exact form of the compromise, however, is hard to predict. My reading of past history and current influences leads me to expect that the main economic and government policy decisions will be governed by the second basic trend, the evolution toward integration. The attitudinal pressures for national identity would be satisfied to a large degree as they are being today by measures that protect cultural and national identity along with limited economic measures by which Canadian identity can be preserved with minimum sacrifice to the standard of living. This expectation is based more on intuition than logic, however, and, as in the past, it is likely that the actual course of events in the future will be governed by forces not readily assessed today.

QUESTIONS

1. What reasons are offered for the growing trend in the Canadian public toward less favorable views on foreign investment?
2. What is the relationship of these attitude trends to the transmission of foreign cultural values into Canadian society?
3. How have these attitudes varied across different opinion groups, socioeconomic classes, and political parties? Why have they varied?
4. Given that the future prospects for even more restrictive government policies become a reality, what advice would you offer a United States firm currently actively involved in Canadian markets?

NOTES

1. John Fayerweather, *Foreign Investment in Canada: National Policy Prospects* (White Plains, N.Y.: International Arts & Science Press, 1973). This study was part of the New York University MNC Project supported by a grant from the Sciafe Foundation.

2. Toronto *Daily Star,* 12 February 1972.

3. J. Alex Murray and Mary C. Gerace, "Canadian Attitudes toward the U.S. Presence," *Public Opinion Quarterly* Fall 1972, p. 390.

4. John Fayerweather, "Elite Attitudes toward Foreign Firms," *International Studies Quarterly* December 1972, pp. 472-490.

5. Murray and Gerace, "Canadian Attitudes," p. 392.

6. *Foreign Direct Investment in Canada* (Ottawa, Canada: Goverment of Canada, 1972), p. 416.

7. Toronto *Daily Star,* 4 December 1971.

8. Ibid., 29 December 1971.

9. Ibid., 12 April 1972.

10. George Grant, *Lament for a Nation* (Toronto, Canada: McClelland & Stewart, 1965).

11. Ibid., p. 90.

12. Ibid., p. 63.

13. Ibid., pp. 86-7.

14. *Foreign Direct Investment,* p. 403.

15. Carl E. Beigie, "Foreign Investment in Canada: The Shade Is Gray," *Columbia Journal of World Business* November–December, 1972, p. 24.

16. Mitchell Sharp, "Canada-U.S. Relations: Options for the Future," *International Perspectives* Autumn 1972.

17. *Toronto Globe & Mail,* 21 August 1972.

18. John Fayerweather, "Attitudes of British and French Elite Groups toward Foreign Companies," *MSU Business Topics* Winter 1972, p. 19.

19. John Porter, *The Vertical Mosaic* (Toronto, Canada: University of Toronto Press, 1970), p. 373; "Some Bases of Party Support in the 1968 Election," in Hugh G. Thorburn, ed., *Party Politics in Canada* (Scarborough, Ontario: Prentice-Hall, 1972), pp. 36–37; "Prairie Revolt, Federalism and the Party System," in Thorburn, *Party Politics,* p. 206.

20. House of Commons *Debates,* 9 December 1971, p. 10322.

21. *International Perspectives,* Autumn 1972, p. 22.

22. *The New Environment for Canadian-American Relations* (Montreal, Canada: Canadian-American Committee, 1972), pp. 39–44.

23. *Sovereignty at Bay* (New York, N.Y.: Basic Books, 1971), p. 187.

24. *Foreign Direct Investment,* p. 416.

25. Beigie, "Foreign Investment in Canada," p. 24.

26. Fayerweather, *Canadian Policy.*

Can third world nations become truly economically self reliant while social values and behavioral patterns are continuously transformed to reflect those of developed countries? The author puts forth the arguments that "socio cultural" investments into host countries, by transnational firms greatly influence their business cultures as well as overall societal orientations. These influences are a function of the pervasive impact of foreign dominated media, the unidirectional managerial relationship existing with foreign affiliates, the control of international advertising, and other related forces. Sauvant suggests that the acceptance of Western values and consumption patterns constitutes self-colonizations that can only be avoided through appropriate actions by host countries.

10. His Master's Voice

Karl P. Sauvant
United Nations Center for Transnational Corporations

In the 1950s and 1960s, it was widely believed that the problems of the developing countries were only a symptom of the political status of these states. By the end of the 1960s, these hopes had been shattered. The international development efforts did not deliver what they had seemed to promise. If anything, the gap between north and south had increased. At the same time, it became obvious that political independence is a mere chimera unless based on economic independence. Economic decolonization and development thus came to be viewed with new urgency.

In their search for solutions to these economic problems, the developing countries embraced the concept of individual and collective self-reliance. Self-reliance requires that the political, economic and sociocultural structures created to link colonies to metropolitan countries (in a status of dependence) be altered to link developing countries to one another (in a status of interdependence).

Source: Reprinted with permission from September–October, 1976 issue of *CERES*, published by Food and Agriculture Organization (FAO), Rome, Italy.

The self-reliance discussion led to a realization by top-level decision-makers in the Third World that emancipation from colonial dependence is a multidimensional process. It showed that political independence had to be complemented by economic independence. A third dimension of this process, however, has so far largely been ignored. During the colonial period, the countries of the Third World were not only subjected to political and economic but also to sociocultural colonization. The values and behavioural patterns of important segments of Third World societies had gradually been transformed to reflect those of the metropolitan countries. After independence, hardly any change took place, although the attempt to explore self-reliance as an alternative development model itself constituted a step toward sociocultural emancipation.

The Spread of Television

In general, however, the infused patterns have been maintained and reinforced through a variety of mechanisms. Education has traditionally played an important role. Members of the elite and the middle class were—and are—frequently educated in the major developed countries where, of course, they are also exposed to the life-styles of the host societies. Similarly, domestic education in many Third World countries is based on material imported from former metropolises. Old sociocultural ties are also strengthened by foreign-language broadcasts, newspapers and extensive cultural programs of major developed countries. In addition, local broadcasting frequently draws on whole series of programs acquired from developed countries, and popular music programs in particular are strongly foreign, and especially United States dominated. An even higher degree of import dependence is characteristic of the film industry, a dependence that is virtually total for news films (including for news occurring within the country). Newspapers and magazines, in many of which syndicated United States comics have become fixtures, have to rely for their global news (including about other developing countries) almost entirely on two or three international news agencies (UPI, AP, and Reuters) and their selection of what is newsworthy. (To break this pattern, a number of developing countries decided in 1976 to establish, within the framework of the non-aligned movement, a pool of non-aligned news agencies.)

The most important development in this area has, however, been the spread of television since the end of the 1950s and the beginning of the 1960s, reaching already approximately one fourth of the world population. A high percentage (between one third to two thirds) of the television programs in developing countries—especially during prime time—is important from a few countries, mainly the United States, the United Kingdom, and France. Through television, therefore, an increasing number of persons are exposed, on a daily basis, to the way of life of the main developed countries, to their preconceptions and ideals. Together, all these mechanisms (whose control is usually also highly concentrated) disseminate the values and behavioural patterns of a few major developed countries, which thus keep—internationally or not—the developing nations within the sociocultural orbit of these countries.

A new and important mechanism has been added to those discussed above through the growth of transnational enterprises. The critical point is that foreign direct investment does not involve only capital and technology but is usually also accompanied by sociocultural investments. In the traditional raw-material ventures, this was not a major factor since many of them were capital intensive and frequently located in enclaves not linked to the rest of the country. But with the expansion of manufacturing foreign direct investment in the 1950s, and especially during the 1960s, foreign affiliates became closely integrated into their host countries. In this process, they began to shape the production apparatus of the host economy and increasingly determined what was to be produced by it, i.e., for what type of production the resources of the host country would be utilized.

Sociocultural Investments

Beyond this direct impact, transnationals introduced into their foreign affiliates novel business practices, modes of operation, values, and behavioural patterns—all sociocultural investments. These, in turn, are disseminated in the host country through forward and backward linkages as well as the foreign-affiliate experience of employees. In the first case, foreign affiliates may, for instance, insist on the introduction of new standards, different production methods, etc., on the part of their domestic suppliers. In the second case, their employees—who are constantly being exposed to the foreign-affiliate environment and for whom the frequently foreign-trained or expatriate top management may constitute a model—are potentially very effective transmitters (in a multiplying manner) of values and patterns of behaviour to other spheres of the host society.

The importance of the role of transnationals is, therefore, twofold. One, they directly contribute to the shaping of the production apparatus of the host economy; and two, they can be expected to have a significant impact on the shaping of a host country's business cultures and through it the sociocultural orientation of the society as a whole. On the face of it, the changes thus introduced may be beneficial in that they contribute to the industrialization and modernization of developing host countries. Transnationals would then play the role of dynamic agents of change, expediting socioeconomic development and bringing to this task the vast resources of their global networks and their ability to combine various factors of production in an economically efficient way. Before such a conclusion can be drawn, however, a closer look has to be taken at the kind of change that is being introduced, promoted and disseminated. This, in turn, requires a brief examination of the nature of the linkages between foreign affiliates and their headquarters, their choice of production and the content of the transmitted values and behavioural patterns.

A Unidirectional Linkage

The linkages between foreign affiliates and their headquarters are characterized by the former's very high responsiveness to headquarters policies, which is due to a variety of formal and informal control mechanisms. Most significant among these are majority ownership of foreign affiliates by the parent enterprise; prerogatives of headquarters in key decision-making areas of their affiliates; and the presence of expatriate personnel in top managerial positions of the affiliate, which not only exercises a valuable control function but also fulfills, as noted above, an important social model function vis-à-vis members of the indigenous society. The unidirectionality and asymmetry of this relationship, already inherent in a hierarchical business organization, is further accentuated by the absence of any representation of the interests of foreign affiliates (or host countries) in parent enterprises; the latter are almost exclusively owned and managed by home-country nationals and in no way reflect the international involvement of the enterprise system as a whole.

Thus, central to the nature of the relationship between headquarters and foreign affiliates is the fact that the linkage between them is not only strong but clearly unidirectional and consequently asymmetrical. In this situation, headquarters are free, within the boundaries of global economic rationality, to determine the production of their foreign affiliates. Naturally, this choice will take into account two important factors. The first (excluding export-platform operations), is the nature of the local market—or more precisely the part of the market that has purchasing power. This means the small elite and middle class, i.e., groups that can be expected to have most thoroughly internalized the values and wants of developed countries. The second factor concerns product development by and production processes of transnationals. Both are based on research and development (R & D) conducted almost entirely in home countries and reflect the factor endowments of the same countries. Both are geared primarily to the satisfaction of the wants of consumers in developed countries. Naturally, transnationals prefer to utilize these experiences when establishing themselves in developing countries.

Misallocation of Resources

The choice of production for affiliates in developing countries is therefore largely a combination of the production and R & D experiences of the parent enterprise on the one hand and the wants of the small elites and middle classes in host countries on the other. The problem is that both factors reflect the relative abundance of developed countries and not the absolute poverty of developing ones, the wants of consumers in developed countries and not the needs of large proportions of the population in developing countries. For instance, transnationals in developing countries use skilled, capital- and energy-intensive production processes, and not unskilled, labour-intensive ones; they concentrate on luxury and advanced consumption industries and not on agriculture; they serve the individual wants of some, and not the collective needs for essential goods and services of most. Consequently, the direct impact of transnationals (and of domestic enterprises imitating their methods) on the production apparatus of developing host economies tends to lead to a misallocation of scarce resources and, in a large perspective, tends to keep the host economy on an inappropriate development path. Furthermore, most of these patterns of production keep the host economy dependent on inputs from abroad because both demand and supply orient themselves at markets and capabilities of a higher level of development.

Built-in Obsolescence

Closely linked to the question of choice of production is the question of the content of the transmitted values and behavioural patterns. As suggested above, they influence local managers in foreign affiliates and in the operations attached to them through forward and backward linkages, and shape the foreign-affiliate experience of employees in general. Again, given the nature· of the linkage between foreign affiliates and headquarters, they are home-country values and behavioural patterns, reflecting, in other words, the possibilities of an economy and a society at a different level of development and endowed with different factors of production. More concretely, they include—especially in their American variation—a strong preference for a free enterprise system and, therefore, opposition to state intervention; exploitation of resources as soon as discovered; planned obsolescence; product innovation and differentiation; emphasis on packaging and branding; and increased consumption through mass-marketing techniques, including want-creation, style changes and hard-sell advertising.

Among these characteristics, those pertaining to and resulting from advertising are of special interest because they concern differences that at least until recently (and to a limited degree even still today) distinguish American from non-American business philosophies. The differences revolve around "product orientation" and "market orientation," and the implications of these two approaches for the production process. Product orientation—still typical for some non-American enterprises—ideally places the major emphasis on cost consciousness and on the production of relatively durable goods with long life cycles, designed to satisfy recognized consumer needs. Research and development, product development and so forth are geared to this objective. The resulting product is then put on the market where it finds its customers. Thus, to use Veblen's terminology, emphasis is on "workmanship" and not on "salesmanship." In the United States, these priorities have come to be reversed in the time since the Second World War. Emphasis is placed on salability and consumption—as opposed to conservation—and sales, marketing and advertising considerations tend to determine research and development, product development and production. "Product management" plays a key role in this approach. Often, product management is aimed at limiting the life span of a product, for instance through frequent changes in its design and appearance (but not in its function or purpose). Built-in or planned obsolescence, as well as the deliberate creation of wants and needs, is the logical culmination of this policy; and advertising, obviously, is one of its most important tools.

The content of the values and behavioural patterns transmitted by transnationals—especially as pertaining to business culture—therefore further supplements and supports the observations made at the end of the preceding section. In fact, these observations can be further amended to read that the business philosophy on which the production patterns in question are based is being internalized by local management and local employees. Thus, not only the products and the production methods of transnationals but also the business philosophy underlying them tend to be inappropriate for developing countries.

Following Its Clients

Advertising plays a crucial role in the process of want-creation. It appeals directly to a society's value-orientations, manipulating especially its consumer values. But the function of advertising—especially if accompanied also by public-relations activities—is not merely to sell products but to sell ideas. And these ideas are promoted, of course, in the interest of the client—in particular the budget-strong transnational client. Advertising, therefore, is an important mechanism to maintain and further develop the want-oriented demand patterns in developing countries, thereby supporting corresponding production patterns.

The acceleration in the transnationalization of production in the 1960s made it imperative for the advertising industry—as a service industry—to follow its globally expanding clients. This move was greatly facilitated by the parallel spread of television to developing countries. Frequently, agencies established abroad started out with a few major clients already served by the parent agency at home. Given the dominant position of United States-based transnationals in international direct investment, their special preference for the usage of advertising, and the superior know-how and experience of United States advertising agencies, it is not surprising that American shops acquired a prominent position in international advertising. In fact, discussing international advertising is discussing the transnational operations of United States agencies.

International advertising—an industry whose volume was estimated at $33.1 thousand million in 1970—is almost entirely a United States industry: twenty-one of the twenty-five largest agencies in the world are United States agencies (or strongly linked with them), and most of them generate about half of their billings abroad. Moreover, while United States agencies (or agencies with a strong United States partner) are omnipresent, major non-United States shops are either entirely domestic (Japan) or of only regional significance (Western Europe). The dominant United States position becomes apparent from the table, which documents the presence, in 1973, of foreign affiliates among the largest shops of the forty-five developing countries for which information could be obtained. In all countries, and for each of the one hundred thirty agencies on which data was available, foreign ownership—whether majority or minority—means (with one exception) that the parent agency is either entirely North American or has strong United States participation. More specifically, in twenty-nine of these countries, the largest advertising agency is foreign majority-owned and in an additional four countries foreigners have acquired an often substantial minority interest. In all, in only twelve of forty-five countries is the biggest agency entirely owned by nationals. A similar pattern prevails for the other rankings. Of the total one hundred thirty agencies, nearly two thirds are foreign majority-owned, 9 percent have foreign minority participation, and less than 30 percent are entirely in national hands. Furthermore, only a very limited number of agencies account for most foreign shops. The Interpublic Group of Cos. (with McCann-Erickson as the predominant partner) alone controls about one fifth of all foreign majority-owned shops. If SSC and B. Inc., J. Walter Thompson Co., I.M.A.A., and Grant Advertising are added, this share increases to close to two thirds; and if five further parent agencies are added, nearly 90 percent of all foreign shops are accounted for. (It should be noted that a similar pattern prevails in developed countries.)

Foreign-oriented Wants

The pattern-setting potential of foreign affiliates of transnationals in their various linkages with the host country thus receives powerful additional support from advertising, with the converging result of creating, maintaining or further reinforcing home-country values in developing countries.

Just as it has been realized that political independence cannot be achieved without economic emancipation, it also has to be realized that economic independence is, to a certain extent, a function of sociocultural emancipation. The values and patterns of behaviour acquired during the colonial era and especially the consumption patterns created, maintained or reinforced by transnational advertising agencies do not reflect the conditions of developing countries. Rather, they reflect the wants and the abundance of developed countries. At least for the time being, these wants can only be satisfied through continued inputs from abroad. Consequently, economic dependence on countries and institutions that can help to fulfill these foreign-oriented wants continues and is reinforced. At the same time, scarce domestic resources are siphoned off and squandered for production and in processes that do not provide for basic goods and services for the great majority of the population.

As long as transnationals can simply transfer their production and production process experiences to developing countries and as long as a ready market awaits them or is allowed to be created, it cannot be expected that this pattern will be broken by the companies. After all, their purpose is to make profits, not to promote development. It can also not be expected that all of the values and behavioural and consumption patterns under discussion can be avoided altogether; some of them may be unavoidable concomitants of industrialization. In fact, and to go one step further, they may be unavoidable concomitants of production carried out by profit-seeking institutions. To the extent that this is the case, it is not so much (or not only) the foreign or domestic status of an enterprise that is responsbile for its non-social production, but rather the profit-seeking character of the institution itself. However, given that transnationals are most advanced in this area, they can be expected to introduce, magnify, and/or cultivate such patterns.

An Algiers Declaration

Nevertheless, what can be expected is that foreign affiliates adapt themselves to meet specific demands of developing countries, be it for sociocultural identity or for the appropriate use of scarce economic resources. The initiative for breaking the pattern of dependence, however, has to be taken by host countries. In particular, they have to reorient their consumption patterns toward local conditions and persuade transnationals—which will continue to play an important role in the socioeconomic development of the Third World— to reorient their production and production processes in a similar manner.

Economic self-reliance requires sociocultural independence. The acceptance of the values, behavioural patterns and especially consumption patterns of a few developed countries constitutes self-colonization. If sociocultural emancipation does not take place, if industrialization continues to orient itself toward the demand and supply situation of these developed countries, the economic development of the Third World will remain dependent development. And this, in the final analysis, will hinder the achievement of political independence. What is needed is an Algiers declaration and progam of action for sociocultural emancipation.

QUESTIONS

1. How are economic and social-cultural self reliance interrelated?
2. What does the author mean by the term "socio cultural investment"?

3. Do you agree with the author's position on what constitutes a "product" as opposed to a "market" orientation? Discuss.
4. What steps can a host country take to minimize the impact of Western values and consumption patterns on its social fabric?
5. Do you agree with the author that the values of developed nations are not appropriate for Third World countries? Why?

ANALYSIS OF OVERSEAS OPPORTUNITIES: CONCEPTUAL ISSUES

The environmental factors explored in the previous section present many pitfalls to international marketers if not properly assessed. Marketing research like the marketing variables that are derived from it, must also be specially adapted to the markets being investigated. Although conceptually the research process is similar across national boundaries, operational differences must be taken into account. The purpose of the articles included in this section is to familiarize the reader with the major issues associated with conducting international marketing research. The lead article by C.P. Rao outlines the tasks confronting market researchers overseas in terms of the types of information problems that will be encountered and the implications for specific marketing decision areas. These problems are further explored in the selection by Robert Green and Phillip White that focuses on the methodological issues inherent in cross cultural research. The practitioner viewpoint on international marketing research is dealt with in the following article by Lee Adler. Special attention is given to the ways the difficult decision of selecting and working with independent research suppliers in foreign markets is made.

The assessment of overseas marketing oppor-
tunities is a difficult and challenging task.
The author provides some basic guidelines
for market researchers on the types of in-
formation needed, the relevance to specific
decision areas, available sources, and ap-
plicable methodologies. Since research in
foreign environments often requires special
cultural insights, attention is also focused
on how a firm might contact and screen out-
side suppliers.

11. A Multi-Level Approach to Researching Overseas Markets

C. P. Rao
University of Arkansas

In recent years, as a result of various pressures acting on them, many United States companies are increasingly participating in the export trade. However, for many of these companies export is a sporadic activity, undertaken on an opportunistic basis. The amount of planning effort made prior to entering foreign markets is limited. In such a situation, exporting cannot become a continuous and a sustained activity. "Perhaps the biggest mistake that a manufacturer can make in the development of his export business is to permit it to develop on an opportunistic basis—to let the foreign demand for his product force the development and direction of his export business."[1]

In order to make exporting a sustained and continuous activity, it is necessary to undertake systematic planning on a long-term basis. This kind of strategic planning creates a framework for making operating decisions with relation to marketing in foreign countries. It is obvious that accurate information about the market variables is an essential input for systematic planning.

Source: Printed with permission of the author.

Export Marketing Research can provide these inputs and facilitate decision making at various organizational levels.

Perhaps, a clear understanding of the differences between export and domestic marketing would aid appreciation of the important role played by research in successful export ventures. This is not intended to suggest that there is any fundamental difference between export and domestic marketing. The basic principles remain the same in both the cases though the perspective in which they are viewed changes substantially. Firstly, the distance between an exporter and his customers is ordinarily much wider than in the domestic market.[2] This distance primarily connotes the marketing distance rather than the physical distance. The marketing distance is created by intermediaries standing between the exporter and the ultimate consumers of his products and the cultural distance arising out of the fact that these consumers are members of another culture and society. All these distances, together produce an information gap that must be overcome if a company is to plan its export sales rationally. A clear understanding of the information required to fill up this gap is of paramount importance.

Dimensions of the Information Required for Export Decisions[3]

Economic: Many differences in the marketing system existing in various countries originate from the differences in the economic levels of the countries—i.e., from the differences in the standards of living. In the nations that are merely at subsistence level, the marketing system in economic terms is simple as there is little flexibility in buyer choices. As the level of economic development rises, the consumers seem to get an increasing amount of discretionary buying power and such societies offer a great many marketing opportunities. However, rather than the level which the economy of a particular nation has reached, economic dynamism of the society is of greater relevance to marketing decisions. In a stagnant society consumption patterns tend to become set and the whole marketing process becomes a routine supply operation.

Political: The controlling role of the political organization arises from the laws and regulations that the government enforces to direct the country's economy. Although there is a great deal of variety among different types of laws and regulations enforced by various governments, the basic political philosophies that underlie these are limited in number. Therefore, an understanding of the political forces operating within a country is extremely useful for the foreign manufacturers in terms of getting the required insights in the country's basic legal framework.

Cultural: A country's social, educational and religious systems critically influence its marketing system. Apart from influencing buyer-seller relations, these cultural variables have a crucial impact on product-policy. The importance of cultural variables becomes apparent when one finds that substantial differences exist between the consumer preferences in two countries like France and England that otherwise are similar in terms of their economic level and the ideologies underlying their political structure. The Britons have a strong preference for tea whereas the French prefer coffee and the consumption of tea in France is comparatively negligible. Even in the case of industrial products, where the product preferences of the consumers are "rational", these variables play an important role in structuring the selling organization and the related policies. Data about the cultural characteristics of countries is probably most difficult to obtain as it defies attempts at quantification. Also the common tendency to view a foreign culture in the framework based on one's own cultural environment very often results in a certain amount of insensitivity which vitiates a clear understanding of the critical cultural variables.

Planning Process and Relevant Information Collection Functions

As explained earlier, market research is a tool for systematic planning. It is, therefore, important to understand the planning process involved in export marketing that would lead to the various stages in which the information collection function can be undertaken.

The number of world-markets being very large, it is neither possible nor advisable for any one company to cater to all of them. A selective approach is necessary in the choice of export markets and therefore identification of market opportunities becomes an important function. On the basis of preliminary screening it is possible to eliminate many unsuitable countries from the large number of available alternatives. After narrowing down the number of alternatives, a more detailed analysis should be carried out to identify various segments of the market and to determine the sales potential of these segments. This analysis would lead to a final selection of export markets. Having made this selection, *export objectives* can now be set up and strategic planning of the various elements of marketing mix necessary to achieve these objectives can be undertaken. The next step in planning involves making this strategy operational by initiating a number of operational decisions through sales and profit budgeting, manpower planning, etc.

This process of strategic planning is continuous and needs a constant review in the light of the changes in environmental conditions. A continuous feedback from the markets is therefore necessary to introduce appropriate changes in the original plans.

The description of the various stages in the planning process suggests the necessity of different informational inputs at each stage. We shall now take a closer look at these informational inputs and the manner in which they need to be supplied.

Information Needs for a Preliminary Screening of Marketing Opportunities

Preliminary screening, as explained earlier, helps to identify the export markets which warrant further investigation. This kind of screening needs to be done as quickly and inexpensively as possible and therefore the techniques involved in the analysis must necessarily be simple. Initially, it is possible to eliminate a number of alternatives on the basis of very obvious political or geographical disadvantages.

The *limitations of resources* also eliminate some of the marketing opportunities. Similarly certain aspects of the company policy would automatically limit the choice of export opportunities.

The remaining markets can be evaluated on the basis of an appraisal of their trade statistics, which are published by the United Nations and International Monetary Fund on a regular basis. From this source it is possible to find out the extent to which the target country imports a particular product or a product group. In appraising a country's imports, it is advisable not to rely merely on the latest figures. It is necessary to consider the imports data for at least four to five years to arrive at any reliable conclusions. Again, the exporter's product may not be mentioned separately in these statistics, as for the sake of convenience these sources group a number of products in one category. However, it is usually possible to locate the import class containing the exporter's products and the data regarding the whole class can be useful in preliminary screening. This grouping of products may at times make it necessary to use the sources other than U.N. and I.M.F. bulletins.

As a next step in the screening procedure, foreign countries can be classified by the size of the imports of the exporter's commodity or the commodity group. The countries that import very insignificant quantities of the product then may be eliminated. However, many times small imports do not always indicate insignificant markets. Therefore, as a precaution, it may be necessary to go into the reasons behind a country's limited imports. Sometimes the trade restrictions imposed by the target country cause the stagnation of imports. In such a case it will be necessary to be specially alert to further developments about these restrictions because very often they are removed after some time. Usually small imports may be an indication of the low consumption of the particular product. In such a case, most often, further consideration can be avoided. At the same time, the possibility of stimulating higher consumption through promotional efforts cannot be ruled out completely. This kind of effort requires considerable commitment of the resources which only international giants like Singer Sewing Machines and Coca Cola have been able to undertake. This only points out that even at the stage of preliminary analysis, information available from the external sources needs to be evaluated by using the availability of resources as one of the yardsticks.

Apart from the U.N. and I.M.F. publications the trade data of world markets can also be obtained from the sources available in each individual country. However, the U.N. and I.M.F. sources are convenient to use for the purposes of preliminary screening for the following reasons: (1) the data published by the agencies like U.N. or I.M.F. is presented in some international currency (usually United States dollars). Consequently, no efforts are necessary to convert the currencies on a uniform basis for inter-country comparisons; (2) this data can be purchased at a very nominal cost by subscribing to the bulletins which these agencies publish.

After the preliminary screening only a handful of export markets would be left which would merit further investigation. These markets should be subjected to a much closer scrutiny.

Detailed Analysis of Export Opportunities

The preliminary screening process described above mainly attempts to answer two questions viz., (1) Is there any need for the product in the target country; (2) Is there any demand for the product in that country? However, these are not answered in sufficient depth. What needs to be done now is to find out the extent of demand or the extent of need. In other words the question to be answered is whether the market can support the company's product.

For this kind of analysis it is necessary to *sift* a great deal of economic and statistical information available about the countries that qualify for further investigation after the preliminary screening. The following information is necessary for this analysis:[4]

1. Population by language, religion, ethnic groups: population statistics tell us the make-up of the market. Who the people are, where they are and what distinguishing characteristics they have. Usually, it is desirable to have as homogeneous a market as possible within one country. Diversity of consumers creates serious problems in terms of distribution and promotion. These problems can be solved only by expanding huge resources for which the company may not be prepared. The population characteristics, therefore, point out some of the problems likely to be encountered in marketing the product in that country.
2. Population by regions and centers—with growth rates: This data can point out if there is any regional concentration of the potential consumers and whether there is any possibility of marketing the product selectively to only some of the groups.
3. Size of National Income and rate of growth: National Income is an indication of the level of economic activity within the country. The rate of growth of national income effectively shows whether the country is prospering and whether the total purchasing capacity of the country as a whole is expanding sufficiently to spur the marketing activity.

4. Size of Disposable Income and income distribution: disposable income is an important measure of what people have to spend. This is what is left after they have paid their taxes. The data about consumer expenditure habits is also very useful in order to find out the discretionary purchasing capacity of the population. Also the pattern of income distribution within the population points out the relative importance of different income groups to the marketer and helps to delineate the existing segments of the market. Many times the nature of the product itself restricts the relevance of certain income groups to the marketer. For instance, in developing countries consumer durables like refrigerators can be purchased only by the higher income groups. Only a country that has a significant number of population falling in this group would be relevant to a refrigerator manufacturer desirous of exporting his product.

5. Imports, Exports and the domestic production of the product: (Domestic Production + Imports) – (Exports) gives the consumption figures for the country that provide an aid for demand estimation.

On the basis of above information it is possible to grade the countries under consideration according to the scope they are likely to provide for marketing the product under consideration. It must however be emphasized that it is not always possible to penetrate the markets which appear lucrative on the basis of economic considerations. As explained earlier various considerations other than the economic *shape* export opportunities. Some of these derive from the status of the monetary system operating within the target country whereas others are of a purely political nature. Some of the important considerations that a researcher has to take into account are given here.

1. Foreign Exchange Position: scarcity of foreign exchange in the target country restricts the scope of export trade with it. For instance, although there is considerable scope for exporting automobiles to India, no foreign manufacturer can possibly take advantage of the situation because there is a severe foreign-exchange shortage in the country. If there is a shortage of foreign exchange in the target country, it is extremely important to understand the priorities adopted by the government in allocation of this scarce resource. However, while exporting to such a country, the exporter must realize that the shortage of foreign exchange, sooner or later would force the government to start the manufacture of the product domestically. It will, therefore, not be advisable to enter such a market if the initial investment is going to be very large.

2. Stability of the currency: if the currency of the target country is unstable, it will be frequently devalued. This would always result in the consumers paying more for the imported goods. Consequently the demand estimates will have to be reviewed. This would lead to many uncertainties for the exporter.

3. Political and Governmental factors:
   (a) Consistency of government's policies
   (b) The nature of political relationship between the target country and the exporter's country
   (c) Presence or absence of price controls
   (d) Patentability of the product in the target country

The importance of the above considerations is obvious and need not be explained any further.

On the basis of above-mentioned analysis, it will be possible for the exporting firm to take a policy decision about the markets on which it would like to concentrate its marketing efforts. It must, however, be clarified that this kind of decision can only be taken by the top management. The researcher provides all the data to this group of executives along with his comments to enable them to make the right decision.

Also, the information collection function that has been explained so far, pertains to the planning done prior to actual entry into the market. This is, therefore, mainly what can be called desk research. This kind of research can be undertaken by any company as it involves little out-of-pocket expenditure. The usual claim that systematic export can be undertaken only by very large organizations does not appear to be very true. It is possible for an exporter to collect a great deal of information about the target countries without undertaking any expensive field surveys.

Some of the information inputs described earlier will not be very relevant for planning exports of industrial goods. In such a case the problem of determining the potential will be considerably simplified. For instance, an exporter of textile machinery will not need information about the business indicators like disposable income, distribution of income and patterns of consumer expenditure. His approach would be much more direct because the number of his potential customers is stricly limited. He would be interested in knowing about the exact number of textile units within the country, the kind of equipment installed in these units and their purchasing procedures, etc. Also he would be very much concerned about the availability of technical personnel for erection and servicing of the machines sold. Although the specific information inputs may be of a different nature, the basic planning process remains unchanged.

Collection of Commercial Intelligence

After taking a decision about which foreign markets the company intends to explore, it is necessary to collect all the available information about the commercial operations in those countries. This commercial intelligence would consist of the following broad areas:

1. Import Regulations: This would include information about import licenses, quotas and exchange allocations, methods of valuing imports

for customs, for preferential tariffs through membership in trade blocks, trade agreements, preferences for certain countries, import taxes and turnover taxes, other non-tariff barriers (health regulations, etc.,) anti-dumping law and practice.

2. Port and Transport Facilities: in this area, it is necessary to collect information regarding the major ports, the warehousing facilities available in these ports, cost of warehousing, port taxes and fees, unloading delays, status of internal road and rail transport system, cost and advantages of various forms of transport.

3. Distribution patterns: common types of importers, import practices, marketing channels (how goods move from the importer to the actual user), regional distribution centers, compensation mechanism for the entitites handling goods, nature of retail outlets, nature of competition among the wholesalers and retailers, local or foreign origin bias of consumers and government, packaging practices, characteristics of salesmen and compensation methods, profitability of wholesalers and retailers.

4. Credit: credit terms normally extended by importers, credit terms normally extended by local manufacturers, credit terms normally extended to the retailers, extent of credit competition among suppliers, level and nature of installment buying.

5. Advertising: level of techniques, responsiveness of buyers; local manufacturers, wholesalers, retailer attitudes; percentage of sales spent on advertising; largest agencies, their billings and clients; services offered; major media; cost of major media; ad agency compensation techniques; tie-in promotions.

6. Legal: rules of competition on collusion, discrimination against certain buyers, promotional methods, exclusive territory agreements; retail price maintenance law; law about cancellation of distribution or wholesaler agreements; packaging laws; warranty laws; price controls and limitations on mark-ups or mark-downs; patent, copyright and trademark laws.

In the domestic business, it is necessary to find out as much information as possible about the competitors and their products. Similar information needs to be collected for the export markets as well. Who are the competitors, what kind of marketing organization do they have and how does *this fit into their world organization,* what is the nature of their relationship with the government, who distributes their products, what sort of advertising and promotional methods do they use, what kind of price structure do they have—these are some of the questions about the competitors which need to be answered satisfactorily.

This kind of commerical intelligence can best be obtained by a perceptive export executive if he visits the overseas markets. If this is not possible, this information can be obtained through other sources. A great deal of information can be collected on an information basis from the overseas customers that the company may already have, or from the foreign-based suppliers of raw materials, from the personnel employed in foreign embassies, from the executives of some other noncompeting company which may be selling its products in the target countries and from the foreign students. Needless to say, a first-hand collection of the information is always more desirable. Informal sources can be used only as a last resort.

Field Surveys for Information Collection

The information collection process described so far was based mainly on the secondary sources. This kind of information collection, it would appear, does not conform to the *trite* ideas about marketing research. Somehow, marketing research is always equated with expensive and sophisticated surveys, audits and interviews. However, the function of business research is to provide reliable information needed for efficient decision making at the minimum possible cost. Therefore a great deal of information collection deserves to be termed as Marketing Research though it may not involve glamourous methods of collecting the data through field surveys.

This is not to deemphasize the role of field surveys as a method of information collection. As a matter of fact, such surveys are an extremely valuable aid in ensuring that the product as it is marketed will find consumer acceptance. Especially, the influence of cultural variables on the marketing plans can never be fully understood without a systematic consumer survey. "An internationally-minded management examined deliberately and systematically the products it intended to market within a country X from the point of view of the environment of that country. Major environmental factors considered in relation to the design of a given product were:"[5]

Level of technical skills	Product simplification
Level of labour cost	Automation of manualization of the product
Level of Income	Quality and price change
Climatic differences	Product adaptation
Isolation	Product simplification and reliability improvement
Differences in Standards	Recalibrating the product and resizing
Availability of other products	Greater or lesser product integration
Power Availability	Resizing the product
Special Conditions	Product redesign and invention

As can be easily seen all except the last environmental factor can be understood without conducting any field survey. However, this last factor, viz., special conditons is an agglomeration of the special socio-cultural aspects of the environment that can be a crucial determinant of overseas marketing plans.

Very often the products to be marketed in foreign markets need to be subjected to some degree of modifications to be fully acceptable because of the fact that different people have different expectations about the quality and the durability of the product and the kind of price that they are willing to pay for it depends upon these expectations. Also, usually the products serve certain secondary purposes (status symbols) and these secondary purposes are a function of the socio-cultural environment of the country. *Obviously enough*, a marketer must be aware of the consumer expectations from the product to be able to fulfill them and this kind of awareness can rarely be achieved without consumer surveys.

The Use and Selection of Marketing Research Agencies

It is unrealistic to expect that a company will always find it possible to undertake the kind of field investigation mentioned above without any outside help. Especially, in a foreign country, language would always pose problems. It will therefore be necessary to take help of a marketing research agency in such assignments and at times even for the sort of desk-research mentioned earlier.

The first step in the selection of a marketing research agency to do such work is to obtain an adequate list of existing agencies. Such lists can be obtained from various national and international societies and associations that group together marketing analysts as individuals or marketing research agencies as corporate entities.

Having established the agencies that are operating in any given market, the next problem is selecting the most appropriate one for the research in view. The first task is to find out their fields of specialization. Some, for example, will engage uniquely in consumer marketing research and others in industrial marketing research. Direct contact should be made with a number of agencies that have specialized in the desired area.

The agencies need to be questioned about their research facilities, the number and qualifications of their research staff, the range of their research activities and their research turnover. Sometimes, the international affiliations and facilities of the agencies will be important because such affiliations enable them to undertake research in a group of countries. In addition they should be asked the names of their past clients who can be approached for an opinion on the quality of work they have already done. An important point to bear in mind is that staff turnover in such agencies can be high. If specialization in a certain field is claimed it should be verified that the individuals who built up the special know-how have not left the organization. It is also important to talk directly with those who will undertake the work, and not just to their superiors. The way people talk about a problem, whether it is research methodology in general or the marketing problems of a specific product is usually revealing of their capacity for clear analytical thinking.

These initial contact and discussions should make it possible to prepare a short list of the research agencies. At this stage it would be necessary to ask for a written research proposal. This research proposal should deal with:

a definition of the research aims.
the details of research methods that would be utilized.
an estimate of the cost of the work.

The comparison of the proposals submitted by various agencies should lead to further elimination of some of them. However, it would not be advisable to eliminate an agency merely because its price was somewhat high.

It is quite possible that discussion with an agency will lead to a reformulation of the problem, and the potential client should be open to this. It may be that the wrong questions were being posed; or that a more fundamental problem concerning product availability needed to be clarified before marketing research could be justified; or that within the field of marketing research certain aspects needed more and others less emphasis.

Close cooperation and contact between agency and client is necessary throughout the research in order to avoid final disappointment—a not infrequent occurrence. A useful precaution that can sometimes be taken to avoid disappointment is to commission a part of the project on a pilot basis. If this is successfully accomplished, further work can be authorized with greater assurance of ultimate satisfaction.

Organizing Feedback from the Market and Forecasting the Demand

In the earlier part of this note, it was mentioned that the operational strategy for export needs to undergo continuous change in keeping with the changes in the environmental conditions. Very often, the entry of a new competitor or the appearance of a new substitute for the exporter's product disturbs the balance of market forces. The foreign manufacturer should be able to adjust himself to such changes in the market equilibrium.

Such adjustments are possible only when there is a regular flow of information from the operating level to the policy-making level. Market research, therefore, is a continuing process and does not cease after the entry into the export market. The methods used for such a feedback will be more or less similar to what we use in the domestic markets. Demand forecasting is one of the important areas which would very directly depend upon the feedback from the markets. Forecasting with relation to foreign markets can at times be somewhat trickier than the forecasting in domestic markets. As a great deal of information collected by the researcher can be needed for forecasting, the problems involved in the process are treated below at some length.

Forecasting gives a time dimension to quantification. The first task in forecasting is to isolate the variables on which demand depends. These may in turn depend upon further variables. Correlations between variables can be worked out for the past and projected forward; but there will always be an assumption made about the behavior of some of these variables in future. The question is how valid these assumptions can be.

In effect it is necessary for the exporter to try to find out to what extent the forces that have operated in the past will remain valid for the future. It is because the demand is derived from factors more fundamental than are visible at first sight, that the kind of field research earlier described becomes necessary. An exporter may often be unaware of the basic forces shaping demand. Awareness of these basic forces can result only if he goes to the wholesalers, retailers and consumers to understand the change that is taking place.

One way of becoming certain about the future is to use one country's past to reveal another country's future.[6] This is possible to some extent because all countries of the world are strung out at different stages of development. It is reasonable to expect that the process of development will take countries through experiences already traversed by others. Thus in the case of a product whose consumption in Western Europe is rising, like citrus juice, it is useful to know when a saturation point is likely to be reached. A comparison of per capita consumption in Europe with those in North America may show how far or how near this point is, though differences in national consumption habits have to be borne in mind. This kind of comparison is a useful tool for the market analyst.

The most difficult variables to take into account in forecasting are those concerning the development of technology. The great strides made by chemical industry have been responsible for the onslaught on traditional materials that to a great extent come from the developing countries. Synethetic rubbers have cut into the market for natural rubber; synthetic fabrics have limited the growth of cotton fabrics industry. It is virtually impossible to foresee such developments, though once the invention is known, it may be possible to forecast its effects.

A forecast is not a once-for-all activity. It is valid only when it is made. A systematic review of the variables and the assumption used in forecasting is very necessary.

Who Should Undertake Research

Research for overseas markets can be undertaken at various levels. It will neither be possible nor advisable for an individual firm to undertake every kind of information collection activity mentioned in this note. An individual manufacturer, therefore, must learn to make a judicious use of the government agencies, industry and trade associations and co-operative selling organizations.

QUESTIONS

1. Discuss how one would undertake a preliminary screening of marketing opportunities.
2. Discuss how the information cited as part of the detailed analysis of export opportunities can be related to marketing mix decisions.
3. How would a firm go about evaluating the quality and competence of outside suppliers that would assist it in conducting market reserach in foreign countries?

NOTES

1. Root, Franklin R., *Strategic Planning for Export Marketing,* (Scranton, PA: International Textbook Company, 1966), pp. 1-13.

2. *Ibid.,* pp. 18-24.

3. Fayerweather, John, *International Marketing.* (Englewood Cliffs, N.J.: Prentice Hall, 1965), pp. 5-15.

4. Stuart, Robert Douglass, *Penetrating the International Market.* (New York, N.Y.: American Management Association, 1965), pp. 25-39.

5. Robinson, Richard D., "The Challenge of Underdeveloped National Market," *Journal of Marketing,* vol. 25, October, 1961, p. 22.

6. Keegan, Warren J., *Multinational Marketing Management,* (Englewood Cliffs N.J.: Prentice Hall, Inc., 1974), pp. 190-196.

An increasing number of cross-national studies are being reported in the consumer behavior literature. However, a review of this research suggests that many of the methodological issues involved in the conduct of cross-national research are being ignored. This paper presents some of the most fundamental considerations that are involved in studies of cross-national consumer behavior, and suggests methods of incorporating them into research projects.

12. Methodological Considerations in Cross-National Consumer Research

Robert T. Green
University of Texas

Phillip D. White
University of Colorado

The field of consumer behavior has evolved rapidly in a relatively brief period of time. The depth as well as the breadth of the research on consumer behavior has been impressive. However, most of the research in the area has one common limitation: it is culture bound. Nearly all consumer studies have been conducted in the United States. Thus, the principles that have been developed are associated only with United States consumer behavior; the theories that have been derived can legitimately be used to describe, predict, or understand consumer behavior only in the United States.

The unicultural perspective that characterizes consumer research places constraints on the development of the field. The natural conclusion to be drawn from the recognition of this current inadequacy in consumer research is that more cross-national research should be conducted.[1] However, the conduct of cross-national research cannot be viewed as a mere extension of domestic research. As soon as the decision is made to conduct research

---

Source: Reprinted from the *Journal of International Business Studies* Fall/Winter 1976.

in more than one nation, the researcher is faced with a myriad of problems that often do not have to be considered in the conduct of purely domestic research. Failure to recognize these considerations can place severe limitations on the potential contribution of a cross-national research project.[2]

The past five years have witnessed an increasing number of cross-national consumer studies.[3] Attention has been focused primarily on the decision-making processes of ultimate consumers[4] and of industrial buyers.[5] In addition, studies have been reported concerning product perceptions,[6] repeat buying habits,[7] innovator characteristics,[8] and consumer information systems.[9] There are also several cross-national consumer research projects currently in progress.[10] Presumably, the results of these studies will provide a base for future studies conducted in the area. Yet, many of the studies contain major drawbacks owing to the methodological procedures they employed.

The primary objective of this paper is to identify and explain the major methodological considerations which should be incorporated into cross-national studies. An understanding of these issues is crucial to the conduct of cross-national research because in many instances results will be rendered useless if the investigators are unaware of the subtleties involved. The secondary objective of the paper is to provide prospective cross-national researchers with a set of sources to which they can refer for detailed information about the individual issues.

Methodological Considerations

The specific issues of concern to cross-national consumer researchers include the functional equivalence of the phenomena being studied across nations, the cross-national equivalence of the concepts and research instruments being employed, the comparability of the samples in each nation, and the translation of the research instrument into different languages. These methodological issues are all highly interrelated, but for purposes of exposition are considered individually in the following sections.[11]

Functional Equivalence

"Obviously, if similar activities have different functions in different societies, their parameters cannot be used for comparative purposes."[12] This statement provides a concise expression of the problem of functional equivalence that confronts cross-national researchers. Some of the most common variables and situations employed in consumer behavior studies are not functionally equivalent across nations. Many products tend to perform different functions in different nations; bicycles provide basic transportation in some countries, but are essentially recreational in others. The act of shopping does not always perform the same function in all countries. In France shopping is reputed to be an integral part of the housewife's social life, whereas in the

United States shopping tends to be considered a chore. Thus, a cross-national study that involves measurement of some aspect of consumer behavior while purchasing a particular product or while shopping could be dealing with functionally non-equivalent situations. Any differences ascertained in responses could not automatically be attributed to national differences on the variables being measured, since it may be equally plausible that the differences were caused by the functional non-equivalence of the product or the buying situation.

The issue of functional equivalence is particularly critical in the cross-national testing of consumer behavior theory. The identificaton of cross-nationally valid relationships which enable greater understanding or prediction of consumer behavior demands explicit consideration of the functional equivalence of all aspects of the research project. However, the area of cross-national consumer behavior has probably not reached the point where this type of hypothesis testing is possible, since so little is known about the functional equivalence of purchasing-related phenomena across countries. Therefore, a primary objective of current cross-national consumer research may be the identification of functionally equivalent and non-equivalent phenomena through basically descriptive studies. The results of such descriptive work can provide the input for future theory development.

Functional equivalence may not be a necessary requirement for cross-national research conducted for primarily managerial purposes. In many cases business managers may be concerned mainly with purchase response under well-defined and relatively discrete conditions. For instance, the manager may wish to know only whether consumers in Country A respond to a certain advertising theme in the same way as consumers in Country B. In this case, the manager would be interested in discerning the effectiveness of the particular theme, and functional equivalence may not be an issue. However, even then, identification of possible functional differences may be a useful byproduct of the research.

Conceptual Equivalence

Another consideration in cross-national research concerns the equivalence of the concepts which are employed in the countries being investigated.[13] This consideration recognizes that many concepts are culture bound and are inappropriate for use on a cross-national basis.[14] The results from a cross-national research project may be uninterpretable if they are based upon concepts which apply in one way in some countries and in a different way—or not at all—in others. Problems of this type can arise from the conceptual base of a study. Similarly, conceptual equivalence can be an issue in the selection of terms that are employed to measure certain items (which will be discussed below with respect to translation problems).

Problems in conceptual equivalence might arise in cross-national consumer research when testing the role that certain sociological or psychological constructs play in purchasing behavior. For instance, a conceptual equivalence problem might arise if one were to employ a cognitive consistency theory in a cross-national study of consumer behavior. A primary assumption of cognitive consistency theories is that people do not voluntarily hold discrepant attitudes. Such an assumption may be valid in the United States but may not apply in other nations. Thus, the concept of cognitive consistency may be culture-bound, without conceptual equivalents in some other nations and inappropriate for use in some cross-national research.

The preceding discussion is not intended to imply that cross-national research that employs social and behavioral science theories developed in the United States should be avoided. The examples are used to illustrate the point that the concept employed in a cross-national study should be applicable in the nations being tested. Research that is basically exploratory or descriptive may not need to establish conceptual equivalence in the design stages. However, this consideration should be incorporated into the interpretation of any cross-national differences uncovered by the research.

Instrument Equivalence

The development of valid and reliable instruments that measure the phenomenon being studied is a difficult task in any research project. However, the additional variables which must be considered in the conduct of cross-national research make instrument development even more complex. The cross-national researcher should be careful to employ measures that test the same phenomenon in each of the nations being studied. The researcher should also ensure that the translation of the instrument into each language is as precise as possible. While both of these issues appear straightforward, the problems they present to the cross-national researcher can be difficult to resolve. The following discussion addresses each of these issues individually and presents the major considerations involved and the methods that have been devised to overcome the associated problems.

Measurement Equivalence   Once functional and conceptual equivalence has been established, the problem becomes one of devising a research instrument that adequately measures the phenomena under study in each of the nations being investigated. The validity problems that arise when the phenomena are not appropriately measured in each nation are obvious. Ideally, the researcher would construct a single instrument that provides an equally valid measure of the phenomenon under investigation in each nation. However, this is rarely possible. Even if a phenomenon is functionally and conceptually equivalent across nations, it is often the case that the phenomenon is manifested differently in each nation.[15] For instance, consider this problem with respect to the cross-national measurement of affection, an idea frequently expressed in promotional campaigns. While the concept of affection is probably universal, and while the function affection performs is probably similar across nations, the exact form which affection takes in each society differs considerably. Therefore, cross-national instruments that employ the identical measures of such phenomena may not provide data which permit reliable comparisons to be made.

The preceding discussion identifies one of the major problems associated with the construction of testing instruments for use in cross-national research. There is no ideal solution to this problem, but several approaches exist to cope with it. Cross-national researchers may employ one of the two general types of measures in their studies: *emic* or *etic*.[16] Emic instruments refer to tests constructed to study a phenomenon only in the context of a single society. Etic instruments are culture-free, and the identical instrument (properly translated) can be employed in all (or a number of) nations.[17]

The application of the emic approach to cross-national research would require that individual instruments be constructed to measure a particular aspect of behavior in each nation. The instrument employed in each society would likely be different, since the object of investigation will probably be manifested in different ways across nations. Thus, perfect cross-national comparison may be difficult; but the particular aspect of behavior will have been isolated in its own national setting. Virtually all instruments to date that have been constructed to measure aspects of consumer behavior are emics. They have, for the most part, been devised in the United States and have employed assumptions that pertain to this country. The measurement of the same concepts in other countries may require significant alterations in these instruments in order to obtain reliable measurement of the phenomenon under investigation.

An etic instrument is multinational in its application and permits direct comparisons on the same variables across nations. The difficulties involved in the development of etic instruments are manifold. The problems surrounding the construction of "culture-free" (or, at least, "culture-fair") tests to be presented to different groups within a nation are difficult to overcome.[18] These problems are compounded when developing a single test that applies across several very different national societies.

Several methods are available that can be used to determine the reliability and validity of cross-national instruments. For instance, Triandis, et al., suggest that separate tests be developed in each nation to measure a phenomenon, and then to examine the correlations that exist between scores on the instruments and other variables in the nations being studied.[19] Other cross-national researchers have employed factor analysis to determine the reliability and validity of their instruments, and factor analytic techniques have been developed that have potential applications for this purpose.[20] However, factor analysis has also been shown to have certain problems and limitations in this area.[21] Further reliability and validity techniques are available from a number of sources.[22]

Few standard tests have been developed that are appropriate for use in more than one nation without modification. Those which have been developed include Cattell's 16PF,[23] Gough's California Psychological Inventory,[24] Osgood's Semantic Differential,[25] and certain social desirability scales.[26] However, none of these measures are universally applicable. Consumer researchers engaged in cross-national studies will probably have to rely upon instruments which could not be considered etic, but which serve the purpose of identifying the similarities or differences in the phenomenon being investigated. One possible strategy in this regard is to employ the same test in all nations, even though it was developed in only one of the nations, and to "tease" out the reasons for differences which may be uncovered.[27] Such an approach might be criticized for being "pseudo-etic,"[28] but the results obtained from such an instrument could provide some basic understanding where none existed before, or they could provide the basis for future hypotheses.

In most cases, however, research instruments will have to be altered to some extent from nation to nation. At the very least, certain classification items will have to be different in each nation, since educational systems vary widely, income levels are highly discrepant, etc. Research instruments may also have to consider such differences as might exist in the availability of items (e.g., products) used in the study, in the media that can be employed in each nation, and in the literacy of the respondents. Thus, in most instances cross-national research instruments will have to be somewhat individualized for each nation (emic), a fact which can cause interpretation problems. However, the results of such studies can provide valuable insights into cross-national consumer behavior; but it is important that the limitations of this approach be clearly understood and reported with the results.

Instrument Translation   The development of the instrument is generally followed by translation into the language of the nations in which the instrument is to be administered. The achievement of instrument equivalence depends upon proper translation. Thus, caution must be exercised in the translation process. Caution is particularly necessary due to the number of subtle pitfalls that exist in obtaining a good translation.

One problem frequently encountered is that terms cannot be directly translated into another language and still retain their full meaning.[29] For instance, the word "tough" in English may contain several nuances in its use that makes perfect translation difficult to achieve. A related problem may occur if an equivalent for a term does not exist in another language. The Spanish term "machismo," for example, is impossible to translate into Enlgish because an equivalent term does not exist. Further translation problems may arise from the use of idiomatic expressions or if some terms employed in the instrument are outside the range of experience of the sample. An example of the latter problem might be found with respect to the term "supermarket." While the term itself is capable of being translated into several languages, it is probable that many people in other countries have not been exposed to a supermarket in the American sense of the term—if at all. Thus, such experiential differences could influence the results obtained in a cross-national project and must be considered in the translation process.[30] The importance of a good translation implies first that the original instrument should be written in easily translatable English.[31] It also suggests that researchers should provide evidence to support claims that their instruments were equivalent in all languages in order to avoid the plausibility of rival hypotheses to explain the results obtained.[32]

Several methods of translation can be employed by cross-national researchers, the most common of which is *direct translation*.[33] In this method a bilingual translator simply translates an instrument from one language into another. Although it is the simplest, least time consuming, and least expensive method of translation, direct translation is fraught with problems. Basically, the researcher who employs direct translation cannot be certain about the quality of the translation. All of the problems noted above may have occurred in the direct translation unbeknownst to the researcher.

To overcome many of the problems of direct translation, cross-national researchers often employ a process called *back translation*.[34] In this process a research instrument is first translated into another language by one bilingual translator, and then translated back into the original language by a second bilingual translator. Back translation allows the researcher to identify many of the problems that might arise by noting the discrepancies between the original instrument and the retranslated instrument. Corrections can be made where discrepancies exist, and the back translation process may be repeated. Thus, back translation is an iterative process which ends when the researcher is satisfied that all forms of the instrument are equivalent.[35] The success of this process depends upon the use of skilled translators who are familiar with the particular dialect of the sample to which the instrument is to be administered.

Direct translation and back translation are generally used when an instrument developed in one country is to be employed in other countries. As noted previously such an approach is often labeled "pseudo-etic" and subject to the problems of functional, conceptual, and measurement equivalence. While a competent back translation can overcome some of these problems, it will not resolve all of them. Werner and Campbell suggest that the only way to completely overcome translation problems is to construct the instrument in all of the nations included in the study and to incorporate items from each nation into the instrument.[36] This process is called *decentering* and usually results in a considerably longer instrument.[37] In addition, the time and expense required to perform this process may be prohibitive to most researchers. However, it is perhaps the most highly regarded technique for the development of a cross-national research instrument.

Sample Selection

To help ensure against alternative explanations of differences in results, the researcher should select samples in each nation that are as closely comparable as possible.[38] One way to achieve sample comparability is to draw a truly representative sample from each nation under study.[39] However, such a sampling procedure can be difficult and expensive and often not feasible (judging from the infrequency of its use in even deomestic studies). In addition, consumer researchers may not be interested in surveying two entire populations, since large portions of those samples may not be pertinent to the investigation. Also, representative samples in each nation may exhibit extreme variation which could make cross-national comparisons difficult.

A commonly employed sampling technique in cross-national studies involves drawing the samples from an identifiable subgroup of the countries' populations.[40] For instance, samples of students in two or more countries might be employed, or samples of middle-class housewives might be drawn. The use of samples from subgroups of the populations will limit the generalization of the findings but can provide an indication of the types of similarities and differences which exist between nations. However, when samples from subgroups are employed, the researcher must exercise extreme caution to ensure that the subgroup samples in each nation are comparable.[41] If noncomparable samples are employed, then differences found between the samples can be attributed to the differences in the characteristics of the samples as well as to national factors.

The achievement of perfect sample comparability can be difficult. It is virtually impossible to select samples in two or more countries that share all the same traits. For example, middle-class housewives in the United States and Mexico will differ in terms of their absolute level of income and, perhaps, education. Salesmen in the United States and many other countries may differ in terms of social class. Students in lesser developed nations are likely to be drawn from higher levels of the social strata than students in the more economically advanced countries. Thus, no matter how hard the researcher works to achieve sample comparability, there will usually be some types of differences between the samples. Manaster and Havighurst suggest that cross-national researchers should attempt to hold age, sex, social class, and rural-urban residence constant across samples.[42] It may be impossible to hold these factors constant all of the time, but any lack of comparability in the samples should be reported as a limitaion and incorporated into the interpretations of the data.[43]

Conclusion

Emphasis on cross-national consumer behavior patterns is a natural direction for international marketing research to take. It will have both theoretical and practical benefits. However, the potential contribution of these cross-national studies will be a function of the quality of the research conducted. This paper has presented the most basic methodological problems encountered by cross-national researchers and the principal means of coping with these problems.

In addition, a number of references have been provided on each issue for those who want to pursue individual aspects in greater detail. These considerations should be incorporated into cross-national research projects to ensure reliability of the findings.

QUESTIONS

1. Differentiate between functional, conceptual, and instrument equivalence.
2. Discuss how researchers might achieve sample comparability in cross-national surveys.
3. What are some of the problems facing researchers in trying to ensure comparable measurements of consumer behavior across different countries?

NOTES

1. J. Engel, D. Kollat, and R. Blackwell, *Consumer Behavior* (Second Edition). (New York, N.Y.: Holt, Rinehart and Winston, Inc., 1973).

2. The term *cross-national* is often used interchangeably with the term *cross-cultural* in describing the type of research discussed in this paper. The former term will be used here since the paper is concerned with consumer behavior research conducted across national boundaries. Cross-cultural research can refer to the study of two or more subcultures within a country as well as research across countries.

3. Cross-national research projects are being defined as including: (1) studies conducted by the same authors in more than one country at roughly the same point in time; (2) replications of previous studies by researchers other than the author conducted in previous time periods; and (3) studies conducted outside of the United States, the findings from which have been inferred as being applicable to this country. In addition, consumer research is considered to include studies of both industrial and ultimate consumers.

4. H. Davis, and B. Rigaux, "Perception of Marital Roles in Decision Processes," *Journal of Consumer Research*, Vol. 1, June 1974. pp. 51–62, D. Hempel, "A Cross-Cultural Analysis of Husband-Wife Roles in House Purchase Decisions," *Proceedings*. Third Annual Conference, Association for Consumer Research, 1972, pp. 816–829, D. Hempel, "Family Buying Decisions: A Cross-Cultural Perspective," *Journal of Marketing Research*, Vol. II, August 1974, pp. 295–302; C. Safilios-Rothschild, "Family Sociology or Wives' Family Sociology: A Cross-Cultural Examination of Decision Making," *Journal of Marriage and the Family*, Vol. 31, May 1969, pp. 290–301; W. Silverman, and R. Hill, "Task Allocation in Marriage in the United States and Belgium" *Journal of Marriage and the Family*, Vol. 29, May 1967, pp. 353–359.

5. H. Hakansson and B. Wootz, "Supplier Selection in an International Environment— An Experimental Study," *Journal of Marketing Research*, Vol. 12, February 1975, pp. 46–51, D. Lehman and J. O'Shaughnessy, "Difference in Attribute Importance

for Different Industrial Products," *Journal of Marketing*, Vol. 38, April 1974, pp. 36–42.

6. J. Arndt, "Haire's Shopping List Revisited," *Journal of Advertising Research*, Vol. 13, October 1973, pp. 57–61; I. Cunningham, R. Green, and W. Cunningham, "The Effectiveness of Standardized Global Advertising A Cross-Cultural Study," *Journal of Advertising*, Vol. 4, Summer 1975, pp. 25–30; A. Nagashima, "A Comparison of Japanese and U.S. Attitudes Toward Foreign Products," *Journal of Marketing*, Vol. 34, January 1970, pp. 68–74.

7. A. Ehrenberg and G. Goodhardt, "A Comparison of American and British Repeat-Buying Habits," *Journal of Marketing Research*. Vol. 5, February 1968, pp. 29–33.

8. R. Green and E. Langeard, "A Cross-National Comparison of Consumer Habits and Innovator Characteristics," *Journal of Marketing*, Vol. 39, July 1975, pp. 34–41.

9. H. Thorelli, H. Becker, and J. Engledow, *The Information Seekers*, (Cambridge, Mass.: Ballinger, 1975).

10. S. Comas and J. Sheth, "Cross-Cultural Measurement of Generalized Opinion Leadership," paper presented at the 82nd Annual Convention of the American Psychological Association, New Orleans, September 1974; H. Davis, "Cross-Cultural Comparison of Family Roles," paper presented at the 5th Annual Convention of the Association for Consumer Research, Chicago, November 1974; J. Plummer, "Comparative Life Styles of the Industrial States," paper presented at the 82nd Annual Convention of the American Psychological Association, New Orleans, September 1974; J. Sheth and S. Sethi, "Theory of Cross-Cultural Buyer Behavior," Working Paper No. 115, College of Commerce and Business Administration, Univeristy of Illinois at Urbana-Champaign, 1973.

11. Cross-national research has a rich tradition in the fields of cultural anthropology, psychology and social psychology, sociology, and political science. However, due to the differences in the aspects of behavior with which each discipline is concerned, there tend to be variations in the methods employed and the problems encountered. Since the variables considered in consumer research are most similar to those employed in psychological and sociological research, this paper will be concerned mainly with the problems and considerations of cross-national research in those fields.

12. N. Frijda and G. Jahoda, "On the Scope and Methods of Cross-Cultural Research," *International Journal of Psychology*, Vol. 1, No. 2, 1966, p. 116.

13. R. Sears, "Transcultural Variables and Conceptual Equivalence," in Bert Kaplan, ed. *Studying Personality Cross-Culturally*, Evanston, Ill.: Row, Peterson and Company, 1961, pp. 445–455.

14. J. Berry, "On Cross-Cultural Comparability," *International Journal of Psychology*, Vol. 4, No. 2, 1969, pp. 119–128.

15. R. Sears, *op. cit.*

16. The terms *emic* and *etic* were coined by Pike (see K. Pike, *Language in Relation to a United Theory of the Structure of Human Behavior*, The Hague: Mouton, 1966) and were derived from the linguistic distinction between phonemics and phonetics. The study of phonemics examines the sound employed in a particular language, while phonetics" . . . attempts to generalize from phonemic studies in individual languages to a universal science covering all languages" J. Berry, *op. cit.* p. 123). For a discussion of the use of emic and etic research in cross-cultural studies, see R. Brislin, W. Lonner, and R. Thorndike, *Cross-Cultural Research*

Methods, New York, N.Y.: Wiley, 1973; and H. Triandis, R. Malpass, and A. Davidson, "Cross-Cultural Psychology," *Biennial Review of Anthropology,* Palo Alto, CA: Annual Review, Inc. 1971.

17. R. Anderson, "On the Comparability of Meaningful Stimuli in Cross-Cultural Research," *Sociometry,* Vol. 30, June 1967, pp. 124–136.

18. N. Frijda and G. Jahoda, *op. cit.*

19. H. Triandis, R. Malpass, and A. Davidson, *op. cit.*

20. L. Gordon, "Comments on 'Cross-Cultural Equivalence of Personality Measures,' " *Journal of Social Psychology,* Vol. 75, June 1968, pp. 11–19; L. Tucker, "Some Mathematical Notes on Three-Mode Factor Analysis," *Psychometrika,* Vol. 31, September 1966, pp. 279–311.

21. D. Peterson and G. Migliorino, "The Uses and Limitations of Factor Analysis in Cross-Cultural Research on Socialization," *International Journal of Psychology,* Vol. 2, No. 3, 1967, pp. 215–220.

22. L. Eckensberger, "Methodological Issues of Cross-Cultural Research in Development Psychology," in John R. Nesselroade and Hayne W. Ruse, eds., *Life-Span Developmental Psychology: Methodological Issues* (New York, N.Y.: Academic Press, 1973), pp. 43–64; H. Gulliksen, "Methods for Determining Equivalence of Measures" *Psychological Bulletin,* Vol. 70, December 1968, pp. 534–44; G. Manaster and R. Havighurst, *Cross-National Research: Social-Psychological Methods and Problems.* (Boston, MA: Houghton Mifflin Company, 1972); A. Przeworski and H. Teune, "Equivalence in Cross-National Research," *Public Opinion Quarterly,* Vol. 30, Winter 1966, pp. 551–568; A. Przeworski and H. Teune, *The Logic of Comparative Social Inquiry.* (New York, N.Y.: Wiley, 1970).

23. D. Butt and E. Signori, "Personality Factors of a Canadian Sample of Male University Students," *Psychological Reports,* Vol. 16, June 1965, pp. 1117–1121; R. Cattell and F. Warburton, "A Cross-Cultural Comparison of Patterns of Extraversion and Anxiety," *British Journal of Psychology,* Vol, 52, February 1961, pp. 3–15; E. deAndrade, D. Alves, and J. Ford, "A Comparison of North American and Brazilian College Students' Personality Profiles on the 16PF Questionnaires," *International Journal of Psychology,* Vol. 4, No. 1, 1969, pp. 55–58; B. Tsujioka and R. Cattell, "A Cross-Cultural Comparison of Second-Stratum Questionnaire Personality Factor Structures—Anxiety and Extraversion—in America and Japan," *The Journal of Social Psychology,* Vol. 65, April 1965, pp. 205–219.

24. H. Gough and H. Sandhu, "Validation of the CPI Socialization Scale in India," *Journal of Abnormal and Social Psychology,* Vol. 68, May 1964, pp. 544–547; H. Gough, "Cross-Cultural Validation of a Measure of Asocial Behavior," *Psychological Reports,* Vol. 17, October 1965, pp. 379–387; H. Gough, G. DeVos, and K. Migushima, "Japanese Validation of the CPI Social Maturity Index," *Psychological Reports,* Vol. 22, February 1968, pp. 143–146; J. Levin and E. Karni, "Demonstration of Cross-Cultural Invariance of the California Psychological Inventory in America and Israel by the Guttman-Lingoes Smallest Space Analysis," *Journal of Cross-Cultural Psychology,* Vol. 1, September 1970, pp. 253–260; T. Nishiyama, "Cross-Cultural Invariance of the California Psychological Inventory," *Psychologia,* Vol. 16, June 1973, pp. 75–84.

25. D. Heise, "Some Methodological Issues in Semantic Differential Research," *Psychological Bulletin,* Vol. 72, December 1969, pp. 406–422; L. Jacobovitz, "Comparative Psycholinguistics in the Study of Cultures," *International Journal of Psychology,* Vol. 1, No. 1, 1966, pp. 15–37; C. Osgood, G. Suci, and P. Tannenbaum,

The Measurement of Meaning, Urbana, Ill.: University of Illinois Press, 1957; C. Osgood, "Studies on the Generality of Affective Meaning Systems," *American Psychologist,* Vol. 17, January 1962, pp. 10–28; C. Osgood, "Exploration in Semantic Space: A Personal Diary," *Journal of Social Issues,* Vol. 27, No. 4, 1971, pp. 5–64; Y. Tanaka, T. Oyama, and C. Osgood, "A Cross-Cultural and Cross-Concept Study of the Generality of Semantic Space," *Journal of Verbal Learning and Verbal Behavior,* Vol. 2, December 1963, pp. 392–405.

26. P. Baltes, K. Eyferth, and K. Schaie, "Intra- and Inter-Cultural Factor Structures of Social Desirability Ratings by American and German College Students," *Multivariate Behavioral Research,* Vol. 4, January 1969, pp. 67–78; C. Consalvi, "An Item and Factor Analysis of Danish, Lebanese, and United States College Student's Responses to the Marlowe-Crowne Social Desirability Scale," *Journal of Cross-Cultural Psychology,* Vol. 3, December 1972, pp. 361–372.

27. N. Frijda and G. Jahoda, *op. cit.,* p. 118.

28. H. Triandis, R. Malpass, and A. Davidson, *op. cit.*

29. R. Brislin, W. Lonner, and R. Thorndike, *op. cit.*; A. Przeworski and H. Teune, *op. cit.*

30. L. Sechrest, T. Fay, and S. Zaidi, "Problems of Translation in Cross-Cultural Research," *Journal of Cross-Cultural Psychology,* Vol. 3, March 1972, pp. 41–56.

31. R. Brislin, "Back-Translation for Cross-Cultural Research," *Journal of Cross-Cultural Psychology,* Vol. 1, September 1970, pp. 185–216; R. Brislin, "Translation Issues: Multi-language Versions and Writing Translatable English," *Proceedings,* 80th Annual Convention of the American Psychological Association, 1970, pp. 299–300; R. Fink, "Interviewer Training and Supervision in a Survey of Laos," *International Social Science Journal,* Vol. 15, No. 1, 1963, pp. 21–34; E. Nida, *Toward a Science of Translating,* (Leiden, Netherlands: E.J. Brill, 1964); E. Scheuch, "The Cross-Cultural Use of Sample Surveys: Problems of Comparability," in Stein Rokkan, ed., *Comparative Research Across Cultures and Nations,* (Paris: The Hague Mouton, 1968), pp. 179–209; A. Treisman, "The Effects of Redundancy and Familiarity on Translating and Repeating Back a Foreign and Native Language," *British Journal of Psychology,* Vol. 56, November 1965, pp. 363–379.

32. R. Brislin, W. Lonner, and R. Thorndike, *op. cit.*

33. L. Sechrest, T. Fay, and S. Zaidi, *op. cit.*

34. R. Brislin, *op. cit.*; R. Brislin, W. Lonner, and R. Thorndike, *op. cit.*; O. Werner and D. Campbell, "Translating, Working Through Interpreters, and the Problems of Decentering," in Raoul Naroll and Ronald Cohen, eds., *A Handbook of Method in Cultural Anthropology,* (New York, N.Y.: Columbia University Press, 1973), pp. 398–420.

35. R. Brisin, *op. cit.*

36. O. Werner and D. Campbell, *op. cit.*

37. F. Berrien, "Cross-Cultural Equivalence of Personality Measures," *Journal of Social Psychology,* Vol. 75, June 1968, pp. 3–9; L. Gordon and A. Kikuchi, "American Personality Tests in Cross-Cultural Research—A Caution," *Journal of Social Psychology,* Vol. 69, August 1966, pp. 179–183; L. Gordon, *op. cit.*; H. Triandis, R. Malpass, and A. Davidson, *op. cit.*

38. F. Berrien, "Methodological and Related Problems in Cross-Cultural Research," *International Journal of Psychology,* Vol. 2, No. 2, 1967, pp. 33–43; R. Brislin and S.

Baumgardner, "Non-Random Sampling of Individuals in Cross-Cultural Research," *Journal of Cross-Cultural Psychology,* Vol. 2, December 1971, pp. 397–400; N. Frijda and G. Jahoda, *op. cit.*; W. Lamber and O. Klineberg, *Children's Views of Foreign Peoples: A Cross-National Study,* (New York, N.Y.: Appleton-Century-Crofts, 1970).

39. G. Almond and S. Verba, *The Civic Culture: Political Attitudes and Democracy in Five Nations,* (Princeton, N.J.: Princeton University Press, 1963); F. Frey, "Cross-Cultural Survey Research in Political Science," in Robert T. Holt and John E. Turner, eds. *The Methodology of Comparative Research,* (New York, N.Y.: The Free Press, 1970), pp. 173–294.

40. R. Brislin and S. Baumgardner, *op. cit.*

41. *Ibid.,* R. Brislin, W. Lonner and R. Thorndike, *op. cit.*

42. G. Manaster and R. Havighurst, *op. cit.,* p. 161.

43. J. Berry, *op cit.*

*The problems, goals, and methods of re-
search conducted overseas and domestically
are similar. The author contends, however,
that cultural, social, economic, and other
differences create some 'special wrinkles' in
international marketing research. Examples
of how these factors on the conduct of research are presented and steps to take to
avoid potential pitfalls are explored.*

13. Special Wrinkles in International Marketing Research

Lee Adler
Farleigh Dickinson University

Once upon a time, marketing abroad was a cinch for American firms. Overseas markets were regarded as dumping grounds for surplus goods, quality
rejects, or last year's unsold fashions. The small number of United States
companies that recognized long-term opportunities abroad realized profits
disproportionate to sales volume.

Today, of course, international marketing has changed a great deal,
thanks to a number of developments: the growing size of overseas markets,
the greater sophistication and aggressiveness of foreign marketers, the growing spirit of nationalism, and the rapid escalation of labor costs and other expenses abroad. As a result, United States-based multinational firms must
tool up to deal with a new array of troubles. Obviously, marketing research
is one tool that enables marketers to keep up with turbulent, intensely competitive markets.

The problems, goals, and methods of research overseas are no different

Source: Reprinted by permission from *Sales & Marketing Management* magazine. Copyright © 1976.

from those in the United States. What differs is the detail, and that's crucial because of cultural, social, economic, linguistic, and other differences. Let's examine some of these special wrinkles:

National Differences

A *Reader's Digest* study of consumer behavior in Western Europe once astonished everyone by reporting that France and West Germany consumed more spaghetti than Italy. The reason for this curious finding was that the question dealt with packaged and branded spaghetti. Many Italians buy their spaghetti loose.

Economic Differences

Market segments vary so drastically between countries and even within the same country that there are different requirements for designing market studies. For example, the market for many common packaged goods—foods, over-the-counter drugs, cosmetics, etc.—is limited to the upper social strata in many developing countries, in contrast to the high usage levels in the developed lands. Thus it's wasteful to include nontarget segments in probability samples.

Cultural Differences

These may necessitate sharp variations in research design. For example:

> In England, Germany, and Scandinavia, beer is generally perceived as an alcoholic beverage. In Mediterranean lands, however, beer is considered akin to soft drinks. Therefore, a study of the competitive status of beer in Northern Europe would have to build in questions on wine and liquor. In Italy, Spain, or Greece, the comparison would have to be with soft drinks.

> In Italy, it's common for children to have a bar of chocolate between two slices of bread as a snack. In France, bar chocolate is often used in cooking. But a West German housewife would be revolted by either practice.

> A third of all German and Dutch businessmen take their wives with them on business trips, as opposed to only 15 percent of their English and French counterparts. As a study for one hotel delicately put it, the criteria each group uses in judging hotels and the services they offer clearly are likely to be different.

Market Environment Differences

Factors to take into account include the following:

competitive situation

legal constraints

physical distribution facilities

tariff and other import regulations

traditions in such things as selling policies and practices, pricing, discounts, customer service, and technical aid

geographic concentration

media configurations

Differences in Research Facilities and Conduct

In the United States, we're accustomed to ever-increasing use of the telephone for survey research. But this is scarcely possible in most other countries, even advanced ones, because of both the low incidence of telephone ownership and the quality of service. Even in the United Kingdom and West Germany, only about one-third of the households have phones. Mail surveys are easily conducted in the United Kingdom and Germany, but high illiteracy rates in Italy and Spain rule against successful mail studies there.

Cultural differences also affect research methods. For instance, it's relatively easy to get groups of working-class women to attend focussed group interviews in England and Germany. But in southern Italy or Spain a recruiter would be regarded with suspicion. Before accepting, the women would probably have to consult their husbands and possibly the priest.

Long questionnaires do not seem to be much of a problem in the United States if handled intelligently. But they don't work in Hong Kong, where everyone seems to rush breathlessly about. In Brazil, even short questionnaires have a way of becoming long because Brazilians are conscientious about answering honestly and fully.

In some countries, as in the United States, it's hard to interview men during the day. But they may be interviewed readily in the early evening, or, surprisingly, in the early morning. In other countries, notably the Moslem and Asian lands, there may be some resistance to in-home interviewing, and respondents must be plied with questions on the doorstep or in the street.

The raw material for drawing area probability samples varies considerably from country to country. In some countries, reliable electoral registers, local maps for selecting blocks and planning interviewers' routes, and auto registration lists are available. In other nations, they're not.

Locating these lists is also a factor in research administration. In Great Britain, a central electoral register is maintained in London for the entire country. In Italy, voter lists are kept in each commune, of which there are over 9,000. Even in Britain, it's impossible to draw a practical sample of A, B, and C social class members (roughly the top third, socioeconomically) because there is no equivalent of United States Census Bureau block data.

These are just some of the special considerations to keep in mind if you or your research department are planning overseas studies. Obviously, special expertise is required.

I outlined above the cultural, economic, and technical factors that make international marketing research different from domestic research. Now, I'll explain how to avoid the problems that multinational marketers commonly experience in managing the research function.

But there is one thing to consider first. In the United States, we often insist, rightly, on comparability of research methods in order to achieve comparability of results. However, in conducting multinational studies, exactly the reverse may be true. To get the comparable results that we want, we may have to use different methods. Overseas, although comparability at the data-collection stage may be technically tidy, it may also defeat the objectives of the study. Questionnaire, sample design, and field work methods may all have to be different to attain comparable results. In other words, comparability is concerned with ends, not means.

This point is important. Achieving comparability calls for a high degree of centralized planning, control, and analysis of data. If your company can supply this caliber of coordination, you may be able to get by with using a local agency for field work. However, if your international research capability is limited or nonexistent (a common enough state of affairs), you need strong support from the research agency you select. That is likely to come from a centralized multicountry agency, although there are also affiliations of research houses operating under one banner that provide adequate central planning and control.

The need to respect national differences may appear to clash with this stress on centralization, but the conflict is more apparent than real. An able central agency will know how to judge national factors so as to avoid cultural booby traps. The thing to avoid is innocently sending the same questionnaire and field work "specs" to a group of independent local agencies and then expecting a cohesive result. Also, don't operate on the principle of "leave it to the local boys; they know best." Sometimes they do, but often they're slaves to their own prejudices and misconceptions; or they may have their own self-interest to serve.

Useful sources of information in choosing a research agency include the following:

> Associates, friends, and fellow (noncompetitive) executives experienced in that country. These are the best sources.

> Directors of research agencies, such as the ones published by the European Society for Marketing and Opinion Research, the British Market Research Society, and the American Marketing Association.

> Local associates, suppliers, and other business connections such as your company's local manager, importer, or the

like; advertising agencies; government bureaus; telephone directories, many of which have Yellow Pages or the equivalent. Note that ad agencies may offer research services themselves, which may make them either potential suppliers of research or biased informants.

If you can swing it, it's a good idea to make an on-site visit to each prospective agency. The research field generally is less mature abroad than in the United States, and you'll find that agencies run the gamut from highly qualified, full-service organizations to hustlers and charlatans. If you can't visit the countries yourself, you have two alternatives: (1) Select a multi-country agency and let its home office assume full responsibility for the local efforts. (2) Retain an independent international research consultant. There are a small number of these men, and they usually have served as international research executives with large corporations before hanging out their own shingles. They will either know the houses abroad or know how to find out about them in jig time.

Some other useful practices:

Put all research plans, proposals, and contracts in writing. The more lavish the detail, the better the chances of avoiding misunderstanding later on.

Check on fluency in English, especially if the research firm is to write the final report. Beware of the trap of "reasonable fluency." There are even well-known semantic pitfalls between "English" English and "American" English.

Agree on timetables in advance and in writing. Check progress frequently against due dates. Remember that Americans' sense of time differs from that of many foreigners. Americans are inclined to think of time as an enemy to be killed, a conspirator to be outwitted, or a long-distance runner to beat. Most foreigners, mercifully for them, are more relaxed about time.

In scheduling studies, beware of calendar, seasonal, and religious differences. For example, in the Mideast, at least five calendars are used and they all differ considerably from our Gregorian system.

Look into differences in research ethics. They vary widely from country to country. In a number of European countries, ethics are at least as stringent as in the United States. Some overseas researchers, however, do not hesitate to work for competitive clients concurrently, and others even sell a client's confidential data to competitors.

Have a representative present, if possible, when interviewers are being briefed, and have him examine the results of the first one or two days' field work. This may avoid some research horrors. Other stages of a project can, of course, be handled by mail or phone.

With respect to your own staff, if the volume of work warrants, I would recommend that your research department have a separate, well-qualified international unit, even if it's a one-man band. However, if your department is organized along product, divisional, or functional lines, international projects may logically be assigned to each specialist.

The problem, of course, is that they are not likely to build up a body of experience that way. Obviously, international research is sufficiently different to require separate treatment. You will find that the more you can treat it on its own terms, the better it will serve you.

QUESTIONS

1. Which of the special considerations identified by the author would have the greatest effect on a firm's international marketing effort? Why?
2. How does the author suggest contacting, evaluating, and criticizing an outside market research agency in conducting international research?

ANALYSIS OF OVERSEAS OPPORTUNITIES: APPLICATIONS

The profiling of overseas markets can be perceived as the outcome of numerous secondary as well as primary research efforts. The selections in Part IV are intended to cultivate an appreciation of the complex and often subtle differences that would be uncovered by researching different foreign markets. The countries highlighted by the following readings represent the most important future growth areas for international marketers. Given the emerging world economic situation it is not surprising that the Middle East has been widely studied. One article in this section, by Jack Kaikati, looks at Saudi Arabia and the unique character of its marketing environment. The other articles attempt to develop a similar perspective for Japan, Western Europe, the Eastern bloc countries, and the People's Republic of China. In each of these articles the authors describe the existing and emerging opportunities in these markets and the problems associated with their actualization. A number of case histories of successful, and not so successful, ventures by United States firms in these environments serve to further illustrate the challenges confronting international marketers.

This article explores the opportunities for marketing in Japan through the identification of major consumer consumption trends. A description of the past and present Japanese distribution system is developed along with an identification of key considerations in formulating strategies to deal with the Japanese trade.

14. Marketing Opportunities and Marketing Strategies in Japan

Masaru Yoshimori
Systems International Incorporated

Marketing Opportunities in Japan

Perhaps a direct method to illustrate market opportunities in Japan would be to review what merchandise items were best-selling in 1973. *Nikkei Ryutsu Shimbun*, a specialized distribution trade newspaper, published last December, a list of such merchandise. This will give some idea on general consumer trends in Japan.

A. Non-Polluting Warm-Air Heater

Warm-air heater is non-polluting type fired either by gas or oil. Air intake and exhaust gas pipes are extended outside the home into the open air, so that room air is kept clean. Nearly all the production of 400,000 units have been sold out.

Source: This article is reprinted from MANAGEMENT JAPAN, Vol. 8, No. 2, 1975, published by INTERNATIONAL MANAGEMENT ASSOCIATION OF JAPAN, INC.** Japanese National Committee of CIOS-World Council of Management.

B. Tennis Racket
    Despite production increase of 30 percent against previous year, shortage of supply has been seen. Tennis specialty stores were opened.
C. Imported Large-Sized Refrigerators
    50,000 units of large-sized refrigerators over 400 ℓ capacity mostly from the United States were imported, which is 400 percent up against 1972.
D. Imported Wine
    Annual imports from nearly all wine producing countries exceeded well over 10,000kℓ or 300 percent increase over previous year.
    According to a wine importer, a limited number of Romane-Conti was initially priced at ¥100,000 but ended up with ¥250,000 and still all was sold out.
E. Black-Shaft Golf Clubs
    10,000 clubs were sold. The highest-growth item in the golf supplies.
F. Do-It-Yourself Kits
    Market of 240,000 million yen. Growth expected as 5-day week becomes established.
G. High-Grade Ice Cream
    Home-size packages are selling +20 percent over last year. Selling even in the winter. Borden of U.S.A. set this pattern by selling a high-priced package (¥450 for 450cc).
H. Mail Order Catalogs
    200,000 copies of Sears Roebuck and 50,000 Quelle mail order catalogs were sold during the first year of their operations in Japan.
I. Chandelier
    +30 percent over previous year. For private home and commercial use. Luxury trend of interiors.
J. Electronic Cooking Range
    +55 percent over previous year with 900,000 units sold. Owned by 10 percent of households still a luxury but is one most promising appliance.
K. 4-Channel Stereo
    +40 percent over previous year, with 70,000 million yen sold. Popular among young people.
L. Korean Ginsen
    2,000 million yen sold in a boom for Chinese-medicine and for the health-conscious.
M. Furs
    Sales almost doubled since previous year with the most popular price line around 50,000 yen.
N. Bicycles
    +33 percent—Anti-pollution and energy crisis. More than one unit now owned per household.
O. Multi-Function Radio
    Second-hit item offer tape recorders for the youth market. Some brands were sold out.

P. Games
   "Billionaire game" and "Survival game" reflecting situation of current life were sold in a volume of 200,000 even among adults.
Q. Prefabricated Steel Storage Units
   660,000 mini-storage houses were sold due to lack of carpenters.
R. Overseas Vacation Trips
   Continued to be growth sector with two million tourists participating.
S. Mini Calculators
   +250 percent against previous year with four million units sold.
T. Passenger Cars
   +22 percent over 1972 for passenger cars with 2,630 thousand units sold
U. Diet Food
   Non-sugar, non-salt food items and others now constitute ¥2,000 million market. Pharmaceutical manufacturers are entering the market one after another. High growth potential.
V. Digital Clocks
   +100 percent over 1972. High novelty appeal.
W. "Joconda" Reproduction
   Sudden boom created by planned public display of this painting in Japan in 1974 as a result of Premier Tanaka's visit to France. A reproduction with framework cost approximately $33.
X. Snoopy (Characters Items)
   Used for stuffed animal toys, greeting cards, etc. long-lasting one-point mark.
Y. Membership Leisure Club
   Club-Mediterrance type leisure clubs made a more or less satisfactory initial success.

This array of merchandise and services is quite indicative of the prevailing consumer pattern and trends. These are 11 leisure-related merchandise (B, E, F, K, N, O, P, R, W, X, Y), three health-oriented items (A, L, U), five housing-related items (C, I, J, Q, V) and three luxury or "good living" merchandise (D, G, M).

Following are expected changes in the Japanese consumer environment:

A. More free time due to 5-day week system
B. Emphasis on good living rather than hard work
C. Detachment from tangible merchandise and more value on satisfaction from intangible services and activities (leisure, education, sports, etc.)
D. Increased income resulting in desire for more quality and luxury
E. Increased disposable income of the younger generations
F. Individualization of tastes
G. Growing awareness for health-care
H. Westernization of life style
I. Continuous education

These trends in consumer tastes and environment are increasing on projected to increase market opportunities for the following group of products and services:

Convenience Goods
  Examples: Pre-cooked food, Natural food
Luxury Goods
  Examples: Furs, Cosmetics, Foreign gourmet items
Leisure Goods
  Examples: Tennis rackets and wear, Gardening equipment, Amateur
      carpenter set
Health-Care Goods
  Examples: Diet food, Athletic equipment, Emotion control pharma-
      ceuticals
Housing-Interior Goods
  Examples: Bed, Stereo Set, Carpets
Educational Goods
  Examples: Foreign language learning machine, Desk-top computers
Services
  Examples: Fast food, Travelling

Current Position of Japanese Distribution System

Historical Evolution

Transition of marketing power among manufacturers, wholesalers and retailers in Japan and the United States seem to imply that there is a certain universal pattern of evolution in the development of distribution system.

One important yardstick to measure a stage of development of a distribution system would be channel leadership. Channel leadership is defined as a control exercised by a channel member—manufacturer, wholesaler, or retailer—over final consumer prices, over brandnames and over selection of distribution channel.

Review of Japanese and United States evolution of channel leadership indicates the following three steps of shifts in the channel leader.

First Stage: Wholesaler   In an earlier stage of economic development, manufacturing industries are still small in scale, limited in production capacity and lacking in significant technological innovations. They are too busy with production to be concerned with marketing.

Retailers, on the other hand, are mostly small family operations. Means of transportation and telecommunications are underdeveloped. Under these conditions, it was easier for wholesalers to dominate both manufacturers and retailers.

In Japan, wholesalers continued to be channel leader until around 1955 when Japan took off for a mass consumption society. Increased production volume backed up by technological innovations and strengthened financial position put manufacturers in a relatively stronger position vis-à-vis wholesalers.

In the United States, this stage continued until the end of 1800's during which general stores were major retail institution served by general merchandise wholesalers who were often engaged in foreign trade as well.

Second Stage: Manufacturers   Gradually, manufacturers grow in production capacity and company size. Some of them supply their products for the national market under their own brandname. Increased production capability dictates manufacturers to expand their market area. Wholesalers who are operating in a relatively limited local market find themselves less and less qualified to perform their functions in a manner satisfactory to manufacturers. The power shifts from the whoesaler to manufacturer.

In Japan, relative decline in wholesaler position started in the last 10–15 years and the United States, as early as in 1900.

Third Stage: Retailers   Retailers here refer to large-scale retailers such as supermarket chains, general merchandising store chains, variety stores, etc. Nowhere in the world has the change of channel leadership from manufacturer to retailer taken place so early and in such a scale as in the United States. Already at the beginning of this century, grocery chains like A&P and Kroger, variety store chains such as Woolworth and Kresge, mail order operations of Sears Roebuck or Montgomery Ward were highly developed. These large-scale retailers were operating on low margin—high turnover basis and dealt directly with manufacturers to bypass wholesalers to enable discount sales. In 1925, A&P had 14,000 store units and Woolworth had 1,420 store units to cite a few examples.

Direct purchase by large-scale retailers from manufacturers drove traditional wholesalers and independent small retailers into a difficult position. Through 1920's–30's existence of wholesalers was seriously questioned and challenged and majority of textiles wholesalers, for instance, went into bankruptcy.

It is interesting to note that Japan has been undergoing a similar evolution as lately as in the last 10–15 years, and that the first supermarket store was opened in Tokyo in 1955. Popular observation that the Japanese distribution scene is 20–30 years behind United States development is derived from this situation.

Characteristics of Japanese Distribution System

Longer Channel

As has been discussed, emergence of large-scale retailers and increased position of manufacturers is a relatively recent post-war phenomenon in Japan.

Wholesalers, therefore, are still playing an important role in the Japanese distribution system.

According to Japanese Government statistics, total wholesaler sales volume is four times the total retailer sales volume, whereas a corresponding figure is 1.7 for West Germany, 1.3 for Britain, 1.1 for France and 1.4 for the United States. The larger this multiplier is, the longer is the distribution channel.

Another way to look at the length of channel will be how much percentage of total retailer purchase is made directly from manufacturers. In Japan, this is only 3.4 against 20 percent of the United States. Japanese retailers buy 92 percent of their merchandise requirements from wholesalers (including captive marketing companies of manufacturers), whereas this is only 23 percent in the United States.

There is a definite tendency, however, that these lengthy distribution channels are becoming shorter. Reflecting competition among manufacturers in their strive to increase their market share, manufacturers are increasingly concentrating on larger wholesalers for distribution of their products. Wholesalers in turn are competing among themselves to increase sales volume and to improve their bargaining position with manufacturers.

As a result, smaller secondary and tertiary wholesalers are finding it increasingly difficult to survive. Latest census of commerce conducted by Japanese Government indicates that as of May 1972 small wholesalers with 1–2 employees decreased by 3.5 percent in number against 1970.

Mass retailers, particularly supermarkets and other chain stores are purchasing in increasing volume from manufacturers, bypassing wholesalers as mass retailers' sales volume is growing at a very high rate.

Fragmented Retail Outlets

In comparison with many Western nations, Japan has smallest average number of employees and smallest population per retailer. Average Japanese retail outlet has 3.1 employees compared with 6.1 of the United States, 5.1 of Britain, 5.4 of West Germany and 3.4 of France. In terms of population per retail unit, Japan has 74 while United States has 144, Britain 110, West Germany 138 and France 104. This shows that a Japanese retail shop is smaller and caters to smaller number of customers than any other nations mentioned.

Position of large-scale retailers is still less important compared with that of other nations. In 1972, self-service chains and department stores represented approximately 25 percent of total retail sales volume (excluding restaurant sales), whereas the corresponding figure was 30.6 for the United States already in 1960, 42.7 percent for Britain in 1961 and 25.6 percent for France in 1962.

Large-scale retailers, however, are strengthening their position, with self-service chain store registering a growth of 52 percent in 1972 over 1970 and department stores 35 percent in the same period. Independent stores have been constantly decreasing in their share against a steady increase of both types of large stores.

Emphasis on Personal Relationships

Japanese distribution scene is characterized by the fact that personal relationships and traditional trade practices often go before economic rationale. For instance, manufacturers who do not any longer require wholesalers find it most difficult to do away with them. On the one hand, wholesalers feel that they helped manufacturers grow to their current position when manufacturers were small and badly needed wholesaler services such as financing, warehousing, etc. For manufacturers to deal directly with large supermarket chains, therefore, is an act of "ingratitude" from the point of view of wholesalers. Wholesalers thus regard their position not as a pure economic function but as a sort of vested interest which is not geared to what they actually perform.

One consequence of this situation is that manufacturers are paying a margin to wholesalers even if sales has been materialized with, for example a supermarket chain without comparable services from the wholesalers. If a manufacturer refuse to pay such a commission, wholesalers usually react violently, saying that this is an infringement of their interest. "No work, No pay" principle is certainly not pronounced in the Japanese distribution.

Another example is how allowances are granted to wholesalers. In Japan, manufacturers do not disclose how allowances are calculated, so that wholesalers do not know exactly how much they can get. Here, allowances are something like a favor given unilaterally by a feudal lord to its subjects.

Emphasis on personal relationships is reflected on the fact that a formal contract is quite often not exchanged but a commitment is made verbally instead. This means that personal relationships are more valuable and more binding than a written contract.

Distribution Channel

Channel Selection

Distribution channel varies from commodity to commodity and therefore a study on a specific product by product basis is indispensable to obtain a meaningful picture.

Channel selection is subject to following factors:

a. Corporate policy to control the channel
b. Investment requirements to set up and operate the channel
c. Purchase volume of customers
d. Company's capability and financial, manpower resources
e. Relative marketing and financing capability of middlemen
f. Product characteristics: breadth of product lines, complexity, physical dimensions, perishability, frequency of sale, speed of style change, unit

cost and profit, geographical concentration of consumers, after-service requirements, etc.

g. Competitive situation

A rule of thumb for the channel selection is that convenience goods require longer channels and specialty goods shorter channels, with shopping goods positioned in between.

Typical Patterns of Distribution Channel

A typical channel of distribution comprises primary, secondary and often tertiary wholesalers.

Primary wholesalers are usually located in Tokyo, Osaka or other major cities and are also called national wholesalers or central wholesalers. Secondary wholesalers are operating in medium to large local cities and purchase their requirements from primary wholesalers for resale to tertiary wholesalers. Tertiary wholesalers supply merchandise to local retailers.

The Japanese distribution channels can be categorized into three basic patterns.

Direct Distribution   One is direct distribution type, whereby goods are distributed from manufacturers directly to final consumers. This type of distribution system is the shortest and takes the form of door-to-door sales, mail order sales and sales made by manufacturers' own retail outlets.

Tupperware's home party system and Avon Cosmetics' Avon Lady sales system fall under this category. Teijin, one of major textile manufacturers, has been setting up mens apparel stores. This distribution pattern, however, is not common in Japan, chiefly because marketing cost for manufacturers tends to be substantially higher than other types of distribution channel.

For industrial goods, particularly technically sophisticated machinery and equipment, direct distribution system is extensively utilized.

Single-Stage Distribution   The second type of distribution channel is single stage distribution. Under this formula, manufacturers sell to retailers who in turn sell to final consumers. This channel pattern has been gaining in importance in Japan since mass retailers made their rapid growth in the last several years as mentioned earlier. As there is no wholesaler involved, manufacturers and retailers can obtain profit margins which otherwise would have been secured by wholesalers. Manufacturers, moreover, can exercise a tighter control over price, sales promotion and other marketing activities, as they can directly influence retailers.

Another advantage for manufacturers is their direct exposure to the market, so that market reaction and information is more easily fed back to manufacturers.

This marketing channel type is suited for fashion items which have to reach consumers with minimum time to avoid risk. This channel type is also appropriate when profit margin is too small for wholesalers to be interested in.

Needless to say, these advantages have to be evaluated against possible disadvantages. Manufacturers must take into account that their distribution cost may be higher if retailers are small. Manufacturers must also have more salesmen to take care of retailers. They have to collect payments from retailers at their own risk and account.

Multi-Stage Distribution   The third marketing channel is multi-stage distribution, whereby one or more than one wholesalers are involved between manufacturers and retailers. This is the predominant pattern of distribution channel in Japan.

For instance, tooth paste is first distributed from manufacturers to 30 primary wholesalers which are located in large cities such as Tokyo and Osaka. These primary wholesalers sell to 2,500 to 3,000 secondary and tertiary wholesalers mostly operating in local cities who serve approximately 200,000 retailers throughout the nation including 2,000 mass retailers.

Advantages of this type of distribution method include the possibility of manufacturers to sell a large lot of merchandise since purchase volume of wholesalers is substantially larger than that of individual retailers. Manufacturers can also easily cover the national market through wholesalers without incurring expenditure for hiring own salesmen. Another advantage is that manufacturers do not have to adjust production volume to demand fluctuations at retailer level, as wholesalers normally keep the merchandise as a buffer stock.

Disadvantages associated with this distribution pattern are that wholesalers do not necessarily work in the same manner as the manufacturers expect them to work. Manufacturers are furthermore hampered from getting first hand information on the market when wholesalers are poor information transmitters.

Marketing Strategies

Use of Existing Distribution System

First consideration is whether a foreign firm should be involved in marketing activities on its own by establishing a wholly-owned marketing and/or production company in Japan. Some criteria of decision-making have been discussed under II.2., Part A.

Given complicated and fundamentally different system of distribution in Japan, however, most foreign firms entering the Japanese market are recommended to utilize existing Japanese partner who has strong established marketing network.

Building and operating a sales network takes a heavy initial investment and time which only companies with strong financial resources could sustain. This applies particularly to convenience goods which require extensive coverage of retail outlets and therefore wholesalers.

For example, Warner Lambert, one of major United States pharmaceuticals manufacturers, has been marketing very successfully its Schick razor products through Seiko's extensive and excellent retail outlets. It is interesting that Warner Lambert does so though it has its own subsidiary in Japan.

Another example is General Foods, one of largest United States foodstuffs manufacturers. General Foods' Japanese subsidiary has recently sold 50 percent of its equity to Ajinomoto, Japan's top manufacturer of monosodium glutamate, instant soup, salad dressing, etc. Ajinomoto has a very strong marketing network throughout Japan, covering 3,000 wholesalers, 5,000 supermarkets and 120,000 independent retail outlets. It is of interest to note that General Foods, after several years of operations in Japan on their own has decided to count on Japanese company's established sales channels to increase its market share.

Ajinomoto has also been producing and marketing with success Knorr instant soup of Switzerland.

Quite often, this type of arrangement works to the satisfaction of both foreign and Japanese parties. From the foreign company's point of view, heavy initial expenditure and difficulty for setting up marketing network can be nearly completely eliminated.

Timing and Balance of Promotional Activities

Promotional schemes are generally divided into in-channel and end-consumer promotion. In-channel promotion is geared to motivating wholesalers and retailers through margins, rebates, detailing services, etc.

In Japan where wholesalers still play an important role, incentives sufficiently competitive with competing manufacturers are of great importance. This is particularly so, as foreign companies have to motivate wholesalers to pay greater attention to this newly introduced products over other competing lines.

End-consumer promotion is advertisement and other schemes such as premiums geared to motivating consumers.

Manufacturer's detailing force is also a crucial factor of in-channel promotion. Nestle (Japan) is one of the foreign subsidiaries who have made a spectacular initial success by deploying extensive detailing services. Nestle was the third runner with 6 percent of market share after General Foods (42 percent) and Morinaga (43 percent) in March 1961, when instant coffee was introduced on a full-scale basis to the Japanese market. Nestle staged vigorous detailing activities which covered visit to retailers for explanation, advertisement, ordertaking, advice on mass display, provision of posters, sticker, hangers and other POP tools. Coupled with this in-channel promotion was heavy end-consumer advertisement which was estimated at 3–4 times the expenditure of General Foods.

With this promotional strategy, Nestle came to the top position in market share of 40 percent in July 1962, or in less than one and a half years, whereas the market share for General Foods and Morinaga fell to 22 percent and 20 percent respectively.

Wholesaler Strategy

Most successful foreign firms in Japan are utilizing wholesalers to their advantage. While Japanese distribution channel is certainly long, one cannot ignore the reality. In many cases, direct selling is more expensive and time-labor consuming for a newly formed foreign company. Particularly for convenience foods, that require extensive store coverage, wholesaler's role should not be underevaluated.

Nestle did rely on primary, secondary and tertiary wholesalers in marketing its instant coffee. Nestle's sales team called retail outlets to render various services mentioned earlier. Orders placed with detail people were credited with wholesalers. This very "Japanese" approach won Nestle a dominant market position which is now 70 percent of the market.

Yamazaki-Nabisco, a joint venture between United States Nabisco and Yamazaki Bakery has also been successful by marketing through wholesalers and existing wholesalers.

In selecting wholesalers, approach should better be made to a limited number of outstanding wholesalers. Smith Kline and French has been often cited in Japan as a successful case of wholesaler strategy. SKF appointed 35 wholesalers for marketing its Contac 600 in an exclusive franchised territory. This is a good contrast with most of Japanese pharmaceutical manufacturers who have more than one wholesalers competing with each other in the same territory on the same product.

Institutional Market

Consideration should be given to initially approach mass retailers and institutional market. This strategy is advantageous in the sense that relatively limited number of customers with high purchase volume reduces initial difficulty, financial outlays and risk for developing extensive sales network on a national basis. A certain foreign manufacturers of carpet tiles has also been extremely successful by initially selling to an institutional market such as hotels, golf clubs, and bowling centers. Distribution cost is quite often directly influenced by the number of accounts, so that concentration on a smaller number of institutional customers with higher purchase volume is conducive to an effective and sound distribution strategy especially at an early stage of Japanese operations.

Non-Traditional Channel

Foreign firm should also look at non-traditional marketing channels. A case in point would be toiletry goods such as soap, detergent and tooth paste. Selling through toiletry goods wholesalers has been the traditional distribution channel for this type of goods. Pharmaceuticals wholesalers, however, should be able to play an equally or more important role, because 21 percent of the total retail sales of tooth paste, for instance, is realized by pharmacies. This channel is all the more interesting from the standpoint of manufacturers because pharmaceuticals wholesalers are larger in size and retain more professionally qualified salesmen than toiletry goods wholesalers. Pharmacies are also in need of diversifying their merchandise mix, as they will find it increasingly difficult to rely only on pharmaceuticals as more and more of them become prescribed items reflecting a change in Government medical policy.

QUESTIONS

1. How do Japanese channels of distribution differ from channels existing in the U.S.?
2. What basic marketing strategies does the author identify for penetrating the Japanese market? Do these differ from strategies that would be practices in the U.S.? Why?
3. How can the changes projected for the Japanese consumer environment impact on international marketing opportunity for U.S. corporations?

Saudi Arabia is the world's largest producer of petroleum and as a result represents the second most rapidly growing import market between Europe and Japan. This article describes the dimensions of the Saudi Arabian market environment in terms of prevalent business practices and major marketing opportunity areas contained in the five-year economic plan. Of particular interest is the discussion of governmental constraints on the promotional mix variables.

15. The Marketing Environment in Saudi Arabia

Jack G. Kaikati
Southern Illinois University

The Kingdom of Saudi Arabia was established in 1932, following a period of unification of most of the Arabian Peninsula by King Abdal-Aziz ibn Al Saud.[1] Today the Kingdom is rapidly gaining stature as an economic and political leader in world affairs. This new leadership role has been exercised in the following events.

Saudi Arabia is one of the founders of the Organization of Petroleum Exporting Countries (OPEC). In September 14, 1960, five leading oil exporting countries—three Arabs (Iraq, Kuwait and Saudi Arabia) and two non-Arab (Iran and Venezuela)—founded OPEC for the purpose of coordinating the common oil interests of developing countries whose economies depended primarily on oil exports.

From this modest and seemingly innocent beginning, OPEC has become the toughest and most powerful cartel in history. As of 1975, OPEC membership list was expanded to accommodate thirteen member countries, with

---

Source: Reprinted with permission of the *Akron Business and Economic Review*, (ABER), Summer 1976.

a majority of seven Arab countries.[2] Member countries currently span three continents: six are in the Arabian-Persian Gulf: (*Abu Dhabi,* Iran, *Iraq, Kuwait, Qatar* and *Saudi Arabia*); four are in Africa: (*Algeria,* Gabon, Lybia and Nigeria); two in Latin America (Ecuador and Venezuela); and one in the Far East (Indonesia).

The cartel implemented a unified price policy and raised the price of oil until it reached unprecedented heights. The cartel's power has further increased due to the world's oil demand situation that has changed a buyers' market into a sellers' market. For example, United States imports of oil grew by two and one-third times between 1970 and 1973, from 1.5 million to 3.5 million barrels a day.[3]

On the political front, OPEC became more conspicuous during the 1973 October War when Saudi Arabia led other Arab countries in implementing an oil embargo against the West as part of the warfare against Israel. This oil embargo resulted in what is currently referred to as the "energy crisis."

As a result of OPEC's past and present economic successes, the rest of the world is witnessing a sudden flow of petrodollars into one of the least populated corners of the globe. Not since the shipments of gold and silver from the Americas to Spain during the colonization period of the sixteenth and seventeenth centuries has there been a comparable transfer to resources from one part of the world to another.

Current published reports estimate that OPEC countries have earned $90 billion in oil revenue during the year 1974.[4] A more detailed breakdown is presented in Exhibit 15-1 which reveals that Saudi Arabia is the richest of the cartel members. Already a vast construction boom is getting underway in the Kingdom, a boom that will create new cities, replace camel tracks with paved highways across deserts, and industrialize coastal villages.[5]

The promise of jobs and contracts associated with such a construction boom is attracting a swarm of European, Japanese and United States companies that are anxious to tap into the growing pool of Saudi Arabian oil money. An increasing number of these companies are encouraging their executives to take intensive courses in the Arabic language in order to overcome the handicap of bargaining through middlemen.[6]

Economically speaking, Saudi Arabia is not merely the richest of the OPEC countries, it is the world's largest current producer of petroleum with proven oil reserves for the future estimated at about ninety-three billion barrels (about one quarter of world reserves). In addition to its economic fortunes, the Kingdom also commands special respect among the world's 471 million Moslems because it embraces Islan's two holiest cities, Mecca and Medina.

Since Saudi Arabia represents such a growing and important market for various goods and services, a description of the Saudi marketing environment should be of interest. Therefore, the objective of this article is three-fold: (1) to provide background information on Saudi Arabia, (2) to discuss a

EXHIBIT 15-1

Estimated OPEC Oil Revenues and GNP

Country	Population (million) 1973[1]	Oil Revenues (million U.S. $) 1973	Oil Revenues (million U.S. $) 1974	Non-oil Exports (million U.S. $) 1973
Arabian-Persian Gulf:	50.7	13,900	56,900	1,463
Iran	31.2	4,100	17,400	864
Iraq	10.4	1,500	6,800	22
Kuwait	1.0	1,900	7,000	
Qatar	0.2	400	1,600	577[4]
Saudi Arabia	7.8[3]	5,100	20,000	
Abu Dhabi[2]	0.1	900	4,100	
Africa:	77.4	5,300	18,700	663
Algeria	15.4	900	3,700	270
Gabon	0.5	100	400	N.A.
Lybia	2.1	2,300	7,600	106
Nigeria	59.4	2,000	7,000	287
Latin America:	17.7	2,900	11,400	1,232
Venezuela	11.2	2,800	10,600	1,232
Ecuador	6.5	100	800	N.A.
Far East:	124.0	900	3,000	1,923
Indonesia	124.0	900	3,000	1,923
Grand Total	269.8	23,000	90,000	5,281

[1] Population figures extrapolated from 1971 data as shown in World Bank Atlas.

[2] Member of the United Arab Emirates.

[3] This does not reflect Saudi Arabia's most recent population census of 4.3 million.

[4] This figure represents the combined non-oil exports of Kuwait, Qatar, Saudi-Arabia and Abu Dhabi.

Source: Adapted from *IMF Survey*, Vol. 4 (February 3, 1975), p. 38.

few of the many features of the Saudi marketing environment, and (3) to stress the problems foreign firms encounter in selling there.

One of the major obstacles to this undertaking is the lack of reliable, easily interpreted data. Very few statistical time series are available which can be used to trace developments through time. To overcome this obstacle, parts of this article will be supplemented by informed opinion. Another minor obstacle is that most of the Saudi statistics are compiled on the basis of the Hijri (Moslem) year which is 11–12 days shorter than the Gregorian calendar year.

Background

Area and Population

Saudi Arabia is the largest country in the Middle East and occupies about four-fifths of the Arabian Peninsula. Some undefined boundaries result in estimates of the total area of the Kingdom ranging from 600,000 to 850,000 square miles, or about one-fifth to one-fourth the area of the continental United States. Saudi Arabia is bordered on the north by Jordan, Iraq and Kuwait; on the northeast by the Arabian Gulf[7]; on the east and southeast by Qatar, United Arab Emirate and Oman; on the south by the People's Democratic Republic of Yemen (Aden); on the southwest by the Arab Republic of Yemen (Sana); and on the west by the Red Sea.

The first census recently completed shows a native population of only 4.3 million compared with the usual external estimates of some eight million and earlier Saudi estimates of 5 million.[8]

Although Saudi Arabia is less populated than the United States, it would be misleading to consider it solely or primarily from the standpoint of an area population relationship. Some important differences from American demography exist. Largely because of climatic restrictions and the location of the oil deposits, the country's 830,000 square miles has been unevenly inhabited. At one time most of the population were desert nomads. But shortly after the discovery of oil in 1938, nomads poured into the oil fields to become drillers, mechanics and clerks.

Nowadays, about one-fifth of the Saudi Arabians are still nomads and the majority of the population is concentrated in the principal cities: Riyadh, Jedda, Mecca, Medina and Dhahran. In addition, Jedda has a highly visible foreign community, as does Dhahran, center of the oil industry. Foreigners are discouraged from living in the capital, Riyadh, an extremely conservative and religious city. Therefore, foreign embassies are located in Jedda, and ambassadors and other embassy officials must shuttle between Jedda and the capital to conduct their business.

Climatic Conditions

Saudi Arabia is one of the driest places in the world. Rainfall averages four inches a year in most parts of the kingdom; but some interior deserts may have no rain for as long as twenty years. In the summer, temperatures of over one hundred ten degrees are common in such population centers as Riyadh, Jedda and Mecca and even higher temperatures are experienced in other major cities.

Because of this sparse rainfall, Saudi Arabia lacks rivers. Agriculture is limited to dry stream beds (wadis), where wells tap subsurface water-bearing gravels and a few places where water is available. Historically, the wadi network determined the location of the settled population, the course of caravan routes and the location of commercial centers. These same climatic conditions also worked to keep the herding population nomadic, as the search for water and vegetation was almost constant. At the present time, only 3 percent of the total area of Saudi Arabia is devoted to agriculture. The crops produced are confined to dates, with some barley, rice, vegetables and assorted fruits.

Political and Legal System

The country remains an absolute monarchy but it has moved gradually toward a ministerial system of government. Constitutionally, the King rules in accordance with the Sharia, a sacred law of Islam.[9] A Council of Ministers appointed by the King makes decisions by majority vote, but these require royal sanction. There are no political parties and no parliament. Saudi Arabia has no diplomatic relations with any communist state and opposes the encroachment of communist influence into the Arabian Peninsula.

The legal system is also based on Koranic law. For example, a hand is cut off after the third conviction for theft; adultresses are stoned to death; and major crimes are punished by beheading. Recently, the assassin of King Faisal was beheaded in a square jammed with more than 10,000 spectators. To deter crime, the public is invited to watch execution of sentence. Not surprisingly, the crime rate is exceptionally low and streets are safe to walk at night.

Social and Cultural Changes

Saudi Arabia's entry into the modern world has not been easy. When television was introduced in the late 1960s, irate citizens attacked the station and called TV "the work of the devil." Nowadays, Saudi viewers have particular fondness for American programs like "Lucy," "The Virginian," "Bonanza" and various wrestling programs. However, all television programs are tightly censored to eliminate scenes of kissing or drinking alcoholic beverages.

On another occasion several years ago, citizens marched on Riyadh and stoned the Ministry of Education in protest against a girls' school being established in the town of Buraida. Now the town has found the education of women so much to its liking that it is asking for another girls' school. Moreover, the Saudi community is becoming more tolerant with women's mode of dress. Even though Saudi women still are veiled in public, they are not shrouded in black from head to toe, as in the past.

Other social changes also are taking place. Even though Saudi puritanism bans alcohol as well as public movies, films are viewed by many Saudis in their living rooms through projectors purchased in Saudi shops. Then too, the role of the moral police has changed. Not long ago, the "mutawien", the moral police, had authority to halt people on the street to enforce religious laws. Their primary duty now is to make shopkeepers lower their shutters and stop work during prayers—which takes place five times daily.

The Consumer Market

Saudi Arabia has a unique social class structure. For all the country's wealth, there is virtually no middle class in the Kingdom. One expert explains the class structure in Saudi Arabia in the following words:

The class structure resembles a knitting needle stuck in a pancake. There is a very small, well educated elite, a minute middle class (in the Western sense) below that, a vast mass of illiterate, unskilled nomads or peasants forming the lower class.[10]

Currently, Saudi Arabia is witnessing the emergence of a new middle class.[11] Moreover, life for the ordinary Saudis is improving. Demand for labor is so heavy that the wages of even unskilled laborers have jumped from $2 a day to $5. Generally, home loans are available, and medical care and education through university level are underwritten by the government. With gas selling at a modest 13¢ a gallon at service stations, it is not surprising that auto imports tripled in 1974.

Price data are collected and published by three major agencies: (1) the Central Department of Statistics (CDS), (2) the Saudi Arabian Monetary Agency (SAMA), and (3) the Ministry of Agriculture. In January 1973, CDS started publishing data on retail prices in five major cities covering 250 commodities. The nature of the sample used by CDS is not clear, however, and the absence of "weights" makes a meaningful interpretation of such data rather difficult. SAMA prepares quarterly retail and wholesale price data on seventy-nine commodities in the city of Jedda. The Ministry of Agriculture prepares periodical retail price statistics on selected agricultural commodities distinguishing between imported and locally produced goods.

Mainly on the basis of these data, CDS prepares annual estimates of wholesale price and cost of living indices. Exhibit 15-2 depicts a very mild rate of inflation of about 1.8 percent per annum in the wholesale price index for the period 1963-64—1971-72. Within this index, "food" and "construction materials" seem to have risen the fastest, at the average annual rate of 2.3 percent and 2.4 percent respectively. Exhibit 15-3 indicates that the cost of living index also has risen at about 1.5 percent per year with food items rising at slightly higher rates. However, these indices probably underestimate the price increases, especially in more recent years when rates of inflation abroad accelerated.

In order to counter the inflationary pressures of imported goods, the Saudi government introduced at least four measures. First, a number of tariffs were either abolished or reduced effective May 1973 on a wide range of goods. Second, the Kingdom implemented a 5.1 percent revaluation of the

EXHIBIT 15-2

Wholesale Price Index

Year	Food	Textile	Fuel	Construction Materials	Miscellaneous	General Index
1963/64	103.5	97.3	95.3	104.2	98.4	101.7
1964/65	105.2	90.3	92.9	105.5	99.7	101.7
1965/66	108.4	90.5	90.9	106.9	102.3	103.7
1966/67	113.9	92.8	91.1	116.4	102.3	108.5
1967/68	113.5	92.4	90.9	123.8	104.2	109.2
1968/69	116.0	90.9	90.3	125.1	107.2	110.7
1969/70	110.3	94.2	89.4	136.4	102.7	114.2
1970/71	119.9	95.4	102.1	135.2	102.6	116.1
1971/72	124.6	104.2	87.7	126.5	104.4	117.1
1972/73*	129.5	106.5	92.5	136.3	107.5	123.2

*Estimates.

Source: *Central Department of Statistics, Ministry of Finance and National Economy.*

EXHIBIT 15-3

Cost of Living Index in Urban Areas*

Year	Food	Housing	Clothing & Footwear	Miscellaneous Goods & Services	General
1963/64	103.9	103.6	102.0	100.1	102.8
1964/65	104.2	106.7	96.2	100.5	103.2
1965/66	106.0	109.7	97.9	100.5	104.8
1966/67	111.4	112.1	90.2	100.9	107.0
1967/68	110.2	118.2	89.6	104.2	108.7
1968/69	116.0	120.7	96.7	104.3	112.5
1969/70	114.6	122.2	96.1	105.5	112.7
1970/71	116.3	121.2	97.7	108.5	113.8
1971/72	119.5	123.5	99.2	111.1	116.2
1972/73	122.4	124.6	101.1	114.5	118.5

*For households with average income of SR 600 per month.

Source: *Central Department of Statistics, Ministry of Finance and National Economy.*

Saudi Arabian Riyal in August 1973. Third, the government is subsidizing basic commodities in order to cushion the effect on the consumer. Finally, the King has urged Saudi businessmen to keep prices of essential commodities within the reach of consumers and to help the government to control inflation.[12]

The Economy

The economy of Saudi Arabia defies classification in the traditional academic categorization of either "developed" or "underdeveloped". The rapidity of change has contributed to the blurring of distinction; the Saudi economy combines extreme features of both classifications. The very high per capita income, a strong annual growth rate, and a consistently favorable balance-of-payments situations are all indicators of a developed economic status. Yet, on the debit side of the development ledger there are equally striking examples of underdevelopment, such as the overdependence on imports of capital goods and consumer products, an inadequate indigenous supply of technical skills and labor, and the near-total reliance of the economy on a single product.

Prior to the discovery of oil in 1938, the country's largest source of wealth was pilgrims' expenditures. Even though pilgrimage is no longer the major source of revenue, the government still pays considerable attention to it. The government allocated approximately $285.7 million to improve facilities and services in the pilgrimage centers of Mecca, Medina, Taif and Jedda. Remarkable improvements were made during 1975 because that year included the "Friday" pilgrimage (i.e., the climax of the pilgrimage falls on a Friday). For those pilgrims who made the journey last year, it counts as seven pilgrimages. Since such an opportunity arises only every nine years, the Saudi authorities estimated some three million pilgrims have arrived in time for the season which began in December, 1975. It is important to note that Friday is the sabbath in Moslem countries, so the "weekend" is Thursday afternoon and Friday.

Currently, the Saudi economy still is based on the free enterprise system and relies heavily on foreign trade. While oil accounts for the major part of the Saudi exports and foreign exchange earnings, the Kingdom imports most of its daily needs and industrial requirements. Consequently, Saudi Arabia now ranks as the second most rapidly growing import market between Europe and Japan (the first import market is Iran).

Saudi imports have reached unprecedented heights; imports have registered a growth of 44 percent between 1972 and 1973 following an increase of 28 percent during the previous year. It is tentatively estimated that imports in 1974 have doubled since 1972. During the first half of 1973 imports from these countries amounted to SR 2,313.1 million (approximately $660.8 million) as compared with SR 1.531.4 million (approximately $437.5 million) in the corresponding period of 1972, implying a growth of about 51 percent. This was a natural consequence of the increased economic activity in the country as a result of significantly expanded government expenditures. Now, looking at the origins of these imports, it is clear that the largest increases were in the imports from Japan (SR 407.7 million or $116.4 million), followed by the United States (SR 182.1 million or $52 million).

The New Five-Year Plan

The new Five-Year Plan (1975–1980) calls for an expenditure of approximately $142 billion for economic development.[13] This figure is ten times larger than the first plan (1970–75). The main objective of the plan is to transform Saudi Arabia into one of the world's most advanced countries by reducing its dependence on oil, building up and diversifying the industrial sectors, and expanding education and the social services. Overall, the plan envisages a 13.3 percent growth rate for Saudi goods and services outside the oil sector.

A more detailed breakdown of the Saudi development plan reveals that the biggest single item (around $24 billion) is for defense spending. Since this huge sum matches Iran's military spending, it appears that the Saudi monarchy is seeking to contain Iran's political ambitions in the region.

On the economic front, the state oil organization, *Petromin,* which would provide the basis for most of the industrial development, would be allocated $13.85 billion to finance massive projects for oil refineries, petrochemical complexes and gas treatment and liquefaction plants. Most of the industrial development would be concentrated in the eastern region at Jubail.

Moreover, $9.7 billion would be spent on water projects, $1.14 billion on agriculture, and $1.7 billion on electricity. The plan provides for a vast expansion of communications, including the construction of 8,500 miles of surfaced roads, with airports at all the major towns and 2,000 miles of new power cables to bring electricity to the most remote villages.

Major developments also were planned in the social and public sectors. $20.85 billion would be spent on education, and the number of schools would be increased from 3,335 to 5,318. The number of hospital beds would be almost tripled, rising from 4,000 to 11,400 and 270,000 new homes would be built.

In addition, a Real Estate Development Fund (REDF) has been established with a capital of $571 million. The aim of the fund is to speed up the development of real estate in various Saudi towns. The management of the fund is empowered to provide loans up to 70 percent of the construction costs of private houses, subject to an upper limit of $86,000, and 50 percent of the cost of housing complexes and buildings, subject to an upper limit of $2.85 million.

Severe Unresolved Problems

Despite its riches and purchasing power, not everything is rosy for Saudi Arabia.[14] Most of the doubts about the Saudi's ability to realize the Plan's objectives center on the massive manpower requirements of the Plan. The Saudi labor force is not larger than 1.5 million[15] and that estimate is probably putting it too high.

One observer has estimated that in 1967 most establishments operated at less than 50 percent of their capacity and that the rates of shutdown, operating costs, and management turnover were high. He attributes these difficulties in large part to the lack of a skilled labor force and a well-established indigenous managerial class.[16] Another expert provides two reasons for the shortage of competent Saudi labor:

First, the average Saudi male considers most physical labor demeaning. He would rather be a taxi driver or work in some other service type of employment than be a plumber, carpenter, brick layer or hold any other "blue collar" job. Second, the government's employment policy encourages school dropouts. It is easy to find relatively well paying government jobs requiring little formal education. Thus, boys tend to acquire a minimum level of education and then drop out of school for a government job rather than continue to forego income and stay in school.[17]

It is estimated that more than 500,000 foreign technicians, teachers and workers would be needed to carry out the plan. Consequently, entry regulations for foreign workers have been eased to combat the growing labor shortages.[18] Other measures are also being taken to encourage both skilled and unskilled workers to go to Saudi Arabia. For example, income tax on foreigners has been abolished altogether, the only deduction from their earnings being the five percent social welfare tax (the "zakat").

The current Saudi plans are also limited by the existing infrastructure. Although road and port construction are proceeding rapidly, the pace must be tripled to meet demands of the combined civilian and military programs outlined in the second plan. A surcharge is already in effect for ocean shipments to Jedda (where tonnage is up over 50 percent over 1973) and congestion is becoming more and more serious in Dammam.

Finally, Saudi Arabia's progress depends not only on strengthening its manufacturing, agricultural, and extractive industries, but also on developing a sound marketing system. The present marketing structure cannot cope with the growing volume of goods. All the existing marketing institutions need to be generally upgraded. Probably such a development will have to be done by a new generation of marketers who are better-trained to operate on a larger scale. Above all, the Saudi Universities should recognize marketing as a major subject area in the curriculum of the future.

Channels of Distribution

Channels of distribution are similar in type to those in the United States. The most common channel for manufactured products is the orthodox manufacturer-wholesaler-retailer-consumer. However, there are two major elements which dominate the channels of distribution. First, although the kingdom adheres to the free enterprise system, there are not many things in Saudi Arabia the royal family does not have a hand in, or an eye on. The second factor is the concentration of business interests in a small number of hands. In Jedda, Riyadh and Dammam, a "clutch" of families have established a grip over government contracts and virtually all the channels of distribution. These prominent families can almost be counted on the fingers of one hand: the bin Ladins, the el Gossaibs, the Ali Rezas, the Sherbatlys, the bin Zaghers, the Juffalis, Gaith Pharaon and Adnan Kashoggi. Because of the major role played by such formidable families in the channels of distribution, they can be referred to as channel captains.

To illustrate the importance of these prominent families, let one trace the role of the Juffali family.[19] Ahmed Juffali and his two brothers have expanded their business by branching out from their father's carpet business into electric utilities, imported appliances, telecommunication and cement manufacture. Moreover, they represent at least thirty western companies in Saudi markets, including Daimler-Benz, IBM, Bell & Howell, Babcock & Wilcox, and Volkswagon.

Nowadays, these channel captains are being sought by United States, European and Japanese corporate executives bearing lavish joint venture deals. The Saudi channel captains are being courted because they will benefit from the huge amount of money that will begin to pour as the new five-year plan moves into high gear. The Saudis are equally interested in joint ventures because the foreigners bring in technology and managerial skills. Although Saudi channel captains do not lack capital, they prefer foreign investment in joint projects to ensure the necessary technical and management expertise to make the project successful.

Having emphasized the importance of those prominent families in the Saudi channels of distribution, it is also important, at this point, to examine the types of business establishments in Saudi Arabia. In 1967 the Central Department of Statistics conducted a survey which classified Saudi business establishments by major economic classes and geographic regions.[20] The survey reveals that commercial and service establishments outnumber manufacturing establishments on a ratio of approximately three to one. Out of a total of 43,616 business establishments in the Kingdom, about 66 percent were service and commercial activities and 21 percent manufacturing. Within the commercial group, two types of activities account for 71 percent of the group: (1) retail trade in food, beverages and consumption goods account for 53.8 percent; and (2) retail trade in textiles, clothes and home furnishings account for 17.2 percent.

The survey also reveals that of the 43,616 business establishments in the Kingdom, about 50 percent were located in the Western region, 23 percent in the Central region, 17 percent in the Eastern region, and about ten percent in the Northern and Southern regions.

Product Policy

Realizing that the Kingdom ranks as the second most rapidly growing import market between Europe and Japan, some foreign manufacturers are already redesigning their products in order to appeal to the Saudi market. For example, a Japanese manufacturer of desk-top calculators has redesigned his product to incorporate keys using Arabic symbols rather than the usual Western Arabic numerals.[21] Similarly, a British brewery is experimenting with a non-alcoholic beer since Saudi puritanism bans alcohol.[22]

At the same time, some companies are prohibited from selling their products and services in Saudi Arabia. This is due to the restrictions imposed by a blacklist of some Western firms. The 1970 Saudi blacklist which was produced at the Senate's subcommittee on multinational corporations, contained about 1,500 companies, including such big names as Ford, Xerox, Hertz, Helena Rubenstein and Coca Cola. The Saudi list is basically the same as the Arab League official blacklist. The Arab blacklist is not new. It was established twenty-four years ago in Damascus by the Arab League's Arab Boycott Office.[23]

Saudi Arabia has insisted that companies are blacklisted not because they are owned or staffed by Jews but because of sympathy with Israel. Other Arab spokesmen echo a similar explanation. Spokesmen stress that they do not blacklist corporations that conduct routine business with Israel. They balk at activities that will materially strengthen Israel's economy or military capability or that imply an ideological commitment to the Israeli cause. Undoubtedly, a wide range of activities can be interpreted to violate these standards.

At least two factors indicate that the list has attained some degree of success. First, it has prevented the blacklisted corporations from selling their products in most Arab markets where imports totalled more than $5 billion in 1975. Second, some Western corporations were willing to play the blacklist game. For example, Britain's Leyland Motors, which has long been on the blacklist, recently decided to stop assembling truck chassis in Israel so that it can enter the Arab market. More recently, the Anti-Defamation League of B'nai B'rith accused Chase Manhattan Bank of refusing to open a branch office in Israel. Moreover, some 200 Western companies submitted documents to the Arab League's boycott office aimed at proving they shouldn't really be on the list. Currently, the Ford Administration and Congress are considering antiboycott measures which would directly affect Saudi Arabia.[24]

Before a firm initiates any marketing strategy with Saudi Arabia, it is recommended that the company should find out whether it is on the list. One way to find out is to consult the 1970 Saudi boycott list. However, since the 1970 list is somewhat outdated, it is advisable to refer to the monthly Saudi trade magazine *Al-Tijarah* which contains names of companies included in or released from the list. Another way to find out is to write the boycott office in Damascus.

Advertising and Personal Selling

Advertising Campaign

The most important considerations for developing an advertising campaign in Saudi Arabia are the degrees of literacy and the extent of government control over the advertising media. On the one hand, 85 percent of the adult population of Saudi Arabia have had little or no formal education and cannot read or write. On the other hand, stringent government controls are imposed on two effective communication media. This section discusses the major types of communication media in Saudi Arabia and pinpoints those media which are inaccessible to advertisers.

Radio   Currently, there are three state-owned radio stations located in Jedda, Riyadh and Dammam. These stations broadcast local programs in Arabic and they also operate international services in Arabic, English, French, Indonesian, Persian, Swahili and Urdu. Peak listening times for local programs are reported to be between 3 p.m. and 4 p.m. and between 7 p.m. and 9 p.m. In addition to the three government-controlled stations, there is a private station (ARAMCO Radio) in Dhahran which broadcasts programs in English for the entertainment of the employees of Arabian American Oil Company. However, it is important to note that even though the radio is the best-developed channel of communication in Saudi Arabia, it is inaccessible to advertisers. The Saudi government prohibits radio stations from accepting advertising messages.

Television   Another important communication medium is television. TV was introduced into the kingdom by Aramco, which initiated a television service for employees in 1957. Apart from the Aramco station, Saudi Arabia now has five state owned TV stations at Riyadh, Jedda, Medina, Dammam and Qassim, which operate six hours daily. In addition, a number of major stations and relay points are under construction to serve all principal towns. The new five-year economic plan envisages a colored TV in 1980. Even though TV is relatively new in Saudi Arabia, it is becoming an important communication medium as more people can afford to possess one. Current published reports estimate that there are about 122,000 sets in use in the Kingdom.[25] In spite of its ever-growing popularity as a medium of communication, TV suffers from the stringent restrictions imposed on radio stations because the Saudi government bans advertising on TV.

Magazine & Newspapers   As a result of the tight measures levied on advertising in Saudi radio and TV stations, advertising expenditures are concentrated in newspapers, magazine, billboards and direct mail. Exhibit 15–4

EXHIBIT 15-4

Newspapers and Periodicals of Saudi Arabia

	Place & Language of Publication	Circulation
I. Dailies		
al-Bilad	Jedda; Arabic	20,000
al-Medina al-Munawara	Jedda; Arabic	20,000
al-Nadwah	Mecca; Arabic	10,000
Replica	Jedda; English	n.a.
al-Riyadh	Riyadh; Arabic	10,000
al-Ukadh	Jedda; Arabic	3,500
II. Weeklies		
Akhbar-al-Dhahran (Dhahran News)	Dammam;	1,500
al-Dawa	Riyadh; Arabic	n.a.
al-Jazirah	Riyadh; Arabic	5,000
al-Khalij al-'Arabi (The Ababian Gulf)	Al-Khobar;	1,200
Arabian Sun	Dhahran; English	n.a.
News from Saudi Arabia	Jedda; English	22,000
News of the Muslim World	Mecca; English and Arabic	n.a.
Oil Caravan Weekly	Dhahran; Arabic	n.a.
al-Qasim	Riyadh;	1,000
al-Riyadhah	Mecca; Arabic	500
Umm al-Qura	Mecca; Arabic	5,000
al-Yamamah	Riyadh; Arabic	1,000
al-Yaum (Today)	Dammam; Arabic	n.a.
III. Monthlies		
Hajj (Pilgrim)	Mecca; Arabic and English	5,000
al-Manhal	Jedda; Arabic	3,000
al-Mujtama	Riyadh; Arabic	n.a.
al-Tijarah	Jedda; Arabic	1,300

n.a. = Not Available

Source: Adapted from the Middle East and North Africa, 1974–1975 (London, England: Europa Publications, 1974); pp. 605–606.

reveals that there are six daily newspapers and almost a score of periodicals in operation in Saudi Arabia. Exhibit 15-4 also shows that the newspapers *Al-Bilad* and *Al-Medina Al Munaware* enjoy the largest circulation of 20,000 copies respectively. Both are large format newspapers and contain advertisements for various imported and local goods.

In addition to the local newspapers and periodicals, Arabic-language publications from Cairo, Beirut and Baghdad are particularly popular. It is also reported that American news magazines and *Reader's Digest* enjoy relatively wide circulation in the large cities. All important publications are subject to close scrutiny by Saudi Government censors before being admitted.

Sales Promotion   Some firms attempt to supplement their advertisements in newspapers and periodicals by pursuing different promotional strategies. For example, foreign firms in the large trading areas, such as Jedda and Dammam, maintain showrooms and use posters in Arabic for advertising. Other firms have induced "game shows" on television and radio stations to accept contributions in the form of gifts and prizes in return for announcing the contributors during the show.

Over-and-above the governmental restrictions on the various advertising media, Saudi Arabia lacks advertising agencies of the type known to United States firms. The few advertising agencies operating in Saudi Arabia are affiliated with large Beirut-based establishments. Moreover, advertisers have to be careful not to infringe upon moral or religious sensitivities of the highly conservative audience. For instance, it is prohibited to use women, nudity and sex appeal in advertising messages. Moreover, it is against the law to display or advertise publicly any symbols that contain Christian connotations. For example all neon lighting fixtures in the main lobby of a hotel in Riyadh had to be scrapped because they were shaped like crosses.

Personal Selling

Since bargaining still prevails as a business method in Saudi Arabia, most firms and independent shopowners place heavy emphasis on personal selling. The personal exchange between buyer and seller is highly ritualized. Much satisfaction is derived from the bargaining process, which provides an opportunity for those concerned to demonstrate their skills in concluding transactions. Due to the lengthy bargaining process involved in closing a sale, few stores sell goods at fixed prices.

Apart from the highly ritualized personal selling process, the Saudi sales force has another unique characteristic. To the dismay of the Western women liberation movement, women are not allowed to participate in the Saudi labor force. Consequently, all secretaries, receptionists, and salespersons are men. Even the cosmetics and lingerie department of all the stores are staffed by males.

Conclusion and Recommendations

The remaining quarter of this century will be a period of rapid change for the Saudi Arabian economy. The new Economic Development Plan (1975–1980) envisages a 13.3 percent growth rate for Saudi goods and services outside the oil sector, and establishes specific goals in virtually all sectors of the economy. The time is ripe to penetrate and secure a solid share of this second most rapidly growing import market between Europe and Japan.

Before undertaking a business trip to Saudi Arabia, United States businessmen are strongly urged to consult the Bureau of International Commerce (BIC) which can assist United States Firms in many ways with a wide range of services in the field of international marketing. For example, BIC can provide a valuable trade list containing names and addresses of prospective agents, distributors, and end-users of products and services in Saudi Arabia.[26]

Western businessmen also are advised to take into consideration the following Saudi holidays in planning business travel to Saudi Arabia. It is important to note that the Saudi Arabian weekend consists of Thursday and Friday. Business, however, can generally be conducted on Thursday except during the month of Ramadan, the fasting season. Ramadan in 1976 will begin about August 27–28 and end about September 24–25. Business is slow during the day but can pick up in the evening. United States businessmen could plan visits during the period but should be ready to work nights. United States businessmen should also observe the Pilgrimage of Haj season, which will begin about November 2 in 1976. All Saudi businesses are preoccupied with services to the pilgrims, hotels are fully booked and transport facilities are generally overloaded. The Saudi government usually restricts visa issuance during this period.

QUESTIONS

1. Discuss how some foreign marketers have adapted their products in order to appeal to the Saudi market.
2. How do Saudi channels of distribution differ from channels found in the United States?
3. Would you classify the Saudi Arabian economy as developed or underdeveloped? Why?
4. What kinds of modification would a marketer have to make in the development of promotional strategies for the Saudi Arabian market?
5. "The Saudi Arabian new five-year plan is an excellent demand forecasting tool." Discuss.

NOTES

1. Some general introduction to the history of Saudi Arabia can be found in the following sources: Fred Halliday, "Saudi Arabia; Bonanza and Repression," *New Left Review*, (July–August, 1973), pp. 3–26; Raman Kanauerhase, "Saudi Arabia: A Brief History," *Current History*, (February, 1975), pp. 74–79; George A. Lipsky, *Saudi Arabia*, (New Haven: HRAF Press, 1959); Ray Vicker, *The Oil Kingdom*, (New York: Scribner, 1974), Norman C. Walpole et al., *Area Handbook For Saudi Arabia*, (Washington, D.C.: U.S. Government Printing Office, 1971); and R. Bayly Winder, *Saudi Arabia in the Nineteenth Century*, (New York: St. Martin's Press, 1965).

2. Arab countries are in italics.

3. Philip H. Trezise, "More OPECs are Unlikely," *The Brookings Bulletin*, (Winter, 1975), p. 9.

4. *IMF Survey*, (February 3, 1975), p. 38.

5. "Nation We'd Better Get to Know," *Forbes*, (February 15, 1973), pp. 28–30.

6. "Learning the Language of the Arab World," *Business Week*, (August 18, 1975), pp. 105–106.

7. In Saudi Arabia, the Persian Gulf is called the "Arabian Gulf."

8. Anwar Ali, "Al Siasah Al Maliah W-Al Negdiah Fe Al Mamlakah Al Arabia Al Saudiah" ("Fiscal and Monetary Policy in Saudi Arabia"), *Al Belad*, (Daily Newspaper, Jedda, Saudi Arabia), July 23, 1969, p. 5.

9. Soliman A. Solaim, "Saudi Arabia's Judicial System," *The Middle East Journal*, (Summer, 1971), pp. 403–407.

10. Richard N. Farmer, "Organizational Transfer and Class Structure," *Academy of Management*, (September, 1966), p. 208.

11. William Rugh, "Emergence of a New Middle Class in Saudi Arabia," *The Middle East Journal*, (Winter, 1973), pp. 7–20.

12. "King Calls for Action on Inflation," *Middle East Economic Digest*, (November 22, 1975), p. 28.

13. "Saudi Arabian Five-Year Plan (1975-80)," *Middle East Economic Digest*, (August 22, 1975), pp. 28–29.

14. "Aladdin's Troubled Dream," *Forbes*, (February 15, 1976), pp. 28–32.

15. U.S. Department of Labor, Bureau of Labor Statistics, *Labor Law and Practice in the Kindom of Saudi Arabia*, (Washington, D.C.: U.S. Government Printing Office, 1972).

16. Faisal Bashir, *Survey of the Private Industrial Sector in Saudi Arabia* (Riyadh: Central Planning Organization, June 11, 1968).

17. Ramon Knauerhase, "Saudi Arabia's Economy at the Beginning of the 1970s," *The Middle East Journal*, (Spring, 1974), p. 128.

18. "Entry Eased for Foreign Workers," *Middle East Economic Digest*, (April 18, 1975), p. 39.

19. "Saudi Arabia: The New Breed of Empire Builders," *Business Week*, (December 7, 1974), pp. 42-43.

20. Central Department of Statistics, *Statistical Yearbook,* 1388 A.H., p. 181.

21. "Arabic Calculator," *Business Week,* (February 24, 1975), p. 78.

22. "Beer Without Alcohol To Be Made For Saudis," *Middle East Economic Digest,* (October 10, 1975), p. 23.

23. Robert E. Weigand, "The Arab League Boycott of Israel," *MSU Business Topics,* (Spring, 1968), pp. 74–80.

24. "Washington Bridles at the Arab Blacklist," *Business Week,* (December 1, 1975), p. 18.

25. J.M. Frost, ed. *World Radio TV Handbook 1975,* (Denmark: O. Lund Johansen, 1975), p. 322.

26. *Trade List For Saudi Arabia,* (Washington, D.C.: U.S. Department of Commerce, Bureau of International Commerce, October 1975).

This article explores the effects of an enlarged European Economic Community on Euro-U.S. trade. A survey of both European Economic Community and United States firms revealed that most felt that trade will remain the same or increase slightly. The conclusion is drawn that expansion of the EEC from six to nine firms currently poses no threat to opportunities existing in these markets for the United States.

16. Expansion of the European Common Market and Its Effect on the Euro-United States Trade

Venkatakrishna V. Bellur
Northern Michigan University

The European Common Market, also known as European Economic Community (EEC), was established in 1958 by member countries Belgium, France, Italy, Luxembourg, the Netherlands, and West Germany following the Treaty of Rome on March 25, 1957. The community of "six" was enlarged to "nine" when Denmark, Ireland, and the United Kingdom (UK) were admitted as members on January 1, 1973.

The entry of Denmark, Ireland, and the United Kingdom into the EEC at the beginning of 1973 was a milestone in the process of European integration that has been underway since the end of World War II. By 1980, the EEC plans to accomplish a full economic and monetary union. As the community moves toward the "ever closer union of the people of Europe," a new political entity, the United States of Europe (U.S.E.), is emerging. The EEC's expansion could be traumatic for both Europe and the United States. Exhibit 16-1 provides geographic, demographic, and economic profile as a means of comparison of the EEC and the United States.

Source: Reprinted with permission of the author.

EXHIBIT 16-1

A Profile of the EEC and the U.S., 1975

Area, Population, Gross National Product, and Trade	Community of "six"	Community of "nine"	U.S.
Area (thousand square miles)	449.00	589.00	3,600.00
Population (millions)	193.91	258.06	213.61
Gross National Product ($billion)	978.94	1,231.24	1,573.00
Exports ($billion)	240.91	296.56	107.191
Import ($billion)	231.81	299.21	103.44
Percentage of world exports	30.49	37.54	13.57
Percentage of world imports	28.87	37.27	12.88

Source: *Deadline Data on World Affairs,* August 23, (Greenwich, Conn.: DMS Inc., 1976).

Monthly Bulletin of Statistics, December 1976, (New York, NY: United Nations, 1976),

Between 1963–71, economic growth in terms of increase in the Gross National Product (GNP) at constant prices was most rapid in the Netherlands and France—more than 55 Percent. It varied between 44–48 percent for Denmark, West Germany, Italy, and Belgium. Growth in GNP was slower in three countries: Ireland, 37 percent; Luxembourg, 31 percent; and the United Kingdom, 23 percent. For the "nine" as a whole, the total productivity went up by 43 percent over the same time span, as compared with 35 percent in the United States.[1]

The trend in the EEC growth is continuing. The population in the enlarged community was estimated at 257.7 million in mid-1974. The GNP increased from $1,057 billion in 1973 to $1,158 billion during 1974. The per capita GNP of EEC countries was $4,495 in 1974. The growth in real GNP for 1975 was approximately 2.5 percent, and the projection for 1976 indicates a growth in real GNP ranging between 3.0–3.5 percent.[2]

Since 1958, the EEC has been the fastest growing sizable market for American exports. In 1958 the community imported 2.808 billion units of account (UA) worth of goods from the United States, while exporting 1.664 billion UA there. In 1972, the community of "six" imported 8,585 billion UA from the United States and exported goods to the tune of 8.321 billion UA to the United States. For the enlarged community, the corresponding figures in 1972 were imports of 11.900 billion UA from the United States and exports of 11.713 billion UA to the United States.[3]

Western Europe is more important to the United States as a customer than the United States is to Europe. In 1972, 30.5 percent of Western Europe's exports arrived in the United States. The EEC countries accounted for approximately 23.9 percent of total United States exports and the United States imported 8.2 percent of EEC exports.[4]

The EEC of "nine" imported from the United States $17,972 million worth of goods in 1973, and this went up by 31.5 percent in 1974. The United States share of total imports, which was $15,772 million worth of goods in 1973, went up by only 20.3 percent in 1974. These figures indicate that the enlarged community's imports from the United States are going up at a much faster rate than its exports to the United States.[5]

The expansion of EEC might have some significant impact on United States business. To assess the impact of the enlarged community on United States firms, Duerr conducted a survey of 135 senior international executives of United States companies operating in Europe. The results of the survey indicated that the executives expected the expansion of EEC to benefit all parties, that is, both the EEC and United States companies.[6] Since Duerr's study did not consider the attitude of businesses and industries located in the United States and EEC, and involved in export and import activities, a study in this direction was needed. Therefore, this study was designed with the major objective of determining the effects of an enlarged EEC on: (1) export of goods and/or services from the United States to the "nine" Common Market Countries; (2) import of goods and/or services from the "nine" Common Market Countries into the United States; (3) goods and/or service categories, marketing of which might be affected due to the admission of the three new member countries; and (4) to determine the awareness of the United States and EEC exporters and/or importers of the expansion of EEC and their attitude towards the effects of expansion of Euro-U.S. trade. It was believed that the objectives also might provide some answers to questions related to the future of the Euro-American trade relationship.

Research Procedure

To accomplish the objectives of the study it was necessary to gather information from firms that were involved in export and/or import activities and were located in both the EEC and the United States. Consequently, two sets of similar questionnaires were developed and tested to make sure that the questions were specific, brief, and clear. The questions were arranged in a sequence to provide an easy flow of responses.

The specific topics covered in the questionnaire pertained to: (1) type of business/industry operated; (2) type of product and/or service exported and/or imported; (3) the length of time the firm had been involved in export and/or import activity; (4) percentage of total exports and/or imports exported to or imported from the EEC and vice versa; (5) annual value of exports and/or imports; (6) awareness of the expansion of EEC; and (7) the direction in which the exporters and importers felt that the Euro-American trade would be affected because of EEC expansion. The firms were also asked to identify the product category in which the trade might be affected. The standard industrial classification (SIC) was used to classify the products exported and/or imported by the firms participating in the survey.

Five hundred questionnaires were mailed to the firms located in the "nine" EEC countries during October 1975. The firms were randomly selected from the import/export directory of each country. In some cases, Denmark, for example, the embassy provided the addresses of the firms involved in export and/or import activity with the United States. The package mailed to the firms contained: (1) a letter of introduction requesting the cooperation of the firm, (2) the questionnaire, and (3) a self-addressed envelope. No stamped envelopes could be included in the package because there was no way of getting stamps from all the countries for that purpose. This was emphasized in the letter of introduction to make the firms realize that it was difficult to enclose a post paid, self-addressed envelope.

It was surprising to note that eighty-four usable responses were received, about a 17 percent return rate. The responses were coded, tabulated, and analyzed. Wherever necessary, chi-square values were estimated to determine the statistical significance of the data.

To obtain information related to the objectives of the study from the United States firms, one thousand questionnnaires were mailed during November 1975. The firms were selected randomly from the 1975 edition of *American Register of Exporters and Importers*. The package mailed to these potential respondents contained: (1) a letter of introduction requesting the cooperation of the firm, (2) the questionnaire, and (3) a self-addressed postpaid envelope to facilitate return of the completed questionnaire.

A total of 148 completed questionnaires, representing a 15 percent return rate were received. The data were coded, tabulated, and analyzed, as was done with EEC data.

Findings

The finding will be discussed under two main sections: (1) analysis of information obtained from EEC firms; and (2) analysis of responses from the United States firms.

European Economic Community

Type of Business/Industry Operated and Type of Product Exported and/or Imported

Most of the firms surveyed were operating businesses/industries related to: (1) food and kindred products; (2) chemicals and allied products; (3) fabricated metal products, except ordinance, machinery, and transportation equipment; (4) machinery, except electrical; (5) electrical machinery, equipment, and supplies; (6) transportation equipment; and (7) professional, scientific, and controlling instruments; photographic and optical goods; and watches and clocks. Of the eighty-four firms that listed the type of business/industry operated, only eight, representing slightly more than 95 percent of the total responses, listed the items they exported to the United States. Only sixty-six firms, representing 79 percent of the total response, indicated the items they imported from the United States.

Estimated chi-square value was highly significant for the data related to the type of business/industry operated and to: (1) type of product exported, and (2) type of product imported. Also highly significant was the relationship between the type of product exported and: (1) type of product imported, and (2) the product that falls under the SIC category in which the Euro-U.S. trade will be most affected. The relationship between type of product imported and the product that falls under the SIC category in which the Euro-U.S. trade will be most affected was, however, significant only at $p < 0.05$.

Eighty-two firms, representing approximately 98 percent, answered the question, asking whether they were involved in both export and import activities. Of that number, forty-eight firms or 59 percent reported that they were both exporters and importers. The remaining 41 percent were either exporters or importers.

Number of Years in Export and/or Import Business, Annual Value, and the Percentage of Total Exports to and Imports from United States

Answers of firms to the question on length of time they had been involved in exporting and/or importing activities and how long they had been exporting product(s) to the United States showed that the majority of firms had been involved in export and import activities for twenty-five years or longer. Further, the data revealed that forty-five of the seventy-seven firms in the export business, representing approximately 58 percent, were exporting their product(s) to the United States. Of that number, about 25 percent had been involved in export to the United States for twenty-five years or longer.

With regard to the annual value of exports and/or imports, it was interesting to note that the annual value of exports was less than $10 million for approximately 72 percent of the firms involved in exporting. The annual value of imports was less than $10 million for approximately 81 percent of the firms. Furthermore, it can also be seen that the number of firms with an annual export and/or import value of $50 million or more represent 9.9 and 7.7 percent, respectively. Thus, the distribution of firms with regard to annual export and/or import values is highly skewed.

Eighty-three firms responded to the question concerning whether they exported product(s) to the United States, and fifty-three of these, representing 64 percent, answered yes. This indicates that a larger number of firms responding to the survey were exporting their product(s) to the United States.

When asked what percentage of their total exports was exported to the United States and what percentage of their total imports came from the United States, forty-six and twenty-four firms, respectively, provided answers. The data showed that approximately 78 percent of the firms exported less than 15 percent of their annual exports to the United States. With regard to the imports, it was interesting to note that about 33 percent of the firms were importing 25 percent or more of their total annual imports from the United States. This clearly indicates that both the EEC and the United States are benefiting by trading with each other.

Awareness of Expansion and Its Effects on Euro-U.S. Trade

Since the major objective of the study was to determine the effects of EEC expansion on Euro-American trade, a number of questions were included in the questionnaire to ascertain awareness of the expansion and its effects on Euro-U.S. trade.

Eighty-two firms responded to the question on the awareness of EEC expansion. Of that number seventy-three firms, representing 89 percent, said that they were aware of the expansion, and the rest exhibited a lack of awareness.

In response to whether they felt that the expansion will affect the Euro-U.S. trade, out of seventy-five firms replying, thirty-seven or 49 percent said that it will affect trade. The remaining thirty-eight firms or 51 percent indicated that the EEC expansion will not affect the Euro-U.S. trade.

Two attitudinal statements included in the questionnaire were intended to ascertain the direction in which the respondents felt the Euro-U.S. trade might be affected. Almost an equal number of firms, fifty-three and fifty-two, respectively, responded to the statement on imports and exports. Most importers and exporters believed that the Euro-U.S. trade will either remain at the present level or moderately increase. Exhibit 16–2 provides a breakdown of responses to the two statements. Estimated chi-square value for the relationship between the attitude towards changes in imports and exports was highly significant.

Only fifty out of eighty-four responded to the question asking in which product category Euro-U.S. trade might be affected. Of that number 28 percent mentioned capital goods; 42 percent, consumer durable goods; and the remaining 30 percent, consumer non-durable goods. Thirty-six firms provided an example of a specific product that would fit into the above three product groups. The example provided by 59 percent of the firms represented the following items: (1) transportation equipment; (2) machinery, equipment and supplies; and (3) food and kindred products.

The United States

Type of Business/Industry Operated and Type of Product Exported and/or Imported

The data related to the type of business/industry operated by the firm, and the type of product exported to and imported from the EEC showed that

EXHIBIT 16-2

Attitude of EEC Firms Toward Change in Imports and Exports

Attitudinal Statement	Number of Firms	Percentage
Imports from U.S. to EEC will:		
a. greatly increase	2	3.8
b. moderately increase	21	39.6
c. remain the same	22	41.5
d. moderately decrease	8	15.1
e. greatly decrease	—	—
Total	53	100.0
Exports from EEC to the U.S. will:		
a. greatly increase	2	3.8
b. moderately increase	22	42.3
c. remain the same	25	48.1
d. moderately decrease	2	3.8
e. greatly decrease	1	2.0
Total	52	100.0

most firms were operating businesses/industries related to: (1) food and kin-dred products; (2) chemicals and allied products; (3) machinery, except elec-trical; (4) electrical machinery, equipment, and supplies; and (5) professional, scientific, and controlling instruments; photographic and optical goods; watches and clocks. Data on export to and import from the EEC revealed a similar pattern with regard to the product(s) exported and/or imported.

Of the one hundred forty-eight firms that listed the type of business/industry operated, only one hundred five firms, representing approximately 71 percent of the total responses, listed the items that exported to EEC. Only eighty-one firms, representing about 55 percent of the total responses, listed the items they imported from the EEC.

Estimated chi-square value was highly significant for the data related to the type of business/industry operated and: (1) type of product exported, and (2) type of product imported. The relationship between the type of product exported and: (1) type of product imported; (2) attitude towards exports from United States to EEC; and (3) attitude towards imports from EEC to United States was also statistically highly significant. The relation-ship between type of product imported from EEC and attitude toward ex-ports from United States to EEC was highly significant. However, the relationship between type of product imported from EEC and (1) attitude towards imports from EEC to the United States, and (2) product that falls under the SIC category in which the Euro-U.S. trade might be affected were significant only at $p < 0.05$.

The question regarding involvement in both export and import activity was answered by one hundred forty-five firms. Of that number, forty-six firms, representing approximately 32 percent of the responses said that they were in both export and import business. The remaining 68 percent were either in the export or the import business.

Number of Years in Export and/or Import Business, Annual Value and the Percentage of Total Exports and Imports from the EEC

Responses to the question concerning the length of time firms had been involved in export and/or import activities and had been exporting to EEC revealed that most firms were involved in export and/or import activities for twenty-five years or more. Also, most of them (36.2 percent) had exported their product(s) for the same time period.

With regard to the annual value of exports and/or imports, it was interesting to note that the annual value of exports to and imports from EEC was less than $5 million for 80 percent and 82 percent of the firms, respectively. Less than 10 percent of the firms reported an annual export value of $50 million or more. The firms reporting an annual import value of $50 million or more represented less than 5 percent. There were very few firms distributed within the $5–50 million range. Thus, similar to EEC firms, the distribution of firms with regard to annual export and/or import values is highly skewed.

A total of one hundred twenty-seven firms responded to the question pertaining to whether they exported their product(s) to the EEC. Of this number, seventy-two firms, representing about 57 percent, answered affirmatively. The remaining 43 percent said they did not.

When asked what percentage of their total exports was destined for the EEC, and what percentage of their total imports came from EEC, a total of seventy and forty-eight firms, respectively, responded. The majority of firms either exported to or imported from EEC 25 percent or more of their total exports and/or imports.

Awareness of Expansion and Its Effects on Euro-U.S. Trade

The question of awareness of EEC expansion was answered by one hundred forty firms. Analysis of the responses revealed that one hundred thirty-one firms, representing about 94 percent of the responses, were aware of the expansion. When asked whether they thought that the expansion of EEC will affect the Euro-U.S. trade, one hundred eighteen responded. Seventy firms, representing 59 percent, said it will have an effect and the remaining 41 percent indicated that it will have no effect.

Two attitudinal statements were included in the questionnaire to ascertain the direction in which the respondents believed the Euro-U.S. trade will be affected. Statements related to the imports from EEC to United States, and exports from United States to EEC was answered by ninety-nine and one hundred twelve firms, respectively. Exhibit 16–3 provides a breakdown of responses to the two statements. It can be seen that most United States exporters and importers believed that the exports and/or imports will either remain the same or moderately increase. The relationship between the attitude towards changes in imports and exports was highly significant.

Only seventy-two out of one hundred forty-eight firms responded to the question as to which product category in the Euro-U.S. trade might be affected. Of this number about 40 percent mentioned capital goods; 32 percent, consumer goods; and the remaining 28 percent, consumer non-durable goods. Fifty-four firms provided an example of a specific product that would fit into the above product groups. Classification of the example provided by 84 percent of the firms represented the following items: (1) machinery, except electrical; (2) transportation equipment; (3) food and kindred products; (4) textile products; (5) fabricated metal products, except ordnance, machinery, and transportation equipment; and (6) professional, scientific and controlling instruments; photographic and optical goods; watches and clocks.

EXHIBIT 16–3

Attitude of U.S. Firms Toward Changes in Imports and Exports

Attitudinal Statement	Number of Firms	Percent
Imports from EEC to U.S. will:		
a. greatly increase	3	3.0
b. moderately increase	33	33.4
c. remain the same	51	51.5
d. moderately decrease	10	10.1
e. greatly decrease	2	2.0
Total	99	100.0
Exports from U.S. to EEC will:		
a. greatly increase	5	4.5
b. moderately increase	47	42.0
c. remain the same	48	42.8
d. moderately decrease	12	10.7
e. greatly decrease	—	—
Total	112	100.0

Summary and Conclusion

Europe and United States have been trading partners for centuries. Creation of the Common Market during the late 1950s was the beginning of the integration of Europe into an economic and political entity that might one day be strong enough to compete with the United States. The Common Market of "six" was expanded into "nine" by the addition of three new members—Denmark, Ireland, and the United Kingdom. It is certain that in due course of time, the present "nine" will be expanded to include many more. The direction in which Western Europe is moving might have some impact on the Euro-U.S. trade at present and the Euro-U.S. relationship in the years ahead. As a result this study was designed with the major objective of determining the effects of an enlarged community on the Euro-American trade. The specific objectives were, however, to determine the impact of an enlarged EEC on: (1) exports of goods and services from the United States to the "nine" Common Market countries; (2) import of goods and services from the "nine" Common Market countries into the United States; (3) goods and/or service categories, marketing of which might be affected due to the admission of the three new member countries; and (4) to determine the awareness of the United States and EEC exporters and/or importers of the expansion of EEC and their attitude towards the effects of expansion on Euro-U.S. trade.

Five hundred and one thousand questionnaires, respectively, were mailed to the firms involved in import and/or export activities in EEC member countries and the United States. Approximately 17 percent of the questionnaires mailed to EEC firms, and 15 percent to United States firms were completed and returned. Analysis of the responses indicated that most EEC and United States firms were involved in the import and/or export activities pertaining to: (1) food and kindred products; (2) chemical and allied products; (3) fabricated metal products, except ordnance, machinery, and transportation equipment; (4) machinery, except electrical; (5) electrical machinery, equipment and supplies; (6) transportation equipment; and (7) professional, scientific, and controlling instruments; photographic and optical goods; and watches and clocks. There was a statistically highly significant relationship between the type of business/industry operated and the type of product(s) imported and/or exported. Most firms had been in the export and/or import business for twenty-five years or longer and for most, the annual value of exports and imports was less than $10 million.

Most firms were aware of the expansion of the Common Market and indicated that the Euro-U.S. trade will either remain the same or will moderately increase because of expansion. The categories of products in which they felt the trade might be affected were those which they either imported or exported.

It is fair to conclude that the EEC expansion poses no threat to the

Euro-U.S. trade at present. This can be supported by the data that are available, which indicate a moderate increase in trade between United States and EEC. That supports the findings of this study.

QUESTIONS

1. What is the European Economic Community?
2. How important have EEC markets been to United States firms in the past?
3. Why do you think an expanded EEC is not perceived as a threat to Euro-U.S. trade?

NOTES

1. European Community, No. 165, (Washington, D.C.: European Community Information Service, May 1973), p. 3.

2. "Market Profile—European Economic Community (EEC)," *Overseas Business Reports,* OBR 75-59, (Washington, D.C.: The U.S. Department of Commerce, December 1975), pp. 2-3.

3. *The European Community and U.S.A. in 1973,* Pamphlet P-49, (Brussels, Belgium: Statistical Office of the European Communities, November 1973), p. 22.

4. "Trade Patterns of the West 1972," *News Release, Bureau of Public Affairs, Department of State, Media Service* (Washington, D.C.: U.S. Govt. Printing Office, August 1973), p. 2.

5. "Market Profile—European Economic Community (EEC)," *op. cit.,* pp. 2-3.

6. Michael G. Duerr, *The Expanded EEC and U.S. Business* (New York: The Conference Board, Inc., 1974), pp. 1-12.

Eastern bloc countries have recently begun to apply techniques that closely resemble what is practiced in the free world as marketing. The author discusses the emergence of marketing activities from a historical perspective and the types of adaptation that characterize socialist marketing. The implications for western marketers of the practice of marketing by socialist countries are also raised.

17. Marketing in Eastern European Socialist Countries

Charles S. Mayer
York University

Eastern European Socialist countries have recently "discovered" marketing as an important tool to bolster their economies. While their form of marketing is not identical to that practiced in the West, its emergence is important for three reasons. First, it raises the question of why marketing surfaced in an economy that viewed it as a "non-productive cost." Second, socialist marketers are attempting to develop practices consistent with their philosophy of what is *socially desirable* at a time when western marketing is under attack for its lack of responsiveness to social needs. A philosophical underpinning for western practice could be welcomed. Third, the emergence of marketing in a socialist world gives the semblance of closure between two competing forms of economic organization. How real this closure is, and how far it will progress, is important to future relationships between East and West.

Source: Reprinted by permission from the January, 1976 issue of the *University of Michigan Business Review*, published by the Graduate School of Business Administration, The University of Michigan.

This paper will discuss the emergence of marketing from a historical point of view and the various aspects of socialist marketing which show the path of development.

Marketing in a Free Enterprise Society

In order to compare socialist marketing to our western system, it is important to extract the essence of marketing as we practice it. There seem to be five fundamentals in western marketing:

1. The central organizing principle of production and distribution is consumer satisfaction (the marketing concept).
2. Consumer satisfaction is derived from both goods and services.
3. The market is composed of different segments, each with its own needs and wants.
4. The profit motive brings forth new goods and services.
5. The standard of living of an individual is uniquely determined according to the satisfaction of *his* needs and wants.

Marketing in a Traditional Socialist Economy

Marketing has a completely different starting point under traditional socialism. The teaching of Marx, Engels and Lenin offer some insight into the role of marketing. Their views seem to be in direct contrast with the five fundamentals of western marketing:

1. Supply creates its own demand (Say's Law).
2. Only goods have labor content value; services and other marketing activities add nothing (Labor Theory of Value).
3. Consumer communes are viewed as uniform.
4. The output of society is distributed to its members not in relation to productivity, but according to needs.
5. The standard of living is determined and administered centrally.

The goals of the socialist economy are implemented through central planning. When particular problems manifested themselves under a rigidly-conceived central plan, the resulting dissatisfaction with the system of central planning led to many of the marketing changes discussed in this paper.

Developments in the Socialist System

In 1930, the GOSPLAN (the central planning agency in the Soviet Union) dealt with but a few hundred products. By the early 1950s, this number had risen to about 10,000 with at least 5,000 listed in detail in the annual plan. Needless to say, the planning process had become very complex and difficult to manage centrally.

The first attempt at decentralization was a form of regional decentralization, attempted by Kruschev in 1956. However, that solution was not satisfactory and was abandoned eight years later. During this time, the USSR had arrived at the stage where consumers were becoming restless about their non-participation in the productive benefits of their economy. Some attention had to be paid to producing a variety of consumer goods. But what goods to produce?

With the "luxury" of discretionary consumer income, inventories of undesirable goods began to accumulate. Thus, some attention had to be paid to the requirements of the market. Prices could not be used to clear surpluses because they were based on labor content. Yet, the emergence of shortages and black market prices of scarce, desirable goods, and the simultaneous emergence of excess inventories of other goods, clearly indicated that prices should reflect both production costs and consumer preferences. The need to estimate carefully the consumer demand in those fields which were deemed socially acceptable became an important aspect of production planning.

State trading companies also became more insistent that manufacturers' obligations not end when goods were delivered to the trading company. The insistence surfaced in the emergence of contractual agreements with the productive enterprises, including, in the case of dissatisfaction contractual penalities to be assessed against the manufacturers. In other words, the responsibilities of the manufacturer were expanded from meeting production quotas to the level of sales and sometimes beyond.

The need for adaptive behavior at the manufacturing level became clear. These enterprises had to respond rapidly to changes in the marketplace to correct flaws in the plan—more rapidly than was possible under central planning.

Growing foreign trade also created problems in planning. With increased trade among the socialist countries and between East and West, price could no longer reflect the labor costs in one country; they had to be comparable to trading block or world prices. For this reason, emphasis on internal cost reduction began to surface. To this point, there had been little incentive at the enterprise level for cost reduction, since this would only result in price reduction, not volume sales increases. Now, lower costs were the only means of obtaining foreign contract sales.

All these factors underscored the need to decentralize some of the decision-making to the manufacturing level. A desire for a new rationale of socialist economic structure, alternately known as the economic reform or the new mechanism, soon emerged.

The New Mechanism

Generally attributed to Professor Liberman of the Soviet Union and some of his colleagues, a new rationale was, in fact, adopted between 1965 and 1970 by all socialist countries: Profitability was the new yardstick of enterprise efficiency. Under this yardstick, the central plans could be more aggregated and operate through regulatory means. Individual enterprises would be able to determine how they wished to operate within centrally-defined "socially desirable" constraints. Enterprise efficiency could be measured by profits. ("Profit" calculations under the socialist system do not include rents for capital, productive resources or land, nor does depreciation form any part of productive costs. Also "socialist profit" is not an unlimited concept, but is constrained at the upper end to about 15 percent above "planned profit.")

The main change under the new mechanism was the end of detailed planning by the central agency and, in its place came more detailed, locally-determined planning. The overall control of the economy remained with the central planning agency.

Centrally Controlled Regulating Mechanisms

Socialist central planners create a five-year plan, a one-year plan, and a fifteen-year plan. Among these, the five-year plan is the most important and goes into the greatest amount of detail. The one-year plan interprets the goals of the five-year plan for the current year, while the fifteen-year plan guarantees that that inter- and intra-sectoral growth takes place at a balanced rate.

The plans provide for the regulation of individual enterprises through four specific means:

1. Direct means. Since the replacement of plant and equipment is not provided through depreciation, the enterprise must continually seek ministerial approval. Accordingly, the central agency has a strong direct impact on what equipment the enterprise will receive and the research and development it is able to undertake.
2. Indirect means. The central authority, operating through several different agencies, can control both the amount of credit available to a specific enterprise and the amounts of rent and taxes it must pay.
3. Indirect administrative means. Regulation may also be effected through administrative controls. For example, a firm may or may not be licensed to carry on international trade. At a lower level of regulation, a firm may be denied a building permit to carry on required expansion.
4. Direct administrative means. Controls can also be exercised through direct administrative orders. The central agency, acting as the owner of the enterprise, gives specific instructions which are binding on the directors of the enterprise.

The planning agency further affects the ability of individual enterprises to maneuver by controlling such figures as rate of growth, the rate of consumption relative to the rate of growth of the economy, the rate of accumulation (savings) and the productive/non-productive sector ratio. By enforcing such ratios for the whole economy, it can affect the ways in which individual enterprises behave.

Additionally, various incentive schemes have significant impact on the activities of an enterprise. Among these are direct payments, tax rebates, subsidies and differential rates of profit retention.

Within these centrally determined regulations and in the specific area where an enterprise is permitted to function, the enterprise has some leeway to increase its productive efficiency and hence its profitability. In its attempt to operate efficiently, the enterprise may make use of marketing tools.

Marketing Research

It should not be surprising that marketing research plays a large role in a socialist economy. While it is not all in the same direction and with the same focus on marketing research in the free enterprise countries, those areas in which marketing is used are highly developed and extremely well implemented. Under planning, the need for marketing research is vital. It is carried out by large national institutions of marketing research. These agencies service the planning board, the ministries, manufacturing enterprises and, to an increasing extent, foreign marketers.

The research institutes specialize in forecasting demand for specific goods and in obtaining data for and working with econometric models. Attitude research and various behavioral research is much less important.

The number of studies conducted as well as the sample sizes of specific studies can be quite large. In Hungary, for example, the National Institute of Marketing Research operates six panels of 3,000 families each, with questionnaires mailed every two or three months and with 90 percent cooperation rates. The statistics descriptive of this panel operation are sufficient to cause envy to western marketing researchers.

There are some interesting ways in which marketing research is used in a socialist country. First, the information obtained from consumers may be used in normative as well as descriptive ways. For instance, if it is determined from a consumer panel that a specific family's income has reached the proper level and if, from its inventory of durable goods, it is evident that this family could use, say a television set, then the planning authority might decide to build them a television set. The authority would organize television production in such a way that the family could obtain a television. Even if that particiular family wanted a washing machine more than a television (provided that washing machines are not manufactured in sufficient quantities), it becomes difficult for the family to obtain one. Therefore, it is quite likely that the television purchase planned for the family becomes a real purchase by the family.

Marketing research is especially important in a socialist country because the system is less flexible in adapting to wrong market estimates. If, in fact, a plan has been drawn which required the manufacture of a specific number of frying pans, the system is not sufficiently sensitive that frying pan production could be halted prior to the fulfillment of the plan. Accordingly, the cost of a wrong decision is high and the amount of shortages or excess inventory is significant when the research is wrong.

The Product

The type of production is regulated by the central planning authority. For example, it was determined that the economic production level of automobiles in Hungary is somewhere between 200,000 and 300,000 units per year. Simultaneously, it was determined that the demand for automobiles in Hungary is somewhere between 20,000 and 30,000 units. Accordingly, Hungary could not economically justify its own automobile production. Rather than build its own automobiles, Hungary has entered into reciprocal agreements with its trading partners whereby Hungary supplies many of the other countries from its large bus factory and in turn buys its autos from the other countries. Similar examples can be found in other areas of production. Each country will attempt to specialize in types of production where it has an advantage and avoid other specific areas.

When demand manifests itself there is no guarantee that demand will be satisfied. A product may emerge to satisfy the demand or certain acts may be taken to temper the demand. For example, there may be a promotional campaign to show that that particular good is not "socially acceptable."

Since products tend to be generic as opposed to branded, lack of competition keeps the level of product quality quite low. There are, however, recognizable differences among products depending on what factory produced them. There seems to be a form of brand competition among products based not on brands, but on the factor of origin.

Service associated with products is also low, especially at the distribution stage. Long lines seem to be the accepted mode of acquiring goods in socialist countries. While there has been some improvement in services they are still far from acceptable to a Westerner. However, the satisfaction one receives from a particular service is heavily tempered by his expectation of that service. Therefore it is quite possible that socialist consumers are satisfied with the level of service they receive.

Products from the West have had a strong impact on product quality in socialist countries. They are freely available in some of the socialist countries and certainly can be seen in all socialist countries. While they are beyond the purchasing ability of most of the population, they do influence their expectations and aspirations. Thus, western goods create strong pressure for improvement of socialist goods.

There are, however, important factors in socialist countries that prevent the emergence of new products. First, it is not clear that an enterprise could charge a higher price for a superior good. If superiority means higher costs but not higher prices, it is evident that an enterprise would not wish to move in this direction. Second, a new product might require changes in the production line. Since managers have learned how to live with their existing production lines and to make a "reasonable profit" with them, they are reluctant to make changes which leave them open to a reassessment of costs by the ministry. If that reassessment is less favorable, they will have a more difficult time earning profits.

Pricing

Initially prices represented the labor content value and were strictly determined by the central authority. Recently, however, prices are determined on the basis of both costs and social desirability. Socially desirable products, such as drugs, cultural activities, community services, transportation and housing, are highly subsidized in order to maintain a low price. Others, such as alcohol, tobacco, luxury goods and jewelry, are deemed socially undesirable and are heavily taxed. In addition to direct taxation, goods also bear a "circulation tax" which is differentiated from product to product. In Hungary, for example, the circulation tax on sugar is 2 percent, on wine 20 percent, and on beer 30 percent. Heating fuels carry a negative circulation tax (i.e., they are heavily subsidized).

   If the government fixes prices, it should also insure that the goods are available. It is in this area that the central planners have generally failed. For example, housing is one of the socially desirable goods as defined by the government. It is heavily subsidized and rental prices run as low as $15 per month for an apartment. Nevertheless, people are willing to pay up to $40,000 to purchase a condominium apartment. How can this phenomenon be explained? The answer is found in the lack of availability of adequate housing in the rental market. Incidentally, one of the reasons governments have permitted the appearance of condominium housing in the socialist countries (which, after all, is private ownership) is that housing prices deviate greatly from building costs. While it was a principle of government that prices on housing should remain low, government could not afford to make additional housing available at these prices. Hence the condominium.

   Some countries are experimenting with fully floating prices or with prices that can move within a predetermined range. For example, in Czechoslovakia about 6 percent of commodities have market-determined prices, while in Hungary the figure is 23 percent and in Yugoslavia, 50 percent.

   With controlled prices, the profit potential varies widely from industry to industry. Accordingly, the use of profit as a yardstick of industrial performance is open to major difficulties, many of which have yet to be faced by socialist countries. Most of these manifest themselves in capital-intensive industries such as the generation of energy. These are the very same industries in which the profit motive is criticized as ineffective in the western countries.

One of the major issues of the world today is inflation. While the socialist countries are struggling to administer their inflation and keep it at an "acceptable" level, it is a difficult task. Some of their resource input prices are rising heavily, and tourists can create havoc in a market that has unrepresentative prices. Of all the differences between the two systems, price determination is probably the one which characterizes most clearly the fundamental differences in philosophy.

Promotion

The level of advertising, point-of-sale effort and packaging quality is far below that in the western countries. The role of promotion is seen to be educative or informational, not to create competition among (for them) non-existent brands.

Promotion is a seriously under-utilized tool in socialist countries. With a generic good like linen, for example, Argunov[1] reports an interesting experiment in the Soviet Union. Through special promotional techniques including displays, television advertising, fashion shows and persuasive advice, the sales of a product during a two-week test period were increased by a factor of 10. Accordingly, it is not unlikely that promotion will play a much greater role in the socialist marketing systems of the future.

Promotion can also be used in the socialist system to harmonize the purchasing patterns of consumers with the social rationality of the planners. Instead of producing a good that is in demand, advertising can be used to diminish the demand for the product. If advertising can increase the desirability of a product it can also decrease its desirability. We are just beginning to attempt this in the West, as exemplified by the campaigns against cigarette smoking. When the central agency has virtually unlimited funds, it can sponsor negative advertising as part of its quest to achieve its goal.

Personal selling, as can be expected, is at a low level of development, especially in the industrial area. There are simultaneously few sellers and few buyers. Much of the production of an enterprise is committed, sometimes by plan, for significant periods in advance.

Distribution

The distribution system in socialist countries is surprisingly ineffective. "Surprisingly" because there is great potential for organizing socialist distribution systems efficiently. Since all distribution channels are owned by the same agency, many of the optimizing models employed to some extent in the West could have greater impact in socialist countries. For the time being, however, queues, out-of-stock products and over-stock inventories are common. So are inefficiencies in regional distribution.

Experiments are being undertaken with privately-owned small retail stores. These can be usually easily identified due to their neatness, cleanliness, longer hours of operation and generally better service atmosphere.

Since retail outlets are also judged on their profitability, and since the product mix available to similar outlets is identical, further improvements in service can be safely predicted.

The Future of Marketing in the Socialist Countries

From the foregoing it can be seen that there has been considerable closure between the marketing systems of the free enterprise countries and the socialist countries. Some of that closure may have come from the free enterprise system moving closer to the socialist system. A good example would be price controls on fuels during the energy crisis. While the technologies of marketing in both systems are moving closer together, it may be misleading to predict that the socialist countries will become more capitalistic through the introduction of the profit motive. Certainly their major differences remain.

It is important to bear in mind that the point of departure for the two systems is totally different. First, while the free enterprise system has lately concerned itself with developing a sufficient market to clear the goods it is capable of producing, the socialist system still is attempting to continue to increase its productive capability. Hence one system is market-oriented, while the other is still production-oriented. Second, the emphasis in the free enterprise system is on the individual while the socialist system tends to focus on the social aggregate. Third, the goals of individuals are self-determined in the free enterprise system, while they are centrally determined in the socialist system according to socially acceptable criteria. Fourth, the free enterprise system is far more responsive to market needs than a centrally planned system.

One reason the study of socialist marketing is important to western marketers is that the socialists are trying to harmonize a philosophy of what is socially desirable with the satisfaction of demand from the marketplace. In the free enterprise system, the primary focus has been on responding to those demands from the marketplace. This has caused some problems in the social arena. Many of the problems discussed in the West, such as the use of disposable containers, develop from the fact that the system is market responsive without recognizing the consequences of delivering what may be socially undesirable.

Most analysts of socialist marketing are careful to point out the major differences between the two systems. Some claim that, due to the difference between the points of departure and the underlying emphasis of socially-determined goals, the technology of socialist marketing will approximate the technology of western marketing but the two systems will always remain quite dissimilar. Others have argued that at a particular stage of industrial development the logic of the industrial system is such that marketing systems tend to converge.

In my opinion, planning and the profit motive do not mix. While planning may limit the role of the profit motive, as soon as managerial efficiency is judged on the basis of profits, a consumer-orientation must emerge. The plan, itself, will be perceived as a constraint on earning profits. If this is so, then the "marketing concept" (the orientation of the business enterprise towards satisfying the needs of the customer) will succeed where other forms of diplomacy have failed—that is, in bringing together the two ideologies of social organization that divide the world today.

QUESTIONS

1. Why have socialist countries begun to apply marketing techniques?
2. How have central planners used such concepts as marketing research, product development, pricing, promotion and distribution?
3. Do you see future marketing practices undertaken by socialist companies more closely approaching the marketing practices of western countries? Why?

NOTES

1. M. Argunov, "What Advertising Does," *Journal of Advertising Research*, December, 1966, pp. 2–3.

How will the economic growth goals of the People's Republic of China affect the opportunities of American firms? This article explores the staggering potential represented by Peking leadership to increase Chinese imports in a host of industrial and agricultural areas. A number of obstacles that must be removed, if the United States share of these imports is to grow, are identified and discussed.

18. The Coming Leap Forward in China Trade

Julian M. Sobin
*International Minerals
and Chemical Corporation*

The People's Republic of China is on the growth trail. The Peking government will give the highest priority to orderly economic development in the years ahead.

This should mean an enlargement of China's role in world trade, with renewed Chinese investment in oil for export and more purchases of advanced technology and capital equipment from the West and Japan.

Pronouncements in the Chinese press underscore a new emphasis in Peking on foreign trade expansion.

"The facts eloquently prove that foreign technology makes China stronger," said a joint declaration by China's new leadership group in the "People's Daily."

Material Incentives

Mao Tse-tung's successor, Hua Kuo-feng, says his administration will brook no interference with economic growth. Management of the economy will be

Source: Reprinted from *Nation's Business*—July, 1977.

entrusted to qualified planners, and the bestowing of higher wages as rewards for fulfilling production quotas will be reintroduced.

Chinese officials say production schedules were seriously undermined in the past, slowing the growth of Sino-Western trade, as a result of a downgrading of managerial efficiency and emphasis by the "gang of four" on such nonmaterial incentives as awards of red flags. The "gang of four" includes Mao Tse-tung's widow, Chiang Ching, and her three closest allies: Chang Chun-chiao, vice premier and chief armed forces commissar; Wang Hung-wen, number three in China's Communist Party; and Yao Wen-yuan, a member of the ruling Politburo. All were arrested last fall.

Now that a new set of economic reforms is being implemented, China's production will increase, Chinese trade officials are saying, and so will her exports and imports.

Profit Motive in Farming

As a further incentive to boost production, Hua is expected gradually to ease restrictions on the amount of communal land set aside for private cultivation and to approve a return to a system of limited rural free markets which will provide Chinese peasants with profit for produce they grow on private plots.

Confirming the economic direction of China's new regime are key appointments and the reemergence into prominence of figures long associated with economic development based on profitability and extensive commercial exchanges with the West.

Wan Li, the minister of railways who lost his job last year, has been reinstated. He was ousted because he tried to deal with railway labor problems by raising wages and offering other material incentives—a cardinal violate of the old policies. Hsiao Han, who supports a policy of buying from abroad, has been named to the top post in the Ministry of Coal Industry.

On the way back is Kang Shih-en, who was ousted as minister of petroleum and chemical industries because he favored intensive development of China's oil resources in order to underwrite acquisition of technology and capital equipment acquisition from the West and Japan. The appearance of his name on the committee which planned Mao's funeral presages his rehabilitation.

In addition, Party Vice Chairman Le Hsien-nien and former Deputy Prime Minister Teng Hsiao-p'ing, both of whom favor a rapid program of economic modernization based on extensive commercial exchanges with the West, played pivotal behind-the-scenes roles in helping Hua Kuo-feng assume power last October. It is only a question of time until both are given major assignments in the new administration.

Those who doubt that Hua Kuo-feng will prove durable enough to put his economic intentions into effect overlook the fact that he enjoys the backing of powerful regional military commanders and of Defense Minister Yeh Chien-ying.

United States Share is Small

Imports arranged at China's semiannual Canton Trade Fair last autumn surpassed the import levels at previous fairs, a confirmation of the intent of China's economic planners to increase purchases from abroad. Total business transacted—both import and export deals—was in the $800 million range.

While statistics for the spring trade fair last April and May are not yet available, it is clear that China's purchases again reached record levels and that total business transacted exceeded the total transacted at the previous fair.

The volume of business transacted by United States firms was minimal at both fairs: about $50 million last autumn and some $60 million in the spring. The largest Sino-American trade contract signed at either fair was a United States sale of polyester fibers worth approximately $10 million.

Total United States exports to China were about $470 million in 1973, $819 million in 1974, $303 million in 1975, and $135 million in 1976. During these years China's total imports averaged about $7 billion annually.

In fact, China accounts for no more than one percent of United States exports. And the United States acccounts for no more than 2.5 percent of China's annual exports of about $6.5 billion.

Japan Leads

Meanwhile, Japan and Western Europe hold 25 percent and 15 percent of the China trade, respectively.

Japan, of course, enjoys cost advantages in the Chinese market because of geographic proximity. But United States businessmen eager for more trade with China need not be overly concerned about this. Experience has shown that distances will not deter the Chinese from buying anywhere in the world. They never hesitate to switch orders from Japan to manufacturers in Europe, for example.

What stands in the way of Sino-American trade growth are a number of obstacles, the removal of which would require either a political leap leading to full diplomatic relations or a step-by-step approach.

These obstacles include this country's current inability to provide Export-Import Bank financing; the lack of direct commercial banking relations with the People's Republic of China; the absence of direct shipping and airline connections between the flag carriers of China and the United States; and the lack of most-favored-nation tariffs on Chinese goods imported to the United States. Duties on Chinese goods are 100 to 300 percent higher than those on goods from countries to which we grant most-favored-nation status.

The Frozen Assets Issue

Eximbank financing and direct banking relations and shipping connections will not be possible until settlement of the frozen assets issue is achieved.

(Assets totaling $196 million and $78 million were seized by the Chinese and American governments, respectively, in the early 1950s.) This is because private claimants might seek redress through the courts by attaching ships, aircraft, or other Chinese property which came into the United States.

High officials of the Peking government have indicated a desire for negotiations on the frozen assets issue, even without full normalization of diplomatic relations.

China's Staggering Needs

The Chinese seem to wish to follow the step-by-step approach in easing constraints on Sino-U.S. trade. At the same time they have given clear indication that, barring unusual and unforeseen circumstances, they will insist on formal diplomatic relations before permitting a significant rise in trade with the United States.

China's industrial and agricultural requirements to carry out her avowed modernization plans by the year 2000 are staggering, and there should be a significant role for American industry in this modernization process.

The Chinese requirements include substantial purchases of manufacturing machinery and even of complete plants; telecommunications equipment; transport equipment, such as heavy trucks, tractors, and other special-purpose vehicles for construction, mining, agriculture, and forestry; aircraft and aircraft components to upgrade the nation's civil aviation fleet; railway vehicles; and ocean freighters.

China needs chemical fertilizers—China's agricultural productivity must be increased by 26 percent over the next ten years to meet demand from her population, which is growing at the rate of 1.25 to two percent annually. And China needs oil drilling machinery to develop her vast oil resources. China earned nearly $1 billion from crude oil exports in 1975 and more than $500 million in 1976. She lowered her oil prices last year in order to capture a greater share of the oil market, especially in Asia.

Quakes Reduce Steel Output

Also, China needs metals—especially copper, nickel, lead, and steel—and metal products.

The tragic earthquakes which devastated the northern city of Tangshan last August substantially increased the Chinese market for foreign steel. Tangshan's Kailuan coal complex of seven mines produced enough coking coal to support the output of ten million tons of steel, about half of China's total production in 1976. Chinese planners had counted on their country's steel production rising to an average of about 35 million tons annually over the next few years to help complete mechanization of agriculture by 1980, a key priority of China's fifth five-year plan (1977–1981).

With the reduction in steel output caused by the destruction of Tang-shan's coal mines, China will have to increase purchases of steel; steel products, including bars, seamless tubing, hot rolled plate and sheet; tractors; and water pumps.

Chinese Trade Minister Li Chiang recently reiterated a promise of significant growth in Sino-U.S. trade if full diplomatic ties between Peking and Washington are established.

A Sino-American bilateral trade agreement also would remove impediments to trade growth. Whatever course the Carter administration decides to take on these complex issues, it can rely on a substantial reservoir of friendship which has traditionally existed between the Chinese and American peoples.

QUESTIONS

1. Why has the Chinese leadership turned towards imports as a means of achieving economic growth?
2. How can the United States government reduce the obstacles for American businessmen in dealing with the Chinese market?
3. What American industries stand the greatest to gain as a result of more liberalized trade with China? Why?

PRODUCT STRATEGIES

The focal point of the marketing mix, whether it be a domestic or international marketing venture, is a firm's product/service offering. What product or services sold by firms domestically can be adapted to foreign markets? Is international uniformity possible for a firm's product/service lines? How are product or service attributes perceived and influenced as they are introduced abroad? These and other questions regarding the formulation of product/service strategy are addressed by the selections in this section.

Warren Keegan in his classic article on multinational product planning provides a strategic framework to assess the many alternatives resulting from the interdependent factors of product/service attributes, company resources, marketing mix support variables, and target market characteristics. The second article, by Vern Terpstra, explores the advantages and disadvantages of locating R & D facilities abroad and offers some generalizations for further study. The following article by Jose De LaTorre illustrates the adaption and use of the product life-cycle concept in formulating multinational marketing strategies. The section concludes with an interesting treatment of a product/service issue that is becoming increasingly vital to world economic development—that of technology transfer. In this article, Ladman discusses the impact of exporting technology to less developed countries, and how the process can be improved to increase the benefits of both the exporter and the recipient nations.

Formulating an explicit product strategy for international expansion is one of the major untapped opportunities facing headquarters' executives of multinational companies. This article identifies strategic alternatives and shows how to select the most effective strategy given any particular product-company-market mix.

19. Multinational Product Planning: Strategic Alternatives

Warren J. Keegan
George Washington University

Inadequate product planning is a major factor inhibiting growth and profitability in international business operations today. The purpose of this article is to identify five strategic alternatives available to international marketers, and to identify the factors which determine the strategy which a company should use. Exhibit 19-1 summarizes the proposed strategic alternatives.

Strategy One: One Product, One Message, Worldwide

When PepsiCo extends its operations internationally, it employs the easiest and in many cases the most profitable marketing strategy—that of product extension. In every country in which it operates, PepsiCo sells exactly the same product, and does it with the same advertising and promotional themes and appeals that it uses in the United States. PepsiCo's outstanding interna-

Source: Warren J. Keegan, "Multinational Product Planning: Strategic Alternatives". Reprinted from *Readings in International Marketing*, January 1969, pp. 58–62, published by the American Marketing Association.

EXHIBIT 9-1

Multinational Product-Communications Mix: Strategic Alternatives

Strategy	Product Function or Need Satisfied	Conditions of Product Use	Ability to Buy Product	Recommended Product Strategy	Recommended Communications Strategy	Relative Cost of Adjustments	Product Examples
1	Same	Same	Yes	Extension	Extension	1	Soft drinks
2	Different	Same	Yes	Extension	Adaptation	2	Bicycles, Motor-scooters
3	Same	Different	Yes	Adaptation	Extension	3	Gasoline, Detergents
4	Different	Different	Yes	Adaptation	Adaptation	4	Clothing, Greeting Cards
5	Same	....	No	Invention	Develop New Communications	5	Hand-powered Washing Machine

tional performance is perhaps the most eloquent and persuasive justification of this practice.

Unfortunately, PepsiCo's approach does not work for all products. When Campbell soup tried to sell its United States tomato soup formulation to the British, it discovered, after considerable losses, that the English prefer a more bitter taste. Another United States company spent several million dollars in an unsuccessful effort to capture the British cake mix market with United States-style fancy frosting and cake mixes only to discover the Britons consume their cake at tea time, and that the cake they prefer is dry, spongy, and suitable to being picked up with the left hand while the right manages a cup of tea. Another United States company that asked a panel of British housewives to bake their favorite cakes discovered this important fact and has since acquired a major share of the British cake mix market with a dry, spongy cake mix.

Closer to home, Philip Morris attempted to take advantage of United States television advertising campaigns which have a sizable Canadian audience in border areas. The Canadian cigarette market is a Virginia or straight tobacco market in contrast to the United States market, which is a blended tobacco market. Philip Morris officials decided to ignore market research evidence which indicated that Canadians would not accept a blended cigarette, and went ahead with programs that achieved retail distribution of United States-blended brands in the Canadian border areas served by United States television. Unfortunately, the Canadian preference for the straight cigarette remained unchanged. American-style cigarettes sold right up to the border but no further. Philip Morris had to withdraw its United States brands.

The unfortunate experience of discovering consumer preferences that do not favor a product is not confined to United States products in foreign markets. Corn Products Company discovered this in an abortive attempted to popularize Knorr dry soups in the United States. Dry soups dominate the soup market in Europe, and Corn Products tried to transfer some of this success to the United States. Corn Products based its decision to push ahead with Knorr on reports of taste panel comparisons of Knorr dry soups with popular liquid soups. The results of these panel tests strongly favored the Knorr product. Unfortunately these taste panel tests did not simulate the actual market environment for soup which includes not only eating but also preparation. Dry soups require fifteen to twenty minutes cooking, whereas liquid soups are ready to serve as soon as heated. This difference is apparently a critical factor in the soup buyer's choice, and it was the reason for another failure of the extension strategy.

The product-communications extension strategy has an enormous appeal to most multinational companies because of the cost savings associated with this approach. Two sources of savings, manufacturing economies of scale and elimination of product R and D costs, are well known and understood. Less well known, but still important, are the substantial economies associated with the standardization of marketing communications. For a company with worldwide operations, the cost of preparing separate print and TV-cinema films for each market would be enormous. PepsiCo international marketers have estimated, for example, that production costs for specially prepared advertising for foreign markets would cost them $8 million per annum, which is considerably more than the amounts now spent by PepsiCo International for advertising production in these markets. Although these cost savings are important, they should not distract executives from the more important objective of maximum profit performance, which may require the use of an adjustment or invention strategy. As shown above, product extension in spite of its immediate cost savings may in fact prove to be a financially disastrous undertaking.

Strategy Two: Product Extension— Communications Adaptation

When a product fills a different need or serves a different function under use conditions identical or similar to those in the domestic market, the only adjustment required is in marketing communications. Bicycles and motorscooters are illustrations of products in this category. They satisfy needs mainly for recreation in the United States but provide basic transportation in many foreign countries. Outboard motors are sold primarily to a recreation market in the United States, while the same motors in many foreign countries are sold mainly to fishing and transportation fleets.

In effect, when this approach is pursued (or, as is often the case, when it is stumbled upon quite by accident), a product transformation occurs. The same physical product ends up serving a different function or use than that for which it was originally designed. An actual example of a very successful transformation is provided by a United States farm machinery company which decided to market its United States line of suburban lawn and garden power equipment as agricultural implements in less-developed countries. The company's line of garden equipment was ideally suited to the farming task in many less-developed countries, and, most importantly, it was priced at almost a third less than competing equipment especially designed for small acreage farming offered by various foreign manufacturers.

There are many examples of food product transformation. Many dry soup powders, for example, are sold mainly as soups in Europe but as sauces or cocktail dips in the United States. The products are identical; the only change is in marketing communications. In this case, the main communications adjustment is in the labeling of the powder. In Europe, the label illustrates and describes how to make soup out of the powder. In the United States, the label illustrates and describes how to make sauce and dip as well as soup.

The appeal of the product extension communications adaptation strategy is its relatively low cost of implementation. Since the product in this strategy is unchanged, R and D, tooling, manufacturing setup, and inventory costs associated with additions to the product line are avoided. The only costs of this approach are in identifying different product functions and reformulating marketing communications (advertising, sales promotion, point-of-sale material, and so on) around the newly identified function.

Strategy Three: Product Adaptation— Communications Extension

A third approach to international product planning is to extend without change the basic communications strategy developed for the United States or home market, but to adapt the United States or home product to local use conditions. The product adaptation-communications extension strategy assumes that the product will serve the same function in foreign markets under different conditions.

Esso followed this approach when it adapted its gasoline formulations to meet the weather conditions prevailing in foreign market areas, but employed without change its basic communications appeal, "Put a Tiger in Your Tank." There are many other examples of products that have been adjusted to perform the same function internationally under different environmental conditions. International soap and detergent manufacturers have adjusted their product formulations to meet local water conditions and the characteristics of washing equipment with no change in their basic communications approach. Agricultural chemicals have been adjusted to meet different soil conditions as well as different types and levels of insect resistance. Household appliances have been scaled to sizes appropriate to different use environments, and clothing has been adapted to meet fashion criteria.

Strategy Four: Dual Adaptation

Market conditions indicate a strategy of adaptation of both the product and communications when differences exist in environmental conditions of use and in the function which a product serves. In essence, this is a combination of the market conditions of strategies two and three. United States greeting card manufacturers have faced these circumstances in Europe where the conditions under which greeting cards are purchased are different than in the United States. In Europe, the function of a greeting card is to provide a space for the sender to write his own message in contrast to the United States card which contains a prepared message or what is known in the greeting card industry as "sentiment." European greeting cards are cellophane wrapped, necessitating a product alteration by American greeting card manufacturers selling in the European market. American manufacturers pursuing an adjustment strategy have changed both their product and their marketing communications in response to this set of environmental differences.

Strategy Five: Product Invention

The adaptation and adjustment strategies are effective approaches to international marketing when potential customers have the ability, or purchasing power, to buy the product. When potential customers cannot afford a product, the strategy indicated is invention or the development of an entirely new product designed to satisfy the identified need or function at a price within reach of the potential customer. This is a demanding but, if product development costs are not excessive, a potentially rewarding product strategy for the mass markets in the middle and less-developed countries of the world.

Although potential opportunities for the utilization of the invention strategy in international marketing are legion, the number of instances where companies have responded is disappointingly small. For example, there are an estimated 600 million women in the world who still scrub their clothes by hand. These women have been served by multinational soap and detergent companies for decades, yet until this year not one of these companies had attempted to develop an inexpensive manual washing device.

Robert Young, Vice President of Marketing-Worldwide of Colgate-Palmolive, has shown what can be done when product development efforts are focused upon market needs. He asked the leading inventor of modern mechanical washing processes to consider "inventing backwards"—to apply his knowledge not to a better mechanical washing device, but to a much better manual device. The device developed by the investor is an inexpensive (under $10), all-plastic, hand-powered washer that has the tumbling action of a modern automatic machine. The response to this washer in a Mexican test market is reported to be enthusiastic.

How to Choose a Strategy

The best product strategy is one which optimizes company profits over the long term, or, stated more precisely, it is one which maximizes the present value of cash flows associated with business operations. Which strategy for international markets best achieves this goal? There is, unfortunately, no general answer to this question. Rather, the answer depends upon the specific product-market-company mix.

Some products demand adaptation, others lend themselves to adaptation, and others are best left unchanged. The same is true of markets. Some are so similar to the United States markets as to require little adaptation. No country's markets, however, are exactly like the United States, Canada's included. Indeed, even within the United States, for some products regional and ethnic differences are sufficiently important to require product adaptation. Other markets are moderately different and lend themselves to adaptation, and still others are so different as to require adaptation of the majority of products. Finally, companies differ not only in their manufacturing costs, but also in their capability to identify and produce profitable product adaptations.

Product-Market Analysis

The first step in formulating international product policy is to apply the systems analysis technique to each product in question. How is the product used? Does it require power sources, linkage to other systems, maintenance, preparation, style matching, and so on? Examples of almost mandatory adaptation situations are products designed for sixty-cycle power going into fifty-cycle markets, products calibrated in inches going to metric markets, products which require maintenance going into markets where maintenance standards and practices differ from the original design market, and products which might be used under different conditions than those for which they were originally designed. Renault discovered this latter factor too late with the ill-fated Dauphine which acquired a notorious reputation for breakdown frequency in the United States. Renault executives attribute the frequent mechanical failure of the Dauphine in the United States to the high-speed turnpike driving and relatively infrequent United States maintenance. These turned out to be critical differences for the product, which was designed for the roads of France and the almost daily maintenance which a Frenchman lavishes upon his car.

Even more difficult are the production adaptations which are clearly not mandatory, but which are of critical importance in determining whether the product will appeal to a narrow market segment rather than a broad mass market. The most frequent offender in this category is price. Too often, United States companies believe they have adequately adapted their international product offering by making adaptations to the physical features of products (for example, converting 120 volts to 220 volts) but they extend United States prices. The effect of such practice in most markets of the world where average incomes are lower than those in the United States is to put the United States product in a specialty market for the relatively wealthy consumers rather than in the mass market. An extreme case of this occurs when the product for the foreign market is exported from the United States and undergoes the often substantial price escalation that occurs when products are sold via multi-layer export channels and exposed to import duties. When price constraints are considered in international marketing, the result can range from margin reduction and feature elimination to the "inventing backwards" approach used by Colgate.

Company Analysis

Even if product-market analysis indicates an adaptation opportunity, each company must examine its own product/communication development and manufacturing costs. Clearly, any product or communication adaptation strategy must survive the test of profit effectiveness. The often-repeated exhortation that in international marketing a company should always adapt its products' advertising and promotion is clearly superficial, for it does not take into account the cost of adjusting or adapting products and communications programs.

What Are Adaptation Costs?

They fall under two broad categories—development and production. Development costs will vary depending on the cost effectiveness of product/communications development groups within the company. The range in costs from company to company and product to product is great. Often, the company with international product development facilities has a strategic cost advantage. The vice-president of a leading United States machinery company told recently of an example of this kind of advantage:

> We have a machinery development group both here in the States and also in Europe. I tried to get our United States group to develop a machine for making the elliptical cigars that dominate the European market. At first they said "who would want an elliptical cigar machine?" Then they gradually admitted that they could produce such a machine for $500,000. I went to our Italian product development group with the same proposal, and they developed the machine I wanted for $50,000. The differences were partly relative wage costs but very importantly they were psychological. The Europeans

see elliptical cigars every day, and they do not find the elliptical cigar un-
usual. Our American engineers were negative on elliptical cigars at the outset
and I think this affected their overall response.

Analysis of a company's manufacturing costs is essentially a matter of identifying potential opportunity losses. If a company is reaping economies of scale from large-scale production of a single product, then any shift to variations of the single product will raise manufacturing costs. In general, the more decentralized a company's manufacturing setup, the smaller the manufacturing cost of producing different versions of the basic product. Indeed, in the company with local manufacturing facilities for each international market, the additional *manufacturing* cost of producing an adapted product for each market is zero.

A more fundamental form of company analysis occurs when a firm is considering in general whether or not to pursue explicitly a strategy of product adaptation. At this level, analysis must focus not only on the manufacturing cost structure of the firm, but also on the basic capability of the firm to identify product adaptation opportunities and to convert these perceptions into profitable products. The ability to identify preferences will depend to an important degree on the creativity of people in the organization and the effectiveness of information systems in this organization. The latter capability is as important as the former. For example, the existence of salesmen who are creative in identifying profitable product adaptation opportunities is no assurance that their ideas will be translated into reality by the organization. Information, in the form of their ideas and perceptions, must move through the organization to those who are involved in the product development decision-making process; and this movement, as any student of information systems in organizations will attest, is not automatic. Companies which lack perceptual and information system capabilities are not well equipped to pursue a product adaptation strategy, and should either concentrate on products which can be extended or should develop these capabilities before turning to a product adaptation strategy.

Summary

The choice of product and communications strategy in international marketing is a function of three key factors: (1) the product itself defined in terms of the function or need it serves; (2) the market defined in terms of the conditions under which the product is used, including the preferences of potential customers and the ability to buy the products in question; and (3) the costs of adaptation and manufacture to the company considering these product-communications approaches. Only after analysis of the product-market fit and of company capabilities and costs can executives choose the most profitable international strategy.

QUESTIONS

1. What is meant by "product extension"? Communications adaptation"?
2. Differentiate between product adaption, communications extension, and dual adaptation. Give examples of each.
3. Discuss the strategic considerations involved in conducting a product-market analysis?
4. What are the benefits to be obtained by an international marketer from conducting a product-market analysis?

In all phases of product development, multi-national firms should rely on international inputs to minimize the inherent risks penetrating foreign markets. One way firms can internationalize their product development activity is through the decentralization of R&D efforts. The factors influencing the overseas location and role of R&D facilities are discussed in this article.

A review of existing research and the experiences of a number of companies are used by the author to develop guidelines for future research on the many questions raised.

20. International Product Policy: The Role of Foreign R & D

Vern Terpstra
University of Michigan

The question of what products to sell in foreign markets is the essence of product policy in international marketing. Should we sell the same products we sell domestically or should they be adapted to local conditions? Will our product line be the same abroad as at home, or should we sell a different mix of products in foreign markets? For each company and industry the answers to these questions may be somewhat different.

Theories of foreign direct investment do not address these questions. They seek to explain why the firm will invest and produce in foreign markets without asking what products or businesses the firm will be in in those markets. They implicitly assume that the firm will be producing the same products abroad as at home. This is especially clear in the Product Life Cycle theory, according to which the firm begins foreign production of a product which has reached the mature stage of its life cycle at home.

Source: Reprinted with permission from the Winter, 1977 issue of the *Columbia Journal of World Business*. Copyright © 1977 by the Trustees of Columbia University in the city of New York.

The general answer to the product policy questions raised above is that the firm should sell those products abroad that best help it to meet its objectives, such as market share, growth, and profit maximization. The practical experience of most companies suggests that the products and product lines sold in foreign markets to meet these goals will not be identical to those sold domestically, though there will be a strong similarity.

International marketing would be easier, of course, if a firm's products and product lines were identical in all countries. However, most multinational companies are forced to modify both products and product lines in foreign markets. Many different factors combine to induce such modifications. Among them are differences in use conditions, technical specifications, government regulations, competitive opportunities, and consumer tastes and purchasing power. Because the firm cannot usually automatically extend its domestic products to foreign markets, it faces a critical question in international marketing: how can the multinational firm adapt, develop, or acquire the products appropriate to foreign markets?

Getting Appropriate Products for Foreign Markets: Alternative Strategies

When firms first go multinational, they usually market their domestic products with minimal adaptation to foreign conditions. Another approach is to acquire a foreign firm which has products designed for its own market. Each of these approaches may be satisfactory as an initial method of getting products for foreign markets. For the long run, however, a more sophisticated *business and product development plan* is desirable. In its planning process, the firm must decide what businesses and what markets it wants to pursue. Ideally, this planning and scanning should be on a global basis. Product strategy is an important part of this plan, and that includes a strategy of product development.

It is possible for a firm to get products without developing them itself. One way is to copy products developed successfully by others. Many firms follow this strategy with some success. It is obviously not, however, the strategy of a market leader.

Another way of getting products for world markets is shown by Colgate's approach. Colgate has chosen to market internationally several products that have been successfully developed and introduced nationally by other firms. For example, in many world markets, Colgate sells Wilkinson razor blades for the British company and Pritt Glue Stick for Henkel of Germany.

Colgate president David R. Foster explained: "We've adopted the practice of using someone else's technology and our own worldwide reach." This strategy seems to work well for Colgate but it is not one followed by many other firms. Of course, Colgate also develops internally many of the products it sells.

Most multinational firms do not follow either of the strategies just mentioned. That is, they do not rely on imitation to develop their new products, nor do they market internationally products developed and introduced by others. As a result, the primary way firms get their products for world markets is through internal product development, with acquisition as a secondary method.

International Product Development

If internal product development is the major method used by multinational firms to obtain their international product lines, how do they internationalize their product development activity? Drawing on research in progress, we shall look primarily at the role of R&D in international product development. Research and development are not the whole of the product development process, but they are a major ingredient and the only one considered in the present discussion.

A firm's product development activity should be based on a policy statement to give it coherence and direction. The various product development activities—idea generation, screening of ideas, selection of products for development, and development of the product—should take place within the guidelines of the policy statement. In all of these phases of product development, the multinational firm should have international inputs to assure the international profitability of its products. There are various ways firms can and do internationalize these phases of product development, but we shall look only at the role of R&D in this process.

The Role of R&D

Firms that conduct R&D consider these activities crucial to their survival and growth. From R&D come the new products that will help the firm survive and meet its goals in the future. We want to see how the multinational marketing of the firm affects its R&D practices, and especially the location of its R&D facilities.

Almost all multinational firms began as national firms with their activities concentrated in their home country. Generally, the first international activity of multinationals is marketing, followed later by foreign production. The last activity of the firm to be organized on an international basis—if it is at all—is R&D. Indeed, some multinationals do not conduct any R&D outside of their home country. For most multinationals R&D is much more centralized in the home market than is their production and marketing.

Why this centralization of R&D when the multinationals' marketing and production activities are rather heavily decentralized in foreign markets? A major reason is that the needs and pressures which lead to foreign marketing and production do not apply to R&D. For example, the need to reach customers, to cut costs of production, transportation, or tariffs, and the need to satisfy "buy national" policies have no connection with R&D. Consequently, many firms apparently think they can be successful international marketers with all of their product development activity in their home market. Obviously, the historical development of the company and inertia play a role in R&D policy also. Though products must be developed for world consumers rather than just domestic consumers, many would argue that foreign market requirements can be fed into the domestic R&D activity. For example, it is notable that in 1972, R&D conducted by United States companies for the direct support of their foreign affiliates was only 14.5 percent of parent R&D, but that was equal to 134 percent of their overseas R&D.[1] Most American firms are obviously using their domestic R&D for their international operations.

Let us look at some of the major arguments for maintaining R&D exclusively in the domestic market of the multinational. These arguments assume that centralization of R&D is deliberate policy rather than historical accident.

Arguments for Centralizing R&D Domestically

Critical Mass and Economics of Scale   R&D can be an expensive activity in terms both of personnel and equipment. The domestic market where the firm started its R&D has the best opportunities for economies of scale. It may be difficult to get the critical mass necessary for efficient and effective R&D in foreign markets. Start-up costs and learning time are deterrents to starting up foreign R&D.

Easier Communication and Coordination   There is no doubt that management of R&D is facilitated when carried on in just one country instead of several. Communication and coordination are easier when there are fewer language and cultural barriers to surmount and when there is shorter physical distance to cover. Duplication of effort is less a problem with centralized R&D also.

Better Protection of Know-How   Ideas and techniques coming out of R&D are among the most valued possessions of the firm, and they must be safeguarded. Patents are one means of protecting this intellectual property. Another means is close control over the R&D process and personnel. This control is facilitated by centralizing R&D in the home country.

More Leverage with Host Governments   It is a common business strategy to avoid putting too many eggs in one basket. In the present case that means multinationals may resist locating R&D in a country where they already have production and marketing operations. By withholding R&D from a country, they feel less vulnerable to adverse government action, especially expropriation. If a firm has R&D facilities in a country, it has more to lose, and the country more to gain, in an expropriation.

More Domestic Experience and Expertise   Most multinationals have their longest experience, largest market and greatest expertise in their domestic market. They are further down both the learning curve and the experience curve in their home market. Since R&D must relate to the rest of the firm's operations, it can be argued that greater synergy is possible between R&D, production and marketing in the home market than in foreign markets.

Whatever reasons companies may have for their R&D location policy, the fact is that R&D is highly centralized in the home countries of multinationals. The most comprehensive evidence we have is for United States companies. A government funded study conducted by the Conference Board showed that 90 percent of company expenditures on R&D were made in the United States.[2] No such macro studies exist for other home countries of multinationals but there is evidence that other multinationals behave as the Americans on this score. (Canadian firms may be an exception as we shall see later.) Philips of the Netherlands, and Hoffman-La Roche and Nestle of Switzerland are illustrations. These three firms are large multinationals from small countries. It could be argued that since most of their sales are outside the home country, they would have more reason than American firms to decentralize R&D in the country where they are located.

Why Decentralize R&D Abroad?

Although R&D by multinationals is highly centralized in home markets, many multinationals do conduct R&D in foreign markets. For American firms, foreign R&D amounts to about ten percent of the total, or over one billion dollars annually since 1971. IBM alone spent over $200 million annually on foreign R&D in the early 1970s. There are a variety of external pressures and company motivations for conducting R&D abroad.

Transfer of Technology   Ronstadt studied foreign R&D in seven large United States multinationals and found the major initial corporate motivation to be the transfer of technology to their foreign operations to aid in the production of existing company products rather than in the development of new products abroad.[3] However, the evolution of these units was in the direction of new product development for local or even reigonal or global markets.

Subsidiary Pressures   Multinationals often come to conduct R&D abroad because of subsidiary pressures. For example, local staff might become restive if their status remains that of "just a factory operation" instead of moving toward that of a full-fledged member of the multinational family. In this way, Sperry-Vickers acceded to the demands of European subsidiaries for "a fair share" of R&D. Granting R&D to local operations thus reduces discontent and improves morale in the subsidiary.

Host Government Influences   There are both incentives and pressures by host governments to conduct local R&D. For example, Canada offers financial rewards, which encouraged National Cash Register to begin a new research program in Canada, and helped IBM and Control Data to expand their Canadian R&D. Host governments also try to require multinationals to conduct R&D locally to maximize the technology fallout from their operations. While governments have difficulty in pressuring foreign firms to initiate R&D, they have more success in getting multinationals to continue R&D in the local companies they acquire. For example, Britain feared that Chrysler's acquisition of Rootes would lead to a brain drain to the United States, so the government required as a condition of purchase that Chrysler maintain Rootes' existing R&D activity. Corning Glass maintained and expanded an R&D operation in a French acquisition to keep a promise made to the French government.

Public Relations Value   In addition to improved subsidiary morale and compliance with host governments, there is often a public relations reward in conducting R&D locally. For example, IBM has gained a great deal of favorable publicity as a result of having conducted R&D in Europe, just as Hoechst has in India—a very different environment. Conversely, a firm that refuses to conduct R&D in foreign markets may suffer from bad public relations.

Research Talent and Product Skill Gains   Conducting R&D abroad can be a way of tapping personnel who have sophisticated research talent and specialized product skills, but who are unwilling to leave their home country. This has been important to firms in such science-based industries as electronics, computers, chemicals and pharmaceuticals. For example, even an advanced company like Hewlett-Packard found it advantageous to locate R&D facilities near the Universities of Edinburgh and Stuttgart which exercised world research leadership in certain products of interest to the company. The United States Manufacturing Chemists Association claims that only three of the world's top ten chemical research organizations belong to United States companies and that eleven of the nineteen great chemical innovations of the past thirty years were based on foreign discoveries.[4]

Potential Cost Savings   A further incentive to establish local R&D is potential cost savings in many countries where scientific and technical personnel are paid less than in the firm's home market. For instance, Europe used to be less expensive than the United States, although that appears to be changing. On the other hand, a country like India offers technical skills at modest remuneration compared to Europe or the United States. The Conference Board study found that "there is strong evidence that the performance of R&D overseas is less costly than in the United States."[5]

New Ideas and Products   With R&D in more than one country a greater and more varied flow of new ideas and products may be possible. There are theoretical arguments to support this position on decentralized R&D,[6] a few examples of which can be given here. Research and development personnel in any one country are subject to one set of environmental constraints and influences, while those in other countries are subject to a different set. Monroe Auto Equipment, for example, set up an R&D facility in the Netherlands because American R&D in auto parts is so dominated by General Motors that no one dares to innovate very far from GM design. Europe is a much more fragmented market, and different kinds of product design can be tried, resulting in potential innovations.

Unilever has a deliberate policy of decentralizing R&D. Accordingly, a vice-chairman stated, "By locating R&D activities in a number of countries, an international firm can take advantage of its unique ability to do research in a variety of national environments. The probability of success is increased if there is good liaison betwen laboratories. There is a greater chance of sparking off new ideas."

Wothington Pump's Italian subsidiary in 1975 earned 200,000 dollars in royalties from its American parent because of development originating in the local R&D operation. This is an explicit and notable illustration of the contribution of foreign R&D in one company.

Faster and Better Results   An international division of labor in R&D can sometimes mean faster and more effective results than centralized R&D. In his study of seven United States multinationals, Ronstadt found that part of their expansion of foreign R&D "was based on the need to utilize internal engineering, manufacturing and marketing resources in a large scale effort to develop complete new lines of products."[7] Following this principle, IBM was able to meet its development targets for the System 360 in the 1960s.

More recent examples are Honeywell and Kodak. Honeywell introduced a new five-model computer line in 1974. Development began in the early 1970s with competitive pressures for an early output. The French company was assigned one of the five models for development, and the Italian company another. French and American operations shared responsibility for the critical Model 64. The programming languages and software were shared by the company's British and United States operations. Technical coordination was from Minneapolis. The international division of labor enabled Honeywell to meet its goals for introducing the new line.

For its new instant camera, Kodak required a fast film using a high speed emulsion four times as responsive to light as any then known. An international team began working on this in 1973. It involved one thousand employees in Europe and the United States for one year. The final product used an emulsion developed in England, refined in Rochester, and made commercial with the help of French expertise in emulsion control. This marked another successful collaboration in international R&D.

Greater Sensitivity to Local Markets   Local R&D will be better attuned to local market needs and desires than R&D centralized in a distant and different market. This is especially true with products for which cultural and market considerations play a greater role than purely technical aspects. This applies more to consumer than to industrial goods, but industrial goods are not exempt either. For instance, Otis Elevator conducts R&D on small elevators in Europe because there is no real market for them in the United States. Leroy notes that local market peculiarities are also the reason Alcan's Building Products Division decentralizes its R&D abroad.[8]

An example in consumer goods is Beacham's in Brazil. The local subsidiary felt there was a local demand for a deodorant with a strictly feminine image. The Brazilian staff developed the product and made extensive local tests of the deodorant and perfume element. From these tests the Brazilian company developed and introduced the product. Within one year it was already vying for the number one position in the market.

In automobiles, Ford in Brazil provides an example. For many years, Ford had reasonable success in that country by adapting cars originally made in the United States. Yet Ford's biggest winner was the Corcel, a car produced by local R&D in Brazil.

Continuation after Acquisition   It is likely that R&D obtained through acquisition will be continued by the acquiring firm. Most acquisitions are not made to obtain R&D facilities, but once the R&D is acquired there are strong reasons for keeping it: morale in the subsidiary; government and public relations; and new skills and personnel acquired. Often the acquired R&D is in a product area new to the firm; for example, in Italy Dow Chemical acquired Le Petit in pharmaceuticals, and likewise Gillette acquired Du-Pont in France where Cricket lighters had been developed. Carnation is a company that entered many foreign markets by acquisition, and acquired overseas R&D capability in several new product areas this way.

U.S. Tax Law Changes   For United States firms the attractiveness of expanding abroad can increase with changes in application of United States tax law. Assume an American firm does all of its R&D in the United States but has half of its sales abroad. If the firm can get credit on its United States taxes for only the proportion of R&D corresponding to its United States sales, then, in this case, it has one half of its R&D uncovered. This would give the firm an incentive to move some or all of that uncovered part abroad where it, too, could enjoy a tax savings.[9] This is an oversimplified illustration of a complex topic, but it does indicate the potential influence of tax considerations on R&D locations.

It is possible that some multinationals have not yet addressed the question of whether to conduct R&D abroad, but have merely continued to do all their R&D at home. Many others, however, have had to face the issue either when it was raised by their subsidiaries or foreign governments, or when they acquired a foreign firm with R&D. Rather than responding to such events on an ad hoc basis, the firm can improve its decision making by incorporating

R&D location policy into its overall strategy for international business development. Historically, much of the internationalization of a firm's marketing, production, and especially R&D, has been relatively unplanned. All three activities should be part of the firm's global strategic planning.

This article will offer no solutions to the questions raised. In contrast to the internationalizing of marketing and production, the theories and strategies for internationalizing R&D are relatively underdeveloped. More study is needed by both business planners and academic investigators. As a contribution to that study, the author suggests the following generalizations for further investigation and testing.

Some Generalizations on the Location of R&D

Multinationals conduct most of their R&D in their home countries. The proportion done in the United States by American firms is about ninety percent, but this depends somewhat on accounting practices and definitions.[10] Canadian firms may be an exception to this, since some of them have transferred R&D to the United States.

Increasingly multinationals are conducting R&D in their foreign markets. For all United States firms the amount spent on foreign R&D in 1966 was about 500 million dollars or 7.4 percent of United States expenditures. The amount spent abroad in 1972 was over 1.2 billion dollars or 10 percent of United States corporate expenditures.[11] An industry example is given by the United States drug industry which increased its foreign R&D from five percent of the total in 1960 to ten percent of the total in 1970. The drug industry illustrates both generalizations: most R&D is done at home but a growing proportion is done abroad.

The larger markets of the firm will have the earliest and largest share of the multinationals' foreign R&D activity. For American firms, this means primarily Canada and Western Europe, with Brazil the leading host country in Latin America. In fact, three countries account for almost two-thirds of the overseas R&D of United States companies—Canada, the United Kingdom, and Germany.[12] European firms conduct above average amounts of R&D in the large United States market. And Canadian based multinationals have even transferred significant segments of R&D to the United States from Canada. At the same time, multinationals conduct only limited R&D in developing countries, though the amount is growing. For United States firms the proportion of foreign R&D conducted in the less developed countries rose from 1.8 percent in 1966 to 3.3 percent in 1972. For less developed countries, Ben-Porath has discussed the implications of size and level of development for investment in R&D.[13]

For a country to become an R&D location it must have sufficient scientific and technical personnel. If it has these, it may be a small or less developed country and still attract R&D. Swedish SKF chose Holland as the location of a major R&D center. Cyanamid chose the Philippines for a regional R&D center. In both cases personnel considerations were critical. On the basis of size and availability of personnel, India is a good candidate. On the other hand, General Motors developed its Basic Transportation Vehicle in the United States because of a lack of qualified personnel in the target markets.

Acquisition of foreign companies is a major means by which multinationals initiate or expand foreign R&D. This is true even though the major reason for the acquisition usually has nothing to do with R&D but is primarily a means of market entry. Firms tend to keep the R&D they acquire. Ronstadt's study of seven United States multinationals found that 25 percent of their foreign R&D was in facilities acquired when they bought local firms and then continued their R&D activity.[14] Britain's Imperial Chemical Industries acquired Atlas Chemical in the United States and not only continued its R&D but switched over to the United States some products that were being developed in Britain.

Frequently the acquisition represents a new area of R&D for the firm: for example, Braun and small appliances for Gillette; Knorr and soups for Corn Products Company. Another inducement to the acquisition of foreign R&D is that R&D abroad is ahead of United States R&D in some product areas. Some examples in pharmaceuticals are the following: Smith Kline & French bought the Belgian lab that developed the Rubella vaccine for measles; Merck, an R&D leader, paid out 5.9 million dollars in royalties for drugs developed abroad while receiving only 4.9 million dollars.

Industry and product line are variables in this decision. There is more decentralization in consumer goods than in industrial goods. Whenever local market characteristics, adaptation, and testing are important, there is more local R&D than when technical considerations predominate. For example, there is more decentralized R&D in food than in non-food consumer goods; more decentralization with automobiles than with tractors or diesel engines; more with pharmaceuticals than with chemicals. However, the evidence also suggests that there is no product or industry in which technical factors are the sole influence. A good example is the chemical industry which, though highly technically oriented, usually needs some decentralization of R&D, especially at the development end. This can be seen in the experience of Cyanamid, Dow, and DuPont, among others.

Host government pressures and incentives do influence the location of R&D. Some examples were given earlier. There is evidence that several countries have had some success in attracting local R&D by multinationals, for example Britain, Canada, France, Spain, Brazil, and India.

An important variable in the decentralization of R&D is the divisibility of R&D as a corporate activity. It is divisible on at least two bases: one is by product line, and the other is by the nature or level of the R&D.

Product Line R&D Decentralization   R&D decentralization by product line is especially common when a multinational enters a new product area by acquisition. The examples of Carnation, Corn Products Company, Dow and Gillette have been cited earlier. However, R&D decentralization by product line also occurs apart from acquisition. Many multinationals have a policy of decentralizing R&D by division or product line. Corn Products Company has its R&D for industrial products centered in its Belgian subsidiary. Imperial Chemical Company assigns to ICI-Europe the research on fibers and polymers, and to ICI-America the basic research on resins, pharmaceuticals and specialty chemicals, with all the other areas being covered by ICI-UK. In the computer field, Burroughs, Honeywell, and IBM all do significant R&D abroad for varied parts of their product line.

Decentralization by Level of Technology   Generally, the simpler the technology and the closer to the development end of the R&D spectrum, the more multinationals will decentralize. Ronstadt found the primary reason seven major United States multinationals established R&D abroad was to help transfer technology from the parent to the subsidiary.[15] Kacker found that twenty-six United States firms in India did almost no basic research but concentrated on applied research to determine the feasibility of using local materials in the firms' products.[16] Cordell found that multinationals' R&D in Canada is also primarily of the support or application variety.[17] Hood and Young find the same thing with regard to United States multinationals in Scotland.[18]

Crookell notes, "When the product has a high technological content, the subsidiary usually depends on the parent for the basic research . . . . When the technology content of the product is low, the skills of the sub may be sufficient to develop it alone. For example, Canadian General Electric introduced a lawn trimmer in Canada. The parent company didn't follow this so CGE was able to secure access to the United States through G.E.'s extensive distribution system".[19]

Once foreign R&D is established by the firm, it tends to evolve away from technology transfer and adaptation toward more basic research and product development. Many of the forces behind the initial establishment on foreign R&D cause it to evolve in the direction of greater sophistication. The work of Leroy and Ronstadt confirms the author's findings here. Hewlett-Packard's foreign R&D began as technology transfer but evolved rather quickly into product development to the extent that over one-fourth of H-P's overseas sales are of products developed locally. Many of Ronstadt's respondents stated that the best incentive they could offer their R&D people was the opportunity to become involved with more challenging technology. Technical service work was not demanding enough to challenge and retain their best people.[20]

Foreign R&D follows foreign direct investment and tends to be associated with manufacturing operations. Firms do not usually establish foreign R&D units in isolation. Foreign manufacturing is the first presence of the firm abroad, usually after some export experience. Later in the firm's international development may come foreign R&D. This R&D is almost always associated with manufacturing operations because its initial purpose is to aid in the transfer of technology from the parent firm. This has been noted in the Creamer, Leroy and Ronstadt studies, but it is also verified in the experience of most multinationals.

The longer the firm has been engaged in international business and the larger this business is relative to the total, the more decentralized is the firm's R&D. This has been shown for the United States pharmaceutical industry and can be illustrated in the case histories of most multinationals. Leroy found it to be almost a part of the growth pattern of the United States and Canadian multinationals he studied.[21] It is verified in the experience of United States companies in England also.[22]

Conclusions

From our discussion there emerges no simple model to help a firm decide whether to conduct foreign R&D. There are strong arguments both for centralizing and for decentralizing R&D in the multinational company. An individual or case approach may be necessary in this decision. We have identified many of the variables a firm must consider. The question has been made more urgent for American firms because of recent interpretations by the IRS. The issue of R&D location is becoming more pressing for all multinationals, however, because of the demands by the third world for increased technology transfer in the New International Economic Order. Further research can aid decision making in this area.

QUESTIONS

1. What strategy alternatives are available to a multinational firm seeking to introduce products in foreign markets?
2. What are the arguments for maintaining a centralized or domestic R&D function?
3. What are the arguments for decentralizing R&D abroad?
4. What factors determine the feasibility of firms locating R&D facilities in foreign countries?

NOTES

1. Creamer, D.B., *Overseas Research and Development by U.S. Multinationals,* 1966–1975, New York, The Conference Board, 1976, 7.

2. *Ibid.,* 4.

3. Ronstadt, R.C., R&D Abroad, unpublished dissertation, Harvard University, 121.

4. *Multinational Chemical Companies,* New York, Manufacturing Chemists Association, 1974, 8.

5. Creamer, *op. cit.,* 6.

6. See for example: Jewkes, J., *et al., The Sources of Invention,* New York, St. Martin's Press, 1959.

   Arrow, K., "The Economic Implications of Learning by Doing," *Review of Economic Studies,* Vol. 29, No. 80, (1962), 155–173.

   Hollander, S., *The Sources of Increased Efficiency,* Cambridge, Massachusetts, MIT Press, 1965.

7. Ronstadt, *op. cit.,* 186.

8. Leroy, G., *Multinational Product Strategy,* New York, Praeger, 1976, 105–106.

9. Conversation with Michael Lake, Tax Manager, Clark Equipment.

10. Creamer, *op. cit.,* 4.

11. *Ibid.*

12. *Ibid.*

13. Ben-Porath, Y., "Some Implications of Economic Size and Level for Investment in R&D," *Economic Development and Cultural Change,* (October, 1972), 96–103.

14. Ronstadt, *op. cit.,* 120.

15. *Ibid.,* 121.

16. Kacker, M., *Marketing Adaptation of U.S. Firms in India,* New Delhi, Sterling Publishers, 1974, 43.

17. Cordell, A.J., "Innovation, the MNC and Some Implications for National Science Policy," *Long Range Planning,* (September, 1973), 22–29.

18. Hood, N., and S. Young, "U.S. Investment in Scotland," *Scottish Journal of Political Economy,* (November, 1976), 279–294.

19. Crookell, H., "The Transmission of Technology Across National Boundaries," *The Business Quarterly,* (Autumn, 1973), 52–60.

20. Ronstadt, *op. cit.,* 175.

21. Leroy, *op. cit.*

22. Hood and Young, *op. cit.,* 286.

How can international marketers better monitor the performance of their products in worldwide markets? The author presents an interesting case for the application of product life cycle conceptual framework as a means of evaluating international marketing strategies. The implications of identifying product characteristics and specifying their relationships to corporate and marketing strategies are also explored.

21. Product Life Cycle as a Determinant of Global Marketing Strategies

Jose de la Torre
INSEAD

There can be little doubt of the increasing importance of the international environment for United States enterprises. In the last four years we have witnessed two major crises in the international monetary system, considerable advances in East-West economic relations, and a significant rise in foreign investment flows into the United States. In 1971 the United States suffered its first trade deficit since 1888 (reaching more than $6 billion in 1972), touching off significant protectionist sentiment in various quarters, and resulting in the introduction before Congress of numerous pieces of restrictive legislation. The outlook for the future continues to be rather pessimistic as imports of oil, gas, and other fuels will reach staggering proportions.

For the marketing executive concerned with global markets, these developments strike at the core of his area of responsibility. What factors determine the degree of international competitiveness of his various product

Source: Reprinted by permission of the publisher and the author from *Atlanta Economic Review* September–October, 1975, pp. 9–14.

lines? How can consumer needs in different environments best be met? Which products should be produced in which countries to supply which markets?

This article discusses a framework which allows the international marketing executive to evaluate his products' performance in world markets and, more importantly, to predict changes in their performance over time. By having some concept of future trends in relative competitiveness, the firm can anticipate any changes in strategy necessary to reduce its exposure to changing trade patterns. The use of the same framework also is illustrated as an aid in assessing the suitability of a particular marketing strategy which has evolved in one market to other markets the firm may wish to enter.

The concept of *product life cycles* certainly is not new to marketing students or practitioners. Application of the S-shaped growth curve to sales forecasting can be found as early as 1922.[1] What is relatively new is the attempt to expand its use as a marketing tool to include the international dimension.

Traditionally, the product life cycle has been viewed as having four distinct stages:

Introduction—A new product (or concept) is introduced to the market on a very limited basis and subject to changes in design and technology. Demand is small and growing slowly. Advertising expenditures are high as a percentage of sales (increased awareness is being sought), channels are courted to stock the product and push it, and a skimming price strategy is most probable.

Growth—If the product makes it past the early stages, demand begins to accelerate at increasing rates. Competition becomes a critical factor as others try to copy or improve on the product, and brand differentiation begins to develop. Promotional strategy shifts to establishing brand preferences among old and new customers alike. Larger production runs and technological advances permit lower prices; while unit margins may decrease, total profitability reaches its peak during this period.

Maturity—Demand grows at a decreasing rate, or stabilizes according to external factors such as substitutes, replacements, and growth rates in population and income. The market is saturated with producers engaged in substantial communication expenditures aimed at maintaining market share. Product differentiation on the basis of either price or marginal product changes, or both, is critical for survival. Competition takes its toll of marginal producers resulting in higher industry concentration.

Decline—Over-capacity and a decrease in per capita demand signify the end to all but a few efficient producers, who often lower promotional expenditures and spare each other any further grief. The product is allowed a graceful exit from the public mind.[2]

Although most products follow such a cycle, their individual behavior differs widely. Consumer goods, especially certain fashion items, often have short life cycles that might skip a stage. For example, the hula-hoop craze of the early 1950s had a total of one summer's duration, exhibiting no introductory or mature stages. Other products, notably basic industrial goods, may experience a long life cycle in which maturity consists of a slow creeping growth in sales over time. The shape of the cycle curve also can be influenced by direct action. A firm may, for example, promote more frequent or varied usage among present users, or it may seek new users in new markets or through new applications of the basic material. DuPont's experience with nylon demonstrates the feasibility of all these strategies. In the absence of these efforts, nylon consumption would have reached a saturation level of 50 million pounds of annual consumption by 1962. Instead, consumption in that year exceeded 500 million pounds as the market for nylon expanded to tires, carpeting, clothing, and so on.[3]

Discussion of life cycles typically has been limted to changing marketing characteristics. Yet many other aspects of the product or its manufacture also are subject to significant variations throughout the life cycle. Exhibit 21-1 summarizes how some critical product, production, and industry characteristics change over the cycle, among which the following stand out:

1. Early *technology* typically is unstable and untried. Changes are frequent, but technology stabilizes as product acceptance increases and the opportunities for product modification and innovation decrease. The near monopoly status and control over patents, which characterize the early period, also yield to greater diffusion of knowledge over time.

2. At the introductory stage *production* is carried out in small batches, employs multipurpose equipment, and is product centered. The competitive scramble that follows brings about search for lower manufacturing costs through value engineering, process innovations, longer production runs, and greater use of automation. Eventually, mass production techniques prevail.

3. The relative use of *capital* in the production process over time is related to the foregoing discussion. In the early stages, product-centered runs and the uncertainty attached to any manufacturing process argue for little investment in capital equipment. The situation is reversed, however, at the mass production stage.

4. Following the same reasoning, *labor* intensity is higher at the early stages, before any significant capital substitution takes place. However, the skill distribution of the labor force also varies substantially during the cycle. A high concentration of scientific and engineering personnel characterizes the manufacturing process for new products. In contrast, semiskilled and unskilled workers make up the majority of the diminished labor content involved in manufacturing each unit of the mature product.

Trade and Policy Implications

The United States market is particularly suited for new product introductions because of its large population and high income per capita.[4] It is not

EXHIBIT 21-1

Summary of Product Characteristics Throughout the Life Cycle

Characteristics	Stage of the Life Cycle		
	Introduction	Growth	Maturity
Technology	rapidly changing and adapting to consumer preferences	few product variations of importance with various degrees of refinement; process innovations critical	both product and process stable; no major design innovations of importance
	closely held by innovating firm; no licensing or sale	patent variations decrease monopoly of technology; some diffusion and licensing	readily available and transferable
Production	product centered	shifting to process	process centered
	short runs; prototype manufacturing	larger runs; mass production introduced although techniques may differ	long runs; stable processes
Capital	low use of capital; multipurpose equipment	increased utilization	high investment in specialized equipment
Industry structure	innovating firm leads, with others entering field to capitalize on success	large number of firms; many casualties and mergers; growing integration	number of firms declining with lower margins
	know-how principal barrier to entry	financial resources critical growth	established marketing position principal barrier to entry
Human inputs	high scientific engineering and marketing skills	financial and production management necessary to reduce costs	unskilled and semi-skilled labor; marketing
Marketing and demand structure	sellers' market	balanced market	buyers' market
	low price elasticity; "snob appeal"	growing price elasticity	high price elasticity for individual producers
	high introductory marketing effort in communication and awareness	beginning product differentiation; distribution critical	high brand and product differentiation may appear through various means
	high monopoly prices	increased competition reducing prices	lower prices and margins

uncommon to find a high incidence of product innovations introduced to the marketplace much in the same manner described previously.[5] During these early days, the producer feels a strong need for close association with his market. He seeks to minimize the costs of interacting with customers and suppliers, and among the firm's various units (e.g., marketing, R&D, engineering, and production), precisely at the time when such communication is critical for dealing with rapidly changing market and technological conditions.

During this time foreign demand also develops, particularly in those countries with income to those prevailing in the United States. This foreign demand is satisfied through imports from the United States since local production neither exists nor is yet contemplated. At this time,

$$\text{(A) } C_E > C_{US} + t_{US \rightarrow E} + d_E.$$

That is, the cost of manufacturing abroad, Europe, for instance (C_E), is greater than the United States manufacturing cost (C_{US}), plus transportation from the United States to Europe $(t_{US \rightarrow E})$, plus European import duties and/or other nontariff restrictions (d_E). Manufacturing costs at any location are principally a function of:

Volume, which in turn is a function of the size of the local market, population, income, and so forth.

Technological complexity, of both product and process.

Economics of scale, which are dictated by the nature of the product and the process technology available.

Factor costs, such as the cost of capital and of various skill categories of labor.

Absorptive capacity, in terms of the country's ability to absorb and utilize the given technology.

Availability of *external economies.*

A critical observation is that all of these factors are dynamic in nature. As the United States market expands, unit costs and prices decrease, and technology stabilizes and becomes more accessible. But foreign markets also are growing, and with it their ability to undertake local production. The time comes when inequality (A) is reversed (point P_E in Exhibit 21-2). At this point, given some tariff protection and lower factor costs overseas, foreign production can compete with United States imports even though operating at smaller volumes. The exporting firm must now choose between loss of its export markets or investment in foreign production facilities.

Exports from the United States grow more slowly after this point as still other advanced countries follow suit in manufacturing the product internally. United States exports will shift to the smaller developed and the less developed countries (LDC) with markets still too small to justify local production. The new producers in Europe and Japan may not yet compete

EXHIBIT 21-2
U.S. TRADE IN THE PRODUCT LIFE CYCLE

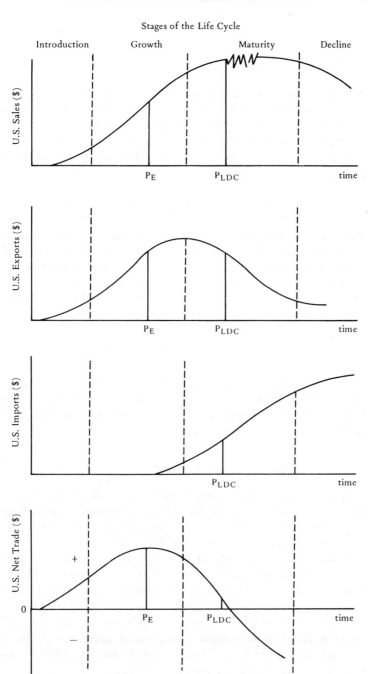

with United States goods in these markets, where both face similar tariff and transportation obstacles. Hence,

$$\text{(B)} \quad C_{US} + t_{US \to LDC} + d_{LDC} < C_E + t_{E \to LDC} + d_{LDC}$$

and the United States will continue to hold a lead in these markets for some time.

As demand in Europe and other advanced countries exceeds minimum requirements to achieve economies of scale, their lower factor costs will give these producers the necessary edge to compete with United States production in third markets, that is, inequality (B) will reverse also. In fact, as European and Japanese producers expand their markets through exports, the time may come where,

$$\text{(C)} \quad C_{US} > C_E + t_{E \to US} + d_{US}$$

and the United States begins to import the now maturing product. Negative United States trade balances in that product category will soon follow.

Eventually, developing countries will commence production (point P_{LDC} in Exhibit 21-2) as they, too, have expanding markets served by imports. An upward adjustment of the "d" factor (tariffs and other forms of protection in the LCDs) in

$$\text{(D)} \quad C_{US} + t_{US \to LDC} + d_{LDC} < C_{LDC}$$

will result in the necessary economic justification for local manufacturing. The model predicts further that these countries, having the lowest labor costs of all, eventually will dominate world markets in mature standardized products, and

$$\text{(E)} \quad C_{US} > C_E > C_{LDC} + t_{LDC \to US/E} + d_{US/E}$$

where $t_{LDC \to US/E}$ indicates transportation cost to the United States and Europe, and $d_{US/E}$ indicates tariffs and other forms of protection in the United States and Europe. Certain textile products, shoes, furniture, and leather products are but a few examples of this trend.

This model, as all generalizations, is subject to errors of oversimplification. Many products never enter the trade cycle for reasons of high transportation costs, specialized production, or limited demand. Also, market segmentation permits two-way trade flows in similar products, as in the case in automobiles (the United States exporting style, luxury, and size and importing economy, low maintenance costs, and maneuverability). Nevertheless, the general pattern is sufficiently valid to warrant its use for policy recommendations at both the national and corporate level.

National Policy

Space considerations render impossible an adequate treatment of the implications of the product life cycle model for national policy, but a few observations are in order. First, the United States must maintain a continuous stream of innovations if it is to sustain a surplus cumulative trade balance. Whether this is possible, as the experience of the last two years seems to contradict, depends on many underlying factors, among which four stand out:

1. The rate of innovation in the United States as compared with that prevailing in Europe, Japan, and other advanced countries.
2. The rate of technological diffusion and of absorptive capacity in other countries.
3. The differential rate of growth between the United States and foreign incomes.
4. The relative rate of change of factor costs—principally changes in wage rates, productivity, inflation, and the exchange rate.

The evidence seems to indicate that recent trends in most of these factors have been against the United States. For example, most European countries and Japan were expanding R&D expenditures as a percentage of GNP during the 1966–1971 period, while the United States percentage declined.[6] Foreign licensing of technology to the United States during the last five years has increased faster than United States licensing overseas. Also, United States export prices increased by 18 percent in 1966–1971, compared with increases of 9 percent for Japan and 12 percent for Germany. This was due primarily to the adverse effects of low productivity increases coupled with rapid inflation in the United States during that period.

Policies are needed which go beyond seeking currency realignments and reduction of trade barriers, although these constitute desirable elements of a comprehensive program. Yet, if the combined effects of high price inflation and low productivity vis-à-vis our trading partners is not reversed, only a constant stream of current adjustments can maintain United States international competitiveness.

A dynamic long-term approach is required to a problem which is basically evolutionary in nature. The 1974 Trade Act takes a step in that direction by recognizing that the United States can maintain domestic production of certain mature product lines only at considerable cost and protection. Thus, while favoring generalized tariff preferences for developing countries, it calls for national assistance to firms and employees in the low-technology, mature end of the product spectrum.

United States inventiveness must be rejuvenated. An increased flow of new products in frontier technology areas (e.g., pollution control equipment) will contribute substantially to a positive trade balance. Innovation in production processes will improve United States productivity and lengthen the

cycle by increasing United States competitiveness overseas. Measures and incentives aimed at promoting a greater flow of R&D funds will contribute
more than any other single factor to the long-term competitiveness of the
United States in world markets.

Corporate Implications

Most companies are subject to similar cycles which determine their competitiveness in the international arena. New products exhibit significant
export potential; older, mature products are subject to intense foreign competition. A knowledge of the cycle characteristics of a product allows the
firm to plan in advance not only a marketing strategy to meet domestic competition, but appropriate strategies to meet foreign challenges domestically
and abroad.

This does not imply that the firm must sit impassively as "nature takes
its course" in world markets. The firm may innovate in product design, seek
new users, or seek new markets among the less developed countries, and in so
doing superimpose a new cycle on the old one. It may rely on a strategy of
new product development. It may undertake process innovations that,
through increased productivity, prolong the firm's cost advantage in world
markets. It may attempt to differentiate its products to secure brand loyalty
or other similar advantages over the cheaper competition. Alternatively, the
firm may attempt all of these strategies in various degrees. Or, as has been increasingly the case, the firm may attempt to obtain maximum returns by
following an international logistics policy geared to the life cycle model.

This last strategy holds considerable promise for the firm. Export markets for new products allow greater unit cost reductions and quicker amorti-
zation of development costs than would be possible from domestic sales
alone. As the product matures and foreign demand increases, the company
can extend the benefits derived from its marketing and technical know-how
by entering foreign markets with production facilities, preempting similar
moves by United States or other competitors. As costs become critical in the
competitive struggle and the domestic market is threatened, the United States
firm is in an ideal position to exploit its knowledge of the United States
market and its established domestic distribution channels by moving manufacturing of mature standardized products to low-wage developing countries.
The United States electronics and apparel industries have followed such
policies with great success over the last five years. By following this sequence
of strategy adjustments, the firm can maximize returns over the life cycle
and minimize the risks of being surprised by competitive moves.

Marketing Program Implications

Marketing literature often has discussed the dilemma between standardization and adaptation in international operations.[7] The incentives for stand-

ardizing marketing programs on a global basis are significant, e.g., lower unit design costs and easier monitoring of performance. Yet the international competitive road is littered with the remains of those that stood firmly against the challenge of local adaptation.

A recent study that looked into more than 200 cases of international "blunders" by United States companies bears witness to the dangers of a homogeneous strategy.[8] Over 53 percent of all the blunders identified and documented by the researchers were in the marketing area. If consumer product industries were isolated from the rest of the sample, the incidence of marketing errors rose to over 75 percent. Most significantly, nearly all of these blunders occurred when the firm introduced one of its domestically successful products into a new foreign market. The lesson seems to be: beware of success lest it cloud your vision.

Whether or not adaptation is required, and (more critically) to what extent, is a complex but vital decision falling squarely on the shoulders of the executive with responsibility for foreign market entry. A number of analytical frameworks have been suggested to assist him in his task. In all of these it appears that the transferability of a standard marketing package is dependent on the interrelationship between two factors:

The degree of dissonance between the two environments as measured by (a) differences in consumer behavior, in turn determined by a host of sociological, cultural, economic, and political factors; and (b) differences in institutions, such as the media, the legal and regulatory environment, or the existence of appropriate channels.

The nature of the product, that is, how it is or might be used, the needs it satisfies, whether these are basic or culture-bound, its substitutes, and so on.

Levels of Adjustment

An analysis of the blunders data, as well as these other studies, seems to indicate that there are two levels of potential adjustment and that these may be treated differently. The first level we might call the "elementary adjustment." This is limited, for example, to some simple changes in the product (e.g., change voltage from 110 to 220), channels (e.g., increase number of outlets due to lower sales volume per outlet), or communication (e.g., translation and cultural debriefing) strategies. This elementary adjustment assumes that the basic home country strategy is adequate and transferable and needs only some fine tuning.

The requirements of this first stage of adjustment are comparatively simple. A check is made for legal considerations affecting the use of copy materials, advertising claims, and so forth; an experienced linguist is contracted for the necessary translations, always observant to the danger of making a cultural faux pax; media selection is adjusted to its availability, quality, and impact, as is channel selection; and prices, budgets, and other administrative details are brought in line with competitive factors and profitability considerations.

Although apparently simple, many serious errors have been committed at this first level. A national producer of soft drinks had the company's brand name impressed in Chinese characters which were phonetically accurate. It was discovered later, however, that the translation's literal meaning was "female horse fattened with wax," hardly the image the company sought to portray. General Motors' copywriters in Europe found out to their chagrin the "Body by Fisher" had been translated in their Flemish ads to the equivalent of "Corpse by Fisher."

The second level of adjustment, however, requires some fundamental rethinking of the product's place in the new market, quite separately from any previous successes experienced in the home or other markets. It is at this level than an analysis based on comparative life cycle considerations can be most useful. A classic example of an ill-fated transfer illustrates the importance of these considerations.

In late 1965 Polaroid introduced the Model 20 "Swinger" Land Camera in the United States at a suggested retail price of $19.95. This model placed Polaroid for the first time in the mass market for inexpensive cameras (less than $50 retail), which accounted for over three-fourths of all still cameras purchased yearly in the United States. The results were phenomenal. Polaroid sales jumped by over 50 percent in 1965 and by nearly 60 percent in 1966. The company reported more than five million Swinger cameras sold by "sometime in 1969."

Polaroid had designed a product aimed at this mass market. It was simple and inexpensive. Extensive national advertising (nearly 6 percent of sales in 1965 and 1966) displayed these features prominently, capitalizing on the previously established reputation of Polaroid and its concept of instant photography. Television accounted for nearly one-half of the total advertising budget, and the emphasis on Swinger advertising shifted from the earlier educational message to a low price and "swinging" appeal. Distribution was made directly to over 15,000 retailers, including many, such as drugstores, that had never carried Polaroid cameras before. Discounters often offered the Swinger at prices well below the suggested retail price (as low as $14), featuring it as a promotional item or loss leader.

In September 1966 Polaroid France, S.A. introduced the Swinger to the French market. With the concurrence of its United States advertising firm, Polaroid France's marketing program for the Swinger was patterned closely after its successful United States counterpart. The price was set at 99 FF ($19.90). Advertising and promotion was heavily emphasized, although the lack of commercial television required a shift in the relative allocation of the promotion budget. Dealers were encouraged to demonstrate the cameras and in-store sales demonstrations were arranged, although trade margins were kept to a minimum on the assumption of large volumes. In essence, the strategy consisted of a well-planned, internally consistent pull effort similar to that which had propelled United States sales of Polaroid to record heights.

Yet there were substantial differences between the French and United States camera markets. In general terms, the French market was much smaller and more heavily skewed toward the lowest price ranges (less than $10) and toward the older, wealthier segments of the population. Specialty stores, where personal contact was critical, accounted for over 75 percent of all camera sales. Most significantly, studies conducted by the company's research staff had shown that in early 1966 fewer than 5 percent of French consumers demonstrated "proved awareness" of the Polaroid concept of photography. This compared with a level of awareness of 85 percent in the United States. This fact combined with the lack of television exposure—believed to be the major factor in the rapid sales expansion experienced in the United States—to render the company's successful United States strategy ineffective in France. Conditions in the French market required a different approach, one based on developing both consumer awareness of the product concept and the distribution capability required for a mass-market merchandising effort.

There are many other examples. A major United States food company introduced its soup concentrates to the Dutch market on the assumption that the transition from canned soups to concentrates would be made without difficulty. After a period of poor sales performance, the company came to the realization that insufficient attention had been paid to the product's stage in the life cycle. Consumers who purchased the soup concentrate would simply heat the contents as they did with ordinary canned soups. As a result, they questioned the strong taste and the higher price compared with a similar-sized can of regular soup. The company had tried to skip the early stages of the cycle unsuccessfully.

This is not to imply that one would automatically revert to an earlier strategy when seeking new markets. But simple elementary adjustments may not be sufficient to ensure success in the transplant. The comparative use of the product life cycle concept allows the firm to analyze the validity of its "proven" strategy when transferred to a new environment in which market conditions may differ substantially and in critical ways from those prevailing at home. The use of this concept, in conjunction with the other necessary analyses, should contribute to a better fit of strategies to markets.

QUESTIONS

1. What is the product life cycle?
2. How do the major characteristics of a product change over the course of its life cycle?
3. How can knowledge of these changes be used by international marketers in developing strategies?

NOTES

1. One of the earliest references to its use is found in Raymond B. Prescott, "Law of Growth in Forecasting Demand," *Journal of the American Statistical Association,* December 1922, pp. 471–479, as reported in Robert D. Buzzell, "Competitive Behavior and Product Life Cycles," in *New Ideas for Successful Marketing,* edited by John S. Wright and Jac L. Goldstucker (Chicago, American Marketing Association, 1966), pp. 46–68.

2. There are many references in marketing literature to this concept. Some utilize more than four stages, but the basic model remains the same. See, for example, Theodore Levitt, "Exploit the Product Life Cycle," *Harvard Business Review,* November–December 1965, pp. 81–94; Chester R. Wasson, *Product Management: Product Life Cycle and Competitive Marketing Strategy* (St. Charles, Illinois, Challenge Books, 1971), pp. 81–94; and John E. Smallwood, "The Product Life Cycle: A Key to Strategic Market Planning," *MSU Business Topics,* Winter 1973, pp. 29–35.

3. See Levitt, "Exploit the Product Life Cycle," pp. 89–90.

4. One of the first expositions of this theme can be found in Louis T. Wells, Jr., "A Product Life Cycle for Industrial Trade?" *Journal of Marketing,* July 1968, pp. 1–6. For a detailed and more theoretical coverage of the subject, see Wells, ed., *The Product Life Cycle and International Trade* (Boston, Harvard Business School, 1972).

5. The relationship of income, education, and other factors to innovation is widely covered in the literature. Two principal characteristics of early adaptors include high income and youth, characteristics typically found in combination within the United States market to a larger extent than in other markets. For a treatment of innovation and its relationship to various consumer characteristics see, for example, E.M. Rogers, *Diffusion of Innovation* (New York, The Free Press of Glencoe, 1962). Whether innovation is in fact a result of attempts to satisfy unfulfilled needs in the marketplace, or, in the Galbraithean sense, demand is created by the innovator post-facto does not alter significantly the concepts developed here.

6. See, for example, Pierre Aigrain, "Trends on Research Funding," *Physics Today,* November 1974, pp. 32–37. It should be noted that while funding levels for R&D in the United States have declined relative to most other advanced countries, the United States still maintains a significant edge in terms of the absolute level of R&D effort, both on a per capita basis and as a percent of GNP.

7. There are many studies dealing with the alternatives open to the company. Three excellent articles are Robert D. Buzzell, "Can You Standardize Multinational Marketing?" *Harvard. Business Review,* November-December 1968, pp. 102–113; Richard H. Holton, "Marketing Policies in Multinational Corporations," *Journal of International Business Studies,* Summer 1970, pp. 1–20; and Warren Keegan, "Multinational Product Planning: Strategic Alternatives," *Journal of Marketing,* January 1969, pp. 58-62. For additional references, see Jac L. Goldstucker and Jose de la Torre, *International Marketing,* Bibliography Series No. 19 (Chicago, American Marketing Association, 1972).

8. David Ricks, Marilyn Y.C. Fu, and Jeffrey Arpan, *International Business Blunders* (Columbus, Ohio, Grid, Inc., 1974).

*From the extended or total product con-
cept, the transfer of technology is an important marketing concern. This article deals
with the policies and issues involved in exporting technology from advanced countries
to less-developed countries. Particular emphasis is placed on pricing and property
rights, technological appropriateness, and
environmental impact.*

22. Technology Transfer to Less Developed Countries

Jerry R. Ladman
*Arizona State
University*

The Problem

The importance of technology in the growth of civilization has been amply
recognized by historians who have labeled progressive stages of human development as the Stone, Bronze, Machine and Atomic Ages. Yet within each
of these ages, the fruits of available technology have been unevenly distributed. This has led to a somewhat uneven pattern of growth of the different civilizations and regions of the world. Thus, over the course of history,
technology in the form of both consumer and producer goods has tended to
be transfered from those countries which have developed the technology to
those which did not have it.

During the Industrial Revolution technological development was concentrated in Western Europe and the United States; thus these regions became
centers of manufacturing activities. In sharp contrast most of the nations of

Source: Reprinted from *Arizona Business* (October 1977), Bureau of Business and Economic Research, College of Business Administration, Arizona State University.

Africa, Asia and Latin America had experienced little technological advancement except in mining and some agricultural production. In accordance with the principle of comparative advantage, trade of manufactured goods and raw materials developed between the industrial nations and the primary materials-producing countries. This pattern continued well into the twentieth century. Technology transfer in this stage was basically in the form of introducing consumer goods developed in the advanced western culture countries via trade to the primary materials-producing countries. To a much lesser extent some production technology was transferred through foreign investment and the immigration of entrepreneurs and skilled labor.

In the latter part of the nineteenth century the technologically advanced countries began to undertake more direct foreign investment—and the associated technology transfer—in the poorer countries. Involved were not only raw materials production, but also transportation, communications and public utilities. The major transfers of technology continued, however, as a result of international trade.

A major change in this trend occurred when the less developed countries (LDCs) which produce raw materials realized, as a result of the severe shocks of World Wars I and II and the Great Depression, that they could not rely on the export of primary products as the engine of growth of their economies. They then turned to industrialization and constructed protective tariffs to encourage domestic manufacturing under programs of import substitution.

The response was twofold. First, foreign firms, which had identified markets in these countries through their previous exports, immediately jumped the tariff barriers and began local production of the same goods. Second, the domestic firms secured licenses from foreigners for the rights to produce and distribute products which had foreign patents and trademarks. Therefore, in this stage the processes of technology transfer not only continued the pattern of introducing western culture style goods to the LDCs but more importantly led to the establishment of manufacturing facilities in these countries utilizing the techniques of the western world. This same pattern continued as the LDCs began to look to regional trade groupings and export markets as additional stimuli for economic growth.

Strong arguments can be developed in favor of a world economic system based on trade in accordance with the principle of comparative advantage as well as international movements of resources. Yet, in the last several decades, concern swelled from critics who argue that such a situation has only led to a dependency of the IDCs on the developed countries (DCs) for imported products, export markets, investment capital and technology. The rise of the multinational corporation (MNC) in recent years has only served to strengthen this position since these large firms exhibit such a strong base of economic power and associated political leverage and influence.[1]

In earlier times the question of technology transfer was largely confined to academic papers. In the 1970s the question of technology transfer from the DCs to the LDCs has become an important issue on the international scene. This is especially true since a number of LDCs have passed new and more restrictive legislation on the subject. The reasons for this increasing importance are readily evident. On the one hand, almost all of modern technology has been developed in the DCs. On the other hand the LCDs recognize the acute need for technological innovation alongside capital investment in their countries in order to increase productivity and generate income and employment. Thus it is only natural that LDCs should look to the possibilities of foreign aid, foreign investment and technology transfer from the DCs as means to foster economic development. Whereas the roles and means of foreign aid and direct foreign investment have long been subject to question and discussion, it is only in recent years that technology transfer has come under scrutiny in international forums.

In response to threatened sovereignty and the alleged abuses of the past, a number of LDCs not only have developed new legislation dealing with technology transfer but also they have turned to the solidarity of groups in international forums in order to try to establish a power base for developing and negotiating norms for foreign investment and technology transfer. Examples include: the pronouncements of former Mexican President Luis Echeverria in his Rights of Nations speech before the 1972 United Nations Conference on Trade And Development (UNCTAD) assembly; the pronouncements of the Group of 77 less developed countries in the UNCTAD; the specific treatment of the subject in Decision 24 of the Andean Group; and the discussion of same in the Articles of Incorporation of the Latin American Economic System (SELA) in 1975. As a consequence, controversy over technology transfer between DCs and LDCs has come to the fore.

An Overview of the Issues

The purpose of this article is to identify and discuss the three key issues that surround the process of technology transfer from the DCs to the LDCs and to examine some of the policy alternatives. First is the issue of the price of technology and the rights of the sellers and buyers of same. This issue captures much of the attention in today's world because it encompasses the current and ongoing negotiations between the DCs and LDCs as well as negotiations involving private industry on both sides with respect to foreign investment and technology transfer. The ominous presence of the relatively new MNC in combination with a long history of alleged exploitation of LDCs by foreign investors and the DCs has led the LDCs to try to obtain investment and technology on much better terms than in the past. Meanwhile, owners of technology in DCs, long accustomed to having much their own way are resisting giving up this advantage. Thus there is considerable ground for negotiation on the terms with which technology will be transferred.

The second issue is considerably more subtle and less clearly understood. It deals with the appropriateness of the technology being transferred. Most technology has been developed in the economic and cultural climate of the DCs. Thus products are geared to mass consumption and a relatively wealthy society; production techniques reflect the relative scarcity of labor and abundance of capital in the DCs. In contrast, the LDCs have large segments of their economies living in a traditional context under conditions of unemployment and poverty. The relative scarcity of capital and abundance of labor suggests the need for labor-intensive production techniques, precisely the opposite that is generally available for transfer from DCs. Thus two basic questions must be raised: Is the type of technology being transferred, as embodied in consumer goods, appropriate? and Is the type of capital-intensive production technology that is being transferred appropriate?

The third issue is also subtle and of considerable long-range importance. It deals with the ecological dimensions of technology transfer. The direct and indirect effects of modern technology in DCs are widely recognized. Technology not only is a heavy user of exhaustible resources but also had created a number of polluting side effects. Thus the issue is what path the LDCs should follow in the evolution of the employment of technology and the consequent effects on the world's scarce natural resources and pollution. In the following sections each of these issues will be discussed with emphasis placed on an understanding of the concerns at hand and on setting forth some policy alternatives.

Rights and Price

Problem

The interrelated issues of the property rights of sellers and buyers of technology and the determination of a price for the technology are at the core of new LDC technology transfer legislation which is designed to protect the interests of the LDCs. The controversial nature of the laws generates strong feelings on both sides that quickly inflame the points in conflict and hence threaten to create conditions of impasse and seriously hinder the flow of technological knowledge.[2]

On the one hand, foreign owners of technology such as the MNCs, are casting about the world for opportunities to undertake foreign investment and its associated technological component or to sell its technological know-how through licensing agreements. The technology available for transfer is typically patented and thus the seller is in the position of having certain monopoly powers over his exclusive information. Therefore the sellers are in a position of not only being able to select to whom they will transfer the technology but also to negotiate from a position of power in determining the price of the technology and the conditions under which it will be employed.

On the other hand, the LDCs recognize the need for additional technology in their development programs. Under the sting of the alleged exploitation of the past, LDC governments are anxious to establish norms for technology transfer which, in their view, are more equitable than those of the past. Yet LDCs recognize, in the presence of competition for foreign investment and technology with other countries, that they must not adopt a drastic and rigid posture for fear of losing the interests of foreign suppliers of technology. Thus the battleground is established. The points in conflict essentially revolve around two distinct but interrelated issues: the property rights of both the sellers and buyers of technology and the price or cost of the technology being transferred.

At the heart of both issues is the philosophical question of ownership. Technology is information and as such embodies different characteristics than more tangible property such as physical goods. Technology is not exhaustible; it can be used over and over again. Moreover, many of the ideas that are contained in a particular technology were not developed by the owner but were gained in part from general knowledge or earlier technologies.[3] Thus the concept of technology ownership, whether protected by patents or not, is a philosophical gray area and as a consequence is subject to considerable negotiation with respect to the rights of both buyers and sellers.

Issues

There are several major points in dispute. First, what technology will be transferred? The owner is in the position of holding all the cards and he may wish to withhold some and thus not transfer his total stock of technological information. Since the buyer does not have this information, he deals in a partial vacuum and may not realize the extent of the technology, or lack of technology, he is purchasing.

Second, what products will be produced with the technology? Can the seller specify the product line to be limited to certain products or can the buyer use the same technology to produce a wider product line?

Third, what limits can the seller impose on the distribution of this product? Can they be exported? If so, they may compete with the seller's own product lines elsewhere in the world.

Fourth, will the buyer also be required to purchase and use trademarks for the products produced? This represents an additional cost to the purchaser.

Fifth, what rights does the buyer have to resell the technology or to make it available to competitors?

Sixth, and related to all of the above, what is the effective duration of any agreement between the buyer and the seller?

The determination of the price of technology is another murky theoretical issue.[4] At its root is the previously mentioned question of ownership: Does the nature of the product suggest that the seller should not expect to extract the price that his monopoly position might permit? Aside from this debatable point, the price that is determined in the marketplace should be one that is mutually satisfactory to buyer and seller. It can be expected that the marginal returns to the purchaser will be quite high, whereas the marginal cost of selling the technology will be relatively low. Thus a process of bargaining must take place in order to determine a price between these two positions. Intrinsically, however, the buyer is at a bargaining disadvantage because he does not have complete information about the technology he is purchasing. It is possible that the seller might choose to withhold information. This aspect, in combination with the sheer economic power of many sellers of technology, places the buyer at a severe disadvantage.

Historically, the sellers have, therefore, been able to establish prices very favorable to themselves. Typically the price of technology under a licensing agreement is based on an initial fee plus royalties based on a percentage of gross sales. Royalties of 3 percent of gross sales may appear on the surface to be quite reasonable but when figured on the basis of the actual value-added by the new production in the technology-purchasing country, they may be considerably higher and appear to be out of line. In the case where technology transfer is embodied in direct foreign investment there may be no technology charge per se; but an implicit price exists in terms of the amount of profits taken out of the country directly through repatriation or indirectly through higher transfer prices and high capitalization of technology on the business's books. The direct and indirect effects both contribute to an outflow of foreign exchange, and the direct effects create a lower tax base. The net effect is higher profits for the foreign investor (technology transferer) and higher costs for the host country through lower income and larger outflows of foreign exchange.

Policies

In light of the basic conflict, broad policy considerations are apparent. First, the LDCs must continue to utilize regional and international groups to espouse their collective interests and to provide a larger base of power to confront the powerful MNCs. This will serve to enhance their bargaining position for both the price and the terms of the technology transfer.

Second, as exemplified by former Secretary of State Henry Kissinger's 1975 speech to the General Assembly of the United Nations, the DCs must also be willing to work out means to facilitate the technology transfer.[5] A logical outcome will be the gradual establishment, by DC and LDC collaboration, of a set of general international norms which will provide guidelines for technology transfer. This should be done in such a way as to take into account the interests of both the buyer and the seller and not be heavily biased in a favor of the latter, which has been so typical of the past.

Third, individual LDCs must continue to develop technology transfer legislation that is more protective of their own interests not only in the context of the price and terms of the technology transfer but also the appropriateness of the technology within the context of the country's development plan. Yet at the same time the legislation should contain enough flexibility to permit the country to negotiate more liberally for technology that is crucial to its development plan and to permit effective competition with other LDCs which are alternate buyers for the available technology. If such policies are followed, a new era of technology transfer will be attained where there will be a harmonious and mutually advantageous marriage between the buyers and sellers of technology but on terms that may be less favorable than each might desire but that will be acceptable to both and workable for a long period.

Appropriate Technology

Issue

The issue of the appropriateness of the technology being transferred unfortunately does not gain the attention that it deserves. Yet in many ways it comes to the core of serious and fundamental problems that most LDCs must solve in order to escape their state of underdevelopment. There are two dimensions of the issue—demand and supply. On the demand side is the type of consumer goods that are being transferred to the LDCs. The western style of culture that is ubiquitously being transplanted around the world, as represented by the products produced, often has the effect of destroying traditional values and supplanting products that are indigenous to LDCs. While, in part, this is desirable, more attention should be given to modifying these products in such a way that will permit these cultures to maintain important aspects of their traditions and thus avoid cultural dependency. Another demand dimension is that many of these modern products have associated capital-intensive production techniques. As a result, their production in LDCs does not lend itself to absorbing labor as would the production of more simple and perhaps traditional products.

On the supply side, appropriate technology deals with production techniques that are more compatible with LDC resource endowments in order to get at the serious problems of poverty, unemployment and income distribution. Recent estimates are that at least 10 percent of the work force in most LDCs are without jobs and that 25 to 40 percent of those who work are significantly underemployed. Moreover it is estimated that 67 percent of the population in LDCs are seriously poor and 30 percent are destitute.[6] Thus strong arguments are made to utilize labor-intensive technology in order to create employment and income-earning opportunities in these countries.

The problem, as mentioned previously, is that most available technology from DCs and MNCs is capital intensive due to the resource conditions in those countries. The policy implication is that means should be utilized to develop technologies more suited to the factor endowments of LDCs. A caveat is in order, however. There are some capital-intensive production processes, for example petroleum refining, for which it is highly improbable that much less capital-intensive techniques can be developed or if they were, that they would be economical. Yet even in these cases there are possibilities of making modifications, such as in handling materials, where more labor could be employed.

Policies

Generalizations about the policy alternative for this issue can be broadly grouped under those for LDCs and DCs. LDCs first need to take serious account of this problem by establishing appropriate technology norms in their development plans. The general lack of such norms to date suggests a strong need for enlightenment of their leadership.

Second, LDCs should give strong consideration to doing away with policies such as concessionary interest rates in credit programs which give subsidies to capital-intensive techniques.

Third, LDCs should consider developing technologies of their own both for types of consumer goods and for production processes. Because this type of applied research is very costly, LDCs might look to programs of international cooperation in order to share the costs for developing technologies that are appropriate and transferable across national boundaries. The international agricultural centers provide a good example of this approach and its benefits.

In the DCs governments can facilitate the development of appropriate technology in several ways. First, foreign aid and technical assistance can be provided to assist the development of such technology by the LDCs. Second, they can stimulate research directly through funded research projects or indirectly through incentives to the private sector. Third, they can develop, as has been proposed in the United States, a technology clearing house which would function as a source of technology both for resurrecting obsolete technologies of DCs, which may be nowadays applicable in LDCs, and for cataloging existing technologies in the world in order to make them available to LDCs.

The private sector in DCs can also make a contribution through conscious efforts to develop products and production techniques that are suitable to LDC needs. The small tractor program of Massey Ferguson and television assembly programs of Phillips are examples of what has been done. Perhaps the most important incentive to encourage such research by the private sector is their recognition of a potential market for these products. Thus if the LDCs effectively demonstrate a need for and exert pressure for such technology, its development will be enhanced.

Ecological Technology

Issue

This issue is common for both DCs and LDCs. It has become increasingly apparent that the modern world in search of technological advancement has created a new generation of problems through the side effect of pollution and congestion. Thus, considerable recent attention has been directed to modification of production processes and the development of consumer goods and a lifestyle that have less pollutive and congestive effects. Perhaps the most articulate proponent to date has been E.F. Schumacher whose book *Small is Beautiful* has received widespread attention.[7]

Another dimension of the problem is that modern technology requires heavy utilization of nonrenewable resources. The doomsday message of the Club of Rome[8] is clear—as the world's population grows and economic advancement occurs, civilization will begin to bump against the constraints of limited resources. Thus unless technology is altered to use considerably lower coefficients of these resources and to reduce the negative ecological side effects and unless the rate of population growth is drastically reduced, the world's average level of living will eventually decline.

LDCs could seriously diminish the negative ecological effects of increased production and reduce the rate of consumption of nonrenewable resources if they were to utilize technology that had low pollutive and congestive side effects and low requirements for exhaustible resources. This, however, is a big order on two accounts. First, much of this type of technology is not yet available and it can hardly be expected that LDCs should or would be willing to wait until such a time as it is available to continue their development. Second, where such technology is available, such as smoke arrestors on factory chimneys, it is expensive and raises production costs and thus requires the use of scarce capital resources which could otherwise be employed in society.The present value of such future benefits may not be very high to a society that is struggling to cope with the more pressing problems of unemployment and poverty. Indeed, it is probably a rare government that would choose to allocate substantial resources in such a manner.

Policies

This is not to suggest that there are no policy alternatives that can be implemented in the meantime. First, as pressures from limited resources and polluting production techniques come to bear more urgently throughout the world, more emphasis will be given to the development of alternate technologies in the DCs which can in turn be transferred to LDCs. Second, LDCs can utilize policies that are harmonious with both the short-run development goals and long-run ecological goals. Examples are regional development programs to avoid excessive migration to the capital cities, encouragement of labor-intensive technology in rural areas to reduce rural-urban migration; subsidies for mass transportation systems and penalties for single automobiles; and plans for urban centers and industrial sites.

Conclusions

In the 1970s technology transfer has emerged as an issue for LDCs. Previously a transfer of technology both in the form of consumer goods and in production techniques took place through foreign trade, direct foreign investment and licensing agreements, but under terms which were largely determined by the owners of technology in DCs. In this decade LDCs have begun to develop norms which would more favor their particular interests. Most of the attention has been directed to the price of the technology and the terms under which it is transferred. While this issue is extremely important in order that the LDCs might reap advantages from technology at a lower cost, longer-term and more subtle issues of the appropriateness of technology and its ecological effects are also emerging.

A number of policy measures dealing with each of the three issues were set forth in this article; several major points emerge. First, while the individual LDCs must develop their own plans and provisions for technology transfer, it is important that they continue to group together as they have done in this decade in order not only to express their concerns collectively but also to form blocks of power which can confront the extreme economic power of the sellers of technology such as the MNCs. Only in this manner will they effectively be able to improve their bargaining position.

Second, part of the responsibility lies with the DCs. They must work to help establish norms for the operations of MNCs which includes technology transfer. Also, as part of their foreign assistance programs, they must direct resources towards the development and dissemination of technology that is more appropriate to the resource endowments of LDCs. Moreover, they have a responsibility to develop technology which confronts the ecological and nonrenewable resource problems and which can in turn be transferred to LDCs.

Thus, for all three issues, the policy prescription calls for individual as well as collaborative action on the part of both LDCs and DCs. Given the need for the international transfer of resources, including technology, it is in their mutual interests to work together. Although conflicts of interest are bound to arise, such as the current negotiations over price and terms, both LDCs and DCs have sufficient self-interest that they will find means to resolve these conflicts and move ahead together to their mutual benefit.

QUESTIONS

1. What is meant by the term "technology transfer"?
2. How does technology transfer relate to the development of marketing strategy?
3. What are the major problems and issues underlying the transfer of technology?
4. How can these problems and issues be minimized by the parties involved in technological transfers?

NOTES

1. See for example: Osvaldo Sunkel, "The Pattern of Latin American Dependence," paper presented at Conference on the Economic and Financial Relations of Latin America with the Industrialized Countries, held at the Colegio de Mexico, Mexico City, December 6–11, 1971, sponsored by the International Economic Association (mimeographed); and Ronald Muller, "The Multinational Corporation and the Underdevelopment of the Third World," in the *Political Economy of Development and Underdevelopment,* ed. Charles K. Wilber (New York: W.W. Norton, (1973), pp. 186–204.

2. Jose de Cubas, *Technology Transfer and the Developing Nations.* (New York: Council for the Americas and Fund for Multinational Management Education, 1974), p. 1.

3. Constantine V. Vaitsos, "Bargaining and the Distribution of Returns in the Purchase of Technology by Developing Countries," *Bulletin of the Institute of Development Studies,* (October 1970), pp. 16–23, reprinted in Gerald M. Meier *Leading Issues in Economic Development,* Third Edition (New York: Oxford University Press, 1976), pp. 413–414.

4. Ibid.

5. Henry J. Kissinger, "Global Concensus and Economic Development," Speech delivered at Seventh Special Session of the United Nations Special Assembly, September 1, 1975 (Washington, D.C.: U.S. Department of State, Bureau of Public Affairs, Office of Media Services), p. 7.

6. International Labor Office, *Employment, Growth and Basic Needs: A One-World Problem* (Geneva: ILO, 1976), pp. 18 and 21.

7. E.F. Schumacher, *Small is Beautiful* (New York: First Perennial Library Edition, Harper and Row Publishers, 1975).

8. Donella H. Meadows, Dennis L. Meadows, Jorgen Randers, William W. Behrens III, *The Limits to Growth* (New York: Signet Books by the New American Library, 1972).

DISTRIBUTION
STRATEGIES

As in domestic marketing, the distribution process for overseas programs involves all those activities related to the creation of time, place, and ownership utilities for industrial and ultimate consumers. The selection, operation, and motivation of effective channels of distribution often are key factors underlying a firm's differential advantage in international markets. So, many activities and the culturally differentiated roles of channel intermediaries make the formulation of distribution strategies a most challenging decision-making area for a firm entering foreign markets. The following articles discuss some of the many facets of an international distribution mix. The first selection has been excerpted from the Department of Commerce's *Guide to Overseas Markets*. It illustrates the types of intermediary alternatives available to domestic exporters, and some useful guidelines for selecting most appropriate channels for a firm's distribution mix. The next article, by Donald Hackett, illustrates the importance of international franchising to United States firms, and explores the rationale as well as patterns of development of overseas franchising relationships. Physical distribution management in an international setting requires special knowledge of complex rate structures, tariffs, and many other unique problems. L. Soorikian's article focuses on the importance of developing management information systems to deal with the costs associated with the existing as well as potential problems facing international decision makers in physical distribution. The last article in this section, by Art Detman, Jr., illustrates how one multinational organization—TRW Datacom—has effectively implemented a marketing subsidiary to deal directly with overseas distributions.

A number of channels of distribution alternatives are available to the international marketer. This article briefly outlines the functions performed by middlemen in an indirect selling situation as well as sources of information useful to managers undertaking channel decisions.

23. Selecting Sales and Distribution Channels

United States Department of Commerce

There are two basic approaches to selling internationally, either direct or indirect. When selling direct, the United States firm deals with a foreign firm and usually is responsible for shipping the products overseas. The indirect method means dealing through another United States firm that acts as a sales intermediary and that normally will assume the responsibility for moving the products overseas.

Indirect Selling

There are several different types of intermediary firms and the manufacturer will have to decide on the type of operation he feels will best be able to sell his products.

Commission Agents—Commission or buying agents are "finders" for foreign firms wanting to purchase United States products. These purchasing

Source: Reprinted from *A Basic Guide to Exporting,* a publication of the United States Department of Commerce (Washington, D.C.: U.S. Government Printing Office, 1976), pp. 2-4 and 8-14.

agents obtain the desired equipment at the lowest possible price. A commission is paid to them by their foreign clients.

Country Controlled Buying Agents—These are foreign government agencies or quasi-governmental firms empowered to locate and purchase desired goods.

Export Management Companies—EMCs, as they are called, act as the export department for several manufacturers of noncompetitive products. They solicit and transact business in the name of the manufacturers they represent for a commission, salary, or retainer plus commission. Many EMCs also will carry the financing for export sales, assuring immediate payment for the manufacturer's products.

This can be an exceptionally fine arrangement for smaller firms that do not have the time, personnel, or money to develop foreign markets, but wish to establish a corporate and product identity internationally.

Export Merchants—The export merchant purchases products direct from the manufacturer and has them packed and marked to his specifications. He then sells overseas through his contacts, in his own name, and assumes all risks for his account.

Export Agents—The export agent operates in the same manner as a manufacturer's representative, but the risk of loss remains with the manufacturer.

In transactions with export merchants and export agents the seller is faced with the possible disadvantage of giving up control over the marketing and promotion of his product which could have an adverse effect on future successes.

Direct Selling

The product involved, and the way it is marketed in the United States, will provide a clue to how it might be marketed internationally; i.e., through a representative, stocking distributor, consignment agent, retail store, or even directly to the end user. The customary business methods and established channels of distribution in individual foreign countries will also have a bearing on how to proceed.

Sales Representatives or Agents—A sales representative is the equivalent of a manufacturer's representative here in the United States. Product literature and samples are used to present the product to the potential buyer. He usually works on a commission basis, assumes no risk or responsibility, and is under contract for a definite period of time (renewable by mutual agreement). This contract defines territory, terms of sale, method of compensation, and other details. The sales representative may operate on either an exclusive or nonexclusive basis.

Distributor—The foreign distributor is a merchant who purchases merchandise from a United States manufacturer at the greatest possible discount and resells it for his profit. This would be the preferred arrangement if the product being sold requires periodic servicing. The prospective distributor should be willing to carry a sufficient parts supply and maintain adequate facilities and personnel to perform all normal servicing operations. Since the distributor buys in his name, it is easier for the United States manufacturer to establish a credit pattern so that more flexible or convenient payment terms can be offered. As with a sales representative, the length of association is established by contract that is renewable if the arrangement proves satisfactory.

Foreign Retailer—Generally limited to the consumer line, this method relies mainly on direct contact by traveling salesmen but, depending on the product, can also be accomplished by the mailing of catalogs, brochures, or other literature. However, even though it would eliminate commissions and traveling expenses, the United States manufacturer who uses the direct mail approach could suffer because his proposal may not receive proper consideration.

Selling Direct to the End User—This is quite limited and again depends on the product. Opportunities often arise from advertisements in magazines receiving overseas distribution. Many times this can create difficulties because the casual inquirer may not be fully cognizant of his country's foreign trade regulations. For several reasons, he may not be able to receive the merchandise upon arrival, thus causing it to be impounded and possibly sold at public auction, or returned on a freight-collect basis which could prove to be costly.

State Controlled Trading Companies—This term applies to countries which have state trading monopolies, where business is conducted by a few government sanctioned and controlled trading entities. Because of worldwide changes in foreign policy and their effect on trade between countries, these areas can become important future markets. For the time being, however, most opportunities will be limited to such items as raw materials, agricultural machinery, manufacturing equipment, and technical instruments, rather than consumer or household goods. This is due to the shortage of foreign exchange and the emphasis on self-sufficiency.

New Product Information Service (NPIS)—This special service, now offered by the Department of Commerce, can facilitate your direct selling effort to potential overseas customers. It enables United States companies interested in selling a new product overseas to submit appropriate data through Commerce Department District Offices for placement in the following media:

A Commerce publication—*Commercial News for the Foreign Service.* This publication is mailed regularly to 240 United States Foreign Service Posts. The new product data is extracted and reprinted in their own individual newsletters that are tailored in design, content, and language to individual foreign markets.

The United States Information Agency's (USIA) *Voice of America.* New product information is selected for its "New Product USA" global and regional broadcasts that cover the world and the USIA's international news service which carries a biweekly "New Products" feature column sent by teletype to 102 nations for placement in relevant overseas trade journals.

Locating Foreign Representatives

How does an exporter locate someone in a foreign country who is qualified and interested in handling his product?

Department of Commerce

One of the most effective and economical ways of locating foreign representation is by utilizing the services of the Department of Commerce. The Department has several aids that are designed to assist the American manufacturer. Some of these are:

THE AGENT/DISTRIBUTOR SERVICE (ADS)

The ADS is used to seek representatives (agents) and/or distributors. The essence of the service is the determination of a foreign firm's interest in a specific United States proposal and willingness to correspond with the United States requester. United States Foreign Service posts supply up to three selected names of such firms together with the addresses and persons to contact.

Charges for this service, as well as ADS application forms, may be obtained from Commerce Department District Offices. International trade specialists at these offices will help applicants prepare their applications. They will give guidance and ascertain that there are not factors barring the desired relationship.

TRADE OPPORTUNITIES PROGRAM (TOP)

TOP is an easy, effective way for a United States company to learn about overseas firms that could act as agents or distributors for its products. The United States company, as a subscriber to TOP, specifies the products and the countries for which it would like to receive notices of overseas representation opportunities. That information is put into the TOP computer.

As representation opportunities are telexed to Commerce from Foreign Service posts, they are put into the computer and matched against the subscriber's information specifications. When a match occurs, the computer prints out a notice of the opportunity that is then mailed to the subscriber. Subscription costs may be obtained from Commerce District Offices.

EXPORT CONTACT LIST SERVICES

The Department of Commerce collects and stores information on foreign firms in a master computer file designated as the Foreign Traders Index (FTI). The file contains information on more than 138,000 importing firms, agents, representatives, distributors, manufacturers, service organizations, retailers, and potential end users of American products and/or services in 130 countries. Newly identified firms are constantly being added to the file while information on previously listed firms is updated frequently. This information is available to United States exporters in the following three forms:

Export Mailing List Service (EMLS). The EMLS consist of special targeted retrievals for individual requesters wishing to obtain lists of foreign firms in selected countries by commodity classification. Retrievals are offered on gummed-mailing labels or on printout and include, to the extent available, the name and address of the firm, name and title of executive officer, type of organization, year established, relative size, number of employees and salesmen, and product or service codes by SIC number. Information on charges for this service may be obtained from Commerce District Offices.

FTI Data Tape Service (DTS). Through this service, information on all firms included in the FTI for all countries (or in selected countries) is available to United States firms on magnetic tape. Users can retrieve various segments of the data in unlimited combinations through their own computer facilities.

Trade Lists. Following is a brief description of two styles of individually printed industry Trade Lists that are available from the Department of Commerce. A free Index may be obtained from Commerce District Offices.

Lists of "State Controlled Trading Companies." Identifies government sanctioned and controlled trading entitites in those countries where foreign trade is conducted through state-owned or controlled organizations.

Business Firms. These lists contain all commercial data available in the automated Foreign Traders Index for selected developing countries.

SPECIALIZED UNITED STATES GOVERNMENT TRADE MISSIONS

These Trade Missions are groups of American businessmen recruited by Commerce from a specific industry to promote the sale of the products or services of that particular industry, or to establish representation in overseas markets. Commerce, assisted by the United States Foreign Service—Department of State, provides detailed marketing information, advanced planning, publicity, and trip coordination. Mission members pay their own expenses and a share of the overseas operating costs, and conduct business on behalf of the firms they represent.

COMMERCIAL EXHIBITIONS

These are trade shows, either wholly sponsored by the United States Government or in which it is participating, where American products may be displayed at low cost to test a market, generate sales, or locate representation.

PRODUCT MARKETING SERVICE (PMS)

This program, initiated by the Bureau of International Commerce in 1975, was designed to provide United States businessmen traveling abroad with "an office away from the office" at any one of the following United States Trade Centers overseas: London, Paris, Tokyo, Frankfurt, Milan, Stockholm, Mexico City, Taipei, Singapore, Sydney, or Tehran.

Essentially, the PMS provides businessmen with office space for up to 5 days; free local telephone service and access to telecommunications; audio-visual equipment and a place to use it; a market briefing, a list of key business prospects, and help in making appointments. Help also will be offered in obtaining secretarial and interpreter services (at the United States company's expense).

The daily minimum charge for this service may be obtained from your local Commerce District Office, which also has information on similar services in Eastern Europe and the U.S.S.R.

COMMERCIAL NEWSLETTERS

Many of the larger United States Embassies and Consulates publish a periodic newsletter that is distributed to the business community they serve. At no cost, it is possible for United States firms to have new products described in this publication so that if a local representative is interested, he may contact the United States firm.

BUSINESS TRAVEL OVERSEAS

For firms wishing to travel overseas to search for a qualified business partner and to gain firsthand knowledge of a country's business conditions, Economic/Commercial Officers in the American Embassy or Consulate can provide considerable assistance—either by way of indepth briefings or by arranging introductions to appropriate firms, individuals or foreign government officials.

United States firms planning overseas business trips and believing advance notification would be useful, should write directly to Foreign Service Posts in countries they plan to visit. They should write at least two weeks before leaving the United States, and should address their communication to the *Commercial Section,* not to an individual officer by name. United States firms should identify themselves by business affiliation and complete address, and indicate the objective of their trip and the type of assistance they desire of the Post *after* arrival. Also, a description of their firm and the extent of its international experience would be helpful to the Post.

Businessmen should consult the list of overseas holidays which is published annually in *Commerce America* (Usually in last issue of each calendar year) prior to planning an overseas business itinerary, as American Embassies/Consulates and foreign business and government offices may be closed on these holidays. A list of the addresses of American Embassies and Consulates may be found in the Foreign Service List, available from the Superintendent of Documents, United States Government Printing Office, Washington, D.C. 20402.

Industry Organized Promotions

Private groups (representing a state, city, chamber of commerce, trade association, industry group, or single industry) occasionally sponsor and finance various types of overseas promotions, one of which is Industry Organized-Government Approved Trade Missions. An IOGA Trade Mission consists of a group of American businessmen who wish to promote the sale of United States products or services, or to establish agents. The United States Department of Commerce assists in planning the mission and coordinating arrangements with United States Foreign Service Posts. A Commerce officials briefs mission members prior to departure regarding business, economic, and political conditions in the country to be visited.

Banks

Banks can be another excellent source of assistance. Acting through their own international department or through the international department of an affiliate bank in the States, it is possible for them to locate, through correspondent or branch banks overseas, reputable firms qualified and willing to represent United States firms.

Service Organizations

Ocean freight carriers, airlines, port authorities, and American chambers of commerce maintain offices throughout the world. Through these offices it is often possible for United States firms to find outlets or representation at no cost or obligation.

Many of these same organizations also publish newsletters or booklets that are widely distributed overseas in which products can be described to attract interested representatives.

Publications

There are many foreign circulation business and travel magazines in which advertising space can be purchased to either solicit representation or publicize products.

Reliability

After locating a potential foreign representative, it is necessary to investigate him to assure he is reliable and reputable before entering into an agreement. It is recommended that at least two supporting business and credit reports be obtained. There are several ways this can be accomplished.

World Traders Data Reports. A business report prepared by the United States Foreign Service—Department of State and available from the Department of Commerce which gives such information as the type of organization, year established, relative size, number of employees, general reputation, territory covered, language preferred, product lines handled, principal owners, financial references, and trade references. It also contains a general narrative report by the United States Commercial Officer conducting the investigation as to the reliability of the foreign firm. Request forms and information on charges for this service are available from Commerce District Offices.

Commercial credit reporting firms such as Dun & Bradstreet, Foreign Credit Interchange Bureau, and Retail Credit Corporation offer similar data.

Another source of credit information is through United States banks and their correspondent banks or branches overseas.

Drawing Up an Agreement with Your Representative

After successfully making contact with a prospective representative and investigating his integrity, financial responsibility, community standing, share of the market, and other product lines which he represents for conflict of interest, the next step is to consider the foreign sales agreement itself.

Basic Items

An agreement of this type can be either relatively simple or detailed. The following basic items normally are included in a typical foreign sales agreement:

> Name and addresses of both parties.
>
> Date when the agreement goes into effect.
>
> Duration of the agreement.
>
> Provisions for extending or terminating the agreement.
>
> Description of product lines included.
>
> Definition of sales territory.
>
> Establishment of discount and/or commission schedules and determination of when and how paid.
>
> Provisions for revising the commission or discount schedules.
>
> Establishment of a policy governing resale prices.
>
> Maintenance of appropriate service facilities.
>
> Restrictions to prohibit the manufacture and sale of similar and competitive products.
>
> Designation of responsibility for patent and trademark negotiations and/or pricing.
>
> The assignability or non-assignability of the agreement and any limiting factors.
>
> Designation of the country (not necessarily the United States) and state (if applicable) of contract jurisdiction in the case of dispute.

The agreement should also contain statements to the effect that the representative will not have business dealings with a competitive firm; reveal any confidential information in a way that would prove injurious, detrimental, or competitive to the United States firm; enter into agreements binding on the United States firm; and all inquiries received from outside the designated sales territory are to be referred to the American firm for appropriate action.

To insure a conscientious sales effort from the representative on behalf of the United States firm, the foreign representative should also agree to devote his utmost skill and ability to the sale of the product for the compensation named in the contract.

For tax purposes, in both the United States and possibly foreign countries as well, the place and time at which title to the merchandise passes from the seller to the buyer can be very important and therefore in certain instances, should be written into the agreement.

At all times, avoid articles which could be contrary to United States antitrust laws. Legal advice should be sought when preparing and entering into foreign agreements.

QUESTIONS

1. Differentiate between direct and indirect selling.
2. What are the major middlemen alternatives open to a U.S. marketing manager utilizing an indirect strategy?
3. What methods exist for a U.S. marketer to carry out a direct selling strategy?

*Expansion into international markets repre-
sents a major growth opportunity for
domestic franchise operations. This article
presents the results of a survey that focused
on the entry motivations, ownership practices, marketing strategies, profit profiles,
and problems associated with United States
franchise operations abroad.*

24. The International Expansion of U.S. Franchise Systems: Status and Strategies

Donald W. Hackett
Wichita State University

In 1975, the franchise method of distribution will account for over $158 billion in retail sales within the United States encompassing a full 27 percent of retail sales.[1] This volume of sales is phenomenal when it is considered that nine out of every ten franchising firms have been established in less than twenty years.

The term franchising has several connotations. The context in which Vaughn describes the term is used in this study. Vaughn defines franchising as "... a form of marketing or distribution in which a parent company customarily grants an individual or relatively small company the right or privilege, to do business (for a consideration from the franchisee) in a prescribed manner over a certain period of time in a specified place." This "privilege" may be the right to sell the parent company's product, to use its name, to adopt its methods or to copy its symbols, trademark and architecture.[2]

The distribution form known as franchising started many years ago in Germany when beer brewers entered into licensing and financing arrangements

---

Source: Reprinted from the *Journal of International Business Studies*, Spring 1976.

for the exclusive sale of various brands of beer and ale.[3] But it is in the dynamic United States economy that franchising has prospered. In 1863, the Singer Sewing Machine Company instituted what was probably the first modern form of franchising in the United States; the automobile and soft drink industries adopted franchising as the principal method of distribution in the 1890's and petroleum producers followed in the 1930s.[4] In 1935, Howard Johnson developed the first franchised restaurant chain.

The franchise industry in the United States began accelerated growth in the 1950s. Such diverse businesses as fast food restaurants, business services, construction, hotels and motels, recreation, entertainment and rental services integrated the franchise concept of distribution into their marketing strategy. Perhaps the most notable example of the franchise industry's growth is McDonald's Corporation. From 1961 to 1971, McDonald's franchise units increased by an astounding 758 percent! The corporation began operations in 1955 and by 1973 rang up sales of $1.03 billion, surpassing the United States Army as the nation's biggest dispenser of meals.[5] The United States Commerce Department estimates that the 1,200 companies comprising the franchise industry will generate sales in excess of $176 billion from some 460,000 establishments in 1975.[6]

The franchising boom began to level off in the late 1960s. With the advent of the 1970s, many franchise systems have found fewer prime locations, increased competition and an unsettled legal environment. Faced with these conditions, companies began to look for opportunities in foreign environments. As recently as 1969, a survey of the International Franchising Association found only 14 percent of the member firms had franchisees outside the United States and many of these were limited to Canada. From this tiny beachhead, American franchisers expanded, and in 1973 the United States Department of Commerce estimated that more than 208 American firms operated over 9,500 franchise establishments abroad.[7] The trend toward international franchising is so well established that it might be described as the second boom in the history of franchising.

The Study

Several prior studies have been concerned with the efforts of United States franchise systems abroad. Walker and Etzel focused on the progress and procedures of United States firms operating in foreign markets.[8] The United States Department of Commerce periodically surveys American franchising firms to develop statistics concerning their international involvement.[9] The United States Department of Agriculture has polled leading fast food firms to determine their foreign expansion plans.[10] Additionally, numerous "how to" articles have appeared in newspapers, trade journals and other publications.[11]

This study examined specific aspects of the internationalization of American franchising firms. Of particular interest to the researchers were (1) the identification of motivations underlying overseas expansion, (2) the geographic location of foreign outlets, (3) the ownership strategy used in international entry, (4) the effect of foreign environment on United States firms' marketing and financial strategies, and (5) the major problems involved in establishing franchise operations abroad.

Data for the study were developed from a nationwide mail survey of United States franchising firms. Several trade and membership lists were integrated to form a master composite mailing list; only automobile and petroleum franchising companies were excluded from the survey.[12] Executives of 719 franchising firms were contacted to determine if their firms were involved in international operations. Special efforts, including personal and telephone interviews, were made to insure response from firms targeted as internationally oriented companies. Usable replies were received from 353 firms giving a total response rate of 49 percent. A total of eighty-five firms indicated involvement in foreign markets and provided the data upon which this study is based.

Results of the Study

A profile of the participating firms is presented in Exhibit 24-1. The respondent firms were classified into nine major categories. The greater number of respondent firms currently involved in international markets, 30.5 percent, founded their enterprises in the period 1960-1964. Closer analysis of the data in Exhibit 24-1 reveals that business services and soft drink systems were rapidly developing in the immediate post World War II period. The majority of fast food, hotel/motel and car rental firms now involved in foreign markets initially began domestic franchising operations during the 1950s and early 1960s. A total of 22.4 percent of the internationally involved firms resided in the fast food group, a statistic that reflects the prevalent and aggressive nature of these firms in the franchising industry. The extensive involvement of other franchise groups such as the soft drink and business service firms also illustrates that overseas entry is an industry-wide occurrence.

The boom in international participation by United States franchise systems is clearly illustrated in the lower half of Exhibit 24-1. A steady, if not spectacular, entry picture is reflected by respondent firms in the periods prior to 1960; but it is in the decade of the 1960s that a major upswing in international participation evolved. This was followed by an even more dramatic surge in the first five years of the seventies. For example, a total of 36.4 percent of the respondent firms launched their initial international venture between 1970 and 1975! Prior to 1960, soft drink and business service firms were the most active overseas entries; fast food, automotive services and hotel/motel systems entered international markets most heavily in the 1960s. Since 1970, the penetration of foreign markets has been widespread among the franchise groups.

As indicated in Exhibit 24-2, size is a factor in international entry. The

EXHIBIT 24-1

Profile of respondent firms involved in international markets

Classification	By Year of Initial Domestic Franchise							
	Pre 1940	1940 1949	1950 1959	1960 1964	1965 1969	1970 1975	Total	Per cent
Automotive Services	0	1	1	3	1	1	7	8.2
Business Services	1	5	1	1	1	0	9	10.6
Car Rentals	0	1	3	2	1	0	6	7.1
Recreation Services	0	0	1	1	1	1	4	4.7
Fast Foods	1	3	6	6	3	0	19	22.4
Retailing (Food)	1	1	1	4	1	0	8	9.5
Hotels/Motels	0	1	1	4	1	0	7	8.2
Soft Drinks	3	4	1	2	0	0	11	12.9
Miscellaneous*	1	5	2	3	2	1	14	16.5
Total	7	21	17	26	11	3	85	100.0
Percent	8.2	24.7	20.0	30.5	12.9	3.5		

Classification	By Year of Initial International Franchine							
Automotive Services	0	0	1	3	2	1	7	8.2
Business Services	2	0	2	1	0	4	9	10.6
Car Rentals	0	1	1	0	1	3	6	7.1
Recreation Services	0	0	0	2	0	2	4	4.7
Fast Food	0	0	0	5	5	9	19	22.4
Retailing (Food)	1	0	0	1	2	4	8	9.4
Hotels/Motels	0	0	0	2	2	3	7	8.2
Soft Drinks	2	2	4	1	1	1	11	12.9
Miscellaneous*	2	1	2	1	4	4	14	16.5
Total	7	4	10	16	17	31	85	100.0
Percent	8.2	4.7	11.7	18.8	20.0	36.4		

*Firms classified in this category included laundries, lawn care firms, art galleries, copy firms, real estate agencies, industrial service companies, and non-food retailers.

systems that completed the questionnaire ranged in size from 21 units to over 5,000 units. As expected, the larger firms accounted for the majority of outlets abroad. Those firms which exceeded 300 units in size accounted for 76.1 percent of the total international units of the respondents. However, one in five of the respondent firms involved in foreign markets had fewer than 75 outlets under contract both domestically and internationally. Taken a step further, 43.6 percent of the firms involved internationally had fewer than

EXHIBIT 24–2

Respondent firm's international participation by size

Parent Firms by Franchise Size	Number of Respondents	Percent of Respondents*	Percent of International Outlets by Size**
Under 49	10	11.8	1.2
50– 74	7	8.3	1.3
75– 99	3	3.5	2.0
100–199	17	20.0	9.1
200–299	14	16.4	10.3
300 or more	34	40.0	76.1
Total	85	100.0	100.0

*Read as 11.8 percent of respondent firms operate under 49 domestic franchise outlets.
**Read as 1.2 percent of total international outlets of surveyed firms are operated by firms with less than 49 franchisees.

200 total units. Based on these figures, it appears large size is not necessarily a prerequisite for global involvement even though the larger firms do currently dominate in total outlets on line.

Exhibit 24–2 indicates that current operations of United States systems are largest in the westernized and industrial nations of the world. Canada has the largest number of United States franchise operations followed by England and Japan. South Africa has a surprisingly large number of units but the majority of these resulted from one drugstore firm's operations. Somewhat surprisingly, West Germany has few United States franchise systems in operation, but unsuccessful attempts by two major firms in the early 1970s slowed the industry's move into this market. Australia, Mexico and Western Europe are also heavily penetrated markets at this early date.

Motivations Behind International Entry

In an effort to identify motivations underlying the decision to expand internationally, each respondent firm was requested to rank in importance eleven motivational statements on a scale from one to five. Initial entry of most respondent firms was prompted by intermediate and long-run market potential rather than by immediate financial gain. As evidence we have the high ranking of statements relating to market potential, and the lower rankings given to financially related statements. A senior executive's early interest was also a factor in many of the international entry decisions. This interest was frequently initiated by prospective or existing franchise holders requesting rights to develop international territories. Once a system was established abroad, its success acted as a catalyst for further international ventures. Respondent firms ranked the statement concerning a "saturated   United

EXHIBIT 24-3

Present and planned international locations of U.S. franchise systems

Region or Nation	Operating	Planned*	Region or Nation	Operating	Planned
AFRICA			LATIN &		
South Africa	993	32	SOUTH AMERICA		
Rhodesia	13	5	Mexico	262	148
Nigeria	9	5	Central America	87	28
Kenya	7	6	Argentina	62	9
Ghana	7	4	Brazil	51	39
Other	32	5	Venezuela	50	10
Area Total	1061	57	Other	78	24
CARIBBEAN	87	34	Area Total	590	258
CANADA	2832	932	FAR EAST		
			Japan	1087	1609
EUROPE			Philippines	50	74
England	1535	259	Malaysia	41	13
Italy	255	19	India	19	2
Germany	162	261	Guam	18	5
France	155	45	Hong Kong	16	8
Spain	134	32	Other	37	43
Scandinavia	101	35	Area Total	1268	1754
Belgium	90	28			
Switzerland	71	19	MIDDLE EAST		
Austria	42	7	Iran	25	5
Portugal	35	8	Lebanon	22	13
Greece	28	6	Israel	18	10
Other	47	14	Other	65	28
Area Total	2655	733	Area Total	130	56
USSR AND			OCEANIA		
SOVIET BLOCK	8		Australia	251	205
			New Zealand	44	31
			Area Total	295	236
			TOTAL	8926	4060

*A total of 32 percent of the respondent firms intentionally skipped the "planned units" column because of uncertain plans or under a claim of proprietary information.

States market" low in influencing their foreign entry decision. Apparently United States franchise systems still view the domestic market with optimism. Few firms credit United States government agencies with any meaningful role in their international entry decisions.

The generalization of agreement among the franchiser groups concerning their motivations for entry were analyzed using Kendall's coefficient of concordance.[13] A significant level of agreement (Kendall's w = .84) was found among the franchiser classifications. This extremely high coefficient indicates the international oriented franchisers significantly agree among themselves on the ranking of motivations.

Ownership Strategy

The overseas expansion by United States systems reflects a variety of ownership strategies. Over 80 percent of the surveyed companies reported that American ownership abroad is allowed and oftentimes encouraged. This strategy is risky in many nationalistic countries and indeed, a number of firms indicated that this policy was under review. Single and multiple ownership policies were split; 58 percent of the respondent firms' international outlets are owned by individual entrepreneurs, and 42 percent operate under multiple-unit ownership. However, in fast food systems, over 70 percent of the foreign units are multiply owned.

One-hundred percent franchisee ownership is the most frequently used entry strategy in international franchising; over 47 percent of the respondent firms use this ownership method. This is in contrast to the trend toward company-owned units in domestic markets.

Six of the nine franchise classifications are dominated by the use of the 100 percent franchisee ownership form. Only the recreation, retailing and hotel/motel systems use other ownership strategies more frequently. The master or area franchise for cities and nations is the next most commonly used strategy. Some 20.7 percent of the surveyed firms employ this method and one franchise classification, recreational services, makes greater use of this ownership mode than any of the others. A total of 17 percent use a company-owned ownership policy. Food retailers rely on the company-owned outlet to the greatest extent while business services and fast food systems also frequently adopt this ownership form. Several firms noted that new markets are tested with company-owned stores prior to beginning major franchising efforts. Joint ownership positions are the least utilized with only 14.8 percent of the firms reporting their use; however, the joint venture arrangement is the most commonly used ownership tactic among the hotel/motel systems.

Most classifications of franchisers utilize more than one form of ownership in international markets. Indeed, ownership strategies are often based on the risk complexion of the nation or region. For instance, since Mexico's passage in 1973 of the Law to Promote Mexican Investment, severe limitations have been placed on foreign investment in Mexico. As a result, many franchisers who once desired to open company-owned stores are moving toward risk avoidance ownership forms such as the joint venture and franchise-owned outlets. On the other hand, in Brazil, profits and royalty payments may be remitted only on capital brought into the country or on "reinvestments" of profits derived from such capital. In this case, franchisers often institute company-owned and joint venture operations in order to repatriate profits from the country.

The respondents acknowledged the influence of risks on ownership policies. The driving force behind 100 percent franchisee ownership, in most cases, was the desire to penetrate markets while avoiding the risk of ownership and financing in the local markets. The master or area franchise form was often selected in those cases where simplicity of control and coordination were primary considerations. Majority joint venture positions were desired by franchisers when the laws of the country required a local national partner and prospective franchisees lacked the necessary financial base. Motivation of the partner, maintenance of some control, lack of available financing and the desire to reduce equity risk were reasons given for taking a minority ownership position.

Marketing Strategy

Firms often develop unique marketing programs for each international market environment. In contradistinction, other firms institute a uniform or standardized approach to international markets. Indeed, much of the franchising industry's success has been attributed to the predictable nature of product offerings and services. Many franchise systems have successfully penetrated foreign markets with little alteration of the domestic marketing strategy; 41.2 percent of the firms reported no major changes in their franchise marketing package for overseas ventures. The soft drink, business services, and automotive product groups are the strongest adopters of the standardized approach while the more visible retailers are more apt to use an adaptation strategy. The greater alteration of marketing strategy takes place in the product area. A total of 25 percent of the companies reported significant alterations of their product or service to better fit local market conditions; however, 70 percent of the fast food group significantly changed product offerings in operations outside the United States. The alterations by fast food groups involved menu additions and deletions as well as changes in esthetics. For example, McDonald's often uses a heavy wood decor in those nations of northern Europe, such as Scandinavia, where wood furnishings have a long tradition. The alteration or change of logos, promotional and color themes, and architecture was reported by another 33.8 percent of the surveyed firms.

Profits in International Markets

The motivation for international expansion of most firms is the initial penetration of potential markets; but the ultimate success of any business venture depends on profits. The increasing and important role international operations play in the franchising industry's financial posture is presented in Exhibit 24–4. The greatest number of firms, 46.4 percent generated less than five percent of their revenues from overseas operations. Surprisingly, one out of every four firms in international markets already generates 5 to 9 percent of its profits from these markets and over 18 percent of the respondent firms derive 25 percent or more of their total corporate sales from international establishments. Those groups which began international operations in the 1950s generated the greatest sales from abroad.

The profit-per-unit data reported by the respondents portray a near-normal distribution. A total of 41.4 percent of the firms reported international profits per unit about equal to their domestic operations; 31.4 percent reported greater profits internationally, and 27.2 percent derived less profit-per-unit from foreign systems. Within the classifications, the fast food, recreational and soft drink systems' profit data were skewed toward greater profit per unit internationally. The automotive and business services, car rentals and hotel/motel systems reported profits which generally corresponded with domestic systems while the miscellaneous group's profits were skewed toward greater profit per unit than the domestic establishments. The retailers' profit pictures were mixed with no established trend.

A profile of the respondents' international sales activities is illustrated

EXHIBIT 24–4

Percent of corporate sales generated by respondent firms' international franchise units

	Less than 5%	5–9%	10–24%	25–50%	Over 50%	Total
Automotive Services ·	1	3	0	1	0	5
Business Services	4	1	0	3	0	8
Car Rentals	2	1	1	0	0	4
Recreation Services	0	2	0	0	1	3
Fast Foods	12	4	0	1	0	17
Retailing (Food)	4	0	0	1	0	5
Hotels/Motels	2	3	0	0	0	5
Soft Drinks	1	1	2	4	1	9
Miscellaneous	6	4	2	1	0	13
Total	32	19	5	11	2	69
Percent	46.4	27.5	7.3	15.9	2.9	100.0

in Exhibit 24–5. Surprisingly, the food retailer respondents led all categories in number of foreign establishments and total sales volume. The greatest contributor to the retailer category was the convenience food store group; however, over one-half of all food retailer establishments were located in Canada. The fast food franchisers trailed the food retailers in establishments and sales volume even though twice as many fast food firms responded. The hotel/motel systems, with the least number of overseas units, led all other groups in sales per establishment by a wide margin. Recreational system registered the lowest average and total sales volume of all reporting groups. Nonfood retailers contributed the greatest sales volume to the miscellaneous category but the heterogeneous nature of this group makes meaningful evaluation difficult.

Problems in International Entry

The problems encountered in foreign markets by franchise firms are similar to domestic business problems but differ in intensity and severity. Respondent firms were asked to rank fourteen problem areas on a one-to-five scale. A free-response space for other troublesome areas was included in the questionnaire. Host government interference and red tape topped the problem list followed by high duties, taxes and monetary uncertainties, logistical control and locational problems. The franchisers agreement on the problems encountered in international markets was also analyzed using Kendall's coefficient

EXHIBIT 24–5

Revenue profiles of U.S. franchise firms' international units (thousands of dollars)

Classification	Number of Respondents	International Establishments	Average Sales Per Establishment*	Total Revenues**
Automotive Services	7	1043	104	$ 108,472
Business Services	9	300	61	18,300
Car Rentals	6	921	141	129,861
Recreation Services	4	108	43	4,644
Fast Foods	19	1367	220	300,740
Retailing (Food)	8	1374	251	344,874
Hotels/Motels	7	301	708	213,108
Soft Drinks	11	803	N/A	N/A
Miscellaneous	14	2709	107	289,863
Total	85	8926		$1,409,862

*Average sales per establishment were estimated from those firms reporting sales data in each franchiser category.
**Estimates based on "average sales per unit" data supplied by respondents.

of concordance. A rather low level of agreement among the franchiser classifications was indicated by the Kendall's w = .40. Not all franchise systems ranked red tape as their paramount problem.

For example, the fast food group ranked location and logistical obstacles first and second, respectively. High real estate costs, especially in Japan and Europe, created major problems for several of these firms. Hotel systems ranked competition as their greatest area of difficulty while business and automobile services ranked servicing of United States made equipment as the major problem. Somewhat surprisingly, the firms ranked problems inherent in "adapting to foreign cultures" low in the problem hierarchy. Not one firm ranked "adapting the franchise package to local market" among its top five impediments in foreign operations. Governmental, financial and logistical difficulties are more ubiquitous and appeared consistently as obstacles in all the franchise group responses.

Several problems frequently spell disaster in international markets. Indeed, 40.3 percent of the surveyed companies reported that one or more of their foreign franchise units had failed. Most franchisers blamed poor management or ignoring established procedures as the cause for their failure. Four fast food systems reported poor locations as the prime factor, while a major restaurant chain pointed to expatriate American managers as the principal reason for its outlet's demise. A soft drink firm and a hamburger franchiser mentioned distance and communication as the main reason for foundering operations while several firms cited the recent economic recession abroad. Finally, one car wash franchiser succinctly stated, "We just didn't do our homework."

Future Trends

The firms currently involved in international markets are highly optimistic. They are making plans for further expansion outside the United States, particularly as other economies adopt western lifestyles and discretionary incomes rise. All the surveyed firms who are active internationally plan to increase the size of their foreign operations and the majority project increases from 150 to 300 percent by the end of the decade.

These plans are illustrated in Exhibit 24-3 under the "planned units" column. Over 4,000 new units are planned worldwide in the near future; Japan with 39.6 percent and Canada with 22.9 percent are targeted for over 62 percent of all planned units. Germany, and to a lesser extent Western Europe as a whole, Australia and Mexico are tagged as major growth areas. Strong interest is being shown in England, representing an area with established trading ties and the Middle East, a relatively new area of international economic interest. Africa and South America, with the exception of Brazil, are not as attractive to American franchisers at this time. Several firms indicated interest in Eastern European nations but few have made serious plans for entry.

Firms were also asked to indicate the nations and regions of greatest growth opportunity in the next five years. Europe was ranked first by 31.2 percent of the respondents followed by the western Pacific rim countries with 24.6 percent. The Middle East polled 18.6 percent for third place. But these figures apply only to firms currently involved internationally. Of those firms not currently involved internationally, 28 percent intend to enter foreign markets in the next five years. Undoubtedly, many other franchisers will be encouraged to consider foreign markets as they observe the successful performance of other systems.

Summary and Conclusions

The results of this survey show that the American franchising industry is experiencing growth in international markets akin to the domestic market boom between 1950 and 1965. Firms, motivated by the desire to penetrate potential growth areas as early as possible, are entering international markets at a spectacular rate. Larger firms, with good profit history in Canada and Europe, have now gained the expertise to do well in more diverse markets and are expanding into the Middle East, Asia, and Latin America. Firms newer to international markets are learning the intricacies of international business and are entering the newer as well as the more established market areas.

In the United States the ownership trend in franchising has moved toward more company-owned outlets; but in international markets the franchisee-owned outlet is the most frequently used ownership strategy. American franchisers do not always alter their marketing packages in foreign cultures; but when altered, most modify the product or service to fit local tastes. Profits from international ventures are mixed with a near normal distribution of firms reporting less, equal or greater profits in comparison to domestic units. Government interference and red tape are the most pervasive problems encountered by United States systems abroad; however, the expansion plans of the respondent firms would indicate that these obstacles are surmountable in most regions of the world and virtually all the firms have greater efforts planned for foreign markets. An overall optimism pervades the industry's outlook for the international arena and greater participation by the industry as a whole seems to be a certainty.

QUESTIONS

1. What factors have most greatly stimulated the entry into foreign markets by United States franchisers?
2. What kinds of ownership strategies have been undertaken by American franchisers?

3. What kinds of problems have been encountered by international franchisers?

4. How can these problems be minimized by the franchiser firms? By the United States government?

NOTES

1. U.S. Department of Commerce, *Franchising in the Economy, 1973-1975* (Washington, D.C.: Government Printing Office, 1975), p. 5.

2. Charles L. Vaughn, *Franchising* (Lexington, Mass.: Heath Lexington, 1974), p. 11.

3. Edwin L. Felter, Jr., ed., *International Franchising Conditions and Prospects* (Denver: Continental Reports, Inc., 1970), p. 3.

4. Vaughn, *Franchising*, p. 12.

5. "The Burger that Conquered the Country," *Time*, September 17, 1973, pp. 84–92.

6. U.S. Department of Commerce, *Franchising in the Economy 1973-1975*, p. 1.

7. Ibid, p. 29.

8. Bruce J. Walker and Michael J. Etzel, "The Internationalization of U.S. Franchise Systems: Progress and Procedures," *Journal of Marketing,* Vol. 37 (April 1973), pp. 38-46.

9. For the latest survey see U.S. Department of Commerce, *Franchising in the Economy 1973-1975.*

10. U.S. Department of Agriculture, "Fast Food Franchises: Market Potentials for Agricultural Product in Foreign and Domestic Markets," reprinted from *The Marketing and Transportation Situation,* ERS 596, (February 1975).

11. For example see Matthew Lifflander, "Looking for New Profits Abroad?" *Business Abroad,* Vol. 94 (September 1969), pp. 9-11 and Matthew Lifflander, "So You Want to Go Abroad," *Franchising Around the World,* Vol. 4 (July/August 1970), pp. 24-29.

12. The composite listing was developed from the *1973-74 International Franchise Association Membership Directory,* Washington, D.C., the *1972 Directory of Franchising Annual,* Newport Beach, California, the *12th Annual Soft Drink Franchise Company Directory,* 1972, Great Neck, New York and *The Franchise Opportunities Handbook, 1973,* U.S. Department of Commerce.

13. Sidney Siegal, *Nonparametric Statistics for the Behavioral Sciences* (New York: McGraw-Hill Book Company, 1956), pp. 229-38.

Effective international physical distribution management is critical to the success of overseas marketing ventures. This article focuses on the universal nature of physical distribution activities, and the need to reorder commercial boundaries to better accommodate the challenges of a changing environment. The author contends that new methods to move products and people are called for if physical distribution management is going to responsibly contribute to the world's energy problems.

25. Planning and Control in International PD

L. Soorikian
International Telephone and Telegraph

The focal point in any discussion of physical distribution management, whether it is national or international, is the issue of controlability or manageability. An astute manager controls most effectively when functions are relevant and its costs visible or measurable. The last quarter century of writing, discussions and demonstrations of success by dedicated practitioners of physical distribution management have established this function's relevance. However, we have failed to establish a universal language for exposing the invisible costs of physical distribution. Is there a universal management accounting system for measuring the costs of:

Untimely delivery—too late or too early?

Reasonableness of "carriage free" or "free-on-board" terms?

Source: Reprinted by permission from *Transportation and Distribution Management*, January–February 1974. Edited from a seminar on "International Distribution and Control" sponsored by the World Trade Institute and the National Council of Physical Distribution Management.

316

"Delivered Price?"

Ship best way?

Unnecessary freight caused by balloon packaging?

Warehouse lay-out that stifles efficiency?

Cost of inventory in transit?

Design that renders product unsuitable for transportation handling or storage?

The value of forwarder services?

Customer satisfaction or dissatisfaction?

Returnable packing?

The wrong location for plant or warehouse?

Knee-jerk reaction to sales mandate to ship within twenty-four hours of order and maintain 100 percent level of service?

Too many warehouses or not enough?

Can there be a great deal of satisfaction when whatever contribution we make to the competitiveness of our products and a favorable balance-of-trade are officially listed as "invisible exports"? I wonder if any of us appreciates the characterization of our serious efforts as "free" such as in "free-on-board."

Let's try to rid ourselves of this word "free" because sooner or later a brilliant economist will declare that if all goods and materials were purchased and sold "free-on-board," then 10 percent of our gross national product would be "free." Then, this being true, no one needs us to waste our time looking after something that is "free."

In a more serious vain, we might ask, what is new about physical distribution, national or international? The answer, of course, is that the forces that determined the locations of our cities, the geographic specialization of industry and the ability to trade, provide service and supply factories and markets.

Accepting the important role and relevance of physical distribution stems from a search for greater efficiency. We have always known about the bits and fragments of a system we generally accepted as parts of many other functions. The system has now emerged as physical distribution management. More recently, we have discovered the opportunities that exist in controlling international physical distribution. For in no other function is there as much waste, duplication and indifference as there is in moving goods from one country to another. If physical distribution is difficult of quantification and measurement in a United States manufacturing company with many plants, warehouses and markets, then you add to this, the complexity of national borders, customs of trade, protective customs, carrier preferences, nationalism, monetary exchange and the urge for filing documents, you can imagine the problem of control.

Here, in international physical distribution, we have the most challenging problems of performance visibility and control. We talk about the total system of physical distribution, subfunctional interrelationships and suboptimization of costs, service and inventories through trade-offs. Yet, buyers and sellers can't readily measure so many variables and continue to make decisions on the basis of time honored phrases that have the word "free" in it. This type of physical distribution control by proxy is too prevalent and it accomplishes only one freedom. It makes the individual, obviously not a PD manager, "free" from having to examine many related activities and costs. Unwillingness, particularly outside the United States, to face the challenge of physical distribution system analysis by industrial firms has given rise to a vast freight forwarding operation.

Forwarders perform a needed and effective service, but, generally, they as well as transportation companies, have done an inadequate job of role-playing in the physical distribution grid that closely ties their operations with all other forms of economic activity. This statement may be unfair, considering that it is the owner of the goods who must plan and control the arrangements for efficient flow and product availability. Yet, efficiency of the total physical distribution system is the object of our analysis. The role that each participant in the system plays or can play becomes significant. There is already evidence of greater integration of planning between the shipper and service elements in international trade.

PD is Universal

Physical distribution has no national boundaries. The activities and subfunctions of physical distribution are universal. We are headed in the same direction in physical distribution in Germany, in Singapore, in Brazil, in Zambia or in the U.S.S.R., as we are in the United States or in trade among nations.

Ten years ago, I could not imagine that the Trans-Siberian Railroad would be competing with the United States Railroads located in another continent and linked to Asia only by water. Yet, intermodal development, the closing of the Suez Canal and rapid industrialization of the Far East has created such competition. Predominance of the Far-Eastern consumer electronics position coupled with container ports in Siberia now move more freight to western Europe than the unfulfilled land-bridge dreams of the United States railroads.

Physical distribution management has one basic mission. That mission is the best allocation of resources to increase the utility of time. As we all know time is money and all activity consumes time. When we consider the life cycle of a product from material source through processing or manufacturing to the consumer, the greatest portion of that life cycle or time is spent in movement or storage—as much as 80 to 90 percent of the time.

Managing the physical distribution functions are so pervasive in basic economic activity that until recently we had taken it for granted—as granted as air that surrounds us and just as difficult to make visible or measure, unless, of course, we introduce pollution. There is no doubt that physical distribution must be managed and controlled. The amount of success we can expect in accomplishing this goal and determining the direction physical distribution management will take, depends, at this juncture:

1. On the realities of accounting as it is generally practiced.
2. On the organizational niche of the PD function.

With very few exceptions, accounting systems and traditional cost centers do not provide the management information necessary for control of physical distribution costs. Dr. Michael Shiff's study entitled *"Accounting and Control in Physical Distribution Management,"* a study sponsored by the National Council of Physical Distribution Management is an excellent beginning. However, the implementation of a PD cost system by industrial companies, particularly outside the United States, has been very slow. We cannot expect to control or manage physical distribution until we can measure it or make its costs visible. After over a quarter of a century of trying to establish the relevance of physical distribution management, I believe that the next 10 years will see a concentrated effort to adapt a physical distribution management information and control system to our individual needs.

We at ITT have developed and tested variations of a basic physical distribution cost reporting system as it applies to product lines and United States or non-United States requirements.

Earlier, I mentioned the pervasiveness of physical distribution activities and the way they cut across other established functional areas. This feature of PD management is the biggest challenge and opportunity for efficiency while at the same time, the main obstacle in rapid progression of its effective management. This brings us to the next major evolutionary stage of PD management growth and direction within the corporate framework over the next dozen years—that of organization. In this area, much will depend on the individual directing corporate PD activities and his knowledge of total business management. Internationally, the problem of organization and the place of the PD manager in the corporate structure is a bit more difficult. The difficulty is one in translation. Direct translation produces rather unusual and lengthy phrases. Therefore, at ITT we employ the physical distribution title and job scope without translating it. But is has taken several years of effort to establish the function and its effective performance. Today, physical distribution councils, organized or regional, national or product line groupings regularly meet and discuss our common interests in advancing the effectiveness of PD activities. These council meetings are not restricted to physical distribution personnel, but include representatives from manufacturing, purchasing, comptrollers and other operational areas.

Perhaps, the more significant contribution we can make in the long run is a bold and imaginative approach to reorder commercial boundaries to meet the needs of 21st century commerce. Already, we have seen evidence of this approach in the formation of the European Economic Community.

The energy crisis itself will tend to reorder our traditional methods for moving products and people. A quarter of the world's energy is consumed in transportation. Physical distribution management cannot escape its responsibility to provide efficient methods for mobility and availability. Without movement, factories will starve.

And in the area of bold approaches, consider a monograph published by Dr. G. Etzel Pearcy, retired chairman of geography at U.C.L.A. Dr. Pearcy urges that the United States be divided into thirty-eight parts instead of the fifty states. He maintains that artificial state boundaries of 18th and 19th centuries may no longer apply to our present and future needs. Sections of the country could be rearranged to make the best use of population density, position of cities, lines of transportation and water availability. He claims that such an arrangement would save the nation $4.6 billion annually. This is not an official endorsement by ITT of Dr. Pearcy's viewpoint. But, Dr. Pearcy's approach really highlights the difficulties facing physical distribution managers in their search for efficiency and control, and it *is* also a challenging and bold approach.

QUESTIONS

1. What are the invisible costs associated with physical distribution management?
2. What does the author mean by the statement "the most important challenge is reordering commercial boundaries"?
3. What trends does the author foresee in physical distribution management?

Selling to overseas markets through a wholly owned marketing subsidiary has proven to be a highly successful strategy for TRW Data Communications. The improved support provided to independent distributors, and the benefits obtained from establishing the company's master distributorship are discussed by the author.

26. TRW Datacom: A Better Idea for Overseas Distribution

Art Detman, Jr.
Sales and Marketing Management

The slowly ebbing worldwide recession notwithstanding, foreign countries still are large and tempting markets for United States makers of high-technology equipment. In this field IBM is, of course, the premier multinational marketer. But what about small companies? They have neither the capital to build a direct selling organization overseas nor the reputation and expertise needed to recruit first-rank independent distributors.

One answer, perhaps unique and certainly unusual, is TRW Datacom International, a wholly owned marketing subsidiary of TRW, the big, multinational conglomerate that is largely a manufacturing company. TRW Datacom, based in Los Angeles, is a master distributor that purchases data-processing equipment from United States companies for resale through a network of foreign distributors that Datacom has recruited and trained and to which it provides marketing support. Datacom's aim is to provide to its distributor network all the things that a well-organized home office would provide to a field sales organization.

Source: Reprinted by permission from *Sales & Marketing Management* magazine. Copyright © 1976.

Not quite three years old, Datacom already has twenty-five distributors selling in about forty countries. In 1975, Datacom's sales totalled about $25 million; distributor sales exceeded $50 million. "It's hard to say what our sales might be five years from now," says Robert L. Ashley, a TRW vice president and general manager of Datacom. "But we think that we should grow, in transfer sales to our distributors, to $100 million. Now, that's not a forecast, but that is a general estimate of the size we expect to be."

Ironically, TRW probably would never have organized this subsidiary if it hadn't been for a small, struggling electronics company in San Antonio that was on the verge of collapse. The story of Datapoint Corp., then known as Computer Terminal Corp., is a familiar one. Founded in 1968, it was strong in engineering, weak in capitalization. Its products—mini computers and data-processing equipment for multilocation systems—were oriented to large end-users such as railroads, insurance companies, government agencies, and chain stores. Because industry-leader IBM leased its equipment to end users, companies like Datapoint also had to lease rather than sell. The more units customers ordered, the farther into the red went Datapoint. Management began a hunt for money.

"We were asked," Ashley says, "if we would be interested in making an investment in Computer Terminal. Now, this is something we generally do not do because TRW is an operating company, not a venture capital firm. But we felt that there were some unique things going on in this company in terms of its new product development, the 'intelligent terminal,' as it was called." He adds, "Also, at that time TRW was attempting to break into the commercial equipment business—data processing, data communication, and telecommunications. This area was, we felt, a gap between our systems activities, which were very expansive, and our components activities, also large and broad."

In that light, an investment in Datapoint appeared attractive. Datapoint products could be (and today are) the heart of some TRW small business and data communication systems. The investment was made, but to protect it TRW agreed to represent Datapoint worldwide, in all markets except the United States. From Datapoint's view, the arrangement was a godsend. It could not afford to sell overseas on its own; yet it desperately needed the cash flow that would be provided by selling to distributors instead of only leasing to end users. As for TRW, the arrangement allowed it to gain international experience in a new market.

The five-year agreement that was signed in 1971 did not create TRW Datacom. Rather, TRW's electronics group was to select distributors that would sign contracts directly with Datapoint. TRW would receive a commission from Datapoint on all units shipped abroad. After two years of hard work, 16 foreign distributors were signed. "Recruiting distributors," Ashley says, "was by far the most difficult problem we had because in almost every instance there were no logical candidates. That is, logical in the sense that they were already doing what we were looking for." Ashley adds, wishing it were otherwise, "Those kinds of distributors just didn't exist in this business."

To find leads, Ashley and his managers enlisted the help of TRW executives overseas and of international bankers. The criteria were stiff. "You see," Ashely says, "with a computer product line such as this, we require that a distributor have not just a strong marketing capability but a very strong maintenance force, software personnel, applications engineers, and systems engineers. We really need a total organization."

Needed: $100,000

Naturally, Ashley was seeking large and successful distributors in related fields. But such distributors weren't always available. Ultimately, TRW also signed small distributors and manufacturers that agreed to form distributorships, and it set up joint ventures—as in Australia—and wholly owned subsidiaries—as in Brazil and Canada.

Lokka notes that the cost of entry for a distributor is at least $100,000. "And even that is quite minimal," he adds. "The distributor has to buy a demo unit. If it's a simple intelligent-entry terminal, that's $10,000. If his market calls for complex, multiterminal Datashare units, the demo could be $80,000. And he needs to double that for spares. So in equipment alone there is a swing of $20,000 to $150,000."

The recruitment of dealers under the original agreement with TRW helped Datapoint, but not enough. In fiscal 1972, on sales of $5.4 million, the company lost more than $2 million. The board of directors, including the two TRW members, agreed it was time for a change of management. In March 1973, they recruited Harold E. O'Kelley, then a group vice president of Harris Corp., the electronics and printing equipment manufacturer.

O'Kelley had a better idea for overseas distribution. He suggested that TRW form an international marketing subsidiary that would handle, on an exclusive basis, all Datapoint products except those acquired through merger and acquisition. In addition, TRW could handle the products of other companies, thereby leveraging its investment. TRW liked the idea, formed TRW Datacom International, and in July 1973 signed a 10-year contract with Datapoint.

"We have the benefit of having all our international sales as full cash, nonrecourse sales, which creates a positive cash flow," O'Kelley says. "And instead of our having to worry about letters of credit, international monetary matters, and the like, TRW does all that. It buys direct from us and resells to the distributor." O'Kelley also changed the domestic marketing system of Datapoint, phasing out distributors and enlarging his direct field sales force. Today, Datapoint has about 60 domestic salesmen and nearly as many systems engineers.

These and other changes have had their effect. In fiscal 1975, ended July 31, Datapoint sales were up 38 percent, to $46.9 million, while earnings rose 32 percent, to $3.1 million. In the first quarter of fiscal 1976, sales climbed 43 percent, to $14.5 million, while earnings jumped 55 percent, to $1 million.

O'Kelley won't say what portion of his sales is to TRW Datacom, but he admits that it's a big and important chunk. Last year $22.6 million of the company's total sales were made abroad, mostly through Datacom but some to another manufacturer for inclusion in systems sold abroad. It's likely that Datacom currently accounts for about 40 percent of Datapoint's sales. Under the 10-year contract, it must account for at least 26 percent in any one year.

"There is a built-in sales quota in the arrangement with TRW," O'Kelley says. "But it's not the usual quota in terms of absolute numbers. Setting a quota over a 10-year period is extremely difficult, of course. I think we arrived at an equitable and perhaps unique solution in that we established a quota by making it a ratio of international shipments to domestic shipments, and that ratio is .35."

The ratio is calculated on the dollar value, at full list price, of domestic units shipped, including leased units and discounted units. For each $10,000 worth of equipment shipped domestically by Datapoint, TRW Datacom must purchase $3,500 worth for international resale. The presumption is that as Datapoint products gain acceptance in the United States, they should gain acceptance abroad. "Conversely," O'Kelley notes, "if we design a product that won't sell in the United States, it's not fair to expect Datacom to sell it internationally. And that is the reason for not setting a sales quota in absolute numbers." However, there is no limit on what Datacom may buy. "Absolutely not," says O'Kelley. "We'll sell them everything we can. We like them."

The agreement changed TRW's position from that of a commissioned middleman to a full-fledged marketing company with sales quotas that presumedly would rise over the years. Ashley established two distributor support centers—the one in London serves distributors in Europe, the Middle East, and Africa; the one in Los Angeles serves distributors in the Western Hemisphere and the Pacific Basin.

As part of its marketing responsibility, Datacom provides distributors with technical training for distributor service representatives; product and market training for distributor salesmen; and technical manuals, sales brochures, and other material printed in English. It places full-page, four-color advertisements (created by Benjamin White & Associates, Los Angeles) in international editions of *Business Week* and *Datamation*. It also acts as a technical and market information clearinghouse among distributors. And, not least of all, it sends its executives into the field to help distributors sell major accounts.

"Sometimes it's necessary to do some sales-oriented analysis of the customer's job to qualify him or to find out what his real problem is," says Thomas F. Cull, Datacom's product sales manager. "And when a big account is involved and the distributor requests assistance, we'll participate directly with the distributor in that presales environment. In fact, every one of us in a management position here participates in the direct selling effort in addition to his specific function assignment. Everyone."

As for the distributor, he is expected to recruit salesmen and technicians and provide them with basic training, translate into the local language whichever Datacom materials seem appropriate, create and place local advertising as he deems necessary, pass on to the customer at least the manufacturer's warranty, arrange for customer financing as needed, and of course sell and service the products. Each distributor is also responsible for his own pricing, and typically he prices his units so as to provide a 35 percent to 50 percent gross margin.

New distributors are signed originally for a year, then renewed for periods ranging up to five years. "In any agreement," Datacom's Lokka says, "we are going to ask the distributorship to perform at a certain level, something that we both consider satisfactory. In the first year we do it in a rather loose structure, with no real pressure on the distributor. After that, we both have a handle on the marketplace and can look out for the next two or three years or whatever to set quotas and so on."

Today, the distributor network covers markets that account for an estimated 90 percent or more of the computer installations in place. Three more candidates are on the verge of being signed. Because the remaining markets are so small, future distributors are likely to be multinational in order to generate sufficient volume. Some small countries might be covered largely at the behest of big United States multinational corporations, which are prime sales prospects that favor uniformity of equipment worldwide and demand local service capabilities.

The recruitment process has been slow and deliberate. "Our selection is in the context of the long term," Lokka says. "I am frequently tempted by the guy who says he's got a big order if we'll name him today. But we don't succumb to that type of thing because we feel that a long-term solution is the answer. We try to choose the distributor who it appears we will be able to work with on a compatible basis over a long period of time." He adds, "Because of the great distance involved it is extremely important that we establish ahead of time that the two companies are compatible in their general business philosophies."

From a personal standpoint, too, such compatibility makes life easier for the Datacom marketers. "For instance," Lokka says, "my wife thinks that the only time I make business calls is when I'm at home. In the morning I'm calling Europe and in the evening I'm calling the Far East."

Datapoint presently accounts for the overwhelming bulk of TRW Datacom sales; a few years ago, it accounted for all the sales. "We excluded other companies in the start-up years because we didn't want to dilute our efforts with the Datapoint line in any way," Ashley says. "This represented a market that was growing very rapidly and where we had more than we could handle in terms of building our organization."

Slowly, TRW Datacom added other products, all compatible from a marketing viewpoint: an optical character reader manufactured by Computer Entry Systems Corp. of Maryland; bank teller terminals, credit-authorization systems, and other financial data equipment manufactured by two TRW divisions; and printers manufactured by Centronics, Inc., based in New Hampshire.

Each agreement is different, and Ashley believes that is one of the strengths of his organization—it combines flexibility with specialization. Datacom can distribute products on an exclusive or nonexclusive basis, worldwide or only in selected markets. Generally, it prefers an exclusive worldwide arrangement. In any event, the products and their markets are all broadly compatible.

"Our general thrust in terms of products," Ashley explains, "is to add products that are complementary to the Datapoint product line. We want products that can be sold and serviced within our existing network. We have put together a great deal of expertise, and we don't want to dilute it by getting into markets or products that are too far afield from our present business."

Like Datapoint, TRW Datacom is growing fast. When Sales & Marketing Management asked one manager if another had just joined the company, the first answered, in all seriousness: "Oh, no. He's been here ten months." From a handful of people thirty months ago, Datacom now has seventy-two employees, forty-five of them at the master distributorship level, twenty-seven in wholly owned subdistributors.

Unsurprisingly, Datacom's table of organization has been in flux. Currently, Ashley has the title of vice president and general manager. Reporting directly to him are a vice president of operations, a vice president of marketing, and a director of business development. Under James L. Kelly, the vice president of operations, are four groups: finance; a sales group that markets Datapoint products to TRW divisions within the United States; sales administration, which includes shipping, export documentation, billing, scheduling, and the like; and distributor operations, the group headed by Lloyd Lokka that works directly with distributors on a day-to-day basis, setting sales goals, recruiting new distributors, and so on. "When I came here," Lokka says, "I said, 'Gee, my job is kind of like that of an international sales manager.' "

The marketing vice president is Melvin R. Wellerstein, and his group provides the distributors with day-to-day marketing support in the areas of pricing, sales training, sales promotion, advertising, competitive evaluation programs, application exchange programs, and direct selling assistance. Wellerstein has some accounts, and so does Kelly, his counterpart in operations.

"You must remember," says one Datacom marketer, "that this is strictly a marketing subsidiary, and so 'operations' really means 'marketing operations.' At Datacom, everyone is in marketing."

The director of business development, Matthew Shapiro, has two responsibilities: recruiting new accounts—United States and foreign—that want Datacom to handle their products, and working with present accounts, such as Datapoint, to develop new products. Says Shapiro: "We feel that we can bring a unique capability to companies that are not yet doing much internationally. We can offer instant access to international markets in a large way through an experienced organization. A small company that is growing rapidly has all it can do to sell in the United States, much less overseas. We relieve it of the need to dilute management efforts in establishing overseas distributors and learning about export-import regulations, customs, insurance, and the like. We also assume all financial risks—bad debts, accounts receivable, and so on—and pay cash to these companies, many of which are leasing in the United States and getting only 2 percent or 3 percent of their money each month. So we think we have a valuable service, and we intend to grow, not only in terms of increased sales of existing products but by bringing in additional products."

The outlook appears bright for doing just that. Aside from the normal difficulties of managing such a fast-growing operation, Ashley appears to have only two long-term problems. One is the health of himself and his top executives. The other problem is the growing protectionist mood of developing countries that have mounting balance-of-payments deficits. To reduce those deficits, they might demand that Datacom manufacture locally some or all of its products instead of exporting them from the United States.

Still, Ashley has good reason to be optimistic. There are literally hundreds of small, high-technology companies in the United States that have good products but no feasible way of marketing them overseas. They had no way, that is, until TRW Datacom International came into being.

QUESTIONS

1. How has TRW benefited from using its wholly owned marketing subsidiary?
2. What does TRW expect from its distributors?
3. What advantages do the distributors receive under the new TRW distribution arrangement?

COMMUNICATIONS
STRATEGIES

The creation of awareness, interest, desire, and action is the universal concern of the communications mix. The coordinating and integrating of communications or promotional mix elements with other aspects of marketing strategy is often more difficult to accomplish in overseas markets. The quality, availability, and scheduling of promotional tools all impinge on the degree of success realized by a product or service. The selections in Part VII illustrate several important considerations underlying the design of an international communications effort. The issue of effectiveness versus efficiency is a fundamental trade-off in the decision to standardize multinational communications strategies. First, Manville provides a listing of caveats which affect selling overseas. The second article, by Peebles, Ryans, and Vernon deals with this problem by advancing a programmed management framework for simultaneous design of advertising strategies for several foreign markets. Governing the standardization or transferability of communications across national boundaries is the degree of cultural homogeneity in existence among neighboring nations. The next article, by S. Watson Dunn, explores the extent to which the European market is characterized by broadly assimilated values, and discusses the implications raised for multinational advertisers. The section concludes with David McIntyre's article on the marketing communications consideration underlying the development of Seven Up Corporation's multinational product positioning strategy.

The environment of international marketing contains many pitfalls for promotional marketing strategies. The author outlines a number of caveats about the political, social, and economic climate of overseas markets that directly impinge on media availability, copy claim effectiveness, protecting brand names and trademarks, and personal selling efforts.

27. Caveats for the Prospective Overseas Marketer

Richard Manville
Richard Manville Research

Thinking about taking your business abroad? Many marketing and legal traps lie ahead for American executives contemplating international marketing. And many of these traps can be avoided.

The cautions below can help the would-be exporter deal with some of the irritations, bureaucratic red tape, contradictory laws, and resultant exasperations that often plague international marketers.

Unless anticipated, such traps can result in setbacks, lost orders, lower sales, or even worse. Minimizing these problems can maximize your chances of success.

Listed below are marketing traps and helpful hints. (There are other problems, such as "cultural gaps," but they represent an entirely separate subject.)

Source: Reprinted from *Marketing News,* March 10, 1978, by permission of the publisher, the American Marketing Association, and the author. Copyright © 1978 by Richard Manville, Westport, CT 06880.

Before going into the traps, however, let's look at some international marketing prerequisites. For one thing, before you market overseas, here are factors you will have to *know* (not guess at) in order to decide whether you can or cannot export successfully:

What products will you offer for overseas sales?

What size of market should you have for your product classification?

Who is—and how strong is—your competition?

Have you determined that your product can hold its own in the country/countries you are thinking about?

What are the size and type of the marketing/distribution structure in that country or those countries?

What are the names of potential overseas trading partners?

Have you ascertained their possible interest in your line?

Have you checked out these potential distributors as to their market coverage, sales ability, and creditworthiness?

Have you made an effort to learn about the country's customs, business, and highlights.

Another set of prerequisites: Before you go overseas you should have made arrangements—two or three months in advance—by writing to the United States commercial consul, telling of your planned visit. In your letter you should have outlined (or asked):

Precisely what you want to sell.

The major uses of the product.

How you market it in your own country.

Whether you want to meet potential importers or agents.

Whether you want a distributor or trade town.

Whether you want an interpreter.

Will local holidays conflict with your visit?

Have you forwarded catalogue pages, labels, prices (approximate, including cost, insurance, freight) to the Bureau of Export?

Have you forwarded credit references?

Have you indicated memberships, if any, in service clubs such as Kiwanis, Rotary, etc. to help establish "fraternal" links?

With these preliminaries out of the way, the hopeful overseas marketer should be thinking about:

Political Climate

The political climate for foreign business involves the importance of "local customs" concerning the facilitation of contracts. Whether it is called "greasing the palm" (U.S.), "rashwah" or "baqshish" (Arabic), or "hui lo" (Chinese), this custom has proven difficult for American companies trying to do business abroad. The Lockheed bribery scandal was but one of several hundred which have surfaced.

What to do about this? As the *New York Times* (Jan. 22, 1978) stated:

. . . Acting under the pressure of U.S. laws, regulations, and public opinion, most U.S.-based multinationals have substantially reduced or eliminated foreign political payments. Small payments to minor officials of foreign governments to induce them to perform their duties expeditiously—generally known as "facilitating" payments or "grease"—appear to be inescapable and continue. They're not prohibited by U.S. law or regulation.

Some American multinationals have changed their mode of transacting foreign business to reduce direct relationships with foreign government officials. Thus, a large electrical equipment manufacturer now produces equipment in certain countries, rather than exporting it from the United States, to avoid the payment of commissions to foreign agents, whose activities it cannot control.

Some organizations have arranged to have their former agents act as principals who buy and sell on their own accounts. This eliminates the payment of commissions and the responsibility for monitoring their use.

Still other companies, particularly engineering and construction firms, have abandoned roles as prime contractors to foreign governments and have become subcontractors to French, West German, Japanese, or South Korean companies.

By these stratagems, American companies have insulated themselves against charges of impropriety, but the practice of making political payments continues in other hands.

In any case it is important to examine the business-political climate of the host country toward a foreign company. Is it friendly or difficult? Don't go by what you think it is—or *was*. Things change. Today Peru *wants* private enterprise; so does Mexico.

As of November, 1977, India told IBM that its products manufactured in India were "not sophisticated enough, nor did it export enough." Therefore India wanted to nationalize that company. It also would not allow IBM to continue majority ownership of its business in India. IBM declined and is leaving that country.

India also told the Coca-Cola Co. that unless it gave the Indian government its formula for syrup it could no longer do business in India. The Coca-Cola Co. now is leaving India. The Indian government, in turn, is now marketing, through the same bottlers, a government-created substitute drink called 77.

Even when the political climate seems hospitable, the cultural or professional climate may be hostile:

Japanese lawyers are trying to exclude two prestigious "foreign" law firms, one an American firm, the other a British (Hong Kong) firm representing British nationals in Japan. These law firms "represent" possible "foreign" competitors in law practice in Japan.

Even local companies can hurt from layer upon layer of bureaucracy when governmental approval is needed. It's doubly difficult for a "foreign" company. In Thailand for example, local law awards local officials 20 percent of any fines the courts impose on a company convicted of wrongdoing.

This incites and corrupts underpaid civil servants. Siam Kraft is being sued for importing raw pulp and not paying duties on "finished goods." Customs people admitted that pulp is a raw material, but the court ordered the company to pay $200,000 in duties. It then slapped on a $3 million fine. If forced to pay immediately, Siam Kraft could fold, reported *Business Week* (Nov. 28, 1977).

Tax Burdens

Study, in advance for each country you are considering as an export market, all the import and other taxes that an exporter has to pay. These include taxes on product, or trade, or consumer level. Also how do these vary, if at all, from the costs of shipping in a totally-assembled product from the United States or, alternately, by using local labor to assemble parts made elsewhere, within the importing country? These taxes—and therefore, your costs—can vary tremendously.

"Local Content" Laws—Will They Affect You?

Become familiar with each country's "local content" laws—those stipulating that a prescribed percentage of the value of a final product must be manufactured locally. Do they apply? Can, or should, you ship into a *third* country, fully or partly assemble there, and *then* ship into the intended country? This could be especially attractive if the proposed "assembly" country has free access to countries in its area, such as those of the Latin American Free Trade Area or the European Common Market.

Do You Know the Foreign Commercial/Fair Trade Practices Laws?

Have you studied not only the market's laws, but also its customs, preferences, and taboos? In Germany, for a single example, putting up window advertising signs without paying government sales tax is not allowed. In some countries, outdoor boards are taxed. Giving away free merchandise or free samples, particularly cigarettes and liquor, is frowned upon in many countries, despite its prevalence in the United States. These "common" United States promotions or sales practices may run afoul of laws in overseas countries.

A special category is represented by the European regulations governing the pharmaceuticals industry. Here are some of these, as reported by Philip J. Brown in *Medical Media Marketing* (September, 1977):

France. A new decree has been introduced which, apart from other measures, profoundly restricts direct mail communications between a pharmaceutical company and a doctor. As one leading manufacturer recently put it, "It will soon be illegal to even send a letter to a prescribing physician."

Germany. A comprehensive new "Medicines Act" took effect on January 1.

Denmark. Restrictions on what can be said came in at the beginning of 1976.

Norway. Already the most severe in Europe, this nation is tightening the screws further.

Sweden has become the first country in the world to enact legislation against most aerosol sprays on the ground that they may harm the atmosphere.

The ban, which will take effect January 1, 1979, covers the thousands of hair sprays, deodorants, air fresheners, insecticides, paint, waxes, and assorted sprays that use Freon gases as propellants. It does not apply to certain medical sprays, especially those used by people who suffer from asthma.

The Swedish government, which has one of the world's most active environmental protection departments, is taking seriously warnings by some scientists that continued release of these chemicals could eventually degrade the earth's ozone layer.

Great Britain. Promotion expenditures for drugs have been running at 14 percent of sales. This had to be down to 12 percent in 1977 and 10 percent by the end of 1978. This is an average for the industry and means that the giants like Merck, Sharp & Dohme and Roche must keep below 4–5 percent, while the very small companies keep to around 30 percent.

Throughout Europe governments are introducing legislation which is designed to severely limit the content, type, and quantity of pharmaceutical promotion. (This type of restriction also applies to promotions for other products—contests, lotteries, etc.)

In Spain a proposed new law aims at reducing all forms of promotion expenditure and severely regulating content.

If you plan to sell pharmaceuticals in Europe, be sure to check, in advance, upcoming legislation from the EEC and become knowledgeable about cartel and monopoly legislation. Dawn Mitchell, Research Services Ltd. (London), reminds us:

You should be aware that in Britain prices and, importantly, price increases for pharmaceuticals, are negotiated between the individual manufacturer and the government. Each year a company has to submit a full financial declaration, showing in great detail all items of income and expenditure. This annual financial return is the basis for all price negotiations, and, although it is part of what we call the Voluntary Price Regulations Scheme, governments use it to keep companies' returns on investment very much in line.

(Restrictions of this type are found in a number of countries and are applied by overseas governments to a wide range of consumer products.)

If restrictions on sales promotion, advertising, and even profits of pharmaceutical companies seem oppressive, let's examine additional marketing traps that await the unwary, the innocent, or the unprepared United States exporter of *other* products who wants to sell overseas:

Poor Timing.

Running sales on local holidays, which may run contrary to local holiday purchase patterns, can result in failing to reach sales targets and profit goals overseas.

Ignorance of Additional "Bogeys"

Selling products with wrong electrical frequency cycles or type of current, or with unfamiliar or incorrect accessories needed, or used, in a local market. Selling electric shavers in the Middle East (regardless of money available) is a problem because of the uncertainty of the electrical service. Selling clothing sizes can be disastrous if you don't label the sizes according to local customs; sizes vary from country to country.

"Cultural" differences can affect sales. One example (Sunbeam, and 30 percent of its profits), came from overseas, and it didn't come easily. Sunbeam was dismayed to discover that although West Germans eat a lot of toast, Italians don't.

There were similar pitfalls with the electric shaver market. "We were the first company to develop the ladies' electric shaver, and success came quickly," the Sunbeam chairman, Robert P. Gwinn, said. "But when we showed it in Italy, we sold relatively few." His explanation: Italian men like their women with hair on their legs.

Misjudging a Market

"Positioning" a company incorrectly in an overseas market—selling "price" in a quality-conscious overseas market, or vice-versa.

Remember, too, that a count of the total population of a country does *not* mean "X" size market in dollars (or local currency) for your product (per capita). *Disposable* or discretionary income and socioeconomic groupings can vary enormously by country.

Another cause of export marketing failures is ignorance or naivete' about foreign distribution/sales channels.

For example, a would-be exporter may not fully appreciate the crucial role that trade shows and exhibits play in a foreign country as a *basic* channel for testing a product, selling a product, or obtaining leads that will get a United States exporter either local, or other foreign importers, distributors, or retailers in one or more countries.

An exhibit in Germany may be attended by would-be *importers* from six to ten additional countries. Prepare your material and "homework" accordingly—know in advance your shipping costs from New York to Hamburg, as well as to Bahrein or Milan.

PCA, a United States-based chain of department store quick-photo departments found, on going overseas, that the effect of its technology-oriented approach to protrait processing on craft-oriented workers in Denmark was a strike, a two month shutdown, and a huge loss. Overseas retailers, too, would not turn over space to the company for a 10 percent sales conversion, resulting in unexpected costs.

Additional mistakes frequently made by exporters may be of omission or commission, when it comes to obtaining distributors in an overseas market. Shipping incorrectly labeled goods *after* having secured an importer or distributor is another frequent error.

Exporters often fail to properly promote their own overseas trade show exhibits to prospective importers, distributors, retailers, or OEMs, via their companies' *own* private mailings and promotion to their *own* lists of overseas prospects.(Don't depend on the trade show mailings! You want traffic in *your* booth.)

A Serious Mistake: Incorrect or Illegal Packaging or Labeling

Inadequate identification, in the failure to correctly identify contents, failure to use the needed languages, or inadequate or incorrect descriptions printed on the labels—all of these or any of them may cause problems. (If in doubt, study carefully your foreign competitors' labels. Learn the elements and languages they include on their own labels for each country.)

Incorrect labeling *can* be serious. Coca-Cola, Italy, found its complete business brought to a standstill because of a judicial order: "A judge in Genoa, today (*New York Times,* November 16, 1977) ordered the nationwide seizure of all bottled Coca-Cola on the ground that its ingredients were not properly labeled. The Magistrate, Mario Sossi, also banned any further distribution or production of bottled Coca-Cola, a $120 million-a-year business in Italy."

The ruling did not apply to canned Coca-Cola which does list the ingredients.

The company claimed the ingredients for the bottled Coca-Cola were listed on the bottle cap; the judge felt that description did not meet Italy's label laws.

Some countries—among them Canada, which requires that the text be in both English and French—can confiscate goods if the rules are not met. France has one of the most stringent requirements. There the law says: "In any offer, presentation, advertisement, written or spoken, instructions for use, specification, or guarantee terms for goods or services, as well as for invoices and receipts, the use of the French language is compulsory."

Germany has exceptionally stringent food laws. In part because the Germans are very health-conscious, it is, for an outsider, exceptionally difficult to enter the health-food market.

Local (Overseas) Food and Drug Laws

Failure to know what ingredients, additives, or chemicals are permitted in the host country can keep your product out of an overseas market. Ignorance is no excuse.

Even if the United States Food and Drug Administration allows a dye or additive in a United States food, that in itself doesn't assure that another country will allow the same ingredient in its food. Check it out by consulting the host country's consular office, asking the United States Agriculture Department's Foreign Agricultural Service, or asking the FDA.

A Common Error

Using poorly translated documents or manuals, either written by classical scholars in the United States *without* a knowledge of local (overseas) commercial, business, or technical terms or, worse yet, publishing instructions in the wrong language—Spanish-language manuals for Brazil.

Typical mistakes by Americans: failure to recognize that Belgium uses two languages; Switzerland has four linguistic ethnic groups; American English is *not* English English. Spain can traditionally be classified into thirteen regions; ten languages are spoken, two of which, Catalan and Basque, are not merely dialects of Castilian but *separate* languages.

Failure to know and cater to local preferences as to size or unit price, or types of outlets at which local customers prefer to buy or the local laws permit, also causes sales failures overseas.

These sales outlets, or sizes of product you sell or make available overseas may be *totally different* from what you might normally "assume," based on long established United States practices. Quite often, against their own interest and against apparent "logic," consumers overseas with modest or low discretionary purchasing power buy smaller sizes—even single units (for example, a cigarette)—in order to stretch a limited budget to buy an item. Even if the *smaller* size or unit does sell for more per gram or ounce than the United States "giant size"!

Furthermore, they might prefer to buy toothpaste from a newsstand, or cigarettes or whiskey from street vendors, as they do today in Beirut.

Things like this naturally affect your decisions as to the channels of distribution you use overseas. But you have to go overseas yourself to have the full impact sink into your consciousness.

Channels of Distribution

Failure to take into consideration the myriad and sometimes (to us) unusual local channels of distribution for your product, which may differ *markedly* from the United States channels, can make for difficulties. In Germany, for example, department stores are important retail outlets for foods. In France, industrial food brokers are very important.

Lack of knowledge of the *marketing* structure of a foreign country. Distribution practices and markups naturally affect the final purchase price.

In Japan, for example, it can take as many as ten "layers" of distribution before the consumer gets a food product from the original supplier through his channels of distribution.

Some Media Surprises

You cannot know the subtleties of consumers' preferred media from a twenty-four-hour visit to an overseas market. Neither can your agency unless it has been in—and has worked in—each country over a period of time.

You've got to work with your local marketing or sales people to really know the local media peculiarities that exist. (Quirks to Americans, but "obvious" to a *local* marketing man/woman.) Some markets are strong on TV— yet available time is incredibly tight.

You give *them* the commercial; *they* tell you, that "When it appears, it will appear." It can be at 2 a.m., mixed in with six or ten other television commercials run back-to-back. That is the government's TV ad policy. (In some countries, all of your advertising—theme, copy, and visuals—must be approved by government agencies.)

Other countries (often those with lower literacy rates) may be called "poster" media countries. But there are no hard-and-fast rules. You've got to know your territory, and you can't know your target country from examining the local media catalogue pages while sitting in your office in New York, Chicago, or Los Angeles.

Some product advertising is prohibited in some media and the pattern of "logic" is sometimes difficult to fathom.

The mix of the press media, strong in most European markets, changes from country to country. General interest magazines are strong in Italy, where the national daily newspaper is very weak—the reverse is the case in the United Kingdom.

Advertising Copy/Symbols

Before you advertise, first check the patent and copyright laws, country by country. You've got to know—before you advertise or package your product—whether your company or brand name is "unspeakably vulgar" when translated. What does your name or trademark symbol, reproduced in the various media of the host country, "mean" to the nationals of that country? It may "communicate" such an absurdity (to an overseas customer) that it can subject your brand name or trademark to derision or produce a violently negative image.

Sometimes, in or out of context, a well-known or highly respected United States brand name or trademark is vulgar, meaningless, difficult, or funny to the local customers. Sometimes your highly prized United States brand name is difficult to pronounce in the foreign language, or is pronounced in such a way that it means a ridiculous word. Or it can have a "poor" or unfortunate implication in a foreign language.

If you're going on TV (overseas) and thinking of using an American commercial, stop before you do. Even hand gestures are far from international, *Business Week* reports. For example, if you form a circle with thumb and forefinger, most Europeans will know you mean, "It's the best" or "It's A-okay," etc. But in some Latin American countries, the same gesture has a vulgar connotation.

(One example in reverse: Japanese firms taking space in United States office buildings try to avoid fourth floors—just as we Americans don't like thirteenth floors. It seems that in Japanese the pronunciation of the number "four" is the same as that for "death.")

Your company's brand name, label, or trademark may have been pre-empted by someone in the overseas country. *Legally.* And you have to market your product in *that* country under a different brand name. Whatever the reason, protect your trade names *immediately* in each country.

You may make claims or competitive statements that are forbidden by law—and thus open yourself to legal damages—in the foreign country. Competitive claims, even if true, are "out" in many countries. Ditto for "comparative" advertising.

"Learn before you burn" about local import laws as they affect your use of television commercials. In Australia, for example, be sure you learn, in advance, whether you can import footage for television commercials and "dub" in the local language and/or package shots; or whether all footage—even though you have it on film—must be refilmed in Australia itself (like reinventing the wheel!).

Target Market Tastes

For each country in which you plan to sell overseas, you've got to *know* the target market. And sometimes illogical as it may seem, the target market varies from one country to the next. In soft drinks, for example, lemon-lime flavors are aimed at the children's market in some countries and at the adult market in another country. (The leading flavor in Columbia is cream soda—as it was several decades ago in New York City!)

In Japan, one of the leading soft drink flavors for several years was grape. With the trends toward pure food and pure drinks (the "natural food" revolution among consumers is as strong in Japan as elsewhere), the leading flavor today is no longer grape but lemon-lime. Reasons: Fewer colorants for grape drinks are acceptable to the governing food law administration in Japan.

"Special Packaging/Shipping Containers?"

Face the realities of packing and shipping time and delays. How long does it actually require to move your goods from your plant to the ultimate local retail outlet? Are your goods perishable? How long will your goods have to wait in port before unloading—regardless of the reason? And does your packing (and packaging) reflect storage habits (and handling) in the proposed export market as to weather, heat, humidity, cold, insects, mold?

How about inadequate, careless, or primitive loading methods or transport? Will your labels "stick"? Will the freight handlers, dock workers or truckers be able to read and understand your English instructions (if you have them) on the ouside of your packing cases: Should they be in the foreign language or symbols also? Yes!

"Who Pays for What?"

What are the local or trade customs in regards to distributor markups? What is the distributor's share (if any!) in your local advertising costs? Ditto for the retailer? Who pays for samples (and shipping costs)? Who pays for factory-training programs? Returned goods? Credit losses? Trade shows? For visits overseas and vice-versa?

Pricing and Costs

Has a proper study been done of competitive costs and pricing? Has *everything* been included? All local taxes? V.A.T. (Value Added Tax)?

In setting your price, even in a prelimianry way (and you should have some estimates, in advance, for your "partner"/distributor negotiations *before* you to to a foreign country), be sure you include, in your pricing, the following cost items of your product for an overseas market (and these items do not include the usual local markups by the local channels—distributor, dealers, etc., which we learn from a study of the market structure in each country):

1. FOB factory price
2. Taxes, if any
3. Travel to depot
4. Freight to port
5. Unloading costs
6. Wharfage
7. Handling
8. Storage
9. Cartage
10. F.F. forwarders
11. Verifications
12. Certifications
13. Foreign invoice
14. Certificate of origin
15. Consular forms
16. Loading
17. Demurrage
18. Freight costs
19. Insurance
20. Landing fees

21. Customs duties
22. Customer's broker
23. Finance/credit carrying charges
24. Cost of special packing or packaging

And in estimating your costs of doing business have you anticipated possible foreign currency losses? For example: H.J. Heinz, the giant American food processor, earned on its foreign operation $83.8 million in 1976 on sales of $1.9 billion. Those earning would have been $94 million if it had not been for foreign currency losses.

Firing Policies?

What are the local rules for getting rid of the local agent or general manager or distributor if he (or they) doesn't work out? The severance-pay penalties in many overseas countries can be costly, no matter how incompetent or rebellious a local agent or employee, or how correct you are in trying to build your business overseas with a new staff. Ask your lawyer; be sure he consults with the *local* authorities in each country.

Advertising costs/payments: It is not rare for an overseas advertising medium to send (upon request), three bills to an advertiser for the same insertion: One bill quotes actual charges to be paid; one bill quotes higher charges for the "benefit" of the overseas corporation which is paying all, or part of, the advertising cost when the bill is submitted for evidence that an ad has appeared; the third bill is specifically designed for the tax collector, masking, for tax purposes, any clues as to how much sales the local advertiser might be doing (the lower the sales, the lower the taxes the local firm pays, based on an "estimated" advertising ratio to sales).

So, while an overseas business relationship almost always comes down to "good faith" and credibility, padded bills are not unknown overseas—just as similarly padded advertising bills have been monitored, for years, by American retail advertisers, working with manufacturers. This has been especially true on co-op advertising costs.

Two books you'll find helpful in getting a "feel" for a foreign country *before* you get there are *Passports and Profits,* published by Pan American World Airways, and *Living Abroad,* published by Brigham Young University.

The *Pan Am Guide to Business Customs in Europe* is also helpful. Some examples: When you visit India or Thailand, you do not shake hands. In Europe and the United States you do, on entering and on leaving. In Europe, last names are proper; in the United States, first names are accepted quickly. Appointment hours in Western Europe and the United States are expected to be kept. In the East, precise appointments are a bit more relaxed.

Finally, Some "Basics"

One of our overseas French colleagues, Daniel Debomey, cautions us to beware of the "marketing structure" differences between the United States and

European countries. The "usual" channels of distribution and price structure, markups, etc., may vary sharply between the United States and any given European country.

"In some cases, the European market can be regarded as one entity, in which country differences are minimal (for example, semifinished products used by very concentrated industries, with only three or four major potential customers in each country). Here the technological level is roughly the same in all major countries of Western Europe. In this type of marketing situation, a producer of goods can consider the European market as a whole," he says.

"In other cases, especially consumer goods, the differences in habits, 'values,' shopping, preparing and eating food, mentalities, and cultures make for profound differences in 'markets.' It is impossible to extrapolate any conclusion from Country A to Country B. Each market has to be dealt with separately."

Some clients find it difficult to understand that the cost of a marketing study in, say, Benelux, (roughly thirty million inhabitants) can be more than double the cost of the same study in France (fifty-five million inhabitants). Belgium and the Netherlands, though they have customs agreements, are two different countries, sometimes with very different distribution and production structures. The cost of a study has little to do with the size or "importance" of a country, says Debomey.

"Another reflection that comes to mind, regarding market research techniques, is the difficulty one sometimes has with clients (most particularly American clients) in explaining that quantitative, structured survey techniques are the only existing techniques, and that they are even sometimes totally inadequate to solve the problem."

A side note to American companies: As you can readily conclude, when you're dealing overseas, even the marketing research executive is perceived differently.

Patent and Copyright Problems

Laws differ in different countries. Your product may not be patentable in some. And you may find yourself in competition with *your* own (worldwide) brand in a country where another company is selling your brand name under its own ownership (having unethically filed *your* brand name before you did!).

Service/Training Problems Overseas

When you have a product requiring repairs—parts and service—the problems of obtaining, training, and holding a sophisticated engineering or repair staff is not an easy one. If your product breaks down, and for whatever reason your repair/service arrangements overseas are *not* up to standard, then *your* product, brand name, and maybe your dealer are going to go out of business, "bad-mouthed" to death.

Price/Credit Terms Competition

If you're selling large capital goods, machinery, or public works construction (dams, bridges, canals, schools, buildings, etc.) you'll quickly find that while "they" want United States equipment, marketing, and know-how—and respect the implied quality upon which American resourcefulness has built its reputation—"they" often buy non-American because of more favorable credit or financing they get from a foreign corporation than from a United States company. Long-term low-interest terms are common sales tools of foreign suppliers, subsidized often by their governments. In such cases, you often can't compete, unless you can offer *your* foreign buyer the best possible financial terms.

Ask your bank about Eximbank medium- and long-term loans to help you compete against foreign subsidized competitors. Also, look into the OPIC (Overseas Private Investment Corp.). Learn if you can tie-in your project or sale with a United States investment package.

QUESTIONS

1. What environmental factors must an international marketer take into account before entering an overseas market?
2. How can these environmental factors affect a firm's international promotion strategy?
3. What kinds of training programs can be developed for a firm's international salesforce to make them more effective in overseas markets?
4. How can market research assist international promotional strategies in avoiding the pitfalls identified by the author?

The issue of standardized versus localized strategies for international promotion has long been debated. This article attempts to develop a programmed management for simultaneously determining and implementing effective advertising campaigns in several market areas. Basic guidelines illustrated through an actual case history are presented to assist the international marketing manager.

28. Coordinating International Advertising

Dean M. Peebles
Goodyear International Corporation

John K. Ryans, Jr.
Kent State University

Ivan R. Vernon
Baylor University

Academicians and practitioners alike have debated the desirability of standardized vs. locally tailored international advertising campaigns.[1] This dialogue has continued for well over a decade, and yet we seem little closer to complete agreement than when the issue was first joined. Perhaps the problem is that we are asking the wrong questions.

Practically speaking, neither an entirely standardized nor an entirely localized approach is necessarily best.

Proponents of the standardized approach often seem to assume that the firm's home office has the right answers, that it can develop the one best campaign for all the countries in which its products are marketed. Too often, these advocates also assume that the home office, once it has arrived at the "best" campaign, is *capable* of imposing its will upon its foreign subsidiaries, branches, or other operating divisions. Such power, however, is often lacking. Even though a multinational firm may possess such power

---

Source: Dean M. Peebles, John K. Ryans, Jr., and Ivan R. Vernon, "Coordinating International Advertising." Reprinted from the *Journal of Marketing*, January 1978, pp. 28–34, published by the American Marketing Association.

over its operating divisions, the very use of authority may in itself result in a less than optimal implementation of the standardized campaign by subordinate units.

On the other hand, a purely localized effort has faults. Local autonomy may result in failure to utilize knowledge and expertise accumulated over many years by the parent firm. Widely differing local campaigns may yield disparate messages of varying degrees of effectiveness. This schizophrenic approach may well backfire because of differential message exposure on the part of consumers who travel freely among foreign market areas. This problem is particularly acute in Europe, much less so in South America and Asia. In addition, local autonomy creates a situation in which production costs may mount rapidly. The opportunity to effect economies of scale is reduced. Also, excessive local autonomy may create a situation in which overriding corporate objectives are not met or perhaps even considered.

Seven General Rules

Many of the criticisms of standardized campaigns have been misdirected. The development of an effective standardized campaign necessitates careful management and good communications. Without these two key ingredients, a standardized campaign is likely to fail. This can happen even when the advertising objectives are well thought out, and the creative strategy appropriate and well executed. Criticism of the standardized strategy occurs after such a failure misses the mark. The fault is in the implementation, not in the validity of the standardized concept.

Likewise, non-standardized campaigns have failed to achieve corporate-wide objectives. In many cases such failures have resulted from a *laissez faire* management philosophy. The attitude of some MNC's has seemed to be that conducting a non-standardized campaign simply involves relaxing all controls over foreign affiliates and letting them go their own way. Corporations following this approach apparently feel that an effective non-standardized campaign will somehow emerge, one well designed to meet the individual requirements of each foreign market. The resulting failure is then viewed as evidence that the non-standardized *concept* is faulty. Again, the problem may well be one of implementation rather than concept validity.

As stated earlier, perhaps we are asking the wrong questions. Perhaps the question should not be whether or not the campaign is standardized, but rather: How well is the campaign being administered, standardized or not?

It is possible to set forth a few general management rules to govern the conduct of the international advertising effort. These rules are believed to be generally applicable whether or not a standardized campaign is adopted.

Know Your Markets The home office international advertising executive should maintain an ongoing effort to collect market data in each foreign market for his product. There is really nothing exotic about this. Just keep trying to get the same type of information you would want in your home market—customer demographics (age, sex, income level, occupation), shopping behavior, product uses, etc. Differences in individual foreign markets may become apparent when you conduct a comparative analysis of available data. This analysis, incidentally, may give you clues regarding feasibility of a standardized approach, or may clearly signal the necessity of a highly differentiated campaign.

Know Your Foreign Counterparts   Make it a point to know personally the executives in your foreign affiliates, operating divisions, or independent distributorships. It is important to know their strengths and weaknesses, competencies and biases. Obtaining their cooperation will be much easier if you know with whom you are dealing, and they know you. You can also estimate from such first-hand knowledge the degree of cooperation you are likely to receive in the development of your advertising campaign.

Travel in Your Foreign Markets   This point cannot be over-stressed. Most international advertising executives are seasoned passport users. They are no longer thrilled at the thought of flying to Paris, Bonn, or Mexico City. And the responsibility is certainly an easy one to shift to younger and less experienced managers. Too much delegation of foreign travel responsibilities, however, removes the top executive from the concrete reality of foreign market practicalities. It becomes too easy to speculate about a foreign market when the executive conceptualizes it as an abstraction because he is now too far removed to think in concrete terms. Even worse, he may be thinking in terms of yesterday's realities.

Use a Network Agency   It is much better to work with a large international agency having branches in each foreign marketing area than to have to rely upon separate agencies in each area. Use of a network agency enhances coordination of efforts, while use of separate agencies is likely to lead to poor cooperation and lack of communication, prompted by interagency jealousies.

Know Your Foreign Advertising Account Executives   Just as it is good practice to know your foreign counterpart executives, you should know the agency and advertising personnel with whom you work. This rule is desirable whether you use a network agency or depend upon separate local agencies in each marketing area. Insist upon marketing *local* advertising agency account executives. Ask to see samples of their earlier work on other accounts. Learn their style, media biases and preferences, and other unique factors. Familiarity with the agencies permits you to evaluate their campaign suggestions much more realistically. At the same time, the development of a direct relationship will help mitigate the defensive attitude that some agencies develop in the face of parent corporation advertising suggestions.

Use Long Planning Lead Times   A long planning horizon has several advantages. First, it gives you time to work in trips to market areas requiring special attention. Also, the longer lead time encourages foreign ad managers to internalize stated campaign objectives. In the case of non-standardized campaigns they can take the time to develop a campaign appropriately designed for local conditions, yet consistent with overall corporate goals. For a standardized campaign, the longer lead time lets your office get needed data to develop the campaign pattern, and leaves you more time to sell the campaign to foreign divisions.

Maintain Home Office Budget Approval Authority Hold onto the purse strings until you are satisfied that local campaigns are appropriately developed, or until the standardized campaign theme is fully understood and adopted. You can obtain an amazing amount of information from some rather remote parts of the world prior to budget approval. Afterwards communications breakdowns may occur much more readily.

Six-Step Program

It is highly desirable to obtain input from each national market. Thus, local initiative must be stimulated. At the same time, the experience and global perspective of the home office are essential. The management framework utilized should incorporate features aimed at encouraging two-way communication, and it should maximize the likelihood that local ideas will receive a fair hearing, yet permit timely decision making.

Exhibit 28–1 provides a framework for this type of approach. As shown, six major steps are involved.

Marketing and Advertising Strategy and Objectives At this stage, the home office and its subsidiaries should jointly clarify their understanding of the firm's marketing objectives. In this regard, established corporate goals may be paramount. This would be true, for example, in a major new product introduction. Similarly, in any given year the corporation may establish as a parameter the necessity of stressing corporate public relations themes. Other possible marketing and advertising objectives would include increased brand share, repeat purchases, new customers, strengthening of channels of distribution, and larger average order size.

In many cases subsidiary management will be able to offer valid and useful insights regarding proper marketing and advertising strategies and objectives. Particularly useful to the home office is the opportunity to review this type of input from several different countries. Recurrent themes may alert the home office to market problems and opportunities of which they were previously unaware.

Individual Market Input Based upon the home office's reaction to their strategies and objectives, each separate market builds a tentative advertising campaign. The campaign need not be developed to presentation standards, and a media plan is *not* necessary at this stage. However, a sufficient amount of visual material and copy must be prepared to indicate the primary creative

EXHIBIT 28-1

FRAMEWORK FOR PROGRAMMED MANAGEMENT APPROACH

1. Strategy and Objectives

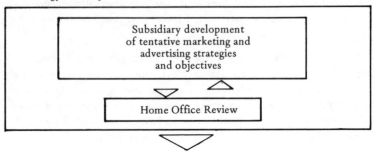

2. Individual Market Input

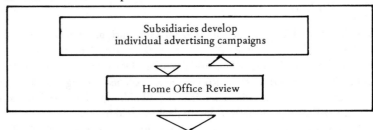

3. Testing

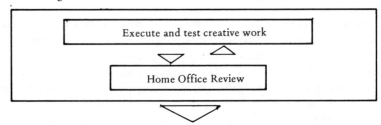

4. Campaign Review

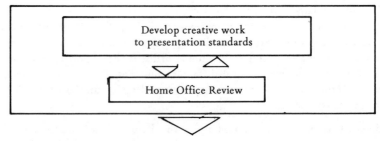

5. Budget Approval

6. Campaign Implementation

thrust of the campaign. The home office will review all the campaigns and offer suggestions.

Testing Each local campaign must be market tested in its particular country. It is preferable to use an independent marketing research firm rather than relying upon subsidiary marketing research departments, or even the marketing research unit of the subsidiary's local advertising agency. The home office will review the test results and offer comments, criticisms, and suggestions.

Campaign Review Based upon market test results and the home office critique of those results, subsidiaries develop their campaigns to presentation standards. Each subsidiary's campaign is then submitted to the home office for review and approval or modification.

Budget Approval Final budget approval for each subsidiary is delayed until the home office is satisfied with its campaign.

Implementation Upon receiving budget approval, the subsidiaries have the green light to move into full-scale campaign implementation. Media commitments may be made, and final production work begins.

The overall campaign resulting from this approach may be highly standardized, or it may be a campaign incorporating disparate elements aimed at unique market conditions. The programmed approach does not *per se* assure one or the other. Rather, the approach taken grows out of the interaction process; it assists in finding the right campaign approaches and it assists management in determining whether one set of appeals can be standardized for the entire market area. This management system also prevents local markets from changing creative approaches too often—and eliminates the possibility of inconsistent or desperate actions by local managers who become overly obsessed by temporary market frustrations.

Example: 1976 Goodyear Campaign

Goodyear International, Inc.'s 1976 campaign, may be cited as an example of a United States-based multinational corporation which has successfully implemented the programmed approach. For several years Goodyear International has relied upon a programmed approach to coordinate the development of a unified advertising program in Western Europe. While the reasons will not be detailed here, experience has shown that customer mobility, media overlap, and many consumer "common denominators" make the programmed approach especially suited to Goodyear International in this area. Goodyear is highly pleased with their managerial framework and expects to continue using it in the future.

Exhibit 28–2 shows the management flow chart utilized by Goodyear to direct and coordinate the development and implementation of their 1976

EXHIBIT 28-2
MANAGEMENT FLOW CHART: 1976 CAMPAIGN DEVELOPMENT

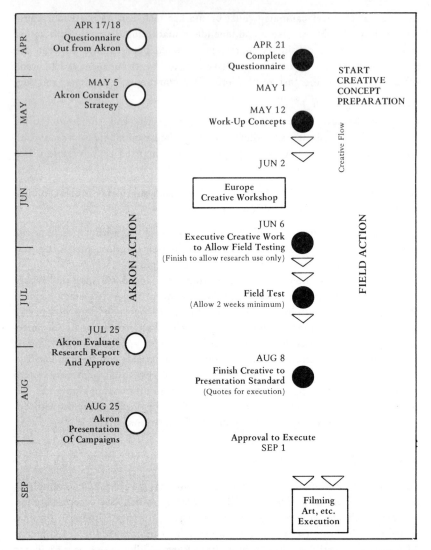

advertising campaign in eleven Western European markets—Austria, Belgium, Denmark, England, Germany, Greece, Holland, Italy, France, Sweden, and Switzerland. The chart, covering the period April–September 1975, was distributed to each European subsidiary. (Such advance planning, i.e., summer for the following year, is obviously necessary for the scale of advertising employed by Goodyear International.) The chart is also furnished to each country's network advertising agency, all members of Interpublic Group's Campbell-Ewald International. All personnel involved were made aware of the importance of adhering to deadlines established via the flow chart.

Shown on the chart are two sets of responsibilities—home office and subsidiary actions. The light-shaded nodes denote home office (Akron) activities, and the dark-shaded nodes indicate subsidiary (field) activities.

The flow of activities moves through discrete sequential steps from field input regarding strategy and objectives (in April) to home office approval to execute the approved campaign (in September).

The procedure and planning dates indicated by the framework are described as follows:

April 17. The home office forwarded to each field office a questionnaire requesting a one-year marketing plan covering the 1976 period. The local office finished documents, due in Akron on May 5, that cover objectives, strategy, and general theme of the local advertising campaigns. This stage proved extremely valuable. Preparation of this report assisted the subsidiaries in clarifying and formalizing their own thinking and gave the home office insight into both the unique and common problems facing each market area.

Notice the two flow paths through the chart. The flow path on the right (creative flow) signifies the fact that the field offices may initiate their creative work immediately upon dispatching their marketing plans to the home office. *They did not need to wait until receiving home office comments prior to beginning this work.*

May 5. The home office began its review of the subsidiary plans on this date, completing their review by May 12. The home office provides each local office with a detailed critique of their individual plans. This review enabled Akron to detect and correct weaknesses in subsidiary market planning in such areas as product and brand name emphasis, media strategy, and other broad policy areas. In the 1976 campaign, for example, the home office found that several field areas were taking a short-run attitude toward sales growth and had not grasped the corporate market expansion strategy.

May 12. This was the final date designated for the subsidiaries' receipt of home office market plan critiques. These local offices, which by this time had already initiated their creative work, studied the critique and incorporated home office comments and suggestions into their campaigns. The subsidiaries then spent the last half of May working up their campaign themes and rough artwork to field presentation standards.

June 2–6. The European creative workshop, attended by the home office international advertising executive, the advertising managers from the six largest European markets, Interpublic's Campbell-Ewald representatives from each market area, Campbell-Ewald's European coordinator, and creative people from the agency's United States headquarters focused upon overall

European policies and objectives. Each market informally presented its advertising plans and creative concepts to the other attendees. A loose, informal atmosphere prevailed, encouraging a free and open exchange of views, opinions, and concepts.

The creative workshop, held in a European resort area, has proven to be a highly successful communications forum where a sense of unity of purpose is sought. Quite often the workshop results in improving all the campaigns. One or more markets may discard their original ideas in favor of suggestions offered by other markets or in recognition of an overriding corporate objective. The workshop offers the headquarter representatives an opportunity to re-establish direct contact with foreign market representatives and advertising agency representatives. The workshop also enables the Campbell-Ewald European coordinator to work directly with local agency representatives collectively, as a special account group. The agency coordinator and Akron executives in effect act as informal leaders of the client-agency symposium.

June 6–July 25. Following the creative workshop, the individual markets developed their campaign proposals more thoroughly, based upon inputs obtained during the workshop. During this development stage, the "co-chairmen" traveled and worked with individual markets. Revised campaign concepts were then to be refined to a stage sufficient to permit consumer testing. This meant that artwork and storyboards were to be developed sufficiently to convey the advertising message in a market test environment.

Next, the individual market areas field tested their campaigns. Each market area utilized independent marketing research organizations for this work rather than performing the test work themselves or permitting their local advertising agency offices to do the work. In general, three to four versions of the campaign were tested, using four to six consumer focus groups for each version of the campaign.

Psychological probing was utilized on occasion to determine underlying consumer attitudes toward the campaigns being tested. The market testing focused upon one of Goodyear's identified key markets, men in the 20–40 age bracket. (The target market in the more affluent European countries tends to be somewhat younger than in less affluent countries. The German key market, for example, tends to be somewhat younger than the Italian market.)

July 25. This was the deadline for the formal presentation of the various comprehensive campaigns to the Akron home office. The Campbell-Ewald coordinator traveled to Akron to present all the foreign market campaigns along with market test results. At this stage, he had available television storyboards, experimental films, and other roughs adequate to fully present each market's campaign concept. The coordinator, in effect, presented the campaigns including each market area's reasoning for developing its campaign and for altering it in accordance with market test results.

This formal presentation was made to an assembled group of home office corporate executives and advertising specialists, who had the opportunity to ask questions and make further technical and policy suggestions. The end result was home office approval of the campaign, with possible suggestions for further modifications.

August 8. Home office approval of the research results and the campaign themes permitted the subsidiaries to now begin to develop the campaigns to finished presentation standards, incorporating any modifications needed as a result of the home office review of research results. The individual market areas now must also develop media schedules, campaign cost estimates, and proposed advertising budgets. This work had to be completed in time for a final review in Akron by August 25.

August 25. The home office reviewed the campaigns, generally suggesting some changes even at this late stage. The home office also reviews each country's overall campaign plans—media schedules, media mix, advertising budget, etc.—and may request changes in these areas as well. The creative flow line, as shown in Exhibit 28-2, was actually released on August 8. The subsidiaries thus were free to develop finished creative work beginning at that time. Therefore, this second review by headquarters tended to focus more heavily upon implementing strategy (media planning and budgeting) than upon creative content. The Akron home office did, however, review such finished artwork as was available at this date. Corporate headquarter's advertising executives eventually reviewed *all* finished creative work for approval prior to release to the media.

September 1. This was the deadline established for home office approval and funding of each market campaign. This approval permitted the subsidiaries to begin making the financial and other commitments necessary to implement the campaign during the following calendar year, 1976. From this point on, Akron continued to monitor local market performance. Each market is required to furnish quarterly progress reports, samples of materials produced, and consumer research reports in the form of trend data.

Conclusion

The programmed management approach is recommended as a useful framework for the coordination of international advertising campaigns. It cuts through the "standardized vs. localized" debate and offers a method for determining and implementing effective advertising campaigns in several market areas simultaneously.

It offers the home office the opportunity to standardize certain aspects of the campaigns, if this appears desirable, while at the same time permitting maximum flexibility in response to differing market conditions. This approval greatly facilitates communication between the home office and each foreign market, and also among the individual foreign markets. This communication process and the other safeguards built into the programmed management approach, such as the creative workshop and the required independent market research, help to assure that effective campaigns are developed, and insuring that valid corporate policies and objectives are implemented.

The programmed management approach represents a hybrid prototype—a cross between close corporate control and local option management. The result is a product of teamwork, a blending of effort by corporate, local market, and agency representatives. The end result is an effective international advertising campaign, one well designed to meet local market conditions, and yet in harmony with long-range corporate objectives.

As the Goodyear International 1976 campaign development illustrates, a high level of interaction between home office and subsidiaries is necessitated under the programmed management approach. Both the home office and local advertising representatives (and their agencies) are required to "defend" their positions and stand the test of peer and superior criticism. The final objective, of course, is the development of the most effective campaign these joint inputs can produce.

QUESTIONS

1. What are the basic arguments underlying the use of a standardized versus localized approach to international advertising?
2. What general management rules are offered by the authors for conducting international advertising?
3. What problems can you see in applying the six-step programmed management approach outlined in the article?

NOTE

1. Arthur C. Fatt, "A Multi-National Approach to International Advertising," *The International Advertiser*, September 1964, pp. 17–19; John K. Ryans Jr., "Is it too Soon to Put a Tiger in Every Tank?" *Columbia Journal of World Business*, March–April 1969, pp. 69–75; Robert T. Green, William H. Cunningham, and Isabella C. M. Cunningham, "The Effectiveness of Standardized Advertising," *Journal of Advertising*, Summer 1975, pp. 25–30; Steuart Henderson Britt, "Standardizing Marketing for the International Market," *Columbia Journal of World Business*, Winter 1974, pp. 39–45; and Ralph Z. Sorenson and Ulrich E. Weichmann, "How Multinationals View Marketing Standardization," *Harvard Business Review*, May–June 1975, p. 38.

How transferable or standardized can promotional strategy in international marketing be? The author attempts to survey the extent to which European consumer values are becoming national in character, and the impact this may have on multinational marketing planning.

29. Effect of National Identity on Multinational Promotional Strategy in Europe

S. Watson Dunn
University of Illinois

After fifteen years of disappearing trade barriers, internationalizing of consumer tastes, and general praise for such supranational organizations as the European Economic Community, there are signs that Western European countries are reemphasizing their national identities. For example, France has chosen to deal separately with oil-exporting countries and has avoided joining other countries in buyers' cartels. Prominent Britishers of both major parties have during 1974 and 1975 urged withdrawal from the EEC. At the same time Scotland, looking forward to the fruits of North Sea oil exploration, talks of breaking away from the United Kingdom. Such traditionally thorny issues as agricultural support policies, currency exchange levels, and labeling of wine have in recent years caused even more friction than in the past. Recent economic problems in each country have tended to accentuate nationalistic tendencies.

Source: S. Watson Dunn, "Effect of National Identity on Multinational Promotional Strategy in Europe." Reprinted from the *Journal of Marketing,* October 1976, pp. 50–57, published by the American Marketing Association.

One major problem confronting multinational marketers is whether a reorientation in politics and culture will lead to a reorientation in consumer tastes. Will the European consumer increase her preference for products made in her own country and catered specifically to her national tastes? To what extent will appeals to national identity become more effective than those that emphasize foreign origin?

Evidence that there may be a reemphasis on national identity in consumer tastes in Europe comes from marketing as well as from politics. For example, most major United States multinational corporations have suffered serious marketing failures in Europe in recent years, and there is no evidence that the failure ratio is lessening.[1] In fact, it may well go up as executives try to compensate for the reduced acceptance of innovations in the domestic market by increasing product introductions abroad. Other evidence of renewed national identity comes from some of the recent research studies on European marketing, from the warnings of veteran multinational marketers, from the decline in importance of international media in Europe, and from language *faux pas* ("Body by Fisher" became "Corpse by Fisher" in some translated versions, and Pepsi's "Come Alive" came out instead "Come out of the grave").

This article will examine several research studies that concentrate on the transfer of marketing strategy, including two recent ones supervised by this author. The objective is to determine the extent to which consumer tastes are becoming more national in character and how such changes are likely to affect multinational marketing planning and the transfer of promotional strategy.

Past Research on Marketing Transferability

Much past research has supported either complete transferability or complete tailoring of promotion to the needs of a particular country. A devotee of the first school is Erik Elinder, a prominent Swedish marketing executive, who reported that savings-bank promotions were used all over Scandinavia with equal success. His investigations led him to predict that the same campaign could be used anywhere in Europe and that it was a waste of effort and money to custom-tailor promotion to each country.[2] Along these same lines, Gordon Miracle maintained that: "the requirements of effective communication are fixed and cannot vary with time, place or form of communication; therefore the same approach to communication (that is, the same approach to preparation of messages and selection of media) can be used in every country."[3]

In a field study of advertising transferability in Europe and the Middle East conducted during the 1960s, this author found that successful United States print advertisements were surprisingly transferable.[4] Several French and Arabic versions were created by professionals and tested under controlled field conditions in Paris and Cairo. Those literally translated with accompanying American illustrations were almost as successful as those carefully designed by creative experts of the country. This was true in the case of all three measures of effectiveness that were applied. These were, however, strongly visual, and they promoted consumer products that varied little in positioning from country to country.

On the other hand, several researchers have stated that approaches should be tailored to each country. Anthropologist Edward T. Hall has emphasized the barriers involved in one culture trying to communicate effectively with another.[5] Claude Marcus and Jean Max Lenormand, top advertising executives in France, have maintained that one must tailor promotion to specific markets—especially when dealing with the Franch market—and that anyone who assumed otherwise was taking unnecessary risks.[6] John K. Ryans, Jr. has questioned whether Esso's much acclaimed universal campaign was really all that universal.[7]

Other research studies have ended up with a more middle-of-the-road recommendation in an attempt to isolate those factors that determine when to standardize, when not to standardize. For example, Robert D. Buzzell compiled a table that summarized the four types of obstacles to standardization and their application to each major element of the marketing mix. He suggested that the right balance of local autonomy and central coordination might come from a careful weighing of the pros and cons of standardization and from a careful estimate of the revenue and costs resulting from alternative transfer strategies.[8] On the basis of his supervision of the marketing portion of the Harvard Business School multinational studies program, Richard Holton decided that sequential game theory was a most promising approach to unraveling the complexities of multinational marketing strategy.[9]

In a study of marketing practices of United States-based multinational firms in Europe, Aylmer found that local managers enjoyed a good deal more autonomy in making advertising decisions than they did in other areas of marketing.[10] He singled out two variables as good predictors of how autonomous the local manager would be: (1) the importance of the international versus the domestic operations: and (2) the prestige of the local affiliate. A study by Donnelly indicated that the degree of centralization depended heavily on how important advertising managers thought cultural differences were (i.e., the more important the cultural differences, the more decentralized the strategy).[11]

In a comprehensive study of 27 United States– and Europe-based multinational firms, Ulrich Wiechmann found that advertising tended to be more decentralized than other marketing functions and that advertising strategy varied more from firm to firm than did other functions.[12] He emphasized more strongly than previous researchers the importance of: (1) corporate acculturation (assimilation of company philosophy by foreign managers); (2) systems transfer (a uniform framework for marketing planning): and

(3) cross-border planning and budgeting. Like many of his predecessors, he concluded that the more culture-bound the product (e.g., food) the more difficult it is to transfer promotional strategy. In a comparative study of consumer buying habits in France and the United States, Green and Langeard found substantial differences between consumers in the two countries and suggested that marketing programs would probably have to be revised if they were to be transferred to France from the United States.[13]

Reassessment of European Markets

By the early 1970s, the opinions of many marketing executives moved away from the earlier optimism about painless transfer of marketing strategy. For example, marketing executive Paul Griffin cited several failure stories in a talk before the Primary Club of London in 1972:

> Maxwell House, billed as "the great American coffee" spent a potful to find out that Germans have little respect for "American coffee."
> Procter & Gamble found that Crest's fluoride appeal meant little or nothing to the English public.

Another indication that national differences might be increasing was the change in the media picture in Europe. International consumer media have all but disappeared, as magazines such as *Playboy* and *Cosmopolitan* have turned to local editions in the major European countries, an approach that *Reader's Digest* has followed successfully. Another successful approach seems to be the publication of identical editorial content in various languages—a practice followed by *Vision/Europe,* which is published in English, French, German, and Italian. A recent study of European media by Foote, Cone & Belding pointed out that "The *International Herald-Tribune* is about the only true remaining international news medium [in Europe] with a large circulation."

Wind, Douglas, and Perlmutter have suggested that the concept of the world as one big market (geocentric approach) has been greatly overrated.[14] They believe instead that the polycentric (subsidiary overseas acts independently of the parent) or regiocentric (region acts autonomously) approach is preferable.

Tom Sutton, executive vice-president of J. Walter Thompson and a long-time internationalist, pointed out that the "people are alike" theory has become a dangerous oversimplification.[15] The hitherto equalizing effect of affluence and establishment of international standards of consumption, he pointed out, may well boomerang as customers search for differences through consumption. He suggested that international campaigns will be of lesser value in the future and that local tailor-made advertising will become more effective.

Evidence from Two Recent Studies

Two studies supervised by this author shed some additional light on the changing nature of promotional strategy in Europe.[16] Both were designed to find out how marketing executives of large United States-based multinational corporations make decisions regarding the transfer of promotional strategy.

Study I: Importance of Environmental Variables

In the first of these studies, a cross section of multinational decision makers was asked to assign relative weights to certain environmental variables that might be used in making transfer decisions.[17] These variables were gleaned from past research studies, from the marketing literature, and from relevant theoretical works. Executives were contracted either in person or by mail and were asked to rate, on a scale of one to seven, some 194 variables that might be used in formulating advertising strategy. The completed ratings were returned by mail to the author. The objective of this phase of the study was to reduce the variables to a smaller number of meaningful dimensions. Consequently, a factor solution was obtained using principal components with a varimax rotation. The 31 variables listed in Exhibit 29–1 reflect the factors in order of decreasing importance.

The sample used to weigh the original 194 variables was drawn from a list of decision-making executives in leading United States multinational firms (those in which at least 15 percent of total sales were from outside the United States). The list was compiled by the author from various directories and personal contacts, but it was confined to executives who were (1) responsible for at least a major part of the promotional decision making of their firm, and (2) in a top or middle-management position in the firm. Executives contacted were chosen at random from the list, and seventy-one executives from thirty-five leading firms replied (68 percent of those contacted). Although the number of respondents may seem small by some standards, it should be noted that the factoring was used primarily to generate groups of variables for further study. The resulting groups turned out to be quite homogeneous in terms of variable meaning.

To isolate differences in the perceived importance of these dimensions for the creation of strategies for developing versus developed countries, a second set of the questionnaires was prepared. The thirty-one master factors were listed for each, and a new group of subjects was asked to rate them (again on a scale of one to seven). The second sample, chosen in the same manner, consisted of ninety respondents (62 percent of those contacted), one-third of whom had replied to the first questionnaire. Replies from new and old respondents turned out to be quite similar. Respondents were asked to indicate the relative importance of each factor in transferring creative strategy to (1) a typical developed foreign market, and (2) a typical developing market. From these data, eight master factors were extracted. Those

EXHIBIT 29-1
Thirty-one environmental variables useful for formulating advertising strategy

Rate of economic growth of country
Per capita income and distribution of income
Average size of household
Level of literacy
Level of education
Vocational training
Social class structure
Attitudes toward authority
Attitudes toward the U.S.
Degree of nationalism in country
Attitudes toward achievement and work
Attitudes toward risk taking
Attitudes toward wealth and monetary gain
Similarity of ethical and moral standards to U.S.
Availability of time on commercial broadcast media
Adequate coverage of market by broadcast media
Availability of satisfactory outdoor media
Availability of satisfactory print media
Independence of media from government control
Political organization and stabiliy
Import/export rate of country
Legal restraints on advertising within the country
Availability of prototype campaigns
Relative importance of visual versus verbal in ad message
Experience and competence of personnel in foreign subsidiary and distributor
Experience and competence of personnel in foreign agency or branch of U.S. agency
Eating patterns and customs
Importance of self-service retailing
Import duties and quotas in country
Development and acceptance of international trademark or trade name
Applicability of products' theme or slogan or other markets

for the developed country—which would, of course, be applicable to Europe—
are summarized in Exhibit 29-2.

Research Findings The most significant findings of this study were the
following:

1. Decision-making executives, in spite of their frequent disclaimers to the
   contrary, do have in mind certain environmental factors when they
   decide to transfer promotional strategy.
2. There is somewhat more consistency among decision makers than one
   might expect, at least among those in this sample of consumer goods
   companies that are experienced in multinational marketing.

EXHIBIT 29-2

Master environmental factors for consumer goods companies in a developed country

Factor Number	Description of Factor
I	Level of education; level of literacy
II	Attitudes toward: risk taking, achievement and work, and wealth and monetary gain
III	Experience and competence of personnel in foreign agency of branch of United States agency; experience and competence of personnel in foreign subsidiary or distributor
IV	Degree of nationalism in country; attitudes toward the United States
V	Rate of economic growth of country; per capita income and distribution of income; import duties and quotas in country; development and acceptance of international trademark and trade name
VI	Eating patterns and customs; importance of self-service retailing
VII	Attitudes toward authority; social class structure; applicability of product or slogan to other markets
VIII	Independence of media from government control; availability of satisfactory media

3. There is no reason to believe that consistency in assigning weights leads to consistency in the use of campaigns in various markets. Instead, it seems to indicate that analytical tools for discerning meaningful differences are developing, and localization can become more sophisticated.

Study II: Field Interviews in Europe and the United States

A follow-up field study was designed to probe the whole process of promotional decision making, including nonenvironmental as well as environmental variables that might influence decisions. Focused interviews were conducted with seventy-eight decision-making marketing executives in thirty major multinational companies. Approximately half of the interviews took place in the United States with the other half distributed among the United Kingdom, France, Germany, Switzerland, Belgium, Holland, Denmark, and Sweden. None of the seventy-eight respondents had been asked to fill out the mail questionnaire in previous waves of this study, and all were chosen on the basis of their decision-making role in a major firm. Of the thirty firms, twenty eight were United States based and two were Europe based. During the interview, certain hypotheses drawn partly from the results of the mail questionnaire were suggested and a general interview guide was followed. These provided some structure and served as a jumping-off point for further exploration as promising areas of investigation opened up. Flexiblity was needed, since a complicated mix of companies, products, management styles, and distribution patterns was involved. Included were, on the one hand, such diversified firms as Colgate-Palmolive and, on the other, those such as Avon that concentrated most of their promotional efforts on a single line of products.

Certain parameters were, however, established for the selection of companies. Companies that had been covered in previous case studies by the author were included where possible. It was thought that meaningful comparisons between the middle 1960s and the early 1970s could thus be made.[18] Many executives from these companies had participated in the rating of environmental factors described earlier in this article. Most were package goods firms and all depended on advertising and related promotions as major ingredients in their marketing mix both in the United States and abroad.

An attempt was made in the case of the multibrand companies to compare foreign promotional strategy of successful and not-so-successful brands. Four tests of success were used: (1) gross sales trends during the past five years; (2) net income during the past five years; (3) opinions of their fellow businessmen solicited during interviews by the question, "What two or three United States companies are doing the best job in your country?"; and (4) opinions of European executives given in answer to, "What advertising campaigns do you consider to have been particularly good? . . . and particularly bad?" The last question was one of many in a lengthy questionnaire sent to over 7,000 European business executives in late 1973 in connection with a study of their attitudes toward advertising.[19]

The question on "particularly good" multinational campaigns did not, unfortunately, stimulate many mentions. Only thirty-seven multinational campaigns were cited as "good" by at least three respondents. Of these, only three were for United States companies or brands. And of the fourteen listed as "particularly bad" only two promoted products of United States multinationals. One was for a household cleaner and the other for a detergent. One would have to conclude that campaigns of United States multinationals did not make a very strong impression pro or con on European executives.

Research Findings The proportion of companies using basically the same advertisements abroad as at home was less in 1973 than in 1964. Even in the case of cosmetics, soaps, and drugs (companies that have traditionally tried for a similar image and product position from country to country), there was a higher proportion of firms making major changes in 1973 than in 1964. Included in this classification are such sophisticated international marketers as Unilever and Procter & Gamble, which are among the biggest users of research and multinational market planning but which also attempt to preserve a degree of local autonomy. However, local autonomy was generally greater in the developed markets than in the developing ones, and the movement toward local autonomy often represented a disenchantment with superficial similarities that have led in the past to undue standardization. Some blamed it simply on the tricky crosscurrent of rising nationalism.

A basic cause of this increased local autonomy is a substantial increase in the sophistication of the European marketing executive—who is more likely today than ten years ago to be a European rather than an American.

As Harry Clark, Jr., senior vice-president for international at J. Walter Thompson, points out, one would not try today to run in Austria a German campaign created for Germany even though it might well have 40 percent penetration of the target group in Austria. Instead, it would be better to leave it to the multinational marketing executive in Vienna, who could "quite rightly see some of the differences between an Austrian housewife and her counterpart even in Munich, only several hundred kilometers away" and who would insist that the advertising directed to Austrian housewives be specifically created for them.[20]

The interviews indicated that this new sophistication stems mainly from the factors listed in Exhibit 29-1—particularly value systems, availability of media, degree of government control, and nature of the creative message. Two that do not appear on the list are product positioning and consumerism. Yet the interviews revealed that companies were collecting more evidence on product position within each market, depending less on the product type as viewed from the United States home office.

Consumerism and advertising regulation vary substantially from country to country. Although both are on the rise almost everywhere, they tend to reflect the environment of the country and thus contribute to differences in promotional opportunity. For example, strict controls were found in the high per capita income countries of Scandinavia, as compared with more lenient regulation in low per capita Italy and Greece. In such countries as Sweden and Norway, both the laws and their administration tend to be quite strict.

Message variables turned out to be even more important in determining transferability than Exhibit 29-1 might imply. This may be a result of the appeal or theme. The Ajax white tornado was less successful as a symbol of power than the Esso "Tiger in Your Tank." Coke's "Things Go Better with Coke" and a number of variations proved transferable, but "It's the Real Thing" has been difficult to use in many markets. Ultra-Brite's flying kisses and the sexy girl who throws them aroused an adverse reaction in Belgium. This approach and the theme "Give Your Mouth Sex Appeal" were dropped; "Nice to Have Sex Appeal" was substituted, but recognition in Belgium still leveled out at 12 percent—low for this type of product.

Sometimes creative transferability is a function of technique. Libby made a commercial for less than $20,000 to be used by its subsidiaries around the world. To avoid problems in localizing it, the commercial featured a clown, pantomime, and the simple story of the clown enjoying Libby food products.

Eight companies used prototype campaigns and promoted them strongly to subsidiaries. However, these seemed to be pushed less in the early 1970s than in 1964. Colgate-Palmolive and Procter & Gamble depend heavily on international advertising experts who act as advertising consultants to their subsidiaries around the world and help them adapt themes, execution, and even research techniques to local conditions. They find this approach more satisfactory than reliance on a prototype campaign or on pattern books.

Sales promotion themes and techniques were easier to transfer than advertising campaigns according to a majority of the respondents. The firms felt they could more easily profit from economies of scale in the case of sales promotion and were less likely to run into national cultural barriers. This finding tends to bear out the results reported by Aylmer and Wiechmann. The principal problem was the difference in legal regulations from country to country.

The more astute of the MNCs are accepting added controls as inevitable and are taking steps to cope with them (e.g., setting up committees to monitor consumer activism and proposed regulation, working with Council of Europe committees on harmonization of laws). Today's Western European businessperson does not seem discouraged by increasing regulation. Although he strongly favors self-regulation and enforcement of an ethical code, the European businessperson is much less terrified by government regulation than his counterpart in the United States.[21]

Research is used only slightly more today as a major input into decision making than it was in the 1960s. The package goods firms are the biggest users—with a little more emphasis today. Syndicated research is used, of course, but there are many complaints about how expensive it is (especially for probing markets with only a limited potential) and considerable doubts as to the accuracy of much of what it reports. None of the companies studied had made major changes in its research budget in recent years; instead, almost all kept the budget at a constant percentage of sales and made special allocations for new product introductions or other special projects.

Approximately two-thirds of the executives thought nationalism or emphasis on national traits would increase and that promotion would have to be modified to adapt to it. Executives queried in Europe were more likely than those in the United States to emphasize national trends. Executives of multinational corporations operating in France expressed this viewpoint more emphatically than those in other countries. They believed executives back in headquarters tended to underestimate the need to adapt marketing strategy to the French consumer. Executives in Germany were, however, almost as emphatic on this point.

When European executives were asked to name campaigns they considered truly multinational, most were hard put to be specific. Most frequently named were Coca-Cola and Volkswagen. One said that there were really *no* multinational campaigns—only different degrees of similarity. Another said that multinationalism existed only in *production* in Europe—never in marketing. He maintained that marketers were misled by the ease of standardizing production into believing they could also standardize marketing strategy.

The studies indicated also that Western Europe was never quite as homogeneous as some of the avid multinationalists believed and that the so-called multinational campaigns were never quite as standardized as many home-office executives thought. Some marketing executives do not really know what is and is not being transferred across boundaries. In some instances, this is a case of planned decentralization. In others, it is the result of poor communications, which could well cause problems when the international marketing competition gets a little rougher and nationalism increases. There is a common tendency for an executive at the United States headquarters to believe that there is more standardization than actually exists.

Similarly, multinational executives think they have more control over marketing than they really have. This difference in perception of control was emphasized by one United States executive working in Europe, who said:

There are really four different ways in which executives perceive home-office control—all different. There's the perception of the European manager here in Europe, the perception of the European manager back at the home office in the States, the perception of top management back in the States, and the perception of that same top management when they come to Europe. The only time I would consider making a major change in policy is when the home office boss is here in Europe—and never when he and I are back in the States.

The changes in national attitudes make it more important than ever before to improve both the quantity and quality of information flowing to the United States home office from abroad. In some companies, fooling the United States bosses is partly chauvinism, partly a game. The French marketing manager of one large United States-Based company told the author proudly: "We did not use a single commercial prepared by New York last year [1972]." He maintained that they were too unsophisticated for the European audiences, too much like those used by his firm in the United States, and not different enough from those of his major competitor. "We used a few of the American commercials in the North African market," he added disparagingly. The New York office had reported earlier that the same print advertisements and commercials with minor variations were being used in all Western European countries. Obviously, the information system within the company was not working very efficiently.

Conclusions and Recommendations

These two surveys indicate that there is indeed a resurgence of national identity in Western Europe. The European executives of the United States-based multinationals and the executives of the two Europe-based multinationals feel this most strongly. However, there was also evidence that many multinationals are slowing down on the transfer of promotional strategy and are trying to replace overstandardization with a more sophisticated approach. This trend is not viewed as a reversion to old-fashioned nationalism either culturally or politically. Instead, it seems to represent a search for symbols—including products, services, and the ads that promote them—which reflect that identity. This does not mean that all international campaigns need to be discarded. For example, Coca-Cola has been successful at coming up with themes that lend themselves to internationalization with only minor adaptations. Multinational marketers who can figure out how to reflect national identity in their ads will progress the most in the next decade.

Although the concept of "national identity," like "nationalism," is at best a fuzzy one, some clues as to how to pin it down and what information researchers should look for develop from the two research projects discussed here. These may be useful benchmarks in predicting how much modification is needed in a particular country.

The most important types of information needed are the following: product position, wealth and achievement, experience of personnel, degree of political nationalism, rate of economic growth, eating patterns, attitudes toward authority, character and availability of media, and consumerism. Keeping up with consumerism trends means understanding and cooperating with government, educational, and political leaders in most countries as well as soliciting information from consumers. Many prominent and successful MNCs have a fairly continuous flow of information on these factors. Few have gone as far as weighing the factors according to country, product, or some other variable and constructing an index, but there is a definite feeling that they lend themselves to some quantification.

The more successful multinationals were strong on planning, with fact books for each country, specific objectives for each country, specific rules for preparing plans, and stipulations for both yearly and longer-term plans. The methodology of planning is one area where fairly standardization seems to work.

Staffing key positions in local subsidiaries with strong, well-trained, well-paid nationals seems to provide better information and a stronger identification with the local market. In several firms covered here, well-qualified third-country nationals appeared to be doing a remarkable job of adapting to the problems of nationalism.

Prominent by its absence in appraising transferability is cross-cultural theory. The decision makers come through mainly as pragmatists; when they use conceptual approaches, they are likely to describe these in pragmatic terms.

The very success of some of the past multinational advertising campaigns may well have contributed to the rise of national tastes. One finds resentment at the sameness of the Coca-Cola campaigns, the sameness of the McDonald's stores, the sameness of the Holiday Inns and Howard Johnsons. The more people think marketers put them together in one big mass, the more they try to prove they are different. Nationals are starting to look inward as well as outward even though many of the multinational campaigns by most standards remain quite successful. The best approach is to preserve some covert multinationalism in the campaign but to add a deft touch that is distinctively French or British or Italian. . . .

QUESTIONS

1. What does the author mean by the statement "Consumer tastes are becoming more national in character"?
2. What has research on the transferability of marketing strategy revealed?
3. What are the major conclusions drawn by the author on the transferability from the analysis of the two recent surveys?
4. What are the implications of these conclusions for international marketing managers?

NOTES

1. David Ricks, Marilyn Y. C. Fu, and Jeffrey S. Arpan, *International Business Blunders* (Columbus, Ohio: Grid Publishing Co., 1974), Chap. 2.

2. See Erik Elinder, "How International Can Advertising Be?" in *International Handbook of Advertising,* S. Watson Dunn, ed. (New York: McGraw-Hill Book Co., 1964), pp. 59–71; and Arthur C. Fatt, "The Danger of 'Local' International Advertising," *Journal of Marketing,* Vol. 31 (January 1967), pp. 60–62.

3. Gordon E. Miracle, "Internationalizing Advertising Principles and Strategies," *MSU Business Topics* (Autumn 1968), pp. 29–36.

4. S. Watson Dunn, "The Case Study Approach in Cross-Cultural Research," *Journal of Marketing Research,* Vol. 3 (February 1966), pp. 26–31; S. Watson Dunn, "Cross-cultural Research by U.S. Corporations," *Journalism Quarterly,* Vol. 42 (Summer 1965), pp. 454–457; E. S. Lorimor and S. Watson Dunn, "Use of the Mass Media in France and Egypt," *Public Opinion Quarterly,* Vol. 32 (Winter 1968–69), pp. 679–687; E. S. Lorimor and S. Watson Dunn," Reference Groups, Congruity Theory and Cross-Cultural Persuasion," *Journal of Communication,* Vol. 18 (December 1968), pp. 354–368; E. S. Lorimor and S. Watson Dunn, "Four Measures of

Cross-Cultural Advertising Effectiveness," *Journal of Advertising Research,* Vol. 7 (December 1967), pp. 10–13.

5. Edward T. Hall, *The Silent Language* (New York: Doubleday & Co., 1959).

6. Claude Marcus, "France," in *International Handbook of Advertising,* S. Watson Dunn, ed. (New York: McGraw-Hill Book Co., 1964), pp. 375–385; and J. M. Lenormand, "Is Europe Ripe for the Integration of Advertising?" *International Advertiser,* Vol. 5 (March 1964), p. 14.

7. John K. Ryans, Jr., "Is It Too Soon to Put a Tiger in Your Tank?" *Columbia Journal of World Business,* Vol. 4 (March-April 1969), pp. 69–75.

8. Robert D. Buzzell, Can You Standardize Multinational Marketing?" *Harvard Business Review,* Vol. 46 (November-December 1968), pp. 102–113.

9. Richard H. Holton, "Marketing Policies in Multinational Corporations," *Journal of International Business Studies,* Vol. 1 (Spring 1970), pp. 1–20.

10. Richard J. Aylmer, "Who Makes Marketing Decisions in the Multinational Firm?" *Journal of Marketing,* Vol. 34 (October 1970), pp. 25–30.

11. James E. Donnelly, Jr., "Attitude toward Culture and Approach to International Advertising," *Journal of Marketing,* Vol. 34 (July 1970), pp. 60–62.

12. Ulrich S. Wiechmann, "Integrating Multinational Marketing Activities," *Columbia Journal of World Business,* Vol. 9 (Winter 1974), pp. 17–23; and Ralph Z. Sorenson and Ulrich E. Wiechmann, "How Multinationals View Marketing Standardization," *Harvard Business Review,* Vol. 53 (May-June 1975), pp. 38 ff.

13. Robert T. Green and Eric Langeard, "A Cross-National Comparison of Consumer Habits and Innovator Characteristics," *Journal of Marketing,* Vol. 39 (July 1975), pp. 34–41.

14. Yoram Wind, Susan P. Douglas, and Howard V. Perlmutter, "Guidelines for Developing International Marketing Strategies," *Journal of Marketing,* Vol. 37 (April 1973), pp. 14–23.

15. Tom Sutton, "Advertising at the Crossroads," *Advertising, Marketing and Media Weekly,* July 18, 1974, pp. 30–31.

16. Both studies were funded in part by a grant from the American Association of Agencies Educational Foundation and in part by the University of Illinois at Urbana-Champaign.

17. See Steven Eli Permut, "Decision-Making of the Multinational Executive: A Research Paradigm," *Journal of the Academy of Marketing Science,* Vol. 2 (Summer 1974), pp. 508–522.

18. Dunn, same as reference 4 above.

19. This research project was conducted in conjunction with the University of Manchester Institute of Science and Technology and was supported by the Marsteller Foundation. See S. Watson Dunn, "European Executives Look at Advertising," *Columbia Journal of World Business,* Vol. 9 (Winter 1974), pp. 26–32, for a summary of the major findings.

20. "Europe—Tops in Solving Ad Problems," *Media Decisions,* Vol. 9 (October 1974), p. 16.

21. Stephen A. Greyser and Bonnie B. Reece, "Businessmen Look Hard at Advertising," *Harvard Business Review,* Vol. 49 (May-June 1971), pp. 18 ff. for the U.S. viewpoint; Dunn, in reference 19 for the European viewpoint.

Can positioning strategy be employed in an international marketing context? Although the possibilities for multinational positioning are somewhat limited because fewer brands are marketed on a worldwide basis, the author contends that positioning can be every bit as effective as it has been in the United States. The positioning concept is explored in the article along with illustrations of its potential applications abroad.

30. Multinational Positioning Strategy

David R. McIntyre
J. Walker Thompson Company, Inc.

The 1970s have been heralded as the "Age of Positioning." That is, positioning your product, which can be either a brand or service, in the minds of prospective consumers by taking into consideration the strengths and weaknesses of not only your brand but those of your competitors as well. We have seen this positioning concept, which emphasizes market strategy rather than creativity, work in quite a few instances in North America, i.e., Avis Rental Car System "We're Number 2" campaign and "7UP, the Uncola" campaign to name two classic examples.

The concept, however, although used in some individual European countries, has not been used extensively on a multinational basis. Admittedly, the possibilities for multinational positioning are limited because fewer brands are marketed on a worldwide basis, language barriers exist and local regulations prohibit any reference, implied or otherwise, to competitors.

Source: Reprinted with permission from the fall 1975 issue of the COLUMBIA JOURNAL OF WORLD BUSINESS. Copyright © 1975 by the Trustees of Columbia University of the City of New York.

Nevertheless, a multinational positioning strategy can be just as effective as it has been in North America because of the important similarities which exist in the world marketplace. To support this statement, let me back up somewhat by explaining the positioning concept and how it evolved in the United States. The case will then be made for a more effective use of the positioning strategy on a multinational basis by using 7UP as an example.

To correctly position a product, an "outward" examination of the market must be made to accurately determine what is happening there. It is imperative to know first what consumers think of the product, and, secondly, how it is perceived vis-à-vis major competitors. If a company's marketing department has not gone through this soul searching process recently, the results may be surprising. What seems to have been a sound strategy three or even two years ago, could actually be detrimental to the brand's growth in today's economic climate of retrenchment.

This outward approach is a considerable departure from the 1950s in North America when a company's strategy was to simply look "inward" at their own product in terms of how many units could be sold. These were the days when only a few brands competed in most product categories and a little hard sell television advertising would generally result in a sales increase. A case in point is the cigarette industry. Twenty years ago there were only six brands on the United States market. Camels, Chesterfields, Lucky Strike, Old Gold, Philip Morris and Pall Mall. Today, there are literally scores with more being introduced each year.

The devastating effects of World War II plus lack of commercial television retarded the development of most consumer products in Europe. However, by the early 1960s, our European marketing counterparts had caught up. As more and more products were being introduced through TV advertising on both sides of the Atlantic, hard sell competition for a smaller share of each market caused the advertising industry to seek new methods of getting their message across to consumers. Each brand had to have an image. Remember the successful worldwide Esso gasoline campaign "Put a Tiger in Your Tank". Here was an ingenious strategy which used an animated tiger to build an image for an unromantic product like gasoline. Most of us can also recall the one-eyed man in Hathaway Shirt ads and Commander Whitehead of Schweppes.

Just as the "Me Too" brands killed the hard sell era of the 1950s, the "Me Too" brands crowded in and eventually brought an end to the image era of the 1960s. In overseas markets where commercial television advertising exists without rigid government controls, the same situation prevails. By 1968 the noise level of television advertising became so loud with this type of image advertising, the some companies realized that by looking "outward" into the marketplace through consumer research studies, they would find that consumers subconsciously related some brands to others according to the position it holds in their minds.

We all know that the human mind is a very complex organ . . . yet in some ways it is rather limited. One of these limiting characteristics is its peculiar inability to readily recall more than one major event related to a particular subject. For example, most of us can easily recall the first time we drove a car alone. We can also probably remember the first airplane ride we took and the first boy/girl we kissed. These recollections are fairly easy, but now try remembering the second or third time you drove a car alone, flew in an airplane or the boy/girl we kissed. If these events come to mind as quickly as the first, then your recall facilities are better than average.

Let me carry this train of thought one step further by asking you to again recall certain things which related to these first happenings . . . such as the year and make of the first car you drove alone, the destination of that first airplane ride or your exact location when that first kiss was experienced. If you're like most people, the answers will come to mind almost immediately because they directly relate to something which occupies a strong "first" position in your mind. This same principle applies to the position a particular brand occupies in the consumer's mind.

Let me illustrate this point by using 7UP as a case study. In 1967 when The Seven-Up Company's product-oriented "Wet & Wild" campaign failed to stop the brand's declining market share, a focus group study revealed that even though consumers knew 7UP was a soft drink, they did not think of it as such. With the cola segment of the market, led by Coke and Pepsi, accounting for a whopping 60 percent share and both major brands spending over $50 million to promote a similar image for two products which look and taste somewhat alike, it was no wonder that the word "cola" became generic to mean soft drink. The problem for 7UP was clear . . . it had to convince consumers that it was a soft drink just like cola but different. This could not be accomplished by attacking cola's strong position directly with cola type advertising like the Wet & Wild campaign. Since cola occupied the leading soft drink position in consumers' minds, 7UP had to relate to this strong position in terms they would readily understand . . . by positioning itself as an alternative to cola, or as "The Uncola".

This, of course, has been a tremendous success story for The Seven-Up Company but let's relate it to the Brand's overseas position. Although there are many differences between the New York Metro market and the large Southern California area most United States product managers will look for the similarities, or common denominators, in planning strategy for a national advertising campaign. The same principal also works in international markets. There are more similarities among worldwide consumers than dissimilarities. In addition to the basic human physiological need for food, shelter, etc., most people have similar psychological needs such as achievement, status, recognition within peer groups, etc. The human mind seems to work in much the same manner for Malaysians and Nigerians as it does for Americans and Europeans.

Another universal factor which strengthens the argument for an international positioning strategy is the "noise level" on commercial media. Most overseas markets have commercial television, radio, newspapers, etc., which accept advertising. Many countries, even in developing regions, have also experienced a rapid increase in the number of consumer products being introduced during the past ten years . . . an explosion similar to that experienced in the industrial nations. In observing the rapid, universal increase in television advertising rates, we strongly suspect that the "noise level" or number of products being aimed at consumers via television, is also approaching United States and European saturation levels. Because of these two major similarities, I believe that the concept of positioning is just as usable in Manila, Johannesburg or Cairo as it is in New York.

Let's look more closely at 7UP's international position vis-à-vis major cola competitors. In 1973 we re-examined our market position by analyzing the annual bottler marketing plans. These individual market plans serve as the cornerstone for the entire corporate planning procedure, while marketing programs vary from country to country, the planning process, i.e., updating existing market conditions, identifying opportunities and formulating action plans, is highly standardized.

The first step was to segment these markets according to existing brand strength and potential development to re-define where our major markets were. In doing so, we clearly saw that 80 percent of the total overseas business came from only eighteen of the seventy-nine countries where 7UP is marketed.

By eliminating the top three markets which have well staffed subsidiary offices that produce their own national advertising campaigns, and therefore do not rely on St. Louis headquarters for television commercials, fifteen major markets remain which account for 30 percent of the total business. Although thought was given to adding three or four additional markets to this list where the Brand is presently weak but the potential is great, it was decided not to because a solid Brand base is needed to successfully launch a new advertising campaign in this particular instance.

Once it was determined where the major markets were, the next step was to analyze them to find where the opportunities lay. In this endo-market analysis, we found three interesting common denominators:

> Twelve of these fifteen markets were dominated by either Coke or Pepsi or both to the extent that ten of these markets showed cola share of market exceeding 40 percent.

> The 7UP Bottler in most of these markets had developed the Brand over the years into a leading competitive position.

> Most of these 7UP Bottlers had extensively used previous series of multinational film commercials and the Brand has a positive image on which a new campaign can be built. The 1973 image in these major markets probably equaled 7UP's comestic image prior to the introduction of the Uncola campaign in 1968.

In addition to these endo-market similarities there were two other extra-market factors which presented additional opportunities for 7UP:

> Coke, Pepsi and 7UP have universal package designs and trademarks. Additionally, the flavor category into which both cola products belong is a part of their brand names. This allows both competitors to be collectively referred to as "Cola".

> Both cola competitors market products which are similar in taste, similar in looks and share similar brand images perpetuated by all those years of using boy/girl/fun activities type commercials.

All of these endo and extra market factors provide 7UP with the opportunity to exploit Coke and Pepsi's traditional sameness in these cola dominated markets.

In late 1973, this problem/opportunity was turned over to our advertising agency. J. Walter Thompson was asked to create something which would communicate 7UP's unique position to people of diverse cultures, intelligence levels and varying degrees of sophistication. A new campaign had to be amusing, yet not contain anything which could be interpreted as denigratory towards our cola competitors.

Because 7UP's market position was very similar to the Brand's 1968 position in the United States, thought was first given to exporting the Uncola campaign. This proved not to be practical because the slogan could not be translated into other languages and still retain its special meaning. However, the strategy behind the campaign, that is to position 7UP in consumers' minds as a unique, untraditional, alternative to cola had definite possibilities.

In place of the untranslatable Uncola slogan, J. Walter Thompson created an unusual character who lives in a little greeen box. The activities of this amusing visual device cuts across many levels of sophistication to develop a style very distinctive from cola. In effect the Uncola campaign strategy is being used on a multinational basis but in a somewhat modified form.

In those three major markets where colas do not dominate or where 7UP is the market leader, a small change in the copy lines of the voice-over film track will enable 7UP to be positioned merely as an untradition, fun soft drink with no mention of cola.

Now that 7UP is midway through its second year of this campaign, it becomes important to try and measure what effect "Green Box" has had on Brand sales. Even under the best of conditions this is a difficult chore with often questionable results. Compounding the problem of comparing sales results for 1974 over 1975 is the sales dampening effect of depression and inflation experienced by most oil importing nations over the past eighteen months plus last year's worldwide sugar shortage. Nevertheless, we selected ten national markets which used our "Green Box" campaign during the months of May, June and July of 1975 and compared them to sales over the same period in tén other markets of comparable size which used different advertising or promotional material. The difference was significant even after we made adjustments for market variations.

The ten "Green Box" markets showed a 16 percent sales increase for the three month period of 1975 compared to the same period in 1974. Those ten markets which used other material showed an 8 percent loss in sales over the same time period.

Although these figures are impressive they become somewhat qualified because of the major variables involved. Nonetheless, we are encouraged enough to commission a multinational, qualitative research project to try and determine through focus group sessions in four countries if "Green Box" is being understood by consumers and is reaching its creative objectives. If these results prove positive we will continue the concept into 1976 and beyond.

In summary, there is little doubt that the positioning concept has been used successfully in North America. I contend that this same concept can be used with equal success on a multinational basis as long as the same consistency is exercised in the use of the Company's trademark/brand/packaging as is practiced in the United States. An example would be the The McDonald's Corporation. They continue to use their famous double arch in international markets which signifies quality hamburgers plus fast, friendly service. McDonald's can position itself against the slow, old-fashioned, take-your-chances-on-quality foreign competitors. Another example would be L'eggs panty hose which will enter the international field in 1976. I see no reason why they cannot use essentially the same dynamic packaging and name trademark overseas to position itself as a quality product against existing (locally made) competitors.

These strategies were used by both companies to gain a strong market position in the United States . . . and they can be used with equal success overseas. The world is growing "smaller" all the time. Television satellite broadcasting, inexpensive group travel plans, etc. have all contributed to this shrinking phenomenon. In the process we have found that there is really very little difference between worldwide consumers. They all want quality products which will enhance their personal prestige at an affordable price. This is the universality of the average consumer with disposable income. An advertising strategy which has proven to be successful in one country has a fairly good chance of being successful in another. That's what multinational positioning is all about.

QUESTIONS

1. What is meant by product positioning?
2. Do you agree with the author's contention that positioning is applicable to international marketing?
3. How was a positioning strategy developed by 7UP?
4. What other brands do you think would be able to use the positioning approach?

PRICING
STRATEGIES

Pricing is a particularly critical and complex marketing decision variable in overseas markets. The reason being that it ultimately impacts on the ability of an organization to sustain its international marketing ventures. At the same time the uncertainties created by what often appear as entirely unpredictable costs, competition, and demand forces pose numerous pitfalls for pricing strategists. The readings chosen for this section will hopefully develop a framework for understanding international pricing processed by describing the problems encountered and tactics practiced by overseas marketers. The lead article by Arpan reports on the results of a comprehensive survey of the pricing decision factors considered, and the resulting strategies of non-United States multinational firms. The results from Arpan's study are compared to results from previous research conducted on United States multinational firms and some interesting contrasts are drawn. The second selection by Kressler explores different perspectives on the controversial topic of uniform pricing for foreign markets. The concluding piece in this section is concerned with the influence of international commodity agreements on market power and price setting for increasingly scarce resources. Kirpalani describes different types of commodity agreements, their rational, and the global economic implications.

How are corporate pricing strategies decided for international markets? The author presents a summary of research performed on certain elements of the pricing practices of multinational corporations. A thorough investigation of past research on United States multinational firms first was undertaken to identify problems and procedures encountered in pricing international sales. These findings served as basis for comparison of the research results on non-United States multinationals.

31. Multinational Firm Pricing in International Markets

Jeffrey S. Arpan
Georgia State University

Pricing considerations in international business operations are not only more numerous than those in strictly domestic ones, but also more ambiguous and risky. A selling firm must consider at least two different sets of laws, two competitive markets, the reactions of two sets of competitors, and two governments. Each of these considerations is comprised of a number of components which may also vary in importance and interaction over time. Thus, the firm selling internationally is confronted with two different and constantly changing market collages. It is not surprising that determining prices for international sales is such a difficult problem, even for the occasional exporter.

Successful pricing is a key element in the profitability of any business operation, domestic or international. As a result, pricing policies and procedures are largely secretive information areas for virtually all firms. The cloud of secrecy enshrouding pricing can also cover practices of a quasi-

---

Source: Jeffrey S. Arpan, "Multinational Firm Pricing in International Markets," from SLOAN MANAGEMENT REVIEW, Winter 1973, pp. 1–9. Reprinted by permission.

illegal, often outright illegal, nature, making it doubly difficult for outside researchers to obtain information.

Definition and Limitations

The research sample consisted only of multinational firms, that is, firms which have direct investments in at least two countries. Firms which strictly export were excluded for two reasons. Pricing policies and procedures for internal sales (intracorporate pricing or transfer pricing) usually affect those for sales in final markets, whether they be to nonaffiliated firms or directly to consumers. Since exporting firms, by definition, cannot make an international intracorporate transfer, their pricing practices would not be similarly affected. Secondly, pricing policies of export firms are likely to be different from those of multinational firms because the reasons behind the sale are often quite different. The exporter may sell simply because of excess capacity reasons, because a nondomestic buyer has run short and needs an emergency purchase, or for a number of similar, less planned occurrences. Exports and imports among the parents and subsidiaries of multinational firms, however, are essentially parts of their production, marketing, and financial planning process. Despite the exclusion of strictly exporting firms from the research sample, the considerations in pricing sales to nonaffiliated buyers (which are discussed later in this paper) apply equally to exporters and to multinational firms.

As used in this paper, pricing refers to the value determination process for a good or service, and encompasses the determination of interest rates for loans, charges for rentals, fees for services, and prices for goods. International markets refer to markets located outside the national boundary of any particular country, regardless of whether the buyer is affiliated or not with the seller.

The research upon which this paper is based had certain limitations. Only 60 of the 145 non-United States firms surveyed responded, and the data gathered on United States firms by previous researchers were not perfectly comparable in all respects. Nonetheless, the findings of this research are important because they represent the first investigation of pricing in international markets by multinational firms of different nationalities, and they provide a number of interesting questions for future research. It should also be pointed out that members of eight large international accounting firms participated in the study, making invaluable contributions in the form of substantive and analytical comments on the study's initial findings.

The Theory of International Pricing and Prices

In Ricardo's world of free competition and perfect knowledge, each country specialized in the production and sale of those goods in which it had a comparative advantage. Allowing free mobility of goods, labor, and capital, the net result of free trade was factor price equalization, goods price equalization, and the maximization of total world utility. Even without factor mobility, the end results were the same so long as goods were allowed to move freely. Uniform prices and pricing practices were both a theoretical and socially desirable result.

Although an oversimplified version and analysis of the classical theory of comparative advantage and free trade, the above does provide a base starting point for analyzing present pricing practices in international markets.

The Reality of International Prices and Pricing

Whether or not there ever existed purely competitive firms and markets is at best a theoretical, highly conjectural debate. Few experts would argue that today's world of international commerce is an example of such a market. The nonexistent, noninfluential governments of classical theory are omnipresent today. Trade activity is now highly managed and controlled by governments, firms, and banks. Governments use a host of trade and investment policies to restrict or encourage the extent, nature, and timing of international transactions.[1] The large corporations which dominate today's commerce can employ practices—such as dumping, price discrimination, and intracorporate pricing—to exploit their monopoly advantages in both domestic and international markets. Similarly, the international banking community affects trade and investment by altering credit policies, interest rates, and the amount and types of international services it offers. In sum, today's world of imperfect competition and knowledge gives ample opportunity and incentive for multinational firms *not* to price uniformly.[2] The following sections contain the more realistic sides of the pricing problems in international markets, including many noneconomic considerations.

Factors Influencing Price Determination

For a truly multinational firm, its overall international competitive position is its major consideration in determining prices, for prices determine revenue, and revenues along with costs determine profits. Although profit maximization in a world of uncertainty is not possible—and in modified form may be only one of a number of corporate objectives—profit considerations continue to be the major element in virtually all company decisions. A multinational firm must consider not only the profitability of its investments in both domestic and nondomestic markets, but also the ways in which these investments affect each other. To give an example, an American firm making a collusive agreement with a German firm to divide markets in Germany might ensure its competitive and profit position only to have suit brought against it via the extraterritorial reach of American antitrust law. Another example would be the use of intracorporate pricing to maneuver profits out of high tax rate countries into lower ones. The foreign subsidiary can sell at or below cost to its parent and sister subsidiaries in lower tax rate countries, thereby showing a loss in its local market, but contributing significantly to the profits of the buying members of the firm.

International Sales

Viewed in this light, two separate types of international sales must be considered in terms of their effect on the firm's competitive position. The first involves sales to nonaffiliated buyers (that is, entities not part of the corporate family), and the second involves sales to members of the family. In the first case, about which considerably more information and research is available, such factors as buyer needs, tastes, purchasing power and practices, and income and demand price elasticities are very important.[3] The exit prices of goods and services largely determine the market share and profitability of the firm in that particular market, and serve as the starting point for overall company considerations (see the discussion, below). Local income and turnover taxes, rates of inflation, and practices of competitors are also of major importance. Additionally, divisional performances and evaluation techniques become important when the firm operates strictly on a profit center basis, particularly when intracorporate or interdivisional sales are substantial.[4]

Both the local profitability and competitive position of the subsidiaries as they sell to nonaffiliated groups are usually less important then the subsidiaries' contribution to the profitability and competitive position of the *overall* corporation. This contribution, however, is not always synonymous with the increased profit and improved competitive position of the parent. In some instances, the parent company itself may desire to show losses, preferring to have profits accrue to its subsidiaries in lower tax rate areas. The pricing considerations related to this "contributing to the whole" concept, which primarily involves intracorporate pricing, is an area about which there is very little known.

The Internal Pricing Structure

Intracorporate prices essentially are based on costs or on market prices.[5] The former begin with some internally calculated cost—such as full cost, variable cost, or marginal cost—and usually have added to them a percentage markup (such as 10 percent) that allows some margin of profit to accrue to the selling unit. The latter begin with an established market selling price, and the products usually are sold at that price minus a discount to allow some margin of profit for the buying division (such as market price less 10 percent).

The derived prices of the two methods converge at a certain percentage markup and markdown, but cost based prices allow greater flexibility because the cost base itself may be changed in addition to the percentage added on. This flexibility factor is particularly important in international business because of the complexity and dynamics of world market considerations. For example, as competitive conditions become more severe, the percentage markup or cost base may have to be reduced to allow the firm to maintain its market share.

Alternatively, if under a currency rationing system the local government suddenly reduces the amount of foreign currency available to the firm for purchasing imported manufacturing inputs, the parent company can respond by lowering its selling prices to the subsidiary. In so doing, the subsidiary can continue production without serious disruption. Furthermore, since price manipulation is tantamount to revenue manipulation, cost based prices are better suited for maneuvering income and profits to low tax rate areas and achieving a number of other corporate objectives, some of which are mentioned below.

The Company Objectives

The overall competitive and financial position of the firm must be the major consideration for any policy, and transfer pricing is no exception. In fact, intracorporate sales can so significantly alter the financial results of global operations that they comprise the most important ongoing area of decision making for large multinational corporations.[6] Not surprisingly then, transfer prices are set by the firm's major financial officer, usually the financial vice-president or comptroller, and parent company executives uniformly are unwilling to allow much participation by other department or subsidiary executives.[7]

Exogenous Variables

A number of exogenous environmental factors determine the results of any particular transfer pricing strategy chosen; income taxes and the various degrees of competition facing the firm are the two most important ones. Customs duties, export subsidies and tax credits, exchange controls, inflation, and future changes in foreign exchange rates are also usually considered, but they vary much more in relative importance with individual firms and over time.[8] Consider the dilemma facing an Italian firm with a subsidiary in a country with high income tax rates, high *ad valorem* tariffs, price controls, exchange rationing, restrictions on profit remittance, and a banking system which loans on the basis of a firm's yearly profitability. High transfer prices on goods shipped to the subsidiary and low ones on goods imported from it will result (*ceteris paribus*) in minimizing the subsidiary's tax liability and getting more money out of the host country. The same procedure also will result in higher duties, reduce the competitive position of the subsidiary (due to higher input prices), reduce the amount of goods the subsidiary can import, and possibly reduce the ability of the subsidiary to borrow locally due to lower profits.

The problems grow geometrically as additional subsidiaries located in countries with different environmental characteristics are added. The firm inevitably faces trade-offs. It must weigh the importance of each factor in each environment, and each environment against the others. Here are no easy answers, no simple decision rules. As an example, consider an American multinational firm with subsidiaries in England and France. Certain conditions in England may call for low cost-based transfer prices, while others suggest the desirability of high market price based transfer prices (as in the Italian firm example mentioned above). Assume that the firm decides to use the market price orientation. Next assume that the environmental conditions in France make a cost-based, low transfer pricing system desirable. To utilize the two different pricing systems would not only take considerable amounts of bookkeeping—probably resulting in considerable confusion—but might also be in violation of American antitrust laws prohibiting price discrimination. If forced to select only one system orientation, the firm must analyze each system's costs and benefits to the world corporation as a whole.

Endogenous Variables

The policy adopted also will be tempered by a number of internal objectives and policies peculiar to each firm. If the firm operates on a profit center basis, some consideration must be given to the effect of transfer pricing on the subsidiary's apparent (but arbitrarily determined) profit performance. It is hardly fair to judge a subsidiary's profit performance as poor if it had been decided in advance that that subsidiary would be a net source of funds (that is, show a loss). The subsidiary, in so doing, would contribute more to the overall profit position of the firm than by showing a profit in its country. To take another example, if the firm has as one of its objectives being a good citizen of each country in which it operates (to minimize possible negative confrontations with host governments), market prices for transferred goods would be more appropriate because they are construed to be the most equitable and least manipulated. This consideration, however, must be weighed against the possible financial gains foregone by not manipulating prices. Thus, the multinational firm must attempt to balance not only external environmental factors but internal objectives as well.

With both external and internal factors changing over time, the decision process becomes even more complex. It is not surprising, given the complexity of the problem, that the comptroller of one multinational firm stated that expediency was the major criterion for determining intracorporate prices in his firm! Nor is it surprising that most firms surveyed use only one basic orientation (cost or market); changes in the markups or markdowns are less disruptive to management control and evaluation system, and less likely to be noticed by governments than changes in the overall system orientation.

The Influence of Corporate Size

Although there are innumerable variations on the two basic transfer pricing orientations, the very large multinational firms use predominantly cost-based systems. The larger the firm and the spread of its international activities, the greater are the opportunities for, and advantages of, manipulating prices. Therefore, greater flexibility of cost-based transfer prices becomes an advantage. The use of this price flexibility almost always necessitates the keeping of separate records (books) utilizing market price equivalents for subsequent management performance evaluation, but the additional cost is judged to be worthwhile. The large multinationals do more income maneuvering and, as a result, are much more concerned with transfer price determination and its subsequent effects.

Operating in monopolistic or oligopolistic markets gives these large multinationals additional protection from the competitive pressures which otherwise might influence the selection of a transfer price orientation or particular profit margin on sales. For smaller firms that cannot differentiate their products enough to justify a departure from a widely known market price the choice of orientation essentially is made for them. This is particularly the case for smaller American firms since Section 482 of the Internal Revenue Service Code specifies the use of market prices (if they exist) for intracorporate sales.

The Influence of Culture

The cultural background of parent company executives also often influences the choice of orientation. The internal objectives mentioned earlier in this paper are largely conditioned by cultural attitudes and views of business and the world in general.[9] As a result, several distinct national patterns exist for the small to medium size multinational firms.[10] On the whole, non-United States firms use more market-based systems, while United States firms use predominantly cost-oriented ones.[11] This pattern is by no means universal, however. The English, French, and Japanese firms exhibit preferences for cost systems, while Canadian and Scandinavian firms prefer market systems. The Italians, Germans, and Dutch tend to use combination systems. The precise extent to which these national preferences can be attributed solely to cultural factors is open to some question. For example, other variables such as firm size, industry characteristics, and managerial sophistication make it difficult to state unequivocally that a particular French cultural trait is the unique cause of French multinational firms' preferences for cost-based transfer pricing systems. Nonetheless, their fervor in seeking to avoid paying taxes explains why the French prefer the cost-based prices—this form of transfer pricing allows them to maneuver income to low tax rate areas more easily. Similarly, the tax determination and collection procedures in Italy are so complex and ambiguous that the Italian multinational firms prefer to maximize income in Italy. A combination system is utilized wherein transfers from subsidiaries to parents are priced low (at cost). The next result is that the major profit from each sale ends up in the parent company.

The English preference for cost-based systems is not based as much on tax considerations as on those considerations pertaining to return on investment calculations. The English banking community demands a specific return on investment before making a loan to finance subsidiary creation or expansion, and then watches closely the real rate of return at the end of the year. English firms thus make certain that both the final rate of return is equal to the promised rate, and that cost-based transfers permit large adjustments more easily.

Finally, the Germans' apparent lack of interest and concern with regard to transfer pricing can be explained in terms of their emphasis on the fixed asset position and long run stability of the firm. Since transfer pricing is mostly related to short run profit performance and involves principally current assets, it is not of major concern to German managers.

The above are only a few examples of the ways in which culture influences the selection of an intracorporate system. Yet, despite cultural preferences for any given system orientation, the ability to utilize that system is becoming increasingly contingent upon the attitudes and surveillance techniques of the national governments involved.

The Influence of Governments

For a considerable period of time, the magnitude of the effect of intracorporate pricing—in both real and potential terms—was unknown to many governments. As these governments became distraught over their loss of tax revenues or over the negative effects of competition suffered by strictly local producers, they became aware of the many manipulative possibilities transfer pricing affords. As a result, considerably more attention now is accorded transfer prices both into and out of these countries. Increasing emphasis is being placed on the "fairness" of the transfer price, and on regulations specifying market prices. Fair market prices are perceived to be those prices that would be arrived at by two unaffiliated parties, neither allowing the other to take an advantage. Although these governments often have difficulty in ascertaining a market price for a particular good, their concern and surveillance are making it increasingly difficult, and in many cases legally dangerous, for firms to use cost-based prices.

Conclusions and Implications

The obvious conclusion about the international pricing practices of multinational firms is that there is presently very little that can be concluded. This somewhat confused tautology is indicative of the real world confusion over pricing in international markets. There are almost too many influencing factors to consider: some general, some specific; some exogenous, some endogenous; some static, some dynamic; some isolated, some interrelated. As is often the case, the attraction is also the danger; the international environment offers many advantages that can easily become disadvantages. Many firms do price quite successfully, however, and have done so for a number of years and under many different conditions. Thus, there is still a great deal of research to be done in this area until the "secrecy of pricing" becomes the "science of pricing." Until that time, researchers should continue to investigate along the following lines:

1. What are the real ranges in which price manipulation is possible?
2. What is the real magnitude of price manipulation: the number of firms, their volume of sale, their degree of manipulation?
3. When exactly do corporate size and the percentage of international operations diminish cultural influences?
4. Are there differences in practice which can be strictly explained on an industry basis?
5. What factors do pricing executives really consider as opposed to what they may say they consider?

QUESTIONS

1. How does the "reality" of international pricing vary from classical economic theory?
2. What is the relationship of corporate size and pricing practice? Culture? Government?
3. Differentiate between an exogenous and endogenous variable. How do they both affect pricing practices?

NOTES

1. Examples of these policies are tariffs, quotas, international agreements, currency controls, licensing rules, subsidies, and tax policies.
2. For example, see Kressler.
3. For example, see *Solving International Pricing Problems*, McCalley and Rutenburg.
4. For example, see Boyd, Boyer, Mauriel and Anthony, and Fremgen.
5. For a good discussion of the many variations of these two orientations, see Dean, Shillinglaw, Cook, and Greer.
6. See Zenoff and Zwick, and Arpan.
7. See Arpan.

8. See Shulman, *Solving International Pricing Problems*, and Arpan.

9. For studies focusing on these types of cultural influences on management styles and attitudes, see Haire, Ghiselli, and Porter, Grannick, and Clark and Mosson.

10. For a more detailed discussion, see Arpan.

11. This was the consensus of the participating members of the international accounting firms.

REFERENCES

1. Arpan, J. *International Intracorporate Pricing: Non-U.S. Systems and Views.* New York, Praeger Publishers, 1972.

2. Boyd, R. "Transfer Prices and Profitability Measurement," *The Controller.* Vol. 29 (February 1961).

3. Boyer, J. "Intracompany Pricing's Effect on R.O.I. Analysis," *Financial Executive,* Vol. 34 (December 1964).

4. Clark, D.G. and Mosson, T.M. "Industrial Managers in Belgium, France, and the U.K.," *Management International,* Vol. 7, no. 2-3 (1967).

5. Cook, Paul Jr. "New Techniques for Intracompany Pricing," *Harvard Business Review,* Vol. 35 (July–August 1957).

6. Dean, J. "Decentralization and Intra-Company Pricing," *Harvard Business Review,* Vol. 33 (1955).

7. Fremgen, J. "Measuring Profit of Part of a Firm," *Management Accounting,* Vol. 47, no. 5, sect. 1 (January 1966).

8. Grannick, D. *European Executive.* London, Wedenfield and Nicholson, 1962.

9. Greer, H. "Divisional Profit Calculation—Notes on the Transfer Pricing Problem," *N.A.A. Bulletin,* Vol. 43, no. 11, sect. 1 (July 1962).

10. Haire, M., Ghiselli, E., and Porter, L. *Mangerial Thinking,* New York, John Wiley & Sons, 1966.

11. Kressler, P. "Is Uniform Pricing Desirable in Multinational Markets?" *Akron Business and Economic Review,* Vol. 2 (Winter 1971).

12. Mauriel, J.J. and Anthony, R.N. "Misevaluation of Investment Center Performance," *Harvard Business Review,* Vol. 44 (March–April 1966).

13. McCalley, M.I. "Pricing in the International Market." In: Reed Moyer (ed.), *Changing Marketing Systems,* Chicago, AMA. 1967.

14. Rutenburg, David. "Three Pricing Policies for a Multi-Product, Multinational Company," *Management Science* (April 1971).

15. Shillinglaw, Gordon. *Cost Accounting: Analysis and Control,* revised edition. Homewood, Illinois, Richard D. Irwin. (1967).

16. Shulman, James. "Transfer Pricing in Multinational Business." Doctoral dissertation: Harvard Business School, 1966.

17. *Solving International Pricing Problems.* New York, Business International, 1966.

18. Zenoff, D. and Zwick, J. *International Financial Management.* Englewood Cliffs, New Jersey, Prentice Hall, 1969.

Uniform pricing for overseas markets is a subject of great controversy in international marketing circles. This article explores legalistic, economic, host country, and marketing perspectives on the practice of price discrimination versus price uniformity by multinational organizations.

32.   Is Uniform Pricing Desirable in Multinational Markets?

Peter R. Kressler
University of Akron

There is a raging controversy today among lawyers, economists, and business-men as to the desirability of uniform pricing in multinational markets.[1] The crux of the dispute is that lawyers utilize one yardstick in measuring this activity; economists, yet a different one; and businessmen employ one or the other as the situation warrants.

From a legalistic viewpoint, uniform pricing is emphatically desirable in multinational markets. In fact, legal attempts to bring about price uniformity in multinational markets are contained in: (1) the United States Antidumping Act of 1921, as amended;[2] (2) Article VI of the General Agreement on Tariffs and Trade (GATT) of 1947;[3] and (3) the International Antidumping Code of 1967.[4]

According to the 1921 Act, foreign products are "dumped" in the United States market, provided: (1) a product is sold in the United States at a lower price than that for which the same or a similar product is sold in the country of origin; and (2) this lower-priced, imported product injures or

---

Source: Reprinted with permission of the *Akron Business and Economic Review (ABER)*, Winter 1971.

threatens to injure a United States industry. If the authorities' investigation finds both price discrimination and injury present, an antidumping duty must be levied. This assessment must equal the difference between the lower import price and the higher foreign price; in effect, this is tantamount to the imposition of uniform pricing policies on the foreign seller.

These concepts used by the United States to determine an act of "dumping" were incorporated into Article VI of the GATT in 1947.[5] Twenty years later, these same ideas were reaffirmed in the International Antidumping Code. In expounding upon the provisions of Article VI, the Code defined some of its terms and detailed certain administrative and investigative procedures—all of which slightly modified earlier United States practices.[6] Notwithstanding such minor alterations, the historical evolution of these measures clearly indicates that the general trend has not changed.

From an economic viewpoint, uniform pricing is definitely not desirable in multinational markets owing to the existence of imperfectly competitive market structures—pure monopoly, oligopoly, and monopolistic competition. Such differences are not reflected in the various antidumping measures.

To investigate the pricing strategies of a pure monopolist, let us examine the case in which the firm[7] wants to sell its product in the home market, as well as in one foreign market.

In this two-market case, assume that the domestic demand for the firm's product is given by the line D_2 in Exhibit 32-1 and the foreign demand for

EXHIBIT 32-1

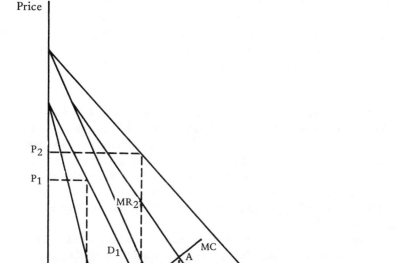

the same product is depicted by line D_1.[8] The marginal revenue curve associated with each demand curve is indicated in Exhibit 32–1 by MR_2 and MR_1. The monopolist must now decide upon the optimal combination of price/output for each of the two markets. The derivation of the optimal price/output combination for each market is a two-step process—determination of the total output and its allocation between the two markets. To ascertain the optimal output, one laterally sums the two marginal revenue curves—line ΣMR. At the point of intersection (point A of Exhibit 32–1) of the aggregate marginal revenue curve and the marginal cost curve of the total output, the monopolist reaches the optimum point of production OQ.

To maximize profits, the monopolist will allocate the total output OQ to achieve marginal revenue AQ in each market. Consequently, it will charge price P_2 and sell quantity Q_2 in the home market, and charge a lower price P_1 and sell quantity Q_1 in the foreign market. In short, the firm will *discriminate* between the buyers in the home and foreign markets.

Multilateralizing, the monopolist maximizes profits by selling the product in different markets at different prices. Mathematically, this process is stated $MC_{\text{total output}} = MR_1 = MR_2 = \ldots MR_n$.

In turning to the price/output decisions of firms in an oligopolistic market structure, one discovers that the force of mutual interdependence influences all decisions which removes such industries from the realm of strict marginal analysis.[9]

Relying upon a hypothetical example to illustrate a possible pricing policy of oligopolists in multinational markets, suppose that Industry Z is composed of the "Big Three" firms—A, B, and C, accounting for 50, 30, and 15 percent of sales, respectively.

Company A has long been accepted as the dominant firm, and, thereby, recognized as the price leader in this industry. This company might well use a cost-plus basis to determine its pricing policy. Also assume, "A" adjusts the markup factor in its pricing policy to take into account the different demand elasticities for the product, thus establishing an industry-wide pricing policy.

As Company A enters various foreign markets, it may find itself still the price leader within each foreign market, but may be confronted with a more elastic demand than that encountered in its home market. This results in a downward adjustment of price. Should "A" face a more inelastic demand for its product, it will adjust its price upward. In short, Company A will have to evaluate each international market on its own merits. It would, then, determine different percentage markups in each market to take advantage of the particular elasticities.

Company A entering that foreign market in which it is a minority supplier must accept the prevailing prices if it wishes to remain. In this instance, "A" may have to lower its prices "to meet the competition";—thereby forcing a reallocation of its overhead costs. It, of course, may find itself entering a foreign market in which higher prices prevailed, requiring like price adjustments.

Companies B and C may also find themselves in any one of these or other combinations of circumstances, thereby choosing pricing policies appropriate to the dictates of each foreign market.

Like the monopolist, a firm in an oligopolistic market structure also finds it advantageous to *discriminate* in different markets.

We now turn to the pricing strategies of firms in the third market structure—monopolistic competition. In contrast to pure monopoly in which one firm produces the entire output of a highly differentiated or unique product, and to oligopoly in which a few firms account for most of the output of a moderately differentiated product, monopolistic competition includes a large number of firms, each maintaining a small share of the output of a slightly differentiated product. Consequently, the pricing policies of each firm in this market structure are independent, and can be based upon marginal analysis. Variations in price/output decisions by any one firm will go unchallenged because the impact is minimal, i.e., consumers will be drawn from each of the other firms, causing virtually no demand variations on any one firm.

A monopolistically competitive firm's highly elastic demand curve, as well as its marginal revenue and cost curves are graphed in Exhibit 32–2. This firm can maximize its profits by resolving its price/output problem according to marginal analysis—MC=MR. Thus, the firm will produce quantity Q_1 and charge demand price P_1.

In evaluating each foreign market, the firm may find that there exists different demand elasticities than that encountered in the home market. Hence, it behooves the firm to take advantage of these different demand elasticities by charging the appropriate price in each market. The firm would find such a pricing pattern beneficial to pursue; again, mathematically, where

EXHIBIT 32-2

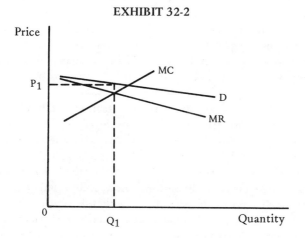

$MC_{\text{total output}} = MR_1 = MR_2 = \ldots MR_n$, but in this market structure, the firm has only a slight degree of latitude in its ability to practice *price discrimination*.

The pricing strategies followed by firms in any one of the imperfectly competitive market structures are not reflected in the various antidumping measures cited in Section 1 of this paper. In fact, pursuit of discriminatory pricing policies might well cause the firm to run afoul of these measures.

As stated in the first section of this paper, "dumping" is defined as the act of selling a product in a foreign market at a lower price than that at which the same or similar products are sold in the country of origin. Ultimately, the market value in the country of origin is determined by a "constructed value" which is the average costs of production including a reasonable allowance for general expenses, as well as for profits. Hence, the measures impose the stricture of uniform pricing strategies world-wide.

From a businessman's point of view, the desirability of uniform pricing in multinational markets depends upon his circumstance and market structure. A businessman who wants to prevent foreign competition to preserve his market position will look at the problem from the legalistic viewpoint. On the other hand, the businessman who wishes to sell his products internationally and utilize his market structure to his advantage will view the problem from the economic perspective. Thus, there are two different yardsticks for measuring the same activity.

These two different yardsticks can best be illustrated by an example using four parameters: (1) a purely domestic United States firm "E"; (2) a multinational United States firm "F"; and (3) and (4) their foreign counterparts "G" and "H," respectively.

Within the boundaries of the United States, "E" finds itself in one of the three imperfectly competitive market structures. This firm will attempt to determine its price/output combinations with a view toward profit maximization via one of the economic strategies detailed in Section II of this paper. Firm E ignores foreign trade until confronted with imports that are substitutes for its differentiated product. The influx of imports will precipitate a reaction—the invoking of legalistic measures in defense of its market share.

Firm E reacts in an attempt to avoid the inevitable changes occasioned by the appearance of imports. Imports reduce "E's" market share—it now faces a more elastic demand for its product. Imports may also force "E" to operate in a different market structure. If, in fact, Firm E had been a national monopolist before the presence of imports, it will, by definition, become a firm in an oligopolistic market structure. Likewise, the same change might also confront "E" had it operated in either an oligopolistic or monopolistically competitive market structure, though "E" in the latter market structure will never become purely competitive.[10] As a result of imports, "E" must redefine its pricing policy in accordance with the new market conditions.

Firm F, not unlike Firm E, will pursue a pricing policy in its home market in compliance with the dictates of the elasticities of demand. In contrast to

Firm E, however, Firm F sells its products in many foreign markets. As detailed in Section II, "F" will employ the appropriate economic rationale in its optimal pricing policy; *price discrimination* is an integral part of such policies. Quite to the contrary, when Firm F's role becomes that of the encroached-upon party in its home market, it has several options that it may exercise in defense of its market position. It may, as could Firm E, invoke legalistic measures. If, however, Firm F expects retaliatory actions in one or more of its foreign markets, it may well resort to economic measures instead of legalistic ones to minimize the impact of imports. Or, Firm F may elect a combination of both legalistic and economic measures.

Obviously, foreign Firms G and H, when placed in United States Firms E and F's respective positions, can be expected to react in the same manner as the like United States firm.

From a nationalistic viewpoint, a government protects its industries from foreign competition. The "Infant Industry" argument is the only economic one that may be applied temporarily to protect an adversely affected industry. However, protectionists leap upon more politically motivated rationale, including self-sufficiency, maintenance of the United States standard of living, etc., in attempting to substantiate their arguments. Hence, uniform pricing "becomes" desirable.

From a free-trade vantage, one arrives at a far different conclusion. From the economic viewpoint, there is no rationale for uniform pricing in multinational markets. In fact, as discussed in Section II of this paper, *price discrimination* is an essential characteristic of the pricing policies of firms in the three imperfectly competitive market structures.

Furthermore, in a given national economy, one has a particular market structure, but the market structure may well be different in a world-wide model. As the geographic dimension of an industry is redefined from a nationalistic to an international one, there is economic justification for *price discrimination*.

QUESTIONS

1. What is meant by "uniform pricing for multinational markets"?
2. Contrast the legal, economic, marketing and nationalistic viewpoints on uniform pricing.
3. What are the advantages and disadvantages of uniform pricing to multinational organizations?

NOTES

1. Controversy is indicated in such recent articles as: "U.S. Importers Worried by Treasury Crackdown," *Christian Science Monitor,* (May 29, 1971), p. 10. "Did SKF Sell Out to the Enemy?", *Business Week,* (July 10, 1971), pp. 22–23. "Electronic Warfare," *Fortune,* (September, 1971), p. 47.

Specifically, the following exemplary cases are noted:

"Tariff Unit Studies Marble Import Curbs," *Wall Street Journal,* (March 19, 1971), p. 26.

"Antidumping Inquiry on Mexican Sulphur Begun by Treasury," *Wall Street Journal,* (April 7, 1971), p. 26.

"British Ceramic Tile, Japanese Glass Found Anticompetitive," *Wall Street Journal,* (April 8, 1971), p. 30.

"Japanese Textiles Officials Dismiss as Groundless U.S. Dumping Charges," *Wall Street Journal,* (May 17, 1971), p. 11.

"Commission Rules Pig Iron Imports Harm U.S. Makers," *Wall Street Journal,* (June 16, 1971), p. 16.

"Canadian Revenue Unit Affirms T.V.-Set Dumping by Japan and by Taiwan," *Wall Street Journal,* (July 8, 1971), p. 17.

"Matsushita Lawsuit Denies Japanese TVs are 'Dumped' in U.S.," *Wall Street Journal,* (July 9, 1971), p. 9.

"France, Germany, Italy Ruled to have Dumped Glass at Unfair Prices," *Wall Street Journal,* (August 4, 1971), p. 13.

"Japan TV-Set Makers Told to Raise Prices 5% on Exports to U.S.," *Wall Street Journal,* (August 6, 1971), p. 3.

"Antidumping Probe Slated for British Needle Tips," *Christian Science Monitor,* (September 2, 1971), p. 8.

2. 19 U.S.C. 160-173.

3. Contracting Parties to the General Agreement on Tariffs and Trade, *Basic Instruments and Selected Documents,* Vol. IV, (Geneva: 1969), pp. 1-78.

4. Contracting Parties to the General Agreement on Tariffs and Trade, *Legal Instruments Embodying the Results of the 1964-1967 Trade Conference,* Vol. V, (Geneva: June, 1967), pp. 3692-3718.

5. John B. Rehm, "The Kennedy Round of Trade Negotiations," *The American Journal of International Law,* (April, 1968), p. 428.

6. The reader interested in pursuing this issue further is referred to U.S. Congress, Senate, Committee on Finance, *International Antidumping Code, Hearing,* 90th Cong., 2nd sess., June 27, 1968.

7. In a monopolistic market structure, the firm is, by definition, the industry.

8. For additional analysis, cf.,

Joe S. Bain, *Pricing, Distribution, and Employment,* revised, (New York: Henry Holt and Company, 1953), Chapter 9.

Joan Robinson, *The Economics of Imperfect Competition,* 2nd ed., (New York: St. Martin's Press, 1969), Chapters 15 and 16.

Alfred W. Stonier and Douglas C. Hague, *A Textbook of Economic Theory,* 3rd ed., (New York: John Wiley and Sons, Inc., 1967), pp. 172-181.

9. William Fellner, *Competition Among the Few,* (New York: Augustus M. Kelley, 1965), Chapter 1.

10. Delbert A. Snider, *Introduction to International Economics,* 4th ed., (Homewood, Illinois: Richard D. Irwin, Inc., 1967), pp. 246-248.

The stability of prices in international trade can be greatly affected by the imbalance of supply and demand in world commodity markets. The author presents an analysis of the market power implications derived by nations entering into international commodity agreements. Existing and proposed commodity agreements are described as well as the recommendations for stabilizing producer commodity export earnings.

33. Commodities: Importance, Market Power, and Feasible Solution

V. H. Kirpalani
Concordia University

World commodity exports amount to some $225 billion a year, which is equivalent to 25 percent of world exports, 4 percent of world GNP and close to 15 percent of Third World GNP. OPEC exports some $125 billion a year. Other Third World countries export about $60 billion worth of commodities and the First World, notably the United States, Canada and Australia, export the balance $40 billion. The main consumer is the First World, producing two-thirds of world GNP.[1]

Commodity prices tend to fluctuate widely for two major reasons. One, the nature of the supply/demand interaction system with low price elasticities in the short-term and much higher price elasticities in the long-term. The difference in price elasticities over time is basically caused by the considerable time it takes to respond to price changes, but the time lag phenomena is also a feature on the demand side. The tendency to price oscillation is illustrated through the workings of the dynamic cobweb model.

Source: Printed with permission of the author.

393

Suppose for some reason, climatic or disease, crop output falls to Q_1, a level below the equilibrium and assumed full operating capacity at Q_0. Price then rises to D_1. This decides commodity producers rationally or expectationally to increase supply capacity. Substitute products also enter and add to supply. When this incremental capacity is operational, greatly augmented supply appears at S_1, and causes price to fall to D_2. The low price occasions a later capacity run down which leads to S_2 supply availability. This is one variation of the cobweb model. Agricultural food commodities are particularly prone to unplanned supply fluctuations.

The second major reason is that the demand for commodities is a derived demand, dependent on final demand at the end user level for the product made from the commodity. In high consumption free market economies such final demand is a function of per capita incomes, prices, the prices of substitute goods, tastes and promotion. It is thus inherently unstable. Moreover, this instability is magnified at the derived demand level. A recent study shows that if GNP deviates 1 percent from a steady norm, commodity prices alter by over 4 percent.[2] Demand shifts are the usual cause of price changes for industrial raw materials, metals and minerals.

Consumers are interested in assured commodity supplies at stable prices. Many Third World producers, however, in the spirit of OPEC, want to transfer income from the rich countries to themselves through raising commodity prices. Further, there is the especial case of a number of developing countries who rely on their primary commodity sales for a very large proportion of their export revenues, so that unanticipated fluctuations in these revenues can lead to major disruptions of development planning.

The objective of this paper is to make recommendations which would help consumers and producers. In order that the recommendations be viewed constructively it is helpful to sketch the background pertinent to the assessment of producer market power and the various commodity arrangements tried. The paper has four sections.

1. Gives the production, consumption and export picture by important commodity.
2. Analyzes the history of commodity agreements, cartel possibilities and market power.
3. Discusses arrangements that are currently being proposed.
4. Draws conclusions and makes recommendations.

Production/Consumption/Exports

Commodities can be relevantly placed into the three groups of oil, agricultural products and metals/minerals. OPEC members account for over 60 percent of world oil production and 90 percent of exports valued at $115 billion annually. The other 40 percent of oil production mainly occurs in

North America and the North Sea. However, the United States imports some $40 billion a year due to its high consumption and need to conserve domestic reserves. Other large net importers are industrialized Western Europe and Japan to the tune of $35 billion, and the Third World, excluding OPEC, also at about $35 billion.[3]

Agricultural Products and Minerals:

Overall the industrialized countries have a larger share of world trade in non-oil basic commodities than the developing countries. In the grains, citrus and soyabeans the industrialized countries dominate. Also the world's two largest producers of coal, iron ore, copper and phosphates are the United States and the U.S.S.R.

The importance of a wide range of commodities is indicated in the following Exhibits. As can be seen in Exhibit 33-1, Third World countries produce three quarters or more of the total output of bananas, groundnut, palm oil-kernels, coffee, cocoa and tea, jute, sisal and rubber; coconuts and pepper. Moreover, they are the major exporters of these commodities and of rice, raw sugar, cotton and logs.

Further, Exhibit 33-2 shows that a number of Third World countries are heavily dependent for export earnings on one commodity. Noteworthy are the dependence of Panama and Honduras on bananas, Uganda and Columbia on coffee, Ghana on cocoa, Bangladesh on jute, Sri Lanka on tea, Zambia, Chile and Zaire on copper, and Bolivia on tin.

Given the importance of commodities in world trade and their affects on economic development price stabilization emerges as an important objective. Increasingly, however, commodity arrangements are being discussed as a vehicle for compensation finance to maintain commodity producers export earnings, aid giving and a help for economic development. Also, in the long-term potential commodity scarcity looms as a world problem and therefore a global need, in a space ship economy, is to plan global output. The history of commodity arrangements and the possibilities of cartels are worth investigating in context.

Commodity Arrangements, Cartels and Market Power

International commodity arrangements have gone through four phases.[4] The first was from 1918-1929. A number of different cartel type schemes, of multinational producer firms or national agreements operated by producing governments came into operation. These emerged because of the decline in demand from 1914-1918 wartime peaks and the increased instability of prices caused by volatile industrial demand and a shortage of international shipping.

The second phase was from 1929-1939. The Great Depression caused commodity prices to fall. Previous arrangements embodied insufficient

EXHIBIT 33-1
Selected commodities: world production and exports by country group 1974–76 (volumes: global shares in percentages)

		Production			Exports			
		Industrial Countries	Centrally Planned	Developing Countries	Industrial Countries	Centrally Planned	Developing Countries	Exports as % Production
Grains:	Wheat	39.3	42.0	18.7	80.5	14.6	4.9	20
	Maize	65.8	10.0	24.2	68.1	3.7	14.2	12
	Other Coarse	47.0	0.3	52.7	N.A.	N.A.	N.A.	
	Rice	37.9	5.3	56.8	34.5	15.2	50.3	2
Sugar:	Raw	29.3	24.0	46.7	29.3	0.9	80.3	27
	Citrus Fruits	56.5	2.6	40.9	67.7	1.9	32.4	14
	Bananas	2.7	0.7	96.6	0.4	2.7	96.9	N.A.
	Soyabeans	68.3	26.6	5.1	90.3	6.7	3.0	15
	Groundnuts	10.1	13.9	76.0	9.7	4.4	85.9	9
	Palm Oil	—	—	100.0	3.1	—	96.9	49
	Palm Kernel	—	—	100.0	0.1	—	99.9	45
Beverages:	Coffee	—	0.1	99.9	1.9	—	98.1	77
	Cocoa	—	—	100.0	2.1	—	97.9	79
	Tea	7.0	17.9	75.1	6.8	23.9	69.3	38
Fibres:	Cotton	20.9	32.0	47.1	23.2	13.8	63.0	30
	Jute	—	—	100.0	8.0	—	92.0	21
	Sisal	—	—	100.0	8.5	—	91.5	87
Rubber:	Natural	—	—	100.0	—	—	100.0	89
	Coconuts	—	—	100.0	2.4	—	97.6	38
	Pepper	40.0	15.0	45.0	0.3	—	99.7	N.A.
	Tobacco	30.0	30.0	40.0	35.0	12.0	53.0	24
	Plywood	81.4	9.4	9.2	58.0	10.8	31.2	13
Logs:	Hardwood	40.0	21.6	38.4	36.0	0.6	63.4	15
Metals:	Copper	40.0	17.0	43.0	32.0	10.0	58.0	30
	Aluminum	80.0	15.0	5.0	95.0	—	5.0	18
	Zinc	60.0	22.0	18.0	60.0	17.0	23.0	26
	Lead	46.0	28.0	26.0	82.0	—	18.0	24
Tin (Concentrates)		3.0	—	97.0	13.0	—	87.0	26
	Bauxite	28.0	12.0	60.0	29.0	—	71.0	25
	Chromium	26.0	33.0	41.0	30.0	33.0	37.0	50
	Manganese	25.0	30.0	45.0	40.0	25.0	35.0	30

Sources: F.A.O., World Metal Statistics; The Economist; UNCTAD, Document TD/B/C,
1/166, 1974; U.N. Yearbook of International Trade Statistics.

EXHIBIT 33-2
Countries heavily dependent on exports of a commodity

	Country's Exports as % of		
	World Exports		Country's Own Total Export
Rice	U.S.A.	30	Thailand 20
	Thailand	17	
	China	12	
Sugar	Cuba	23	Phillipines 17
			Cuba N.A.
Bananas	Ecuador	18	Panama 55
	Honduras	16	Honduras 45
	Costa Rica	13	Ecuador 31
	Panama	11	
Coffee	Brazil	30	Uganda 59
	Columbia	14	Columbia 53
			Ivory Coast 30
			Angola 27
			Brazil 23
Cocoa	Ghana	29	Ghana 59
	Nigeria	22	Cameroon 26
	Ivory Coast	13	Ivory Coast 19
	Brazil	12	
Jute	Bangladesh	57	Bangladesh 34
	Thailand	30	
Tea	India	27	Sri Lanka 56
	Sri Lanka	26	Kenya 11
			Bangladesh 10
Rubber: Natural	Malaysia	52	Malaysia 30
	Indonesia	20	Sri Lanka 19
			Liberia 18
			Indonesia 12
Copper	Zambia	11	Zambia 93
	Chile	11	Chile 77
	Canada	11	Zaire 69
	Zaire	7	
Tin	Malaysia	49	Bolivia 55
	Thailand	12	Malaysia 19
	Indonesia	9	
Crude Fertilizers:			
(Phosphates)	Morocco	52	Togo 32
	U.S.A.	14	Morocco 23
	Togo	8	Tunisia 17
	Tunisia	6	

Sources: F.A.O., World Metal Statistics, Metal Bulletin Handbook.

monopoly power and ability to restrict supply. New intergovernmental agreements, such as those for tin, rubber and wheat, emphasized quantitative restrictions, which gave producers the possibility of exercising monopoly power. Consumers reacted with some hostility. Yet even before World War II, this monopoly power was being weakened by a broadening in the substitution in use of some commodities and the development of synthetic fibres and plastics.

The third phase ran from 1945–62. Commodity prices rose as consumer demand accelerated after World War II and further rose during the Korean War. But after this war producers wanted interference with the open market as the terms of trade for commodities versus manufacturers deteriorated by over 15 percent from 1954 to the mid 1960s.

The fourth phase is from the mid 1960s. The UNCTAD group of 77, actually made up of 113 developing countries, has put forward the general principles that measures ought to be designed to increase and stabilize commodity export earnings at equitable and renumerative prices and, a naturally acceptable relationship be maintained between the prices of manufactured goods and primary products.

Commodity agreements can be of various types depending on the amount of producer-consumer cooperation, whether the objective is price stabilization or export earnings stabilization, and the extent to which the agreement is a vehicle for aid giving and help for economic development. Cooperation is a spectrum which starts from the zero base of a pure producer cartel. A number of Third World producers are trying the cartel route, imbued with OPEC results. Therefore it is worthwhile examining the fundamental conditions for major success of a producer cartel. These conditions would seem to be the following:

1. The cartel club must have a large share of world exports.
2. Relatively inelastic demand and supply govern the commodity in the short-term and over time.
3. There is fairly low product substitution competition.
4. Cartel members have relatively similar costs of production.
5. The economic interests of cartel members are fairly homogeneous, with reliance on these commodity exports and the ability to sustain losses about equal.
6. Cartel member governments are politically stable and in control of their private sectors.

First and Third World producers differ markedly on conditions 4, 5 and 6 above. This has meant a rather low community of interest between them. Therefore, attempts at cartels have mainly involved only those commodities for which the major producers are Third World countries.

OPEC has been the outstandingly successful Third World cartel. This cartel to a significant extent fulfills the six conditions outlined earlier. OPEC members account for over 60 percent of exports.[5] Demand and supply are relatively inelastic, product substitutability fairly low and costs of production similar in the short-term. Governments are in control of the oil sector and member economic interests are also fairly homogeneous. In the longer term as the demand for oil becomes more elastic at high prices the cartel could well break and prices slide. The reason is that, among OPEC countries, there are some with large populations and low incomes such as Algeria, Ecuador, Indonesia, Iran, Iraq, Nigeria and Venezuela which can spend all the money they earn from oil exports on economic development. On the other hand there are some with small populations and bloated incomes like Libya, Kuwait, Qatar and the United Arab Emirates which earn about 25 percent of OPEC revenues, far more than they can reasonably spend. The former group would want to keep their earnings up by supplying more.

The real answer to whether or when the cartel will break probably lies with Saudi Arabia, a country with a population of only eight million people and one fifth of the Free World's proven reserves. How far, that is, may Saudi Arabia be willing to shoulder the burden of production cuts while the main benefits from high prices go to other producers.

Can a successful Third World producer cartel be formed for other commodities? Is there any other commodity that meets the fundamental conditions outlined earlier.

Agricultural Products

These products as candidates in market power terms for possible Third World cartels fall into four groups ranging from the least likely to the more possible. These are:

1. grains, sugar, citrus fruits, cotton, oilseeds, and products
2. rubber, jute, and sisal
3. tropical beverages and foodstuffs including coffee, cocoa, tea, and bananas
4. timber and pepper

In the case of grains, the industrial countries, mainly the United States and Canada, are large producers and suppliers while the centrally planned economies and the Third World are large consumers. Any attempt to raise grain prices would require the co-operation of not only the United States and Canada but Third World importers.[6] Cartels, therefore, are doubtful.

In the case of sugar the industrial countries produce 40 percent of world sugar, mainly in beet sugar form, while the Third World produces sugar from sugar cane. The bulk of world consumption occurs domestically where sugar is grown and exports constitute only about 30 percent of production.

World trade in sugar is highly integrated. The so-called world market is residual to the complex of special arrangements between various groups of countries which account for half of world exports. The most important arrangements are the United States Sugar Act, the Cuba-U.S.S.R. bilateral agreement and the Commonwealth Sugar Agreement. The tendency to self sufficiency in the beet sugar producing countries creates serious difficulties for Third World cane exporting countries. For instance, the enlarged EEC (European Economic Community) is already in surplus.[7] Given the large number of sugar suppliers, the producers do not possess a harmony of interest and would not be likely to form a cartel type alliance.

A producer's alliance with respect to citrus fruits and cotton seems equally unlikely in the forseeable future. Spain, the United States and the E.C. produce over 50 percent of world citrus fruit output. Any restriction of Third World supplies in these circumstances would probably encourage domestic production in the First World. With regard to cotton, the United States is the leading producer and this itself makes it unlikely that any cartel could form.

For entirely different reasons, the producers of oil-seeds and oils from them, are unlikely to join together to raise earnings. This group of products is varied and it is virtually impossible to isolate the market of any one product because they are to a certain extent substitutable and face competition as well from synthetic substitutues for industrial uses. Rather than trying to increase export earnings by curtailing supplies, Third World countries who are the main producers except for soyabeans where the United States dominates, would be better served in the long run by stabilizing supplies.

The basic feature of the markets for rubber, jute and sisal is that each one of them is faced with intense competition from synthetic substitutues made in the industrial countries. The situation today is that around two thirds of the rubber market has been captured by synthetics; the share of jute is declining rapidly in sacking and carpetbacking which are two of its principal uses; and synthetics have replaced a lot of sisal in the important rope, packing twine, baler and binder twine markets. While the natural materials continue to enjoy some special advantages these attributes alone are not sufficient to ensure their market share position. Any attempt to cartel would provide further stimulus to synthetics.

The tropical beverages group of commodities including coffee, cocoa, tea and bananas are exclusively produced and exported by Third World countries with the exception of tea of which some one fifth is produced by China. It should therefore in principle be possible to cartel. However, because of the highly developed and complex marketing network, which is largely in the hands of intermediaries based in the industrial countries, the producers' alliances have so far proved ineffective. Unlike coffee or cocoa, a substantial amount of tea is used by the Third World. Some 50 percent of tea is consumed and 25 percent imported by Third World countries. Since the 1950s, however, several African countries have become new major producers of coffee and tea. These countries view the market quite differently from the traditional suppliers, and seem to want to expand market share rather than cartel.[8]

Third World commercial production for banana export is controlled by powerful multinationals which organize the planting, harvesting, shipment and distribution of the fruit abroad. Moreover banana supplies are spread all over the world. In view of the above and the heavy dependence on bananas of some poor and small countries it seems very doubtful that the producers either possess or can exploit cartel strength.[9]

The share of the Third World in the production of logs and plywood is relatively small but it accounts for more than 90 percent of world export of hardwood logs and 40 percent of plywood. Tropical Latin America has been a relatively unimportant source of hardwood export. Some 70 percent of timber produced in Tropical Africa is exported mainly to Western Europe. This area is currently facing serious supply problems, partly because the easily accessible resources have been almost fully exploited and partly because of the difficulty in supplying species which are currently in demand. By far the largest and most rapidly growing source is Tropical Asia made up of the Philippines, Malaysia and Indonesia. Most of the exports from this region go to Japan, Korea and Taiwan in the form of logs. The marketing in this region is relatively independent of the other regions so an alliance among the Asian producers is possible.

Pepper is another cartel possibility. World production is concentrated in India, Malaysia and Indonesia which together account for around 80 percent of world exports with Brazil accounting for the bulk of the balance. In a sense, pepper seems to combine all the favourable conditions for a Third World cartel. It is produced by a limited number of countries and faces no direct competition in the importing countries. No producing country is overly dependent on this commodity and expenditure on pepper in household budgets is quite small. Pepper can be stored without danger of deterioration. Further the price of pepper in importing countries represents only about 10 percent of the final retail price of the ground and packaged product.[10]

Metals and Minerals

North America is a leading producer of copper, zinc, lead, iron ore, and natural phosphates thus cartels are unlikely to succeed. For example, CIPEC the Third World copper cartel has failed to keep prices up, as have the iron ore producers association. The demand for cobalt and tin is relatively price elastic in the long-term, in large part because of the ready availability of substitutes. Nickel and tungsten for cobalt, and many end use substitutes for products which require tin.

A cartel exists for bauxite, which has successfully raised the price by over 150 percent since 1974. However, bauxite is a plentiful material. Many countries, including the United States have thousands of years of reserves of aluminum bearing clays and ores. Moreover, the hunt to locate and mine more expensive sources of bauxite, for example, in Brazil and Cameroon, has been intensified. Thus the chances are fairly good that within five years the cartel will collapse. Lastly, chromium and manganese are possible cartel candidates but both would require the active participation of South Africa and the Soviet Union, plus Rhodesia for chromium and a number of countries including China for manganese.[11]

It is apparent that Third World cartels, except for oil, have very little chance for success in any major commodity over the long-term; although bauxite and tin are cases where monopoly strength has been exercised in the short-term. It seems obvious that some form of producer-consumer co-operation seems preferable to cartel attempts. A consideration of these schemes follows.

Proposed Commodity Arrangements

The various schemes being advocated can be placed in the following four categories:

1. Indexing commodity prices to the cost of manufactured imports purchased by the Third World from the First World.
2. Multilateral government commitments to buy and sell given quantities.
3. Buffer stocks.
4. Compensatory finance to maintain/raise producer export earnings.

Indexation

This proposal suffers from economic and equity drawbacks. Indexation freezes relative prices but not absolute ones. In today's increasingly interdependent world, with global exports over 15 percent of global GNP, versus a comparative 10 percent figure in the early 1950s, it reinforces the passage of inflation from one country to another.[12] Third World commodity producers will eventually be worse off because of the economic problems caused by inflation. Moreover, it mixes up aid with trade where the aid may not be a function of need. Nigeria, for instance, would receive a lot based on indexing of its export prices of oil, tin, cocoa, palm oil and timber. While Chad and India who are net commodity importers would suffer.

Multinational Government Buy/Sell Commitments

This proposal is unlikely to be workable. Obstacles would arise in the First World market economics. Most commodity trading and user industries in these markets are in the hands of the private sector. Government buying and selling of non-strategic commodities would interfere with the domestic market and arouse opposition. Purchasing governments would run the danger of being left with large stocks if private industry switched to substitutes.

Buffer Stocks

The argument for buffer stocks are that they are price stabilizing and that this stability is beneficial to consumers and producers. The expressed hope is that buffer stocks are self financing. The manager buys when prices fall to the minimum and sells when they rise to the maximum. If target prices are well judged, the financiers never have to pay anything beyond the initial contribution to stock piling. Historically, however, buffer stocks have never been large enough to control price fluctuations.

Buffer stocks have not been profitable. Can they be? And further are they needed because the open market fails to take into account relevant costs and/or benefits. Almost all commodities today have futures markets. The *raison d'être* of professional speculation is to stabilize price to the extent possible given dynamic exogenous economic factors. If there are no restrictions on speculation that impede this role, then there would seem to be little reason to suppose that a buffer stock manager could improve on the market. Other rationale for a buffer stock are then that futures markets do not induce an optional degree of stability since capital gains tax considerations may limit the effectiveness of professional speculation; some speculators enter the futures markets to profit on currency movements unconnected with the commodity in question; long-term price stability requires that buffer stocks be carried which would support prices at a level that encourages adequate investment in supply capacity.

Against this there is the possibility that inflexibility in buffer stock management policy may lead to actions detrimental to profitability. Further, the overall direct benefits are realized largely by producers. Consumers therefore will inevitably have to bear some of the costs. In today's world where there is a growing substitutability in use of many commodities and synthetics, consumers do not seem to want to be locked in to paying a higher minimum price than necessary. Moreover some research indicates that price stabilization may be harmful to export revenues if shifts in demand were the cause of price instability.[13] Overall it is unclear whether buffer stocks are a useful answer for commodity problems.[14]

UNCTAD has proposed a $10 billion common fund for eighteen commodities to be financed by consumers and producers. The present version of the scheme is a fund of $6 billion, which would amount to between 10–15 percent of the export value for the ten core commodities. The assumptions are that the fund would be the primary source of finance for individual commodity arrangements; should set guidelines on such matters as target prices, size of buffer stocks and other measures of supply management; and is empowered to intervene in commodity markets in exceptional circumstances. UNCTAD estimates that up to $5 billion would be required for buffer financing since some buffer stocks would be repaying the fund when others were borrowing. The remaining $1–$1½ billion could provide long-term loans for commodity programmes calling for diversification and rationalization.[15] Parts of the First and Third Worlds view this as an attempt to build cartel strength and transfer resources to selected Third World nations. Further, it is questionable whether the fund management could efficiently judge price stability levels and handle 10 commodities. Moreover, UNCTAD has not made clear how the fund would respond to the entry of new producers.

Compensatory Finance

Such schemes attempt to stabilize producer export earnings through compensatory finance. They are designed to maintain the import capacity of individual developing countries but without directly affecting the prices of goods. Two schemes of this kind already in existence are the IMF facility and STABEX operated by the EEC.

The IMF facility is particularly aimed at countries whose exports revenues depend heavily on one or very few commodities. A country seeking assistance, in addition to ordinary drawing rights, must demonstrate that export short-falls of a short-term, nature which are largely attributable to circumstances beyond its control are causing balance of payment difficulties. It must also undertake to cooperate with the IMF in finding a solution to these difficulties. The STABEX scheme applies to the 46 Third World countries which have signed the EEC convention. For most of these countries it relates only to their commodity exports to the EEC. Moreover the aid does not have to be repaid. The IMF scheme bases compensatory finance on a short-fall in the total exports, commodity plus other products, of the Third World country, and therefore it is conceptually a macroeconomic aid scheme. Its provisions, unlike STABEX, do not tend to disturb trade patterns by stimulating attempts to divert trade from one market to another in order to manipulate the benefits of the scheme. The drawback of export earnings stabilization is that it does not directly result in microeconomic benefits at the commodity production level.

Conclusions and Recommendation

Except for oil, Third World market power to cartel commodities is extremely limited, especially over the longer run. Free market forces have traditionally been unable to contain price fluctuations. Neither have buffer stocks financed by producers had much success, partly due to their limited size. Of the present proposals, indexation of prices would facilitate the makings of a classic inflationary helix and is thus unacceptable. Government agreements to buy and sell non-strategic commodities would evoke opposition in First World market economies. The UNCTAD Common Fund buffer stock is difficult for many to accept because it could become a privileged safeguard for selected commodity producers and exert monopoly strength against all consumers, many of whom are relatively poor Third World countries. Besides it is questionable whether the Fund could improve on future price markets, and successful management of ten core commodities is doubtful. Thus the recommendation proposes an integrated compensatory finance scheme. But it does not deal with oil, since OPEC is an especial case and seems to be working out its interface with consumers on an orbit of its own.

Recommendation

The recommendation is to build individual commodity agreements on an adapted model of the International Coffee Agreement of 1976 for at least all commodities for which, as shown in Exhibit 33-2, Third World countries are major exporters. These agreements to be within the canopy of a compensatory finance scheme. Thus the scheme may cover eleven or more commodities.

The compensation finance recommendation is for export earnings stabilization in SDRs for each commodity for each producer, at a level in each current operational year based on an average of the past few years. The number of past years to be dependent on the period required for capital investment in supply to yield output. The compensatory finance to come from all consuming countries, except those Third World countries who are net importers of all commodities in the total scheme. The finance to be raised by governments from general revenues, similar to the manner in which First World Official Development Assistance is raised. The finance to be a non-repayable grant and to be channelled through a multilateral organization such as the World Bank, who would monitor that the funds are used by the recipient for improving the particular commodity's supply capability. The specific microeconomic purpose would be to the inefficiencies of unused resources and/or improve supply capacity in production, distribution, inland transport or ports in the producer country concerned. If they are not so used the finance would cease.

The Coffee Agreement is between the major importing countries and forty-three exporting countries. The objective is to reduce price fluctuations and induce producers to build up reserves. The agreement rests on export quotas which will be suspended in times of scarcity.[16] The adaptation to the Agreement proposed for the commodities in the scheme is to permit a cumulating 2 percent of global export each year to be reserved for new producers. Thus in ten years 20 percent of export could come from new sources.

It is thought that such an approach is fruitful. Futures markets would play their role in controlling price fluctuations given knowledge of the commodity agreements. Participating producers in the particular agreements would carry stocks, because of export quotas, and due to the aid from compensatory finance. New producers would be allowed entry in an orderly fashion. The First World would be assured of more adequate supplies and would aid economic development in the Third World in commodities where the comparative advantage for the Third World country is established. Over time the First World should consider adjusting market access, which the World Bank estimates could lead to an increase in Third World agricultural exports of some $4 billion annually by 1980.[17] Also, in line with the New

International Economic Order, the First World could, in a phased manner, encourage Third World producers to value add and export a commodity based intermediate product. It is expected that overall this proposal will increase equity without markedly reducing economic efficiency. The costs would have to be researched but a prior does not seem to be reason to suspect that they would exceed the benefits.

QUESTIONS

1. What is an international commodity agreement? What types are there? How do they affect pricing decisions?
2. What trends have been observed over the years with respect to commodity agreements?
3. What factors govern the success of a producer cartel?
4. Why does the author recommend a compensatory finance arrangement as the most workable commodity agreement?

NOTES

1. United Nations, *Yearbook of National Accounts Statistics,* 1974, Vol. II (New York: U.N. 1975) and International Monetary Fund, *International Financial Statistics* (various months 1977).

2. Report on research by the Commodity Research Unit "The Raw World" *The Economist* (October 23, 1976) p. 25.

3. United Nations, *Monthly Bulletin of Statistics,* (various months 1977).

4. Christopher Rogers, International Commodity Agreements, *Lloyds Bank Review,* April 1973, pp. 33-45.

5. "The Oil Story" *The Economist,* (April 26, 1975) pp. 36-37.

6. Food and Agriculture Organization: *The State of Food and Agriculture* (Rome: FAO 1973).

7. Ian Smith "Sugar Markets in Disarray": *Journal of World Trade Law,* (January-February 1975) pp. 41-62.

8. Food and Agriculture Organization, *Agricultural Commodity Projection 1970-80,* (Rome: FAO 1971).

9. Food and Agriculture Organization, *The World Banana Economy,* Commodity Bulletin Series 50 Part I (Rome: FAO 1971).

10. Irfan ul Haque "Producers Alliances Among Developing Countries *"Journal of World Trade Law,* (September-October 1973).

11. Sanford Rose, "Third World Commodity Power Is a Costly Illusion", *Fortune* (November 1976) pp. 147-150.

12. United Nations, *Yearbook of International Trade Statistics,* (New York: U.N. various years).

13. Ezriel M. Brook and Enzo R. Grilli, "Commodity Price Stabilization and the Developing World", *Finance and Development,* Vol. 14, No. 1, (March 1977).

14. C. L. Gilbert, "Does it Pay to Stabilize Commodities?", *The Banker* (October 1976) pp. 1427–1429, and P. T. Bauer and H. Myint, "The Hidden Costs of Commodity Price Stabilization", *The Banker*, (October 1976), pp. 1423–1426.

15. "Big Brother Buffer Stock", *The Economist,* (December 4, 1976) pp. 116–118.

16. *Consumer Reports,* (March 1977), p. 135.

17. UNCTAD, *Report of the Committee on Commodities,* TD/B/432, TD/B/C.1/140, Supplement No. 2 (New York: U.N. 1973).

PLANNING AND IMPLEMENTING MARKETING PROGRAMS

The essence of international marketing management is the development of appropriate objectives, strategies, and plans that culminate in the successful realization of foreign market opportunities. The future environment of the world marketplace will be marked by accelerating change requiring new managerial approaches. To be sensitive to the demands of tomorrow's decision, environment requires a familiarity with the managerial systems presented in operation. The readings in this section have been chosen to provide such a familiarity. In the first article, by Yoram Wind, Susan P. Douglas, and Howard V. Perlmutter, the different orientations towards overseas markets are described and a conceptual framework to analyze and formulate international marketing strategies specified. The next article, by Jagdish N. Sheth, takes an in-depth look at the multinational marketing planning process and suggests how improvements over current practices can be made by devising a more formalized process. William K. Brandt and James M. Hulbert, in the section's third article, investigate the relationship between marketing strategy and organizational structure in United States, European, and Japanese multinational firms. The section concludes with an illustration of the rationale used and the problems experienced by the public telecommunications industry in launching strategies in international market environments.

The formulation of international marketing strategies is requiring more sophisticated management approaches due to the increasing importance of international business operations. The authors examine the relevance of the E.P.R.G. framework (ethnocentrism, polycentrism, regiocentrism, geocentrism) as a guideline for international marketing strategies.

34. Guidelines for Developing International Marketing Strategies

Yoram Wind
University of Pennsylvania

Susan P. Douglas
Ecole des Hautes Etudes Commerciales

Howard V. Perlmutter
University of Pennsylvania

One of the most striking trends in business has been the growing internationalization of business operations.[1] An increasing number of companies are operating on a global or regional rather than a national scale. Thus, new parameters are added to management decisions calling for a rethinking of organizational strategies and planning procedures. Marketing is no exception to this rule. International marketing managers are asking themselves how they should cope with the new scope of operations, and whether they can apply domestic strategies to international markets.

Some guidelines to these and other issues may be provided by the modified E.P.R.G. schema.[2] This framework identifies four types of attitudes or orientations toward internationalization that are associated with successive stages in the evolution of international operations—ethnocentrism (home country orientation), polycentrism (host country orientation), regiocentricism (a regional orientation), and geocentrism (a world orientation). These

Source: Yoram Wind, Susan P. Douglas, and Howard V. Perlmutter, "Guidelines for Developing International Marketing Strategies." Reprinted with permission from the *Journal of Marketing* April 1973, pp. 14–23, published by the American Marketing Association.

attitudes are assumed to reflect the goals and philosophies of the company with respect to international operations and planning procedures with regard to international operations.

In the ethnocentric phase, top management views domestic techniques and personnel as superior to foreign and as the most effective in overseas markets. As the company begins to recognize the importance of inherent differences in overseas markets, a *polycentric* attitude emerges. The prevalent philosophy in this stage is that local personnel and techniques are best suited to deal with local market conditions. This frequently gives rise to problems of coordination and control, resulting in the adoption of a regiocentric position. *Regiocentrism* recognizes regional commonalities and leads to the design of regional strategies. At the extreme, this orientation may lead to *geocentrism* which is characterized by the attitude of "the best man for the job" irrespective of national origin.

The implications of this schema for the functional areas of production, finance, and manpower have already been examined.[3] This article explores the use of the E.P.R.G. framework as a guideline for planning and developing international marketing strategies. In particular, it is concerned with (1) examining the implications of each orientation in terms of marketing strategies, and (2) assessing the conditions under which international marketers are likely to adopt these orientations and associated strategies.

Two exploratory studies were undertaken to investigate these issues. The first analyzed the perceptions of international executives in a large multinational firm toward alternative marketing strategies hypothesized to be associated with different international orientations. The second, based on interviews with senior marketing executives in ten United States companies, examined their evaluations of the appropriateness of the different international orientations and implied strategies to specific management objectives and individual company situations. While both of these studies were exploratory in character and based on very small sample sizes, they nonetheless provide some general indications concerning the relevancy of the E.P.R.G. framework in providing guidelines for marketing strategies.

The E.P.R.G. Framework and Marketing Decisions

A key assumption underlying the E.P.R.G. framework is that the degree of internationalization to which management is committed (or willing to move toward) affects the specific international strategies and decision rules of the firm. Based on this assumption and the nature of the E.P.R.G. orientations, hypothetical profiles of typical marketing strategies associated with each orientation may be inferred.

Ethnocentric Orientation

In the *ethnocentric company,* overseas operations are viewed as secondary to domestic operations and primarily as a means to dispose of "surplus" domestic production. Plans for overseas markets are developed in the home office, utilizing policies and procedures identical to those employed in the domestic market. Overseas marketing is most commonly administered by an export department or international division, and the marketing personnel is composed primarily of home country nationals.

No systematic research is conducted overseas, and no major modifications are made to products sold in overseas markets. Prices are calculated on the same basis as in the home market, with the addition of overseas distribution costs. Promotion and distribution strategies are similar, to the extent possible, to that employed in the home country. The sales force is trained and hired in the home country. It operates from a home country base, and there is likely to be strong reliance on export agents.

Polycentric Orientation

In the *polycentric stage,* subsidiaries are established in overseas markets. Each subsidiary operates independently of the others and establishes its own marketing objectives and plans. Marketing activities are organized on a country-by-country basis, and marketing research is conducted independently in each country. Separate product lines are developed in each country, and home country products are modified to meet local needs. Each subsidiary establishes its own pricing and promotion policy. The sales force in each country is composed of local nationals, and the channels of distribution are those traditionally used in each country.

Regiocentric and Geocentric Orientations

In the *regiocentric and geocentric* phases the company views the region or the entire world as a potential market, ignoring national boundaries. The firm develops policies and organizes activities on a regional or worldwide basis. Marketing personnel include people from the region or from any country of the world. Standardized product lines for regional or worldwide markets are developed, and pricing is established on a similar basis. Promotional policy is developed regionally or worldwide to project a uniform image of the company and its products. Regional or global channels of distribution are also developed.

Empirical Support for E.P.R.G.

An exploration study was recently conducted to provide some initial insight into the validity of this framework.[4] The perceptions and preferences of international executives toward the current and future appropriateness of each of these alternative orientations and associated strategies were assessed. The sample consisted of forty key international executives of one large United States firm whose product line is composed of frequently purchased household items.

Each respondent was presented with a set of four alternative strategies (one for each orientation) for each of fifteen marketing decision areas. For example, for the brand name decision (orientation in parenthesis), the set was as follows:

> Branding policy in overseas companies stresses the parent country as a unifying feature but not necessarily the origin of the parent country (ethnocentric).

> Each local company brands products on an independent basis and consistent with local country criteria (polycentric).

> Overseas companies brand products uniformly within a region (regiocentric).

> A worldwide branding policy exists only for those brands which are acceptable worldwide (geocentric).

Respondents were then asked to select the statement that best described (1) the firm's current international marketing policy, and (2) the most appropriate future strategy for the firm (i.e., the "ideal" strategy). The frequency distribution of responses for the current and desired situation are shown in Exhibits 34-1 and 34-2. These tables suggest that the polycentric orientation is the dominant current approach across all fifteen marketing decisions. Use of the polycentric approach is particularly pronounced in the case of price, customer service, market research, and channels of distribution, and least marked in the case of brand name and product quality. In both these decision areas ethnocentric approaches were used by one-fifth and egocentric approaches by one-third of the sample. When considering the *desired* approach, however, a substantial shift in preference occurs from the polycentric approach to a regiocentric and geocentric approach. For seven out of the fifteen decision areas, geocentrism is viewed as the ideal by the majority.

The executives' responses were then subjected to a multidimensional scaling analysis, using the TORSCA and PREFMAP programs to examine further the interrelationship between the various marketing decisions and their associated international orientations.

The results of this analysis suggest that (1) each orientation does appear to be perceived as a distinct orientation: on both maps each orientation—vector—is clearly separated from the others; (2) as in the simple frequency analysis, considerable differences seem to exist between the present and desired approach for this company; and (3) the type of orientation considered appropriate for both the current and desired operations of the firm differs depending on the specific decision area.

These findings and the specific position of each decision relative to the four orientations should be viewed, however, only as tentative and illustrative. The pilot study suffered from several severe limitations including a small sample size, incomplete data, and possible bias toward geocentrism (which stems from its intuitively greater appeal). In addition, no cross validation was

EXHIBIT 34–1

Frequency of selecting different international orientations as best descriptors of the firms current international marketing activities. (row percentage)

Decision Areas	Ethnocentric	Polycentric	Regiocentric	Geocentric
Market Measurement & Forecasting	5	72	21	2
Market Segmentation	24	53	19	5
Market Research	7	78	10	5
Product Development	9	58	14	19
Product Design	21	61	4	13
Product Quality	16	48	5	31
Customer Service	12	81	1	6
Product Mix	19	68	9	4
Brand Name	22	43	4	31
Price	4	86	6	3
Sales Promotion	13	72	1	14
Advertising	10	67	0	22
Channels of Distribution	6	77	2	15
Sales Administration	13	63	11	14
Marketing Control	10	61	24	1
Cumulative Profile	13	66	9	12

undertaken. Nonetheless, the study does provide some initial support to the hypotheses: (1) The E.P.R.G. framework is *relevant* for describing both current and desired international marketing decisions; (2) distinct international orientations (E.P.R.G.) are presently employed in international marketing operations; and (3) different international orientations are appropriate for functionally different marketing decisions.

E.P.R.G. Orientations and Organizational Characteristics

Once the relevance of the E.P.R.G. framework is accepted as a guideline for developing international marketing strategies, it should be determined (1) which orientation should be adopted, and (2) under what circumstances should each orientation be employed.

A second exploratory study was undertaken to examine the conditions under which different E.P.R.G. marketing strategies are appropriate. The study was based on unstructured in-depth interviews with senior international marketing executives from ten United States corporations. The importance of their overseas operations varied from over two thirds of the company's sales to only a small volume of export business.

EXHIBIT 34–2
Frequency of selecting different international orientations as best descriptors of the desired international marketing strategy (row percentage)

Decision Areas	Ethnocentric	Polycentric	Regiocentric	Geocentric
Market Measurement & Forecasting	2	69	16	13
Market Segmentation	12	38	18	33
Market Research	1	65	16	18
Product Development	3	45	14	38
Product Design	5	40	10	45
Product Quality	6	35	9	51
Customer Service	4	60	10	26
Product Mix	1	57	18	24
Brand Name	7	36	13	43
Price	0	67	12	21
Sales Promotion	5	45	7	43
Advertising	8	43	5	45
Channels of Distribution	1	39	19	41
Sales Administration	6	31	15	49
Marketing Control	6	30	25	36
Cumulative Profile	4	47	14	35

Respondents were asked to describe their company's current strategies, the rationale underlying these strategies, their planned strategies, and their opinions concerning alternative E.P.R.G. strategies. The results of these interviews were content analyzed and categorized under the various E.P.R.G. positions.

Ethnocentric Position

The results of these interviews suggest that the ethnocentric position appears most appropriate when the absolute or relative volume of overseas sales is insignificant. In these situations product modifications are generally viewed as uneconomic. As one executive states, "We simply can't afford to produce different products for foreign buyers," that is, the cost of conducting extensive overseas research or of tailoring marketing policies to specific international customer requirements may not be justified by the low anticipated revenue. Hence, in these circumstances it may be most appropriate to export to countries with similar characteristics to those of the home country.

A similar approach was taken by an executive of a large consumer goods company concerning the development of marketing strategies for the introduction of an established product into new markets. He pointed out that in some cases the size of the potential market was so small that it was not worth the research effort or time to determine the most effective strategy. Similarly, separate advertising appeals and messages were only developed for an individual market if sales in that market were sufficiently large to support the additional cost involved. Otherwise appeals and themes developed in other countries were used. It was presumed that if these had been successful in another market, there was a strong possibility that they might also be effective in the new market.

The major advantage of the ethnocentric approach is that it entails minimal risk and commitment to overseas markets. No international investment is required, and no additional selling costs are incurred with the possible exception of higher distribution costs. On the other hand, lack of research concerning overseas markets and insufficient attention to their specific needs suggests the possibility of lost opportunities for the firm.

The ethnocentric position may be appropriate for a small company just entering international operations or for companies with minimal international commitment. On the other hand, it may not be the most desirable approach for companies interested in expanding their international operations. Executives in several of the large companies interviewed indicated that their company initially had an ethnocentric orientation toward international operations. However, the need to adapt to differences in national markets in order to expand sales generally led to the establishment of separate marketing organizations in each country or region. In many cases, the ethnocentric position appears to result in lack of attention to the needs and interests of international customers, i.e., a minimal degree of marketing orientation. Only in a few instances, notably in small companies, is an ethnocentric attitude associated with systematic selection of target customers with similar needs and interests to those of domestic customers.

Polycentric Orientation

Consistent with the findings of the first pilot study, most executives interviewed tended to regard the polycentric position as currently the most desirable one. Market conditions in various countries were thought to differ significantly, and adaptation to these differences was considered to be critical in the development of marketing strategies. This was thought to be most effectively accomplished through autonomous marketing organizations in each country developing and administering the country's marketing strategies.

Several executives felt that local nationals had a better understanding and awareness of national market conditions than home office personnel. One head office executive said, "I don't presume to tell the Germans how to sell to the German." Another executive considered that at the current stage in the company's evolution, knowledge of the country and local market conditions was critical. This generally entailed national marketing organizations run by nationals of the country. Another executive suggested that the polycentric organization was the most effective means of motivating management. If the marketing manager in each country is responsible for policy decisions and for profits in his area, he was viewed as most likely to be motivated to promote company interests and to develop market potential.

Several problems regarding coordination and control of marketing activities were felt to result from polycentrism. First, the autonomy of national marketing organizations tends to result in a failure to coordinate marketing policies throughout the world. For example, considerable duplication often occurred with regard to the development of advertising appeals. Furthermore, it can also lead to competition between two national marketing organizations for sales in a third country. In one case, ideas developed by one national marketing organization had been adopted by a competitor and used against a subsidiary in another country.

Several executives felt that some of the problems associated with polycentrism might be reduced by centralizing and coordinating strategy development in the home office. For example, major advertising strategy themes could be developed in the head office and circulated to subsidiaries. Managers in subsidiaries were often convinced, however, that a significant difference existed between their customer interests and needs and customers in other countries. Thus, they tended to reject standardized strategy as unsuited to their particular country. Similarly, unique legal restrictions and barriers, differences in national distribution systems, and other environmental conditions in their country or area led managers to emphasize these idiosyncratic characteristics and to develop unique marketing policies and strategies. This may be an appropriate approach if in fact differences between countries are greater than within countries. The growth of cross-cultural communication and emergence of similar subcultural groupings across countries (e.g., the teenager's subculture) suggest, however, that the polycentric orientation may not be the most desirable approach in the future.

Regiocentric and Geocentric Orientations

Some significant advantages were thought to be inherent in the regiocentric and geocentric positions. Since these orientations imply the identification of regional or global market segments crossing national boundaries as well as the development of standard policies throughout a given segment, they may provide improved coordination and control. Geocentrism was viewed as entailing high costs in collecting information and administering policies on a worldwide basis. In this respect, the regiocentric appeal was generally viewed as more economical and manageable. In both cases, however, national environment constraints may restrict multinational operations and make the approach infeasible. For example, national differences in laws and currencies may severely hinder any practical implementation of this "world market" perspective.

The impact of these national environmental differences is considered in most cases to be more critical with respect to marketing activities than for production and finance activities.[6] Thus the geocentric position may be more advantageous for production and research development than for marketing. In fact, several executives suggested that geocentrism was infeasible due to the earlier mentioned attitudes of the local subsidiaries. Since some subsidairies were convinced that different marketing policies were required for each country, movement toward global or even a regional policy development was virtually impossible.

Another executive suggested that the problem of implementing global and regional strategies was primarily one of information, timing, and relative market size. Once sufficient information and understanding of national market conditions was obtained, target segments could be identified on a regional or worldwide basis cutting across national boundaries. Then a regional or even global marketing strategies could be developed and aimed at selected target segments.

In brief, the desirability of the particular international orientation—E, P, R, or G—seems to depend on several factors: the size of the firm, experience in a given market, the size of the potential market, and the type of product and its cultural dependency.

Size of Firm For a small firm, the most desirable approach is likely to be that associated with ethnocentrism—focusing on overseas customers who have needs and interests similar to domestic customers. Larger firms, on the other hand, are more likely to have adequate resources to investigate overseas markets and to find it economical to adopt a poly, regio, or geocentric approach.

Experience in Overseas Markets For firms just entering overseas markets, an ethnocentric approach entails minimum risk, though further development or involvement in international markets will require movement to the polycentric or geocentric position. Similarly, adoption of geocentric strategies requires considerable knowledge and experience in various different national markets.

The Size and Degree of Heterogeneity of the Potential Market Where the potential market is small relative to the domestic market, the design of separate strategies may be uneconomical. As overseas sales grow, segmentation on a country-by-country basis becomes feasible. As sales of national segments increase, further segmentation within each country may take place, and policies aimed at similar segments within different countries may be coordinated on a regional or worldwide basis.

The Nature of the Product Products embedded in the life style or cultural patterns of consumers may be less susceptible to the development of global policies. For example, personal grooming products and food may have to be modified to suit differences in taste. Although the basic appeal is to the same needs, a different presentation of these appeals may be required. For industrial products, on the other hand, there may be no difference in customer interests or response.

The most appropriate E.P.R.G. position will, therefore, depend on the individual company, its objectives, and the specific market situation. While some executives feel that the polycentric type of organization is currently the most appropriate, the problems associated with this type of organization are being recognized. In some cases this results in interest in moving toward regiocentrism or geocentrism in regard to certain types of marketing decisions. In general, however, national and cultural differences are considered to be too great to permit substantial movement toward these positions at least in the near future.

Any international orientation may thus be selected and used to provide guidelines for developing marketing strategies, depending on the organization's desired degree of international involvement.

The E.P.R.G. Framework and Marketing Orientation

Whereas the E.P.R.G. framework suggests appropriate strategies relative to the desired degree of international involvement, it does not take into consideration how these strategies are developed. Assuming that the marketing concept is equally relevant for domestic and international operations, a company should be concerned not only with the degree of internationalization, but also the degree of marketing orientation. In other words, the analysis of consumer interests and the interests and objectives of channel members should provide the basis for developing international marketing policies.

The relationship between the degree of international orientation and marketing orientation were examined based on the data from the second pilot study. This analysis suggests that with the possible exception of ethnocentrism, the extent to which a marketing-oriented approach is adopted does not depend on the level of international involvement, i.e., a polycentric, regiocentric, or geocentric firm can employ a high or low degree of marketing orientation. Furthermore, the degree of marketing sophistication of a domestic firm does not imply that its international marketing operations (whether ethnocentric, polycentric, regiocentric, or geocentric) will also be highly sophisticated.

Adoption of an ethnocentric approach generally implies that customer behavior and interests in overseas markets are not investigated. Consequently, this orientation is generally associated with a low degree of marketing orientation. Some exceptions may occur, however. An example is the small firm which deliberately focuses its efforts on similar customers in domestic and overseas markets. Apart from such cases, given the heterogeneity of demand in overseas markets, any investigation of overseas markets seems likely to result in a movement away from this position.

Whereas polycentrism appears compatible with a high degree of marketing orientation, the extent to which marketing strategies are based on customer interests and characteristics may depend on the individual subsidiary and its marketing sophistication. For example, one subsidiary may have a high degree of marketing orientation whereas another's marketing orientation may be minimal. Similarly, a country-by-country segmentation, which is typical of polycentric companies, may be the wrong strategy if no significant differences exist between customers in different countries, or if the behavior of customers within a country is highly heterogeneous.

The relative lack of information available regarding international customer characteristics and their responses to marketing variables suggests that at least currently the geocentric position may imply a low degree of marketing orientation. Emphasis on the production and distribution savings association with a standardized marketing strategy may result in a tendency to ignore differences among world customers. This may, however, depend on the particular product, the degree of heterogeneity among world customers, and level of market segmentation. Where similar segments with similar interests and needs can be identified in different countries such as, for example, data processing requirements of banks, a geocentric approach may be coupled with a high rather than a low degree of market orientation.

Thus consideration of both the level of international orientation and the degree of marketing orientation is required to provide useful guidelines for the design of a firm's international marketing strategies. The level of international orientation determines the firm's desired level of involvement in international operations and the appropriate unit of analysis for developing marketing policies, i.e., by region, country, or world. The degree of marketing orientation, on the other hand, determines the specific analytic approach to be used. Regardless of the level of international involvement, a company's international operations should always reflect a high degree of marketing orientation. This implies that the company follows a rigorous marketing approach of examining its markets—individual markets in the polycentric stage, regional markets in the regiocentric stage, and world markets in the geocentric stage—and identifying relevant target segments. Product, price promotion, and distribution strategies are then designed to meet the needs and wants of these target segments.

Once the firm has determined its desired degree of involvement in international operations, it should then move toward a high degree of marketing orientation within the boundaries of the given international orientation. This idea is summarized in Exhibit 34-3. In some cases, a careful analysis of the market may precede the selection of the desired level of international involvement.

A company's position on two key dimensions of marketing and international orientation cannot be determined by observing its actions. Observing a common advertising strategy in several countries does not reveal, for example, whether the company is (1) an ethnocentric company implementing the same campaign it is using in the home country; (2) a polycentric company which decided after considerable study to use the same advertisement in each country; or a (3) regiocentric or geocentric company following a unified regionwide or worldwide advertising strategy.

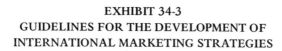

EXHIBIT 34-3
GUIDELINES FOR THE DEVELOPMENT OF
INTERNATIONAL MARKETING STRATEGIES

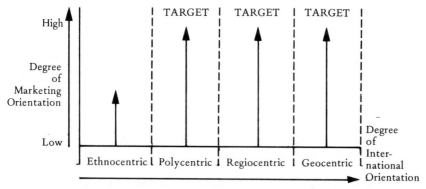

One may, therefore, use as indicators for the degree of international marketing sophistication the extent and nature of marketing research activities, the inputs used and process followed in making the marketing decisions, and the nature of the marketing organization (structure, communications network, etc.).

Conclusions

Despite the limitations of the two exploratory studies reported here, the findings provide some initial empirical insights into the implications of the E.P.R.G. framework for international marketing strategies and its usefulness as a guideline for international marketing decisions.

First, the degree of international orientation alone does not appear to provide sufficient guidelines for developing international marketing policies. Assuming that a firm also strives to achieve a high degree of marketing sophistication, the appropriate approach to developing marketing strategies must also be considered.

Second, there appears to be no single superior or dominant international orientation. Despite the widespread popularity and intuitive appeal of geocentrism, its desirability and feasibility as a guideline for marketing operations appear questionable at least in the current international environment. Lack of adequate and comparable information on customer characteristics and response patterns within countries suggests that it may imply a somewhat low degree of marketing orientation. Polycentrism or regiocentrism with improved regional coordination of national marketing strategies at regional and corporate levels may thus provide a more appropriate approach. Ethnocentrism is appropriate in a limited number of situations, but may imply a low degree of marketing sophistication.

In general, the advantages and disadvantages of a particular orientation vary considerably with the individual company's financial situation, product line, and size of potential overseas markets. These affect the costs and bene-fits associated with each position and thus its desirability to the company. Each company must, therefore, evaluate independently the desirability of each position and select the most appropriate degree of international orienta-tion in light of its own market situation and objectives.

Furthermore, the appropriateness of a given orientation tends to vary according to the specific marketing decision area. For example, while regio-centrism or geocentrism may provide an appropriate organizational base for distribution, logistics, and product policy, high costs may be entailed in adopting such an approach for customer service or promotional activities.

However, no definitive conclusions may be drawn due to the exploratory character of the studies. Further study of the impact of different environ-mental and intracompany factors on the costs and benefits of the various international positions and the implications of different international orienta-tions is needed. Hopefully such research will shed better light on the inter-national marketing operations of the multinational firms of the seventies.

QUESTIONS

1. Differentiate between an ethnocentric, polycentric, regiocentric and geocentric orientations to international marketing.
2. What conditions govern the adoption of each E.P.R.G. orientation? What are advantages and disadvantages of each orientation?
3. How can the E.P.R.G. framework be used in developing marketing strategy?

NOTES

1. See, for example, David S. Leighton, "The Internalization of American Business—The Third Industrial Revolution," *JOURNAL OF MARKETING,* Vol. 34 (July, 1970), pp. 3–6.
2. Howard V. Perlmutter, "The Tortuous Evolution of the Multinational Corporation," *Columbia Journal of World Business,* Vol. IV, (January-February, 1969) pp. 9–18.
3. Howard V. Perlmutter, *Functional Studies Using the E.P.R.G. Categorization: Types of Headquarters Orientation Towards Subsidiaries in an International Enter-prise,* Technical Memo B.R. 3:2, Division for Research and Development of World-wide Institutions, Wharton School, University of Pennsylvania; and David Heenan, "The E.P.R.G. Approach to the Manpower Development Function," Working Paper 1972, Wharton School, University of Pennsylvania, Philadelphia.
4. The study was designed by Howard Perlmutter and the data collected by David Heenan.
5. The respondents aggregated data which resulted in a 15 x 4 matrix was converted to a 15 x 15 decision similarity matrix. This matrix served as the input to the

TORSCA multidimensional scaling program. The output of this phase was then submitted together with the aggregated international orientation vectors (15x4 for the actual and 15x4 for the desired data) to the Carroll-Chang PREFMAP program. These and other multidimensional scaling procedures are discussed in Paul E. Green and Frank J. Carmone, *Multidimensional Scaling and Related Techniques in Marketing Analysis,* (Boston: Allyn & Bacon, 1970).

6. A similar point of view is often taken by academicians. See, for example, Millard H. Pryor, "Planning in a World-Wide Business," *Harvard Business Review,* Vol. 43 (January-February, 1965); and Robert D. Buzzell, "Can You Standardize Multinational Marketing?" *Harvard Business Review,* Vol. 46 (November-December, 1968).

Although the financial rewards from international marketing ventures are substantial so are the associated risks. The author offers a multinational long-range planning framework that can be used by marketing strategists to better control these risks. Current planning practice of multinational corporations are reviewed in the process of describing the model components.

35. A Conceptual Model of Long-Range Multinational Marketing Planning

Jagdish N. Sheth
University of Illinois

In the last two decades, we have witnessed an enormous expansion of multinational business among many corporations headquartered in the United States. By 1969, the United States Corporations were participating in more than 30 percent of total world trade, were importing products valued in excess of $40 billion dollars and exporting products valued in excess of $26 billion dollars. Correspondingly, the direct foreign investment shot up from less than $8 billion dollars by 1950 to more than $70 billion dollars by 1970. Finally, most of the top United States Corporations, according to the Fortune Magazine Survey, today depend on foreign markets for their sales and profits.

Is this growth in multinational business likely to continue for the United States Corporations? A number of factors suggest that the future growth of United States Corporations in terms of multinational business will be less than spectacular hereafter. First, a large part of private foreign investment was related to the economic aid programs during the reconstruction days following World War II. The virtual monopoly experienced by the United

Source: Reprinted by permission from *Management International Review*, No. 4–5, 1972.

States Corporations during that time period is rapidly vanishing as many advanced economies are rebuilt and as the spirit of nationalism begins to pervade increasingly among newer nations. Second, many other foreign countries are participating in multinational business notably West Germany and Japan. The character of their industries is also beginning to take the multinational shape so that the technological gap today is either nonexistent or very rapidly closing in most industries. Third, markets for products in both advanced and less developed countries are rapidly becoming mature with sufficient number of entries from local indigenous companies. Both the political and economic considerations encourage these companies to survive and grow sometimes at the expense of foreign corporations. Finally, and most importantly, the United States Corporations have sadly neglected the marketing orientation in their multinational business activities. During the period of spectacular growth, their attention has been diverted mostly to the transfer of technology to other countries and to the estimation of risks in commiting financial and managerial resources to the new opportunities. Without the temporary competitive advantages of monopoly protections and technological gap, this neglect of marketing orientation is clearly the most vulnerable aspect in the likely decline of United States postion in multinational business.

At the same time, if history can be of any guide, it is equally inevitable that the United States multinational corporations will become more marketing-oriented. After all, this has been the experience in the domestic market for most companies in the early fifties. Unfortunately, the luxury of historical evolution of marketing orientation in multinational business is likely to entail some rude awakening for many United States Corporations. I think there are several compelling reasons which dictate that immediate attention should be paid in incorporating modern marketing thought in multinational operations. First of all, profits from foreign markets have, to a large extent, disguised the enormous failures in the domestic markets prior to the marketing orientation. There is no comparable "buffer" activity that will bear the burden of losses in multinational business due to lack of comparable marketing orientation. Second, private foreign investments are, by definition, more complex because financial and legal complexities are widely different in foreign countries and subject to rapid change. This implies that without the support of market place and its loyalty, it is difficult to survive. Fourth, the type of lobbying support prevalent within the United States to thwart governmental actions is generally not available in most foreign countries. The only support that one can effectively rely upon is to build market loyalties among customers by proper marketing orientation. Finally, the ultimate opportunity lies in the vast populations outside the United States. A planned modern marketing orientation is likely to go a long way to effectively take part in this opportunity.

This paper provides a conceptual framework for planning multinational marketing. The framework is useful for large-scale corporations doing business in several countries, and it is primarly a long-range planning model. The various activities and flows within the rectangular box constitute various aspects of modern multinational marketing. The small boxes outside the rectangle are the environmental aspects, which constantly influence the marketing process. The solid lines represent direct flow of activities within the marketing process whereas the broken lines represent continuous feedback and interchange between various marketing activities. The environmental influences are depicted with crossed lines. The rest of this paper describes the conceptual model for developing multinational marketing planning.

In my view, multinational marketing should begin first with the assessment of buyer needs and expectations on a world-wide basis. It should not, therefore, begin after a product concept is developed or after the pro-

EXHIBIT 35-1
A CONCEPTUAL MODEL OF LONG-RANGE
MULTINATIONAL MARKETING PLANNING
MODELE CONCEPTUAL DE PLANNING DU MARKETING
DANS LES SOCIETES MULTINATIONALES
EIN BEZUGSMODEL DER LANGFRISTIGEN MARKETING-
PLANUNG DER MULTINATIONALEN UNTERNEHMUNG

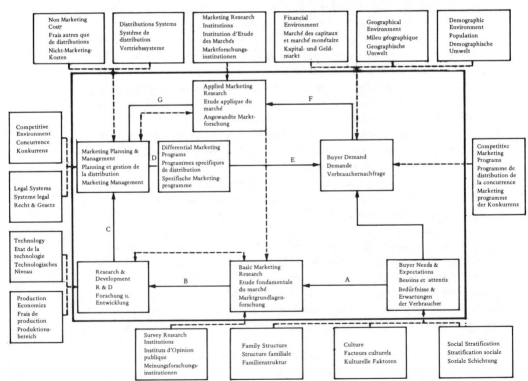

duction facilities are erected. Implicit in this statement, I am pointing out several limitations in the current practice of multinational operations.

First, there is no systematic and continuous assessment of buyer needs and expectations in the current practice of most corporations. Most of the marketing research is post-facto; to find out whether a new concept or product developed by R and D will be acceptable to the customers. Even if there is any effort to assess buyer needs before the concept is developed, such an effort is typically ad hoc. I am suggesting a continuous research effort to systematically monitor present and changing needs of the market place.

Second, the present practice is to do marketing research on country-by-country basis. In addition, most multinational marketing decisions are centered around the question as to whether the company should extend its marketing program to newer countries or adjust it to suit the local conditions. While such a practice was probably quite appropriate during the colonial days and may be useful even today for exporting or trading companies, it tends to be myopic in the long-run. In fact, it is not difficult to trace a number of failures in multinational activities directly to this practice.

A world-wide systematic and continuous assessment of buyer needs and expectation is likely to point out that (a) potential markets are mostly in the metropolitan areas especially in the less developed countries, (b) clustering metropolitan areas both within and between countries is more meaningful from marketing viewpoint, and (c) probably we shall find greater similarity between metropolitan areas across countries than within countries.

Third, the assessment of customer needs and expectations should be based on data collected at the micro level, namely the household or the business unit. The present practice is to assess potential demand from secondary data which are aggregate and typically historical. While these data are useful to some extent, experience has shown that they can easily mislead the conclusions particularly because of their aggregative nature.

Finally, contrary to the current marketing practice, the emphasis in the conceptual model is on the customer needs and not on the product. It is my belief that this focus on customer needs is more enduring a concept and tends to avoid the myopic tendency which a company is likely to fall into as its products become mature in their life cycle.

The world-wide assessment of buyer needs and expectations should be done by establishing a longitudinal panel in selected geographical areas. The selection of specific geographical areas should be based on clustering of all the geographical areas of the world in terms of their similarity on the environmental factors such as political stability, market opportunity, economic development, cultural unity and legal barriers in doing business with the area. The geographical areas can be countries or preferably metropolitan areas.

The model shows that buyer needs and expectations are likely to be determined by culture, social stratification and family structure. The differences in buyer needs and expectations are, therefore, likely to be found between geographical areas with varying dimensions on these three factors. Similarly, over a period of time, these factors are likely to change perhaps rapidly in many countries, bringing about corresponding changes in buyer needs and expectations. The reader is referred to Howard and Sheth (1969)[1] for a discussion of ways in which these factors determine buyer expectations.

We must distinguish between basic marketing research and applied marketing research. Just as there was no basic research and development two decades ago in most companies, there is today no basic marketing research activity. In the long-range planning, basic marketing research is essential. My view is that the world-wide continuous assessment of customer needs and expectations should be the responsibility of basic marketing research staff. Furthermore, this activity should be centralized at the corporate level in the multinational corporation to maintain world-wide perspective.

In monitoring buyer needs and expectations the basic marketing research is likely to perform at least the following things: First, it will bring to bear professional and systematic effort to provide a common understanding of market place needs in place of ad hoc and often incomparable research presently focused on products. Second, it will make explicit the assumptions of R and D about the market needs in developing new products, and therefore, subject to examination and criticism.

Finally, it will act as the bridge between the R and D expertise with respect to technology and production economics and the unfulfilled needs and expectations of the market place.

The basic marketing research is likely to vary its procedures in assessing buyer needs and expectations from one geographical area to another due to differences in sophistication and availability of survey research institutions. For example, in some countries telephone interviews may be impossible because only a few possess them whereas in other countries mail questionnaire may be less useful due to illiteracy and postal facilities. There is, however, sufficient knowledge available today on cross-cultural survey research to enable the company to establish a viable basic marketing research unit.

The role of Research & Development (R and D) is to attempt to convert specific recommendations from the basic marketing research into viable product offerings by taking into account technological and production economics considerations. The recommendations from basic marketing research can be as simple as packaging changes to as complex as developing a new concept from scratch. In the model, therefore, R and D is envisioned to be market-oriented instead of technology-oriented. The latter unfortunately is the more common reality in today's multinational corporations.

I am also suggesting that the organizational importance and de facto power of R and D be neutralized by the establishment of the basic marketing research unit. Ideally, R and D people will provide technological and economic expertise and the basic marketing research will provide psychological and marketing expertise in the common objective of matching people's needs and expectations with mass production facilities. In view of the interdependent roles between R and D and basic market research, the model assumes a feedback look between the two activities. For example, R and D develops a new packaging scheme based on the recommendations from basic marketing research. The new packaging scheme is then tested by the latter with recommendations to modify if market reactions are not satisfactory and so on. I presume considerable interaction between the two entities at least until the test marketing phase of any new product introduction is completed.

The concrete proposals as outcomes of the joint efforts of R and D and basic marketing research are recommended to marketing management. In addition to the routine activity of monitoring relative position of existing products in many markets, the marketing management must spend considerable time in reviewing new proposals. This will enable it to maintain the dynamic element and be prepared to make quick decisions when a change is demanded due to some abrupt change in the market environment.

The role of marketing management is analogous to that of the diamond cutter. It must attempt to convert the concrete opportunities dug up by both R and D and the basic marketing research units in terms of profitable and societally useful means of satisfying buyer demand. It is, therefore, a very crucial role, and following the analogy, not many concrete proposals will become viable modules to achieve corporate goals.

Just as considerable skill and experience is required to become a good diamond cutter, the marketing management also requires considerable experience and skill in decision-making to cope with a large number of environmental factors. These factors are classified as (1) competitive structure, (2) legal environment, (3) nonmarketing costs and (4) distribution system. Since these factors are widely known and discussed in many books, we will not elaborate on their importance here. The only relevant point to make here is that these factors are likely to vary widely from one segment of the market to another segment, whether the segments are based on clusterings of countries, metropolitan areas or some other entities.

The output of managerial decision-making will result in specific marketing programs on a world-wide basis. The marketing programs are likely to be differentiated from one segment of the world market to another segment. This differentiation will be with respect to both the budget allocations and the specific emphasis of marketing mix elements.

The specific marketing programs should be designed based on the concept of world segmentation. Unlike differentiating markets on a country basis, the most viable and profitable segmentation basis seems to be the examination of underlying factors that determine buyer demand. These factors can be broadly classified as buyer expectations and buying climate. The first factor was briefly discussed before and it is based on culture, social stratification and family structure. The second factor (buying climate) is primarily based on financial factors (disposable personal income, asset holdings, etc.), geographical factors (temperature, humidity & altitude; tropical vs. temperate climate, etc.) and demographic features (size of family, age distributions of family members, life cycle of family etc.).

Below is a scheme of differentiated marketing programs based on segments which differ in either buyer expectations or buying climate or both. If the differences are primarily with respect to buying climate, the company must adopt differential product (size, packaging, variety, quality, etc.) and distribution (direct selling, self service, length of middlemen chain, etc.) strategies from one segment of the world market to some other segment. On the other hand, if differences are primarily in terms of buyer expectations, the company must adopt differential promotion (different advertising appeals, different media, different display promotions, etc.) and pricing (price thresholds, price-quality relationship, etc.) strategies. If both the buyer expectations and buying climate are different, a completely differentiated marketing program will be needed for each segment of the world market. Exhibit 35-2 gives a summary of differential marketing programs. The reader is referred to Sheth (1972)[2] for a fuller discussion of these strategies.

In the model, therefore, differential marketing programs are considered essential. However, it is suggested that these differential marketing programs should not be based on national sovereignty of the countries in which a company markets but must be based on the buyer demand characteristics.

The demand for a company's products at the micro level is likely to be determined by a number of factors in addition to buyer needs and expectations. The three environmental factors which often break the relationship between buyer needs and buyer demand are (1) financial environment, (2) geographic environment, and (3) demographic environment. They were briefly described in the last section. A fuller description can be found in Howard and Sheth (1969).

In addition, buyer demand for a specific brand can be influenced by the company's differentiated marketing effort. This effort, however, will be relative in its success depending upon the competitive marketing effort. In general, one can safely assume that (1) if the company's marketing programs are based upon proper assessment of buyer needs and expectations and (2) if the

EXHIBIT 35-2
DIFFERENTIAL MARKETING PROGRAMS FOR
SEGMENTED WORLD MARKETS

| | | Buying Climate | |
		Same	Different
Buyer Expectations	Same	Universal Marketing Programs	Differential Marketing with respect to: Product & Distribution
	Different	Differential Marketing with respect to: Advertising & Promotion and Pricing	Fully Differentiated Marketing Programs

differential marketing approach is adopted, the company can effectively communicate the market customers about its products.

The assessment and continuous reporting of buyer demand is the function of applied marketing research. In addition to company's own records, this entity must understand and record market demand at the micro level. Fortunately, a number of syndicated marketing research services such as MRCA or Atwood Panels are available so that the applied marketing research does not have to set up its own data collection activities.

A second major activity of the applied marketing research is to carry out experimentation with differential marketing programs including the test marketing activities. It is my hope that this applied marketing research will perform similar liaison function between marketing management and market demand as does the basic marketing research between buyer needs and company's Research & Development.

What are the implications of the conceptual model presented in this paper? First of all, the model encourages the multinational corporation to examine the world as potential market place. As such, piece meal and trial-and-error efforts of the present multinational expansion is given a more systematic orientation. This will in turn enable the company to avoid costly mistakes in one part of the world and take advantages of opportunity present in some other part of the world.

Secondly, the model emphasizes greater customer-oriented marketing planning. A number of benefits arise from this orientation. For example, product failure rate is considerably diminished, better marketing and merchandising effectiveness is attained, and more stable pattern of continued success is derived. All of these benefits have been demonstrated in the domestic marketing.

Third, the model points out the need to go beyond aggregate secondary data. Often, irrevocable marketing decisions are based on either poor or irrelevant information with the consequences that marketing success is still more by accident than by design.

Finally, the model puts in proper perspective the role of marketing research in multinational business operations. It has been neglected so far and more than optimal reliance has been placed on the capability of R and D to provide insights on market desires.

QUESTIONS

1. What are the limitations identified by the author in the current planning practices of multinational organizations?
2. How does the author suggest that the role of R & D be defined in the planning process?

3. How would marketing programs for different world market segments be influenced by the buyer expectations and the buying climate? Give illustrations.

NOTES

1. John A. Howard and J. N. Sheth, *The Theory of Buyer Behavior,* John Wiley & Sons, 1969.

2. Jagdish N. Sheth, "Relevance of Segmentation for Market Planning," paper presented at the ESOMAR Seminar on Segmentation and Typology, May 10-12, 1972, Brussels, Belgium.

*Multinational marketing strategy is directly
and indirectly affected by a firm's organizational structure. The nature of the relationship between the elements of strategy and
objectives, organizational arrangements, and
other parent-subsidiary characteristics are investigated through a survey of multinational
subsidiaries operating in Brazil. The authors
conclude that organizational structure appears to be an important intervening variable
between the parent company's nationality
and subsidiary strategy. In developing suggestions for conducting future research the
article also presents an in-depth description
of subsidiary strategy and organization of
North American, European, and Japanese
multinationals.*

36. Organizational Structure and Marketing Strategy in the Multinational Subsidiary

William K. Brandt and James M. Hurlbert
Columbia University

The relationship between organizational structure and marketing strategy has
long been recognized as a key determinant of company performance, and
appears to extend to the overseas operations of multinational corporations.
This paper reports on organizational structures and marketing strategies in
sixty-three foreign subsidiaries of North American, European and Japanese
multinational corporations. Specifically, the following issues are addressed:

1. To what extent does subsidiary organization structure coincide with
   the organization structure or nationality of the parent company?
2. What types of marketing objectives are established by subsidiary management?
3. How are the elements of strategy affected by objectives, organization
   structures and other characteristics of subsidiary and parent?

Source: Reprinted from *Proceedings of the American Marketing Association,* No. 37,
Spring-Fall, 1975, pp. 320–325. Published by the American Marketing Association.

BACKGROUND

Organizational structure for marketing has been widely recognized as an important problem area, and recommendations have reflected the need to modify existing structures in response to marketing objectives and strategies. Empirical research on the topic has also emphasized the impact of organizational structure on marketing practice.

The multinational subsidiary offers an exciting setting in which to explore the development of organizational structures and marketing strategies. With few exceptions, existing research has dealt with the home-office perspective. However, at the subsidiary level the strategies, systems and organizational structures suggested or dictated by the home office are likely to be moderated by the marketing environment of the subsidiary's host country.

Method

Sample Selection

The information for this paper is part of a larger study which included personal, structured interviews with managers of eighty MNC subsidiaries operating in Brazil. During the study we questioned sixty-three chief executives and sixty-two marketing managers, focusing on different issues for each type of manager. The chief executive was interviewed first and in forty-four subsidiaries the marketing manager was subsequently questioned. In nineteen cases a second interview was not feasible and another firm of like nationality and industry was substituted.

The sample of subsidiaries was selected in stages. First, Brazil was chosen because it offered a large, single-country market with substantial foreign investment from North America, Europe and Japan. Second, six manufacturing industries with heavy foreign investment were selected.[1] Finally, the leading foreign-controlled firms in each industry were identified and contacted, and in all but one case the interview was granted. In some industries smaller competitors were added to balance the sample by nationality.

Company Characteristics

Among the sixty-three subsidiaries for which the chief executive was interviewed, twenty-eight had home offices located in West Germany, Great Britain, France, Italy, Switzerland, Sweden, Finland, and the Netherlands, and will be referred to as European for purposes of the present discussion. Twenty-four were headquartered in the United States or Canada and will be termed American Companies, and the remaining eleven were Japanese.

Exhibit 36-1 reports that the 1972 annual sales of the Brazilian subsidiaries in the sample ranged from one to 725 million dollars. The average sales figures for the American and European subsidiaries were almost identical with median sales of 54 and 52 million dollars, respectively. Sales for the

EXHIBIT 36-1
Sales of participating companies

Nationality[a]	Sales of Brazilian Subsidiary (Millions U.S. $)		World-wide Sales of Parent Company (Millions U.S. $)	Overseas Sales as Proportion of World Sales[b]
	Median	Range		
American	54	(5-350)	2600	26%
European	52	(1-750)	1300	67%
Japanese	6	(2-35)	1100	20%

[a]American includes companies headquartered in the United States and Canada. European include West Germany, Great Britain, France, Italy, Switzerland, Sweden, Finland, and the Netherlands.

[b]Overseas sales include exports and overseas manufacturing, excluding intra-company transfers.

Japanese subsidiaries, most of which were established after 1965, averaged six million dollars. The worldwide sales of American parent companies were, on average, twice the size of the European companies and two-and-one-half times the size of the Japanese companies. Thus, given the equal size of European and American subsidiaries in Brazil, subsidiary sales as a proportion of world sales were higher for European firms (3.6 percent) than for American (2.6 percent), or Japanese companies (0.8 percent.).

Organization Structures of Parents and Subsidiaries

Three quarters of the subsidiaries were organized on a functional basis, with three or more directors or vice presidents each responsible for a functional area such as marketing, finance, production, administration and others. One out of six was organized around product groups or divisions, while the remaining eight percent had a mixed form combining both structures.

Subsidiaries using a product-division structure in Brazil were apparently modelled on their parent's domestic structure: virtually all subsidiaries with product divisions also had divisionalized structures in the home country. Among those subsidiaries with pure forms of product divisions, all were American, primarily producers of packaged goods or pharmaceuticals. Several European and one Japanese firm used a mixed structure with both product and functional responsibilities at the top management level.

We ascribe the relative scarcity of product-division structures in Brazil to two related factors. First, most Brazilian subsidiaries are small and relatively undiversified when compared with their parent's domestic operations. Second, the subsidiaries and the Brazilian market in general are still relatively "young" in their development with the results that the marketing emphasis forcuses on penetration more than diversification.

Subsidiary Marketing Organization

Marketing Responsibilities

In three fourths of the subsidiaries, marketing functions were grouped together to form a "unified" department. In these companies marketing research, advertising, channel management, pricing and market developing activities were under the domain of a marketing or commercial manager.[2]

A "unified" structure for marketing was most common among consumer goods manufacturers, but was also more prevalent in American subsidiaries. Japanese subsidiaries, in particular, tended to divide marketing activities among several people or departments, with little apparent integration.

The title of the top "marketing" executive also appeared to make little difference in terms of actual responsibilities. While most were titled "marketing manager," others were called "commercial director" or "sales manager." Use of the marketing manager title, however, certainly gave no reliable indication of marketing orientation or sophistication.

Production Management

Although only 17 percent of the subsidiaries were organized by product divisions, 63 percent of American and 42 percent of European firms had product or brand managers within the marketing organization. Consumer-goods companies and firms with Brazilian sales exceeding 50 million dollars were far more likely to use product managers.

New products were seldom the responsibility of product or marketing management: only one third of American and 15 percent of European and Japanese subsidiaries developed new products within the marketing department. Makers of packaged goods were more inclined to follow this practice, perhaps because new product introductions often involve minor modifications, low capital investments, or product ideas imported from home-country divisions. In most subsidiaries the responsibility for new products rests with engineering or research departments, far removed from marketing.

Most subsidiaries based their business plans on some form of marketing research, but less than three out of four had an internal department to handle this activity. Marketing research departments were more common for larger firms and for manufacturers of consumer products. The size factor may explain why only one Japanese firm had a market research department, but it is not clear why fewer American subsidiaries had internal departments compared with the Europeans.

Sales Force Management

For three-fourths of American and European subsidiaries the sales organization was responsible to the marketing or commercial manager. Most Japanese firms and the other remaining companies separated marketing and sales, in effect giving equal rank in the organization to the sales manager and the marketing or commercial manager. This separation was most common in industrial companies where the sales force is generally considered the key promotional tool. The sales forces were organized either by product specialty (52 percent) or by region (39 percent). Only two companies organized specifically by customer type, though in some instances organizing by product specialty achieved the same result. Differences between European and American sales forces were minor, but because many Japanese firms sold a narrower product line, they tended to organize on a geographic basis.

Marketing Objectives and Strategies

Choice of product-market emphasis and development of marketing objectives and strategies are the core of the marketing job and a key element of corporate strategy. In Brazil the design of marketing strategy has played a crucial role in recent years. Whereas financial and production problems were the major preoccupations in the sixties, 60 percent of the chief executives interviewed felt that marketing decisions were most crucial to their firms' success during the past five years. Perhaps this helps to explain why these same executives devoted 40 percent of their time, on average, to marketing problems.

Marketing Objectives

The marketing objective should stipulate in explicit, concise terms what the firm hopes to accomplish during the next planning period. Despite the use of formalized planning systems in most subsidiaries, many executives had difficulty specifying their primary marketing objective for the coming year. The responses were a mixture of broad goals, operating objectives, strategy statements and even specific tactics or programs. Nevertheless, it was possible to group the statements into four general categories.

Maintaining or increasing market share was the principal objective for nearly half the sample. By adding "growth in sales" to this category, almost two-thirds were stating objectives in terms of penetrating or developing existing markets. Although three fourths of the subsidiaries were evaluated on the basis of profits, only eight percent mentioned profits alone as the primary objective. This suggests that most chief executives agreed with the maxim that profits are not a useful operational objective. Another 21 percent, however, mentioned profits in conjunction with some other objective, such as market penetration. Considering the tremendous market protential for most products in Brazil, penetration objectives seem entirely reasonable.

Another alternative to growth is through new market or product development, a category we label "diversification." One fifth of the executives claimed that this was their principal objective. Several noted that competitive pressures were forcing them to search for new products or markets, a condition mentioned most often by consumer-products companies.

Some classes of objectives were strongly associated with particular company characteristics. American firms, for example, tended to stress diversification objectives more than the other subsidiaries. Organizational structures within the marketing department were also linked with objectives. Exhibit 36-2 reports that companies using product managers within marketing were significantly more likely to include profits in their objective statements. Even more striking is the relationship in Exhibit 36-3 between penetration objectives and the presence of an internal marketing research department. From these results it appears that companies with penetration objectives place their growth emphasis on developing and segmenting an existing market, rather than technological innovation. For these firms market knowledge and technology become a crucial resource, which is reflected in the organizational structure.

Strategic Emphasis

By examining the marketing plans it was often impossible to identify a clear-cut statement of strategy. Instead we attempted to identify the strategic emphasis by asking marketing managers which decision areas would be most cricital in helping them achieve the marketing objective previously stated. The decision areas included sales force, advertising, sales promotion, distribution, pricing, new market development, and new product development.[3]

Looking at these decision areas by nationality of the MNC, we observe in Exhibit 36-4 that sales force decisions were emphasized by European and American subsidiaries whereas the Japanese focused on pricing and developing new markets. Despite the small number of Japanese responses for this question, the results seem consistent with their situation in Brazil: the Japanese subsidiaries are still small and are therefore compelled to expand their markets and later their product line in order to grow. A low-price strategy proved effective for their export development some years ago, and it appears that a similar strategy may be a central thrust of their expansion into overseas manufacturing.

The subsidiary's strategic emphasis also showed some relationship to its organizational structure. Firms with functional structures stressed sales force decisions, while those with product divisions concentrated more on new products and sales promotion (Exhibit 36-5).

Because the relationships noted above may be explained by many other variables, multiple regression analysis was used to isolate the relative effects of organization, nationality, type of industry and marketing objectives on each decision area.[4] The dependent variables were coded one if the decision area ranked first or second most important among the seven alternatives; otherwise it was coded zero.

The findings for sales force decisions complement the tabular results showing that organizational structure, nationality, industry type and objectives were significantly related to the importance of sales force decisions. Subsidiaries with divisionalized structures, those using product managers, makers of consumer products, and the Japanese placed less emphasis on sales force strategy. Firms which stressed diversification and profitability objectives concentrated more on the sales force when compared with those adopting penetration objectives.

The results for other decision areas were less encouraging: with the exception of low-capital intensity, no other variable was significantly related at the .05 level to the remaining decision areas. While it may be that these decisions were truly not related to variables included in the model, problems of interviewer performance, questionnaire design and response error may be responsible.

EXHIBIT 36-2
Marketing objectives and product management organization

Primary Marketing Objective	Product Management Organization	
	Used	Not Used
Profit Included	11	3
Profit Not Included	12	21
$X^2 = 7.0, \text{ld.f., } p < .01$		

EXHIBIT 36-3
Marketing objectives and presence of internal marketing research department

Primary Marketing Objective	Internal Marketing Present	Research Department Not Present
Market Penetration Mentioned	20	1
Market Penetration Not Mentioned	15	11
$X^2 = 6.75, \text{ld.f., } p < .01$		

EXHIBIT 36-4
Strategic emphasis by nationality of parent company

| | Nationality of Parent Company | | |
Decision Area	American	European	Japanese
Sales Force	38%[a]	58%	0%
Sales Promotion	17	33	17
Advertising	33	17	17
Pricing	30	21	50
Distribution	17	21	17
New Markets	25	17	50
New Products	29	25	33
Number of cases	(24)	(25)	(6)

[a]Table should be read: 38 percent of American subsidiaries reported that sales force decisions were first or second most important to achieve the marketing objective.

EXHIBIT 36-5
Strategic emphasis by organizational structure of subsidiary

| | Organizational Structure | |
Decision Areaa	Divisionalized	Functional
Sales Force	18%[a]	53%
Sales Promotion	46	26
Advertising	27	18
Pricing	36	26
Distribution	18	16
New Markets	36	24
New Products	46	24
Number of cases	(11)	(38)

[a]Table should be read: 18 percent of divisionalized subsidiaries reported that sales force decisions were first or second most important to achieve the marketing objective.

Conclusion

This survey of MNC subsidiaries illustrates the need and potential for empirical research which investigates the relationship between marketing strategy and organizational structure. The results observed are far from conclusive but they do suggest promising areas for future research.

For example, the parent company's nationality may well influence subsidiary behavior in some fashion, but we should be cautious in generalizing that "European MNC's tend to . . ., while Japanese do . . ., and Americans behave . . ." Further analysis may show that the influence of nationality operates through an intervening variable like organizational structure. Thus, while particular nationality groups may prefer certain structural forms, it may be organizational attributes rather than nationality *per se* which relate to strategic objectives of the subsidiary. This certainly appears to be the case for the types of standardized marketing programs sent from home office: organization and strategy play a far greater role in the programs received than does nationality of the parent company.

The research results also suggest approaches for broader investigations of strategy and structure. Developing an effective marketing strategy requires a matching of company resources and market opportunity. Studies such as the PIMS project suggest that there are large payoffs to appropriate choice of strategy, yet little research is available to help identify the capabilities needed for different strategies, or the organizational structures best suited to execute them.

Finally the study offers several methodological insights for future research. Contrary to prior warnings we experienced no problems gaining access to top subsidiary management of any nationality group. The chief executives in Brazil were contacted directly without prior home-office approval, and in no case was an interview refused. The nature of the interview should be specified precisely during the initial contact.

Stereotypic fears about the candor and helpfulness of certain nationality groups were largely baseless in this study. Subsequent validations indicate that no one nationality group was more or less truthful in their descriptions of company activities and performance. Candor during an interview is more a function of the manager's personality and the interviewer. The interviewer's position, knowledge and ability to "trade" assistance for information are crucial to the success of such interviews.

Questionnaire design for executive interviews demands careful attention to the ease of verbal execution, as opposed to visual execution. Structured questions are possible but ranking or rating scales with more than three or four items should be used with caution. Although pretests with scaled questions ran smoothly in the United States, they were sometimes difficult to administer overseas.

QUESTIONS

1. What do the authors mean by the term *organizational structure*? What factors do they classify as organizational structure attributes?

2. What is the nature of the relationships between organizational structure and marketing strategy?
3. How can these relationships be applied by executives in formulating multinational marketing strategy?

NOTES

1. Industries represented included both consumer and industrial products viz. motor vehicles and major components, electrical and telecommunications equipment, pharmaceuticals, consumer-packaged goods, office equipment, and textiles.

2. Sales force and new product development responsibilities were specifically excluded from these functions. In brand management or high technology companies, respectively, these functions are often separately organized.

3. Executives were asked to rank each of the seven areas in terms of importance for their principal product line. Most were unable to rank the seven areas but could easily rank the first two or three decision areas.

4. A regression analysis using a 0-1 dependent variable is equivalent to two-group discriminant analysis, and the regression coefficients are a linear multiple of the discriminant coefficients.

REFERENCES

1. Ansoff, H. Igor. *Corporate Strategy*. New York: McGraw-Hill, 1965.

2. Brandt, William K. and James M. Hulbert, "Marketing Strategy in the Multinational Subsidiary: The Role of Headquarters," in *Making Advertising Relevant: Proceedings of the American Academy of Advertising, 1975.*

3. ————. "Patterns of Communications in the Multinational Corporation: An Empirical Study," *Journal of International Business Studies,* forthcoming.

4. Brooke, Michael and H. Lee Remmers. *The Strategy of Multinational Enterprise.* New York: American Elsevier Publishing Co., 1970.

5. Carson, David. "Marketing Organization in British Manufacturing Firms," *Journal of Marketing,* 32 (April 1968), 34-9.

6. Chandler, A.D. *Strategy and Structure.* Cambridge, Mass.: MIT Press, 1962.

7. Corey, E. Raymond and Steven H. Star. *Organization Strategy: A Marketing Approach.* Boston: Division of Research, Graduate School of Business Administration, Harvard University, 1971.

8. Farley, John U., John A. Howard, and James M. Hulbert. "An Organizational Approach to an Industrial Marketing Information System," *Sloan Management Review,* 13 (Fall 1971), 35-54.

9. Franko, L.G. *European Business Strategies in the United States.* Geneva: Business International, 1971.

10. Hill, Richard M. and James D. Hlavacek. "The Venture Team: A New Concept in Marketing Organization," *Journal of Marketing,* 36 (July 1972), 44-50.

11. Luck, David J. "Interfaces of a Product Manager," *Journal of Marketing,* 33 (October 1969), 32-6.

12. Keegan, Warren J. *Multinational Marketing Management.* Englewood Cliffs: Prentice-Hall, 1974.

13. Kotler, Philip. "A Design for the Firm's Marketing Nerve Center," *Business Horizons,* 9 (Fall 1966), 63-74.

14. Levitt, Theodore, *Marketing for Business Growth.* New York: McGraw-Hill, 1974.

15. *Management of New Products.* 4th ed. New York: Booz, Allen & Hamilton, Inc., 1965.

16. Newman, William H., C.E. Summer, and E.K. Warren. *The Process of Management.* 3rd ed. Englewood Cliffs: Prentice-Hall, 1972.

17. Robbins, S.M. and R.B. Stobaugh. *Money in the Multinational Enterprise.* New York: Basic Books, Inc., 1973.

18. Sallenave, Jean-Paul. *La Strategie de l'Enterprise face de la Concurrence.* Montreal: Les Presses de l'Universite de Montreal, 1973.

19. Schoeffler, S., R.D. Buzzell and D.F. Heany, "Impact of Strategic Planning on Profit Performance," *Harvard Business Review,* (March-April, 1974), 137-45.

20. Snyder, W. and F.B. Gray. *The Corporate Marketing Staff: It's Role and Effectiveness in Multi-Division Companies.* Cambridge, Mass.: Marketing Science Institute, 1971.

21. Kahn, George and Abe Shuchman. "Specialize Your Sales Force," *Harvard Business Review,* 39 (January 1961), 90-8.

22. Schollhammer, Hans. "Long Range Planning in Multinational Firms," *Columbia Journal of World Business,* 6 (September-October 1971), 79-86.

23. Stopford, John and Louis T. Wells. *Managing the Multinational Enterprise.* New York: Basic Books, Inc., 1972.

24. Turner, Ronald E. "Product Priorities Within a Multiple-Product Marketing Organization," *Journal of Marketing Research,* 11 (May 1974), 143-50.

25. Vernon, Raymond. *Sovereignty at Bay.* New York: Basic Books, 1971.

The formulation of international marketing strategy requires the consideration of numerous complex variables. This article illustrates how critical market characteristics such as demand growth factors, technology changes, cost rationalizations, and others impinge on the marketing strategies for international public telecommunications. A number of implications for marketing of other products and services are also raised.

37. Competitive Marketing Strategies for International Public Telecommunications

Gary L. Jordan
University of Connecticut

Governmental bodies are increasingly encountered during the implementation of marketing strategies. These organizations act as entrepreneurs through government-owned industries, regulators of business activity, providers of wide-ranging services to their citizens, and as customers. The issue then is: What is the significance of these various government functions to marketing executives and strategic planners? According to the late Wolfgang Friedmann these functions are undergoing major structural changes and thus the balance of public and private power is shifting.[1] These changes should be of interest to market planners for many products. Direct sales to government agencies are increasingly important in many countries and joint ventures and co-production agreements involving governmental partners are increasingly observed. In most developing countries government officials are involved in equipment purchases for the basic industries of mining, steel, power generation, and commercial transportation. Much the same can be said for France, Italy, and the United Kingdom as well.

Source: Printed with permission of the author. Copyright 1978 by Gary L. Jordan.

Better understanding of this phenomenon can be gained by studying individual industrial markets. Public telecommunications is an example since it covers the communications facilities and services provided by public authorities in various countries. It is of special interest for studying governmental involvement in marketing since the government groups act in all of the functional roles mentioned. The competitive strategies used in marketing to the government depend in turn on the market characteristics encountered.

Many of the supplier companies to the international public telecommunication markets are well known to marketing practitioners: L.M. Ericsson (Sweden), ITT (United States), Siemens (West Germany) Plessey and General Electric Company (United Kingdom), and Nippon Electric, Oki, Hitachi, and Fujitsu (Japan). Inclusion of the United States market adds Western Electric and General Telephone and Electronics. These are full-line companies which can install tele-networks for customer countries.

It is the purpose of this paper to improve the understanding of the role played by the governments in the capital goods marketing process by reference to the market for international public telecommunication systems. This is then an industry case approach to the study of the effects which specific governmental organizations have on the marketing process. The competitive strategies used must have a close relationship to the objectives and implementation actions of these organizations. The critical market characteristics are first described and then the competitive strategies being used by the above international supplier group are set forth and inter-related.

Critical Market Characteristics

The above competitor group must continuously assess market information on a wide range of factors, but these can be classified under four critical market characteristics that are:

A. Demand growth factors
B. Technology changes
C. Cost rationalizations
D. Buyer decision criteria

The factors that are subjected to continuous information scanning are set forth in the following sections along with some of the current measures therefor. Four market characteristics compose the environment for the above companies.

Information inputs are required for each of the market characteristics A-D. The first three characteristics all converge on D. Buyer Decision Criteria, which is controlled by the customer country's telephone administration, usually referred to as a PTT for post, telegraph and telephone. The country's economic development objectives are shown as dominant to the element D criteria since these are viewed as having a controlling influence. The supplier company then sets its competitive strategies, and analyzes operating results.

The strategies chosen then depend upon the identified market characteristics. The factor must be reassessed by new information inputs if sales and profit goals are not met.

The information presented in this paper is from both published and un-published sources. It includes secondary sources and information obtained through interviews of selected telecommunication industry personnel. The competitive strategies being used by the supplier firms are viewed as the dependent variables and characteristics A-D in the marketing environment are seen as independent variables.

Demand Growth Factors

The main market growth (independent) factors are: (1) the demand for ordinary telephone service, (2) the need for improved quality of service, (3) vastly increased data traffic growth, (4) the need to enhance economic development by providing for convenient, low-cost telecommunication services, (5) decreasing use costs per voice circuit, and (6) the evolution of information processing societies in the industrial countries. Each of these factors will be commented upon, but first it is of interest to know the world size of the telephone market, and its classification. It has been estimated at about $20 billion per year by a leading Swedish business publication and nearing the $50 billion mark by Robert La Blanc, a leading industry analyst at Salomon Brothers in New York[2]. The greater difference in these two esti-mates probably depends upon the type of equipment taken into considera-tion since this market is composed of specific equipment markets. The dif-ferent equipment markets have been classified as:

Public exchange stations: transit and local

Local lines network

Public subscriber telephone sets

International exchange stations

Long distance transmission equipment

— Ground trunk lines

— Ground station microwave links

— Satellite microwave links

Private branch exchanges

The focus in this paper is on the first of these categories. One of the principal measures for gauging market activity for the first three categories is to deter-mine the number of mainlines installed. Each of these link at least one main telephone set with a local exchange station. Globally there are about 20 mil-lion main lines being installed per year on a base of an estimated 360 million telephones for a 5.5 percent overall growth rate. The consumption of tele-communications services is another measure of market activity and shows that business and industrial usage of these services has been increasing at much faster than this 5.5 percent/year rate.

A publication of the International Telecommunications Union (ITU), for example, indicates that in the machine building industry in the United States the consumption of telecommunication services increased by a factor of 10 for the period of 1947 to 1964, while the value of its production rose by a factor of only 2.7.[3]

The *demand for ordinary telephone services* depends heavily upon the two factors of existing telephone density and need to lower service costs. France furnishes the clearest case for both factors when compared to a group of some of its EEC partners (West Germany, United Kingdom, Italy, and Holland). The 1971 French telephone density was 15/100 inhabitants while the cost of obtaining the basic telephone service was one hundred and seventy-nine hours/year for the average worker.[4] The comparison group had telephone densities of from eighteen to twenty-four and service costs in the range of sixty-eight and eighty-seven hours/year. The demand growth for the current 1974-79 period is 23 percent in France compared with 8 to 11 percent in the defined group.[5] This is due to the ambitious $20 billion telenetwork program in France for the period 1976-1981. Lack of phone service and/or high service costs appears to generate political pressure for public investments in the telecommunication network of a country. The developing countries have very urgent needs when the 1970 telephone densities like those of 2/100 inhabitants for Brazil, 0.2 for Indonesia, and 0.1 for Nigeria are considered. Saudi Arabia recently entered into contracts for about 2 billion dollars with a group composed of LM Ericsson, Philips, and Northern Electric (Canada), although a substantial part of this amount will be used for local building contracts.

The *quality of service* factor that also fuels growth relates to long queuing times for dial tones (indicating unavailability in the switching channels), signal weakening, cross-talk and nonvoice signal interferences. These translate to needs for improving both switching gear and transmission components.

One *data traffic growth* study was made for Europe in which 1972 was used as a base year and projections were made out to 1985.[6] The prediction is for growth from an index value of one in 1972 to over eleven in the 13-year period. This prediction included both computer data and voice telephone flows. This large index forecasted value can be compared against the 2.5 index value for all inland and outgoing international telephone calls. In the United States AT&T is apparently projecting a 26 percent per year compound growth rate in data transmission revenues for the 1970s.[7] Thus the data traffic growth is a heavily weighted factor for demand growth in telecommunications at least in the industrial countries.

It is generally believed that a communication infrastructure is needed for *economic development*. Statistical studies have shown a high correlation of telephone usage with economic activity. For example, GNP per capita and telephone density showed a correlation of $r = 0.93$ for fifty-eight countries for 1960.[8] The point is that modern telephony makes economic development achievable within a more acceptable time frame.

The equipment suppliers are able to provide transmission links to the various PTTs at *decreasing costs* when measured in *per voice circuit* units. This in turn allows the telephone administrations to price the tele-network services so that increased network usage is economically attractive for network users. The main reason for this cost decrease is the ability to transmit many voice conversations over the same communication link. This is accomplished by compressing the transmission signals through a process known as multiplexing. For the greatest cost efficiencies digital signals are used for multiplexing by first converting the voice frequency signals that are made by speaking into the receiver to a series of electronic pulses which can be handled at lower cost.

Another factor is that the present industrial countries are rapidly becoming *information processing societies.* The labor force in these countries shows increasingly high proportions of workers who are engaged in intangible information processing occupations. The 1975 figure in the United States was 46 percent.[9] It is clear that such a labor force in which nearly one-half of the workers must read, write, talk, calculate, and decide in their jobs must have a low-cost, efficient telecommunications system. Japan in fact has a national commitment to develop an "Information Society". The United States, Canada, United Kingdom, and Sweden are also examples for this demand factor.

Technology Changes

The ability to vastly increase the signal carrying and switching capacities in the tele-network has been one of the main results of the present electronic revolution. The principal technical advances have been: (1) Signal switching by stored computer program control (SPC); (2) Pulse code modulation (PCM) for conversion to digital signals; (3) Use of solid state components.

SPC which was experimentally used in the early 1960s is being increasingly demanded by nearly all telephone administrations. The use of a software program to switch telephone line connections has advantages over the electro-mechanical switching frames that were extremely complex series of automatically operating mechanical switches. The first is that maintenance and corrections are largely simplified to alternations in the software programming. The controlling computer can even be instructed to locate the malfunction positions. Fewer maintenance people, although more highly skilled, are required. The SPC switching works via digitalized signals that are generated by pulse code modulation through a technique of sampling the voice analog signals produced by speaking. The conversion of voice signals to digital pulses is convenient because the same tele-network gear can then handle these together with the computer data traffic which also operates in digital form.

The use of digitalized signals via PCM then led to heavier use of microwave links of both ground station and satellite types. Data transmission costs outside the terrestrial-bound telecommunication network is dropping rapidly as further detailed below. IBM has already satellite-linked its North American and European laboratories.

The use of solid state components has permitted advances such as solid-state switching in which there are no moving mechanical parts and a great reduction in equipment size and power consumption. These components have permitted maintenance economies since they are less subject to failure than parts requiring precise mechanical movements.

Cost Rationalizations

One of the results of the technology revolution is that the signal handling capacity and efficiency in both transmission and switching equipment are being increased at a rapid rate. This means that for a given tele-network voice circuit the use costs are decreasing. The PTTs can arrange the rate structures to encourage full time use of existing links by both business and household subscribers.

A good example of decreasing costs of providing such services is in the data for satellite links. The Comsat INTELSAT series started with Early Bird (I) in 1965 at a cost/voice circuit/year of $23,000. INTELSAT II and III were placed in geosynchronous orbit in 1967 and 1968 respectively at cost levels of $11,000 and $1,600/voice circuit/year, respectively. INTELSAT IV drops the cost to $618 and Generation V planned for a 1978 launch is expected to drop it to an estimated $58.[10] The corresponding cost for the WESTAR satellite of 1974 is about $210. These figures are for the investment cost of building and launching the satellites—the space segment of the linkage costs.

Buyer Decision Criteria

The most important criteria within element D is the customer country's development objectives. Other key criteria are: The PTT method of equipment assessment, its pricing policy, and political and constraining factors.

Economic development objectives can vary throughout the steps of:

a. arranging for only basic business telephone service to be provided by purchasing a package of equipment and services from one or more supplier companies—the PTT as a provider of services and as a customer,
b. acquiring telecommunication equipment production technology and beginning to perform assembly and testing functions,
c. taking the next step to further increase employment and increase the value-added by starting parts manufacturing—the PTT as an entrepreneur,
d. acquiring even more technology and producing a higher percentage of the country's telecommunication gear and services, and
e. placing the country's producing companies in the position to compete for export business in the international markets—again acting as an entrepreneur,
f. creating an information processing society.

The least developed countries are of course at objective a. Brazil could be characterized as holding objective c for the new generation of computer switched exchanges but being at e for the older electromechanical gear. France's leading telecommunication company, Thompson–CSF, in which the government has controlling ownership has recently acquired control of both an LM Ericsson and an ITT subsidiary in order to take in sufficient knowhow to leap up to objective e for even the new SPC exchanges.

Equipment assessment can be performed by a PTT through a well-staffed technical group as in the case of Canada, Sweden and Australia whose government telecommunication offices have required world-wide reputations. Other PTTs rely heavily on the judgments of these leading offices and thus they operate assessment of the suppliers' technical offerings through a system of "transferred confidence". It is also essential that the home country of each supplier purchase its equipment as proof of technical reliability.

Pricing policy for most PTT's comes down to minimizing losses at the local service level and maximizing long distance and international service revenues so as to make the tele-network operate at an overall small return.

Internal *political factors* require the local household fee structure to be kept low while business usage will tolerate much higher fees. Most developed countries have shown decreasing real telephone rate changes for basic telephone services from 1963 to 1975. One study shows an average real rate reduction of about 30 percent over this time period in twelve European industrial countries plus Japan.[11] This shows that the PTTs are passing some of the savings of cost rationalization on through to the users. Hence they are acting as benevolent providers. An external political factor said to affect purchase decisions of developing country PTTs are the past purchases of equipment for colonial-linked suppliers. Other countries such as West Germany, and Japan have reserved markets which are not available to non-national suppliers.

The principal *constraining factor* as usual is the investment capital for the physical plant. The industrial and rapidly developing economies are able to self finance their tele-networks from revenues but the LDC's must depend on international debt and grant funds sources such as the World Bank, Arab Development Fund, United States AID, and the Inter-American Development Bank. The suppliers are also required to help alleviate this problem by extending purchase credit for six to sixteen years.

Supplier Competitive Strategies

The strategies that have been adopted by the equipment suppliers set out in the introduction have been organized in terms of Exhibit 37–1 in which performance reliability and local government involvement are viewed as critical. Connections exist between these two strategies and the others either through activity flow lines or feed back links. The strategies classified within each block in this diagram are strongly interlinked but can usefully be discussed by starting at the left side of Exhibit 37-1 with *equipment choice.*

EXHIBIT 37-1
SUPPLIERS COMPETITIVE STRATEGIES MODEL

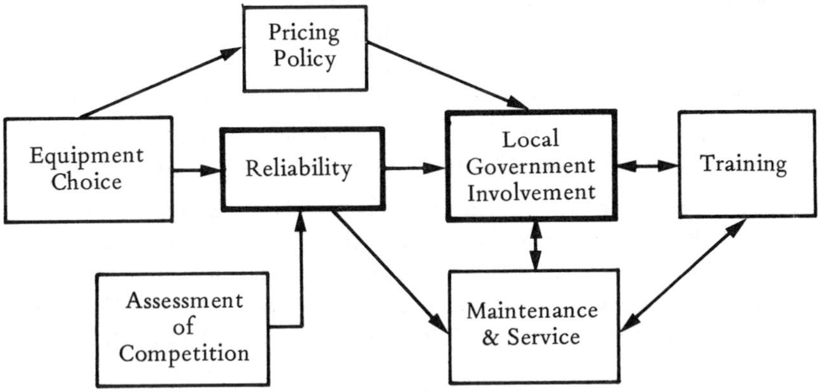

Equipment Choice

Among the more basic choices for equipment purchases that PTTs must wrestle with are: (a) computer controlled switching *vs.* electromechanical gear; (b) if computer switching is used will it be with contact point reeds or solid state switches; (c) ground trunk wires or ground microwave or satellite microwave for long distance links; (d) analog (voice frequency) or digital (pulsed) transmissions.

There are many companies selling various components for each choice in addition to the full-line companies which can handle entire tele-network in-stallations. Therefore an initial strategic choice for each supplier is: What type of equipment should be pursued in R&D efforts? A main avenue of technical competition has been in the development of faster, more reliable signal switching gear. The technical changes, starting in the 1920s with motor driven rotary switching racks, proceeded through several stages of electro-mechanical exchanges and has now come to the all-electronic stage of solid-state switching stations in which there are no moving parts. Most of the SPC switching stations in the present hotly contested contract competition have electro-mechanical reed switches, but are otherwise fully electronic. All major public exchange competitors have developed their version of an electronic exchange. The most recent European entry is the AXE for local exchanges. ITT has the Metaconta transit station. Nippon Electric Company now has the NEAX-61 which apparently can be adapted for either local or transit use. Plessey of the United Kingdom has had its electronic Pentex exchange in operation for over ten years in England.[12] Philips has the PRX 205, Siemens the EWS, Northern Telecom the SPI and GT&E the 1-EAX.

Even the smaller PTTs seem to prefer the new SPC exchanges. This phenomenon appears to be related to the previously mentioned maintenance savings, but it also involves an appreciation of some of the special properties of these exchanges in that:

a. Pulse code modulation (PCM) can then be used which allows lower cost signal compression. The different conversations are sampled and inter-leaved in a non-interferring manner, to achieve this improvement.

b. No interface converters (called modems) are necessary on the switching exchanges to convert digital signals being received from the subscriber equipment to and from analog signals which have normally been switched through the voice channel exchanges. Thus the exchanges are compatible with data traffic flowing between remote terminals and central computers.

The PTTs acting for their governments have regulatory power to specify the technical characteristics that equipment must meet to be acceptable to it and hence usable within its system. This regulatory power can have an irreversible effect on the development of the telecommunication systems. The govern-ment as a regulator is more than just customer choice. It locks in future sales as well.

The new electronic exchanges all work via stored program control, SPC, which means that each competitor has had to become at least, in part, knowl-edgeable in computer manipulation. Some have gone further and have merged with computer makers or have accomplished the same by other routes. It would seem to be a great advantage to be viewed now by the evaluating PTTs as having competence in the three fields of computers, their solid state com-ponents, and telecommunications. Companies fitting this pattern are:

Nippon Electric Company

Siemens

Hitachi

Philips

Exhibit 37-2 shows the three overlapping technical areas just described.[13] The four companies above have reputations for relatively large overlap areas (shown by crosshatching).

Both ITT and Ericsson seem to have steered away from deep computer involvement. It is then difficult to see how these two companies while they are the current market share leaders could offer complete expertise to set up a computer utility integrated with a host country's telecommunication network.

Assessment of Competition

Each supplier must continuously judge its standing relative to the field of competitors. This field is changing in composition. Several changes in the United States and in several other countries appear to be creating new rivals. Two separate events appear to have set the stage for the entrance of new United States suppliers. The first is that in the United States the regulatory agency, the Federal Communications Commission and the reviewing courts have since 1968 attempted to stimulate competition in communications. This has occurred through the "Carterfone" decision which allowed interconnec-

EXHIBIT 37-2

KEY TELECOMMUNICATIONS TECHNICAL AREAS – 1977

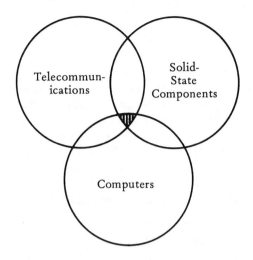

tion of non-Bell devices onto the AT&T network. The result has been the rapid growth of a vigorous new class of suppliers, particularly in the PABX, private automatic branch exchange, interconnection business. Corporations setting up new installations or revising telephone systems are no longer required to install Bell equipment. Many of these new PABX are SPC, solid-state switched devices which could easily be modularized and offered as small (1000-5000 line) public exchanges. Indeed, LM Ericsson has begun to modularize its AXE system so why not the same development from the PABX side.

Another FCC and court decision pattern, the MCI case, has allowed the emergence of specialized communication common carriers. These are carriers for high data traffic loads. These new carriers rent the use of the linkage needed for particular jobs, such as very high through-put on a microwave link once a week for batched data. These carriers may, in time, begin to test the international markets for data traffic equipment.

Another consequence of this "new order" in the United States market is that AT&T now appears to be looking at the international markets. The formation of American Bell International (ABI) in 1976 for such consulting is one step. ABI is providing recommendations for Iran's large program. Western Electric could be a formidable competitor in bidding competition.

Another more interesting market development here is that IBM has formed a joint venture with Comsat and Aetna Life and Casualty Company to engage in microwave telecommunications. This venture was approved by the United States FCC in mid-January 1977. This new company will be able to provide computer services to customers' remote terminals through satellite microwave communications. This is already a threat to ITT and the AT&T Long Lines Division.

The home Japanese market may be reaching a point of saturation at which the domestic suppliers will begin to push for more international business. A Singapore project has recently gone to Japanese companies and they are active in making sales in the Far East and in Africa. Korean and Taiwanese producers appear to be making inroads in the telephone set and cable areas. These entrants will likely intensify price competition.

Some PTT's demand local production participation as a condition of their purchases and these newly created producers can eventually reach export potential. The domestic production facilities being set up by the present suppliers as conditions to win contracts may eventually become competitors rather than remaining customers. Canada's Northern Telecom has already become one of the competitors. France will soon be in the position of a competitor. Brazil already is an exporter to other Latin American markets. Hungary has become a supplier to other COMECON countries following technology transfer from Sweden. Yugoslavia is developing a similar potential.

Reliability

This is a key strategy since the extremely rapid technical changes have outstripped the ability of all but the most highly skilled PTTs to evaluate the wide range of equipment choices. The decision makers in these agencies must be able to form trust bonds with some knowledgeable group. The supplier is one choice if the company can be relied upon to give trustworthy recommendations. There are several stages in this process. When a PTT releases a project request-for-bid the prospective suppliers must first show that they can meet the specifications set out. This is the qualification step or entrance fee and there are always several such suppliers so that sole-source contracts are unusual outside the military area. This requires the supplier to present convincing evidence of technical capability to perform.

The full line companies all have this present performance capability to varying degrees. Demonstrated past expertise is very important in order to stay in the contract award process. Part of the reason is that PTTs do not want to take the additional risks which are associated with newcomers. Questions of delivery times, quality control system functioning, interconnection to the existing network, maintenance, spare parts, and training for PTT operating personnel are all involved. These sum up to *supplier reputation*. It is an all important competitive tool and it is impossible to develop quickly.

Price Competition

Once the bidding supplier has demonstrated proof of technical performance its representatives then enter into discussions with the PTT which has let out the request-for-bid. During this negotiation phase the PTT requirements as to local involvement are specified and the potential supplier must closely study the pricing parameters. An important one, of course, is an assessment of the competition. Occasionally one or more suppliers are rejected from the award competition at this stage based either on technical ability, lack of commitment to provide service and maintenance at later stages, or lack of willingness to permit local involvement. The surviving competitors must carefully assess the likely price spread and adjust its own inputs so as to be just barely the lowest priced supplier who is fully acceptable to the PTT and its other government officials.

Local Government Involvement

PTTs and their associated governments are trying to pursue overall economic development goals when they make telecommunication investments. Often this means requiring some assembly, or testing, or parts production or all three to occur locally. In short the PTT pushes to become the entrepreneur.

Competitively several levels of bargaining are involved.

a. When a host country makes participation in sufficiently large orders contingent on opening a production plant or transferring in needed knowhow these steps must be taken by the supplier or that host country market will be lost.
b. There is usually some supplier who is willing to make the necessary inputs. It is only a question of bargaining position and rate of return.
c. Local production tends to lock in the host country network closer to the participating suppliers equipment. Thus there is a positive drive for the supplier to help the local production desires of the government.
d. Advanced notice of hosts plans for network expansion and local production is critical. Each supplier wants to be the first. Most suppliers have agents in continuous contact with the PTTs to provide an early warning scanning system. This may be giving way to the use of a team of roving top level executives who meet with the PTT management to discuss how they can help with the future development plans.

Maintenance/Servicing Requirements

The supplier must maintain and service his equipment. For if it becomes inoperative he may not get a chance to bid again. The supplier must push the PTT for adequate contract funds here.

One of the supplier's most important assets is a good reputation for the follow-on maintenance and services. Many PTTs know they cannot long survive without this ingredient, but the same applies to the suppliers.

One of the key aspects here is the training of PTT operating personnel to engage in *preventive maintenance*. This is an unknown practice in many countries which do not have a mechanical arts tradition. Thus, the provision of adequate training programs is a critical issue. The major suppliers have mastered this. It represents a barrier to entry by newcomers. The Japanese have not fared well here due to the language problems at the necessary operating levels.

If spare parts are only available for say twenty years after an initial installation of a public exchange then that is its life. All PTT plans for thirty years useful operations are meaningless. Refusal to continue supplying electromechanical parts for the older exchanges will hasten the drive to replace with the new SPC switching gear.

Training Needs

In general, the new SPC electronic systems require much more training by the supplier since greater technical complexity is involved. The new skills needed mean that much closer interworking between the PTT and supplier personnel is needed. Thus continuity of contact, fairness of dealing, and management contracting concepts appear to be important competitive elements.

There are several points remaining for this topic of training needs in view of the previous statements. The major competitors carry this function out in a highly systematic basis. New competitors must learn to do the same.

There is a brain drain effect in that when technicians are trained they leave their developing countries for higher paying jobs elsewhere. Saudi Arabia has pulled such technicians from Egypt, Jordan, Syria, and other Arab countries.

Training is, of course, part of technology transfer and since the training must become more intensive the nonhardware portions of the telecommunications sales should increase. Many of the changes discussed here call for increased attention to the softwares side of the product/service mix in this fast moving industry. Much more intensive and longer term training will probably be engaged in by all suppliers of electronic exchanges.

Linkage of Market Characteristics to Strategies

Information on the independent variable marketing factors is being continuously collected by the full line suppliers. This is then used as the inputs for deciding on competitive strategies as explained in connection with Exhibit 37-1 wherein supplier reliability and willingness to involve local government (or PTT) production participation are critical.

The key market characteristics are the *technology changes* and the *buyer decision criteria* since these are present in each of the strategy blocks of Exhibit 37-1. This indicates that technology utilization is a major variable for assessing intra-industry competitive choices and for determining buyer decisions. It also appears that the buyer decisions cannot be accurately predicted unless the impact of the technology changes on them can be understood. Other markets for technology-intensive products should give consideration to the perceptions of the buyers of the technical choices (and problems) being offered to them. This is particularly true when the buyer is an agency of a developing country and therefore will have economic development as its foremost objective. Willingness to help the buyer achieve this key objective is clearly an important route to making continuing sales over long time periods.

Applicability to other Markets

The market characteristics and competitive strategies identified herein may be of specific interest to students of industrial marketing. Those marketing executives dealing with sales to government enterprises may recognize the pattern of the purchasing agency first being only a customer and then successively becoming a producer for domestic consumption and then for export sales.

The various national governments can discharge some of their pledges to provide services and basic raw materials and energy for the nationals by acting only in the role of a customer as in the case of LDCs buying telecommunication gear. As the officials look for means to promote economic development the role of becoming the entrepreneur seems to be inevitable. The first step is to act as a regulator to define the technical and economic parameters of sales. Then as the experience in the French telecommunications has shown the government will move to expand production through a government controlled, hence favored, company.

The creation of successive generations of technical developments is of course necessary for the suppliers from industrial countries in order to keep ahead of this process. Also the suppliers must be willing to reproduce the productive capability for the past technical development within their customer's definition of economic development. This requires the emphasis of various means of effecting the transfer of technical production and corporate experience and knowledge to the customers. The software portions of the industrial sales for a wide range of industrial products should increase.

QUESTIONS

1. How have demand growth factors and technological changes affected the opportunity to internationally market telecommunications facilities and services?
2. Describe the strategies that have been used by equipment suppliers in response to these changing market characteristics.
3. How has PTT attempted to involve local government in its overseas operations?
4. How can the market characteristics and competitive strategies identified in this article be applied to other types of products and services?

NOTES

1. Wolfgang Friedmann, *The State and the Rule of Law in a Mixed Economy* (London: Stevens & Sons, 1971), p. 104.

2. The first estimate is by Henrik Frenkel, "LM:s bekymmer: Vad gor man med varldens basta produkt?" (LM Ericsson's dilemma: What does one do with the worlds best product?), *Veckans Affarer* (4 augusti 1977), p. 49.
    The La Blanc estimate appeared in Walter Guzzardi, "The Great World Telephone War", *Fortune* (August 1977) p. 144.

3. International Telecommunications Union, *Telecommunications Economic Studies— GAS 5 Manual,* 1976 edition (Geneva: ITU, 1976), Chapter 2, p. 31.

4. *Telecommunication: Sector Working Paper* (Washington, D.C.: World Bank, November 1971), pp. 22–23.

5. *The Economist* 259 (May 15, 1976), p. 86.

6. T. Larsson, "Background Report: I. Key-Address", *Conference on Computer/ Telecommunications Policy: Proceeding of the OECD Conference February 4-6 1975.* (Paris: Organization for Economic Co-operation and Development, 1976), p. 150.

7. V. Schnee and W.J. Gorkiewics, *The Future of AT&T* (Millburn, N.J.: Probe Research, Inc., 1976), p. 171.

8. Artur Attman, Jan Kuuse, and Ulf Olsson, *LM Ericsson 100 Years,* Vol. I (Stockholm: LM Ericsson & Co., 1977), p. 198.

9. Ronald Abler, "The Telephone and the Evolution of the American Metropolitan System" in Ithiel de Sola Pool (ed.) *The Social Impact of the Telephone,* (Cambridge, Mass.: MIT Press, 1977), p. 324.

10. James Martin, *Telecommunications and the Computer,* 2nd Edition (Englewood Cliffs, N.J.: Prentice-Hall, Inc., 1976), pp. 283–89.

11. Ingvar Roos, Dag Norrby, and Ingemar Leijon, "Telephone rates in various countries". *Tele,* Vol. XXVIII, Special Issue 1976 (Stockholm: Swedish Telecommunications Administration, 1976).

12. *Industrial Marketing* 61 (April 1976), front cover.

13. G.L. Jordan, *Report on the International Telecommunications Industry,* (Stockholm: Stockholm School of Economics, IIB, 1978), p. 60.

PROBLEMS AND PERSPECTIVES

International marketing is an evolving discipline and as such will continue to undergo reevaluation and restructuring. Some appreciation of the speed of this evolutionary process can be obtained by reviewing the international marketing scene. The first article by Peter P. Gabriel explores the worldwide economic and social disbenefits associated with the principal international marketing vehicle—the multinational corporation. Next Orville Freeman further elaborates on the social responsibility obligations associated with the tremendous power acquired by multinational firms. The unique moral and legal pressures inherent in the international market environment are treated by Subhash Jain in the section's third article. Jain provides a comprehensive analysis of the international bribery phenomenon and suggests some solutions to the dilemma posed for multinational marketers. Next the problems associated with penetrating the United States market encountered by less developed countries are discussed by Darling and Elsaid.

Since the 1950s, mutinational enterprises have served to promote global economic growth and integration on a scale that might never have been possible by political means. Today, the very nations that have most benefited from the MNCs, as well as others greatly in need of the resources they offer, are busy fencing them in—or out—with all manner of regulations and restrictions. The MNC's survival is not really in danger, the author asserts, but he does foresee far-reaching changes in their future role and mode of operation.

38. The MNC and the Public Interest

Peter P. Gabriel
Management Consultant

By the criterion of sheer growth, the multinational corporation (MNC) is surely one of the most remarkable institutional successes of all time. In barely two decades, it has become, by all accounts, the most formidable single factor in world trade and investment.

Beyond this, the MNC plays a decisive role in the allocation and use of the world's resources in general by conceiving new products and services, by creating or stimulating demand for them, and by developing new modes of manufacture and distribution. Current rates of energy consumption, for example, would be unthinkable without the role of large corporations (most of them MNCs) in the development and expansion of the automobile and electric appliance industries. Indeed, it is the MNCs that largely set the patterns and pace of industrialization in today's capitalist economies. Any major change in current patterns of world resource distribution and use will significantly affect their future; but at the same time, these patterns are unlikely to

---

Source: Reprinted by permission of the January-February, 1971, of the Journal of World Trade Law.

change very much as long as the MNCs continue to manage their operations primarily so as to maximize their shareholders' economic return.

To what extent will MNCs be able to affect resource flows and utilization in the years ahead? If pressures for a major reallocation of world resources are successful, and significant constraints are placed on MNC operations, how would such changes affect the efficiency of resource use? We can begin to think about answers to these questions by looking behind today's trends and assessing their probable future direction.

The Chemistry of Success

Most observers credit the past growth of MNCs to a number of inherent factors. These include their ability to sense and capitalize on production and market opportunities on a worldwide scale, mobilizing their unique technological, organizational and other resources wherever they can earn the highest return; to exploit international differentials in capital and labor costs; to avoid irksome government regulations by operating, so to speak, in the gaps between different national jurisdictions; to minimize taxes through intra-corporate transfer-pricing and other devices; and to gain competitive advantages by extending economies of scale across national boundaries.

Another factor, often ignored by the analysts, is the extraordinarily favorable environment in which the postwar rise of the MNC occurred. During the 1950s and 1960s, just when the MNC was achieving dominance, almost all the industrialized countries and many less developed countries (LDCs) were enjoying unprecedented rates of sustained economic growth. Especially for a foreign company, entering and developing new markets are tasks beset by fewer difficulties in rapidly expanding economies than in relatively stagnant ones.

Equally favorable to the spread of multinational enterprise were certain unique circumstances of the postwar period. Some of these circumstances specifically favored American companies. Quite apart from the nearly prostrate condition of most European industrial firms at war's end, the undeniable superiority of United States management skills (a result of more vigorous competition and longer experience with large-scale enterprise) helped to make the first waves of United States foreign direct investment highly successful, attracting more United States direct investors. At the same time, the increasingly overvalued condition of the United States dollar spurred American corporate investors to acquire overseas production facilities both to serve foreign markets and to fill their own domestic needs for components and finished products. Finally, at least through the Eisenhower years, America's world power and prestige encouraged United States corporations to exploit these advantages to the hilt.

By the late 1950s, with postwar reconstruction largely completed, first European and then Japanese companies entered the world market. They had quickly absorbed American managerial skills while developing highly competitive technologies of their own. As overseas investors, especially in the less developed world, they soon shared with American multinationals the competitive advantages peculiar to large corporations of worldwide scope: superior technical and organizational capabilities, international sourcing and distribution networks, ready assess to capital markets, and so on. Far from displacing the early entrants, the new arrivals further widened investment and market opportunities for MNCs generally.

Moreover, the spread of multinational enterprise benefited from a highly favorable ideological climate. In the home countries of the MNC during the 1950s and early 1960s, large corporations were not yet seriously under attack. Corporate actions were not yet significantly constrained by notions of corporate social responsibility. Issues like pollution, "export of jobs," impending resource scarcities, and indeed the whole controversy over economic growth were just beginning to come to public attention; legislative and regulatory concern was still years away.

In Europe, the full economic impact of this new foreign investment (mostly from the United States) had yet to be felt. But except in De Gaulle's France, the immediate benefits from the injection of entrepreneurship, technology and management skills were too apparent, and commitment to private enterprise too strong, for effective measures to be taken against the growing foreign corporate presence. In fact, as J. J. Servan-Schreiber argued in *Le Défi américain,* American multinationals decisively accelerated European economic integration.

No less favorable to the multinationals during the first two decades following World War II was the climate in the less developed countries. Economic and political dependence were still perceived as two sides of the same coin. International institutions like the United Nations, the World Bank and the International Monetary Fund, were dominated by the industrial nations. All these institutions, along with official foreign-aid agencies and almost the entire academic establishment of the West, were urging the developing nations to adopt economic development strategies based essentially on the Western industrial model.

Under this ideological umbrella, the MNCs flourished. Foreign-aid agencies tended to give short shrift to countries that were inhospitable to private foreign direct investment. The investors—almost all of them MNCs—were widely hailed as engines of growth, purveyors of better standards of living, necessary agents of change.

The worldwide drive for economic development produced its own performance cult. Accepted growth measures highlighted not only success but relative failure—and the laggards in the growth race were usually just those countries that had acted to discourage foreign private investment. Despite much controversy over the cause-and-effect relationships at work here, the view generally prevailed that MNCs were a positive force for economic growth.

A Change of Climate

Today all these conditions have altered drastically. American multinationals as a group have lost most of their advantages over their European and Japanese competitors. Disparities of size and technical capability have narrowed or disappeared. The United States no longer dominates the politics and economics of the non-socialist world. We are witnessing the birth pangs of a new world order, reflecting the continued standoff between the United States and Soviet superpowers, the resurgence of Europe and Japan, and the failure of military force as a means of advancing or protecting Western interests in third-world countries—a failure seen first in the Suez Canal fiasco of 1956 and conclusively demonstrated in the Vietnam debacle nearly twenty years later.

Just as significant have been the changes in the ideological climate. In the MNCs' home countries new standards have been imposed on corporate conduct. Public opinion has become more critical of the corporate pursuit of profit and growth, and government intervention more active. The very legitimacy of the corporation as such is no longer immune to challenge. In the words of one writer: "The corporate institution is undergoing attack from without and suffering lack of confidence within. The ideological foundations of the business society are being severely shaken."[1]

In the less developed countries, meanwhile, the MNCs have been confronted by changes far harsher and more overt. Rising nationalism, mounting political assertiveness toward the rich nations (stimulated by the United States—Soviet stalemate), a pronounced shift to the Left or to populism in most parts of the Third World, the rising expectations and the political ferment generated by the development process itself have steadily eroded the MNCs' welcome.

The impact of these political trends has been reinforced by new thinking about the development process in general and the role played in it by the foreign corporation—in particular, the so-called *dependencia* school of thought associated with the Chilean economist Osvaldo Sunkel. In effect, the proponents of the *dependencia* school argue that the orientation of local enterprises and infrastructures to the needs and interests of MNCs has prevented structural changes in host-country economies that would have led to better utilization of their resources, reduced their dependence on foreign inputs, brought about a far more equitable distribution of wealth and income and created truly indigenous stimuli to development.

National Sovereignty

This new intellectual rationale for curtailing the freedom of private foreign direct investors gained wide currency in the host countries at the same time that the political trends noted above were gathering force. Accordingly,

Third World countries, individually and collectively, have been ever more stridently proclaiming their sovereignty over their own resources, asserting their right to determine how these are being exploited, and insisting on control over the development of their own industries. Almost everywhere in the Third World, beneficent governmental attitudes and policies vis-à-vis the multinational corporation are a thing of the past. Concession agreements have been revoked in the extractive industries, foreign investments in basic industries like public utilities have been nationalized, divestment rules covering all foreign-controlled enterprises are in the process of being implemented by the Andean Pact nations, and subordination of MNC operations to host-country economic development plans has become very much the rule rather than the exception.

The end of MNC dominance in the Third World was perhaps most clearly signalled by the resolution entitled "The Charter of Economic Rights and Duties of States," overwhelmingly passed by the United Nations General Assembly in December 1974. One intent of this resolution is to establish the right of any nation, whenever it perceives its national interest to be at stake, to abrogate any and all agreements and international obligations protecting the interests of foreign investors. Obviously encouraged by the extraordinary success of the Organization of Petroleum Exporting Countries (OPEC), the resolution's sponsors set out to proclaim a new international economic order.

Widespread recognition of the need for a new international order has indeed been an important consequence of the "energy crisis." Signs that all was not well with the existing system had been in evidence at least since the late 1960s. Witness the gradual collapse of the Bretton Woods arrangements for international monetary affairs; the rather abrupt acceleration of worldwide inflation in 1972-73; the emergence of food shortages and other resource scarcities; the dangerous widening of the gulf between the rich and the poor countries; and the repeated failure of public policymakers to deal with these problems within the existing framework. Yet despite all these warning signals it took OPEC's successful quadrupling of oil prices to bring about broad public recognition that the time for a fundamental reordering of international economic relations had finally come.

New MNC Mission

How might such a new order affect the multinational corporation? Although we cannot yet predict the precise outlines of the international arrangements now in the making, there can be no doubt that the MNC will continue to have a vital role. For all the changes in its political and ideological environment, the MNC's inherent strengths as a large-scale, private enterprise remain unequalled. For a long time to come, the technological, managerial, entrepreneurial and logistical capabilities on which modern industry depends will continue to reside mainly in the private corporate sector, where existing industrial knowledge and techniques are continuously being refined and expanded through innovation.

The central imperative of today's technological society, to say nothing of tomorrow's, is the large organization. Only the large organization affords the economies and efficiencies of large-scale operations and specialization in development, production, distribution and delivery that are indispensable to provide the goods and services on which societies (both industrialized and industrializing) have come to depend.

International economic integration, both formal and *de facto,* have made nation-states interdependent, and the MNC is the institutional linchpin of that interdependence, providing three kinds of economic linkages: access to markets as both supplier and seller of raw materials, intermediate goods and finished products; access to the latest generation of technology (in the broadest sense); and international specialization of production through vertical integration across national boundaries.

The real question, then, is not whether the MNC will survive as a centrally managed, global institution, but under what conditions it will continue to perform its unique economic functions. In particular, how will the emerging issue of private corporate power versus the public interest be resolved? The United States, as the largest and most highly developed industrial nation, may well become the first in which this issue is clearly joined. As Blumberg writes: "The fundamental question is the relation between size and liberty. To what extent does the compounded concentration of economic power and control threaten the primacy of political decision-making by democratic institutions and the maintenance of social and political controls over the major centers of power, which are essential components of a free democratic society?"[2]

Viewed in this light, the large corporation is potentially as much under siege at home as abroad. Conceptually there is little difference between, for example, public-interest groups in the United States calling for drastic legal and regulatory reforms to make large corporations "more accountable," and foreign host governments seeking to restrict the freedom of MNCs. Generalizing, we can say that the corporation has attained a size, reach and influence such that its dominant function—a function which must ultimately override the pursuit of private purposes—must be recognized as the private management of public interests. And if this is true of national enterprises, it is doubly true of corporations whose reach is global.

Is Efficiency Enough?

Classical economic theory holds that the conflict between private and public interests is more apparent than real. In this view, the rational pursuit of private corporate benefit, given reasonably free markets, will allocate resources wherever they yield the highest return. Assuming, among many other things, that relative rates of return on resource commitments are proportional to local scarcities of such resources, the economist can prove with mathematical rigor that this process leads to optimal resource allocation—optimal in the sense of maximizing world output and hence world welfare. By this reasoning, the interests of the private corporation and those of the public are, in effect, identical: to support the one is to foster the other.

The trouble with this argument is that it rests exclusively on the criterion of efficiency. Quite aside from the increasingly pressing issue of business's social and environmental effects, negative or positive, it has nothing to say about the *distribution* of world income. And in fact the efficiency criterion has inevitably led MNC investment to favor the rich countries and neglect the poor. Of the more than $90 billion of private foreign direct investment in place by 1966, barely one-third was in developing countries, with petroleum and mining industries accounting for almost half of this portion. This distribution of MNC investments may well have resulted in greater total world output than a distribution skewed the other way. But it is a matter of record that the rich got richer and the poor poorer, relatively, as a result. The remarkable solidarity with OPEC demonstrated by virtually all the developing countries, including those most seriously affected by the explosion of oil prices, is only one of the many signs that the Third World is simply no longer willing to accept this dispensation.

But the notion of a basic identity between corporate and public interests is under attack in other contexts as well. In country after country, market-based criteria of resource allocation and use are being subordinated to socio-economic goals and priorities. Conceived through political processes and translated into national plans and budgets, such goals and priorities increasingly constrain the operating freedom of the private corporation. In the ideological battle between the advocates of the market mechanism and the proponents of central planning, the latter are steadily gaining ground.

Two practical reasons account for this trend. One is the prospect that resource scarcities may significantly change and slow down long-term patterns and rates of economic growth. Should this happen, public intervention seems certain to gain ascendancy over private business decision making as the different claimants on national income compete more and more aggressively for shares of a stagnant or shrinking product.

The other reason for the spread of political interference with the market system is the growing interdependence among economic sectors, as indeed, among nations. This interdependence, largely a consequence of the very power bred by the extraordinary success of the large corporation, gives many private corporate decisions a scope and impact unintended by the decision maker. What is new is not the nature but the consequences of these decisions (for example, the massive, MNC-induced movements of short-term funds during the international monetary crises of the early 1970s), and their concentration in relatively few companies. Similarly, the basic problem of the large corporation, especially the MNC, is not so much socially irresponsible behavior by individual managements as it is the total impact of their aggregate actions. (This impact, of course, is all the greater when these actions are taken in concert, as they frequently are—a result not necessarily of collusion but of identical information sources and similar habits of response.)

In any case, most governments (of whatever ideological stripe) can no longer refrain from concerning themselves with the political and social effects of private corporate decisions in a wide spectrum of areas: employment, prices, industrial development, industrial research and innovation, environmental protection, the country's balance of payments, its competitive position in foreign markets and its dependence on foreign resources. Such concerns are leading them to implement legislative, regulatory and national planning devices that are beginning to transform the private corporation into something like an executive organ of public policy. And the extraterritoriality of the MNCs, far from exempting them from this trend, makes them its first object.

New bargaining patterns

For all this, the large corporation still holds the trump card: Its many skills and capabilities are vital both to the maintenance and continuous development of existing industrial economies and to the creation of new ones. Even Communist countries regard the Western private corporation as an indispensable supplier of superior technological and managerial skills, international sourcing and distribution systems, and a host of other competitive strengths. That, at least, is the evidence of over a thousand agreements between Western companies and socialist economies—from simple "turnkey" contracts to complex "coproduction" arrangements and even joint ventures in third countries with MNCs.

It is essentially these unique assets of MNCs, not their financial resources, around which bargains are being struck. In general terms, the bargaining process may be described as follows:

While corporations compete for foreign investment opportunities, host governments in turn are competing for the benefits that only foreign private investments can supply. The price a given host government will be prepared to pay is a function of three variables: (1) how many foreign firms are competing for a given investment opportunity; (2) how urgently the potential contribution is thought to be needed; and (3) how readily (if at all) the same benefit could be obtained through local entrepreneurship, public or private. The terms acceptable to the MNC on the other hand, will depend on (1) its general need for an investment outlet; (2) the attractiveness of the opportunity in question, compared to others elsewhere; and (3) the extent of its prior commitment to the country concerned (such as an established market position).

It is evident that conditions in the international investment market have turned rather drastically in favor of the host countries. While more and more countries are becoming dependent on technology that only the large multinationals possess, the MNCs in turn are becoming more and more dependent on outlets for that technology. Even in such highly specialized areas as aircraft, nuclear reactors and computors, host countries are now able to shop around for the most favorable terms.

Thus, when the United States government turned down the application of Allende's Chile for credit to purchase Boeing 727s, France offered Caravelles and Russia Ilyushins. When Westinghouse Electric Corporation failed to persuade the United States government to relax its restrictions on the export of nuclear fuel processing technology, Brazil signed a $4.5 billion contract with Kraftwerk-Union and other West German firms. When IBM refused to enter into joint ventures with European companies, Control Data proved more adaptable.

The future framework within which the MNC performs its unique function will in part be shaped by certain trends that have been taking shape during the course of this shift in bargaining power.

> In Canada, Japan, and most developing countries, foreign ownership in individual companies and/or key industries is being limited to minority positions if not proscribed entirely. Current opposition to potential OPEC investments in industrial countries may well foster this tendency.

> Increasingly, in most developing countries, new projects undertaken with MNC participation are being conceived and executed as a part of national development plans, rather than in terms of conventional, market-oriented cost-benefit criteria.

> More and more, the financial risks of such projects are being assumed by host governments and other public agencies rather than private investors.

> The basic function of the MNC is shifting from the mobilization of capital for an entrepreneurial reward to the sale of its corporate capabilities for a managerial reward: pay for services rendered.

Foreseeable Impacts

If these trends continue, two sets of effects already in evidence will be accentuated. First, there will be further changes in the location or the availability of "economic rents" within the MNC's world-wide network of operations. The consequent changes in the structure of profit incentives will be reflected in the design of international corporate systems—which, in turn, affect national cost and price structures.

Second, we can expect an increasing proportion of the decisions governing international resource flows and allocations to be taken by governments rather than private corporations. Hence, more and more of these decisions will tend to be based on political rather than private market considerations.

Even though these changes tend to originate with local developments, the very nature of the MNC favors their swift transmission to other countries covered by the company's global system.

Changes in the sources of the MNC's profits are most apparent in oil and the other extractive industries. Historically, the oil industry's primary source of profits was low-cost crude production, chiefly from the OPEC countries. In order to sell their crude, the international oil companies built worldwide refining and marketing facilities "downstream" through which they could afford to move the finished product at little or no gain, thanks to the huge profits realized "upstream." Successive increases in royalties and taxes levied by producer countries, and their recent move to take over production facilities entirely, have removed the essential incentive for "downstream" subsidization and are forcing the companies to reexamine the practicability of continued vertical integration.

Growing host-government inroads into the MNC's freedom to design its own worldwide systems of production, supply and distribution are not confined to the extractive industries. In manufacturing, some countries are requiring MNC subsidiaries to produce for export in exchange for permission to produce for local markets. Others are insisting on local establishment of research and development facilities, the effective transfer of technology to local competitors, the creation of labor-intensive plants, or the manufacture of products which, though only marginally profitable, are required for national development. Such measures clearly affect not only the profitability of different components of the MNC's network but also their nature, location and development; the international flow of the inputs they need and the outputs they produce; and the associated costs and prices, internal and external.

To be sure, these trends have not been affecting all MNCs alike, nor have all MNCs proven equally vulnerable to government interference with the traditional form of foreign direct investment. The spectrum of susceptibility ranges from oil and other extractive industries as one extreme to high-technology companies like IBM at the other; among countries, it reaches from the pervasively restrictive policies of the less developed states (as well as some industrial economies like Canada, Australia and Japan) to the liberal policies of a country like Germany. But developments over the past few years suggest that the tide is running against the autonomy of the MNC. Its international role is shifting, more perceptibly than its domestic role, from the pursuit of private profit to the management of public interests as defined not by the "invisible hand of the market," nor by multinational corporate officials, but by national political will expressed through government action.

Dilemmas of Adaptation

These changes present the MNC with formidable challenges. It must learn to adapt its worldwide strategies and corporate systems to the requirements and

constraints of national political goals and economic plans. It must accommodate to the new institutional arrangements (like joint ventures and contractual relationships of various sorts and durations) that are displacing the
traditional mode of foreign direct investment. It must face up to the need to
revise or reverse some of its most basic assumptions: complete, long-term
control; the freedom to locate facilities and activities wherever most convenient; and the ability to take full advantage of inter-country cost, tax,
market-price and currency differentials through centrally designed and
managed financial arrangements and transfer-pricing mechanisms.

Is this challenge of institutional adaptation surmountable? The steadily
growing number of innovative devices for the commitment of foreign corporate capabilities in the less developed and Eastern socialist countries suggests that it is. But as these devices succeed and spread, the MNCs will find
themselves facing a far more complex dilemma. To the extent that they become captives of their host countries, they may be forced to act as instruments of conflicting host- and home-government policies. How can an MNC
respond both to Country A's prohibition against exporting jobs and Country
B's insistence on job creation through the export of labor-intensive goods
to Country A (among others)? Or, in the strictly political sphere, to the Arab-
Israeli conflict or the likes of the United States Trading-with-the-Enemy Act?
Whose jurisdiction should be recognized by a company like IBM, which operates in one hundred twenty-six countries overseas, has twenty-three plants
in thirteen countries, and eight development laboratories in as many
countries?

In the halcyon years of the MNC's postwar growth, the implicit answer
to this question could be, in effect: "None—or whichever best serves its interests." Most governments lacked the strength, the independence, or were
too little aware of their own power to challenge the power of the MNCs. In
this setting, MNCs did not only influence national economic policy in many
host countries. They functioned, almost in world government fashion, as a
mechanism for the international allocation of a steadily increasing portion of
the world's resources, including technology. If nationalism had been as potent a
force in the immediate postwar period as it is today, the MNCs would hardly
have attained their present dominance. And, arguably, international trade and
investment and world economic growth would not have burgeoned as they did.

In the event, thanks to American political hegemony, third-world impo-
tence and host-country governmental inexperience in general, the multinationals very largely had the field to themselves—and the way they responded to the opportunity resulted in a degree of global economic integration that probably could not have been brought about by political means.
In so doing, the MNCs had no need to worry about reconciling the conflicting aspirations of different host countries. They could meet any challenge to
their legitimacy simply by pointing to the manifest efficiency of their activities in terms of expanding world product.

Efficiency vs. Expediency

The twin issues of host-country jurisdictional authorities and of the legitimacy of supranational corporate power have now become paramount. As suggested earlier, the position of the MNC vis-à-vis its home country and its many host-nation constituencies is part and parcel of the larger issue of the private corporation in modern society. Both nationally and internationally, the question is this: Should corporations continue to determine patterns of economic growth, resource allocation, income distribution, and a country's degree of dependence on foreign resources and markets, based on the premise that the market choices of amorphous multitudes of consumers ultimately express their social preferences? Or should political decisions intervene? At its root, this is the conflict between, on the one hand, maximizing efficiency alone and, on the other, maximizing a wide variety of social goals of which efficiency is not necessarily the most important—for instance, political autonomy, and the self-determination of national welfare priorities (including the distribution of income and economic opportunity).

Traditionally, the MNC's main claim to legitimacy has rested on the optimization of global economic efficiency through international specialization and central management of production. To the extent that this claim is undermined, the MNC must establish its legitimacy by contributing effectively to the accomplishment of national goals. But, as we have seen, the goals of host countries frequently conflict, and where they do the MNC, as their actual or perceived instrument, can gain acceptance in one country only by sacrificing it in another. For example, where MNCs have yielded to host-country pressure to transfer manufacturing operations from home to host countries, organized labor at home has been able to press that much more effectively for government regulation of MNC international operations.

Public sentiment in the United States and other MNC home countries, which has long favored more government regulation of large corporations in general, is being decisively strengthened by growing public awareness of the MNC's international operations and their domestic repercussions. Most obviously, revelations of corporate participation in political subversion overseas, large-scale bribery, and the use of foreign subsidiaries to conceal illegal domestic activities have been grist for the anti-corporate mill.

The Public Interest Criterion

Given these environmental forces, the larger the corporation becomes (either absolutely or relative to its host environment), the more likely it is to become the manager or agent of public interests defined by government policy rather than private corporate objectives. Left to their own devices and guided solely by standards of globally efficient production, MNCs would not now be building petrochemical manufacturing capacities in OPEC states (almost certainly affecting the potential expansion of their home plants), or steel plants in Africa, or nuclear reactors in Brazil, or a diesel-engine plant in Colombia. All of these projects are underwritten or sponsored by governments; none was initiated by an MNC. All obviously serve goals and purposes other than the maximally efficient utilization of international resources.

The steadily expanding intervention of governments in the decision-making process of multinationals is leading to renewed calls for international agreements to regulate the actions of both companies and governments. But the prospects of firm agreements along these lines appear unpromising: to-day's nation-states are far too diverse in their political and economic interests, their relative economic and social developments, their need for the benefits MNCs can provide, and their willingness to pay the economic and political price of these benefits. Above all, the relative bargaining power of both host and home countries, and their perceived self-interest, are changing too rapidly.

The likelier prospect, then, is that bilateral relationships between MNCs and national governments will continue. Probably with growing involvement by their home governments, individual companies will continue to bargain with host governments for better investment outlets, for access to markets, and over assets already committed. Individual host governments will con-tinue to bargain with multinationals (and, increasingly, their home govern-ments) for their resources and capabilities.

Costs and Consequences

The transfer of private corporate functions of entrepreneurship and risk tak-ing to public institutions that are not directly subject to "the discipline of the market" will no doubt produce some of the worst results prophesied by MNC spokesmen and conservative economists. There will be less efficiency in resource use; indeed, there will be even more significant waste of resources. But the costs of such waste must be seen in perspective. It is at least arguable that in the long run governmental control over MNC investments and opera-tions, particularly by host governments, is more likely than not to expand the effective transfer of real resources and technology where they are most needed, simply by making the MNC both more acceptable and more account-able within the individual country. This situation, if it comes about, might well be less conducive to polarization, especially between rich and poor coun-tries, than the MNC's traditional mode of operation has proved to be.

Obviously, the evolving institutional arrangements for MNC operations cannot safeguard the world from national or international strife. But they are less likely than traditional forms of foreign investment to deteriorate into a *casus belli*. And the costs of resource suboptimization, misallocation, or even outright waste, would be a small price to pay if they could markedly lessen the likelihood of future wars.

QUESTIONS

1. What factors are identified by the author underlying the success of American multinational corporations?
2. What changes in these factors have altered the current "climate" for American multinational corporations?
3. What does the author foresee as the new mission of multinational corporations?
4. What will the future operating framework of multinational corporations be like? What impact will this have on the long term viability of these corporations?

NOTES

1. Philip I. Blumberg, *The Megacorporation in American Society*, Englewood Cliffs, N.J., Prentice-Hall, 1975, p. 177.

2. *Ibid.*

*The demand for a multinational corporation
to undertake careful and objective analyses
of its impact on host countries has never
been greater. This article identifies the large
number of constituencies and array of issues
that a multinational management team must
be sensitive to in developing pre-active rather
than reactive corporate strategies. Illustrations of how positive actions by companies
have contributed to their overseas successes
are also provided.*

39. Analyzing Corporate Impact: Some Innovative Approaches

Orville L. Freeman
Business International Corporation

At Business International we have come to recognize that the multinational corporation, because of its effectiveness and power, has acquired an array of constituencies to which it must be responsive. This is no longer a matter of choice, although of course many choices have to be made about the nature and structure of the response. But failure to recognize that these constituencies exist and warrant a corporate interaction is always costly and sometimes perilous.

We have attempted to pinpoint the publics and issues that represent the major constituencies at this time. The graph in Exhibit 39-1, which was developed for BI's research report on "Corporate External Affairs: Blueprint for Survival," illustrates our findings.

Source: Copyright © 1976. "The Management of International Corporate Citizenship,"
Top Management Report by the International Management and Development Institute
and the U.S. Department of State, Bureau of Educational and Cultural Affairs (now
the International Communication Agency's Associate Directorate for Educational and
Cultural Affairs).

EXHIBIT 39-1
MAJOR CORPORATE CONSTITUENCIES AS IDENTIFIED BY BI

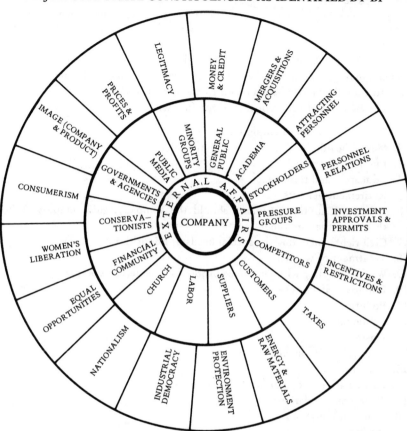

Pre-Action vs Reaction

We are also convinced that it is better corporate strategy to pre-act than to react.

A fine example of pre-action is Caterpillar Tractor Co.'s "Code of Worldwide Business Conduct," which gives that company what in politics would be described as a "platform." From comments and inquiries that have reached us, we know that the Caterpillar Tractor Code has touched a chord in the hearts and minds of the company's constituencies and competitors.

We believe that the drafting of such codes is not only an effective but also a very useful exercise. It prompts a company to examine just what its goals and motives are: what it does; why it does it; how it does it; and what kind of relationships it wants to build, and is building, with all the participants in the corporate enterprise, from employees to customers, stockholders to host and home governments.

The Caterpillar Tractor Code is one innovative approach to appraising the changing external environment and dealing with it effectively. Another is the "social audit," which breaks down a company's many-faceted social activities into measurable categories that can be stated, rewarded, and enforced.

The British Oxygen Company (BOC) has devised such an audit. Its components may be useful to other firms, although of course each company will have to compile its own list and allocate its own priorities.

The BOC social audit consists of the following:

1. Safety and health of employees.
2. Mental health.
3. Employment policies.
4. Education and training.
5. Retirement benefits.
6. Leisure. (Can the company, should the company, guide employees in their use of leisure time?)
7. Civil rights, including the special needs of minorities.
8. Treatment of women.
9. Welfare (dealing with employee problems outside the workplace).
10. Employee attitudes.
11. Pollution.
12. Public safety.
13. Waste.
14. Physical environment.
15. Use of land.
16. Participation in community affairs.
17. Government relations.
18. Consumer relations.
19. Profits.
20. The company's business image.

At Business International we believe that "corporate citizenship" is not only a concept but a reality, with very concrete action points.

For a multinational corporation, acting as a good citizen in both home and host countries is a matter of considerable complexity, but the problem can be distilled into four guiding objectives:

1. To prove by the company's actions the overall value of its business operation in each country in which it is active.
2. To conduct the business of each subsidiary with concern for the national economy of the host country.
3. To maintain communications with the authorities and the opinion groups of each country.
4. To recognize local regulations, traditions, and practices in employee relations, and to provide opportunities for local technicians, professionals, and executives.

The Corporation Balance Sheet

An innovative way of translating these actions into effective communication is "the corporate balance sheet," in which a company or a group of companies present an objective picture of the gains and losses their activities produce for the host country.

Clark Equipment Company

This corporation issues an annual "foreign investment balance sheet" which states, in figures, the company's contributions to host countries in terms of employment benefits (such as salaries and training costs); strengthening of the local economy (e.g., taxes, import duties, purchases from local suppliers, credit granted to those suppliers) and the balance of payments.

Johns-Manville

This corporation is using an interesting approach in Iceland, where the company has a 49 percent interest in a diatomite mining venture, with the government as majority partner. They asked a firm of local consultants to marshall the facts regarding the impact of the venture on the island's regional and national economy and social structure—after three years of operation. The results were stated in a balance sheet going beyond the usual concepts of foreign exchange gains from capital inflows and increased export earnings. The quantifiable factors set forth included: output in quantities and value; the venture's foreign exchange earnings; paid wages; and profit, including interest. Also mentioned were taxes, public charges, and purchases by the plant—of power, finished goods, raw materials, and services. The balance sheet demonstrated that about 40 percent of the investment costs were spent in Iceland with approximately two thirds of the venture's purchases being of local origin.

The report also showed the indirect effects of the project's activities on the immediately surrounding local region—including new home and school construction, increased purchases from local retail shops, tripling of local harbor traffic, and new lighting and central heating systems for the town, plus a marked increase in local tax revenues.

The report indicated that the joint venture was a cornerstone in building up a more balanced and diversified economy in the country as a whole and in the province where the plant was located, with a major contribution coming from increased exports of manufactured goods. Also, the plant was utilizing other Icelandic productive factors to their benefit. Finally, according to the consultants, the greatest benefit to the country over the long term would be the experience gained by Icelanders in the utilization of their own raw materials and geothermal energy.

The findings of the report were favorably mentioned in the local press and on television. When, some months later, a leftist cabinet came to power in Iceland and announced a reorganization of the manufacturing sector, no negative pressures were put on the mining venture and Johns-Manville

EXHIBIT 39-2

The BI checklist

Capital Contributions

1. *Original capital, loans from parent, and reinvested profit,* added to local capital accumulation, speed development, strengthen the local balance of payments.

2. *Trademarks, patents, and know-how* bring in years of research and development.

3. *Local loans* channel savings into wealth-producing projects, stimulate savings.

4. *Local equity capital* channels savings into wealth-producing operations, strengthens the stock market.

Other Contributions

1. *New ideas* represent inputs of technology, new products, marketing organization, business experience.

2. *People trained locally.* Both local managers and technicians, as well as skilled workers, are developed, creating stable middle class, speeding economic development.

3. *Output.* A new venture supplies goods, otherwise unavailable or available at greater expense and/or in smaller quantities, develops local resources.

4. *Import savings* displace foreign exchange losses otherwise incurred to bring in finished goods.

5. *Exports* contribute to country's foreign exchange earnings, provide worldwide marketing network.

6. *Taxes paid* finance government and development.

7. *Wages and salaries* raise employment and living standards, create purchasing power, add tax revenue.

8. *Purchases from ancillary industries* spur local industry, develop diversified local suppliers, in turn raising incomes, tax revenues, and development.

9. *Other local expenditures* stimulate all types of service industries, from insurance and banking to shipping and advertising, raising incomes, tax revenues, and development.

10. *Local dividends paid* strengthen purchasing power, savings.

11. *Stimulus to other foreign investors.* Capital inflow shows confidence in country and encourages further inflow or slows capital flight.

12. *Stimulus to local investors.* A foreign venture enlarges the local market; provides skilled managers, technicians, and workers through transfers among companies; often sets efficiency model; creates confidence in the economy.

13. *Contributions* to charities, education boost social infrastructure.

14. *Working conditions.* Foreign-owned plants usually set standards for worker facilities, plant improvement.

15. *Standard of living.* Foreign ventures make more and better products at lower cost.

Negative Factors

1. *Remittances* of dividends, royalties, fees, interest, and other payments detract from balance of payments.

2. *Materials and components imported,* while cutting import bill for finished products, generally increase overall bill as more semi-manufacturers and raw materials are required.

3. *Damper on local investors.* Fear of "big and powerful" foreign investors sometimes creates antagonism in local manufacturers, who worry about their competitive position.

4. *Lack of local understanding.* Foreign subsidiaries generally are managed in worldwide terms rather than in the interest of any one country (but foreign firms know that success of local operations depends on the stability and strength of the local market).

concluded that it should sponsor a second balance sheet report after another period of years.

Joint Effort in Brazil

Yet another tack was taken by a group of eighteen United States and European manufacturing and banking firms with operations in Campinas, Brazil, who got together to produce a *joint* balance sheet. First, they added up their own employees and the employees of their suppliers of goods and services and discovered that the eighteen investments had created and were maintaining 40,595 jobs, on which another 120,583 people were dependent. That is, more than 161,000 Brazilians were benefiting from the existence of the eighteen operations.

Next, they computed their total annual payroll (Cr 13.2 billion); the total purchasing power created in Brazil (Cr37 billion); the total tax and social charges paid (Cr11.5 billion); and the savings in foreign exchange generated during the year under study ($125.6 million). This total figure reflected the $134.6 million Brazil would have had to spend to import the products the eighteen firms produced and sold in Brazil, plus total exports of $2.9 million, minus imported components and equipment of $12.9 million. The companies presented their results as a contribution to the task of restoring confidence in Brazil's once sanguine investment climate, which has needed reinforcement in the past several years.

Conceptual Checklist

BI has drawn up a conceptual checklist for the development of such corporate balance sheets. It is offered here because we believe that the corporate balance sheet is an innovation whose time has come.

QUESTIONS

1. What does the author mean by a pre-active as opposed to reactive corporate strategy?
2. How can multinational corporations positively and negatively affect the constituencies identified in the article?
3. How can strong "corporate citizenship" contribute to the success of a multinational corporation?

International bribery is currently one of the most difficult ethical problems confronting marketing executives. This article reviews the payoff syndrome in terms of its rationale, types, and the nature of the remedial actions that have been pursued. Implications for marketing managers are developed along with a proposed code of conduct.

40. What Happened to the Marketing Man When His International Promotion Pay-Offs Became Bribes?

Subhash C. Jain
*University of
Connecticut*

Marketers live in a changing environment. They must cope with economic changes, technological developments, changes in life style and political happenings. Additionally, a new type of change has emerged, a change in the morality and ethics of corporate payoffs in generating sales overseas.

Recent disclosures of payoffs by some United States companies in pursuit of overseas sales raise the question of what should be done. Since payoffs have been considered necessary to obtain past contracts, it is now reasonable to expect they can be eliminated? The dilemma facing a marketing executive abroad appears to be irreconcilable. While operating in countries where bribery and kickbacks are an accepted business practice, existence and survival require adherence to a code of ethics different from the one used back home. What may the marketing man do to resolve this dilemma?

Source: Subhash Jain, "What Happened to the Marketing Man When His International Promotion Pay-Offs Became Bribes?" Reprinted with permission from Peter J. LaPlace (editor), *The New Role of the Marketing Professional,* 1978, pp. 138–145, published by the American Marketing Association.

This paper reviews the payoff syndrome, i.e., different forms of payments and the involvement of United States multinational corporations (MCN) in making these payments. The paper deals with payments in violation of both law and ethics which constitute bribes. Over a hundred corporations, some sixty-five of which are on the Fortune 500 list, have revealed making such payments. Further, various solutions such as legislative measures and adoption of a code of conduct, which have been advanced to resolve the payoff problem, are examined. The remainder of the paper deals with the managerial action necessary for resolution of bribery problems. This is based on interviews concerning questionable payments which the author conducted with thirty-five international marketing executives.

Review of the Payoff Syndrome

No other event in the area of international business had drawn more attention in the past two years than the questionable payments to generate overseas sales. It is these payments that led to a variety of charges against monarchs and politicians around the globe. Prince Bernhard of Netherlands was charged for his "unacceptable" behavior in his dealings with the Lockheed Corporation. Prime Minister Tanaka of Japan was indicted on charges of having established a Hong Kong "cover" company to launder illegal funds from Lockheed Corporation. An Italian Premier, A Tory cabinet minister in Britain, a former Defense Minister of West Germany and many others were mentioned as being involved in receiving bribes from multinational corporations for their help in obtaining sales contracts.

While over a hundred United States corporations have confessed to making illegal payments overseas, one corporation that stands out is the Lockheed Corporation. Since 1970, Lockheed has paid $202 million in commissions and fees abroad to obtain $3.8 billion in foreign sales, of which $22 million eventually reached officials of foreign governments or airlines.[1] It should be noted, however, that United States (MNCs) are not alone in making questionable payments. There is enough evidence to suggest that companies like Dassault and Siemens have set a brisk pace in the use of bribery, and there is no indication of Europeans being reluctant to accept bribes.[2]

Why Payoffs?

Why do companies pay huge sums of money to generate sales overseas, and why do people accept such payments? There are two types of factors that lead to such payoffs which may be designated: (a) home-country factors and, (b) host-country factors. Exhibit 40-1 lists factors which lead United States executives to make payments in doing business overseas. Arguments advanced to justify bribes can be grouped into two types. One, the realities of the marketplace desire that such payments be made to best competition and to achieve sales goals. For example, Bowman found that almost two-thirds

---

EXHIBIT 40-1

Home-country factors responsible for bribes

Cost of doing business in certain countries.

An established practice in certain countries no other way to get around.

Encouragement by Pentagon to buy "influence" (to pursue Atlantic Alliance).

Importance of hiring middlemen services in certain countries—to bridge between medieval aristocracies and modern corporations.

Increasing competition in international markets.

Pressure from top management to achieve results.

Opportunity to protect undercover operations via Swiss banks.

---

of the managers surveyed feel under pressure to compromise personal standards to achieve organizational goals.[3] Thus, in their endeavours to meet sales quotas, they resort to payment of bribes. Two, "while in Rome, do as the Romans do," i.e., inherent sociocultural environment of certain countries makes such payments not only desirable but essential. As Bowman states:

> *The fuss about bribery is naive, and that any realistic businessmen knows that bribing is part of the process of bridging two cultures. Where, after all, does bribing begin and end? What is the real distinction between social corruption—the lavish dinner party, the pot of caviar—and the passing of money into secret bank accounts? Both are concerned with creating what Lockheed described in the case of Prince Bernhard as a "climate of goodwill." And Lockheed's generosity in Europe and Japan was in the context of the Atlantic Alliance, which was the accepted policy of all government concerned.*[4]

The host-country factors are summarized in Exhibit 40-2. Unfortunately, American standards of morality and fairness are neither understood nor appreciated overseas. In addition there is a gross misunderstanding about the working of a modern corporation (which is, to an extent, true in the United States as well). To most people overseas, the MNC makes enough money on a deal so that they consider acceptance of a bribe lightly, giving it the label of

---

EXHIBIT 40-2

Host-country factors responsible for bribes

Lure of easy money.

Political involvement in decision making.

Token of appreciation.

Friendly gesture.

Fair "business" deal.

Pressure from vendors.

---

appropriateness via their own customs and practices of gift-giving. Further, the American economic and political hegemony over the world is a matter of jealousy for many people over the globe. These people would like to squeeze as many benefits for themselves as possible, through any feasible means, be it in kind or cash, from an American "institution" that happens to get involved with them. Interestingly, when people demand or accept bribes abroad, they use their own customs and standards; but when a deal becomes public, they are quick to put the whole blame on the American corporation. Surprisingly, more often than not, the Americans are themselves quick to take their own corporations to task for any wrong-doing overseas, whatsoever. Drucker notes:

> The crime of the multinational corporation is that it is not (also) an instrument of American morality. It eludes the populist critic that the multinational corporation cannot fulfill either of these functions because it operates in a myriad of cultures and under diverse environmental-economic, sociological, political, and governmental constraints. In consequence, it must fit itself to the prevailing legal and moral beliefs of the political sovereignty in the country where it operates.[5]

Types of Payoffs

Business bribes are made in different ways and are called by varying names in different parts of the world. Exhibit 40-3 depicts four categories of bribes. The facilitating bribes usually involve small sums of money and can perhaps be ignored. In many countries, facilitating payments are a part of the culture and thus must be lived with to expedite bureaucratic operations and paper work, and to trim the inherent delays. In other words, the facilitating bribes lie outside the present area of serious concern about corporate behavior. It is the middleman commissions, political contributions and cash disbursements which are in violation of both law and custom, and cannot be condoned. No matter whether a country's laws are based on common law or code law, such bribes constitute crimes and are subject to criminal charges. The payment of such bribes is handled through fictitious salary accounts, proceeds of the sale of raw materials, refunds (fees, salaries, commissions), slush funds and so on. Usually payment of such bribes is not entered in the corporate books. Such bribes continue to stimulate concern about corporate behavior.

Remedial Actions

Basically, five different types of actions have been proposed to assure ethical conduct by multinational corporations with reference to questionable payments. These are: regulatory, legislative, diplomatic, code of conduct, and corporate action.

EXHIBIT 40-3

Major types of bribes

a. Facilitating
   Payments

Disbursement of small amounts in cash or kind as tips or gifts to minor government officials to expedite clearance of shipments, documents or other routine transactions. Example: "In India not a single tile can move if the clerk's palm is not greased. Distribution of *bustarella* (an envelope containing a small amount of money) in Italy to make things move in an inefficient and chaotic social system."

b. Middlemen
   Commissions

Appointment of in-between people as middlemen (agents and consultants) to facilitate sales in a non-routine manner, and payment of excessive allowances and commissions to them which are not commensurate with the normal commercial services they perform. Often, the middlemen may request that part of whole of his commission be deposited in a U.S. bank or a bank in a third country. Example: Northrup Corporation's payment of $30 million in fees to overseas agents and consultants, some of which was used for payoffs to government officials to secure favorable decisions on government procurement of aircraft and military hardware.

c. Political
   Contributions

Contributions which take the form of extortion since they are in violation of local law and custom. Also payments which while not illegal are specifically made with the intent of winning favors directly or indirectly. Example: Gulf Oil Corporation's payment of $3 million in 1971 to South Korea's Democratic Republican Party under intimidation and threat.

d. Cash
   Disbursements

Cash payments made to important people through slush funds or in some other way usually in a third country (i.e., deposit in a Swiss bank) for different reasons such as for obtaining a tax break, a sales contract, or for getting preferential treatment over a competitor. Example: Payment of $2.5 million to Honduran officials by United Brands Company for the reduction of export tax on bananas via Swiss bank accounts.

Regulatory Action

The regulatory action has been promulgated by the SEC vis the completion of two forms titled B-K and 10-K. The 8-K form is required to be completed by companies monthly to provide all financial information which may be considered *material*. The 10-K form seeks detailed information on the previously unreported legal, business and financial activities of a company which may be considered material information from the investor's point of view.

Unfortunately, the term "material" has been defined rather vaguely by the SEC. For this reason, the SEC's action has met with many rebuttals. Assume, for example, that a company with annual sales of $3 billion and net income of $140 million happens to contribute $20,000 to a political party overseas. The $20,000 is trivial for such a large corporation and how disclosure of this payment would help the investor is difficult to understand.

Legislative Action

A variety of suggestions have been made to enact legislation to eliminate overseas payoffs. Some members of the Congress have suggested that bribery overseas be made a crime in the United States. This type of legislation, however, may not mitigate the problem. It would leave foreign nationals employed abroad by United States companies free to disperse money as they see fit.

Senator Frank Church's subcommitttee on multinational corporations would require manufacturers to report all payments to foreign officials in connection with the sale of arms to the State Department. This suggestion may not prohibit payoffs, but would vitually ensure that they become public knowledge. This would simply embarass government officials in foreign countries where such payments may be legal but are discreetly handled. In brief, no legislative action has been worked out that may provide a satisfactory solution to the bribery problem in doing business abroad.

Diplomatic Action

In some quarters it is felt that the Department of State can play a dominant role in preventing overseas payoffs. This can be achieved by making firm statements through diplomatic channels overseas that the United States government will protect United States MNC's against extortionate demands. This route might work if only minor officials and bureaucrats are involved in the payoff "game." But when Presidents, Prime Ministers, Princes and other high-ranking persons are involved; strong statements by the Department of State may backfire.

Codes of Conduct

In many quarters, demands have been made for a form of generally accepted code of conduct for MNCs to follow. In mid-1975, the OECD (Organization of Economic and Commercial Development) assigned its committee on International Investment and Multinational Enterprises the task of developing a code of conduct. At the OECD Ministerial meeting in June, 1976, guidelines were adopted which provide for both multinational corporations behavior and host-country behavior, but carry no sanctions for violators. Specifically, the OECD code for conduct spells out as follows on corporate payoffs:

> *Enterprise should not render—and they should not be solicited or expected to render—any bribe or other improper benefit, direct or indirect, to any public servant or holder of public office. Enterprise should, unless legally permissible, not make contributions to candidates for public office or to political parties or other political organizations.*[6]

Other international and regional organizations have developed instruments regarding norms of corporate behavior. The report of the United Nations Group of Eminent Persons titled "The Impact of Multinational

Corporations on Development and on International Relations" covers various issues related to MNCs in a general but comprehensive way. The United Nations' Commission on Translational Corporations is expected to finalize a code of conduct on transnational corporations in 1978. The Organization of American States (OAS) has also conducted preliminary work on a code of conduct.

The above codes of conduct are too general to fully address the bribery problems which a company may confront in its overseas dealings. Giuzzardi states:

> *The corporations do not defend their actions with the inadmissible argument that "everybody does it." None of them says that it had to act as it did or the corporation would have been hard hit in the competitive struggle. The examples simply represent the actualities of business life abroad. Even in the remotest cultures—Lesotho, perhaps, or Rwanda—there are rights and wrongs on extremes. But how do you judge in the gray areas—where most companies work?*[7]

The following quote from *The Wall Street Journal* makes the point explicit:

> *In France, the export-conscious defense ministry is nicknamed "Ministry of Bribes." Over the years, allegations of payoffs by Dassault, the French aircraft maker, have been aired in the Dutch Parliament, a Swiss military tribunal and the British press.*
>
> *In West Germany, Bonn's tax collectors permit resident corporations to deduct foreign bribes, known as "sonderspesen" or "special expenses"; interviews of German executives by Business International Corporation turned up a finding that "companies dislike the practice, disapprove of it, but adjust to local requirements."*
>
> *In Britain, corrupt payments even to British Government officials qualify for tax deduction.*[8]

Corporate Actions

The question of bribes lends itself to no easy remedies. The adoption of a code of conduct would generally make corporations move cautiously in various matters. Nonetheless, for general reasons, it is hard to believe that a code of conduct will result in infusing a spirit of "total" morality among all concerned.

In an increasingly diverse world, common acceptable standards on matters of value judgement are even more unlikely. To illustrate the point, the U.N. group that is preparing a code of conduct for MNCs is coming under pressure from socialist and Third World nations for a double standard. These countries want the code of conduct to apply only to privately owned multinationals, not state companies. Brazil, (whose state-owned multinationals include Petrobras, the oil giant; Banco do Brasil, the bank of Brazil; and the mining giant, Cia. Vale do Rio Doce) is one country pushing for the double standard. One major unanswered question raised by such a standard would be the position of each major state-controlled multinationals as Britain's British Petroleum, France's CII, and Italy's ENI.[9]

What can corporations do amidst this welter of complex issues and questions? Unfortunately, no simple and effective prescription is at hand. Perhaps the most important implications from all of the foregoing discussions is that each company should devise its own strategy to deal with the bribery problem. There are companies which are competitively well placed via their technological or engineering capabilities. These companies can conveniently resist bribery pressures as a matter of corporate policy. But there are other companies, thousands in number, who lack the size and market position. What can they do to adopt a bold moral stance against bribery and corruption? In their case, the answer is simple. The top management of these companies should establish realistic goals which may be realized by people in the field without compromising to corrupt practices. A number of companies have devised their corporate codes of conduct and implementation programs to prevent unethical practices in their realm of operations. Exhibit 40–4 illustrates Dynalectron Corporation's perspectives in this behalf.

EXHIBIT 40-4

An illustration of corporate policy on payoffs

International Relationships

Recognizing the international nature of our business and our commitment to be good citizens of the world community, the following is a Corporate Statement of Policy regarding payments to foreign government officials or employees:

1. It is against the policy of the Company to authorize, encourage or tolerate unlawful payments by the Company, directly or indirectly, to foreign government officials.

2. The Company shall not knowingly pay or incur liability for, or enter into any agreement or understanding to pay or incur liability for, any unlawful fee, commission, payment or consideration, to any foreign sales agent, representative, or consultant ("foreign representative") or other person that, directly or indirectly, in whole or in part, incures to the personal financial benefit of any foreign government official or employee in connection with or in order to promote or influence the Company's business.

3. The Company has developed a standard clause embodying the policies stated in paragraphs 1 and 2 and will include such clause in all contracts with foreign representatives to the extent not prohibited by the laws of the country or countries in which the contract is performed.

4. The Company has developed and implemented procedures requiring certain levels of review and approval of contracts or other arrangements with foreign representatives, in relation to the amount of the fee, commission or other consideration to be paid by the Company to a foreign representative.

5. Company officers and employees are required to report to the General Counsel any information indicating that a violation of the policies stated in paragraphs 1 and 2 has occurred, is occurring, or appears reasonably likely to occur.

Source: *Corporate Mission and Philosophy of Management* (McLean, Virginia: Dynalectron Corporation, 1977), p. 8.

Developing Managerial Response

In abstract terms there is no excuse for a company to make a bribe. But if one were to probe into the circumstances under which corporations have been placed, one may develop a different perspective of the whole issue. Apparently there are a variety of difficulties involved in coming to grips with the payments problem. Thus, while it is desirable that corporations develop and institute a system to resolve the bribery problem, it must be recognized that the problem may not be entirely averted.

To develop insights into the types of managerial actions which would be appropriate to resolve the bribery issues, thirty-five international marketing executives were interviewed. This section of the paper is based on the information volunteered by these interviews.

The nature of the bribery problem requires a systematic effort to resolve it. Exhibit 40–5 summarizes the action steps which, based on the experience of companies interviewed, would be appropriate to alleviate the payments' problem.

Investigation of Past Deals

An investigation of all past improper payments should be undertaken by a special task force appointed by the top management. This investigation should cover all countries and all levels of the organization and should provide informational inputs in to what circumstances were responsible for bribes and what sort of policy and guidelines would be most appropriate to prevent them in the future.

Corporate Policy

The standards of corporate morality and their adherence must be set and exemplified by the top management. Thus, top management should develop a policy on ethical behavior in the realm of international business. While the

---

EXHIBIT 40–5

Corporate action-steps to resolve the bribery problem

1. Investigation of past deals.
2. Development of a corporate policy.
3. Specific guidelines for people in the field.
4. Institution of an internal control system.
5. Setting realistic performance goals.
6. Institution of rewards-punishment system.
7. Development of programs of recruitment, training and promotion.
8. Communication with trade associations and/or federal government departments.
9. Top management's review.

---

form and content of the policy will vary considerably from company to company, it must exhibit a firm commitment of top management to require an absolute standard of morality. Further, it should be made clear that no deviations from the standard will be tolerated. Care must be taken that the policy is not simply a preamble on honesty and integrity. Such a general statement would be taken for granted without anyone paying any attention to it. At the same time, it should not be excessively rigid or unintelligible. If it is so, it will be ignored, and will force the decision-making to an improper level in the company, increasing both the chances that the decision will be wrong and that any resulting arrangements will be improperly or incompletely reported. The policy should be issued over the signature of the chief executive officer and be widely made available to managerial employees in the company.

Specific Guidelines

In addition to a corporate policy, specific guidelines must be developed for people in the field. The purpose of these guidelines is to help employees who interact with foreign organizations distinguish between acceptable and unacceptable payments. Therefore, the guidelines should be made as specific as possible, illustrate what is permitted and what is prohibited, and indicate the appropriate action to take when in doubt. While the guidelines must be based on the special characteristics of a business and its modes and locations of operations, there are some common areas on which businessmen have considered specific statements necessary. These are shown in Exhibit 40–6. Each executive may be asked to certify in writing that he understands the corporation's guidelines and will comply with them.

Internal Control System

The purpose of the internal control system is to provide a climate and mechanism to assure that the guidelines are adhered to both in content and spirit, and that decisions are made at the proper corporate level. To institute an internal control system, careful plans should be made with a view to (a) maintaining the integrity and reliability of corporate books, i.e., every payment and every transaction with outside parties is reflected on the books of the company promptly, accurately and is duly communicated through the formal financial reporting channels; and (b) restore the efficacy of the system of corporate accountability, i.e., whoever makes the decision in an area knows that he is personally accountable for those decisions and should report all such decisions promptly through channels. In addition checks and balances should be built into the organizational structure so that all financial transactions are reported to the corporate headquarters. Finally, the auditors should be made responsible for discovering and disclosing all improper payments which would have a material effect on the consolidated financial statement.

EXHIBIT 40-6

Guidelines for implementing code of ethics policy

1. A flat prohibition of "offensive" bribery—to win business that would otherwise not be available.

2. A flat prohibition of any "off-the-books" accounts or "slush funds."

3. A clear prohibition of false entries on the books to obscure underlying transactions.

4. A clear prohibition of payments made with the intention that the funds will be used for any purpose other than that described in the documents underlying the transactions.

5. A requirement that employees with information or knowledge of prohibited acts report the matter to the secretary of the corporation, general counsel, or other senior officer.

6. A requirement that managers assume responsibility for communicating policy to all employees under their supervisor.

7. A requirement for a periodic statement by managers that they are in compliance with corporate policy.

8. An appeals procedure encouraging employees faced with questionable situations to seek guidance within the company before making any commitment.

9. An affirmation that "proper" commercial and government relations are to continue, with specific examples of permissible gifts and favors.

10. A commitment that violations of policy or failure to report known violations will result in reprimands, demotion or dismissal of the employee depending upon the circumstances.

Source: James Greene, "Assuring Ethical Conduct Abroad," Information Bulletin No. 12, The Conference Board, November, 1976, p. 16.

Realistic Goals

More than anything else, the top management should be realistic in expecting levels of performance from its managers. In a recent survey at Pitney-Bowes, as many as 59 percent of the managers indicated that they felt pressured to compromise personal ethics to achieve corporate goals. In a survey at Uniroyal, 70 percent of the managers expresses similar sentiments.[10] Clearly, the top management should establish realistic sales and profit goals—goals that can be achieved by current business practices. If the goals are unrealistic, the subordinates will be forced into under-the-table deals to comply with the superior's targets. Top management should emphasize doing only the 'right' thing to encourage ethical behavior among the employees. Even if it costs some business in the short run, the corporation will be better off in the long run.

Punishments and Rewards

Every employee who is guilty of violating the corporate policy on ethics should be subject to "corporate justice, commensurate with the degree of transgression". As has been said by Miller, "the code will be meaningless unless it is carefully monitored and enforced: Individuals, both inside and outside the organization will be watching closely to see if the code represents a sincere expression of company policy".[11] If diversions from the policy are ignored, it will indicate the implicit consent of management to engage in unethical acts. At the same time many corporate executives feel that there should be a way to give some reward or recognition to those employees who stick with the corporate policy on ethics against all odds. It is suggested that widespread news coverage be given to such exceptional conduct. The reward/recognition and its publicity should go a long way in encouraging other employees to stick to their guns. It will also provide a moral lesson for employees in other corporations.

Programs of Recruitment, Training and Promotion

Ethical behavior should become an important ingredient through all phases of a corporation's life. Before expecting its people to respond to moral leadership, the company should create an environment which discourages immoral behavior, finds the best people, pays them well, and provides the working conditions they need.[12] When a person is considered for a position in the company, all attempts should be made to judge his willingness to honor the corporate code of conduct. The corporation should also organize training sessions (with outside help if necessary) to: (1) acquaint its managers with new ethical dilemmas and how these may be resolved; (b) discuss problems managers how to reconcile with the corporate code of conduct and how they came out of these problems; and (c) highlight new solutions to existing ethical questions. Such training will keep employees updated on the state of the art in the area of corporate ethics and also provide an opportunity for them to exchange notes with each other on specific problems. Finally, among other criteria for promotion, due weight should be given to an employee's adherence to the corporate code of conduct.

Communication with Trade Associations and Federal Government

Overseas, an agent may find himself politically harrassed and intimated or facing the complexities and dilemmas of applying ethical precepts in an amoral political environment. How could one monitor what an agent does with his commission? Does he bribe anyone? He might if the environment is immoral and contaminated. For the manager of the multinational corporation, however, monitoring the agent presents both legal and practical difficulties. Perhaps the safest course of action for him is to seek help of the local trade association, or the Chamber of Commerce. If the local people are unwilling to be of help, the United States Embassy may be approached. If the facts of the case warrant it, the matter may even be brought to the knowledge of appropriate department(s) of the federal government.

Top Management's Review

Periodically the top management should review to what degree the policy on ethics is being enforced and implemented. This review can be in the form of a special audit by an independent top management committee or by a committee of outside directors.

The purpose of the review will be to make sure that (a) all payments made to foreign nationals are duly authorized, (b) records are well kept, and (c) internal control procedures are strictly followed. The report of the review committee will keep the top management in touch with what is happening and what further policies may be desirable to enhance corporate morality.

Conclusion

A wise man once said:

> *Experts ranked in seried rows*
> *Filled the enormous plaza full*
> *But only one is there who knows*
> *And he's the man who fights the bull.*[13]

The message contained in the above lines is obvious: Strictly from the viewpoint of moralists, a bribe of any sort is undesirable and should be denounced. Judging it from the viewpoint of the competitive climate of the corporation, however, there are all kinds of pressures—from stockholders, the financial community, and employees—to grow and increase profits. To people at the helm of the corporation with their own reputations at stake, payoffs provide a means of at least temporarily achieving their objectives. Thus considering the problem of bribery in a realistic manner, one must accept that even with the best of ethical programs; it may not be possible to completely eliminate bribes. A conscientious effort, however, could pave the way for the businessmen around the world to learn the virtues and practicality of doing business without bribes.

A recent survey of twenty-five corporations who had disclosed making large questionable payments abroad shows that the refusal to pay bribes had not hurt business. None of these twenty-five firms mention losing a significant portion of its foreign business in the aftermath of forbidding the employees to make any more of them.[14] These findings argue well towards creating an encouraging climate against payoffs.

In conclusion, since promotional payoffs could be contrived as bribes, the marketing man should be careful that they are made in good faith in accordance with the corporate code of conduct and the guidelines on them. In addition, the marketing man should look for new ways to promote his products such as product quality, after sales service and the like, rather than the payoffs.

QUESTIONS

1. Why have multinational corporations used pay-offs as part of their international dealing?
2. What types of pay-offs have been uncovered? Which of these do you consider to be the most outright illegal as opposed to those falling in "gray" areas?
3. What remedial actions do you think would be most effective in combatting overseas pay-offs?
4. If you were the marketing vice president for the international division of a multinational corporation, how would you deal with the pressures for pay-offs?

NOTES

1. "The Unfolding of a Torturous Affair," *Fortune,* 63 (March 1976), 27–8.

2. Sampson, Anthony, "Lockheed's Foreign Policy: Who in the End Corrupted Whom?" *New York* (March 15, 1976), 58.

3. Bowman, James S., "Managerial Ethics in Business and Government," *Business Horizons,* 19 (October 1976), 50.

4. Drucker, Peter, *Management: Tasks, Responsibilities, Practices,* New York: Harper & Row, 1974.

5. *Guidelines for Multinational Enterprises,* Paris: OECD, 1976.

6. Giuzzardi, Walter, Jr., "An Unscandalized View of Those 'Bribes' Abroad," *Fortune,* 63 (July 1976), 182.

7. Landauer, Jerry, "Proposed Treaty Against Business Bribes Gets Poor Reception Overseas, U.S. Finds," *The Wall Street Journal,* 58 (February 28, 1977), 28.

8. *Business Week* (February 7, 1977), 50.

9. "The Pressure to Compromise Personal Ethics," *Business Week,* (January 31, 1977), 107.

10. Miller, Arjay, "Business Without Bribes," *Alumni Bulletin,* Graduate School of Business Administration, Stanford University (Spring 1976), 14.

11. Blumenthal, W. Michael, "Top Management's Role in Preventing Illegal Payments," Conference Board Review, 8 (August 1976), 16.

12. Levitt, Theodore, "Marketing and the Corporate Purpose." *Paper,* Delivered as a part of the Key Issues Lecture Series, New York University, March 2, 1977, 22.

13. Pappas, Vasil, "Crackdown on Bribery Hasn't Damaged Sales, Big Companies Report," *The Wall Street Journal,* 58 (March 2, 1977), 1.

*What problems do foreign exporters en-
counter in penetrating the United States
market? The authors investigate the extent
of foreign export activity by developing
countries and propose several solutions to
the financial and marketing problems faced
by these exporting nations in American
markets.*

41. Solutions to Financial and Marketing Problems Commonly Encountered by Foreign Business Firms Marketing Products in the United States

John R. Darling
Southern Illinois University

Hussein H. Elsaid
Southern Illinois University

An examination of recent literature dealing with export operations clearly shows that the problems encountered by foreign exporters, especially developing countries' exporters, to the United States have not received adequate attention. Glenn Garrison has pointed out some of the hurdles a foreign exporter must overcome in trying to penetrate the United States market.[1] These hurdles are: (1) the importance of on-time delivery, (2) meeting product standards commitments, (3) regional differences in the United States, (4) reluctance of potential customers to buy foreign products and (5) competition not only from American producers but also from other foreign firms. In a study of attitudinal differences between European and United States buyers of both consumer and industrial goods, James Ward has examined seven factors—product range, service, packaging, warranty, lead time, product data and price.[2] He concluded that American buyers were more demanding than the Europeans with regard to five out of the seven factors. The differences were statistically insignificant for price and warranty.

Source: Printed with permission of the authors.

The objectives of this study are: (1) to briefly look at the direction of exports and show the need for more participation by developing countries, (2) to identify financial and marketing problems encountered by foreign exporters, especially developing countries' exporters, to the United States of America and (3) to suggest solutions to these problems.

The Need for More Participation by Developing Countries

Exhibit 41-1 shows the direction of exports for 1970 and 1975. From these data, three observations can be made. First, only petroleum exporting countries (for reasons well known) have enjoyed an increase in their share of total world exports. The other three groupings have suffered a decrease. The developed countries still accounted for about two-thirds of world exports in 1975, although their share had decreased from 71.8 percent in 1970 to 66.1 percent in 1975, or a 7.9 percent drop. However, developing countries suffered a slightly larger drop from 12 percent to 11 percent over the same period, or 8.3 percent decrease in their share. Second, the total exports from both developed and developing countries had grown at an average compound annual rate of 21 percent between 1970 and 1975. However, exports from developed to developing countries increased at a compound annual rate of 22 percent as compared with a 20 percent growth rate for exports from the developing to the developed countries. Third, developing countries trade position deteriorated the most. Their trade deficits increased from $11.2

EXHIBIT 41-1
Direction of exports: 1970 and 1975 (f.o.b. value in billions of U.S. dollars)

		Developed Countries	Developing Countries	OPEC	Centrally Planned Economies	Total[1]
FROM						
Developed	1970	172.5	34.2	7.7	8.4	222.8
Countries	1975	404.1	92.3	46.0	35.1	577.5
Developing	1970	26.4	6.9	1.0	2.9	37.2
Countries	1975	66.0	18.2	5.5	6.7	96.4
OPEC	1970	14.1	2.9	0.1	0.3	17.4
	1975	88.0	23.3	0.5	1.6	113.4
Centrally	1970	7.7	4.4	0.8	19.9	32.8
Planned	1975	24.4	10.3	2.9	48.4	86.0
Economies						
Total	1970	220.7	48.4	9.6	31.5	310.2
	1975	582.5	144.1	54.9	91.8	873.3

[1]Minor discrepancies between these totals and the source's figures for total exports are due to the fact that the latter include certain exports for which the regions of destination could not be determined.

Source: United Nations, *Monthly Bulletin of Statistics* (July 1975 and June 1976), pp. xxiv–xxv, and p. xviii respectively.

billion in1970 to a staggering $47.7 billion in 1975. More than one-half of the deficits was accounted for by trade with developed countries. Based on these observations, one can see the need for greater participation by developing countries in export activities.

A similar conclusion can be reached if the analysis is limited to data on trade between the United States and the developing countries. Exhibit 41-2 shows that in 1975 about 26 percent of United States exports went to developing countries, and United States imports from developing countries accounted for about 24 percent of total imports. The trade deficits of developing countries, excluding Egypt and the OPEC members, vis-à-vis the United States increased from $2.4 billion in 1970 to $5.8 billion in 1975. Egypt's exports to the United States had been negligible, while United States exports to Egypt increased at an average compound annual rate of more than 50 percent from 1970 to 1975.

Thus developing countries are important markets for United States products. In addition, the United States relies heavily on non-OPEC developing countries for raw materials, fish and animal protein and low-cost, labor-intensive manufactured goods.[3] In this last category lies the best prospects for developing countries to increase their exports to developed countries in general, and to the United States in particular.

Research Methodology

In an effort to identify the financial and marketing problems commonly encountered by developing countries in exporting products to the United

EXHIBIT 41-2
Trade between the United States and less developed countries: 1970–1975[1]

		U.S. Exports		U.S. Imports	
		f.o.b. values in millions of dollars	percent of total	f.o.b. values in millions of dollars[2]	percent of total
LDCs (excl. Egypt and OPEC)	1970	10,979	25.40	8,561	22.18
	1971	11,134	25.23	9,205	20.94
	1972	11,858	23.82	11,345	21.20
	1973	17,280	24.22	15,279	22.84
	1974	25,814	26.20	23,715	24.15
	1975	28,164	26.16	22,336	23.76

[1] Countries that are classified as less developed here slightly differ from "developing countries" as reported in the UN Monthly Bulletin of Statistics.

[2] Import data, which are reported c.i.f., were divided by 1.1 to reach f.o.b. equivalents.

Source: International Monetary Fund, *Direction of Trade* (1969–75), p. 230.

States, data were collected from Foreign Trade Commissioners residing in New York, Chicago, Los Angeles and Washington, D.C. These Commissioners represented the embassies and trade consulates of a number of foreign countries from the Middle East, Far East, Africa and South America that are exporters of products to the United States. A stratified random sampling technique was used to secure contact with countries from each of these four geographical areas.

A questionnaire was mailed to one hundred of these potential respondents. A follow-up telephone contact was also made, and a subsequent 67 percent initial response rate secured. Five of the returned questionnaires were unusable, so the response rate upon which the data analysis was made was 62 percent. The respondents were asked to rate the importance of each of the financial and marketing problems noted below with regard to the export of raw materials, light industrial products, heavy industrial products, consumer nondurables and consumer durables from their countries to the United States. A definition (or description) for each of the problem categories was provided.

Export incentives	Shipping and transportation
Market analysis and entry	Billing and invoicing
Sales forecasting	Customer order-handling
Product development	General communication
Product standards	Advertising
Product delivery	Personal selling
Product servicing	Special sales promotions
Brand management	Product packaging
Pricing	Distribution channel relations
Price adjustments	Storage and warehousing
Credit management	Inventory management

The respondents rated each of these problems on a five-point Likert[4] scale ranging from a response "of little importance" to a response "of great importance." The importance of each of the problem categories varied between the different classes of products noted above for each of the countries. However, with regard to manufactured products in general, six problem areas were considered by the authors to be of primary importance. These were export incentives, market analysis and entry, product delivery, general communication, distribution channel relations and pricing. In addition, in a convenience sample of eleven of the questionnaire respondents located in the Chicago area, additional data and observations were gathered in personal interviews. The following sections of this paper will deal with these various problem areas.

Research studies of this nature usually have many limitations. The more obvious limitations of the present study may include such items as the countries selected for inclusion in the project, official positions of the respondents within their embassies or consulates, size of the sample of the respondents, problem areas selected for the study and the issues that typically emerge with a research study that deals with respondent attitudes. However, the purpose of the present analysis is not to focus on this original research data, per se, but to offer points of view whereby the problems so identified can be placed in their proper perspective and dealt with more successfully by foreign exporters marketing products in the United States and its various geographical markets. No effort is made in this paper to exhaust the analysis of these problem solutions, however, but to present them and to focus on some of the ways with which they can be dealt.

Export Incentives

It should be stated at the outset that it is not feasible to completely divorce financial from marketing problems. For example, the problem of competition has both marketing and financial ramifications. An exporter's price competitiveness is, in part, determined by exchange rates and export subsidies.

Generally developing countries have initiated their industrialization programs with the production of import substitutes. The initiation and development of these industries have been accompanied by high tariffs, quotas, exchange controls and other restrictions on imports. These policies have ignored the theory of comparative advantage and led to suboptimal allocation of resources. Most significantly, these policies have tended to discriminate against the development of exports for the following reasons.[5]

1. They typically have supported an overvalued local currency (LC), thus making export products more expensive to foreign buyers.
2. They have supported high prices for intermediate inputs, thus increasing costs of exports. This has been the case regardless of whether the inputs have been imported (subject to high tariffs) or supplied by protected domestic firms.
3. They probably have led to the adoption of a technology inappropriate for the development of exports (e.g., imports of capital equipment generally have been exempted from duties, thus encouraging the use of capital-intensive technology).

Promotion of exports requires that either developing countries terminate the discriminatory policies designed to stimulate import substitution, or compensate the export sector for the existing discrimination. Since the former may not be politically feasible, a coherent system of export incentives has to be developed. Many developing countries have adopted some export promotion measures. However, such measures have evolved over the years in a haphazard fashion so as not to undermine the import substitution protective wall of trade barriers.

Basically an optimal export subsidy policy is achieved when

$$IVA_w = INS$$

where IVA_w (incremental value added in world prices) = incremental value of exports (f.o.b.)—incremental value of intermediate inputs in world prices, and INS (incremental net subsidy) = incremental export subsidy—incremental duties on intermediate inputs. However, other contributions by a given industry (e.g., number and type of jobs it creates) should be considered in formulating the subsidy policy. Furthermore, the spill-over or growth generating effect of an industry on other sectors of the economy should influence the level of official support given to such industry. Thus, this policy is not intended to preclude such benefits. If measurable, the net benefits should be incorporated in an expanded IVA_w.

It should be pointed out that the relevant revenue variable is the value added and not the total value of exports. Using total value would yield a policy biased toward exports with high intermediate input component. The problems inherent in the policy rule have to do with the measurement of both value added and net subsidy.[6] It is the authors' contention that attempts at dealing with these problems would force government officials to consider the relevant policy variables in a systematic way. The main components of a policy of export incentives are: (a) exchange rate, (b) tax and duty concessions and (c) financing and insurance.

Exchange Rate

The problem here is two dimensional: first, what should be the rate(s) level? and second, should a country adopt one or multiple rates? As stated earlier developing countries import substitution policies have supported an overvalued LC. Egypt is a case in point. The Egyptian pound official exchange rate established with the International Monetary Fund (IMF) remained constant at United States $2.30/E. pound through 1972. Subsequently it was upvalued twice (in 1973 and 1974) against the United States dollar, reaching United States $2.55558/E. pound.[7] Clearly this was an artificially high exchange rate for the pound. Such a high rate would not only make exports less competitive, especially nontraditional exports (i.e., other than raw materials), but also would discourage capital inflows and create a host of other problems. In 1977, the Egyptian authorities attempted to deal with this problem by adjusting downward the exchange rate between the pound and the dollar in order to stimulate foreign investments in Egypt.

Most developing countries, however, have opted for a multiple rate system as the answer to the overvaluation problems. Egypt is no exception. Some economists have supported such a policy. They argue that ". . . if no single exchange rate can maximize primary export earnings and simultaneously provide enough inducement to import-substitution and export activity in the industrial sector to ensure overall balance of payments equilibrium, the solution would be to adopt two or more exchange rates."[8] However, a system of multiple rates is inherently unstable. Experience shows why it has not achieved the expected success.[9]

1. The rates have tended to proliferate. This adds to the complexity of the system and makes it difficult to understand by those who are intended to use it.
2. Problems have been created because of shifting products and/or invisibles from one effective rate to another. These shifts may not be due to basic change in government policy, but to the influence of pressure groups or favors.
3. The use of multiple rates generally has created a "black market" in foreign exchange. However, "black markets" invariably exist under most systems of exchange controls. Moreover, it has encouraged residents to try to outsmart the system by falsifying information regarding the source of their foreign exchange.
4. Finally, such a system is difficult to administer and may require costly policing.

Thus, the answer to an overvalued LC does not seem to lie in the adoption of multiple rates. The authors suggest the adoption of a single realistic exchange rate. Such a rate would be based on the underlying economic conditions in any given country. For example, one can build a case for an exchange rate between the United States dollar and the Egyptian pound somewhere from United States $1.25 to $1.50/E. pound. Prior to readjusting their currencies' official parities, many industrialized countries floated for a while (that was before they adopted the present managed float system). A technique that can be helpful in setting a realistic rate. To conclude, measures other than multiple exchange rates should be used to stimulate both export activities and import substitution.

Tax and Duty Concessions

Tax concessions may be granted to exporters either by means of an outright exemption or a reduction in taxable income. Tax rebates are quite common in Western Europe and Japan. In the United States exporters can postpone indefinitely the payment of income taxes on a portion of their export profits through the use of the Domestic International Sales Corporation (DISC). Accelerated depreciation on facilities used for the production of exports can be used as another measure to reduce exporter's taxable income. Regardless of the measure(s) used, policy makers have to guard against the distortions tax concessions can create. These distortions are often caused by the problems inherent in the determination of a product's profitability. For example, the Columbian system of exempting export profits from income taxes ". . . was used to reduce or even eliminate income tax liabilities arising from activities entirely unrelated to export business . . . ."[10]

Duty concessions are granted on imported inputs to be used in export activities. The authors suggest that developing countries avoid the temptation of applying the same concession to all imported inputs. Since low-cost, labor-intensive manufactured goods represent their best export prospects to the United States as well as to other developed countries, concessions should be designed with that in mind. Government officials in developing countries tend to argue against major duty concessions not only for the protection of import substitution, but also because duties may represent a major source of government revenue and administratively less cumbersome than say income tax collection. However, import duty should be viewed in its proper perspective as one variable in an overall policy to stimulate economic growth.

Export Financing and Insurance

The major financing problem encountered by an exporter in a developing country is to secure foreign exchange for imported inputs. This may be due to either lack of adequate working capital or to the nonconvertibility of the LC. Since without such inputs exports may not materialize, government should provide the needed foreign exchange financing either through domestic commercial banks or its own agency. The required funds may be secured from foreign banks. The exporter's repayment schedule should correspond to the timing of export proceeds. This important export promotion measure could be cost-free to the government if the exporter is charged the foreign banks' rate plus administrative costs. On the other hand, it can be used to provide exporters with low-cost financing.

Another export incentive measure is insurance. Any exporter may be exposed to three types of risks, namely credit risk, foreign exchange risk and political risk. Credit risk may be defined as variability in expected net cash flows owing to the failure on the part of the importer to honor credit commitments. Distance and lack of exporters' familiarity with sources of credit information in the United States (e.g., Dun and Bradstreet) complicate credit management. Exporters may perceive a higher degree or risk than actually exists. In many cases the expected value of additional information may outweigh the cost of securing it. Furthermore, this risk may virtually be eliminated by a confirmed irrevocable letter of credit. However, the cost of securing such a letter may be borne by the exporter. Foreign exchange risk may be defined as variability in expected net cash flows due to fluctuations in the relative values of relevant currencies. In developed financial markets, this risk can be transferred (generally at a cost) by covering in the money or forward market. Political risk, on the other hand, may be defined as variability in expected net cash flows owing to abrupt political change. There is a common misconception that this risk exists only in developing countries.

It can be encountered in developed countries (e.g., political pressure by interest groups to effect a change in trade policy toward a given country).

Developing strategies to deal with these risks requires a certain degree of sophistication on the part of the exporter and is likely to impose additional financial burden. This may be a deterrent to the development of the export sector in developing countries. Thus, the authors suggest that insurance coverage (at reasonable rates) be made available to exporters (e.g., the central bank may guarantee exchange rates). Credit, political and to a very limited extent foreign exchange risk insurance are available to United States exporters at concession rates. The need to provide exporters in developing countries with insurance coverage can not be overstated.

Market Analysis and Entry

A major hurdle facing exporters of products to the United States is that of market analysis and entry. In fact, a country with a total population of approximately 220 million, a geographical area of 3.7 million square miles and a GNP of $1,710 billion becomes a formidable prospect for many foreign manufacturers.[11]

Unfortunately, many foreign firms view the United States market in just this manner, rather than considering the United States as being composed of many subgeographical markets. The authors have often heard the remark by foreign business executives that "we contacted a representative in New York, but can't understand why we're not doing more business in the United States." In fact, a common response of Foreign Trade Commissioners in the Chicago area is that many of the manufacturers from their own countries seem to ignore the tremendous market potential that exists in the various geographical markets within the interior of the United States.

According to one set of criteria, there are forty primary trade areas in the United States.[12] These areas are identified and ranked on the basis of the size of their contribution to the total marketing picture of quality and premium priced goods and services. The nine indices used to rank these areas were families with incomes of $15,000 and over, families with incomes of $25,000 and over, families headed by males with incomes of $25,000 and over, owner-occupied housing units valued at $35,000 and over, registrations of moderate and higher priced passenger cars, retail sales, department store sales, women's ready-to-wear store sales and character of stores (a qualitative measure). These 40 primary trade areas in the United States, in rank-order, are shown in Exhibit 41-3.

The forty areas account for 50 percent of the United States population, 65 percent of the United States families with incomes of $15,000 and over, 69 percent of the United States families with incomes of $25,000 and over, 67 percent of the United States families headed by males with incomes of $25,000 and over, 75 percent of the United States owner-occupied housing units valued at $25,000 and over, 59 percent of the United States registration

EXHIBIT 41-3
The primary trade areas in the U.S.

1. New York	14. Minneapolis-St. Paul	27. Indianapolis
2. Los Angeles	15. Pittsburgh	28. Columbus
3. Chicago	16. Seattle	29. New Orleans
4. San Francisco	17. Atlanta	30. Phoenix
5. Detroit	18. Baltimore	31. Rochester
6. Philadelphia	19. Milwaukee	32. Tampa-St. Petersburg
7. Washington	20. Cincinnati	33. Dayton
8. Boston	21. Denver	34. New Haven
9. Cleveland-Akron	22. San Diego	35. Charlotte
10. Dallas-Fort Worth	23. Kansas City	36. Honolulu
11. Miami-Fort Lauderdale	24. Portland	37. Providence
12. Houston	25. Buffalo	38. Louisville
13. St. Louis	26. Hartford	39. Sacramento
		40. Albany

Source: "The 40 Primary Trade Areas in the U.S.," *The New Yorker Magazine* (New Yorker Magazine, Inc., 1974).

of new, moderate and higher priced passenger cars, 46 percent of the United States retail sales, 63 percent of the United States department store sales and 57 percent of the United States women's ready-to-wear store sales.

This listing of major geographical markets in the United States emphasizes the fact that there are many different markets in which entry is possible, although most exporters to the United States seem to convince themselves that they must be represented in the major East coast market areas. Firms located on the East coast often will not adequately represent a foreign manufacturer in other geographical areas. In addition, the primary objective is to "successfully" enter a United States market, and the most attractive opportunities may very well lie in other markets than those located close to the coastal areas. This is especially true since the source (i.e., foreign versus domestic) as well as the degree of competition may vary from one area to the other. A fact that is important to entry strategy, however, often ignored by exporters to the United States. Data are available regarding various types of consumer, industrial and governmental buyers in these markets classified by different characteristics such as number, size, markets served, products handled and buying power. In addition, the authors have assisted numerous foreign business firms in identifying those particular geographical markets in which data indicate a significant market entry or expansion opportunity exists.

Product Delivery and General Communication

Product delivery and general communication with the marketplace are very interrelated when it comes to servicing United States customers. Satisfactory product availability and delivery times depend on adequate information systems to and from the marketplace. Therefore, the manner in which inquiries from potential and existing customers, and the procedures established for handling and processing customer orders usually have a major influence on the successful penetration of the United States market by foreign suppliers.

There is a wide belief among the Foreign Trade Commissioners surveyed that on-time product delivery is one of the most important success-determining factors for foreign business firms marketing their products in the United States. Several of the respondents seemed to question the ability of many of their countries' manufacturers to set and meet acceptable deadlines for delivery to the United States. Several examples cited inquiries from United States manufacturers or wholesale distributors that were apparently shelved for several months before replies were sent. Follow-up requests were also often delayed which disenchanted potential customers, who in turn sought the needed products elsewhere.

Americans are said to be much more demanding than customers in many other national markets with regard to the lead times they demand, not only for product delivery but also for sales proposals. This is especially true when the government is the buyer. But, what does this mean for a foreign supplier? Very simply, it means that when United States markets are entered, production capacity must be adequate to serve the market, and the information systems within the firm and throughout its distribution channels must be refined and developed in order to avoid unnecessary delays in market communication. Numerous examples exist of situations where the demand of the United States market has virtually overwhelmed a foreign supplier.[13] This very point focuses in on the need for the typical foreign supplier to seriously consider entry into only one, or a limited number of geographical markets in the United States in order to establish a success record with which the firm can "roll out" to additional markets. This is a typical market entry strategy used by United States producers marketing within their own country.

Distribution Channel Relations

Too often, the foreign exporter to the United States develops his distribution channel from his place of business forward to the marketplace. For example, the exporter may make a trip to the States, locate an import agent who assures the exporter that a market can be secured; at which point the exporter returns home to await the receipt of orders which often do not come.

The starting point in developing the most effective channel arrangement is a clear determination of the market target for the exporter's marketing effort, and a determination of the needs and preferences of the target place.[14] Where are the potential customers located? What are their information requirements? What are their preferences for service? How sensitive are they to price? From whom do they prefer to buy? Once these questions are answered by means of market research data and intelligence, the exporter is in a position to determine the distribution outlets that can most effectively serve the firm's potential customer markets.

The selection of specific wholesale distribution and/or retail merchants will require the exporting firm to make a number of decisions relating to such factors as the transfer of title and/or possession of the goods, need for continuing relationships, control over distribution, authority over price, number of principals allowed, competitive lines to be handled, types of goods and breadth of line, extent of promotion and selling effort required, amount of credit to be extended and market information to be provided by distribution outlet.[15] Therefore, the services expected of channel intermediaries are important determinants in distribution channel development and relationships.

For most exporters of products to the United States, a visit to the States will be needed to meet with and select the distribution outlets that are to be used in the various geographical markets. Personal contact between buyer and seller is of great importance in marketing goods to the United States. In the so-called "business-like America," personality often makes a big difference.

Information regarding the names and addresses of potential distributors can be secured from the Chamber of Commerce of the different metropolitan markets, and from various trade associations. The authors have generally found the Foreign Trade Commissioners of many countries play an important role in locating and securing distribution outlets. In addition, there are several distribution outlet search firms that serve foreign exporters to the United States. Publications such as that of Dun and Bradstreet Inc. are also of great value in providing operational data on potential distributors.

Pricing

Price must be characterized as a major factor in customer buying decisions in United States markets. United States customers are said to be very demanding with regard to price breakdowns and for specific figures on each component. Price and product quality are often interrelated and United States buyers are often inclined to reduce quality demands for appropriate price reductions.[16]

The most prevalent pricing method found among foreign firms exporting goods to the United States is the cost-plus (or average-cost) method. This method has many drawbacks. Customer demand is often not considered in this method and the prices of competitive products ignored. In addition, cost-plus pricing is based on circular thinking. It is true that cost should be a consideration in setting price. However, price may have a direct effect on costs through a relationship of price, sales volume and cost. Therefore, the foreign exporter of goods to the United States might be well-advised to use a market oriented approach to price determination—a method that gives careful

consideration to market demand (the amount of goods customers will purchase at different price points), competitive market prices, mark-up margins
required to secure the services of market intermediaries and government
requirements, in addition to operational and production costs.[17] Successful
pricing in United States markets usually begins at the final selling point, and
breaks price back down at successive stages in the distribution channel to
the required f.o.b. point of origin price.

Concluding Remarks

The primary purpose of this study has been to identify major financial and
marketing problems encountered by exporters of products to the United
States, and to offer various points of view regarding the different ways by
which these problems can be solved. As such, the authors have focused on
issues relating to export incentives, market analysis and entry, product
delivery and communication, pricing and distribution channel relations.

A system of export incentives has to be as simple as humanly possible.
Moreover, care should be exercised in communicating it to present and
potential exporters. Official policy makers have to be extremely cautious
to avoid excessive subsidies. Excessive subsidies can retard rather than promote economic growth. They can create a vicious circle of self-defeating
inefficiencies. Furthermore, they may induce price cuts as if foreign demand
is infinitely elastic, which may reduce foreign exchange earnings.[18] Frequent
policy changes are destabilizing. Relative financial and political stability is a
prerequisite for long-term planning and, thus, for the success of export
promotion schemes.

Foreign exporters attempting to analyze and enter the United States
market should not treat this market as one homogeneous area, but as a
number of sub-markets. As such, the United States can be segmented into
various primary trade areas for analysis and entry. In dealing with issues
relating to product delivery, general market communication, pricing and
distribution channel relations, foreign exporters would be well-advised
to give careful consideration to the varying demands of customers in the different markets being served. Successful international finance and marketing
strategies evolve from a thorough analysis of the market, consideration of the
environmental factors that surround that market, and an awareness of the
operational inherent constraints to the particular exporting firm.

QUESTIONS

1. What are the major problems encountered by foreign exporters selling
   to United States markets?
2. What kinds of export incentives are held out to encourage greater participation in United States markets?

3. How can the issues raised by the authors be utilized in the development of marketing mixes by foreign exporters?

NOTES

1. Glen Garrison, " 'Making It' in the U.S. Market: How Three Belgian Firms Do It," *Business Abroad* (June, 1970), pp. 34-36.

2. James J. Ward, "How European Firms View Their U.S. Customers," *Columbia Journal of World Business* (Summer, 1973), pp. 79-82.

3. Guy F. Erb, "U.S. Trade Policies Toward Developing Areas," *Columbia Journal of World Business* (Fall, 1973), p. 59.

4. For a more thorough discussion of the Likert method of summated ratings, see Bertram Schoner and Kenneth P. Uhl, *Marketing Research: Information Systems and Decision Making,* 2nd ed., (New York, N.Y.: John Wiley and Sons, Inc., 1975), pp. 270-271.

5. Luc De Wulf and Garry Pursell, "Criteria for Policies to Promote Exports," *Finance & Development* (June, 1976), p. 25.

6. *Ibid.,* p. 27.

7. United Nations, *Monthly Bulletin of Statistics* (September, 1976), p. xiv.

8. Michele Guerard, "Fiscal Versus Trade Incentives for Industrialization," *Finance & Development* (March, 1975), pp. 19-22.

9. For example Pakistan's experience, see Andreas S. Gerakis, "Pakistan's Export Bonus Scheme," *Finance & Development* (June, 1974), pp. 10-13.

10. Jose D. Teigeiro and R. Anthony Elson, "Export Incentives in Columbia," *Finance & Development* (December, 1973), p. 31.

11. See "The Business Situation," *Survey of Current Business* (October, 1976), pp. 1-20.

12. See "The 40 Primary Trade Areas in the U.S.," *The New Yorker Magazine* (New York, N.Y.: The New Yorker Magazine, Inc., 1974).

13. See Glenn Garrison, *op. cit.,* p. 82.

14. Warren J. Keegan, *Multinational Marketing Management* (Englewood Cliffs, N.J.: Prentice-Hall, Inc., 1974), p. 296.

15. See Philip R. Cateora and John M. Hess, *International Marketing,* 3rd ed., (Homewood, Ill.: Richard D. Irwin, Inc., 1975), pp. 494-495.

16. James J. Ward, *op. cit.,* p. 82.

17. Harry A. Lipson and John R. Darling, *Marketing Fundamentals: Text and Cases* (New York, N.Y.: John Wiley and Sons, Inc., 1974), pp. 399-406.

18. Andreas S. Gerakis, *op. cit.,* p. 12.

SELECTED
REFERENCES

PART I. NATURE OF INTERNATIONAL MARKETING

Agman, Tamir and Kindleberger, Charles P. eds., *Multinationals From Small Countries.* Cambridge, Massachusetts: The M.I.T. Press, 1977.

Bartel, Robert. "Are Domestic and International Marketing Dissimilar?" *Journal of Marketing,* July, 1968, pp. 56-61.

Hobbing, Enno. "The World Corporation: A Catalytic Agent?" *Columbia Journal of World Business,* July-August, 1971, pp. 45-51.

Horst, Thomas. "American Multinationals and the U.S. Economy," *American Economic Review,* Vol. 66, May, 1976, pp. 149-154.

"How Kodak Clicked Worldwide on the Marketing Plan for Its Famous Instamatic," *Business Abroad,* June 12, 1967, pp. 31-34.

Keegan, Warren J. "Key Questions in Multinational Marketing Management," *Worldwide P & I Planning,* July/August, 1970, pp. 64-71.

Leighton, David. "The Internationalization of American Business: The Third Industrial Revolution," *Journal of Marketing,* July, 1970, pp. 3-6.

McDonald, Alonzo L. "The MNE; Monkey in the Middle," *The McKinsey Quarterly,* Spring, 1977, pp. 15-31.

Multinational Corporations in World Development. New York, NY: The United Nations, 1973.

"New Study Finds Marketing Factors Exert Most Pull Abroad for Firms," *Commerce Today,* May 28, 1973, pp. 28-29.

Sauvant, Karl P. and Lavipour, Farid G. eds., *Controlling Multinational Enterprises.* Boulder, Colorado: Westview Press, Inc., 1976.

U.S. Foreign Economic Policy and the Domestic Economy, A Statement by the Program Committee. New York, NY: Committee for Economic Development, 1972.

United States Multinational Enterprise. Washington, D.C.: Chamber of Commerce of the United States, 1972.

Vernon, Raymond. *Sovereignty at Bay.* New York, NY: Basic Books, 1971.

_____ *Storm over the Multinationals: The Real Issues.* Cambridge: MA: Harvard University Press, 1977.

Weinshall, Theodore D. "Multinational Corporations—Their Development and Universal Role," *Management International Review,* Number 2-3, 1975, pp. 17-28.

Wriston, Walter B. "The Multinational Company: New Weight in an Old Balance," *Financial Executive,* December, 1973, pp. 18-24.

PART II. ENVIRONMENT OF INTERNATIONAL MARKETING

Barbier, Guy. "Business and Economic Impacts of Multinationals on Developing Countries," *The Arthur Anderson Chronicle,* January, 1977, pp. 19-26.

Boddewyn, J.J.; Enberg, Holger L.; Fayerweather, John; Franck, Peter G.; Kapoor, Ashok; and Ness, Jr., Walter. *World Business Systems and Environments.* Scranton, Penn.: International Textbook Company, 1972.

Hall, Edward T. *The Silent Language.* Greenwich, CT: Fawcett Publications, 1951.

Jones, Robert. "Executive's Guide to Antitrust In Europe," *Harvard Business Review,* May-June, 1976, pp. 106-118.

Kee, Y.T. "Business Across Boundaries: A Laboratory Experiment in Cultural Behavior," *Marquette Business Review,* Winter, 1974, pp. 143-153.

Kizilbash, A.H.; and Maile, C.A. "Export Marketing in a Changing Economic Environment," *Journal of Small Business Management,* January, 1977, pp. 1-6.

Kraar, Louis. "Adversity Is Helping the Japanese Refashion Their Future," *Fortune,* October, 1976, pp. 127-131.

Lee, James A. "Cultural Analysis in Overseas Operations," *Harvard Business Review,* March-April, 1966, p. 106.

Lloyd, Gary E. "Changing Dimensions in International Trade," *Personnel Journal,* March, 1977, pp. 132-136.

Nehrt, Lee C. "The Political Climate for Private Investment," *Business Horizons,* June, 1972, pp. 51-58.

Ozawa, Terutomo. "Japanese Technology: A New Element in International Competition," *Akron Business and Economic Review,* Summer, 1975, pp. 10-16.

Kelley, Lane and Reeser, Clayton. "The Persistence of Culture as a Determinant of Differentiated Attitudes on the Part of American Managers of Japanese Ancestry," *Academy of Management Journal,* March, 1973, pp. 67-76.

Suzman, Cedric L. "The Changing Nature of Export Management," *Atlantic Economic Review,* September-October, 1975, pp. 15-20.

Wadia, Maneck S. "The Concept of Culture in the Analysis of Consumers," *American Marketing Association Proceedings,* Winter, 1967, pp. 186-190.

Welch, Wilfred H. "The Business Outlook for Southeast Asia," *Harvard Business Review,* May-June, 1973, pp. 72-84.

PART III. ANALYSIS OF OVERSEAS OPPORTUNITIES: CONCEPTUAL ISSUES

Ahoroni, Y. *The Foreign Investment Decision Process.* Boston, MA: Division of Research, Harvard Graduate School of Business Administration, 1966.

Bartels, Robert. "Are Domestic and International Marketing Dissimilar?" *Journal of Marketing,* July, 1968, pp. 56-61.

Bastl, Fred J. "Determination of the Export Potential," *Akron Business and Economic Review,* Summer, 1971, pp. 5-9.

Boyd, Jr., Harper W.; Frank, Ronald E.; Massy, William F.; and Zohier, Mostafa. "On the Use of Marketing Research in the Emerging Economies," *Journal of Marketing Research,* November, 1964, pp. 20-23.

Felix, Fremont. *World Markets of Tomorrow.* New York, NY: Harper & Row, 1972.

Gibson, Weldon B. "Appraising the External Environment," *The Management of International Corporate Citizenship,* September, 1976, pp. 9-11.

Keegan, Warren J. "Acquisition of Global Business Information," *Columbia Journal of World Business,* March-April, 1968, pp. 48-59.

Lessing, Lawrence. "Why the United States Lags in Technology," *Fortune,* April, 1972, pp. 69-76.

Liander, Bertil. (ed.) *Comparative Analysis for International Marketing.* Boston, MA: Harvard University Press, 1971.

Miller, Edwin L. "The International Selection Decision," *Academy of Management Journal,* June, 1973, pp. 239-252.

Moyer, Reed. "International Market Analysis," *Journal of Marketing Research,* November, 1968, pp. 353-360.

Murray, J. Alex. "Intelligence Systems of the MNCs," *Columbia Journal of World Business,* September-October, 1972, pp. 63-71.

Piper, Jr., James E. "How U.S. Firms Evaluate Foreign Investment Opportunities," *MSU Business Topics,* Summer, 1971, pp. 11-20.

Sethi, S. Prakash. "Comparative Cluster Analysis for World Markets," *Journal of Marketing Research,* August, 1971, pp. 384-354.

Sethi, S. Prakash, and Holton, Richard. "Review of Comparative Analysis in International Marketing," *Journal of Marketing Research,* November, 1969, pp. 502-503.

Stobaugh, Jr., Robert B. "How to Analyze Foreign Investment Climates," *Harvard Business Review,* September-October, 1969, pp. 100-108.

Van Dam, Andre. "The Future of Global Business Forecasting," *Business Horizons,* August, 1977, pp. 46-50.

Wilson, Aubrey. "Industrial Marketing Research in Britain," *Journal of Marketing Research,* February, 1969, pp. 15-22.

PART IV.   ANALYSIS OF OVERSEAS OPPORTUNITIES: APPLICATIONS

Anderson, Dole. *Marketing and Development: The Thailand Experience.* East Lansing, Michigan: MSU International Business and Economic Studies, 1970.

Arning, H.K. "Business Customs from Malaya to Murmansk," *Management Review,* October, 1964, pp. 5-14.

Bottomley, D.T. "Are Consumers Changing Australian Business Practices?—A Market Research View," *Australian Journal of Marketing Research,* August, 1973, pp. 95-101.

Brand, William K.; Hulbert, James; Dunn, S. Watson; and Schiff, Jack. "The Marketing Revolution in Brazil, The 'Sleeping Giant' Is Wide Awake," *Marketing News,* February 1, 1974, pp. 12-14.

Burke, E.M. "The Practitioner's Role in Tapping Arab Markets," *Public Relations Journal,* February, 1975, pp. 12-14.

Damonerman, Marilyn. "G.M. and Who?" *Forbes,* October 1, 1976, pp. 74-77.

Greer, Thomas V. *Marketing in the Soviet Union.* New York, NY: Praeger Publishers, Inc., 1973.

Hayden, Eric W. "Technology Transfer to the Soviet Bloc," *MSU Business Topics,* Winter, 1976, pp. 11-23.

Hibbert, Edgar P. "Statutory Marketing in a Developing Economy," *European Journal of Marketing,* Autumn, 1972, pp. 155-169.

Searby, Daniel M. "Doing Business in the Mideast: The Game is Rigged," *Harvard Business Review,* January-February, 1976, pp. 56-64.

Terpstra, Vern. *American Marketing in the Common Market.* New York, NY: Praeger, 1967.

Thoman, G. Richard. "How European Banks Can Serve the MNC Market," *The McKinsey Quarterly,* Autumn, 1977, pp. 60-71.

Thorelli, Hans B. "Consumer Information Policy in Sweden—What Can Be Learned?" *Journal of Marketing,* January, 1971, pp. 50-55.

Weigand, Robert E. "International Trade Without Money," *Harvard Business Review,* November-December, 1977, pp. 28+.

——————— , "Selling Soviet Buyers," *MSU Business Topics,* Spring, 1976, pp. 15-21.

Weiss, E.B. "The Third World Starts Emerging as a Big Consumer Market," *Advertising Age,* December, 1973, pp. 45, 47.

Yoshino, Michael. *The Japanese Marketing System.* Cambridge, MA: The M.I.T. Press, 1971.

PART V.   PRODUCT STRATEGIES

Bagley, Barbara J. "Packaging Goods for International Shipment," *Traffic Management,* April, 1974, pp. 56-59.

Cooper, George W. "On Your 'Mark,' " *Columbia Journal of World Business,* March–April, 1970, pp. 67-76.

d'Antin, Philippe. "The Nestle Product Manager as Demigod," *European Business,* Spring, 1971, pp. 44-49.

"How to Avoid Brand Name Bloopers Overseas," *Business Abroad,* July 24, 1967, p. 17.

Introducing a New Product in a Foreign Market, Management Monograph No. 33. New York, NY: Business International, 1966.

Kramer, Toland. "Why Manufacture Overseas?" *International Marketing.* Cincinnati, Ohio: Southwestern Publishing Company, 1964, p. 128-135.

McDonald, Peter. "Packaging for Overseas Markets," *Advertising and Sales Promotion,* January, 1968, pp. 30-32.

Mendez, Alfredo. "Social Structure and the Diffusion of Innovation," *Human Organization,* Vol. 27, No. 3, 1968, pp. 241-249.

Nagashima, Abira. "A Comparison of Japanese and United States Attitudes Toward Foreign Products," *Journal of Marketing,* January, 1970, pp. 68-74.

Reierson, Curtis C. "Attitude Changes Toward Foreign Products," *Journal of Marketing Research,* November, 1967, pp. 48-53.

Schooler, Robert D. "Product Bias in the Central American Market," *Journal of Marketing Research,* November, 1966, pp. 394-397.

Sommers, Montrose and Kernan, Jerome. "Why Products Flourish Here, Fizzle There," *Columbia Journal of World Business,* March–April, 1967, pp. 89-97.

Vernon, Raymond. "International Investment and International Trade in the Product Life Cycle," *Quarterly Journal of Economics,* May, 1966, pp. 190-207.

Ward, James J. "Product and Promotion Adaptation by European Firms in the United States," *Journal of International Business Studies,* Spring, 1973, pp. 79-80.

Wells, Jr., Louis T. "A Product Life Cycle for International Trade?" *Journal of Marketing*, July, 1968, pp. 1-6.

Wortzel, Lawrence H. "Product Policy and the United States Multinational Corporation: Some Emerging Generalizations," *Marketing and the New Science of Planning*, Fall Conference Proceedings. Chicago, Ill.: American Marketing Association, 1968, pp. 89-93.

PART VI. DISTRIBUTION STRATEGIES

Arndt, Johan. "Temporal Lags in Comparative Retailing," *Journal of Marketing*, October, 1972, pp. 40-45.

Bartels, Robert. ed., *Comparative Marketing: Wholesaling in Fifteen Countries*. Homewood Ill.: Richard D. Irwin, Inc., 1963.

David, Michel. "Developments in the Structure of Distribution in France: A Moderate Degree of Concentration," *Journal of Retailing*, Summer, 1965, pp. 34-38.

Goldstucker, Jac L. "The Influence of Culture on Channels of Distribution," *American Marketing Association Proceedings*, Fall, 1968, pp. 468-473.

Handley, George W. "Super Vessels and Marine Insurance in the Next Decade," *Columbia Journal of World Business*, December, 1973, pp. 107-112.

Harvey, John. "European Distribution Systems: Similarities and Differences," *Transportation and Distribution Management*, January-February, 1974, pp. 39-40.

Heskett, James L. and Mathias, Peter F. "The Management of Logistics in MNCs," *Columbia Journal of World Business*, Spring, 1976, pp. 52-62.

Hollander, Stanley C. "The International Retailers," Fred C. Allvine ed., *Combined Proceedings: 1971—Spring and Fall Conferences*. Chicago, Ill.: American Marketing Association, 1972, pp. 271-274.

Hollander, Stanley C. and Boddewyn, J.J. "Retailing and Public Policy: An International Overview," *Journal of Retailing*, Spring, 1974, pp. 55-66.

Kacker, Madhav P. "Distribution in a Developing Economy—Some Emerging Trends and Implications for Strategy," *International Journal of Physical Distribution*, Vol. 7, No. 1, 1976, pp. 30-39.

Langeard, Eric and Peterson, Robert A. "Diffusion of Large Scale Food Retailing in France: Supermarche et Hypermarche," *Journal of Retailing*, Fall, 1975, pp. 48-53.

McCullough, John T. "Containerization: The Intermodal Key," *Distribution Worldwide*, March, 1974, pp. 41-43.

Smith, Howard R. "The Chinese Entrepreneur Overseas," *Journal of Business Research*, April, 1974, pp. 177-189.

Tigert, Douglas J. "The Changing Structure of Retailing in Europe and North America: Challenges and Opportunities," University of Toronto Retailing and Institutional Research Program Working Paper 75-02, January, 1974, pp. 17-20.

Wadinambiaratchi, George. "Channels of Distribution in Developing Economies," *The Business Quarterly*, Winter, 1965, pp. 74-82.

Walter, Bruce and Etzel, Michael. "The Internationalization of U.S. Franchise System: Progress and Procedures," *Journal of Marketing*, April, 1973, pp. 38-46.

PART VII.   COMMUNICATIONS STRATEGIES

Abrahams, Burton R. "Selling Abroad Without Risk," *Sales & Marketing Management,* October 11, 1976, pp. 58-59.

Cantry, Bernard R. "The Evolution of French Media Models," *Journal of Advertising Research,* June, 1973, pp. 19-20.

Chevalier, Michel and Catry, Bernard. "Advertising in France: The Advertiser-Advertising Agency Relationship," *European Journal of Marketing,* No. 1, 1976, pp. 49-59.

Donnelly, James and Ryans, Jr., John K. "Agency Selection in International Advertising," *European Journal of Marketing,* 1972, pp. 211-215.

Donnelly, Jr., James H. and Ryans, Jr., John K. "How American Companies Advertise Overseas," *European Business,* January, 1970, pp. 58-62.

Dunn, S. Watson. "The Changing Legal Climate for Marketing and Advertising in Europe," *Columbia Journal of World Business,* Summer, 1974, pp. 91-98.

"Europe's Admen Go Multinational," *Business Week,* May 26, 1973, pp. 52-54.

Fierlinger, Paul. "Advertising Behind the Iron Curtain," *Advertising Age,* May 21, 1973, pp. 55-56.

Gestetner, David. "Strategy in Managing International Sales," *Harvard Business Review,* September–October, 1974, pp. 103-108.

"The Global Challenges to Advertising," *Journal of Advertising,* Summer, 1974, pp. 21-25.

Green, Robert T.; Cunningham, William H.; Cunningham, Isabella C.M. "Effectiveness of Standardized Global Advertising," *Journal of Advertising,* Summer, 1975, pp. 25-28.

Klippel, Eugene R. and Boewadt, Robert J. "Attitude Measurement as a Strategy Determinant for Standardization of Multinational Advertising," *Journal of International Business Studies,* Spring, 1974, pp. 39-50.

"Massey-Ferguson's Success Story," *Business Week,* February 2, 1976, pp. 40ff.

Miracle, Gordon. "International Advertising Principles and Strategies," *MSU Business Topics,* August, 1968, pp. 29-36.

O'Connor, James. "International Advertising," *Journal of Advertising,* Spring, 1974, pp. 9-14.

Ryans, John. "Is It too Soon to Put a Tiger in Every Tank?" *Columbia Journal of World Business,* March–April, 1969, pp. 69-75.

Ryans, John and Donnelly, James. "Standardized Global Advertising: A Call as Yet Unanswered," *Journal of Marketing,* April, 1969, pp. 57-60.

Sheth, Jagdish N. and Smiljanic, Milan. "Advertising's Image—U.S. and Yugoslavia," *Journal of the Academy of Marketing Science,* Fall, 1973, pp. 167-179.

Snyder, James D. "A Sizzling Market Unveiled," *Sales Management,* May 5, 1975, pp. 41-47.

Weinstein, Arnold K. "Development of An Advertising Industry in Asia," *MSU Business Topics,* Spring, 1970, pp. 28-36.

_____ "The International Expansion of U.S. Multinational Advertising Agencies," *MSU Business Topics,* Summer, 1974, pp. 29-35.

PART VIII. PRICING STRATEGIES

Anderson, Evan E. "Soviet Retail Pricing," *Journal of Retailing,* Summer, 1968, pp. 61–69.

Arpan, Jeffrey, S. *International Intracorporate Pricing.* New York, NY: Praeger, 1972.

Clague, Llewellyn and Grossfield, Rena. "Export Pricing in a Floating Rate World," *Columbia Journal of World Business,* Winter, 1974, pp. 17–22.

Clark, P.B. and Grubel, H.G. *National Monetary Sovereignty Under Different Exchange Rate Systems.* New York, NY: New York University, Graduate School of Business, 1972.

Greene, James. "Intercorporate Pricing Across National Frontiers," *The Conference Board Record,* October, 1969, pp. 43–48.

Hayes, Donald J. "Translating Foreign Currencies," *Harvard Business Review,* January–February, 1972, pp. 6–18.

Leff, Nathaniel H. "Multinational Corporate Pricing Strategy," *Journal of International Business Studies,* Fall, 1975, pp. 55–64.

Lipson, Harry A. and Lamont, Douglas. "Marketing Policy Decisions Facing International Marketers in Less Developed Countries," *Journal of Marketing,* October, 1969, pp. 24–31.

McAlley, Ian M. "Pricing in an International Market," Winter *Proceedings.* Chicago, Ill.: American Marketing Association, 1967, pp. 239–241.

Robbins, Sidney and Stobaugh, Robert B. *Money in the Multinational Enterprise.* New York, NY: Basic Books, 1973.

Shulman, James C. "Transfer Pricing in the Multinational Firm," *European Business,* January, 1969, pp. 33–35.

Shulman, James. "When the Price is Wrong—By Design," *Columbia Journal of World Business,* May–June, 1967, pp. 69–76.

Solving International Pricing Problems. New York, NY: Business International, 1965.

Teck, Alan. "Control Your Exposure to Foreign Exchange," *Harvard Business Review,* January–February, 1974, pp. 66–75.

PART IX. PLANNING AND IMPLEMENTING MARKETING PROGRAMS

Alsegg, Robert J. "Control Relationships Between American Corporations and Their European Subsidiaries," AMA Research Study 107. New York, NY: American Management Association, 1971.

Aylmer, R.I. "Who Makes Marketing Decisions in the Multinational Firm?" *Journal of Marketing,* October, 1970, pp. 25–30.

Ball, Robert. "Nestle Revs Up Its U.S. Campaign," *Fortune,* February 13, 1978, pp. 80–90.

Blue, Jeffrey L. and Haynes, Jr., Ulric. "Preparation for the Overseas Assignment," *Business Horizons,* June, 1977, pp. 61–67.

Buzzell, Robert. "Can You Standardize Multinational Marketing?" *Harvard Business Review,* November–December, 1968, pp. 102–113.

Holt, John B. "Joint Ventures in Yugoslavia: West German and American Experience," *MSU Business Topics,* Spring, 1973, pp. 51–63.

Holton, Richard. "Marketing Policies in Multinational Corporations," *California Management Review,* Summer, 1971, pp. 57–67.

Johanson, Jan and Vahlne, Jan-Erik. "The Internationalization Process of the Firm—A Mode of Knowledge Development and Increasing Foreign Market Commitments," *Journal of International Business Studies,* Spring/Summer, 1977, pp. 23–32.

Keegan, Warren J. "Multinational Marketing Control," *Journal of International Business Studies,* Fall, 1972, pp. 33–48.

_____ , "Multinational Marketing: The Headquarters Role," *Columbia Journal of World Business,* January–February, 1971, pp. 85–90.

Pryor, Jr., Millard H. "Planning in a Worldwide Business," *Harvard Business Review,* January–February, 1965, pp. 130–139.

Rapp, William V. "Strategy Formulation and International Competition," *Columbia Journal of World Business,* Summer, 1973, pp. 98–112.

Reynolds, Clvin. "Managing Human Resources on a Global Scale," *Business Horizons,* December, 1976, pp. 51–56.

Sim, A.B. "Decentralized Management of Subsidiaries and Their Performance," *Management International Review,* No. 2, 1977, pp. 45–51.

Stopford, John and Wells, Louis. "Ironing Out the New Relationships," *Worldwide P & I Planning,* May–June, 1972, pp. 32–37.

_____ . *Managing the Multinational Enterprise.* New York, NY: Basic Books, Inc., 1972.

Van Zandt, Howard F. "Learning to Do Business With 'Japan, Inc.,' " *Harvard Business Review,* July–August, 1972, pp. 83–92.

Weinrauch, J. Donald and Rao, C.P. "The Export Marketing Mix: An Examination of Company Experiences and Perceptions," *Journal of Business Research,* October, 1974, pp. 447–452.

Widing, Jr., J. William. "Reorganizing Your Worldwide Business," *Harvard Business Review,* May–June, 1973, pp. 153–160.

Young, Steven and Hood, Neil. "Perspectives on the European Marketing Strategy," *European Journal of Marketing,* Vol. 10, No. 5, 1976, pp. 240–256.

PART X.   PROBLEMS AND PERSPECTIVES

Amid-Hozour, E. and Somoghi, J. "East-West Trade," *Finance and Development,* June, 1973, pp. 32–37.

Behrman, Jack N. *The Role of International Companies in Latin American Integration.* Lexington, MA: Lexington Books, 1972.

Breckenfeld, Gurney. "Multinationals at Bay," *Saturday Review,* January 24, 1976, pp. 12–30.

Brittain III, Alfred. "The Role of Foreign Investment in the U.S.," *Nation's Business,* March, 1977, pp. 54–56.

The Financing of Exports and Imports: A Guide to Procedures. New York, NY: Morgan Guaranty Trust Company of New York, 1973.

Gabriel, Peter P. "MNCs in the Third World: Is Conflict Unavoidable?" *Harvard Business Review,* July–August, 1972, pp. 93–101.

Kahn, Herman and Brown, William. "A World Turning Point—and a Better Prospect for the Future," *The Futurist,* November, 1975, pp. 284–289.

Kaikati, Jack. "The Phenomenon of International Bribery," *Business Horizons,* February, 1977, pp. 25–37.

Karger, Delmar W. and DeGuzman Dante Q. "Factors Affecting Industrialization of Underdeveloped Countries," *Management International Review,* Vol. 17, No. 2, 1977, pp. 73–85.

Mace, Myles. "The President and International Operations," *Harvard Business Review,* November–December, 1966, pp. 72–84.

Ozawa, Terutomo. "Multinationalism—Japanese Style," *Columbia Journal of World Business,* November–December, 1972, pp. 33–42.

Perlmutter, Howard V. "The Multinational Firm and the Future," *Annals of the American Academy of Political and Social Science,* September, 1972, pp. 139–152.

Root, Franklin R. "Public Policy Expectations of Multinational Managers," *MSU Business Topics,* Autumn, 1973, pp. 5–12.

Ryans, Jr., John K. "U.S. Corporate Involvement in Developing Markets: The East African Example," *Pittsburgh Business Review,* July, 1972, pp. 1–13.

Schollhammer, Hans. "Ethics in an International Business Context," *MSU Business Topics,* Spring, 1977, pp. 54–63.

Sorenson II, Ralph Z. "U.S. Marketers Can Learn from European Innovators," *Harvard Business Review,* September–October, 1972, pp. 89–99.

Technology Transfer and the Developing Countries, Report of the Task Force On Technology Transfer, Chamber of Commerce of the United States, 1977.

Vernon, Raymond. "The Future," Charles P. Kindleberger ed., *The International Corporation.* Cambridge, MA: The M.I.T. Press, 1970, pp. 392–393.

Weekly, James K. and Bardi, Edward J. "A Managerial Perceptions of Exporting Problem Areas," *Baylor Business Studies,* January, 1970, pp. 17–27.

Young, Alexander K. "How the Japanese Trade With China," *Columbia Journal of World Business,* May–June, 1972, pp. 45–56.